# India Infrastructure Report

MW01124292

*Editor*

Sebastian Morris

*Project co-ordinators*

Anupam B. Rastogi, IDFC
Sebastian Morris, IIM (A)
Prem K. Kalra, IIT (K)

# INDIA INFRASTRUCTURE REPORT 2001

## 3iNetwork

Infrastructure Development Finance Company
Indian Institute of Management, Ahmedabad
Indian Institute of Technology, Kanpur

**OXFORD**
UNIVERSITY PRESS

# OXFORD
UNIVERSITY PRESS

YMCA Library Building, Jai Singh Road, New Delhi 110001

Oxford University Press is a department of the University of Oxford. It furthers the
University's objective of excellence in research, scholarship, and education
by publishing worldwide in

Oxford   New York
Athens  Auckland  Bangkok  Bogota  Buenos Aires  Calcutta
Cape Town  Chennai  Dar es Salaam  Delhi  Florence  Hong Kong  Istanbul
Karachi  Kuala Lumpur  Madrid  Melbourne  Mexico City  Mumbai
Nairobi  Paris  Sao Paolo Shanghai Singapore  Taipei  Tokyo  Toronto  Warsaw

with associated companies in

Berlin   Ibadan

Oxford is a registered trade mark of Oxford University Press
in the UK and in certain other countries

Published in India
By Oxford University Press, New Delhi

ISBN  0 19 565634 2

Typeset in Garamond 10.5 on 12 by Excellent Laser Typesetters, Tri Nagar, Delhi 110034
Printed in India at Sahara India Mass Communications, NOIDA
and published by Manzar Khan, Oxford University Press
YMCA Library Building, Jai Singh Road, New Delhi 110 001

# PREFACE

When the Infrastructure Development Finance Company (IDFC) was in its formative stages, I felt that much of its value would depend upon our ability to assimilate relevant knowledge already existing in the area of our interest. Apart from setting up our own policy advisory group to think through problems related to private investment in infrastructure development, we also felt that we ought to be able to scan the broader environment to help us with the task at hand.

Harnessing creative talent by developing research programmes in collaboration with the academic community, was one method of achieving this objective. We visited both IIM, Ahmedabad and IIT, Kanpur to see if there was any interest in the enterprise. To our delight we found considerable enthusiasm for the idea. The result was the founding of the 3iNetwork—as an open network where new like-minded partners from industry, academia, non-governmental organizations, and even the government can come together to realize its mission in a spirit of cooperative endeavour.

The 3iNetwork essentially has a dual role: to identify projects within the two academic institutions to further the process of investment in relevant and appropriate infrastructure projects and; to annually document issues in infrastructure development arising from the evolving political and economic environment in the country. With regard to the first, we are currently funding nine projects, ranging from virtual reality simulation labs to public utility pricing for infrastructure services.[1]

This first attempt by us to document infrastructure issues has resulted in the *India Infrastructure Report 2001*. This report focuses on the policies required to create an appropriate market structure for infrastructure provision and the regulatory framework this implies. We envisage that this enterprise will evolve into a periodic document that records progress in the country as a whole, and in the various states on matters of both policy evolution and project development in infrastructure. We intend this to be a standard work of reference with respect to infrastructure development in India.

IDFC considers itself fortunate to have played the role of a catalyst in this process of bringing together academia and industry to deliberate upon and solve many of today's problems. It is our belief that a free, frank, and open exchange of views is necessary to arrive at the most innovative and workable solutions that will find acceptance among various stakeholders. We are ultimately concerned with processes that yield optimal solutions for the government, encourage private participation in investment and provision of infrastructure services, provide an environment of healthy competition, and, above all offer quality services to citizens. With the right framework and willingness to put people first, systems can work to achieve this objective. We need to ask ourselves one simple question in this context—is it sustainable, and is this in the interest of the consumer? If the answer is 'no' we need to seek alternatives, even if that means eliminating existing structures of governance. Governance is about citizens, for citizens, and has no other purpose. We hope to develop the 3iNetwork into an ever-growing fraternity and, together, make a difference for the people of India.

December 2000                                                                                   NASSER MUNJEE

---

[1] The range of activity could be viewed on the network's portal at *www.3inetwork.org* or at *www.idfc.com*.

# CONTRIBUTORS

| | |
|---|---|
| Samir K. Barua | Indian Institute of Management, Ahmedabad |
| Rakesh Basant | Indian Institute of Management, Ahmedabad |
| Atanu Chakraborty | Directorate of Employment and Training, Government of Gujarat, Gandhinagar |
| Puneet Chitkara | Indian Institute of Technology, Kanpur |
| Keshab Das | Gujarat Institute of Development Research, Ahmedabad |
| Saumyen Guha | Indian Institute of Technology, Kanpur |
| Amita Gupta | Infrastructure Leasing and Financial Services, New Delhi |
| Rekha Jain | Indian Institute of Management, Ahmedabad |
| Ashok Jhunjhunwala | Indian Institute of Technology, Madras |
| Abha Singhal Joshi | Centre for Human Rights Initiative, New Delhi |
| Prem K. Kalra | Indian Institute of Technology, Kanpur |
| T. Madhavan | Indian Institute of Management, Ahmedabad |
| S. Manikutty | Indian Institute of Management, Ahmedabad |
| B. R. Marwah | Indian Institute of Technology, Kanpur |
| M. P. Mathur | National Institute of Urban Affairs, New Delhi |
| Alice Albin Morris | Unnati, Organisation for Development Education, Ahmedabad |
| Sebastian Morris | Indian Institute of Management, Ahmedabad |
| Anish Nanavaty | Infrastructure Development Finance Company, Mumbai |
| Ajay Narayanan | Infrastructure Development Finance Company, Chennai |
| B. P. Pundir | Indian Institute of Technology, Kanpur |
| G. Raghuram | Indian Institute of Management, Ahmedabad |
| Bhaskar Ramamurthi | Indian Institute of Technology, Madras |
| K.V. Ramani | Indian Institute of Management, Ahmedabad |
| M. Y. Rao | PricewaterhouseCoopers and Development Associates Ltd., Bhubaneshwar |
| Vivek Raval | Unnati, Organisation for Development Education, Ahmedabad |
| Dheeraj Sanghi | Indian Institute of Technology, Kanpur |
| Sujata Sawant | Rail India Technical and Economic Services, Urban Transport Division, New Delhi |
| Rajiv Shekhar | Indian Institute of Technology, Kanpur |
| Y. M. Shivamurthy | Infrastructure Development Finance Company, Mumbai |
| V. K. Sibal | Rail India Technical and Economic Services, Urban Transport Division, New Delhi |
| Sidharth Sinha | Indian Institute of Management, Ahmedabad |
| Vinita Sinha | Infrastructure Development Finance Company, Mumbai |
| Geetam Tiwari | Indian Institute of Technology, Delhi |
| Jayanth Varma | Securities and Exchange Board of India, Mumbai |

# ACKNOWLEDGEMENTS

The 3iNetwork had met several times to discuss the proposition of an infrastructure report and its possible contents, before adopting the theme of industry structure and regulation. Freewheeling discussions among engineers, social scientists, and practising managers, gave us much insight and many leads to work and write upon. It is now clear to all of us that the topic chosen for the first report could not have been more timely. Nasser Munjee first articulated the idea that policy and regulatory contradictions stand in the way of the development of several physical infrastructural sectors, especially with respect to private investment. The theme was both broad and unifying. Many more articles than those carried in the report were written. Not all could be included due to the limitations of space and time. Similarly, not all who took active part in the report have written papers. However, their contributions are as important to the success of the report as that of the writers.

There continue to be uncertainties with regard to the likely and intended industry structure and restructuring in many of the infrastructural areas. This in conjunction with today's recession, and institutional and organizational inadequacies, have worked to create a situation wherein a fresh approach to the development of infrastructure is important. If this report is able to outline the necessary national effort to create the basic contours of the 'second round of reform' then it would have served its purpose. We are grateful to IDFC, specifically to Nasser Munjee and Anupam Rastogi who provided us this opportunity.

The need to go beyond stylistic, piecemeal and doctrinaire approaches, to a more thoughtful and pragmatic one is by now obvious to any one involved in the development of infrastructure in India. For example, neither the extreme positions of 'abolish all subsidies', nor its contrary of the continuance of the status quo, are justified. Therefore, reform today poses a greater challenge than what is generally believed. The challenge is not merely political, but also intellectual—we need to deeply worry about the 'incentive compatibility' and the institutional basis of any policy. At IIM(A) many of us have long held this view. We were pleasantly surprised to discover similar thinking amongst our colleagues both at IDFC and IIT(K). We worked together closely as part of the 3iNetwork, and in putting together *IIR 2001*. It became clear to us that the basic problems cut across many of the infrastructural areas. While vested interests do stand in the way of reform, such interests have usually been a creation of perverse incentives and insensitive policy. The need to direct intellectual capital into infrastructure is an important task ahead for our country.

The technological dimensions of this task are perhaps as important as the challenge of institutional reform and incentive compatibility. This is especially so in today's world wherein information technology in its broadest sense has the potential to redraw the very economic fabric of society through change in the many ways of communication. Similarly, cheap, real time measurement possibilities, advances in data storage and mining create scope for constructed markets, light regulation, monitoring and control, direct participation and regulation by people, that are only dimly sensed at this juncture. The telecom sector is being directly turned around by developments in technology, and other sectors will not be able to escape its indirect effects. The aspect of convergence already tends to make obsolete some of the institutional initiatives at a sectoral level. In this world of uncertainty, and where phenomena mutate faster than theory, there is a strong need to get back to the basic principles, to 'respect' the specificities of the particular situation and society.

Such a task is seemingly contradictory, but not as useless as a doctrinaire approach would be. Little can be achieved in a democracy like ours without the participation of people in socially important infrastructure such as roads, dams, and municipal water. Thus, issues such as land acquisition and people's right to know, are part of the debate, requiring resolution. Therefore, we also invited persons outside the network but with experience to join the *IIR 2001* team.

We see this report as a modest effort to understand infrastructure and its problems, with the recognition that there are broader dimensions to the problem. We also hope that at this juncture when the direction to move is not clear, such an approach is rewarding.

The preliminary papers were presented at the writers' workshop held at IIM(A) in mid-August. We thank all the special invitees for their comments and lively participation—Sadashiv Rao, Cherian Thomas, Partha Mukhopadhyay, Jayalakshmi Jayaraman, Janak Talsania, Nirmal Mohanty, and Anupam Srivatsava from IDFC, and Subir Gokarn of the National Council of Applied Economic Research (NCAER). I also thank the IIM(A) faculty who participated in the workshop. To Anupam Rastogi, a special thanks is due for holding together the entire workshop. I am grateful to the team of rappoteurs consisting of Bharat Verma, Vinisha Thaker, Deepa Keskhani, Trupti Patel, and Christina Sullivan Sarabhai for painstakingly recording the highlights of the discussions.

A collective effort such as this one is hardly possible without the involvement of several persons. Devika Fernandes of the IDFC was ready to provide much crucial information and data however ill-defined the requests. Deepa Keshkani, Trupti Patel, and Vinisha Thaker took up the 'back office' operations at IIM(A). They put together the bibliography, the abbreviations and helped me with the manuscript, besides assisting G. Raghuram and Rekha Jain with their papers. Ram Mishra looked after the coordination at IIT(K). Urmil Anjaria, my secretary, worked feverishly to get the various papers in shape. Kavita Iyengar and Shreemoyee Patra at Oxford University Press, Delhi not only did a remarkable job of supervising the entire editorial task within an exceedingly tight schedule but also ensured that I did not slacken on the deliverables. Christina Sullivan Sarabhai saved me much time by copyediting many of the papers.

I would also like to thank Jahar Saha, for encouraging the IIM(A) component of the team in so many ways. My personal indebtedness is also due to Jayanth Varma, G. Raghuram, Sidharth Sinha, Bithin Datta, Rekha Jain, Keshab Das, Anupam Rastogi, Jaya Singhania, Puneet Chitkara, Rakesh Basant, Dheeraj Sanghi, Arun P. Sinha, T. V. Prabhakar, Atanu Chakraborty, Bernard D'Mello, R. Nagaraj, Nasser Munjee, Alice Albin, M. Y. Rao, S. K. Barua, Y. M. Shivamurthy, Anish Nanavaty, Sanjay Dhande, B. R. Marwah, Prem Kalra, K. K. Saxena and Subir Gokarn for the discussions I had with them on various issues in infrastructure. I gained much from these discussions.

Mahesh Vyas gave the team and me the confidence that came from knowing that the database of the Centre for Monitoring the Indian Economy (CMIE) was always available to us. The report owes much to the information provided by the CMIE, and I am indebted to Mahesh Vyas for this.

On behalf of the contributors, I thank all those who have helped us put together this report. However, we alone are responsible for any errors that remain.

SEBASTIAN MORRIS

# CONTENTS

# TABLES

# BOXES

# FIGURES

# ABBREVIATIONS AND ACRONYMS

| | |
|---|---|
| AAI | Airport Authority of India |
| ABT | Availability-based Tariff |
| AC | Access Centre |
| ACP | anti competitive practices |
| ADB | Asian Development Bank |
| ADC | Analogue Digital Converter |
| ADSL | Asynchronous Digital Subscriber Loop |
| ADV | animal drawn vehicle |
| AIMTC | All India Motor Transport Congress |
| AITD | Asian Institute of Transport Development |
| APM | Administered Pricing Mechanism |
| APSEB | Andhra Pradesh State Electricity Board |
| APTRANSCO | Andhra Pradesh Transmission Company, an inheritor company of the APSEB |
| ARV | Annual Ratable Value |
| ARWSP | Accelerated Rural Water Supply Programme |
| BDSL | Basic Rate DSL |
| BDSU | Basic Digital Subscriber Unit |
| BFOT | build, finance, operate and transfer |
| BG | Broad Guage |
| BKPL | Barvani–Kanpur Pipeline |
| BOLT | build, operate, lease, and transfer |
| BOO | build, operate, and own |
| BOOT | build, own, operate and transfer |
| BoP | balance of payments |
| BoT | build, operate and transfer |
| BPSA | Bulk Purchase and Sales Agreement (between central power corporations like the NTPC, NHPC, NPC and SEBs) |
| BSD | Base Station Distributor |
| BSES | Bombay Suburban Electric Supply (Undertaking) Limited |
| BSO | basic service operator |
| BWSSB | Bangalore Water Supply & Sewerage Board |
| CAAS | Civil Aviation Authority of Singapore |
| CAGR | Compounded Annual Growth Rate |
| CAPEX | Capital Expenditure |
| CBD | central business district |
| CBSs | Compact Base Stations |
| CCL | Continental Construction Limited |
| C-DOT | Centre for Development of Telematics |

| | |
|---|---|
| CEA | Central Electricity Authority |
| CEOs | chief executive officer |
| CERC | Central Electricity Regulatory Commission |
| CFC | Central Finance Commission |
| CFSs | Container Freight Stations |
| CIDCO | City and Industrial Development Corporation |
| Ckt Kms | Circuit kilometers |
| CLASS | Customs Local Area Signalling Services |
| CLEC | competitive local exchange carrier |
| CMC | Computer Maintenance Corporation Ltd. |
| CMSP | Cellular Mobile Service Provider |
| CNG | Compressed Natural Gas |
| COAI | Cellular Operators Association of India |
| COMUS | Central Office Mux |
| CONCOR | Container Corporation of India |
| corDECT | Registered DECT of TeNet |
| CPC | Central Power Corporations (NTPC, NHPC, NPC, REC) |
| CPCB | Central Pollution Control Board |
| CPE | Customer Premise Equipment |
| CPHEEO | Central Public Health and Environmental Engineering Organisation |
| CPP | Calling Party Pays |
| CPs | Captive Producers |
| CRS | Commissionerate of Railway Safety |
| CRTC | Canadian Radio, Television and Telecommunications Commission |
| CSO | Central Statistical Organisation |
| CSP | Cable Service Provider |
| CTU | Central Transmission Utility |
| CV | Capital Value |
| DEL | Direct Exchange Line |
| DFIs | Development Financial Institutions |
| DGCs | Distribution-cum-Generating Companies |
| DG-IV | General Directorate of Competition of the European Union |
| DGT | Director General, Telecommunications, OFTEL, UK |
| DIAS | Direct Internet Access System |
| DIU | DECT Interface Unit |
| DLD | Domestic Long Distance |
| DMH | Dandeli Mini-Hydel Project |
| DMRT | Delhi Mass Rapid Transit |
| DNPR&R | Draft National Policy on Rehabilitation and Resettlement |
| DoT | Department of Telecommunication |
| DPC | Dabhol Power Company Ltd. |
| DPA | Dubai Ports Authority |
| DPCs | District Planning Committees |
| DPI | Department of Programme Implementation (of the Ministry of Planning), Government of India |
| DSP | Digital Signal Processor |
| DSU | Digital Subscriber Unit |
| DTC | Delhi Transport Corporation |
| DTHB | direct to home broadcasting |
| DTO | Department of Telecom Operations |
| DTS | Department of Telecom Services |
| DVC | Damodar Valley Corporation |
| ECB | External Commercial Borrowing |

| | |
|---|---|
| ECIL | Electronics Corporation of India Ltd. |
| EDI | Electronic Data Interchange |
| EHV | extra high voltage |
| EIA | environment impact analyses |
| EPA | Environmental Protection Agency |
| ERC | Electricity Regulations Act, 1998 |
| ERR | economic rate of return |
| ETSI | European Telecommunications Standards Institute |
| EW | England & Wales (Pool or electricity System) |
| EWS | economically weaker sections |
| EZEV | Equivalent Zero Emission Vehicles |
| FAC | fully allocated costs |
| FACTS | flexible AC transmission systems |
| FCC | Federal Communication Commission |
| FCVs | Fuel Cell Vehicles |
| FDI | foreign direct investment |
| FERC | Federal Energy Regulatory Commission |
| FIRE | Financing Institution Reform and Expansion |
| FLAG | fibre optic link around the globe |
| FOI | Freedom of Information Act |
| FPI | Foundation for Public Interest |
| FSI | floor space index |
| FSP | fixed service providers |
| GAIL | Gas Authority of India Limited |
| GAPL | Gujarat Adani Port Limited |
| GATS | General Agreement on Trade and Services |
| GDCF | gross domestic capital formation |
| GDP | gross domestic price |
| GDR | Global Depository Receipt |
| GEB | Gujarat Electricity Board |
| GIDB | Gujarat Infrastructure Development Board |
| GIDC | Gujarat Industrial Development Corporation |
| GMB | Gujarat Maritime Board |
| GMSC | Global Mobile Service Carrier |
| GNCTD | Government of National Capital Territory of Delhi |
| GPPL | Gujarat Pipavav Port Limited |
| GRT | gross registered tonnage |
| GSM | Group Special Mobile |
| GWSSB | Gujarat Water Supply and Sewerage Board |
| HBCP | Haldia–Barauni Crude Oil Pipeline |
| HDSU | high bit rate digital subscriber unit |
| HDT | host digital terminal |
| HERC | Haryana Electricity Regulatory Commission |
| HEVs | hybrid electric vehicles |
| HMRPL | Haldia–Mourigram–Rajbandh Pipeline |
| HUAC | high voltage alternating current (transmission) |
| HUDC | high voltage direct current (transmission) |
| IAN | Integrated Access Node |
| IAS | Indian Administrative Services |
| IBPL | Indo-Burma Petroleum Limited |
| IBRD | International Bank for Reconstruction and Development |
| IC | internal combustion |
| ICAO | International Civil Aviation Organization |

| | |
|---|---|
| ICE | Information, Communication and Entertainment |
| ICF | Integral Coach Factory |
| ICSEM | Institute for Catchment Studies and Environmental Management |
| IDC | International Data Corporation |
| IDWSSF | International Drinking Water Supply and Sanitation Decade |
| IETP | Internet Engineering Task Force |
| IEGC | Indian Electricity Grid Code |
| IETF | Internet Engineering Task Force |
| IFC | International Finance Corporation |
| IGIA | Indira Gandhi International Airport |
| ILEC | Incumbent Local Exchange Courier |
| IMO | International Monetary Organization |
| INF | Intelligent Network Forum |
| INSA | Indian National Shipowners' Association |
| IOCL | Indian Oil Corporation Limited |
| IP | Internet Protocol |
| IPP | Independent Power Project |
| IPRs | Intellectual Property Rights |
| IR | Indian Railways |
| IRR | internal rate of return |
| ISDN | International Subscriber Dialling Number |
| ISP | Internet Service Provider |
| IT | Information Technology |
| ITI | Indian Telephone Industries Ltd. |
| ITS | Indian Telecom Service |
| ITU | International Telecommunications Union |
| ITXC | Internet Telephony Exchange Carrier |
| JNPT | Jawaharlal Nehru Port Trust |
| JRY | Jawahar Rozgar Yojana |
| JTM | Jabatan Telekom Malaysia |
| JV | Joint Venture |
| JVC | Joint Venture Company |
| KBPL | Kandla–Bhatinda Pipeline |
| KDA | Kanpur Development Authority |
| KPRC | KP Rao Committee (set up to study bulk tariff) |
| KRC | Konkan Railway Corporation |
| KWH or unit | Kilowatt hours |
| LAA | Land Acquisition Act 1894 |
| LDC | less developed country |
| LEC | Local exchange carrier |
| LEV | Low Emission Vehicle |
| LIBOR | London Inter Bank Offer Rate |
| LIC | Life Insurance Corporation |
| LIG | Low Income Group |
| LNP | Local Number Portability |
| LoC | Letter of Credit |
| LoI | Letter of Intent |
| LPCD | Litres per capita per day |
| LRAC | Long run average costs |
| LRDSS | Long Range Decision Support System |
| LRIC | Long Run Incremental Cost |
| LRMC | Long Run Marginal Costs |
| LSP | Local Service Provider |

| | |
|---|---|
| LT | Laxmi Transformers |
| MAINS | Maritime Information System |
| MCD | Municipal Corporation of India |
| MERC | Maharashtra Electricity Regulatory Commission |
| MGC | merchant (independent) generating company |
| MHV | medium and heavy vehicle |
| MIDC | Maharashtra Industrial Development Corporation |
| MIGA | Multilateral Investment Guarantee agency |
| MIS | Management Information System |
| MJPL | Mathura–Jalandhar Pipeline |
| MLAs | Multilateral Agencies |
| mlpd | million litres per day |
| MMC | Monopolies and Mergers Commission of the UK |
| MNP | Minimum Needs Programme |
| MOEF | Ministry of Environment and Forests |
| MoP | Ministry of Power |
| MoST | Ministry of Surface Transport |
| MOT | Maintain, Operate and Transfer |
| MoU | Memorandum of Understanding |
| MPCs | Metropolitan Planning Committees |
| MRTPC | Monopoly and Restrictive Trade Practices Commission |
| MRTS | mass rail transit system |
| MSEB | Maharashtra State Electricity Board |
| MSO | Multiple Service Operator |
| MSRDC | Maharashtra State Roads Development Corporation Limited |
| MTBE | methyl tertiary butyl ether |
| MTC | Mobile Termination Charge |
| MTNL | Maharashtra Transport Nigam Limited |
| MTW | motorized two-wheelers |
| MV | motorized vehicles |
| MWS | Multi Wallset |
| NABARD | National Bank for Rural Development |
| NBCC | National Building Construction Company Limited |
| NHAI | National Highway Authority of India |
| NHPC | National Hydro Power Corporation Limited |
| NIC | National Informatics Centre |
| NICs | newly industrialized countries |
| NLC | Neyveli Lignite Corporation Ltd. |
| NLDC | national long distance carrier |
| NLDO | National Long Distance Operator |
| NLDS | National Long Distance Services |
| NMHC/NMOG | Non-Methane Hydrocarbon |
| NMVs | Non-Motorised Vehicles |
| NORD pool | The electricity pool of the Nordic countries |
| NPC | Nuclear Power Corporation |
| NTF | National Task Force |
| NTPC | National Thermal Power Corporation Ltd. |
| NZ | New Zealand (Pool or electricity system) |
| O&M | Operation and Maintenance |
| OBC | Other Backward Castes |
| OCC | Oil Co-ordination Committee |
| OERC | Orissa Electricity Regulatory Commission |
| OHPC | Orissa Hydro Power Corporation |

| | |
|---|---|
| optiMA | Registered brand of TeNet |
| OSEB | Orissa State Electricity Board |
| OYW | own your wagon (scheme of the Railways) |
| PAFC | Phosphoric Acid |
| PAP | Project Affected People |
| PCC | Public Common Carrier |
| PCS | Personal Service Communication |
| PCUs | Passenger Car Equivalent Units |
| PDH | Plesiochronous Digital Heirarchy |
| PEMFC | Polymeric Electrolyte Membrane Fuel Cells |
| PGCIL | Power Grid Corporation of India Limited |
| PIL | Petronet India Limited |
| PJM | Pennsylvania, New Jersey and Maryland |
| PLF | plant load factor |
| POL | Petroleum Oil and Lubricant |
| PPA | Power Purchase Agreement |
| PPP | Public–Private Partnership |
| PRCL | Pipavav Rail Corporation Limited |
| PRIs | Panchayati Raj Institutions |
| PSEG | Public Service Electric and Gas Company |
| PSP | Private Sector Participation |
| PSTN | Public Switched Telephone Network |
| PTC | Power Trading Corporation Limited |
| PUC | Pollution Under Control |
| PWD | Public Works Department |
| QP | Quality Problem |
| RAS | Remote Access Switch |
| RBI | Reserve Bank of India |
| RBS | Relay Base Station |
| RC | Restructuring Commission |
| REC | Rural Electrification Corporation |
| RGNDWM | Rajiv Gandhi National Drinking Water Mission |
| RLDC | Regional Load Despatch Centre |
| RMC | Rajkot Municipal Corporation |
| ROE | return on equity |
| ROI | return on investment |
| Ro-Ro | Roll-on-Roll-Off |
| ROW | right of way |
| RPI | Retail price index |
| RT | Remote Terminal |
| RTF | Regional Task Force |
| RTO | Road Transport Office |
| RV | Rateable Value |
| SACFA | Standing Advisory Committee on Frequency Allocation |
| SBM | Single Buoy Mooring |
| SCADA | Supervisory Control and Data Acquisition |
| SCICI | Shipping Credit and Industry Corporation of India Ltd. |
| SEB | State Electricity Board |
| SEBI | Securities & Exchange Board of India |
| SEGW | Secondary Sector (electricity, gas and water) |
| SEZ | Special Economic Zone |
| SGCP | Switching Gateway Control Protocol |
| SMPL | Salaya–Mathura Pipeline |

| | |
|---|---|
| SOHO | Small Office Home Office |
| SPM | suspended particulate matter |
| SPV | Special Purpose Vehicle |
| SRMC | short run marginal cost |
| SRTUs | State Road Transport Undertakings |
| SSA | Secondary Switching Area |
| STA | State Transport Authority |
| STD–PCOs | Subscriber Trunk Dialling/Public Call Offices |
| STM | Syarikat Telekim Malaysia |
| STU | State Trading Utility |
| su | subscriber unit |
| SVC | Static VAR compensation systems |
| TAMP | Tariff Authority for Major Ports |
| TAS | Tattihalla Augmentation Scheme |
| TCI | Transport Corporation of India Limited |
| TCIL | Telecommunications Corporation of India Ltd. |
| TeNet | Telecommunication and Computer Network |
| TEUs | twenty feet equivalent units |
| TIPHON | The Internet Protocol Harmonization over Network |
| TNSEB | Tamil Nadu State Electricity Board |
| ToU | time of use |
| TRAI | Telecom Regulatory Authority of India |
| TRANSCO | transmission company |
| TTSC | Transport, Trading, Storage and Communication |
| UI | Unscheduled interchange |
| ULB | Urban Local Body |
| ULEV | ultra low emission vehicle |
| Unicom | United Telecom |
| UPSBC | Uttar Pradesh State Bridges Construction Company Limited |
| UPSEB | Uttar Pradesh State Electricity Board |
| USO | Universal Service Obligation |
| VAR | Volt Ampere Reactive |
| VoIP | Voice over Internet Protocol |
| VPT | Village Panchayat Telephones |
| VRS | Voluntary Retirement Scheme |
| VSAT | Very Small Aperture Terminal |
| VSNL | Videsh Sanchar Nigam Limited |
| VTS | Vessel Traffic Management or Surveillance Services |
| WILL | Wireless in Local Loop |
| WNP | Wireless Number Portability |
| WPC | Wireless Planning and Co-ordination Wing |
| WS | Wall Set |
| ZEV | Zero Emission Vehicle |

# 1 | OVERVIEW

*Sebastian Morris*

*India Infrastructure Report (IIR) 2001* has several contributors including members of the 3iNetwork, a network of three institutions: the Infrastructure Development Finance Company, the Indian Institute of Technology, Kanpur, and the Indian Institute of Management, Ahmedabad.

In little less than six months since the idea of a report outlining the developments and constraints in infrastructure was mooted, the members and others outside these institutions wrote on sectors and themes that constitute physical infrastructure. The coverage no doubt varies with regard to the sectors. Similarly, not all the important issues that bear on regulation and industry structure have been covered. Thus there should have been more detailed treatment of urban transportation especially the intermodal dimensions. Similarly the constraints imposed by current practices with regard to land use in urban areas are not covered. The housing sector has been entirely omitted. Industrial parks had to be omitted for lack of time and because we were anyway not able to cover the important aspects of land use in urban areas. These are important omissions which we hope would be taken up in later issues of the *IIR*.

Nevertheless, in the chapters here we put forward a picture of infrastructure development in India, reviewing the major developments especially with regard to policy and regulation. We draw out certain themes that are interesting and which help in understanding perversities such as distortionary prices, systematic exclusion of the poor, very inefficient operations, and large allocative failures that run through nearly all the sectors. We also outline the nature of both state and market failure with regard to infrastructure and of the relationship between the two. We also identify, in some sectors more than in others, the restructuring tasks ahead.

The overall theme is 'regulation and industry structure', far more broadly interpreted than is conventional. Indeed, the approach has been to discuss the principal constraints in the development and commercialization of infrastructure. We also show how the two are interlinked in a market economy. The principal constraints, including those of a structural and institutional nature, which we believe need to be overcome for the fast development of infrastructure are also covered.

Thus the conservative approach to macroeconomic policy which may have slowed down growth over the last three years or so and the land acquisition processes which arrest infrastructure development and create dissent against development are discussed. Similarly, the limitations of the principal local bodies (the municipalities) that would have to organize much of the urban infrastructure are also discussed.

Public enterprise, whether structured as a company or operating within government departments, find coverage especially in its potential for commercialization. Government departments and regulatory bodies privatizing public enterprise are also discussed.

In this report—in keeping with the overall objective of the 3iNetwork, viz. to 'lead intellectual capital into infrastructure'—we attempt to go beyond a discussion of current constraints to suggest changes in terms of approaches, institutional reorganization, and appropriate policy. Thus we do not hesitate to point out the possible need for an alternative paradigm with regard to project-affected people. Similarly, we would question the consensus around the need to eliminate subsidies. The bigger problem is the mode of administration of subsidies. Our suggestions are best seen as attempts to bring to the attention of policy makers, developers, and others, fresh avenues for extended consideration.

When the idea of such a report was first mooted, it was felt that problems of infrastructure have an emergent character, as reformers and governments learn to do what is right for the economy and the consumer. Thus the mistakes that had been made and need correction (in the view of the contributors) are discussed. The challenge of private sector involvement runs right through the report. This is not because we feel that the state has no role or only a declining one, but because we are convinced that commercialization, which is more important than ownership, is vital to the realization of both allocative and operational efficiency of infrastructure. And that cannot be realized without either a certain degree of privatization or a reorientation of public enterprise away from rules and guidelines to tasks. We see as more important the feedback effect of some degree of privatization, through the tension for reform that such privatization creates, than the fact of privatization per se. Thereby the 'state failure' that limited public enterprise from delivering can begin to be overcome.

Chapter 2, 'Issues in Infrastructure Development Today: The Interlinkages' (Sebastian Morris), discusses cross-sectoral problems, bringing out interrelationships and interlinkages. The need for reform is real. It is no longer a question of merely signalling to the world at large that the country is ready to open its doors to private and foreign capital. Privatization or commercialization of public enterprise and restructuring of many of the infrastructural areas is an urgent necessity. The fiscal situation is explosive in power and urban services and the opportunities in telecom are too large to be missed, especially for an economy that has shown so much potential in software and remote delivery of services. Transport services are misdirected by highly distortionary prices, and pipelines are held back by improper policy.

The economy would most certainly have entered into a phase of infrastructural shortage, given the slower growth of infrastructure in the 1990s. This arises because of the 'limited capacity of the state to invest' and the private sector's unwillingness to do so, since the expected regulatory and policy clarity has not been obtained. While the resulting costs of denial are undoubtedly large, this relative 'shortage', or 'infrastructure later rather than first', has its own advantages in that the problem of directing infrastructural investments is hardly there. The first priority would be to relax the shortages. Appropriability too could improve. But in many areas the state continues to derive its priorities politically or through planning 'exercises'. More efficient use of infrastructure is also possible today.

The slowing down of infrastructural investments in the 1990s has had negative effects on investment demand in general and is most certainly one of the factors underlying the slow growth of the economy since 1997–8. The economy may have reached a stage where from the demand side a major push in infrastructural investment is necessary. Indeed, the matter may be urgent enough to bring back public investment even though it is known to be inefficient.

The problem is not subsidies per se but their mode of administration. Not a single meeting on infrastructure, especially power and water, takes place without lamenting the subsidies. Their administration in such a manner as to create moral hazard in the organizations providing the service has been an important reason for the failure of public organizations. Although the vested interests against reform are strong, they may not be the groups that are usually identified as such—workers and subsidized groups. The vested interests are more likely to be bureaucrats and politicians who have to give up privileges they have enjoyed as managers and owners. The emphasis on vested interests as a barrier against reform may have been overstated. Reforms have not been too well conceived, and that more than vested interests has limited their scope thus far. The need today is to create the right market structures to take advantage of competition wherever possible, and institute light regulation elsewhere. These are tasks that require high levels of skills and effort.

It is important that public enterprises be allowed to function commercially and towards their primary tasks. The pressures against denial of that freedom have increased. The possibility of privatization indeed improves the prospects for such autonomy, and hence for commercialization of public enterprise in infrastructure. 'Empty solutions' that merely postpone the day of reckoning continue to be generated, as when privatization of State Electricity Boards' (SEBs') assets by selling the same to state-level Public Sector Undertakings (PSUs) is proposed, or a sham privatization is proposed to 'satisfy' a multilateral agency. The days for such behaviour would soon be over.

The myth that low prices are in the interest of the poor needs to be recognized as such and exposed. Low prices have created the problem of slow expansion or stagnation of the service, and hence have kept a large number of the poor as 'outsiders', that is those who are denied the service since they do not even have access. There is a need to distinguish between subsidization of access and subsidization of use, the former being welfare enhancing. Direct subsidization via stamps or coupons is the need of the hour especially in irrigation, drinking water, and electricity. That would allow these services to be viably provided by private capital.

So deep have been the price distortions that investments have been taking place on the basis of such distorted prices. Naturally demand has also been affected. As the reform extricates the system out of these distortions there would be a phase when the true prices and demand would be discovered.

The notion that whenever there is a market failure in the neoclassical static sense, an orthodox price regulation is called for is quite questionable. When in an area like telecom, growth is expected to be rapid because of technological changes and network economies, contestability is high and the orthodox regulatory stance is scarcely appropriate. In telecom, especially, freer entry and more liberal interconnect rules would therefore be justified. Convergence too creates it own opportunity for one industry to ride on another as Internet today can be expected to ride on cable television and high bandwidth cables on existing powerline infrastructure.

The most important structural constraint remains the process of land acquisition. The current process and valuations may not be correct if the specificities of the Indian situation and the fact that the land market itself has been distorted by land use restrictions are taken into account. On land acquisition and resettlement of project-affected people, the law needs to change to create the space for their inclusion in the project as stakeholders. Only this can lower the risk from 'displacement'.

Relevant information about public bodies when available with the concerned public can work wonders in making such bodies and their officials responsible. As such, a genuine right to information Act is necessary for the reorientation of the state to its people and their infrastructural needs.

Chapter 3, 'Regulation of Tariffs and Interconnection: Case Studies' (Sidharth Sinha), brings out three cases of tariff rulings by regulators in India, two in the case of the telecom sector and one in bulk power. The chapter uncovers the underlying assumptions and concerns of the regulator and the regulated, and the limitation of these rulings, to make a critical assessment of the same. Some of the limitations in the defined powers of the regulator and in the existing structure of the industry are brought forth.

Independence of the regulator has gained currency but still remains contested and contingent. The temptation to dilute financial regulation or oversight to allow more lax standards in lending to infrastructure is natural but dangerous. This is discussed in Chapter 4, 'Regulatory Dilemmas in Infrastructure Financing' (Jayanth Varma). The author comes to the conclusion that while credit enhancements and tax support for funds flow into infrastructure would be appropriate, dilution of

standards would not be so. The recent experience of the East Asian countries as well as historical experience would show that there is little need for such relaxations, despite the force with which governments and developers may put forward their arguments. Financial markets, especially debt markets are quick to emerge, when the opportunities arise. The problem with infrastructure is usually, and more certainly in India, with the sector as such—regulatory and policy uncertainties, allocative inefficiencies arising out of government's influence in investment decisions—than in the need for special financial dispensation for infrastructure. This is not to deny the role of credit enhancement and land grants in the case of infrastructure with high social returns.

Chapter 5 discusses the principal structural constraints in infrastructure development in India. As 'independent' regulation emerges in many sectors, there is need to look at the relationship between sector-specific regulators and the competition agencies. There are many reasons why we should have a competition policy, despite the known limitations of the same in a transforming economy. Convergence is an important driver that in the years to come would question the standard prescription of an 'independent' sector-specific regulator. Convergence in India could be driven by both technology, as in telecom as voice over Internet Protocol (IP) becomes a distinct possibility, and by the economies of the 'right of way' which tend to be amplified, given the many clearances and dealings with government bodies that have to be gone through before any network investments can be in place. The first part of Chapter 5, 'Interface between Sector-specific Regulatory Bodies and Competition Agencies' (Rakesh Basant), brings out the conflicts that are likely and flags the loose ends, calling for a more detailed study of possible options.

In 'Political and Bureaucratic Hurdles in Reform and Restructuring' (M. Y. Rao), the history of the birth of the Orissa regulator is brought out by one who not only had a ringside view but was actively involved in the early stages of the reform. The biases and assumptions and the vested interests that had to be overcome in institutional reform for regulation remain just as relevant today. We get a feel of the nature of the state and bureaucracy in India at the provincial level. Most certainly hardening budgets and the crisis-like situation were the drivers for change. Thus threats more than opportunities are going to work in the Indian situation.

An important development in the involvement of the private sector has been the passage of several build, operate and transfer (BOT) laws by state governments. In 'Need for a BOT Law' (Atanu Chakraborty), who had been involved in the design of the Gujarat Infrastructure Act, brings out the salient features and the processes involved in bringing forth the legislation. Limitations apart, such BOT laws bring in the operational efficiency of the private sector into areas of infrastructure that are appropriable in part or full. As many state governments gear themselves for reform, the experience of Gujarat would be of interest. Change is not without its hiccups and opponents. In infrastructure, the 'power of the status quo' is most acute: markets do not naturally exist. They have to be 'created' by design, law, and use of technology. Such unbundling makes the task of government more challenging. As such the capacity and capability of the government is vital to the success of reform and privatization.

'Project Preparation: The Cinderella of Private Sector Participation (PSP)' (Atanu Chakraborty), as its name suggests, laments the relative neglect of this rather painstaking but important task when the state puts forward projects for the private sector. The task is especially important if foreign developers are to be interested in Indian projects. Indian government has to develop the skills to put forth projects that speak the same language that developers and foreign institutional investors expect. Unfortunately, many government departments are still to learn what constitutes the relevant details. The creation of specialized bureaus can only be the first step in the diffusion of the relevant skills for project preparation through the state government system. 'How much more of this Infliction? The Case of the Ahmedabad–Vadodara Expressway' (Amita Gupta and Sebastian Morris) brings out coordination failure of government construction in a large project. Few projects have failed on the same scale as this expressway. The case is archetypical of what happens when a bureaucracy has moved far from the Weberian ideal upon which the case for public provisioning rests. Given the current, entirely dysfunctional systems and procedures within government, the case tells us that the more pertinent question to ask may well have been: 'How did such bureaucracies deliver at all?' The answer we guess may well lie in the work of key persons within the system who are willing to creatively interpret their roles to make things happen. That such persons exist is beyond doubt. The challenge therefore is to energize them as change agents within the state system.

In 'Land Acquisition: Law and Practice', Y. M. Shivamurthy and Vinita Sinha bring out the salient features of the Act. The court rulings which have tended to display much concern for the status of the affected persons are also discussed. Land acquisition has been problematic but its solution does not lie in the new bill, which seeks to curb certain freedoms of the affected persons. Indeed a case is made for a paradigm change in land for infrastructure. No infrastructure, however socially beneficial, can be built on inadequate compensation for those whose land had to be taken away. That argument is valid not only from the point of view of justice but also because significant reductions in the time for acquisition and the risks involved cannot come if every act of acquisition has to become a tussle, as it currently is. On what needs to be done though, there is some divergence in this report itself. 'Land Acquisition: The Case of Poshitra Port' (Alice Albin Morris) documents an ongoing process of land acquisition. The inadequacies in the practice are brought out, as the people experience the process of their lands being acquired by the government. In this case the government has gone through most of the motions as specified, in the letter but not in the spirit of the law.

In 'Environment and Social Risks in Infrastructure Development' Ajay Narayanan makes a case for the land acquisition law to change in keeping with 'case law'. He argues for larger compensation and also some involvement of those affected. The need for the Act to be more in line with the Draft Policy on Project-Affected Peoples of the Ministry of Rural Development is also discussed. Moreover environmental risks of infrastructural projects do not go away with mere adherence to all clearances. Project developers have to do much more, truly reducing if not eliminating the ill effects on the environment and adequately compensating those affected.

The environmental consciousness of the 1970s and the 1980s resulted in a formalistic and clearance-based approach. As the terms of the clearances were systematically violated judicial activism resulted and much opposition from those affected created risks. The response of the state which was doing much of the infrastructural development was more towards bear these risks and costs and suffer as a consequence, rather than to go beyond the law to reduce the risks. Today, with private financial institutions being involved, that approach could possibly give way to true risk mitigation as they realize that mere adherence to clearances is no guarantee of freedom from risk. But has this realization taken root? Not as yet, if the story 'Hotshot Consultants Copy a Report to get Project Cleared' (B. S. Nagaraj, *Indian Express*) is any indication.

What can a harried citizenry, in the face of state failure and widespread corruption, do? Today lack of a right to information constrains the average citizen and when he is really desperate, as when his land is being taken over for 'public' purposes or when a local industry pumps back pollutants into the ground, he has no choice but to agitate. A thoroughgoing right to information law could do much in a democracy, especially in as plural a society as ours. 'The Right to Information as a Tool of Empowerment' (Abha Singhal Joshi) argues that the expectations of citizens have been dashed, as the new bill is more an exercise to deny information while having the form of a 'freedom of information'. It would change nothing and the hoped for instrument for the democratic transformation of society would be one more example of 'tokenism'. Information with regard to local bodies and public processes—expenditure statements, plans, allocations etc.—of local bodies and corporations having a public aspect, when available with the immediate population who are affected by their working, can have dramatic effects on elected and non-elected officials. The pressures for accountable and responsible working can be significant, and that, privatization or not, is vital to the improvement in infrastructure and its orientation towards the customer.

In Chapter 6, 'The Electricity Sector', the lead paper 'Missing Interconnections in the Power Systems' (Puneet Chitkara, Rajiv Shekhar, and Prem K. Kalra) takes a close look at the present proposals and rulings of the Central Electricity Regulatory Commission (CERC), bringing out their limitations and suggesting the direction for change. The contradictions created by institutions like the Power Trading Corporation, given the need for competitive behaviour among sellers and buyers of wholesale power, are drawn out. The electricity grid is in very poor shape with grid frequencies for hours on end being either far above or below the stipulated 50 cycles. The current attempt is to convert a problem of indiscipline (that requires for its solution stiff punitive measures and disconnection) to a commercial schedule of varying rates that give large incentives for adhering to grid rules, as the proposed availability-based tariff seeks to do. Would it work? Not at all, argues Chapter 6. The difficulties in the current framework for interstate trade in power and the problem of 'identifying the culprits for grid failures' are also covered.

In 'Power Sector Reforms and Regulation: The Road Ahead' (Sebastian Morris) the roots of the current problems including the increasing regulatory and policy risks are brought out. The need to directly administer subsidies through a stamps-based system is put forth. No other system would work since anything else would create a situation of moral hazard for the utility in question. More than subsidization it is the vested interests within the SEBs and outside that have stood in the way of reform and restructuring. Leakages are very large and if they could be plugged most SEBs would be commercially viable entities at tariffs close to current levels! That is the principal challenge, and only direct subsidization can succeed in delinking reform from the subsidy question. A model of reform and regulation that brings in competition in generation is proposed in

some detail. The aspects of the market creation processes, the tasks that need to be carried out, the degree of unbundling, the prospects for competition and the management and ownership of transmission, distribution, and generation assets are considered. In any market model the independent power producers' (IPPs') power purchase agreements (PPAs) would become stranded contracts, imposing great cost on consumers. Various options to extinguish such contracts and boldly go towards a market model are put forth. Both parts to the chapter on the power sector argue that in not having brought out a paper outlining the strategy for regulation and restructuring, the government has imposed much uncertainty on prospective investors who have therefore kept away. Even if the details of legislation and the passage of bills would take time, the need for a credible announcement of the kind of system and change the government wants is important. If the right to choose the supplier can be given to bulk buyers, and similarly captive units can be allowed to go on the grid, the resistance from the SEBs and their 'hedging strategy'— to corporatize without any change in the incentive patterns or in ownership, for example—could be broken.

In section 7.1 'The Transport Sector', G. Raghuram provides a birds-eye view of the problems with the various sectors that constitute transportation. The neglect of the intermodal and multimodal aspects and the underinvestments in the sector resulting in 'transport myopia' are brought out. The effect of absurd prices on investment choice and traffic patterns and the huge returns to relaxation of congestion both in rail and road that are possible, especially on the 'golden quadrilateral', are discussed. A schema classifying the various activities is presented. The notions of the 'network', 'rolling stock', 'terminal', service, and regulation are applied across the sectors to result in a meaningful approach for an integrated treatment of shipping, roads, pipelines, airlines, and railways. Marwah's paper Box 7.1.4 highlights the vast returns to debottlenecking roads. Seeming capacity constraints in roads in many situations are due to the lack of the attention to bottlenecks on roads that are prone to arise in the Indian situation—sections of roads that are damaged, frequent use of certain portions by animals and slow moving vehicles, and too many junctions on highways.

'Sectoral Issues in Transportation' discusses in detail each of the sectors to the extent possible given the limitations of publicly available data. Productivity has been improving steadily in the Railways, and the need is really to price their products appropriately and bring about a customer orientation. The Railways could raise their declining share of freight tonne kms by providing logistic solutions especially to large customers. Railway privatization, except at the margins for certain kinds of non-network related services, is seen by the author as not immediately feasible. The logistic aspect which is sensed only when the provider is willing to see the problem of transportation from the point of view of the customer needs to inform change and improvements in the sector. In 'A Relook at Passenger Car Equivalents (PCEs) in the Indian Context', Box 7.2.1, Marwah argues that the standard tool of road designers, the PCE would not work because of the wide variation in vehicle types, so the need to develop easy to use simulation models is very important. If the notion of the PCE has to be retained, for the Indian highways the standard 1210 type truck should be the reference.

'Port and Shipment Management at Singapore Port: The Revolution in the Use of Electronic Data Interchange (EDI)' (K. V. Ramani) in presenting the developments at Singapore port helps to remind us of the distance between our best ports and Singapore. Today Singapore port uses IT and the Web to cut turnaround times from two days to hours!

'At the Crossroads: Creating Pipeline Infrastructure for Oil Products' (Samir K. Barua and T. Madhavan) reviews the development of oil pipelines in India. Pipelines have been held back due to adverse policy and the pressure exercised by the Railways to keep for themselves a large part of the liquid freight movement in India. The present policy of joint ventures and stand-alone companies will not allow pipeline construction to take off. Financial institutions naturally insist on take or pay contracts. The policy has not been sufficiently appreciative of the network nature of pipelines, wherein developments in one segment affect on all other segments. The need to quickly move on to a common carrier mode for regulation and access to pipeline infrastructure is argued for.

'Integrating Coastal Shipping with the National Transport Network' (G. Raghuram) argues that coastal shipping has been constrained by archaic customs and cabotage laws. The potential for coastal shipping, especially in low value bulk items, is at least twice its current levels. When combined with other modes, that is with appropriate strategies to provide connectivity of urban and industrial places to coastal ports, coastal shipping can emerge as the main mode for carriage of bulk between the west and east coasts.

The telecom sector in India has perhaps seen the most rapid changes whatever the yardsticks. 'Review of the Indian Telecom Sector' (Rekha Jain) looks at the major developments in the institutions, policy, regulation, and network and industry since the process of reform began in the early 1990s. NTP 1999 and the earlier NTP 1994 are discussed. The gradual evolution of policy from monopoly to licensed oligopoly and now competition is indeed a most positive development. The pressure on the incumbent as private parties were allowed in has made the incumbent expand its capacity remarkably. At current tariffs and connection charges much of the demand has been met. The challenge therefore is to bring in new demand. How far has the policy succeeded? Not very far, since the high licence fees, the lack of competition in the beginning, the possible denial of network economies to the players, and independent regulation itself may have stood in the way of a rapid fall in prices. While cellular services' have had some success, basic services' privatization remains a woeful failure.

'Looking Beyond NTP 99' (Ashok Jhunjhunwala) argues for a paradigm shift into local and small-scale solutions which alone, in a poor country, can quickly give us the 100 million subscribers aimed at. For such a development to take place, use of Indian technology and breaking out of the bind of interlocking international credit and technology (and equipment) markets are necessary. Appropriate policy that allows the application of such technologies, the unit of licensing to be more flexibly defined, and smaller players to operate is necessary. 'Enabling Telecom and Internet Connectivity in Small Towns and Rural India' (Ashok Jhunjhunwala and Bhaskar Ramamurthi) describes ways to achieve a sudden jump in Internet and telecom usage. Essentially the need is to pursue cost-reducing approaches rather than feature-adding research which has a functionality in the rich countries given high incomes and high telecom densities. Few transnationals would be interested in cost-reducing research since they would have geared up for the biggest and most lucrative markets. 'Number Portability: Why do we need it?' (Dheeraj Sanghi) examines the importance of number portability in the working of the competitive market for telecom services. The steep fall in 1–800 number prices as the US regulators announced a phased plan for number portability is interesting. Despite appearances to the contrary, an early pursuit of number portability can do much for competition in telecom services. The poor also use STD facilities at PCOs and the assumption that STD is used largely by business and the rich is not quite correct. 'STD Calls are Not a Preserve of the Rich' (S. Manikutty) brings this out.

The spatial context of infrastructure could not be as effectively covered in this report as we would have liked. Industrial parks and rural infrastructure, except drinking water, have not been covered here. More importantly, there are, we know, major distortions in the market for urban land. Very severe restrictions in land use, cumbersome processes for changes in land use permits, rent control, and punitive taxes on sale of land create a highly distorted market, wherein the prices that rule are no indication of true social costs or scarcities. Investment decisions based on these prices could carry the distortions further into the economy as has most certainly happened in the larger cities. This problem still remains to be addressed and it is hoped that a future issue of the IDR would be able to take up the topic of urban land and its use. The 74th Amendment to the Constitution (CAA74) that sought to give power, autonomy, and fiscal devolution to urban local bodies is an important focus of the chapter on the spatial context of infrastructure. Financing and Functioning of Urban Local Bodies: A Situation Report' (M. P. Mathur) examines the present situation statistically. It draws attention to the poor fiscal situation, and lack of autonomy despite the changes since the CAA74. Again, quite like the situation with regard to the right to information bill, there has been major divergence between the form and content of the devolution. State governments have 'hedged' the independence of urban local bodies, keeping many important powers at the state level and making other devolutions contingent upon the state governments' own assessment. The urban bodies of the largest cities in any case have had the relevant autonomy and the reasons for their poor performance lie elsehere in competitive politics, in their relationship with state governments, in irrational tariff policies, in poor organizational processes, especially in the confusion of responsibility between the elected and nonelected officials. The promise held out for the smaller municipalities by the CAA74 has been belied. The urban bodies are under much fiscal stress and those without access to revenues from octroi and entry taxes have not even been able to maintain existing levels of service. The only answer is rationalizing user charges and better collection of local taxes. The potential though is very good, but not generally recognized as such, since the paradigm of free water and sewerage is deeply entrenched. 'Local Governance in small towns in Gujarat since the 74th Amendment: First Impressions' (Alice Albin Morris and Vivek Raval) brings out the fact that despite the CAA74 nothing has really changed in four small towns in Gujarat.

'Implications of the 74th Amendment on the Water and Waste water Sector' (Anish Nanavaty) brings out the dismal situation with regard to water in most municipalities. The fact that muncipalities do not have the freedom to chose the organization with whom they can deal to provide water and sewerage services, is a major limitation. They have to necessarily deal with the parastatal bodies of the state government. Responsibility is therefore displaced and poor and indequate coverage

results with the municipalities having little incentive to charge fully to expand the service since that is 'not part of their brief'. In some cases since supplies to industry are under the purview of parastatals rather than the urban bodies, they are also denied good revenues. Coverage of water remains poor and, even worse, the actual consumption by the poor remains woefully inadequate. 'How Low User Charges for Drinking Water Act against the Interests of the Poor' (Sebastian Morris) conceptualizes how low charges actually deny the poor access to water. Low charges with restricted supply create a shortage and the elastic demand of the rich typically 'competes' with the inelastic demand of the poor. In that unequal struggle the poor most certainly lose and suffer 'denial'. Access to and use of sewerage services have been even more skewed. We could not, unfortunately, take a look at the performance of water supply systems, with their large losses and leakages. An average of 40 per cent of water is either lost or illegally diverted. While the rural people should have had easy access to drinking water, at least in such areas as are not severely water scarce, the reality is very different. Pollution, competition from urban areas, and, most importantly, diversion to agricultural use, since drinking water tends to have the least priority, have caused much denial in rural areas. 'Rural Drinking Water Supply: Issues and Strategies' (Keshab Das) outlines the current situation and argues for a pluralistic approach to rural drinking water with private and cooperative efforts supplementing the state. Overdrawal of groundwater for agriculture, especially in water-scarce regions like north Gujarat and Rajasthan, which creates drinking water scarcities is interlinked with the electricity subsidies. Removal of the horse power (HP) based tariffs and the subsidization of pumping can bring down the deadweight losses in the economy. This is brought out in 'Over exploitation of Ground Water can be Overcome by Correctly Pricing Electricity and Diesel' (Sebastian Morris).

In 'Dealing with Drought' (Saumyen Guha) argues the case for storage of water in small reservoirs and ponds with local initiative and involvement of the people. Assignment of water rights will be crucial to the success of such efforts.

Urban transport has characteristics of its own. Urban space, especially central space being limited, congestion cannot be entirely avoided. The density of traffic and population implies that the social cost of private motorized transport is more than the private costs. Besides pollution, congestion creates this anomaly. In the Indian context the different types of road users, ranging from pedestrians (not just moving between two stages or modes of motorized transport) and cycles, besides motorized two wheelers, buses, and cars, impose their own special problems, which planners do not typically understand or incorporate in their designs. Thus in Delhi the fact that buses and cycles share the same road space imposes very large negative externalities on the cyclist. Accident rates for pedestrians and cyclists are very large. When the problem is approached from the point of view of safety, altogether different possibilities suggest themselves to increase the carrying capacity of the transport system of a city like Delhi. These insights are outlined and developed in 'Urban and Inter-urban Road Designs in India: Issues Concerning Mixed Traffic' (Geetam Tiwari). Special lanes for cyclists and traffic separation can greatly increase carrying capacity. In contrast conventional planning which emphasizes flyovers and speedways may actually reduce carrying capacity. The chapter puts forward the basics of a design of city roads and traffic management that is at once humane and efficient, and has wide relevance in bus-based cities like Delhi. The fact that for a long time to come the majority of the Indian population would not be able to afford cars, taken together with the constraint that expensive metro systems are out in this era of state contraction, means that most cities should find the safety-based simulation approach of Tiwari useful.

Delhi's infamous blue/red line bus service stands exposed as the worst possible kind of privatization and has imposed upon the population of Delhi very high accident rates. The irrational routes, the small size of the operators, and the lack of any kind of control over the operators are brought out in 'Bus Transport in Delhi' (B. R. Marwah, V. K. Sibal, and Sujata Sawant). As long as the scam of the Delhi bus system continues there is no hope for privatization of urban bus services. 'Vehicular Air Pollution in India: Recent Control Measures and Related Issues' (B. P. Pundir) critically looks at the strategy of the government to control pollution by specifying the engine type and limits on exhaust gases.

# 2 | ISSUES IN INFRASTRUCTURE DEVELOPMENT TODAY: THE INTERLINKAGES

*Sebastian Morris*

## INTRODUCTION

Infrastructure development is at a crucial juncture in India today. Tentative steps have been taken towards a more pluralistic provisioning, especially by the private sector, and as a result infrastructure as a whole has reached a point of irreversibility. It is no longer possible to go back to the old mode wherein the state, both central and provincial, actively provided the bulk of physical infrastructure. The reason is not that 'the state has no funds', as many believe, but the enormous waste, including the dead-weight losses of the old mode, that stands exposed.

In a broader sense, what has failed is not state ownership per se, but the assumption that in a large market economy many infrastructural sectors could indefinitely be run non-commercially. Yet the steps taken in the 1990s do not necessarily add up to a change in the right direction. Indeed, as I will argue, some of the important changes brought about ostensibly to further commercialization may actually have damaged its long-term prospects. These dysfunctional changes will soon have to be corrected.

### No Longer a Question of Signalling

Even if change necessarily involves signalling, to both the concerned 'public' and the world at large, that India is credibly moving away from its closed door controlled economy, enough time has already passed. Many more pressing priorities beyond mere communication of the intent of change have emerged. The need for action and for demonstration of an ability to address the problems of change as they come along, through the framework of an overall stated strategy, is acute. Thus the viability of the infrastructure business of domestic financial

institutions, encouraged to lend to commercially oriented infrastructure, is itself at stake. The growth rates of infrastructural development in sectors like power, water, and roads have fallen well below the rates achieved in the 1980s.

The question no longer is whether or not to privatize, or, more generally, bring about incentive compatibility, but how to do so. That puts us at a crossroads where one path is a more thought through, sustainable, and socially beneficial privatization and commercial provisioning. The other, which can be tempting to decision makers and lenders alike, is essentially one of 'privatizing' without a proper fiscal and institutional basis which can only lead to a deeper mess and greater catastrophe. That policy makers will make mistakes is inevitable. But that the mistakes should have such major consequences, as has happened in India, is not acceptable. The effect of mistakes on the economy can be minimized, if a direction or a desired state (in the near future) is credibly indicated at the very beginning. Unfortunately, in a country where many policies typically originate from the desk of a harried bureaucrat in the form of a 'note' or paper, inevitably the immediate situation looms very large and ominous. The need for consistency and internal coherence with the change taking place in the rest of the economy is often sacrificed and the long-term value of a contemplated measure could then become a casualty. Added to that, there is the tendency towards 'tokenism' (to show that change is taking place) rather than change which is more difficult to bring about: its design requires the services of experts and many minds and involves many more departments and institutions. This results, often enough, in policies and actions that could be quite dysfunctional to the overall progress of reform. Such ad hocism would not reveal credibly the end state or the direction that is intended. As a result, mistakes in policy even when they are reversed have a much greater negative impact on the economy than they should have.

In many areas of infrastructure, such as telecommunications, power, road transport, and airlines, it is possible and necessary to make long-term commitment, at least to the extent that the government spells out in some manner the state in which it wants the industry to be. In other words, there is then scope for a transparent and risk-reducing change.

There is increased acceptance by workers that change is inevitable and that their collective role should not generally go beyond issues of income and working conditions into questioning or insisting upon particular forms of organizations and particular prices for the services of their organizations. Hence the absence of an announced strategy is disturbing. Surely the argument that the announcements would only have given workers the scope to protest is less convincing today. Even when there are outright statements of commitment to privatization of central public sector undertakings (PSUs), the avoidance of a legislated process of privatization does not augur well. The need to distance the privatization process from the government and its day-to-day exigencies is obvious. In a democracy where the government itself is involved in the details of privatization of particular enterprises, it is inevitable that questions will arise about particular actions and pricing decisions in the privatization process and these will be hotly contested and opposed. The process may then be delayed indefinitely or altogether scrapped. With a credible commitment to fair and corruption free privatization, and by pursuing it through a constitutional or other distanced body, the chances of a successful privatization would, on the other hand, be bright in India today. Indeed, without that distancing and independence of the privatization process, real and quick privatization would not be possible even if the government were fair and worked in the best interests of society.

## THE SITUATION TODAY

### Infrastructure First and Later

The consensus of development economics of the 1950s and 1960s was around balanced growth of various types, including through plans. But very early, Hirschman pointed to the historical experience of unbalanced growth in industrial transformation and to the pressures for growth in other sectors to which the disequilibrium created by the process of unbalanced growth leads. Autonomous growth is hardly ever balanced or broad

based till the industrialization process is virtually complete. Outside the command economies, India has pursued a strategy of growth across the widest possible sectors and with much depth. It is now well known that huge costs were borne in pursuing the same in a closed economy framework. The costs were not only directly economic, but also administrative, resulting in the strengthening of bureaucratic controls and restrictions. The distortions that these unleashed created huge scope for rents. The year 1965, as is widely known, is a watershed in the development of the economy. The structural retrogression (Shetty 1978) that India entered into in 1965 was deep, and some of the major sectors of infrastructure, like the railways and irrigation, were its worst victims. The Indian Railways have never really recovered from the absolute decline in gross capital formation in the mid-1960s. Until 1965, the Mahalanobis Plan, with its emphasis on balance, also therefore attempted to provide infrastructure, prior to its need. The emphasis was on both physical and social infrastructure and the strategy *inter alia* was one of prioritizing infrastructure. That being so, the issue of its direction or allocation was crucial. Given the model which was based on the notion that production and physical allocation to particular sectors could be carried out in great detail, like in the Soviet Union, there could not have been a conceptual problem. This worked very well up to 1965.

### The Redistribution Agenda Emerges

The period from 1965 right up to 1979 was one of very slow growth when much of East Asia overtook India. This long period of stagnation essentially changed the focus of policy and the state, from growth and distribution to redistribution. Many of the sop programmes, the major subsidies, and the very idea that poverty had to be alleviated *separately* from the development process arose in this period as a 'self-evident truth'. In many ways, even after the two decades of good growth in the 1980s and 1990s, the assumptions and world-views formed in this period still haunt policy makers and political parties. Notably the notion that the primary purpose of the state is to carry out redistribution through an ever-expanding bureaucratic apparatus and in a detailed and micro manner persists. It has no doubt come under attack, but it remains unshaken for several reasons.

### The Problematic Growth of the 1980s and 1990s

The growth in the 1980s and 1990s, especially the latter, may not on the whole have been labour absorbing. The long period of nearly eleven years of growth, up to

1990–1 from 1979–80, without much labour absorption by the private corporate sector, was perhaps necessary to recover from the long stagnation period during which excess employment had been hoisted on the private sector through controls, dysfunctional labour movements, and hardly any competition in the market. In the 1990s the public sector showed, for the first time, a decline in employment growth. Employment till then had grown at a virtually autonomous and constant rate since 1965. The shedding of excess labour, though delayed by over ten years, was marked in sectors like textiles and other low value added activities, especially detailed manufacturing, where the public sector had to face competition, especially from smaller firms and the unorganized sector. The vast cost advantage which smaller firms have, due to the 'schism' in the labour market, is compounded by the higher growth rate in wages and lower work and productivity 'norms' in the public sector, even in comparison to the organized private sector.

Growth itself, in the 1990s, while rapid in relation to the stagnation period, was nowhere near the blazing 9–10 per cent per annum of the Chinese economy, now for well over two decades since 1978. The preceding Maoist period had itself witnessed growth at 6–7 per cent! At these growth rates, there is no need for special attention to poverty or subsidization. The poor's interest is integral to the growth process itself and in less than a couple of decades per capita income doubles. The initial near equality of incomes, brought about through the Communist Revolution, which removed at one stroke any possible demand inadequacy, was the engine of growth. To this engine was added a second one in the form of manufactured exports, since the open door policy of 1979. Chinese growth has been thoroughly labour absorbing and, contrary to popular belief, less unequal between regions than that in India! In India the need to specifically provide for the poor (or more correctly to provide sops to neutralize any possible dissent from systematically gathering strength), is therefore a result of the very slowness of growth and its specific character, in that it has hardly been labour absorbing. The schism in the labour market is, of course, one determinant, and a result as well of this specific character of growth.

### Advantages of Infrastructure Following Upon Growth

Clearly the resurgence of the 1980s led to infrastructural shortage which may have deepened in the 1990s. This transition from an infrastructure-led economy to one where infrastructure lags has its advantages! It is important to recognize that as infrastructure, especially that which has a direct bearing on production elsewhere in the economy, is constrained, the benefits to be gained in relaxing these constraints can be large enough to improve appropriability and profitability in its provisioning. When infrastructure follows industrial development, the scope for its private provisioning increases. Indeed, if commercial orientation is not resisted by the state bureaucracy and vested interests of the earlier regime, then perhaps the most important gain in infrastructure following growth is that allocative efficiency need not suffer. This is particularly relevant for a society where systems of patronage continue, without signs of abatement, despite over forty years of the formation of the Plan and a state process of making investment decisions. Investment allocation need not be based on assumptions, models, and exigencies of the planner and the politician. The economy and the market could then determine investments and location choice in a transparent manner. Investments in urban infrastructure, in towns like Tiruppur or Moradabad, bursting with economic activity, and therefore in dire need of infrastructure, would result in stupendous social returns.

### The State's Continued Say in Investment Decisions

Similarly, it is no longer necessary to predict where roads, ports, and railways will be needed. The shortages, scarcities, overloading, etc. are evident. This is so not because economic developments were allowed to lead infrastructural investments per se, but because even after the evidence of shortages, planners and politicians continued to derive their priorities in the old way. Among the worst excesses of mislocation are a steel plant in Karnataka, when in Tacher in Orissa we have (and it was known as such) the world's best site for ore, and paper mills atop hills in the North East. It must be remembered that as early as 1965, Plan-based allocations and decisions with regard to infrastructure were already being corrupted by political exigencies.[1] Indeed during the stagnation period, almost no central public enterprise, however powerful vis-à-vis the government, could have avoided suboptimal decisions, especially with regard to location but also technology and product markets, emerging out of the political process. The economics, in the form of the Plan, served to justify the decisions already taken on political and other considerations.

The tendency of the government to have a major say in infrastructure projects, even when there are shortages and congestion to lead infrastructural activity, is thus very strongly embedded. Even a very progressive BOT law of the Gujarat government has been translated by the state and politics into a set of 'projects' based on the planners' and politicians' sense of priority, rather

[1] For instance, see Das (1997); also Das (1999).

than on demand per se. To the extent that the basket of projects is large enough and there is a clear commitment to involve the private sector, and in the structural details of the project the private sector is not shielded from demand risks, there is scope for the allocation of resources to be driven by the economics. Nevertheless the allocative efficiency gains would be nowhere near what they could have been had visible shortages and constraints driven prioritization of projects.

## The Large Costs of Denial

Infrastructure that comes later has another advantage. Shortages are capable of revealing willingness to pay. The true value of denial and therefore of the true cost of exclusion of the 'outsider' become known. Today the cost borne by the 'outsider' is not equal to the value of the resource consumed by an equivalently placed 'insider', but is closer to his willingness to pay. Water market prices in and around most cities not covered by public supply in India and sales of privately generated electricity by using locally made contraptions hitched to slow speed diesel engines (and increasingly by more standard diesel generator (DG) sets), in places like Patna city even to poor households, tell us a lot about the willingness to pay. At a fraction of these prices, the expansion of many services would hardly require any special measures like subsidies, only an orderly liberalization and removal of other legal hurdles to commercial provisioning and entry. Even suboptimal entry, at least till such time as most of the glaring shortages are overcome, would be better than continued denial.

## Urban Road and Space 'Congestion' and Simulation Approaches

The only exception would obviously be urban road congestion and congestion on metro buses and trains as in Mumbai and Calcutta. This is because urban central space is constrained. There is only so much of it. Here there will have to be planning approaches that use simulation to examine the effects of alternative proposals such as denser packing of office and residential space by allowing a higher floor space index (FSI), or coordinated and asymmetric signals during peak hours. Contemplated bans on personal motorized transport in certain areas, shifting of transport-intensive activities to more 'appropriate' locations and freer land use rules and restrictions could also be examined by the simulation mode. The simulation mode has become increasingly relevant and appropriate not only because sophisticated computers and software are easily available, but also because the notion that the physical design, as also the design of rules, can and often does have consequences

not envisaged by designers is given its due weight. By assigning an 'autonomy' to users and agents (in a stylistic manner no doubt) in simulation models, serious users of such models have an orientation and philosophy quite different from central planners or from planners and architects with their unquestioned a priories.

## Infrastructure Developed Later But With the Willingness to Direct and Shepherd

Commercially oriented infrastructure would ensure that little or no infrastructure remains idle. Thus we would not have empty trains running from Ahmedabad to Rajkot or from Trivandrum to Kanyakumari, just to satisfy some perceived value in trains that 'span the length and breadth of the country', while elsewhere people have to travel packed like sardines.

## Infrastructure Later Conserves Capital

Infrastructure that is created later conserves capital and results in fuller utilization. This can reduce the economy-wide capital–output ratio. It is most pertinent to note that much of East Asia, until recently, was in a situation of infrastructure created later (perhaps more because of the extremely rapid growth of manufacturing). In the 1990s, huge capital inflows allowed it to go in for infrastructure, anticipating (not necessarily correctly) future infrastructural needs. The high risk of lengthening payback periods, even as the tenure of finances was declining, because an increasing part of the funding was from foreign sources, was at the root of the East Asian crisis.

While there are severe shortages, a significant part of existing infrastructure in India is underused or even un-used, such as in cities with overprovisioning of roads but having absurd design, like Delhi, Chandigarh, and Gandhinagar, and roads which only politicians and bureaucrats need, such as those between Gandhinagar and Ahmedabad. Other examples of misdirected resource allocation are plush airports where there are only two flights a day, even as others are woefully short of passenger amenities, and Rajdhani and Shatabdi first classes that run with the occasional government passenger. Such misdirections are so pervasive that the enormity of the costs that they impose are hardly even realized. Due to delays and cost overruns which erode the productive value of savings, public enterprise may have imposed a penalty of as much as 1.5 to 2.0 per cent on the growth rate of the economy! If to that the costs of the underutilized and unutilized infrastructure are added, the growth penalty may have been even higher! Who has borne these costs? Obviously the poor, especially those who are still unemployed, since they, more than others, would have gained through faster growth; and of course the 'outsider', as also perhaps the capitalists. Only the middle classes may not have suffered much, because of their fixed and rising incomes, which do not depend much on the growth in the economy. In fact they have the benefit of cheaper services, including those of domestic servants, in an economy that has little dynamism in creating factory jobs. Moreover they can always rely upon some kind of preferential access to infrastructural services in short supply.

Despite all the benefits of later infrastructure, they arise quite clearly from having fallen behind the theoretically optimum proportion of infrastructure. While this is true, what is being argued is that the informational, governance, and institutional costs of remaining close to or above optimum level can be too large for a transforming economy, with pressures on the state to spread thin the resources for infrastructural investment Other than that it places a greater reliance on the planner and the politician rather than on the market. In the given situation of large-scale state failure in India, the late arrival of infrastructure has its obvious advantages.

## MACROECONOMIC LINKAGES

### *Demand Owes Much to Infrastructural Investments*

Not only in journalistic discussions, but surprisingly, even in academia, the demand aspect of infrastructure hardly ever finds mention. The sectors electricity, gas, and water (EGW) of the Central Statistical Organisation (CSO) and transport, storage and communication (TSC) while constituting barely 10 per cent of the GDP constitute 25 per cent of the gross domestic capital formation (GDCF). This is an aspect of the stage of development of the economy. With better incomes, the contribution of non-input infrastructure like housing and urban services will increase. Composition apart, until the industrialization process is completed and for some time after that, when other infrastructure like housing, shopping malls, and city formation functions improve, the gross domestic capital formation (GDCF) in infrastructure would be larger than its relative contribution to gross domestic product (GDP). Certainly at the stage of development the country is in, productive or input-type infrastructure—power, irrigation, basic water, and sewerage in urban areas, telecom, basic and technical education, roads for trucks and buses, ports and railways—will have to expand at a rate at least corresponding to the growth rate of the economy. In these areas, except possibly telecom, the longer life of assets than those in manufacturing, other services, and the primary sector obviously means that the investment

pressure from infrastructure is a major source of the investment demand in the economy.

Therefore, ceteris paribus, the investments actually made in infrastructure have a major impact on income level via the demand multiplier. Indeed, in barely open economies, like the Indian economy before 1984 and the Chinese economy before 1978, investments in infrastructure (largely in the public sector), along with agricultural output, were the principal drivers of the economy. Today, along with these, exports too have become principal exogenous categories of expenditures for both the economies.

The developments in the 1990s, following the stabilization of 1991–2 and the structural adjustment thereafter, are worth recalling. The tightening budgets of public enterprises, arising out of sharp expenditure reductions, hurt investments in infrastructure, bringing about a significant drop in the rate of capacity additions. Overall, the reduction in public expenditure has fallen in a large measure on investments in general and more particularly on infrastructural investments. As arising out of the liberal strategy of rolling back the state, even after the economy had been stabilized, this was to be expected, since the public sector had a predominant role in infrastructure and tightening its budgets would also affect infrastructure.

### *Rising Private Investments in Manufacturing Masked Decline in (Public) Investments in Infrastructure*

Yet, once the economy stabilized by 1992–3, investments grew very rapidly, despite the relative slowdown in public (and infrastructural) investments. This was because investments as a whole were kept up at earlier rates of growth, or higher, by the very large rise in private investments, largely in manufacturing. While private investments seemed to rise in areas like power, they slowed down after a while and in any case their rise was too small to replace the large shortfall in public investments. At that time in 1996–7, I (Morris 1997) argued that the economy would slow down because exports had been affected by adverse exchange rate policy and the scope for private investment in the aggregate to continue at the earlier high rate was not really there. (Recovery from the recession took two years and even today the pointless defence of the currency and attendant inability to lower interest rates will continue to hold back the growth of the economy!)

The reason private investment could not have risen to fill the void created by the falling off of public investment after 1996–7 is because then (and even as yet) the policy, legal, and institutional clarity, besides the price reform necessary for private sector entry into infrastructure on a large scale had not come. It could not have come quickly, certainly not in India, where change typically has been of the two-steps-forward-one-step-backward variety. The reforms needed for private capital to enter on a large scale will have to be deep and fundamental and involve major shifts away from the current paradigm. Privatization on 'escrow' or 'lease' basis could only have gone thus far. It will, in other words, require the second or constructive stage of reforms.

## Even State Investments in Infrastructure are Better than No Investments

Here it is important to remember that uncertainty with regard to infrastructure (and ideological and financial restrictions on the public sector investing) creates a depressionary pressure. Thus the economy bears a cost and a risk in growing more slowly. In the 1980s, with the state investing (however inefficiently), this demand side factor was not adverse and did not slow down the economy.

## Higher 'Target' Growth for Monetary Policy

Despite this, realized growth rates in the 1990s have not been low. Indeed, they have on the average been only marginally less for the industrial sector than those in the 1980s, and probably higher for the economy as a whole, owing to the faster growth of the services sector.[2] Rather than using this fact to justify conservative macro-economic policies, as the Reserve Bank of India (RBI) has all along been doing, it is necessary to recognize that the achievable growth rates are considerably higher than what is generally believed—possibly even as high as 9 per cent (Morris 1997). Monetary policy, including monetization of fiscal deficit, could have been much more ambitious and exchange rate pricing more aggressive than the general consensus would have it.

A revival of infrastructural investment could indeed force the government and the RBI to accept this higher growth potential of the economy and hence an alternative higher equilibrium, where a 5 per cent overall fiscal deficit is actually sustainable (and possibly necessary) for some years to come.[3] Infrastructural investment will then be higher than that in the 1990s. With money

supply growth faster[4] than in the 1990s and much lower exchange rates, the openness of the economy increases steadily through higher growth of the traded sector at between 50 and 100 per cent faster than the rest of the economy. Inflation may be marginally higher at 7–8 per cent[5] rather than the present 6–7 per cent, but the real interest rate would be lower by at least three percentage points. In that situation, growth would be closer to 9 per cent.

## Economic Revival Requires Infrastructural Investment

The leverage point for change would be both investments in infrastructure, and exports (through the exchange rate), to affect demand positively. Thus, not only from supply side considerations, but even more urgently on account of the demand side, infrastructural investments will have to revive. The matter may be so urgent that if private investments are going to be delayed for the reasons mentioned above and the corrections to relax the constraints are not forthcoming in the near future, a reversion to public investments will be necessary.

## Large Potential for Private Investments

The potential for genuine private investment, with the right kind of reform, is large because of certain interrelated factors. The areas of infrastructure that have functionality at this point (from the supply side, or requirements) are power, telecom, roads, and urban water. All except roads are highly appropriable and much of telecom is possible even via competition modes! There is no problem of excludability in all of these except roads. Even here the build, operate, and transfer (BOT) route will be valid and provide substantial private investment, till such time as bottleneck situations are addressed and relaxed. Thus a crash restructuring of the

---

[2] Higher export growth at least till 1996–7 and an average agricultural growth of 3.2 per cent (from the 1980s' 3.0 per cent) and structural changes towards higher productivity industries may have been responsible.

[3] Applying a suitable growth rate of exports of 15 per cent per annum instead of 10 per cent, a growth rate of the economy of 8 per cent instead of 6 per cent, and an inflation rate of 8 per cent instead of 5 per cent on a standard sustainable primary overall fiscal deficit formula, a figure much higher than the generally assumed 2.30 per cent is arrived at, viz. 4.56 per cent.

[4] Targeting money supply growth may not be the right strategy in India. (For the first couple of years of stabilization, one could grant the validity of monetary targeting.) Even elsewhere, economies like the US—where the money multiplier has been far more stable than in India—have grown much faster by shedding their earlier monetarist conservatism and targeting interest rates.

[5] The assumption that inflation is essentially a monetary phenomenon is not quite correct. At inflation above 9 per cent, money supply growth is no doubt the driving factor. At rates much below, up to about 8 per cent, it is the price of primary products whose supply and demand are both inelastic in the short run that has driven the inflation rate in India. Primary products, especially agricultural, have a volatility which is more than double that of manufactured goods, when we look at monthly data. Thus buffer stocking of food and an incomes policy that links spending to the investment demand will be the solution for the economy. Indeed, a well-thought-out incomes policy has *inter alia* been a facet of high speed growth in East Asia, including that of Japan in the 1950s and early 1960s.

power sector on the lines suggested in this report[6] and opening up of the telecom sector on the lines of the Prime Minister's Office's Draft Bill will be necessary. Similarly, the opening up of the urban water sector, especially distribution, to BOT at least in areas not presently covered, or poorly covered by existing public enterprises or parastatals, will help the urban poor a great deal. The last would no doubt entail that urban bodies have the freedom to act and to initiate opening up the water and sewerage sectors with minimal regulation, limited to standards of safety and possibly a liberal price cap. In roads the decision to set up an autonomous road fund with substantial stakeholding by road users and citizens would make it feasible for the private sector to go beyond toll roads, to own and operate even urban roads. In all these, detailed analytical work to produce requisite legal and contractual documents, as also bills to be tabled in legislative bodies will take time. But the point really is to draft and declare a clear overall strategy that outlines the future course of action and the objective of reform. In a sense what we are saying is that there should be 'equifinality' in government actions to necessarily lead to the announced state of the industry.

## THE APPROACH TO REFORM AND RESTRUCTURING

### State Ownership Did Not Overcome Coordination Failure

It is relevant at this point to recall that one dimension of the state failure that brought about the crisis of the early 1990s was precisely its inability to coordinate across sectors. It may be emphasized that this need for coordination was perhaps the most important reason for state ownership in these sectors in the first place. Indeed, the whole idea of the intersectoral consistency plan that India pursued for over four decades essentially arose out of the recognition of such interrelationships. That the effort has failed is not because the need or the opportunity for coordination and interdependence is any less, but because it has not been adequately and appropriately pursued. Planners did not attempt to translate the desired goals and targets into prices, incentives, and consistent rules, but sought to direct agents through administrative fiat in what was even then essentially a market economy.

### The Mode of State Direction is Important

The option of directives, controls, and administration through parastatals and public enterprises was an easy

[6] See section 7.3 in this report.

one for the bureaucracy. It would have been intellectually demanding to translate the desired goals and targets into prices, taxes, and rules, in a manner that created appropriate incentives for agents and managers to act and move towards the very same goals. The intellectual environment of that period which did not question the state's ability or capacity (or even motivation) to carry out the task of directing and controlling the economy, has certainly been part of the problem. In a short time, certainly by the mid-1960s, the inconsistencies which created rents had backlash effects, resulting in a political and economic structure in which rents and profits were so closely intertwined, as to be impossible to disentangle. For the future, piecemeal approaches are no longer feasible. Thus, even while the decisions and legislations may be slow, the strategy for the change cannot be incomplete if it is to become a credible (and inevitable) guide to the future.

### Commercialization of Investment Decisions is the Real Challenge

The objective of early planners to arrive at some understanding of the contours of a desirable future remains valid in a market economy. But now the attempt ought to be to steer the economy with fewer and less dysfunctional instruments, or even to allow the economy to find its own way. This is the challenge of reform in the Indian context.

It goes without saying that there will be situations where the future is only dimly discerned, where predictability is poor, or even where there are no obvious instruments to lead the economy. In such situations, simple rules that enhance the role of markets, not just in producing and selling but also in investments, i.e. to allow and create conditions for markets to play a bigger role in the allocative process, would be functional to the growth and development of the economy.

The challenge of reform and privatization is really to bring the market process into allocative decisions. Governments everywhere shy away from this role for markets with regard to infrastructure. The Indian state, which has the task of balancing various pressure groups and competing regions, would be most reluctant to concede any reduction in its own role in investment decisions. To bring the investment decisions in infrastructure into the market process remains a challenge in many sectors, especially in sectors where failure arises from lack of excludability. The problem is more important to transforming economies like India, where the task of building basic infrastructure lies ahead.

The shift to privatization of infrastructure from a state-dominated system cannot be easy or sudden. It may not even be necessary to start with. Allowing managers the freedom to manage and organizations the basis to be commercially oriented is good enough. Yet in practical terms the Indian government, at both state and central levels, has not shown the capacity to allow managers of public enterprises to work without political interference. It has also not been able to refrain from setting prices that are unsustainable. Infrastructure with state-dominated provisioning poses the dual challenge of privatization (which it shares with all public enterprises in general) and of overcoming in some manner the 'market failure' that is a characteristic of it. Regulation, detailed or otherwise, and market creation through a clear definition of property rights are important means to overcome market failure. Similarly, creating incentive compatibility through appropriate choices and restrictions on ownership is also a significant means to curb market failure. The market-creating power of high speed and networked computers, when brought to the aid of these approaches, can considerably enhance the process of commercialization of infrastructure.

### Mode of Redistribution is the Problem

The above tasks would be common to reforms anywhere. The Indian situation offers specific challenges which can hardly be understood completely with reference to experiences elsewhere. The context is very important. Often policy makers and analysts complain that change is politically difficult and eminently good measures such as tariff reform and removal of poorly directed subsidies are viewed as impossible without political will. Hence reform is slowed down or altogether stalled . The problem, while requiring a political solution today, may itself have been a creation of the past. For example the decision to subsidize or redistribute may not have been wrong per se, but its mode might be questionable. Thus the creation of the well-entrenched nexus in adulterating and short measuring petrol, diesel, cooking gas and other oil products. These vested interests are a creation of the original ham-handedness of the policy, and are today strong enough to slow down or even stall change.

### Vested Interests Can Be Countered

From comparative studies of the Indian state and the strong East Asian states, we do know that the latter intervened as much, and perhaps even more strongly, than did India. But they showed an ability to be conscious of the 'unintended' and compositional consequences of government direction, unlike the Indian state. They have also tended to periodically correct such consequences. In India, slower state and bureaucratic processes, inadequate coordination across and within

vast bureaus, and perhaps even quicker response of agents to exploit the rent opportunities so created were res-ponsible for the pervasiveness of distortions and rent-seeking behaviour. Eventually, vested interests have evolved. Yet one must not exaggerate the power of vested interests, since there are always others outside the current system of benefits and rent generation, that could be mobilized for change. Potentially, such 'outsiders' are larger in number and await the 'political entre-preneurship' that would mobilize and activate them to be the vanguards of change.

### ILL-CONCEIVED REFORMS

Vested interests may not have been the principal reason for the slowness of reforms in the 1990s. Poor conception and design may be the chief culprits. Additionally, resistance from the bureaucracy and poor credibility of the reformers to carry out reforms in a fair and non-partisan manner have created doubts about their benefits among sections that could potentially have been the most important gainers. The tendency to make do with 'known' persons—retired bureaucrats and judges—rather than bringing in experts and special competencies has also contributed to the slowness and ineptness of certain reform initiatives. Analytically it is not certain that the same forces which pushed for the early reforms (the so-called first stage of the reforms), and gained sub-stantially from them, will not oppose the next stage of the more challenging reforms. There is, therefore, no doubt about the need to find new allies, including those without voices. There may even be need to keep at a distance the elements that supported and pushed for reforms in the first stage. Thus, independent power producers (IPPs), early developers, foreign institutional investors (FIIs), and governments with changeable commitment to the economy could resist change if competition in the broadest sense were to emerge to challenge the profitability of their early investments.

### The Challenge of Constructive Reforms

The early phase of the reform, where the constructive aspect was small, needs to be distinguished from reforms needed now that have to, *inter alia*, construct markets where none existed before. It has also to create new institutions with more appropriate incentive structures and codify simple rules that are conditional rather than absolute. Similarly there is need to clarify and refine property rights and bring about common property management approaches to overcome certain kinds of market failure. While the dismantling of licences, removal of import controls and restrictions, relaxation of entry restrictions for foreign capital and the lifting of the ban on the private sector in certain product markets were all relatively uncomplicated, the changes required today are not so. The problem is not only more complex, but solutions will also depend on the specificities of society, economy, and state capacity. Thus learning from experience elsewhere in the world while important would be far more contingent. There are no simple substitutes for creative approaches. The possibility of being overwhelmed by the received wisdom is large.

## Consumers' Interest as the A Priori Concern of Reforms

In bringing about infrastructural reform today, the emergent and the unanticipated aspects are large. I have already stated, therefore, that the scope and need for a strategy of reform are substantial. What can be the common contents of such a reform? Much of it would, understandably, depend upon the particular sector and the specific possibilities of liberalization, the nature of market and state failure that may exist, and other dimensions of the industrial structure. But certainly, the strategy can always reiterate that the purpose of reform lies in the interest of consumers and society as a whole. Thus reforms should have as their priority consumer and societal interests and not the means or intermediate goals such as privatization, or bringing about independent regulation. Many contradictions which regulators today face would not be existing had the consumer been given primacy.

## External Pressures Alone are Inadequate

Infrastructure sectors such as roads, housing, water supply, and sanitation, which, in contrast to other sectors like telecom or power, use traded goods to a lesser extent in their construction and operation, are, therefore, less likely to be subject to external pressure for change. The pressures would have to come from within, or possibly from development financial institutions (DFIs) and multilateral agencies (MLAs). External private interests would tend to be limited to consulting firms and lenders and it is not always the case that the optimal and sustainable reform is necessary for their projects' success. Project success may well be better assured by certain suboptimal (from a societal point of view) contracts that protect the interest of the lender rather than true reform. The danger of a spate of such suboptimal contracts 'defining', through their practice, the nature of change is large. This is especially so when the change has been driven by the presumption that 'the state has no money'.

## LEVERAGE POINTS FOR CHANGE

### Deregulation and Commercialization to Correct State Failure

A valid issue that arises is: it was state failure that brought about the crisis of the economy and the short provisioning of infrastructure in the first place. And now if the state has an important role in creating appropriate strategies and institutions for regulation, is there any real hope for infrastructure unless state failure is overcome? Even privatization and orderly and correct deregulation would require state capacity. To get a handle on this important question, it is necessary to understand the nature of state failure in India. It is certainly not a failure arising out of incompetence, since even today many individuals within the bureaucracy and those outside, but on call, have all the skills to analyse and find solutions to most problems. Similarly, the average Indian politician is more educated than those in many other countries including the US. State failure is primarily one of incentive incompatibility and the distortions that have followed therefrom. As a result, there is a major mismatch between responsibility and authority. Existing structures, reporting relationships, and processes more generally have resulted in the displacement or dilution of responsibility. Even when organizations of the state have started with concern for the primary task, deterioration along these lines has been common. Corruption in high places is also an important dimension of state failure, but as earlier stated, corruption feeds on the inappropriate design of organizations and on 'policies that create rents'. Despite all that has happened thus far, the Indian state machinery cannot be called 'kleptocratic'.[7]

### Reform Does Not Need 'Ideal' Bureaucracies

Perhaps the most important reason for commercialization and privatization is that commercialized or privatized enterprises demand good and competent processes and structures only within a small part of the overall governmental machinery, possibly not even all the time. Thus, even if the bulk of the public works department (PWD) is corrupt or caught in a quagmire of impotence, a small group, well shielded for a while from dysfunctional bureaucratic and political processes and possibly having the support of the top politician, can push through, for example, a worthy BOT law. Once a few projects go through in a fair fashion and a process is established, the potential of substantial sections of the state machinery to delay and hold back

[7] Many in Africa are indeed so [Leys (1975) & Shivji (1976)].

change is reduced. Indeed, as a result, the pressures on these organizations to change may well increase. Even if they do not change, instead of stalling projects and infrastructure businesses, their activities may then merely add some costs (rent) to them.

It is because of this ability to do with less than uniformly good state systems that commercialization and the private sector's role become vital. If indeed pluralistic delivery takes place, the backlash effects of the same could generally clean up the rest of the machinery, since the returns to corruption fall dramatically as competition emerges and the returns of technology and better management improve. This has already taken place in manufacturing industries in India in the 1990s and it is now beginning to show where independent regulators are fighting to do their jobs.

### All or None Kind of Change is Very Difficult

Even in the most dismal of state systems, there are people who are not corrupt and make honest efforts to pursue the primary task. A wholesale replacement of state administration, even a thoroughly corrupt one, has been rare. A quick change for the better via reform of governance that includes the state machinery has also been rare and is almost impossible without revolutionary political change. The Indian state system is, all said and done, 'fair' in politics, at least to those who have voices (and most do). To 'insiders', that is those with some endowments, it is fair even in an economic sense. Thus the state has a legitimacy which goes beyond the credibility of particular governments and their policies. Moreover, those actively involved in corruption are basically few. Many within the administrative system are in a state of impotence because of the cumulative impact of past mistakes that have brought about incentive incompatibilities and reduced the scope for action. There are many honest civil servants, who even within the current system, are able to take risks pursuing change. Would such groups reach the critical minimum size for large-scale change?

### 'Leverage' Points for Change

Change that starts small but attacks key leverage points of the system has great potential and may even have begun to occur. Ushering in markets and commercialization in infrastructure can build upon such changes to unleash the potential of the economy and its positive feedback effects on the state system. True reform would have such effects. With the economy growing at much higher rates than at present, 'outsiders' could soon become 'insiders' and the returns to corruption could dwindle considerably and the stakes (and capacities) of

those who are victims could become high enough to ensure high costs to corruption. For example, the US was a very corrupt economy in the 1920s, but the economic dynamism of the 1920s gave rise to large-scale improvements in governance. Similar pressures are now at work in China, where 'campaigns', the patent response of the Chinese society to problems, have made examples out of corruption in high places. Corruption can then decline suddenly. That day may not be too far off in India, if it can shake off its current constraints to high speed 'inclusive' growth.

## PUBLIC ENTERPRISE IN INFRASTRUCTURE

### 'Hardening' Versus Performance Budgets

One essential aspect of the reform thus far has been the very significant hardening of the budgets of public enterprises. The central PSUs almost immediately after 1991–2 felt the pinch of cutbacks in budgetary contributions. With a lag, state-level PSUs and local bodies which have a big role in the provision of physical infrastructure also felt the heat. 'Hardening' of budgets can create conditions for task orientation and for tariff reform in the organizations which then have to cope with falling contributions from the state. But thus far to rely on that aspect alone has been quite short-sighted. It has meant that the potential to use related and complementary instruments like variability in the hardening of budgets, performance linking of budgets and resources, discretionary and incentive pay for employees of public enterprises has been missed. Simple hardening of budgets for a parastatal, while salaries of workers and managers alike as employees of the state are protected, is hardly a situation likely to improve efficiency. If a small portion (even additional) of employees' wages and salaries could be linked to performance improvement and to the surpluses or losses reduced, then hardening budgets could work to improve systemic efficiency. There is much variation in the degree of public enterprise performance even when adjusted for differing opportunities. Linking of earnings of employees with performance is then possible. No doubt, these cannot lead to optimal investment decisions per se, till such time as the entity in question itself generates a substantial part of its investment requirements. Similarly, when the enterprises in question do not have their own specific and separate budgets, or when change in one set of enterprises is desired, across the board hardening could result in perverse behaviour. Thus, in many states, state-level PSUs continue to exist and new ones are set up, even as those employing semi-skilled and unskilled workers are closed. This is being done so that bureaucrats and politicians do not lose those 'expense accounts'. The key to the successful working of hardened budgets is stakeholding—of employees and managers—in the future of the enterprise in question. This may help in changing the behaviour of managers; those who are part of a cadre and whose career paths and salaries are almost entirely independent of the performance of the enterprise they manage would be little affected by hardening budgets.

## The Bogey of Social Considerations

Unfortunately, so-called social considerations have loomed large, thwarting and resisting commercial provisioning. One must recognize that, despite over forty years of state-directed and -controlled provisioning with low prices, in the name of the poor, neither regional nor income inequality is in any way less than in many other countries. The spread of modern infrastructure like electricity, piped drinking water, and telephones is well below that in countries like China. More than this fact, the reasons for failure to cover, via publicly provided infrastructure, as much of the population as was desired and expected to be covered remain to be systematically addressed. Low, even very low, prices can only go so far in improving consumption among the poor. The very poor can hardly be expected to consume urban sanitary services or electricity beyond the single bulb and fan, only because these services are cheap. In the long run, income is the determinant of demand and prices only an indication of costs. Thus the problem of access goes beyond infrastructure to development. Very briefly, countries in East Asia which carried out 'one-shot' land reforms, rather than using the state continually to redistribute (as India has been attempting to do), and whose industrializations were labour absorbing have had high rates of income growth and, necessarily therefore, of infrastructure development. Export orientation was an important aspect of their labour absorption. When prices are systematically kept separate from costs for long, then that effect can be recognized as equivalent to a small rise in income, usually smaller than the subsidy value of the subsidized good consumed. It is obvious that there are severe fiscal limits to raising incomes through subsidizes in an economy that has yet to make its industrial transformation.

## Problems of Indian Public Enterprise

The ritualization of processes and institutions meant to bring about functional modes of working, has been most potent in ensuring that no real or substantive change takes place even as the 'form' and symbols of change become ends in themselves. Thus the MoUs between public enterprises (CEOs) and administrative ministries, meant to free top managers from interference by government, have, in India, been almost completely ritualized. Similar arrangements have worked well in other countries, notably France. In India MoUs are paper exercises and ministries are hardly constrained by them. Enterprises show 'good to excellent' performance by soft targeting, and the ritual continues every year with more paper work and an added bureau. Similarly, holding companies which have worked well in Italy to distance management from dysfunctional interference by government have not been successful in India.

## Project Implementation

Typically benefits are overestimated and costs underestimated to show high internal rates of return (IRRs) and benefit–cost ratios. After sanction the true costs slowly emerge and delays in approval of the revised (higher) estimates recoil/turn on the project already under construction, increasing costs beyond what they could otherwise have been. Spreading the funds with the government over a larger number of projects than are feasible without delays results in additional delays and cost overruns. Other organizational inadequacies, especially when the projects are implemented by departments or departmental enterprises, with their poor or inappropriate organizational processes and lack of skills in project implementation, compound the problem. The result is very poor project implementation, with cost overruns in excess of 60 per cent. So project cost estimates are usually underestimates of the true costs, but the realized costs are equivalent to overestimates. If problems of inaccurate estimation of costs have become entrenched and inefficient practices the norm, then the public enterprise cost figures are worse than useless. This again underlines the need for benchmark studies and independent, engineering-based estimates to, if nothing else, circumscribe true costs. Otherwise private parties will be tempted to use the situation to their advantage.

## The Danger of Empty 'Solutions'

The problem of the Indian public enterprises goes far beyond the usual 'agency problem' that state-owned enterprises worldwide suffer from to some degree. There is over-manning, governmental interference at all levels, tolerance of enormous leakage and waste, highly constraining rules, and corruption.[8] In such a situation and when the pressure for reform and improved economic performance (real or token) is strong,

[8] Nevertheless there are remarkable cases that are free of these evils: the National Thermal Power Corporation (NTPC) and Bharat Heavy Electricals Limited (BHEL) would be cases in point.

there is a premium upon the 'clever' civil servant or consultant who can offer seeming 'solutions' that are such in appearance but not in content, allowing the rents in the status quo to continue.

## The Potential for Well-managed Public Enterprises

In a vast ocean of state failure, there are some examples of success of public enterprise and state provisioning: The NTPC as a player in wholesale electricity, the Maharashtra State Road Development Corporation (MSRDC) in highway planning and construction, the Tamil Nadu State Electricity Board (TNSEB) and Metro-water Chennai are reasonably efficient. The one common feature is that their managers have had a greater degree of operational autonomy. Dysfunctional government interference has been kept out in such organizations. This has happened either because the government itself made this 'one exception' as in the case of the MSRDC, or because the organizations' top managers 'fought hard' to negotiate the boundary. And the strength emanating from good performance (itself influenced by the functionality of the interface) would have given more power to top managers than in most other public enterprises. That would have allowed them to thwart repeated attempts by politicians and civil servants to interfere in operational decisions and sometimes even to resist pressures against the commercial interests of the enterprise. Thus, while the model of 'well-performing' public enterprise has largely failed in India, the few exceptions and the reasons for their success allow a more optimistic assessment of public enterprise, suitably restricted. The reasons for the same are many, but perhaps the most important is urgency. State and central governments when confronted with challenging and important tasks have, at least occasionally, been able to bring out the good aspects of state provisioning and ownership, by leaving them to the managers to do the job. Therefore the potential to avoid interference is certainly there.[9]

## Ownership and Commercial Provisioning are Not the Same

A related point is that commercial provisioning of infrastructure is neither synonymous with private provisioning, nor does public ownership necessarily have to be non-commercial in approach. Vast allocative and operational efficiency gains await reformers who can

[9] Indeed, the case for privatization in India rests on the experience that governments have continued to dysfunctionally interfere. Thus the more general solution to public enterprise performance in today's context remains disinvestments below 50 per cent.

push systems and sectors into this commercial orientation, without being orthodox about ownership. In specific situations, ownership, including a certain degree of private participation, is important because certain kinds of commercialization are easy with private participation. Even if the tendency towards dysfunctional interference can be overcome (this is not a problem in France, Italy, China, or South Korea, with much state ownership), the aspect of commercial orientation remains. Hence the crucial task of reformers concerned with restructuring is, in creating the right industry structure, and rules of behaviour both operational and investment that are in keeping with efficiency in situations of imperfect markets or even near market failure. Yet with entrenched vested interests, as in the case of state electricity boards (SEBs), reform may have to start with a change in ownership, or at least with internal incentive mechanisms within 'the existing', or their inheritor, organizations.

## Improvement in Public Enterprise Performance is Crucial to Infrastructure

Prospects for commercialization increase dramatically if improvements in the interface and attenuation of 'agency failure' can take place, because a very large part of infrastructure is in the public sector. More importantly, in crucial areas like public health, education, and perhaps even roads, the private sector would be a difficult option. This is because despite the developments in unbundling arising out of fundamental developments in contracting, technology, and market creation processes that have led to the relative decline of the classical public enterprise and of traditional detailed regulation, these areas have severe appropriability problems.

With pressures for privatization increasing by the day, the case for 'giving managers and workers a fair chance to perform by untying their hands' can also be strongly put. If indeed that happens, then part ownership by employees can be effective in bringing about incentive compatibility within existing organizations. As part of the process of liberalization, controls, fiats and case by case direction gave way to price-based instruments like tariffs and prices were brought closer to international and domestic values. In the second stage of reforms, ownership changes, the removal of distortions created by (past) policies and practices, and the removal of the many 'objectives' and constraints placed upon public enterprises can bring huge rewards. There are immediate opportunities for reformers in setting right dysfunctional interface between public organizations, and in relaxing the commercially restrictive policies on public enterprise. The ownership aspect, or disinvestment, could be considered subsequently and correcting the above distortions lays the grounds for successful privatization. Such a strategy would imply an institutional and managerial approach backed by political commitment. If that seems difficult, despite the obvious opportunity, then the only option is to wait for privatization from above.

## The Need to Eliminate Conflicting Tasks and Constraints

Public enterprises have been saddled with conflicting tasks that go beyond their primary purpose—to provide above market benefits to employees, especially at the lower levels; yet they have no freedom to pay differentially for performance and skills, subsidize and cross-subsidize—sometimes with no limits—encourage small vendors, industrialists, and local enterprise, buy from other public enterprises. They have also to maintain three parallel accounting systems, be subject to government clearance and involvement in the details of investment decisions, be amenable to advice from Parliament, and subject to operational 'guidance' from the government. If these conflicting tasks and constraints are removed, even without major ownership changes some enterprises would be able to commercially orient themselves.

## A Commercialized Public Sector is Not a Contradiction

When it is proposed that public enterprises need not be non-commercial in their approach, it seems like an untenable position to both the old proponents of the socialist model and the neoclassically inclined who believe that public enterprise should be limited to certain sectors with a public goods character. In truth, the reasons for state enterprise could go far beyond the public goods market failure or the natural monopoly situation. Public enterprises in late industrialization have been used to lead developments in particular sectors, especially the 'strategic' sectors of the economy, and to create a domestic capitalist class with the ability to hold its own against foreign capital. In this understanding there is an emergent character to markets, and public enterprise may be seen as force-feeding the development of markets. Thus the market orientation of public enterprise is a crucial aspect of not just reform of infrastructure development but of carrying through a successful industrial transformation.

## Levelling the Playing Field

What would help to bring in commercial orientation of public enterprise in infrastructure? Foremost would be the separation of subsidization from the enterprise providing the service. With regard to electricity, it is argued here that this is the first and foremost issue that needs be addressed. This separation, through the mechanism of direct subsidy, can remove in one stroke the excuse for deviations from commercial orientation and performance. This aspect has already been discussed. Next in importance would be levelling the playing field between public and private enterprises. In reforming countries, across the board budget cuts and opening up of the sector to private capital can often be under special law or directive that does not include existing public enterprises. These may then continue to be burdened under the old constraints and impositions. Thus, until recently, even as the IPPs were allowed equity rates starting with 16 per cent and going up to 30 per cent, and that too with very little business risk being borne by the equity shareholders, the NTPC was forced to take only a 12 per cent return with huge risks and on allowable depreciation rates which were much lower! This kept the NTPC's large debt and equity capacity from being brought to bear on adding to generation capacity, relatively much cheaper than what any of the new private players could offer! Had it been allowed even a 16 per cent return things would have been different. Even today the bias against the NTPC continues. There are similar examples of biases against reasonably well-performing state enterprises whose capacities and capabilities are vital to the development of infrastructure. A certain bias against an incumbent in a network industry like telecom may be desirable, but the bias often goes beyond that needed to change market structures to bring about greater commercial orientation, competition, and incentive regulation.

## PRICING AND SUBSIDIES

### The Tendency to Load an Intermediate Rather Than a Final Good: Inversion in Tariff Systems

In electricity, industry cross subsidises households in many states and agriculturalists in all states. In railways, freight cross subsidizes passengers and suburban traffic, in water, industry again cross-subsidizes households. In power and railways, we have reached a situation where the high tariffs for industrial consumers and for freight, respectively, in turn affect investment decisions! The organizations in question also continue to lose demand. The effects and the nature of these losses are discussed elsewhere. Here the focus is on the political basis for such distortionary tariffs. Price controls are an important aspect in a 'mixed economy' that sets itself a 'socialist goals'. The long years of 'redistribution as the central effort and task of the state and policy', entrenched the tendency to use prices and controls to reward and punish consumers. Thus 'luxury' products like automobiles had a total tax that may have exceeded 120 per cent on manufacturing cost. Even today, total taxes on an automobile may be as high as 90 per cent while the prices for such things as water are abysmally low.

While this may seem consistent with the planned objective of curbing unnecessary consumption to mobilize all resources for investment, in reality during the 1970s and 1980s, high and rising administered prices for inputs of industry have acted as a regressive 'taxation'. Water, electricity, coal, freight charges, and heavy taxes on energy are examples. The inputs used by industry in general cannot on any account be final luxury consumption goods. Thus the tendency to avoid bringing subsidies to bear on the budget, but to allocate them repressively on the economy as a whole, via higher input prices, is similar to the regression in using indirect taxes for revenues. Unfortunately, despite the considerable scaling down and rationalization of indirect taxes, the implicit taxes (in the cross-subsidization) have not only continued, but have even grown. They are all intimately linked to infrastructural services. They have proved difficult to reduce despite the best intentions, because the policy thus far has not explored necessary stepping stone solutions. Such solutions have to delink subsidy from the reform process, and allow the reform of infrastructural sectors to continue. In almost all situations direct subsidization would allow the link to be broken. Subsidy could then be capped and with the gains of reform, it would become a smaller part of the overall economy.[10]

### Subsidization of Access Rather than Use

Subsidization has some value when the external effects are large, as in vaccinations, primary health care, education, encouraging the shift from kerosene lamps to electric bulbs, use of safe drinking water, and such other merit goods. Interesting and relatively robust methods do exist for ensuring that merit goods subsidies can continue to be provided even under privatized or commercialized systems. Besides, subsidization of access rather than subsidization of goods or use of service would provide for greater social value and positive externalities.

### Reform and Subsidies are Not Incompatible

The bogey of merit goods and subsidization has been unfairly used to stall reform by its detractors and

---

[10] See section 7.2 for the design of such a scheme for farmers.

surprisingly even by those who genuinely represent the poor. Herein the problem, besides poor communication, could be one of the reformers and state lacking the credibility to ensure that the benefits of reform are equitably distributed. By insisting upon a roll back of subsidies (which is usually not necessary), reformers have unwittingly played into the hands of those who politicize subsidies to stall reforms. Many sectors of infrastructure, of which electricity is one glorious example, also including urban water, irrigation, hospital services, municipal waste collection, are very badly managed with enormous leakages and waste. The need of the hour is to emerge from the catch-22 situation of subsidies being used to justify existing inefficiencies and waste and these in turn contributing greatly to the 'need' for subsidies, by raising costs unnecessarily! It is rather disturbing that no clear strategy has thus far emerged from official circles on how reform can usefully be dissociated from subsidies and each addressed appropriately.

### Subversion of the Independence of the Regulator

The idea that the regulatory function needs to be separated from the government as a player and provider in a situation of pluralistic supply is almost axiomatic. While the idea has most certainly taken root for the good of the reform process, it is still being hotly contested and subverted, or subtly displaced, as when a clever clause is inserted into the bills creating regulators, to retain unwarranted government control or influence.

### Contracts and Their Appropriateness

The role of contracts in their most general sense increases dramatically with pluralistic provisioning of infrastructure. Earlier, the government, typically through internalization, could work around the imperfections in contracts with its parastatals and/or public enterprise, or even between them. They now become inevitable not only because of ownership changes, but also because wherever possible even state-owned entities need to have their independent (and separate) budgets. They are also essential if performance has to be meaningfully reflected in the accounting statements of enterprises. Tightening budgets also require budgetary coherence with the organization's power to spend and to be held accountable. With enhanced role of contracts, lawyers can be expected to gain, but their gain can be usefully minimized through appropriate, easier, and standard contracts. Very honest and dedicated government officials often take great pride in bargaining hard with vendors and construction contractors. Indeed, one-sided contracts have often been drawn up, whetted by the legal departments of the state or its parastatals, and pushed on to 'helpless' private parties. No contract can ever be complete. So it is probable that such unfair contracts are accepted by private parties only because they have options to cheat or underperform, possibly even in ways that still meet the contract. The simple idea that in all contracts both parties should have some gain and hence a stake in the contract tends to get overlooked. A serious businessman would be concerned if the people with whom he dealt did not have the scope to make money. As the reform process creates the need for contracts and agreements among governments, public enterprises, and private parties of many hues, the issue of their appropriateness, in terms of fairness, match between control and responsibility, incentive compatibility, and specifically the adequacy of 'inside options', becomes urgent. More than legal skill, economic and managerial perspectives need to be incorporated in drawing up contracts.

## Pricing Distortions are Likely to Run Deep

There is a tendency to keep prices artificially low when the service in question is perceived to be a necessity. However, the willingness to pay for necessities is higher, ceteris paribus, than for say 'luxuries'. This is true, for example, of drinking water. However, drinking water is priced lower in relation to water for electricity generation or for industrial use. This can result in perverse allocation and further distortions with investment decisions being based on such prices. Allocation of the resource then has to be made administratively, since market clearing prices are not possible and long-run marginal costs are not reflected in the prices. This set-up would typically result in underprovisioning of drinking water. The poor would have to compete with the rich and the well connected for water allocations, and it is almost a forgone conclusion that they will be the losers. This is the second order effect of price distortions, the first being the effect on consumption patterns and substitutes. It is quite likely that a significant part of public investment has taken place under distorted prices. Extricating the economy from the mess is an important task for the regulatory and restructuring strategy.

## Reform is Also About Cost Discovery

Unfortunately, in infrastructure, there is no easy method like trade liberalization or duty simplification to reveal the true costs. In the case of tradables, cascading multiple and complex duty structures that have hidden the true comparative advantages of many activities are revealed when tariff simplification takes place. In infrastructure,

there will have to be a process of cost discovery as reform and deregulation progress and multiple suppliers emerge. The regulator will have to be sensitive to the possible backlash effects that would have taken the prices far from the correct costs. Thus the true costs when they are revealed could surprise developers, institutions, and the regulator.

## Demand Itself May Have Been Distorted

It has already been discussed why the existing demand, and simple projections based on the same, will not do. As costs are discovered and prices are brought in line with true costs, there will be adjustments of consumption and use to these new prices. Equally important, certain structural developments taking place in the economy may bring about changes in what were earlier considered 'robust income elasticities'. For example, it is widely believed that the income elasticity of the demand for electricity is around 1.3–1.5, given the stage of development the country is in. The Chinese, South Korean, and Mexican experiences in this regard would lead one to believe that at current levels of real (purchasing-power-parity-based) income, India should have the same elasticity that China had in the 1980s (around 1.7). In fact, however, India has a much lower elasticity that is possibly even declining in the 1990s. This is because of the changing composition of the gross domestic product (GDP), which seems to be moving away from energy-using industries, and possibly also widening income inequalities, which reduce the demand for wage and basic good industries. Efficient use of energy by the private sector may also have contributed somewhat to this decline. Only if expansive labour-intensive growth were to take place would elasticity increase.

## REGULATORY STANCES

### The Natural Monopoly Revisited

It is important to understand the changing dimensions of market failure in the light of developments in contracting, technology, and property right clarifications, which give rise to more opportunities for deregulation. By now it is widely accepted that regulators and reformers should take the best possible advantage of the opportunities for market-based solutions.

It would be useful to briefly review the principal types of failure that require intervention by players other than market participants. In so doing, we will go beyond the textbook natural monopoly, since that is only one aspect of market failure. But first, a review of the textbook natural monopoly. The natural monopoly arises out of unit production costs falling rapidly with output and continuing to fall even at the point of equilibrium with supply, so that costs of one player are much lower than those for any other conceivable set of players.[11] Cellular telecom, fixed line telecom, electricity distribution, gas and oil pipelines are typical cases. Profit-maximizing behaviour on the part of the private monopolist would result in dead-weight losses and transfers from consumers to the monopolist, so that the monopolist has to be regulated to result in allocatively efficient marginal cost pricing. At marginal cost prices the monopolist does not recover his cost, so the best solution is a subsidy to the monopolist at marginal cost prices, and the second best is full cost pricing. Ideally, if all costs are known and one can see far into the future, the practical regulator should simply fix prices at long-run marginal costs (LRMC) which would be lower than long-run average costs (LRAC). The charge would then have to be of a two-part type, with the charge for the use as above. And the charge for access or connection, would have to be equal to the difference between LRAC and LRMC. The access charge for consumers would have to be based on a rule such as the Ramsey rule of inverse proportionality to the demand elasticities for particular groups of consumers. But the information condition is always violated. More importantly, the motivation of the regulator to do good cannot be assumed, but needs to be crafted.

### Capital Market Failures

Another condition of market failure arises from the nature of capital and bond markets in developing countries. When income streams, beyond say ten years, are ignored in discounting a project, then capital markets beyond that period do not exist. In such a situation, private parties would not be willing to price a service or a product that arises out of the use of capital assets with an economic life of say twenty-five years at the true social prices, even if there are no appropriability problems. Services of ships, aircraft, office, and rental spaces are typically subject to this 'failure'. But such sectors need not be regulated because when there is competition, it may be assumed that economic profits would be whittled down, even if the industry starts with such profits. In infrastructure, the privatization process, when not accompanied by major efforts to develop local capital markets, would necessarily result in regulators

having to award prices that are higher than the long-run incremental costs had such capital markets existed. The difference could be substantial in such activities as electricity generation, gas pipelines, and arterial highways. The BOT approach helps keep the overall transfers from the economy to the private player to a minimum, but this brings about intergenerational 'transfers' from the present generation of consumers to the next.

### 'Outsiders' and Higher than LRMC Prices

This inadequacy of capital may be seen in a positive light in a less developed economy, because the larger than normal surpluses of the service-providing entity, when invested in the same activity would expand the service at a faster rate than otherwise (with LRMC that assumes that long-term capital markets exist). Many potential users of the service are 'outsiders', not because they do not have the incomes to consume the service, but because there is not enough supply. The 'outsiders' would then be brought in more quickly than otherwise. Recognizing this higher growth aspect (provided the surpluses are invested to expand the service), this intergenerational distortion may actually be worthwhile till such time as there are no 'outsiders'. The 'better' solution would still be for the state, or taxes on the rich, to finance the fastest possible expansion of the service to encompass all current 'outsiders'. But such approaches have proved difficult in all but the most comprehensive state systems—the Soviet Union with regard to housing, China with regard to basic amenities.

### High Growth, Technological Change, and 'Effective' Contestability

The natural monopoly situation warrants active regulation only when there is little or no contestability. Thus, despite passenger airlines with fixed schedules having a natural monopoly character, regulation is known to be an undesirable intervention, since contestability should ensure low enough prices. But many sectors are not contestable enough—water distribution, pipelines, electricity distribution, bulk water—either because the sunk costs are high or because of resource specificity.

'Effective contestability' can improve considerably with high growth. This insight is not usual in standard treatment of the natural monopoly and hence some discussion on the same is carried out in this report. A system of backbone cables or optical fibres providing bandwidth is a natural monopoly at any time, but high growth implies entry, since an entrant needs to use his capacity suboptimally only for a short period. Hence, as long as rapid growth takes place, the need for

---

[11] Strictly, sub-additivity of the cost function over the entire range of the output is necessary for a traditional natural monopoly to exist. Most such industries in the advanced capitalist countries (except those at the frontiers of technical change like computers, biotechnology, and telecom), are slow-growing industries, and as such the orthodox regulatory stance would be appropriate.

regulation is minimal—to lay down interconnection and other standards and possibly not even the access charges. Similarly, rapid technological progress gives rise to falling costs and hence an advantage to entrants, so effective contestability is high. For these reasons, an orthodox regulatory posture with regard to such industries may be misplaced.

Unfortunately regulatory theories are cast in a static framework, and hence are unable to formally comment upon the dynamic situation. In areas like water supply, electricity generation and distribution, and sewerage services, growth of more than 10 per cent per annum or so is not expected. And the expected technical change is modest and inferred a few years in advance. Here the orthodox regulatory stance of attempting to regulate is not inappropriate. Though even here the first attempt should be to overcome market failure through market-creating rules and institutions, or by internalizing externalities, if the source of the failure is externalities, through such measures as attribution, clarity, and markets in such newly created property. This aspect of market creation is dealt with later.

In a situation of costs falling with time, competition, duopoly, or even monopoly with small players actively nibbling at the market share of the incumbent, may well be tolerable, since consumers can look forward to falling real prices, even though these may remain above costs at any particular point in time. Thus if $g_i$ is the growth rate in total factor productivity and $p_i$ is the rate of growth in prices, so long as $g_i - p_i > \sum w_i \cdot (g_i - p_i)$, where $\sum w_i = 1$, the growth of the sector (under no regulation) is increasingly beneficial to consumers. Such a situation would probably also be the best strategy for the policy maker, as long as unregulated growth does not result in adverse effects on safety and on future consumer choice. Maybe the right time for the regulator to step in would be when growth has plateaued off and a few new consumers are being added and the industry has become 'normal'.

### 'Catching Up' Could Result in 'Contestability' For A While

But then what about industries like pipeline networks or distribution systems, which could grow very rapidly in late industrializing economies, as the economies catch up with the advanced capitalist countries? It is not always true that these industries during such a high growth phase need regulation. The gas and oil pipelines business in the US came about over a period of intense and unregulated growth. Similarly, the rail networks in an earlier period. As long as they were growing, there was a 'contestability' of a certain kind. The question is really an empirical one with regard to gas and oil

pipelines in India today. If indeed much of the network has yet to come up (as it would seem in China which is unambiguously on the path of industrial transformation), then regulation should come only after much of the network is in place. The problem in the case of India is that it is not so certain that the economy is on the path of successful industrial transformation, neither can it be said that it is in the pre-take off stage.[12]

### Orthodox Regulation is Not Appropriate for Telecom and Related Industries

In the case of telecom on the other hand, without doubt, there is no space for detailed regulation in India. Telecom is as much at the frontier of technological change in India as it is in the advanced capitalist countries. Moreover, with falling costs and rising incomes, even though much more slowly than in China, the number of families that can afford telephones will rise very rapidly, though not at the stupendous pace of China. Even today, at least a third of all TV-owning households can use telephones. Several factors have prevented the realization of this potential. Under state provisioning the coverage was limited by high costs; the idea of a telephone as a luxury of the idle (when used at homes) stifled the market. Widespread use of telecom had little priority under planning. This itself may have been an effect of the small size of the network.[13] The high cost was *inter alia* the result of inappropriate technology choice, virtually no R&D, and most importantly, massive overmanning in the erstwhile Department of Telegraphs and no competition at all in virtually all segments of the industry, from manufacturing of instruments upwards. With the liberalization of the 1990s and the subsequent rapid growth, the network has now reached a size and coverage where there is little or no pent-up demand at the current high prices. Supply-side relaxations have helped achieve the high rate of expansion (but it is still miniscule in comparison to what China has been able to achieve). Clearly, its further growth depends upon new subscribers whose basis for demand would have to be income growth. On account of income growth, the numbers above the income level where a telephone creates net consumer surplus to the user could grow at more than three times of 4 per cent (per capita income growth), that is at more than 12 per cent per annum

[12] China in contrast is the archetypical late industrializer, others being Japan, South Korea, and Taiwan possibly Thailand, Malaysia, and Vietnam.
[13] Planners realized the value of telephones in business. The preferential allotment of telephones to offices, businesses, shops, nurses, and doctors is a case in point. What they did not realize was that the value of telephones, even to businesses, is a function of the numbers connected, including of general citizens.

(Morris 1999). The major growth would have to come from both a significant price fall and consumer-side network economies. The consumer-side network economies could in turn interact with falling costs.

### Consumer Side Network Economies are the Key to Network Expansion

Thus far, discussions on scale economies in telecom have focused on production-side network economies, that is the aspect of the natural monopoly showing falling costs with the increased size of the network. More importantly, the user side benefits (true consumer-side network effects), begin to operate as more people connect to the network. Thus at today's low penetration levels, those with telephones cannot assume that all shopkeepers or services they deal with have telephones. The lower middle classes, today, do not have a strong need for telephones, especially for local use, because few others in their social groups have telephones. The point is once telephone density among today's lower middle classes reaches about 30 per cent, it will increase by leaps and bounds to quickly reach near full coverage among them. Affordability is not the question here. The middle middle classes were already covered to the extent of 25–40 per cent when the reform began. As such, in a few years of very high growth, possibly as high as 50 per cent in this segment, telephone density may have come closer to being complete among the middle middle classes.

### Bidding would have Prevented Costs and Prices from Falling

Such large network effects arising out of consumer-side economies can result in strategic behaviour, on the part of telecom companies. Unfortunately, in India the bid-based licence fee meant that the monopolist/duopolists in the industry were pushed to the low-level equilibrium of the (short-run) profit maximizing natural monopoly. No regulation at all would most surely have led to very different behaviour early enough. Today, with the licence-fee-based system having gone and the Prime Minister's recent announcements of significant opening up of the sector to entry and competition, and assuming that the announcements are a precursor to full competition[14] in the future, strategic behaviour will almost inevitably be in the direction of low access prices. This will allow the network to expand rapidly, so that the company doing so is in a better position than its rivals. Differential discriminating price behaviour, but

---

[14] The fine print would hopefully bring the much needed competition in all segments.

with a positive end results, will then be almost certain. In other words, there will be strong incentives for serious telecom companies to expand the network even to 'uneconomic' areas, for the purpose of reach and completeness, since these have much value for the high use consumer.

### USO becomes a Bogey Against Competition

The concern of the regulator to ensure Universal Service Obligation (USO) may be unnecessary. Confusion will be created by incumbent state players who are bound to lose market share at least in the next few years to come and by players who came in with the assumption that there would be little or no competition. The competition that is likely even from the incumbent will seem to be predatory once it really begins! But as long as the competing networks adhere to uniform standards, takeovers of weaker firms will ultimately ensure correct duopoly or regional monopoly industry structure, at least for the first leg, that is local loop in wireless or with wires. Those who can drop prices at the right time to suddenly expand the network will win the telecom war in India. In a few years from now, say five, the bulk of the lower middle class will have reached that level of income whereby a phone at home is affordable. Then those who had dropped their prices will become dominant.

### Further Cost Reductions are Possible

There are of course technological developments that could result in an even higher than expected drop in prices: non-proprietary exchanges which can be put together, like personal computers (PCs) with inter-operable cards, would be an important development. If the world agrees to have voice over IP, with priority to voice packets, then long-distance costs could drop dramatically. Similarly, convergence could drive telecom, along with other broadband uses, in ways that are seemingly difficult to predict at this point. But as long as the local loop costs remain significant, the picture of beggars with telephones will remain mythical. It is almost certain that all costs other than local loop costs will fall; the question is when will the fall start? Even in the local loop, the potential of intermediate solutions like the one proposed by Ashok Jhunjhunwala in this report, can actually take the telecom revolution further and possibly even very close to that myth; but only if adopted at least at circle level!

Through a convergence of voice, broadcasting, and Internet use over cable and wireless, through the IP mode, which would also make possible direct-to-home (DTH) broadcasting, the joint effects of one class of users, viz. cable TV users, on Internet computer penetration can be high. Among middle to upper middle class households in India, penetration of the Internet via cable modems would most certainly be very high. Internet would then ride on the costs being borne by the base of cable TV users. As cable modems reach the 20 to 30 per cent of cable subscribers, internet users can in turn drive cable networks to higher quality and star topology. This in turn could drive higher quality cable TV and most importantly downloadable films and entertainment material including conventional broadcasts, but with a flexibility over viewing times and of course material. All this means that the bandwidth is for quite some time to come going to be short, despite some expectations to the contrary, and therefore huge investments in bandwidth are likely.

Do ceiling prices as the regulator currently rules, have a role? Indeed they do, as long as the dominance of the Department of Telecommunications (DoT) is not whittled away and strategies of firms do not inevitably shift to network expansion. When that happens, most of the effective prices will be significantly lower than past cost based-prices!

## Appropriate Regulatory Stances

The discussions in the preceding pages leads to some general propositions: (1) When growth and technological change is rapid, as it is in the case of telecom (defined broadly), there is little role for the traditional regulatory stance. More than price regulation, what is important is to keep entry costs low and not frown upon consolidations that are cost reducing. Such consolidations typically occur after bouts of competition and fast growth of the network. (2) In other sectors with slower growth but with the potential for much faster growth than the rest of the economy, it may still be possible to hold back regulation, to allow players to grow and dominate portions of the industry. The bulk gas pipeline networks and retail distribution networks in cities, could be cases in point. More detailed empirical investigations are called for to be able to take a position on such industries confidently. (3) In less developed countries (LDCs) with as yet little coverage of people, the focus should shift from prices to growth of the service. There is an automatic 'hedge' here for the policy-maker concerned with welfare. If coverage is growing rapidly, then surely the prices cannot be wrong. They may still have deviated from the optimal (in the sense of a static optimum), but no regulator can possibly have all the information to do the tight-rope walking that the traditional regulatory stance demands. (4) In sectors with massive undercoverage and a large number of 'outsiders' who would typically pay very high prices

in alternative high cost provision—private water markets for instance—or who do without the same—for example electricity in villages and towns of Bihar—rapid expansion could take place with deregulation. Allowing many kinds of players with little or no territorial or ownership restrictions, including public enterprises relatively free of governmental control in operational decisions, municipal corporations and others, has a functionality that arises out of increased coverage. If higher rates than costs are allowed to be charged and most importantly, the surpluses above allowed rates are constrained to be invested in the service,[15] then rapid expansions can take place. Of course once near complete coverage or coverage of all who can afford[16] has been reached, prices would have to be regulated more traditionally.

## Cross-sectoral Dimensions Need Recognition

Therefore the resolution of problems of infrastructural sectors, while seemingly amenable to a sector by sector treatment, because the peculiarities of each sector are quite significant, may not in reality be so. Thus, transport modes need to be seen together when the emphasis shifts from the developer, the provider, the regulator or the administrator with his need for administrative convenience, to the customer, as it should in any meaningful commercial orientation. Similarly, the services and goods of the oil, gas, electricity, pipelines, and tankers sectors need to be seen together. Telecom, value-added services, wireless and internet services, and even broadcast sectors, 'converge' from a technological and consumer use standpoint. It is not only because of technological convergence but also due to the more mundane and usual dependence of sectors on each other in terms of inputs, outputs, substitutes, and complements that the need for coordinated treatment can be ignored only at a great cost to the economy.

## Opportunities for 'Leapfrogging'

Reform of infrastructure creates opportunities for 'leapfrogging' and for innovations in technology and design when the space for multiple providers, including private players, is created. But realization of such opportunities is not automatic. There may well be pressures to the contrary. A reform, overly influenced by transnational equipment and technology suppliers in interlocking arrangements with private funds (and home country

[15] Such investments need not necessarily be in the same region.

[16] Those who cannot afford, if their number is too small, as is the case in the advanced countries, can be subsidized. In slowly growing LDCs, their number is too large for subsidization to be a solution. Income growth, and therefore high speed growth of the economy, is the only solution.

banks), does not augur well for innovative, intermediate, and possibly more appropriate solutions. This is especially so in situations where technology changes rapidly—telecom, for instance—or where the use of the service has a great deal of local specificity—road and water systems, for example. Unfortunately, the potential of Indian technology and creativity to find solutions to the typical problems of infrastructure, like measurement systems for vehicular traffic, lane separation in multiple lane highways, design of the local loop, standardized and non-proprietary architecture to drive down telephone exchange costs, and innovative designs for duplicable and self-sustaining private schools, is only beginning to be considered with the seriousness that it deserves.

*Innovation in Institutional Design*

Innovations which take advantage of certain behavioural patterns, unique to the society are also possible in the design of institutions and contracts. Thus the existence of successful cooperatives in many areas of economic activity and a vast number of industry associations, including those specific to the location and estates, gives rise to the potential for cooperative financing and management of certain services like power and water. At a time when regulatory clarity and policy are evolving, such arrangements could have much value. Such approaches and innovation could have played a wider role, had reformers started with the objective of solving problems and in a consultative manner.

## THE CONSTRAINT OF LAND AND ENVIRONMENT

*Land and Infrastructure in India*

Land and environment, especially the displacement of people affected by projects, have been at the forefront of the media, popular consciousness, and in public interest litigation, including in the apex court.

Despite all that has been said, it is important to discuss the environmental context for infrastructure development. It was in the early 1980s that the Ministry of Environment and Forests came into the limelight, as it became the one single ministry 'responsible' for the bulk of the delays in public sector projects, which had to necessarily obtain environmental clearance. Delays in obtaining clearances from this ministry were as large as five to seven years. Coal, rail, transmission, and hydel power projects were most severely affected. The notion that 'no forests be lost', resulted in the ministry insisting upon the transfer of equivalent amount of land to the Forest Department, whenever use of forest land under

the Department was involved in a project. Thus land under the Forest Department was by definition 'forest land' whatever its actual state may have been. Many infrastructural projects were held up for proposing to use even highly degraded 'forest land'! This formal legalistic approach when strictly adopted, resulted in vast delays and cost overruns, without in any way protecting forests, since the reasons for the loss of good forests lay elsewhere. The principal reason was illegal felling by organized groups, more often than not with the connivance of the department officials! Other factors were poor and archaic forest management practices of the Department and the interruption of the 'natural' process of ecological succession and regrowth due to pressure from people for grazing and marginal cultivation.

*The Forest Bill and Reactions*

The late 1980s saw the New Forest Bill, which attempted to protect forests by circumscribing the rights of forest dwellers and other poor people dependent upon forests, rather than by attempting to address illegal felling and poor management practices squarely. However, the government could not have its way, since opposition to the Draft Forest Bill was strong. Alternatives revolving around the involvement of local people, joint management of forests, complete ban on felling in certain regions, and the need for biosphere reserves were forced upon the government by agitations and protests. Also, with earlier movements like the Chipko and Apiko entering the public idiom, the pressures on the government to change were large. Consciousness of the need to protect forests is now widespread among the intelligentsia and the media. This positive development took place over a remarkably short period of time and its effects began to be seen in the (possible) slowdown in the rate of loss of forest cover in the 1990s.

*Movements Against Dams*

Simultaneously, with this ideological development, championing the rights of project affected peoples (PAPs) began in many parts of the country, the Narmada Bachao 'Andolan' and the movement against the Tehri Dam in the Himalayas being examples of the more forceful of these. Such movements succeeded in good measure in focusing attention on the (external) costs borne by those affected and displaced from their dwellings and habitat and served to considerably improve the rehabilitation package for those displaced. However, the movement has most certainly gone beyond the interests of people affected by the dams and the environment (in the sense of non-wasteful and conscientious use of natural resources) to a virtual dissent on development. Indeed, the agenda to help the displaced people may not have been the principal one, even to start with, in the private perspective of some of its leaders. Logic and fact no longer have a place in the 'debate' on the Narmada, as governments and 'pro-Narmada' groups have begun to realize. The issue has most certainly gone on to the emotional and ideological plane. Undoubtedly, the hold of the anti-dam protagonists and their nebulous 'alternative development' idea is strongly emotive. Significant numbers of the intelligentsia share their understanding and approach, however alien it is to the people who are actually affected.

### Post-modernist Roots

It is this ideology that is at the root of the environmental risk linked to all land using infrastructure. And even if particular projects and firms are able to avoid or bypass its worst excesses, the country as a whole has borne huge costs. The power of this ideology stems from its post-modernist character and origins. It has important support among many. Today, possibly the majority of the intelligentsia are post-modernist in Western societies. They can indulge in the luxury of aggressive environmentalism now that the good life is assured in the West. That prior generations in the West had carried out their own industrialization at stupendous and often unnecessary environmental cost, in the light of which the environmental damage in countries like China with high speed industrial growth pales into insignificance, is conveniently forgotten. The slowness (yet not stagnation) of the Indian economy has meant that ideas (from the West), including post-modernist areas, have a tendency to take root among sections of the intelligentsia ahead of their time, in terms of the stage of development of the economy! Thus labour movements with demands for labour standards not inferior to those in the West, took root with barely 15 per cent of the labour force having been absorbed in modern industry.

### Middle Classes May Be Ambivalent to Expansive Growth

Similarly, for sections of the elite, especially for the middle and upper middle classes with fixed incomes unrelated to the level of economic activity, growth is not critical to lifestyles or even incomes. Most opinion makers fall into this group. High speed growth is important for competitive and capable capitalists and for the poor who are still 'outsiders'. The appeal to the value of indigenous lifestyles and 'protection of local or tribal culture' is functionally (to the transformation process) no different from sugar-coating the continued exclusion of the 'outsider'. When post-modernists from the West, with their vast resources, work together with the local intelligentsia and in alliance with people like the tribals and the very poor who thus far have not had a chance to be part of the developmental process, a powerful force is forged. Against this force, the resources of governments, businesses, and developers are meagre.

### Governments are Handicapped

Indeed, governments, especially state governments, have a particularly severe handicap emanating from corruption—the standard 5–15 per cent cut in all capital forming public expenditure—which makes them shirk from making available information for 'modernists' and others to defend the case of development more forcefully. The tainted image of the state and its obvious failure in not being able to internalize the negative externalities of development projects that displace people from their land, or degrade the environment, makes it an interested party. Therefore, it has hardly any credibility when it attempts to influence public opinion, even when its facts are right!

### MLAs and NGOs are Already 'Green'

So infectious has been this post-modernist ideology that much of the Left, since the fall of the Soviet Union, has turned 'green'. The majority of the non-governmental organizations (NGOs) are anti-development in orientation and even the World Bank has turned green at one end and become orthodox at the other end. It is not at all accidental that countries with higher growth rates and egalitarian initial conditions (East Asian and China) do not have any significant post-modernist opinions and not many NGOs with an anti-development disposition. Not only that, they also have had better record of protecting the environment.

### Need for an 'Economic Approach' to Land and People

The solution, therefore, is in higher employment-generating growth and in policies, rules, and institutions that internalize the environmental costs of growth, more particularly those of people displaced and affected by projects. The land acquisition process and the process of rehabilitation of project affected people, as they exist today, even when carried out by the state in accordance with the rules, are generally problematic exercises. Neither the stance of the NGOs as elaborated in the Draft Policy on Rehabilitation and Resettlement (DNPR&R), nor its antithesis, viz. the Draft Bill on Land Acquisition (brought about with the intention of speeding up land acquisition for infrastructural development) is in the right direction. The problem with the latter is not, as one critic stated that the Draft Bill is economic in approach, but that it is not sufficiently so. It retains all the elements of the colonial 1884 Act, which is almost entirely a political statement of the overriding powers of the state with respect to land. The Draft Policy on the other hand though with many good features is far too ambitious. To do justice to it in its entirety would be tantamount to arresting development.

## Current Problems in Land Acquisition

Major critiques of land acquisition, now that 'market rates' or better are being paid, are as follows: (1) Public purpose has been so broadly interpreted in actual practice as to include nearly all commercial activity, not just activities such as building of roads which may not have other significant land use options, defence and security projects, or projects of great social benefit like dams and irrigation projects. Even industrial projects which have wide flexibility in the land they could use are interpreted as 'public purpose'. Indeed, in the competition for attracting investments, states like Gujarat have acquired land for all kinds of commercial activities, to be handed over to the investor. (2) Excess land is acquired. (3) The processes are such that cornering of the land takes place especially in land-abundant areas, where therefore the benefits of appreciation are denied to the original (often poor) owners of the land. (4) The focus on land means precluding from compensation those who do not own land as such but are dependent for their livelihood upon the local economy, working as daily labourers, petty service providers, and traders, who are rendered jobless with the destruction of the local economy. (5) Making rather too much rest on the wisdom of the collector has the potential to backfire in the face of organized opposition from those whose lands are acquired, especially in areas where land is dear and intensively used. (6) All these claims are generally true and the current refinements speed up acquisition by short-circuiting the process of announcement, declaration, and hearing for compensation and award. (7) Even when market prices are paid, the authorities go by record books. These are typically understated and reduce the burden of a very onerous stamp duty!

## Market Prices are Distorted

While the awarding of market rates has been accepted by even the detractors of the Bill as a positive development, there are problems here which may help explain why acquisitions have still been problematic. Land acquisition remains a protracted process in most areas except in places like coastal Gujarat and Kutch with very little agricultural productivity and low population density. The problem may well lie in two related factors.

A market price for land, as much as for assets, assumes tradability of land. Agricultural land is typically not tradable for non-agricultural use except through costly processes of application for grant of government permission. As such, the market price is one that takes into account the restrictions in use. The benefits of higher values to industrial use (given higher productivity of land in industrial use) does not spill over to all land currently in agricultural use. As such, land prices (of agricultural land) do not include the probability of industrial or non-agricultural use at much higher prices. All the benefit of the higher price accrues to the land designated (or 'released') by the government for non-agricultural use from time to time. In land acquisition, therefore, the true prices would have been substantially higher than the prior prices. But given the acquisition process that goes by past prices, owners are not able to benefit from the same. Hence there is a 'loss' to the landowner, resulting in his opposition to the acquisition process. In case the government chooses to go by the prices prevailing, say, two years after the announcement, then for such prices to exist trade in land after the announcement of acquisition has to take place. That would mean opening the door wide to speculative cornering of land by those in the know, even before the decision is formally announced.

Clearly, to minimize understatement of land values in transaction records, low duties are a must. This would actually help develop the market for land, which would work to the interest of all landowners including small landholders.

Similarly many states restrict agricultural landownership to 'farmers'. Thereby, the only beneficiaries of prior (to official announcement) information in land acquisition are politicians, who in their status as 'farmers' do not have to compete with other 'speculators'. More importantly, not only is the market for land constrained by land use as outlined earlier, but by restrictions on the 'identity' of the buyer.

Typically, in areas with poor productivity in alternative use, especially agriculture, but with much industrial dynamism, the problem is usually one of excess acquisition and cornering of lands by those connected to the government and in the know. In areas with high productivity and high density of population, as in Goa or Kerala, the problem tends to be of opposition to land acquisition.

## Need for Direct Negotiations

A more open negotiation process of land acquisition, with 'all or none' deals offered by developers and others requiring land, would be appropriate. Most commercial projects which have flexibility in the land they can use ought not to go through the state for land acquisition. Instead, private purchase based on a bargaining approach would be right. The acquirer does not face monopoly and the owners of the land always have the option of alternative use. Private acquisition would have to be brought under a policy whose principal dimensions could be as follows:

(a) The acquirer necessarily makes a uniform base price offer for the land. Otherwise he could get land cheap by offering differential rates, or even create negative externalities for most owners, by first acquiring a small amount of land at high prices.

(b) Similarly, farmers and the village as a whole should have to *collectively* deal and negotiate with the potential acquirer within the framework of a policy that is fair to the landowner and ensures him some gain out of the enhanced value of the land. Typically, when land is so acquired, the details of the subsequent pollution mitigation and safeguards, buffer zone, charges payable in case of occasional pollution, other arrangements such as jobs, and coverage of non-owners who are dependent upon the local economy should go into a contract between the acquirer and the 'village' or collective body. The government should bear the onus and cost of ensuring implementation, as it does in the case of any business contract. This will no doubt increase the cost of land, but will thereby result in its optimal use. The risks will then truly come down. Fighting existing high risks by creating an 'anti-people' law is certainly not the solution. Public acquisition with the social purpose clause should be used only in such cases where the land required is specific.

India, with one of the highest population densities, has to be particularly careful about the externalities in industrial use of land. The high cost of land that such a process would reveal, would mean that polluting industries would go to such places where costs are low.

## Displacement and Environmental Impact Need to be Conceptually Separated

Interestingly most activists and commentators on land acquisition have tended to see environmental damage and the hardships and displacement of PAPs together, to weave a thesis of 'development being anti-poor'. In reality, the environmental costs of development by way of pollution, degradation of forests, and loss of species have to be conceptually seperated from the costs to the people displaced. It is the colonial, almost anti-people land acquisition practice that hurts people most and invite major protest. With better land acquisition—one wherein the displaced gain most—the 'dissent on development' of post-modernists would find less takers.

## THE RIGHT TO INFORMATION AND PRESSURES FROM BELOW

### Right to Information and Responsible Local Governance

Beyond the rights of the displaced, the constructive contribution of environmental and people's movements has been to draw attention to the need for information to be publicly available. Information is currently monopolized by the state and is occasionally and selectively available to groups and journalists, but not generally to the common man. Particularly difficult to come by are data on government spending at local level, especially pertaining to infrastructure and subsidies.

The MKSS's (Mazdoor Kisan Sanghatan Sangh's) long years of struggle for the poor showed to the people, the politician, and the bureaucrat the power of information in the right hands (people) as regards government activities. This was long before it had become popular in academic and journalistic circles to ask for the 'freedom of information bill'. Organizations now realize that in the Internet world driven by information, information access can be a potent way to empower people and embed responsibility. Similarly, there has been a slower realization that the value of data is a non-linear function of its size and coverage, increasing rapidly with the number of attributes and the population, in commercial settings. In Rajasthan, under the initiative of the Tilonia group, the MKSS, with the active involvement of the people in general, forced the government to concede to making available information on such records as local expenditure on schools, wages, wells, buildings, etc. incurred by local and state governments.

In the 'jan sunwai', in which publicly under video official records were read, some officials even publicly admitted to widespread corruption and fraudulent practices. The specific details, the prima facie evidence, and the public aspect of this 'jan sunwai', had the effect of creating a people's movement for information. The movement, by its very nature and objective and entirely democratic and legal tools, was powerful enough to include wide sections of society, even officials in their individual capacity. The Tilonia Group led by Aruna Roy and others had discovered a most potent leverage point for change in governance and in society as a whole in the form of the 'jan sunwai' and the focus on relevant information per se. With the Internet and an Appropriate Right to Information act on the lines suggested recently (see Godbole, 1999 and section 5.8), the same strategy has the potential to reduce corruption considerably. Why so? Very briefly, given democracy and the need to balance the interests of many competing groups, the Indian state has a strong need to appear to be fair, even when it is not. While the democratic and people's constitution charges the state machinery with the responsibility for certain social and publicly beneficial tasks, it also makes it accountable to the people. In actual practice, the fact that the economy has excluded many and archaic and despotic rules and laws have continued—the Official Secrets Act and the Land Acquisition Act, for example— means that 'form of fairness' in administration can be exposed rather simply by opening up government papers.

Thereby the hiatus between the form and the content becomes tense and either one has to give way. So a 'right to information bill' is most likely. Yet the initial processes are likely to be tortuous, and the government in power, however sincere it may be, will find itself under severe pressure from the bureaucracy and the average politician to give the bill the form of a freedom or right to information bill, while in reality loading it with so many constraints and special situations considerations for denial as to render it impotent. There is therefore, the real danger that a bill which nobody but officialdom and the corrupt want gets pushed. From the viewpoint of infrastructural development, information regarding state and local bodies when regularly and routinely available to the people, should do much to reform governments, especially in their enterprise and regulatory dimension. Nothing could be better for commercial provisioning and for good governance which engenders local (and general) development. Given the democratic fabric of our society, this right to information becomes a necessity for real change that brings in the 'outsider'.

# 3 | REGULATION OF TARIFFS AND INTERCONNECTION: CASE STUDIES

*Sidharth Sinha*

This chapter provides three detailed case studies of tariff and interconnection regulation in the telecom and power sectors: rebalancing of telecommunication tariffs, interconnection between fixed and mobile networks, and availability-based tariffs for central generating stations.

In the telecommunication sector the existing tariffs enable the operators—Department of Telecommunications (DoT), Mahanagar Telephone Nigam Ltd. (MTNL), and Videsh Sanchar Nigam Ltd. (VSNL)—to earn reasonable rates of return. In fact, according to some observers the current returns may be excessive, especially if one takes into account the potential for improvements in efficiency. However, as in most other countries, which are in the initial stages of moving from a monopolistic to a competitive market structure, the tariffs are not cost based. National and international long-distance calls subsidize monthly rentals or access charges. Subscribers pay higher call charges on a slab basis as the number of calls increases; and rentals and call charges for rural subscribers are lower than those for urban subscribers even though the cost of rural coverage is significantly higher. Such cross subsidies are unsustainable in a competitive environment. Therefore the first major task of the Telecom Regulatory Authority of India (TRAI) was to rebalance tariffs and simultaneously provide for alternate funding of Universal Service. The first case study describes and evaluates the tariff rebalancing exercise. A brief description of the tariff rebalancing exercise undertaken in the United Kingdom (UK) is also presented.

Fixed and mobile networks are both complementary and competitive. For the incumbent fixed line monopoly operator there is an increase in revenue from the new traffic generated by the cellular network. At the same time, there is a loss of revenue due to existing or potential fixed line traffic migrating to the cellular networks. Therefore the incumbent fixed line operator does not have a clear-cut incentive to negotiate a fair interconnect agreement with the relatively smaller cellular networks. Apart from this, there is also the possibility of the fixed and mobile operators colluding, given the monopoly characteristics of both fixed and mobile call termination. Hence there is need for some regulatory oversight, if not full regulatory intervention, in the case of fixed mobile interconnection. The second case study discusses the TRAI's attempts to arrive at a fixed–mobile interconnection arrangement, especially in the context of a transition to the calling party pays (CPP) regime. As it turns out, the TRAI order was struck down by the court, precipitating amendments to the TRAI Act and the replacement of the Chairman and all TRAI members, except one.

The third case study examines the Availability Based Tariff (ABT) Order of the Central Electricity Regulatory Commission (CERC) for central generating stations. The order is directed at resolving problems of grid indiscipline. The instrument is a two-part tariff structure, with penalties for deviating from scheduled generation and drawals. While there is little controversy about the CERC's objective and the basic design of the tariff structure, NTPC, the party most affected by the order, has objected to the target availability norms and the nature of incentive payments embedded in the two-part tariff. These aspects of the two-part tariff were motivated by CERC's attempts to raise certain benchmarks in order to improve the efficiency of NTPC's operations. The resulting stand off between the CERC and National Thermal Power Corporation (NTPC) illustrates the difficulties in providing incentives for efficiency in an essentially non-competitive

BOX 3.1

### Background to Tariff and Interconnection Regulation

The aim of price regulation is to achieve in a situation of monopoly the economic efficiency outcomes of competitive markets. Economic efficiency ensures the supply of welfare maximizing amounts of goods/services (allocative efficiency) in the most cost-efficient manner (productive efficiency). In a dynamic context it also calls for a process of continuous innovation and productivity improvements. In addition to providing the economic efficiency outcome of competitive markets, price regulation is often required to serve social objectives (e.g. distributional concerns) and operate within political constraints (e.g. uniform nationwide pricing requirements).

Economic theory provides two basic frameworks for price regulation—Ramsey prices and contestable market prices. Both these frameworks point to the need for taking into account demand side factors, in addition to costs, in setting prices, especially in a situation of significant joint and common costs. Neither of these approaches requires allocation of joint and common costs. However, regulators have traditionally been reluctant to set prices based on demand characteristics, especially demand elasticities, and have preferred to set prices equal to fully allocated costs (FACs). In recent years there has been a move away from historical and short-term costs to a cost concept described as Long Run Incremental Cost (LRIC) which uses forward looking costs taking into account expected changes in technology and productivity. A further development has been the use of 'price caps' where the regulator specifies the average price increase for a basket of services. The flexibility for fixing individual prices is left to the operator, with prices often subject to caps and floors. The use of both LRIC and price caps represents attempts by the regulator to provide incentives for improvements in efficiency and productivity.

The main problem in price regulation is the informational disadvantage of the regulator vis-à-vis the regulated firm. The principal–agent relationship between the two gives rise to familiar problems of 'moral hazard' (hidden action) and 'adverse selection' (hidden information). The regulator (as principal) would like to set prices that induce the regulated firm (the agent) to act in a particular way. For example, if the regulator knew what the firm's cost would be, were it productively efficient, she could set prices to cover these costs and force the firm to be efficient in order to sustain itself. In practice, the regulator will never have enough information to use this approach. The regulator may be able to audit the firm's costs *ex post*, but he cannot tell what they will be *ex ante*, and he will never know what they might have been if the firm had taken actions to reduce them. In part this is because an outside regulator will never know as much as the firm, but the firm itself may be genuinely uncertain about its cost *ex ante*.

Given these problems with 'conduct regulation' it is desirable to move to a competitive structure so that less reliance needs to be placed on the imperfect mechanism of regulation. Price regulation is then seen only as a temporary measure and in fact may be designed with the explicit objective of moving to a competitive structure. In fact regulation may be unnecessary even in the case of natural monopoly if there is competition from other modes of providing the same service. This has been referred to as 'intermodal competition' in the transportation sector where the term is used to describe the rivalry between railroads, road transport, pipelines, and water transport, all of which compete for freight traffic. If intermodal competition is strong enough, regulation may be unnecessary even if one or more mode of transport appears to have the structure of a natural monopoly. In the case of telecommunications a good example of emerging 'intermodal competition' is that between voice telephony and internet telephony or between wireline and wireless telecommunication. It is also possible to separate or 'unbundle' the natural monopoly and competitive segments of a business so that competition may be introduced in the competitive segments while the natural monopoly segment is subject to regulation.

Apart from the regulation of prices of final services there is the question of access pricing when a market dominated by a single operator is being opened up to competition. For example, in the telecommunications sector, in countries with high teledensity the incumbent operator is likely to have all potential customers connected to its network. Even in countries with low teledensity a substantial portion of the potentially more lucrative customers are likely to be connected to the incumbent's network. Given the substantial cost of being connected to a network most users will be connected to only one fixed and/or only one mobile network. As long as a user is connected to a given network, that network has a monopoly over the 'local loop' for providing access to that user. New entrants would require this access for providing services either in competition with the incumbent or completely new services. Users connected to other fixed line or mobile networks would also require this access.

The resulting situation can be conceived of as a 'network of networks' encompassing both complementary vertical and competitive horizontal relationships. In the case of complementary vertical relationships, interconnection is mutually profitable and the exclusion of rivals is not consistent with profit-maximizing behaviour. This would be the case if the two operators provide complementary components which need to be bundled together to provide end-to-end service to the customer. It would also be applicable in the case of two similar networks each with its own 'captive customers'. However, in these cases while there is little incentive for excluding the other it is possible for the access charge to be used as a collusive device. When networks offer substitute services then there is incentive for each network to try to prevent the other from bringing its service to the consumer. The dominant operator may then use its monopoly position over some bottleneck facilities, e.g. the local loop, to prevent others from providing the substitute service, by not offering interconnection at all or only on highly unfavourable terms. In both cases there is need for regulating the terms of interconnection provision.

system. There is a limit to the extent to which tariff structure design can achieve the efficiency outcomes of a competitive market strcuture.

## CASE 1. REBALANCING OF TELECOM TARIFFS

The TRAI initiated the consultation process for fixing telecom tariffs in Novermber 1997, with the release of its consultation paper on Concepts, Principles, and Methodologies. Until then tariffs had been set by the DoT with periodic revisions. The last tariff increase of around 20 per cent had been implemented in May 1994. Since 1982, tariffs·had been growing at a compound annual growth rate (CAGR) of approximately 8 per cent, almost at par with the long-term inflation rate. As in most other countries, tariffs are characterized by significant cross-subsidies. In its second consultation paper of September 1998 the TRAI argued that cross-subsidies were unsustainable in a competitive environment and would result in inefficient allocation of resources. Therefore the primary objective of the first tariff review process was to rebalance tariffs and move them closer to costs. However, it was pointed out that some deviation from cost-based prices would continue in order to encourage access to and use of basic services.

### Cost Estimation

Regulators across the world are increasingly using long-run incremental cost (LRIC) instead of the traditional fully allocated cost (FAC) for costing of services. The term long run in the context of LRIC refers to a period long enough for all of a firm's costs to become variable or avoidable. Incremental costs are the additional costs, usually expressed as a cost per unit, that a firm will incur as a result of producing an additional quantity of the good or service. The relevant increment is the entire quantity of the service that a firm produces, rather than just a marginal increment over and above a given level of production. Incremental costs are, therefore, forward looking and not historical or embedded costs. The TRAI would have preferred to use LRIC, but given the lack of relevant information it decided to use FAC as a starting point. The TRAI has attempted to cost the various basic services by allocating all capital and operating costs across four categories—rental (or access), local calls, long-distance calls, and international calls. The costs that are allocated are:

### CAPITAL COSTS

The capital costs of the *local network* determine the cost of rentals. The costing uses a capital cost per line of Rs 31,000. This includes the cost of the local network

as well as the long-distance network. The cost of the local network is estimated at Rs 23,250 or Rs 25,000. The balance is the cost of the long-distance network. The estimate of capital cost per line is based on a study by Industrial Credit and Investment Corporation of India (ICICI) Consulting, 'Revenue shortfall on account of uneconomic subscribers in DoTs fixed line network'. Since the DoT does not maintain any cost data centrally, they were collected from a sample of ten secondary switching areas (SSAs). The data revealed that even though there is no significant variation across exchange systems there is wide variation in cumulative capital expenditure (CAPEX) across SSAs. The cost per direct exchange line (DEL) ranged from a low of Rs 12,400 in Coonoor, Tamil Nadu to Rs 45,207 in Gwalior, Madhya Pradesh. The variation in cost was attributed to improper allocation of 'other costs' and due to differences in the geographical terrain. It was then decided to obtain 'updated' cost data from five SSAs, separately from rural and urban DELs. Ultimately, cost data from three SSAs, backed up by DoT officials' judgements, were used to arrive at national-level cost data.

The capital cost for long-distance transmission is allocated between long-distance and international calls (both incoming and outgoing) on the basis of minutes of traffic. This estimate is based on the ICICI estimate of transmission cost to the next highest exchange. An alternative estimate is obtained on the basis of the breakup of the DoT's Annual Plan Allocations, 1992–3 to 1997–8 (Table A II.2 of Consultative Document). According to this about one-fifth to one-fourth of the capital cost of the local network was accounted for by long-distance-related capital costs.

### OPERATING COSTS

The DoT has provided figures for operating costs and the total number of metred calls for the year 1996–7. The basis of the break-up of operational costs between local and long distance is not provided. The exact breakup of metred calls across the three categories is not available. Information on the minutes of international traffic is available from the VSNL since this information is necessary for settlement payments. The TRAI has estimated the number of minutes of local and STD calls using informal estimates of pulse duration and distribution of total number of metred calls across the three categories.

The operating costs for the local network are allocated across local, long-distance, and international minutes of traffic since the local network is used by all calls. The operating expenses related to the long-distance network are allocated between long-distance and international minutes of traffic.

CAPITAL AND OPERATING COST OF VSNL OPERATIONS

This represents the cost of international transmission and switching and is assigned exclusively to international call minutes. These costs are based on an International Telecommunications Union (ITU) study on 'The Changing International Telecommunications Environment: Country Case Study India', prepared by Tarifica (UK) and Indian Institute of Management, Ahmedabad (IIMA) (India).

*Determination of Rental and Usage Charges*

Rental and usage tariffs have been determined in the following manner:

RENTALS

The rentals proposed by the TRAI are based on the actual current rentals, adjusted for inflation and increase in real gross domestic product (GDP) per capita, since rentals were last revised in 1993. There is a 50 per cent adjustment for the cumulative price increase for the period March 1993 to March 1999. An additional adjustment of 15 per cent is made for increase in real GDP per capita during this period. Therefore the proposed rentals are not directly related to the estimated costs. This was motivated largely out of a concern that low user subscribers would drop out of the network at cost-based rentals.

LOCAL CALLS

The tariff for local calls is based on the operational cost of the local network allocated to local calls. The call charge for the first 500 metred calls per month in a billing cycle for rural subscribers is less than the lowest estimated cost-based charge without any margin. The corresponding call charge for urban subscribers (again without margin or with a small margin) is equivalent to that estimated with average call-holding time of 2.8 minutes. With a call holding time of 2.5 minutes, this tariff would be below cost. For calls in addition to the first 500 metred calls per month in a billing cycle, a margin of 20 per cent has been provided above the upper limit of the cost-based charge with holding time of 2.8 minutes. This also provides a margin on the upper limit of cost-based charges estimated for an average holding time of 2.5 minutes.

LONG DISTANCE CALLS

The long distance tariff is based on the allocated costs of the local and long distance networks as well as the cost of rentals which is not recovered through rental charges.

INTERNATIONAL CALLS

The tariff for international calls is based on the allocated costs of the local and long distance networks, the excess of cost of rental over rental charges, the costs of international transmission and switching, and the 'settlement rate' payment to the foreign carrier.

The major features of the TRAI's 1999 tariff order are:

• There is an increase in rentals, mainly to account for inflation and growth in real GDP per capita, since rentals were last revised in 1993. However, rentals continue to be below the FAC.

• There is an increase in local call charges.

• The tariff for domestic and international long-distance calls has been reduced. However, these continue to be above cost in order to cover the deficit on rentals.

• The TRAI devised a category of 'low user subscribers', those making up to 1000 calls bimonthly, which constitutes about 70 per cent of the total subscribers. The rental for this category will remain unchanged for the period April 1999 to March 2002, even though it is scheduled to increase for other categories of consumers.

• With regard to usage charges, for the first 500 calls (except for free calls) the charge is Re 0.80 per call for rural areas and Re 1.00 per call for urban. For calls above 500 per month the charge is Rs 1.20 per call.

• The order provides tariffs for the year 1999–2000 as well as for 2000–1 and 2001–2.

A standard tariff package provides basic services at the tariffs specified in the schedule, and includes the specified number of free calls. Subscribers must have the option of getting basic services at the standard tariff package, that is at tariffs and free call allowance specified in the schedule. In addition, the service provider may offer 'alternative tariff packages' to subscribers. In the alternative packages, items for which tariffs are specified in terms of a ceiling will continue to be subject to the specified ceiling. Items for which a specific amount of tariff is shown in the schedule (for example rentals and call charges) may have any alternative tariff in the 'alternative tariff package'. Similarly, an alternative free call allowance may be provided in an 'alternative tariff package'.

Tables 3.1–3.5 give the charges for basic telecom services before the TRAI order, those proposed by the order, and those implemented by the DoT. The TRAI tariffs are for 1999–2000. As already pointed the TRAI also determined tariffs for 2000–1 and 2001–2.

*Implementation of Tariff Order*

The DoT strongly opposed the reduction in long-distance and international charges and argued that this

TABLE 3.1
Bimonthly Rentals in Rural and Non-rural Areas

| Capacity of Exchange | Rural | | | Non-rural | | |
|---|---|---|---|---|---|---|
| | Existing | TRAI | New | Existing | TRAI order | New |
| Less than 100 | 100 | 140 | 100 | 100 | 240 | 140 |
| 100 to 999 | 100 | 140 | 100 | 150 | 240 | 240 |
| 1000 to 29,999 | 200 | 240 | 200 | 200 | 240 | 240 |
| 30,000 to 99,999 | 275 | 360 | 275 | 275 | 360 | 360 |
| 1 lakh to below 3 lakh | 360 | 500 | 360 | 360 | 500 | 500 |
| 3 lakh and above | 380 | 500 | 380 | 380 | 500 | 500 |

TABLE 3.2
Call Charges for Rural Areas (no. of monthly calls)

| Rate/pulse | Existing rates | TRAI order | New rates |
|---|---|---|---|
| Free | 125 | 75 | 125 |
| Re 0.60 | 126–225 | | 126–225 |
| Re 0.80 | 226–250 | 76–500 | 226–250 |
| Re 1.00 | 251–500 | | 251–500 |
| Rs 1.20 | 501–1000 | 501 & above | 501 & above |
| Rs 1.25 | | – | – |
| Rs 1.40 | 1001 & above | – | – |

TABLE 3.3
Call Charges for Urban Areas (no. of monthly calls)

| Rate/pulse | Existing rates | TRAI order | New rates |
|---|---|---|---|
| Free | 75 | 60 | 75 |
| Re 0.80 | 76–250 | – | 76–200 |
| Re 1.00 | 251–500 | 61–500 | 201–500 |
| Rs 1.20 | – | 501 & above | 501 & above |
| Rs 1.25 | 501–1000 | – | – |
| Rs 1.40 | 1001 & above | – | – |

TABLE 3.4
STD Call Charges Per Minute (peak rates)

| | Existing (at Rs 1.40 per call) | New (at Rs 1.20 per call) |
|---|---|---|
| Above 50 km and up to 100 km | 7.00 | 6.00 |
| Above 100 km and up to 200 km | 10.50 | 6.00 |
| Above 200 km and up to 500 km | 21.00 | 15.60 |
| Above 500 km and up to 1000 km | 28.00 | 21.60 |
| Above 1000 km | 42.00 | 30.00 |

TABLE 3.5
International Call Charges (at Rs 1.20 per metred call)

| | Existing | New |
|---|---|---|
| SAARC and other neighbouring countries | 42.00 | 30.00 |
| Countries in Africa, Europe, Gulf, Asia, and Oceania | 70.00 | 49.20 |
| Countries in the American continent and other places in the western hemisphere | 84.00 | 61.20 |

would have an adverse impact on its revenue and profitability. The TRAI argued that while the 'volume of STD/ISD calls is likely to increase by at least 10 to 25 per cent, if not more', overall, with the exception of the first year, the tariff rebalancing is likely to be revenue neutral. As per the Explanatory Memorandum of the TRAI Order, 'In the first year of new tariffs, there is likely to be a surplus for the service provider. In the second year, there is likely to be a surplus or a small deficit. In the third year, the reduction in DoT revenues might be about 3–5 per cent.'[1] However, in response to the DoT's concerns the TRAI agreed to review the impact of tariffs at the end of one year, that is April 2000.[2]

The DoT implemented the order with some concessions for rural and low-user urban categories, namely there was no increase in rental or call charges for rural or low-user urban subscribers and the free call limits were not decreased from existing levels. However, this was not a problem as the rates in the TRAI order were only caps or floors and operators had the flexibility to offer better rates. Long-distance rates were reduced in line with the TRAI Order.

*Assessment of Tariff Order*

One of the factors behind the general move for tariff rebalancing/reduction is the profitability of the DoT. According to the TRAI, many consumer groups were of the view that the DoT's profitability was too high and that a decrease in revenues was justified. The TRAI appeared to agree with the consumer groups and argued

[1] Telecom Tariff Order, 1999, Annex A, Explanatory Memorandum.

[2] The DoT in its Annual Report for 1999–2000 has noted, 'Consequent to the revisions in tariffs and rentals, the revised estimates of revenue for the year 1999–2000 were lower by Rs 2082 crores than the budget estimates for the year. Thus, during the year, a reduction in surplus from Rs 8840 crores to Rs 6389 crores is anticipated.' At the request of the government the second phase of tariff revisions scheduled for April 2000 has been put in abeyance while the TRAI completes the review process.

that, 'it is true that the DoT surpluses are significant but the authority's opinion is that at the present stage of India's telecom development, it is necessary for the DoT to have substantial surpluses for expanding the network and to meet other social obligations'. There are two problems with this argument. First, surpluses are not necessarily the only means of financing growth. High growth firms rely on internal surpluses as well as external debt and equity to finance growth. Second, surpluses essentially represent a return on investment and, hence, must be evaluated in a corresponding manner. In the case of the DoT, it must be noted that even if its surplus appears large in absolute terms at about Rs 7000 crores in 1995–6, in terms of return on capital employed it is only about 20 per cent. Moreover, this is on a pre-tax basis since the DoT does not pay any taxes currently. In terms of return on equity the profitability of the MTNL and the VSNL, both with significant private shareholdings, is much higher. Therefore, the question of the level of surpluses that is justified must be separated from the level of funds required for investment. In essence, the responsibility of the regulator is not to provide for a particular level of revenue or surpluses, but only a return on capital which is commensurate with the level of risk of the business given a reasonable level of efficiency of operations. Once the business is able to achieve this level of return, capital for new investment may be expected to flow in from external sources.

In spite of the concern about the DoT's surpluses the order considers the impact of the rebalancing only on the DoT's revenues. Its impact on costs and, therefore, profitability is not considered. For example, given the likely increase in traffic, because of the higher elasticity of demand of STD/ISD, costs are likely to increase, which could have a negative impact on profits, even if there is no adverse impact on revenues. This points to the need for developing a model of profits rather than just revenues. Such a model will also have to take into account the possibility of improvements in efficiency of operations and corresponding reduction in costs.

Overall, the TRAI is faced with a severe information problem, which is unlikely to be resolved so long as the DoT continues to function as a government department with no commercially relevant management information system. The tariff order is based on extremely tentative cost and usage information. The analysis uses 'representative' cost estimates for the current capital costs of the local and long-distance transmission networks. Operating cost estimates are based on historical costs. Finally, allocation of costs is based on extremely speculative estimates of the number of minutes of local,

STD, and international calls.[3] Improvements in efficiency have also not been considered.

This problem of cost and usage data is likely to persist as long as the DoT is not corporatized and does not adopt a commercial accounting and management information system. The Indian telecom sector, perhaps, has the unique distinction of being a government department regulated by a regulatory authority. In most cases the government department is at least corporatized, with some time frame for privatization, prior to regulation. This has several implications for price regulation. Price regulation in general, and incentive-based regulation in particular, assumes a commercial orientation on the part of the regulated firm. This is not possible without at least coporatization of the DoT. Of course, corporatization by itself is unlikely to be adequate if there is no autonomy of operations and introduction of private shareholding. Without corporatization and commercialization the DoT will be unable to produce the kind of information that is required by the regulator for meaningful regulation or in fact that would be needed for efficient management of any commercial organization.

Along with the corporatization of the DoT there is need to introduce competition in the telecommunication sector as rapidly as possible. Even with competition the need for regulatory oversight and intervention will not disappear. The regulator will still have to deal with issues related to interconnection, predatory pricing, collusion, and universal service. However, competition will alleviate some of the information problems and eliminate the need for detailed service by service calculations of costs and tariffs. It may then be possible to move to selective price cap regulation. Competition will also force the pace of tariff rebalancing by creating the right incentives for the incumbent.

So far the attempt to introduce competition in fixed line services has been a non-starter. Three rounds of tenders since June 1995 for a licence in each circle have resulted in licences being issued for six circles only. Against these licences, services have been commissioned in three circles—Madhya Pradesh, Maharashtra, and Andhra Pradesh—with a total subscriber base of about 100,000 as of January 2000. The New Telecom Policy

---

[3] The estimate of domestic long-distance minutes provides a good example of the problems with the TRAI's estimates. In its consultation paper on tariffs the TRAI estimated the total number of long-distance minutes ranging from 8 to 11 billion minutes (p. 66, para. 53, Annex 2) as of 1996–7. In contrast, its consultation paper on 'Introduction of Competition in Domestic Long Distance Communications' provides an estimate of 26 billion minutes for 1998–9 (p. 24, para. 100, Tables 3–8). This estimate is subject to certain caveats but these are unlikely to make a significant difference.

1999 (NTP 1999) provides for several measures for encouraging competition in fixed line services. Most importantly, the licence fee regime has been replaced with a revenue-sharing arrangement. However, competition for circle fixed line services has now been inextricably linked to the opening up of national long distance services.

An important constraint to tariff rebalancing and introduction of competition is the existing mechanism of financing of universal service through cross subsidies in tariffs. Competition limits the ability of an operator to finance the Universal Service Obligation (USO)

through cross-subsidies. The relatively high prices for certain consumer groups or services leads to the well-known problem of 'cream skimming' by possibly less efficient competitors. This creates additional distortions and threatens the viability of the USO provider. According to the NTP 1999, the resources for meeting the cost of universal service would be raised through a universal access levy which would be a percentage of the revenue earned by all the operators under various licences. The TRAI has recently released a 'Consultation Paper on Universal Service', which evaluates the various options for universal service contributions.

---

BOX 3.2

### Rebalancing Tariffs with Price Caps in the UK

The UK government announced in 1982 its intention to privatize British Telecom (BT) (intact as an integrated dominant firm). Simultaneously, Mercury, a subsidiary of Cable and Wireless, was licensed as a national network operator in competition with BT. In November 1983, a year before privatization, the government announced its 'duopoly policy' according to which, for the next seven years, only BT and Mercury would be licensed to operate a nationwide network with fixed links. This duopoly policy also prevented cable TV companies from providing telecommunication services.

INITIAL PRICE CONTROL (1984–9)

The licence issued to BT under the Telecommunications Act of 1984 provided for price control on BT's services. For a five-year period, the price of an index of BT's services could not increase in any year by more than RPI – 3 per cent. The basket of services included all switched inland calls and exchange line rentals. The weights attached to each regulated service in calculating the price index in any year are proportional to their respective contributions to turnover in the previous year. The prices of international calls, leased lines, customer premises equipment, etc. were outside of the price control formula.[4] The price control effectively covered about 50 per cent of BT's revenues. In addition to the RPI – 3 per cent average price constraint, BT gave an undertaking that it would not increase domestic rental charges by more than RPI + 2 per cent in any year. No such undertaking was given in relation to local call charges.

BT used the opportunity provided by the price control to rebalance charges by increasing rentals and local call charges and reducing long-distance charges. The rebalancing corrected existing cross subsidies but was also driven by competition from Mercury. Since Mercury's strategy was primarily aimed at business users, who make a high proportion of peak-time long-distance calls, there was an incentive for BT to reduce charges in this area in particular. As a result of this rebalancing, residential customers saw an increase in their bills in real terms, in spite of an overall RPI – 3 per cent constraint on prices. The Office of Telecommunications (OFTEL) investigated the price increases and concluded that the rebalancing up to 1986 was justified, but that there was no need for further rebalancing. Questions were also raised about BT's profits, even though its prices were within the RPI – X per cent constraint. The regulator published an assessment of the appropriate rate of return for BT, concluding that the then observed level of 18 per cent on book value was about right.

1988 PRICE REVIEW

The 1988 price review determined the regime of price control for the period 1989–93. The duration of the review period was reduced from five to four years, to reflect the uncertainties involved and BT's own investment-planning horizon. The regulator also emphasized that any mid-term review should be limited to major unexpected events outside the company's control. The main conclusions which were agreed with BT were:

- a tightening of the main cap from 3 to 4.5 per cent;
- an increase in the scope of control to include connection charges and operator-assisted calls;
- continuation and formalization of the RPI+2 per cent cap on residential rental charges, and its extension to include connection charges;
- a requirement that BT introduce a low user scheme.

---

[4] International calls, though known to be highly profitable, were not a serious candidate for inclusion at that time, perhaps reflecting the government's unwillingness to provide issues of international liberalization at a time when only the USA was clearly pursuing similar policies. (Beesley and Littlechild 1989).

The low-user scheme gives customers the option of cheaper rental charges together with thirty units of free calls, with calls in excess being charged at a higher rate.

DUOPOLY REVIEW

The government initiated a duopoly review in 1991, with the expiry of the government's commitment not to licence fixed-link network operators to compete with BT and Mercury. The resulting white paper concluded that the duopoly policy should be ended, except in respect of international operations in the short term. In addition, cable TV companies were now allowed to offer telecommunications in their own right. In addition mobile operators were permitted to provide fixed link service.

As a part of the white paper the X in the main cap was increased from 4.5 to 6.25 per cent and international services also came under control, with an immediate 10 per cent reduction in international charges. This was in response to public concerns about the high returns BT was earning on international calls, estimated by OFTEL as over 80 per cent on capital employed. As a result of these changes, regulated services accounted for about 70 per cent of BT's turnover. Apart from the RPI + 2 per cent cap on exchange rentals, a new cap on the median customer's telephone bill of RPI − 7 per cent was introduced. Because of this constraint on rebalancing between call and rental charges, BT argued that without a requirement on competitors to make adequate payments towards its access deficit there would be unfair and inefficient cream skimming.

1992 PRICE REVIEW

The 1992 price review determined the price control regime for the period 1993–7. Its main conclusions were:

- a tightening of X in the main cap from 6.25 to 7.5
- a continuation of the RPI + 2 per cent cap on domestic and single-line business exchange-line rentals
- a stipulation that no individual prices (other than the above exchange-line rentals) increase by more than RPI in any year
- any quantity discounts offered by BT would not count when assessing BT's compliance with the RPI − 7.5 per cent price cap
- BT's low user scheme should be strengthened
- Investment targets, including digital services reaching 99 per cent of the population, should be attained by the end of the price control period.

1995 POLICY STATEMENT ON COMPETITION

As a result of the consultation following the July 1995 policy statement, 'Effective Competition: Framework for Action', the RPI + 2 per cent constraint on BT's exchange line rental charges was removed. This was a significant deregulatory step, encouraging BT to develop innovative packages of call and rental charges which could offer greater freedom of choice to the consumer. This also required BT to nominate one package as a reference tariff against which compliance with the RPI − X per cent cap could be measured.

1997 PRICE REVIEW

In the 1997 price control review OFTEL concluded that, in the past, price control benefits had gone disproportionately to profitable customer groups where BT faced competition. This included not only business customers but also high spending residential users.

Average effective value of X for 1990–1 to 1995–6

|  | per cent |
| --- | --- |
| Official price control | 6.6 |
| All residential customers | 4.2 |
| First 80 per cent of residential customers | 2.7 |
| Top 20 per cent high spending residential customers | 5.7 |
| All business customers | 9.3 |

This is the joint result of the higher levels of competition faced by BT for business and high-spending residential customers and the higher levels of profitability of these services. Price control in future was to be focused on groups with the least access to competition and, therefore, most need of protection. This is defined as the first 80 per cent by spending of residential customers and small business customers. The tariff review made the following proposals:

- A formal price cap of RPI − 4.5 per cent covering those services currently controlled, applied using only the revenues and calling patterns of the first 80 per cent of residential customers by bill size.
- BT would be required to offer a package for business customers which would provide call charges no higher than those

used for calculating adherence to price control in the residential market, and line rental increases of no more than RPI per year.

This structure was considered the best way of ensuring that price-cap regulation was provided to those who needed it most while giving BT greater freedom in areas where competition was already effective.

OFTEL'S APPROACH TO SETTING X

In the case of OFTEL the price cap is set by using a financial model which is used to project forward costs, revenues, and capital employed for the services within each tariff basket. If a large proportion of costs and fixed assets are shared between activities inside and outside the proposed price control baskets, the coverage of the model may need to be expanded to include all those activities where there is potential for costs or assets to be shared. Based on the forecasts derived from the model, a range of values of X is chosen for each price control so as to allow the firm to earn an acceptable expected rate of return by the end of the control period. In order to model the financial performance a number of parameters will need to be estimated:

- potential growth in demand for each service and the firm's share of each service market;
- the relationship between the costs and volumes of output produced;
- the scope for improvement in productivity;
- future movements in input prices;
- the allocation of overheads and fixed assets to the price-controlled business, after taking into account expansion of non-controlled business.

However, as pointed out by OFTEL,

The selection of a precise X for the purpose of RPI – X formula is in the end a judgement. It is necessary to assess where, within the range of values suggested by the modelling set out above, the right balance is struck between price protection for vulnerable customers and the efficiency levels that are reasonable for the UK industry. It is also a duty of the Director General to take account of the need for BT to be able to finance the services which it is obliged to provide. A key consideration in arriving at the value of X is the fact that the best protection for customers and the best spur to higher efficiency will be competition.

*Conclusions from the UK Price Cap Experience*

In the initial phase of price regulation the emphasis was on tariff rebalancing, while maintaining overall financial viability. However, the speed and extent of rebalancing was left to BT, subject to the RPI – 3 per cent constraint and additional RPI + 2 per cent constraint on rentals. The overall RPI – 3 per cent constraint included both the monopolistic access provision and local calls as well as the relatively competitive long-distance calls giving rise to the possibility of predatory cross-subsidization. Given the existing cross subsidization in the opposite direction this was not viewed as a problem in the initial stages. However, the regulator was aware of this possibility and placed informal constraints on the rebalancing, in addition to the formal price control.

Once substantial rebalancing had been achieved, and constraints on entry removed with the duopoly review, the regulator increasingly turned the focus of price control to low-spending residential and small business users—markets with low competition. As early as 1988, BT was required to introduce a low cost low-user scheme. Following the duopoly review, a new cap of RPI – 7 per cent on the median customer's telephone bill was added. Apart from this the 1992 price review stipulated that no individual prices (other than exchange line rentals) increase by more than RPI in any year. These additional caps on all charges while continuing with the RPI + 2 per cent cap on exchange line rentals constrained BT's ability to rebalance tariffs. The cap on exchange rentals was finally removed in 1995. The 1997 price review recognized that there was adequate competition for business and high-spending residential customers. Further price protection was, therefore, to be limited to the lowest spending 80 per cent of residential customers and small business customers.

The UK experience of telecommunications illustrates the use of the RPI – X method of regulation in an industry with rapid technological change and an industry structure which is constantly evolving towards increasing competition. The RPI – X method of fixing a maximum price path for an exogenously fixed interval of time provides the incentive for continuous exploitation of new technology to reduce costs. Simultaneously, the RPI – X method can be easily targeted towards those aspects of the business where regulation is most needed. In principle, rate-of-return regulation can similarly be targeted, but the practical difficulties of disaggregated rate of return measurement would impose a considerable burden.

The UK experience also demonstrates that RPI – X is not a passive form of regulation where the regulator need get active only once in five years or so. OFTEL has been fairly active and the explicit rules of price control have been supplemented with implicit regulation. Price regulation has broadened and tightened over time to take account of changing industry conditions. This has happened not only at the times of formal price review but also between price review. Contrary to the rate-of-return regulation, which provides only a single number—the rate of return—for regulation, the RPI – X approach provides a number of elements—the X factor, the control period, the coverage of the basket, and sub-caps. It is possible for the regulator and the regulated firm to reach an agreement on a package of these elements even if there are disagreements on individual elements.

## CASE 2. INTERCONNECTION BETWEEN FIXED AND MOBILE NETWORKS

Cellular services in India started in September 1995 in the metros and December 1996 in the rest of India. Currently, there are eight operators in the four metros and 34 in eighteen circles. As of March 2000, the total cellular subscriber base in the country is 1.96 million, with a 40:60 split between the metros and circles. Mumbai and Delhi together account for 671,597 subscribers—approximately 35 per cent of the all India total. Table 3.6 gives the growth of mobile subscribers over the last three years.

TABLE 3.6
Number of Mobile Subscribers

|  | Metros | Circles | Total |
|---|---|---|---|
| April 1997 | 349,605 | 18,509 | 368,114 |
| April 1998 | 557,948 | 355,921 | 913,869 |
| April 1999 | 519,571 | 693,809 | 1,213,380 |
| April 2000 | 824,850 | 1,137,937 | 1,962,787 |

*Source:* Cellular Operators Association of India (COAI).

Interconnection between fixed and mobile networks is critical for mobile operators, given the large proportion of total traffic either originating or terminating on the fixed network. As shown in Table 3.7 such traffic accounts for almost 93 per cent of the total traffic in the metros and 85 per cent of the total traffic in the circles.

TABLE 3.7
Minutes of Usage 1998–9 (millions per annum)

|  | Mobile to PSTN | PSTN to mobile | Mobile to mobile | Total |
|---|---|---|---|---|
| Metros | 324.0 | 351.0 | 53.0 | 728.0 |
|  | *44.5* | *48.2* | *7.3* | *100* |
| *Circles* |  |  |  |  |
| 'A' | 75.28 | 104.82 | 26.67 | 206.77 |
|  | *36.4* | *50.7* | *12.9* | *100* |
| 'B' | 209.3 | 145.55 | 51.18 | 406.03 |
|  | *51.5* | *35.9* | *12.6* | *100* |
| 'C' | 17.31 | 7.6 | 5.7 | 30.61 |
|  | *56.6* | *24.8* | *18.6* | *100* |
| All Circles | *48.2* | *37.1* | *14.7* | *100* |

*Source:* TRAI.

*Note:* Figures in italics are percentages.

### Licensing of Cellular Mobile Services

In December 1991, the DoT invited competitive bids from private sector companies for non-exclusive digital mobile licences, for a 10-year period, extendible by 5 years, in the four metropolitan cities of Mumbai, Delhi, Calcutta, and Madras. Up to two licences would be awarded for each of the four metros with the DoT reserving the right to offer cellular services. The licence fee for the first three years was a given parameter, while the licence fee from the fourth year onwards was fixed at Rs 5000 per subscriber (based on unit call rate of Rs 1.10) subject to a minimum total amount. The per subscriber figure was later revised to Rs 6023 based on the revision in the unit call rate. Along with the licence fee, call charges were also a given parameter and the bidding was for the lowest rental to be charged from customers. The evaluation was on the basis of financial strength, experience of the partners, committed rollout, and lowest rentals. At the end of the tender process, the value of lowest rental was fixed at Rs 156 per month and eight licenses were issued.

In the case of each of the twenty circles (usually contiguous with states), the DoT invited tenders for two non-exclusive licences. Rentals and call charges, as applicable to metros, were given parameters and the bidding was for the levy (to be converted into licence fee after selection). Each bidder had to quote a stream of annual licence fees for the licence period and the evaluation was to be done on the basis of the present value, arrived at by discounting the stream of payments at a specified discount rate. The bidders selected for each circle were asked to match the licence fee quoted by the highest bidder. As a result of this process thirty-four licences were issued in eighteen circles. Many observers considered the winning bids extremely high and unsustainable.

The cellular licences set the maximum tariffs that could be charged. The maximum monthly rental charge was Rs 156 per month; in addition a refundable security deposit of Rs 3000 and an activation fee of Rs 1200 were fixed. The standard airtime charge was Rs 8.40 per minute, with peak hour rates double and off-peak rates half the standard rate. This charge applied to both incoming and outgoing calls.

Cellular licences did not provide for an interconnect agreement. This was perhaps because cellular operators were treated as 'franchisees' and not 'access providers'. Cellular licences permit the operator to interconnect with the DoT or MTNL fixed line network and, within the same service area, with another fixed line service provider. However, long-distance connections, both domestic (outside the licensed service area) and international to a VSNL gateway, are required to be made through the DoT or MTNL network only. For mobile to fixed calls, the mobile operator collects from the mobile subscriber the airtime charge as well as the local and long-distance charges incurred on the fixed networks. This call charge is assessed from the point of interconnection between the fixed and the mobile networks. The fixed line charges are paid to the fixed line operator on a monthly basis. For fixed to mobile calls the fixed line operator collects the appropriate fixed line charges and the mobile operator collects the airtime charges from the mobile subscriber receiving the call.

The NTP 1999 of the Government of India provides for a new policy framework for cellular mobile service providers (CMSPs) which implies certain changes in their licence conditions. Most importantly the NTP 1999 replaces the payment of licence fees to the government by a revenue-sharing scheme. The other important features of the new policy are:

• direct interconnectivity between licenced CMSPs and any other type of service provider (including another CMSP) in their area of operation including sharing of infrastructure with any other type of service provider shall be permitted;
• interconnectivity between service providers in different service areas shall be reviewed in consultation with the TRAI;
• the CMSP to be allowed to directly interconnect with the VSNL after opening of national long distance from 1 January 2000;
• the CMSPs to be permitted to provide mobile telephony services including permission to carry their own long distance traffic within their service area without seeking an additional licence.

## Cellular Tariff Restructuring

Cellular tariffs were restructured along with the restructuring of fixed line tariffs. The main reason for restructuring cellular tariffs was that the monthly rental of Rs 156, as specified in the cellular licence, was not only lower than the monthly rental for the alphanumeric paging service, but was also lower than the two highest categories of fixed line service. Simultaneously, the airtime charge was too high. This had resulted in a large number of low-usage subscribers who were a 'net cost' to the operators. Therefore, the major objective of the tariff restructuring was to bring the monthly rental closer to the fixed costs of the network and airtime charges closer to operating costs. In addition the TRAI wanted to introduce a CPP regime 'with the intent to boost usage of the network'.

The TRAI estimated the cost of access and airtime for fixing cost-based rentals and airtime usage charges. The cost of access was based on capex per subscriber. The cost of airtime was based on operating expenses. The TRAI used cost information provided by cellular operators. Actual data had been provided for the two years 1996-7 and 1997-8 and projections for the

following four years. Rentals and airtime charges were calculated using capex and operating expense forecasts for 1999-2000 and 2000-1.

Using the median estimate the TRAI fixed a rental of Rs 600 (earlier Rs 156) and airtime charge of Rs 6 (earlier Rs 16.80) per minute as price caps. The proposed price cap tariffs constituted a 'standard package' always available to subscribers. Operators were free to offer alternative packages with higher rentals and airtime charges than those in the standard package. The TRAI postponed implementation of the CPP system to August 1999 since 'the DoT had indicated that it will take some time to make the technical adjustments required to implement the CPP system'.

## Fixed-Mobile Interconnection

As already pointed out there is no interconnect agreement between the DoT/MTNL and cellular operators. Cellular operators and the DoT/MTNL have been engaged in discussions on an interconnect agreement since 1996 but no agreement has so far been reached. The two major issues that need resolution are: (a) multiple points of interconnection and (b) interconnection access charges.

### MULTIPLE POINTS OF INTERCONNECTION

Cellular operators, especially in circles, would like multiple points of interconnection since it enables them to carry calls on their network to the maximum extent possible and thereby minimize fixed line charges for both originating and terminating calls. On the other hand, the DoT would prefer a single point of interconnection and to charge STD rates for originating and terminating calls to and from the mobile network. The DoT issued an order in January 1997 directing that intra-circle calls would be charged at the pulse rate of 8/16/24/32 seconds. This implied that the peak rate for a fixed to mobile call would be equivalent to about 24 local calls. The DoT argued that with a single point of interconnect, fixed to mobile traffic in a circle would have to travel an average of 100–200 km on the DoT long-distance network before being handed over to the cellular network at the single point of interconnect. The charges specified by the DoT were the STD rates for the 100–200 km slab. The DoT also argued that the higher strata of society like businessmen, corporate organizations etc., which form the core of revenue earning source of DoT through high STD calling, are also the potential target customers for cellular mobile service. A local call tariff for fixed to mobile will be very lucrative. All their STD calls within a circle will get converted into local calls. This will completely wipe out the revenue base of not only DoT but also the basic service operators to whom the government is shortly going to issue licenses for operating fixed telephone service.

Finally, the DoT pointed out that fixed to mobile calls provide additional value to the fixed line caller by being able to contact the mobile subscriber 'possessing no knowledge of the mobile holders' whereabouts within the circle'. Moreover, the fixed caller has the option of using the fixed network to (try to) contact the mobile subscriber. 'It is up to the fixed caller to make a need based, economic choice of the various options.' (Later on, in the CPP dispute, the DoT would take a stance contrary to this view.)

In response to the DoT tariff notification, cellular operators approached the High Court of Delhi, which stayed the DoT order. However, with the issue of a government notification constituting the TRAI, the Court directed the DoT and cellular operators to approach the TRAI for a resolution of their dispute. The TRAI issued an order in April 1997 directing DoT 'that subject to technical integrity of the network and technical feasibility, to grant both-way connectivity at points of interconnect and multiple Global Mobile Switching Centres (GMSCs) to the cellular operators, as they may require'. With multiple points of interconnection the basis for charging fixed to mobile calls at STD rates would be eliminated. However, cellular operators continue to complain that the TRAI order is not being followed by the DoT. For example, according to them, 'the Department of Telecommunication Services (DTS) is insisting that only one interconnect per secondary switching area (SSA) will be permitted.'

*Interconnection Access Charges*

In the second consultation paper on Telecom Pricing (9 September 1998) the TRAI stated that interconnection charges include payment for a link established between two networks (set up cost) and for the use of the interconnection provider's network facilities (usage charges). The TRAI further clarified that interconnection prices are, in general, based on costs, and/or are charged in the form of revenue sharing between the interconnecting operators. 'While the proportion of revenue shared is normally a result of negotiations, in certain instances it is based on the interconnection costs incurred by the interconnecting operators.' It is in this context that the first interconnection regulation is titled, 'The Telecommunication Interconnection (Charges and Revenue Sharing) Regulation 1999'. In this order, charges related to 'set-up costs' have been specified as interconnection charges. These include charges for leased circuits and port charges. Leased circuit charges had been determined in the first tariff order and

port charges have been specified in this order. Usage charges in the interconnection order are specified as revenue-sharing arrangements.

In the interconnection order, the TRAI was careful to specify that

the revenue sharing arrangements are interim, and are not based on detailed cost analysis. Application of an access/ carriage charge regime will provide more *logically tenable* usage charges. . . . Till any access/carriage charge is implemented, a system of revenue sharing must be in place to give effect to the commercial relationships arising through interconnection.

For basic services the following revenue-sharing arrangement was specified largely based on the interconnection terms specified in the licence for basic services:

• Bill and keep for local calls.

• For domestic long-distance calls the originating service provider pays Re 0.48 per unit of measured call. This is equivalent to 40 per cent of the highest per call charge of Rs 1.20.

• For international calls the originating service provider pays Re 0.66 per unit of measured call. This is equivalent to 55 per cent of the highest per call charge of Rs 1.20.

For calls between the cellular mobile and fixed line networks the revenue-sharing arrangement is the same as specified in the original licence. The revenue-sharing arrangement was expected to change with the implementation of the CPP regime. In the second consultation paper the TRAI had suggested that the cellular mobile operator should retain a percentage of the revenue earned from long-distance and international calls. However, in the final order the TRAI refrained from taking any action on this for the following reasons:

• Basic service providers have an access deficit to make up from long distance and international call charges. Cellular operators have no such requirement since profitability has been built into the specified tariffs that are based on median cost estimates (and not on lower estimates based on costs of an efficient provider).

• Tariff forbearance has been specified for supplementary services, which is an additional source of revenues.

• Tariff flexibility has been offered for cellular mobile tariffs for long-distance calls made within the circle.

Cellular operators continue to press for sharing of STD and international call charges on the grounds of parity with basic services operators. As an interim arrangement they would like the interconnection access charges for fixed service providers to be made applicable to cellular operators as well.

## CPP

TRAI'S CONSULTATION AND ORDER

In the second consultation paper on Telecom Pricing (9 September 1998) the TRAI had suggested a changeover to a CPP regime. In the mobile to mobile case the transition would be accompanied by a 'sender keeps all' policy. However, such a policy would not be appropriate for fixed to mobile calls because of the asymmetric costs of the two networks. Hence a migration to CPP would have to be accompanied by a suitable interconnection policy. In the consultation paper the TRAI specified a charge of Rs 3.90 per minute for a fixed to mobile call with the revenue shared between the fixed and mobile operator in the ratio of 15:85. This arrangement was based on two considerations:

• At Rs 3.90 per minute the fixed to mobile charge would be about nine times the fixed to fixed charge. In Europe the corresponding average ratio was about thirteen times.

• A 15:85 sharing would ensure that the fixed line operator overall received the same revenue as that for a fixed to fixed call.

However, in the first tariff order the TRAI postponed the implementation of the CPP regime to August 1999, mainly because the DoT had indicated that it would take some time to make the technical adjustments required to implement the CPP system.

One major and immediate outcome of the NTP 1999 was the replacement of the licence fee regime by an interim revenue share of 15 per cent. The government would take a final decision on the percentage share on the basis of the TRAI's recommendations. Since the licence fee forms a part of the costs incurred by service providers, a migration to the revenue-share regime required a review of the cost-based tariffs specified in the first tariff order. The TRAI combined this review, along with an assessment of the introduction of a CPP regime, in consultation paper No. 99/4 of 31 August 1999. In this paper the TRAI proposed reduction in rentals and airtime charges. It also modified its earlier proposal of Rs 3.90 per minute for local calls from the fixed to the mobile network with a 15:85 sharing between fixed and mobile operators. It now proposed a charge of Rs 2.40 for the first two minutes and Rs 1.20 for each successive two minutes, with equal shares for the fixed and mobile operators. This reduction was done in response to several comments on its earlier proposal stating that the fixed to mobile tariff was too high and would discourage fixed to mobile calls.

In the consultation process, following the release of the consultation paper, a number of operators claimed that their position would be adversely affected by the proposed tariffs. Cellular operators also expressed concern that the relatively low fixed to mobile tariff would encourage a call-back phenomenon where mobile subscribers would call fixed line numbers and then be 'called back' by the fixed line subscribers in order to save on airtime charges. However, the TRAI felt that the data provided by the parties to support their claims were not appropriate. The TRAI decided that it would continue its examination of the corrected information. Simultaneously, on a purely interim basis, it would notify certain tariff reductions together with the introduction of the CPP regime.

The TRAI announced the new tariffs in the Telecommunication Tariffs (Fifth Amendment) Order dated 17 September 1999. For cellular mobile services the rentals were reduced from Rs 600 to Rs 475 per month for metros and Rs 500 per month for circles. Airtime charges were reduced from Rs 6 to Rs 4 per minute for metros and Rs 4.50 for circles. With the implementation of the CPP airtime charges were applicable only for outgoing minutes. For calls from the mobile to fixed network, as before, the mobile subscriber would pay, in addition to the airtime charge, the relevant charges for the fixed network. The fixed network charges would be collected by the mobile operator and passed on to the fixed network operator.

For local calls from the fixed to mobile network the order specified a charge of Rs 2.40 for the first minute and Rs 1.20 for each successive minute. This was exactly double the charge specified in the consultation paper. The main reason cited for this increase was to reduce the possibility of call-back from fixed to mobile and at the same time, provide a higher total revenue for sharing. However, the TRAI clearly stated that it would not like the fixed to mobile call charges to be as high as suggested in the second consultation paper on tariffs. As stated by the TRAI, the tariff balances two objectives: 'Keeping low the charge for this premium call by basic service subscribers, while providing a reasonable amount of revenue to cellular mobile network to partially substitute for the revenue loss on account of removing the incoming call charge for cellular mobile, and to pay for utilizing the network.'

Revenue sharing arrangements between fixed and mobile operators were specified in the accompanying Telecommunication Interconnection (Charges and Revenue Sharing—First Amendment) Regulation 1999. This specified the payment of a mobile termination charge (MTC) to the mobile operator of Rs 1.60 for the first minute and Re 0.80 for each successive minute. This represents a 1/3:2/3 share between fixed and mobile operators. The TRAI reiterated that this arrangement was temporary and would be replaced the following year by a cost-based access/usage charge. Table 3.8 summarizes the two TRAI proposals in the consultation papers and the final order.

objection was not dealt with satisfactorily by the TRAI in the Explanatory Memorandum accompanying the Inter-connection and Tariff Orders regarding the CPP.

Apart from the issue of revenue loss and increase in costs, the MTNL also argued that the TRAI 'had no power and/or jurisdiction to issue or to make

TABLE 3.8
Tariffs in Various Consultation Papers and TRAI Orders

| Call duration | 1 minute | | | 2 minutes | | | 3 minutes | | |
|---|---|---|---|---|---|---|---|---|---|
| | Cons. paper 98/3 | Cons. paper 99/4 | Order 9/99 | Cons. paper 98/3 | Cons. paper 99/4 | Order 9/99 | Cons. paper 98/3 | Cons. paper 99/4 | Order 9/99 |
| Total cost | 3.90 | 2.40 | 2.40 | 7.80 | 2.40 | 3.60 | 11.70 | 3.60 | 4.80 |
| PSTN share[a] | 0.60 | 1.20 | 0.80 | 1.20 | 1.20 | 1.20 | 1.80 | 1.80 | 1.60 |
| Cellular operator share | 3.30 | 1.20 | 1.60 | 6.60 | 1.20 | 2.40 | 9.90 | 1.80 | 3.20 |

[a] PSTN: Public Switched Telecom Network

LEGAL PROCEEDINGS

Legal proceedings against the TRAI orders were initiated by a consumer organization, Telecom Watchdog. It filed a public interest litigation against the orders arguing that the implementation of the CPP would cause an increase of 100–200 per cent in tariffs from fixed line calls. The MTNL joined the proceedings by filing a writ petition asking for a stay on the CPP regime. The MTNL's main objection was that even as the CPP regime would lead to a decrease in its revenue, compared to the pre-CPP regime, it would have to incur additional costs in order to implement the CPP regime. The additional cost was attributable to upgradation of the fixed network, bill collection charges, and bad debts. The MTNL complained that the TRAI had not taken this into account in spite of several submissions.

The MTNL's argument about a decrease in revenue can best be understood with reference to a specific example. According to the MTNL, the average holding time of a fixed to mobile call is 54 seconds. Consider a one-minute duration fixed to mobile call. Assume that the caller is in the highest slab rate of Rs 1.20 per metred call. Under the TRAI Order, the MTNL will collect Rs 2.40 from the caller and pay Rs 1.60 to the mobile operator, with a net retention of Re 0.80 for the minute. In the pre-CPP regime the call would have been charged as a local call for Rs 1.20 with no payment to the mobile operator. In this sense the MTNL stands to lose Re 0.40 compared to its earnings in the pre-CPP regime. If the fixed line caller is in a lower slab rate, for example Re 1.00 per metred call, then the net retention for a 1 minute call will be Re 0.40 as against Re 1.00 in the pre-CPP regime. The MTNL had raised the same point earlier in its response to the consultation paper on the CPP. However, according to the MTNL, this

regulations to regulate arrangement amongst service providers of sharing their revenue'. Such a power 'would have the effect of over-riding the powers and functions of licensor and to rewrite contracts between the parties. Such an interpretation would be contrary to the intention of the said Act'.

The court decided to first address the question of whether the TRAI has the power to 'issue any Regulation which affects the rights of individuals under contracts or which seeks to override terms and conditions of licenses issued by the Central government to various parties'. If the court held that the TRAI *did* have this power then the TRAI would consider all objections and suggestions of the parties and decide afresh whether or not the CPP orders require any modification.

While addressing the question of the powers of the TRAI the court concentrated on Section 11 of the TRAI Act, which lays down the functions of the TRAI. The Telecommunication Interconnection (Charges and Revenue Sharing—First Amendment) Regulation 1999, which specifies the revenue sharing arrangement under the CPP, had been issued by the TRAI in exercise of power under clauses (c) and (d) of subsection (1) of section 11 of the TRAI Act. These clauses are here reproduced:

*11(1)(c):* Ensure technical compatibility and effective interrelationship between different service providers.

*11(1)(d):* Regulate arrangement amongst service providers of sharing their revenue derived from providing telecommunication services.

The court argued that by issuing the Revenue Sharing Regulation, while exercising powers under clauses 11(1)(c) and 11(1)(d), the TRAI had altered the licence conditions of the cellular operators. However, under the Act the

TRAI does not have powers to alter the terms and conditions of licences. Under clause 11(1)(b) of the Act it merely has the power to recommend terms and conditions of licence to a service provider. The court also pointed out that clause 11(1)(d) only empowers the TRAI to regulate revenue-sharing arrangements among service providers. The TRAI can intervene only in the event of service providers being unable to reach an agreement.

Section 14 of the Act also provides the TRAI the authority to settle disputes on matters, among others, relating to revenue-sharing arrangements between different service providers. The court argued that if the TRAI had powers to issue regulations (regarding revenue sharing) which were binding on service providers and/or upon the central government then everybody would be bound to follow those regulations and the question of adjudicating a dispute would not arise.

The court struck down both the Tariff Amendment and the Interconnection Amendment Orders as they related to the CPP regime. However, it suggested that the TRAI should take suitable steps to ensure that the benefits of the change in the licence fee structure are passed on to consumers even if the accompanying CPP regime is not implemented. Cellular operators agreed to implement the reduced tariffs without the CPP features.

TRAI ACT AMENDMENT

In January 2000, the government issued The Telecom Regulatory Authority of India (Amendment) Ordinance which amended the original TRAI Act of 1997. Changes were introduced both in the composition and powers of the Authority. In response to the court's ruling in the CPP case, section 11(1) of the Act, outlining the functions of the Authority, was amended. Section 11(1) now consists of two parts, (a) and (b). Part (a) defines the purely recommendatory functions and part (b) other functions. In part (b) the following new clause has been inserted:

*11(1)(b)(ii):* notwithstanding anything contained in the terms and conditions of the licence granted before the commencement of the Telecom Regulatory Authority (Amendment) Ordinance, 2000, fix the terms and conditions of interconnectivity between the service providers.

The amendment also altered the procedure for settlement of disputes. In the original Act all disputes between service providers, or between service providers and a group of consumers were to be adjudicated by a bench constituted by the TRAI Chairperson. The amendment provides for the establishment of an Appellate

Tribunal, known as the Telecom Disputes Settlement and Appellate Tribunal. In addition to the disputes mentioned in the earlier Act, the Tribunal would also adjudicate disputes 'between a licensor and a licensee'. It would also 'hear and dispose of appeal against any direction, decision or order of the authority (i.e. TRAI) under this act'. Decisions of the Appellate Tribunal can be appealed against only in the Supreme Court.

*Concluding Comments*

The TRAI has repeatedly emphasized that interconnection/usage/access charges should be based on incremental costs directly attributable to provision of interconnection/access/usage. So far the only access/usage charge determination made by the TRAI is the MTC for calls from the fixed to mobile network in a CPP regime. In all other cases it has essentially continued with the revenue-sharing arrangements specified in the various licences. In the case of the MTC the TRAI also had to determine the fixed to mobile retail tariff and, therefore, the amount retained by the fixed line operator.

The tariff and revenue-sharing proposals of the TRAI appear to be driven not so much by costs as by the concern to ensure that the tariff is not 'too high' and both cellular and fixed line operators receive a 'reasonable share'. The only possible way to achieve these objectives in a convincing manner is to base them on costs rather than some general notions of affordability and reasonableness. The TRAI realized that its recommendations suffered from this problem and repeatedly emphasized the 'interim' nature of its proposals, with the promise of eventually moving to cost-based rates. The fate of the CPP proposals clearly shows that non-cost-based interim proposals are not sustainable in a transparent regulatory environment. The TRAI could possibly have used its earlier costing of the basic and cellular networks and made suitable adjustments to arrive at cost-based tariffs and MTC. Given the lack of information such charges would still have problems but they would be more acceptable to operators and consumers.

Interconnection arrangements can be worked out either through direct negotiations among operators or specified by the regulator at the end of a consultation process. Even in the case of direct negotiations, the regulator may have to intervene if operators are unable to reach an agreement or if the agreement is not in the interest of consumers. In the CPP case the TRAI adopted the alternative of specifying charges, even though it had been all along encouraging the DoT and cellular operators to negotiate an interconnect agreement. The TRAI's actions were perhaps precipitated by the failure of the DoT and the operators to reach an agreement, and by its own view of the urgency of introducing the CPP regime. However, according to the verdict of the court, the TRAI Act did not give the TRAI the power to fix interconnection charges. The amended Act seeks to remedy this lacuna and provide the TRAI the power to set interconnection charges.

The TRAI has repeatedly emphasized that interconnection or access charges should be based on incremental costs directly attributable to the provision of interconnection or access. Thus far, the only determination on access charges by the TRAI was on the MTC for calls from the fixed to mobile network, in a CPP regime. In all other cases, the TRAI has used the revenue-sharing arrangements specified in the various licences. While determining the MTC, the TRAI also had to determine the fixed to mobile retail tariff and, therefore, the amount retained by the fixed line operator.

## CASE 3. AVAILABILITY-BASED TARIFF (ABT) ORDER OF THE CERC

The CERC was established under the Electricity Regulatory Commissions Act and has been vested with the power to regulate the tariff of generating companies owned or controlled by the central government. The CERC inherited from the central government the task of introducing ABTs. The government had been examining for over five years the reform of the tariff structure of bulk power so as to improve grid discipline and operation. Most of the grid problems are the result of generators and beneficiaries deviating from their respective schedules for generating or drawing power. During peak hours, with excess drawal, there is a drop in frequency, with the reverse happening during off peak hours. In addition there are rapid and wide changes in frequency for many hours every day and frequent grid disturbances causing tripping of generating stations and interruption of supply to large blocks of consumers and distributors of the regional grids. The main reason for lack of grid discipline is the absence of penalties for deviating from schedules. This in turn is related to the overall structure of tariffs.

### Background on Tariffs for Central Generating Plants

The current tariffs for central generating stations are based on recommendations of the K. P. Rao Committee. The committee made a distinction between fixed and variable charges. Fixed charges include all costs other than fuel costs and return on equity. The government has notified the return on equity from time to time. It was increased from 10 per cent to 12 per cent on 21 December 1991 and then to 16 per cent on 1 November

1998. Fuel cost is included under variable charges. The committee laid down norms for all costs, though these have not been reviewed over time as recommended by the committee. Full fixed charges are recoverable if the generation level, including 'deemed generation', is between 5500 and 6000 hours. Assuming a total of 8760 hours during the year, this is equivalent to a plant load factor (PLF) of 62.78 per cent to 68.49 per cent. Deemed generation is the number of hours a generating station is available but forced to back down because of system constraints. Sharing of the fixed cost among beneficiaries is based on actual energy drawals as a proportion of total drawals by all beneficiaries. Variable cost is also based on energy drawals. The system provided for an incentive payment of 1 paise per kwh for each 1 per cent increase in PLF above 68.49 per cent. Penalty for operating below a PLF of 62.8 per cent was a pro-rata reduction in fixed charges recovery, assuming 100 per cent recovery at 68.5 per cent and 50 per cent recovery at 0 PLF.

Fixed charge allocation based on actual energy drawals was perhaps appropriate for perpetual scarcity situations where it was not possible to make available the allotted MW capacity to the beneficiary. There is also no merit order problem during scarcity as all plants are dispatched. However, this fixed cost allocation formula did not help grid operation during surplus situations. Since state electricity boards (SEBs) considered their own fixed costs as sunk costs they always found it more economical to run their plants, even if the variable cost of these plants was higher, so long as the variable cost was less than the total cost payable to the NTPC. As a result a few states having less generating facilities, and dependent on the NTPC, almost always ended up paying a larger share of fixed charges.

In the absence of a compulsory merit order scheduling and dispatch for all plants in the entire region, self-despatch of the plants was resorted to. The K. P. Rao Committee recommendation regarding vesting regional electricity boards (REBs) with statutory powers for backing down of plants on merit order basis, with penalties for non-fulfilment of such directives, was not implemented. This lead to grid indiscipline and inefficiencies, especially in regions with surplus capacities. Other recommendations of the committee such as time-of-day pricing, which could have improved grid discipline and economic efficiency, have also not been implemented.

The central government issued a set of norms in March 1992 to determine tariffs for power plants to be set up by the independent power producers (IPPs) in the private sector. These have subsequently been modified from time to time. The norms provide for full recovery of fixed charges, including 16 per cent return on equity, at 68.5 per cent PLF. In addition, for every 1 percentage point increase in the deemed PLF there is an incentive in the form of an increase in return on equity of up to 0.7 per cent. There is also a penalty, calculated as a pro rata reduction in the recovery of fixed cost for deemed PLF below target level.

### Draft Notification on ABT

Prior to the transfer of tariff regulation powers to the CERC, the central government had been examining for over five years the reform of the tariff structure of bulk power. The government had engaged international consultants to comprehensively study the Indian power sector and recommend a suitable tariff structure. Their report recommended the introduction of an Availability-based Tariff (ABT) structure. The government then constituted a National Task Force (NTF) as well as regional task forces (RTFs) to debate on various issues in the introduction of an ABT. A draft notification, dated 7 April 1999, was ready but before it could be notified the tariff setting powers were transferred to the CERC.

The ABT system seeks to achieve a situation where least cost power is despatched in preference to more costly power (merit order despatch). This becomes difficult without a two-part tariff for all stations. States tend to compare the total cost of central generators with the variable cost of their own stations, since for them the fixed costs of state-level stations are sunk costs. This results in making central generation appear more expensive than state-level stations, even though on variable cost basis the former may be cheaper. The two-part tariff of the ABT, by making the payment of fixed cost a fixed liability of the states, converts it into a sunk cost thereby levelling the playing field between central generators and state-level plants.

Currently beneficiaries are not liable for payment of the fixed cost associated with the share of capacity allocated to them. If a beneficiary decides not to draw any energy he can escape payment of the fixed charge, which then gets paid by the person drawing energy. This is unfair since it increases the cost of energy even for those beneficiaries who may be drawing energy within their entitlements. The two-part tariff of the ABT assures that each beneficiary will be liable for payment of the fixed cost associated with its share of allocated generation capacity.

On the other hand generators have a perverse financial incentive to go on generating even when there may be no demand. This results in high frequency in the grid as is endemic in the eastern region. The ABT will discourage such behaviour by pricing generation outside the schedule in relation to prevailing frequency.

The following are salient features of the two-part tariff proposed by the NTF:

• The return on equity (ROE) is treated separately from all other fixed charges.

• Reimbursement of fixed charges is based on the availability or declared capacity of the generating station. There are measures to check and penalize excess/under declaration of availability. Available capacity is allocated to beneficiaries on the basis of entitlement. Provision is also made for the unallocated central share of power.

• Full fixed cost, excluding ROE, is recovered at 30 per cent availability on pro rata basis between 0 and 30 per cent. ROE is recovered on pro rata availability between 30 and 70 per cent. There is an incentive of additional ROE of 0.4 per cent for each 1 per cent increase in availability beyond 70 per cent and up to 85 per cent. Beyond 85 per cent the incentive is reduced to 0.3 per cent.

• Variable cost payment is based on the scheduled energy demand of beneficiaries.

• There is provision for additional payment of capacity charge in respect of prolonged outage of any unit of a station beyond ninety days of outage.

• The system provides for scheduling of despatch on a daily basis, at least one day in advance, so as to match supply and demand.

• A charge for unscheduled interchange (UI) charge for the supply and consumption of energy in variation from the pre-committed daily schedule. This charge varies inversely with the system frequency prevailing at the time of supply/consumption. Hence it reflects the marginal value of energy at the time of supply.

### CERC Order on ABT[5]

The CERC issued its order on ABT after almost six months of hearings and consultations. The CERC order on ABT differs from the draft notification in certain significant ways.

• It increases the target availability level at which generators will be able to recover their fixed costs and ROE from 62.79 per cent deemed PLF at present to 80 per cent (85 per cent after one year) for all thermal stations, 85 per cent for hydro in the first year and 77 per cent (82 per cent after one year) for National Long Distance Carrier (NLC). The draft notification provided for recovery of annual fixed costs (minus ROE) at 30 per cent availability and recovery of ROE on pro rata basis between 30 per cent and 70 per cent availability. This order provides for payment of capacity charges

---

[5] Availability Based Tariffs Order dated 4 January 2000.

between 0 per cent and target availability on pro rata basis.

• The draft notification had provided for payment of capacity charges for prolonged outages. The order disallows such payments.

• It delinks the earning of incentive from availability and links it instead to the actual achievement of generation. Hence incentives will be earned by generators only where there is genuine demand for additional energy generation unlike the prevailing situation, or as per the proposed draft notification, whereby it is earned purely because the generator is available.

• The draft notification linked incentives to return on equity. However, this order preserves the status quo of 1 paise per kwh for each 1 per cent increase in PLF above target availability. The PLF is based on actual and not 'deemed generation'.

• It introduces severe financial penalties for grid indiscipline along with significant rewards for behaviour which enforces grid discipline for both generators as well as beneficiaries (see also section 7.1).

• The order permits market pricing for the trading of surplus energy by beneficiaries and generators. It urges the Government of India to allocate the unallocated capacity a month in advance so that beneficiaries know their exact share in capacity in advance and can take steps to trade surplus power.

*NTPC's Objections to the ABT Order*

Soon after the release of the ABT order the NTPC requested a review of the following aspects of the order.

Fixation of target availability at 80 per cent for the period 2000–1 and 85 per cent thereafter.

• The government of India policy for IPPs provides for recovery of full fixed charges including 16 per cent return on equity at 68.49 per cent PLF. Most of the private power agreements (PPAs) have also been signed on this basis. The target availability of 80 per cent in the ABT order is inconsistent with this policy. The CERC does not have jurisdiction to set tariffs which are not consistent with declared government policy.

• Some of the IPPs will be selling power in more than one state and will, therefore, fall under the purview of the CERC. The ABT order, which applies only to the NTPC, is, therefore, discriminatory.

• The CERC has given no reason for deviating from the target availability of 70 per cent specified in the draft notification of the Government of India.

• The CERC has not taken into account several factors such as planned maintenance, forced outages, non-availability of fuel for gas-based plants, and 'regulation

on account of non-payment of outstanding dues' in arriving at the 80–5 per cent target availability.

• Target availability norms cannot be set in isolation from other norms such as financial structure, return on equity, depreciation, operations and maintenance (O&M) expenditure, and station heat rate. These other norms have yet to be fixed pending the result of studies commissioned by the CERC.

• Industrywide norms have not been considered in setting the target availability.

Incentive on actual PLF beyond 80–5 per cent.

• In the case of IPPs incentives in the form of additional return on equity are available beyond 68.5 per cent (PLF plus deemed generation). This is equivalent to providing incentives on the basis of availability rather than actual PLF. The ABT order, therefore, discriminates against the NTPC.

• In the ABT order the incentive for performance beyond 80–5 per cent PLF is less than the penalty in case availability is less than 80–5 per cent.

• In the absence of a merit order despatch system it is not correct to base incentives on actual generation instead of availability.

• Marketing of surplus capacity to deficit regions in order to improve capacity utilization is not possible because of transmission constraints.

Pro rata reduction of fixed charges and returns at all levels.

• This is inconsistent with the draft ABT notification, which provides for some recovery of fixed charges in the event of prolonged outages.

Penalty for misdeclaration of capacity.

• There is a need to define misdeclaration and also develop a proper mechanism for implementation. There is also a need to streamline procedures for revision of declared availability on account of factors beyond the control of the NTPC.

*Resolving the Differences*

While the CERC order makes a number of changes to the draft notification, the main point of contention is the change in target availability from 70 per cent to 80 per cent (from 1 April 2000) and 85 per cent (from 1 April 2001). This becomes all the more significant as all fixed charges, *including ROE*, are recoverable on a pro rata basis between 0 and 80 per cent availability. This is in contrast to the provision in the draft notification where fixed charges, excluding ROE, are recoverable 100 per cent at an availability of 30 per cent, and only the ROE is recoverable on a pro rata basis between 30 per cent and 70 per cent. Additionally, the order does not make any provision for fixed charges payment for prolonged outages. Finally, the generator earns incentive payments not just by exceeding target availability but by achieving PLF of greater than 80 per cent, based on actual, and not deemed, generation.

The draft notification availability norm takes into account:

• the NTPC average performance over a period of ten years of approximately 72 per cent;

• that IPPs are allowed full recovery of fixed cost and ROE at an availability of 68.5 per cent;

• all-India average for thermal stations, including the NTPC, of 58 per cent.[6]

Similarly, the CERC has identified target availability as 'the average level a unit is expected to attain' (5.5.2).[7] It has also refrained from setting stationwise target availability 'since it may involve accepting inefficiencies of each unit and the target cannot, therefore, be ideal in all cases' (5.5.7). It also agreed with the NTF observation that 'Performance of NTPC stations should not be compared with that of SEBs old stations while determining target availability for NTPC units' (5.5.5). The CERC used the following information for arriving at the figure for target availability.

• CEA Annual Report figures for 1998–9 of 76.5 per cent PLF for NTPC stations and all India average of 64.6 per cent. 'The average of 75.6 per cent when combined with the experience of deemed generation, would lead to an average availability of around 80 per cent to 85 per cent' (5.5.4).

• Availability of NTPC plants over the last five years. (There are only ranges of availability across various units and no average is mentioned in the order.)

Fixing target availability on the basis of historical average performance is justified to the extent it implies that on an average, across plants and across years, the NTPC will be able to recover their fixed charges, including the 16 per cent ROE. However, this will be true only if the 'penalties' for below average performance and the 'incentives' for above average performance are symmetric. Interestingly, the draft notification satisfied this condition with respect to the ROE. For each percentage point availability below 70 per cent the firm loses 0.4 per cent ROE (16 per cent divided by

40, the difference between 30 and 70 per cent) and for each percentage point availability above 70 per cent (and up to 85 per cent) it gains 0.4 per cent ROE. Therefore, if, *on an average,* the NTPC achieves an availability of 70 per cent its ROE will also be 16 per cent, *on an average.* In this framework not all payments received for availability above 70 per cent are in the nature of incentives. They are merely payments to ensure that, on an average, the NTPC earns its ROE. The 0.3 per cent additional ROE for availability above 85 per cent in the draft notification is more in the nature of an incentive.

In the case of the CERC order, for each percentage point performance below 80 per cent (*availability*) NTPC loses 1/80th of the total fixed costs, including ROE. However, for each percentage point performance above 80 per cent (*actual generation*) it receives an incentive of 1 paise per Kwh. The gains and losses are unlikely to be symmetric. In fact, since the incentives are based on actual generation, they will be realized only at availabilities of higher than 80 per cent, for example 85 per cent, assuming 5 per cent deemed generation. The rationale given for this deviation—PLF instead of availability—is that 'mere availability of the plant without demand cannot justify incentive payment'. (5.4.3) However, as discussed in the preceding paragraph, payments for performance above target availability are not really in the nature of incentive payments. They are to ensure that the firm on an average realizes its full costs and return. In this case, since the gains and losses are not symmetric, it is unlikely that the NTPC will on an average earn its fixed costs even if it achieves, on an average, the target availability of 80 per cent. This point is in fact made in passing in the NTPC review petition. (A.6.s).

Second, differences in the performance of units can arise not only because of differences in efficiency but also because of differences in technology, age, and fuel supply. While differences in efficiency should *not* be considered in setting norms, differences in factors beyond the control of the firm should be taken into account in setting norms or assessing performance against norms. Of these, perhaps, the fuel supply problem is most significant because of problems in gas allocation for gas-based plants. As per Annexure F of the NTPC review petition, the weighted average PLF for the last five years of gas-based plants has been only 57.5 per cent as compared to 76.6 per cent for coal-based plants. There is thus obvious need to separate the gas-based plants and not average them along with the coal-based plants. Perhaps, their target availability could be linked to the availability of gas, including from imported sources.

[6] NTPC Petition No. 2/1999 (3.ii).
[7] This and subsequent figures in parentheses refer to chapter and paragraph nos of the Availability-based Tariffs Order dated 4 January 2000 of the Central Electricity Regulation Commission.

Third, there is the question of how to deal with low probability events, such as prolonged outages, even caused by a 'cyclone'! (5.6.3). It is not appropriate to ignore them just because they are low probability events because, when they do occur, they can impose significant costs on the NTPC. However, it may be difficult to include them in the averages used for working out target availability since they may not have occurred in the sample period used for calculating the average. The approach taken in the draft notification of making special provision for prolonged outages is probably most appropriate. This should be incorporated in the CERC order as well. An alternative, if possible, is for NTPC to take insurance cover for such prolonged outages and include the annual insurance premium in its fixed cost for the year.

Finally, while NTPC performance should not be compared with that of *old* SEB plants, there is certainly no problem in comparing it with other plants, equivalent in terms of availability of fuel and finance. It should not be impossible to find such plant in several parts of the country which can serve as comparison for NTPC plants.

*Conclusions*

In summary the CERC needs to consider the following modifications to its ABT order:

• Separate gas plants and coal-based plants for tariff purposes. The target availability and PLF of 80 per cent is appropriate for coal-based plants, going by the data provided by the NTPC in its revenue petition Annexure-F. Coal-based plants have, on an average (across plants in a year), achieved an equivalent availability factor of 78–85 per cent in each year since 1993–4.

Target availability/PLF of gas-based plants should be linked to gas availability. Of course, the NTPC should be encouraged to explore all possibilities for obtaining adequate gas supplies.

• Target availability may have to be set below the historical average availability to account for asymmetric gains and losses. The incentive aspect should be built in only after the scope for achieving higher availability levels has clearly been established on the basis of detailed technical studies of NTPC plant performance. This could be a part of the CERC norms setting exercise. The structure of the incentive mechanism should also be thought through more clearly. As pointed out, so called incentive payments may not really be incentive payments.

• Prolonged outages should be excluded from the calculation of historical averages. Instead, special provision should be made for prolonged outages as in the draft notification. The possibility of obtaining insurance for such outages should also be explored.

• Overall, in response to the NTPC's demand for 'revenue neutrality' the CERC should emphasize that the ABT system is designed to ensure that the NTPC covers all its costs and earns the 16 per cent rate of return. The obligation of the regulator is to ensure viability and not revenue neutrality. The ability of the ABT system to generate the appropriate ROE for the NTPC can only be demonstrated by simulations or scenario analysis conducted on a financial model of the NTPC. To begin with, such a model could be simple. Over time complexities can be added to make it increasingly realistic. This must be an essential part of the ABT exercise.

# 4 | REGULATORY DILEMMAS IN INFRASTRUCTURE FINANCING

*Jayanth Varma*

## INTRODUCTION

For most of the twentieth century, publicly financed infrastructure was the widely accepted norm. It was only in the closing years of the century that private financing made a huge comeback. Students of economic history know that infrastructure was largely privately financed in the nineteenth century. Now it is becoming increasingly clear that in this, as in many other respects, the twenty-first century will be more like the nineteenth than the twentieth century.

It is now well understood that private capital will have to build a large part of the infrastructure that we need in India over the coming years. However, the private sector can play this role only if it has access to domestic or international sources of financing for both equity and debt. In emerging markets, financing large infrastructure projects can become difficult since financial institutions and markets are not sufficiently well developed. Promoters of infrastructure projects then turn to the government to help them by either

• relaxing the financial regulatory regime for such projects, or

• providing fiscal incentives, direct subsidies or other forms of government support to attract private capital.

This chapter discusses the conditions under which governments should consider either of these two approaches to promoting privately financed infrastructure. It concludes that while both these approaches have potential uses, they are quite often simply 'soft' alternatives to the painful but essential reforms in the regulation of the infrastructure sectors.

## RELAXING FINANCIAL SECTOR REGULATIONS

### Is There a Conflict between Regulation and Development?

A fairly common argument in favour of regulatory relaxation is that financial sector regulators (for example the securities market regulator, the central bank, the finance ministry, and the insurance regulator) should place 'larger national interests' above their own regulatory objectives. After all, the nation needs roads and bridges urgently, and it is argued that a slight laxity in financial regulations is a small price to pay for ensuring that this infrastructure is built quickly. In this view, economic development is the paramount objective for emerging markets, and regulators in these countries have to balance their regulatory and developmental roles.

It is doubtless true that financial sector regulators in emerging markets have a developmental role to play. Often they have to first create and develop the markets and institutions that they are supposed to regulate, and it is not uncommon for a developmental mandate to be enjoined by statute. For example, the Securities and Exchange Board of India (SEBI) Act states: 'It shall be the duty of SEBI to protect the interests of investors in securities and to promote the development of, and to regulate, the securities markets.'

Yet this is far from saying that regulators should compromise fundamental objectives like investor protection in the pursuit of 'larger national interests'. In fact, the developmental role of regulators is, in the ultimate analysis, only a proactive way of ensuring investor protection by actively encouraging the development of institutions and markets that meet investors' needs.

It is here argued that the alleged dilemma of choosing between good roads and sound banks is a non-existent one. It is possible and necessary to have both. It is also argued that if ever one had to choose between the two, one should choose the latter. The reason is simply that a weak financial system would ultimately drag the rest of the economy down with it, and the best infrastructure in the world would then be of little use.

### Is Infrastructure Financing Risk Free?

Another common argument is that infrastructure is so urgently needed and so clearly beneficial to society at large that there are no real risks in infrastructure projects. It is felt that as quasi-monopoly providers of essential services, infrastructure projects are low-risk projects. It is also thought that infrastructure developers are chosen after careful evaluation of competing bids, and that they are unlikely to be fly-by-night operators.

On closer examination, however, one finds that the alleged absence of risks in infrastructure projects is a myth. Part of the reason is that a socially beneficial project may still be quite risky from the investors' point of view. When regulators are asked to dilute prudential safeguards for infrastructure financing, it is useful to keep in mind the various sources of unique risks in infrastructure projects and their financing instruments.

• Demand-side risks arise because infrastructure is the ultimate non-tradable and is characterized by high asset specificity. Demand can be highly price and income sensitive, as was amply demonstrated during the East Asian crisis. Some examples are cited below.

Kuala Lumpur's second international airport became operational at a time when the Asian crisis had depressed air traffic. As a result, the existing airport was adequate to handle the prevailing traffic, and it became apparent that the second airport could profitably have been delayed a few years. Unlike an aircraft, which can be redeployed on a more profitable route, an airport has a high degree of asset specificity—it can serve only its local market.

Bangkok's traffic jams were so legendary that when three alternative mass transit systems were initiated in the mid-1990s, they must have seemed risk-free propositions. But after the Asian crisis, with slower traffic growth and reduced willingness of consumers to pay for convenience during times of economic hardship, it is doubtful whether these projects would be commercially viable. Thailand's cement manufacturers can export their way out of trouble, but the light railway is condemned to live with its local market.

Pakistan's private power projects are all in jeopardy because of insufficient demand and high tariffs resulting from currency depreciation. Power is less of a non-tradable than many other infrastructure products, but its tradability is still limited—India is the only potential buyer of Pakistani power

• Appropriability risks arise because of free rider problems and political considerations. Even if a project is socially beneficial, the benefits may not accrue to the project because of lack of appropriability. For this reason, projects often have to be sufficiently large in scope to allow multiple benefit streams to be appropriated. This of course leads to management risks.

A good example of this is the Canary Wharf project in London that bankrupted the giant construction firm Olympia and York. When the project failed, critics said that Olympia and York had bitten off more than they could chew. Olympia and York replied that, if anything, the project was too small rather than too large. They said that they should also have included a light railroad to increase the marketability of the commercial property that they were building at Canary Wharf.

Another example is the Eurotunnel rail link under the sea between the United Kingdom (UK) and France. Critics argue that one reason for the project's poor performance is the fact that it did not include a road link. However, at the time of awarding the contract to Eurotunnel against competing bidders, one important consideration for the governments was that it had a well-researched and detailed plan with a short construction schedule and committed funding. The road–rail link would have been more expensive, complex, riskier, and more difficult to finance.

• Management risks are significant because project complexity is very high and management often has no relevant experience or track record.

The telecom bidding in India is a good example. Many companies with no track record in this business won telecom licences on the basis of bids, which with hindsight appear too high. The government had to migrate these contracts from licence fees to revenue sharing. There has also been a wave of mergers, consolidation, and restructuring in the industry.

• Some infrastructure projects carry high technical risks because of their technical complexity, possibility of technological obsolescence, and safety/environmental concerns.

Technological risks are well illustrated by the Iridium project which promised satellite telephony anywhere on the planet through a network of dedicated satellites. Rapid advances in cell phone technology, however, reduced Iridium to a niche market too tiny to be economically viable.

• Financial and legal risks arise from non-recourse financing, complex payment mechanisms (for example escrow accounts), and imperfect credit enhancement.

Non-recourse financing means that the debt is secured only by the assets and cash flows of the project itself. The parent company does not guarantee the debt at all.

Escrow accounts are an imperfect form of security, as borrowers can under conditions of financial distress sometimes divert cash flows to non-escrowed accounts, leaving the lender with no effective remedy.

• Instrument-specific risks arise from maturity mismatches, exposure to interest rate fluctuations, restrictions on assignability, and charge creation. Examples of these are given later in this chapter.

With this in mind, I turn to the regulatory issues in different sources of financing.

### Regulatory Issues in Tapping Retail Investors

In most countries, companies can tap retail investors for equity only after they have established a track record. This is not usually possible in infrastructure projects. Many countries exempt infrastructure projects from the track record requirements for listing. One possible justification for this could be that infrastructure projects are typically awarded by government agencies after a careful evaluation of the capability of the bidder. As such, the possibility of fly-by-night operators emerging in this area are somewhat reduced. Nevertheless, this is a conscious sacrifice of investor protection.

Most security market regulators worldwide rely on strong disclosure requirements in ensuring that the public is not misled by issuers of capital. Ensuring effective disclosure in infrastructure projects can be quite challenging:

Not only are the projects themselves quite complex, but they involve complex contracts (for example Power Purchase Agreements [PPAs]), complex legal structures (for example escrow accounts and special purpose vehicles), and complex priority rules and charges on assets.

Complex instruments are quite common in infrastructure financing globally. Sometimes different financial instruments are 'stapled' together so that investors can buy and sell them only as a unit. Different kinds of debt may be stapled together, or debt may be stapled together with a non-detachable equity warrant. Eurotunnel provides an example where the shares of the British and French companies operating the tunnel are stapled together and can be traded only as a unit.

In India, we have seen several public sector infrastructure projects where there have been serious disclosure problems in the prospectus. Consider the following examples:

Irrigation projects promoted by various state governments have issued bonds on the strength of a tripartite agreement with the state governments. Retail investors have had great difficulty in understanding the difference between a government guarantee and the tripartite agreement. Disclosure of the tripartite agreement has left much to be desired.

There have been bond issues that were rated principally on the strength of a letter of comfort from the government. The letter of comfort was neither reproduced in the prospectus nor even made available for inspection.

There have also been municipal 'secured' bonds. These were not really secure in any meaningful sense. All that promised was that security would be created on certain assets. On these assets the corporation obtained, after all due diligence and efforts, the requisite consents and permissions to create the mortgage or charge.

Regulators also insist on effective, continuing disclosure by entities that have raised capital from the public. In an infrastructure project, it is not uncommon for the issuer of security to be a special purpose vehicle (SPV) while the operating company and the ultimate guarantor are totally different entities. Continuing disclosure may mean disclosure by one or more of these entities or it may mean disclosure on a consolidated basis. Some countries (for example Australia) require that all three statements (SPV, operator, and consolidated) be sent to investors so that they can choose which ones to use. While not wholly satisfactory, this may be the best possible solution. In the Eurotunnel example given earlier, UK law requires that investors be given the stand-alone financial statements of the UK company. French law requires a 'horizontal' consolidation of the UK and French companies. Investors thus receive two sets of accounts prepared under different accounting standards.

There has been some talk of infrastructure developers in India wanting to float special purpose mutual funds that would invest only in the debt securities of the promoter. If this were acceded to, it would destroy the diversification that is the hallmark of a mutual fund.

### Regulatory Issues in Tapping Contractual Savings

Much of the literature on infrastructure financing in India refers to the large pool of contractual savings like provident funds, pension funds, and insurance. Unfortunately, tapping contractual savings is not free of regulatory problems.

In case of defined benefit schemes, the sponsor of the scheme guarantees a specified set of benefits (for example lifetime pensions) regardless of actual performance of the investment portfolio underlying the fund. Ensuring the solvency of such funds is notoriously difficult. Globally, there have been several instances of government- and corporate-sponsored defined benefit schemes that have become bankrupt in all but name.

• It is forecasted that the US Social Security system will turn into deficit by around 2010 or 2015.

• Most Japanese companies have large unfunded pension liabilities that they have not so far been required to report on their balance sheets. This must be kept in mind while considering the apparent success of many East Asian countries in using their government-sponsored contractual savings as a vast pool of developmental finance.

• East Asian countries like Malaysia and Singapore mobilized large savings through contractual savings schemes. The governments were able to use these funds quite effectively in financing industrialization and infrastructure development. In trying to replicate this success, we must remember that apart from prudent investment policies, the viability of this model was facilitated by rapid economic growth and by favourable demographics.

In case of defined contribution schemes, the sponsor does not guarantee any benefits. The benefits that the contributor receives depend entirely on the return earned by the investment portfolio underlying the scheme. In some cases, the contributor is allowed to choose between a limited number of investment portfolios managed by the sponsor. The regulatory dilemma here arises because contractual savings involve a significant element of forced savings as well as a pre-emption of these savings into specific investment channels. It is all the more important for the regulator to ensure a reasonable return on these savings. Otherwise, contractual saving schemes could become an instrument of financial repression.

The Indian regulatory regime for contractual savings is based on the archaic and arcane notion of a 'trust security'. As the name suggests, these are the only securities in which charitable trusts are allowed to invest. However, the same investment restrictions apply to provident funds and some other contractual savings vehicles. In India, the definition of trust security is a state subject and does not come under the purview of any of the financial sector regulators. For all practical purposes, the approval of a security as a trust security has been a political decision with little emphasis on investor protection. Maharashtra, which is home to some of the

largest trusts and provident funds, is known to use the trust security approval to ensure subscription for bonds floated by government bodies in Maharashtra. Trust security approval for bonds of comparable risk from government bodies of other states have often been denied or delayed.

### Regulatory Issues in Borrowing from Banks and Financial Institutions

Financing of infrastructure by banks and financial institutions gives rise to three different kinds of regulatory issues.

First, many infrastructure projects require long-term financing. When banks provide such funding, they are exposed to a maturity mismatch, as most of their funding is through short-term deposits. The maturity mismatch is partly a liquidity risk and partly an interest rate risk. Lending on a floating rate basis can mitigate the interest rate risk for the bank but at the cost of creating the same risk for the project. Capital-intensive infrastructure projects are not well positioned to handle this risk.

Because of their long maturity and unique risks, credit appraisal of infrastructure projects is very different from the credit appraisal that banks do for providing short-term credit facilities to industrial borrowers. As a result, only a relatively small number of banks have the appraisal skills required for this purpose.

Large infrastructure projects may breach banks' exposure limits for individual borrowers or industries. This problem arises when banks attempt to fill the gap created by the projects' inability to tap other sources of finance. The problem is also aggravated when only a limited number of banks have the willingness and ability to engage in infrastructure financing.

This is not to deny that banks have a significant role to play in infrastructure financing. The point is rather that they cannot be the sole or even the dominant providers of funds for these projects. However, a project that is able to tap a diverse range of funding options could benefit greatly from timely bank finance. For this to happen, it is necessary to strengthen and reform the banking system (Ferreira and Khatami 1996).

### Regulatory Issues in Tapping Foreign Debt

There is a vast literature on the regulatory issues involved in opening up the economy to external capital flows. An important conclusion in this literature is that opening up the capital account to foreign debt is more dangerous than opening it up to foreign direct investment (FDI) or even to foreign portfolio investment. The East Asian crisis has brought this home in dramatic fashion. East Asian countries opened up their economies to capital inflows (especially debt-creating inflows) while retaining substantial restrictions on capital outflows. This coupled with weaknesses in the financial sector led to the economy as a whole taking very large foreign exchange risks and credit spread risks (Varma 1998).

India has operated a fairly restrictive policy on allowing foreign borrowing. The key element in this has been an annual ceiling on aggregate external commercial borrowing (ECB). This has been coupled with a floor on debt maturity and a ceiling on interest rate spread, which together act as a credit-rating filter. An often heard demand is that infrastructure should be exempt from the annual ECB ceiling. One argument in favour of this has been that the requirement for infrastructure finance is so large that the domestic capital market is simply incapable of meeting this need in the foreseeable future.

The major problem with this argument is that if the infrastructure financing need is indeed so large, not just for the next year or two but for the foreseeable future, then we as a nation cannot possibly afford that infrastucture at all. It is evident that if the financing remains large for several years, then in time its debt service would become equally large (if not larger). If the financing requirement were too large for our economy to absorb, then we would not be able to absorb the servicing requirement either.

The only way out of this would be if the large investments led to a large increase in our debt service capability. Unfortunately, this is not likely to happen because infrastructure tends to produce non-tradable outputs. Unlike an export-oriented factory, which earns the foreign exchange for its own debt servicing, an infrastructure project produces goods and services that must of necessity be locally consumed. This means that financing infrastructure with foreign debt is particularly risky from a macroeconomic point of view. In fact, one could argue that the ECB for an infrastructure project must be subject to even more stringent caps than normal ECB.

Historical experience suggests that dependence on foreign funds for infrastructure is likely to be a short-term phenomenon. There might be a few years during which the need for infrastructure financing is very great and has to be met from foreign sources, but over a period of time this dependence is likely to decrease. In fact, after a few years the infrastructure companies themselves would probably generate significant cash flows and the dependence on outside finance (debt or equity from domestic or foreign markets) would come down. For example, in the United States, railroad companies relied on outside finance for 98 per cent of their capital needs in the 1880s. By World War I, internal sources accounted for 40 per cent of capital needs, and during 1920–40, internal sources provided 95 per cent of the capital needs. In a less extreme form, the same story was repeated in other infrastructure industries like electricity and telephones (Ulmer 1960).

Recent experience of the International Finance Corporation (IFC) suggests that foreign funds account for more than half the project costs in developing countries (IFC 1996). However, the IFC itself recognizes that this is not sustainable and argues that domestic savings intermediated through domestic capital markets would provide a larger chunk of infrastructure financing in the future.

### Regulatory Issues in Tapping Foreign Equity

There are no major regulatory concerns in tapping foreign equity for infrastructure projects. In fact for some sectors, like telecom, foreign equity is very attractive. Dedicated sector funds exist, especially in the United States, for some of these sectors. These funds have distinctive expertise and competence in the sector, and their global experience and diversification enables them to take a view on technology.

Data for IFC-funded infrastructure projects suggest that foreign funding in the form of debt is nearly four times as large as foreign funding in the form of equity (IFC 1996, table 6.2). This is only partly explained by the fact that the projects had an average debt -to-equity ratio of about 1:5:1. Interestingly, the experience in the nineteenth century was not very different. It has been estimated that around 1914, the value of British holding of foreign bonds was about two and a half times the value of British holding of foreign equities (Lewis 1938). Eichengreen (1994) suggests that this bias against equity arises because investors in stocks require a more reliable and comprehensive flow of information as compared to investors in bonds, and because foreigners have greater difficulty in getting this information.

### Regulatory Issues in Tapping the Consumer

There are some distinctive advantages in creating innovative financial instruments that offer preferential access to infrastructure services in return for financing. Preferential access may be in the form of lower cost, guaranteed availability, or superior quality. An extreme example would be a power company that floats bonds whose coupons and redemption are specified not in money terms but in units of electricity. These kinds of instruments

• provide a natural hedge both for the operating company and for the consumer

- are especially beneficial when fixed costs are high and
- provide reliable indicators of demand

However, there could be a possible conflict with sectoral regulatory structures. Many sectoral regulators may take a dim view of the implicit 'bundling' of infrastructure services with financial claims. Abhorrent as these ideas may seem to orthodox sectoral regulators, they do deserve serious consideration in sectors like power, irrigation, and water where a combination of regulatory and state failures makes alternative routes to infrastructure development very difficult. At least in the transitional phase, pending thoroughgoing reforms in these sectors, sectoral regulators should probably permit some degree of bundling of financial claims with infrastructure services.

## GOVERNMENT SUPPORT FOR INFRASTRUCTURE FINANCING

### Alternative Forms of Support

Government support for infrastructure financing can take several forms:

- In India, income tax incentives have been provided either to the infrastructure project itself or to the investors in such a project.

    - Some infrastructure projects enjoy a tax holiday for a few years, but for long-gestation projects this may not mean much in present value terms, as these projects do not expect to make significant profits in the initial years.

    - Interest earned on certain infrastructure bonds has been exempted from income tax.

    - Limited tax breaks have been given for equity investment in certain infrastructure companies.

- Central and state governments in India have underwritten the major sources of risk in some infrastructure projects through guarantees of various kinds.

    - In many power projects, PPAs transfer all demand risks and input cost risks to the government.

    - In some other projects, developers have (with varying degrees of success) been demanding guarantees from the government in respect of projected traffic and other demand parameters.

- In many emerging markets including India, governments have used their directed credit systems to channel funds into infrastructure. India has done this with its banks and insurance companies, while some East Asian countries have used their large state-managed contractual savings pools in this manner.

- Britain has had considerable success with auctions in which competing developers bid for the lowest amount of subsidy that they would accept in return for undertaking a socially desirable infrastructure project that is not privately profitable. This is like an auction of licences except that the licence fee is negative. Just as a company pays the government for the right to undertake lucrative projects (telecom licences, for example), the government pays the company to undertake unprofitable but socially useful projects (a low-traffic railway line, for example).

- The nineteenth century provides plentiful examples of governments providing credit enhancement for or directly subscribing to bonds floated by infrastructure companies.

I shall argue later in the chapter that though negative licence fees represent the most transparent and efficient way of supporting infrastructure financing in a mature capital market, credit enhancement could also have a role to play in a country with underdeveloped debt markets. But before coming to these conclusions, let us take a closer look at each of the tools listed above.

### Income Tax Incentives

In general, income tax incentives represent a blunt and inefficient instrument for promoting any specific economic activity. This is true for infrastructure financing as well. Tax incentives are available equally to the most profitable projects which would have been undertaken even without the tax break. In fact, a tax holiday is most valuable to highly profitable projects! Another difficulty is that the persons who are in the best position to utilize the tax incentive may not be the ones who are best equipped to undertake the desired economic activity. Many tax incentives are most attractive to retail investors, and the project may not be suitable for retail financing.

Above all, tax incentives go against the general thrust of fiscal reform, which aims at a low tax rate with few deductions and exemptions. Tax incentives for financial instruments also distort the capital market and work against the objective of financial sector reforms to create an efficient market free of segmentation.

### Risk Transfer to the Government

In many ways, this route is the worst possible to promote private infrastructure. In fact, when the risks have been transferred to the government, the 'derisked' project is 'private' infrastructure in name only. In economic substance, such derisked projects are simply an expensive form of government borrowing to finance infrastructure. With the major risks assumed by the government, the private sector is provides hardly any risk capital. The capital the private sector provides to such derisked projects is analogous to lending to the government with a risk premium added for residual risks assumed by the project. True, such 'borrowing' does not show up in the government's fiscal deficit, but that is only because the government's accounting does not recognize contingent liabilities at all. In fact, replacing publicly funded infrastructure with derisked privately funded projects is substantially the same as replacing government borrowing with a contingent liability.

The whole idea of private financing of infrastructure is to let capital markets assume a greater role in the allocation of resources. This would happen only if the equity investors in so-called private infrastructure projects bear most of the significant risks and receive the associated rewards. Any attempt to derisk the projects by transferring significant demand-side risks to the government defeats the very objective of private sector infrastructure financing.

After reviewing the IFC's experience in this regard, Bond and Carter (1994) state: 'IFC's experience indicates that it is the combination of risk finance and performance-linked contracts that determines the success of private infrastructure projects. Capital supplied without risk (i.e. government guaranteed) and/or without binding incentives has not had a similar record of success.' It is paradoxical that despite this evidence from its own experience, the World Bank's policy prescriptions for sectors like power in India amount to derisking the project and transferring major risks to the government.

## Directed Credit

Directed credit is largely a pre-liberalization phenomenon. Financial sector reforms seek to reduce the scope of directed credit and to eliminate it eventually. Moreover, directed credit is only a non-transparent way of (quasi) sovereign credit enhancement. Providing credit enhancement directly and transparently has the advantage of not weakening the financial system.

## Negative Licence Fee

If an infrastructure project has a high social but an unacceptable private rate of return, the socially desirable level of investment can be achieved by a transfer payment from the state to the private sector. This is a standard proposition in the economic theory relating to externalities. The theory would also say that the transfer payment should not exceed the amount of the externality itself (the difference between the social and private returns to the project). If this is violated, then projects that earn an unacceptable social rate of return may be undertaken.

The negative licence fee arrived at through a bidding process can potentially achieve this transfer payment. The auction process must include a reservation price (or upset price) to set a ceiling on the transfer payment and ensure that it does not exceed the externality. Of course, cynics would argue that regardless of what economic theory might say, this upset price will in practice be more the outcome of political processes than anything else. The determination of this upset price is therefore the principal difficulty involved in operationalizing the concept.

Another problem that has occasionally arisen in Britain relates to the bankruptcy of the original bidder. Often the project is characterized by high asset specificity, and most of the money that has already been invested in the project may be regarded as a sunk cost. Then it would appear that a small incremental investment made by the state to rescue the project has a huge social return. The government may thus be tempted to provide an additional subsidy to the project to save it from bankruptcy. On the other hand, it could be argued that such an additional subsidy would amount to renegotiating the bids of the original auction and is not fair to other bidders. In a sense, this problem arises from bankruptcy rather than the subsidy itself. More or less the same problem has arisen in India with companies that bid very large (positive) licence fees for telecom licences and then got into financial distress.

## Credit Enhancement

There is a fairly large amount of literature showing that the privately financed infrastructure of the nineteenth century in fact made substantial use of public funds. For example, the UK was the only large country that did not support railway construction with public funds in that century. In a country like the United States, the federal, state, and local governments provided financial support in various forms. They subscribed to some of the Railways' bonds, they guaranteed the interest on some bonds, and they provided the collateral for many bonds through their land grants.[1]

All these forms of credit enhancement made infrastructure bonds more easily marketable to domestic and foreign investors. Yet in almost none of these cases was the government support anywhere near complete. Paradoxically, the only important instance of almost complete government guarantee that reduced the risk

---

[1] See, for example, Eichengreen (1994) and Dobin (1994).

of default to virtually zero was that of the guarantees provided to finance railroad construction in colonial India. These guarantees, which provided clean arbitrage profits to the investor, lacked economic justification and were motivated by political and military consider-ations. The result, of course, was a railway network that revealed scant concern for commercial optimality. Unfortunately, the colonial Indian railroad guarantees have helped to wrongly convince many Indian policy makers and analysts that infrastructure financing re-quires large public financial support.

In drawing lessons from the nineteenth century, we must disregard the colonial Indian experience and inter-pret the experiences of other countries in the light of the following crucial factors:

- In the nineteenth century, financial markets in most of the North American and European countries were still in the process of development. It is significant that the country with the best financial markets and institutions (the UK) did not find it necessary to provide any financial support at all.[2] Thus public support reflects the state of the financial sector even more than the unique characteristics of infrastructure projects.

- A great deal of the difficulty of attracting private capital to the railroads in the nineteenth century stemmed from the fact that this was then a new industry whose economics was totally unknown. Projecting the returns on railroads in unfamiliar terrain must have been as difficult then as projecting the returns on an internet company is today. (The key difference was that unlike today's internet companies, the railroads needed huge amounts of physical investment and therefore lots of funds.) Today countries like India are trying to draw private funds into mature infrastructure projects whose economics is extremely well understood both domesti-cally and globally. This makes the task far easier than the task of the great infrastructure projects of the nineteenth century.

- In many cases, the state provided funds for specific projects more like an economic agent (or rather a collec-tive of economic agents) than like a state exercising its sovereign function. For example, a city that was threatened with being bypassed in railroad route plans often offered money to the railroad to change these plans so as to pass through the city. It was behaving just as any private economic agent would.[3]

- Some forms of public support, like land grants, represented a mechanism by which the project could appropriate the social returns more completely and internalize some of the externalities. For example, when the construction of a railroad leads to a rise in property prices in the vicinity, what we are seeing is a large externality (the landowners garner some of the social benefits of the railroad). The land grant merely served to internalize this externality and bring private returns closer to social returns. Evidently, land grants might have a similar role to play in encouraging private investment in road building in India.

This analysis suggests that the principal argument in favour of credit enhancement as a tool for promoting infrastructure development in India is our relatively underdeveloped bond markets. It is to this that this chapter now turns.

### Development of the Bond Market

Much of the literature on the Indian debt market has a lugubrious air to it. Indeed a very common phrase that one hears is that the Indian debt market is a dead market. Much of the discussion therefore concludes either that the debt market will not develop in the foreseeable future or that the state must somehow bring this market into existence through tax breaks and other regulatory changes.

I believe that while governments can create market-places, the participants create markets. A market comes into existence when a critical mass of economic agents finds it advantageous to transact in that market. In the case of the debt market, three kinds of participants can have the incentive to create the market—the borrowers, the lenders, and the intermediaries. Experience suggests that most often the borrowers have taken the initiative in this regard, just as in most product markets the manufacturers go about creating the market for their products. The reason is simple—the borrowers have the greatest ability to internalize the market creation costs in the form of lower borrowing costs. Having said that, it must be added that the nineteenth century provides some interesting examples of debt markets being created by financial intermediaries.[4] Even in this case, though, the government in its capacity as a major borrower played a vital role in supporting and encour-aging these intermediaries.

---

[2] 'The United Kingdom is the only important country whose railways have been developed practically without public aid,' Dunn (1913).

[3] It is sometimes thought that this practice was undesirable and represented a form of corruption. This is not the case at all. In fact, it was a fairly rational way of choosing a railway route, if

we assume that the cities competed with each other in a more or less 'efficient' market. Interestingly, in Britain, where the central and local governments refrained from supporting the railroads, private local groups took up the task of influencing the route planning (Dobbin 1994).

[4] See, for example, Landes (1956) for more information.

Recent global experience provides ample reason to be optimistic about these markets emerging fairly quickly when the conditions are ripe:

• When the Euro came into existence at the beginning of 1999, many observers were optimistic about the currency but fretted about the lack of a well-developed bond market in the Euro zone. In just over a year's time, while the currency has fared disastrously, the corporate bond market in the Euro, including the high yield market, has exceeded the expectations of most analysts. On most measures, the market now rivals the dollar market. European integration forced large European companies to raise huge amounts of debt to finance their cross-border expansion. With that kind of incentive, a pan-European debt market came to life very quickly.

• When the East Asian crisis struck, corporate debt markets in the region were as close to being non-existent as in India. In the wake of the crisis, companies that had borrowed significantly in dollars were looking desperately to replace them with local currency debt. The banks were weighed down with bad debts and unable to lend. Slowly East Asian companies appear to be creating a local currency bond market. To take just one example, Thailand's largest industrial conglomerate, Siam Cement, was able to raise over US $ 1 billion of local currency bonds in the space of a few months. Of course, it had to design innovative bonds, use several maturity tranches, create arrangements for market making, and so on. But the point is that borrowers with strong incentives will incur these costs.

• During most of the 1990s, South Africa presented the strange spectacle of an economy where the corporate bond market was more liquid and active than the stock market. The Bond Exchange boasted of annual trading volumes equal to several times the total bonds outstanding. Even more strangely, some of the large corporate bonds (particularly public sector corporate bonds) were more liquid than the sovereign bonds of the Republic of South Africa itself. The reason was that these large issuers provided very active market-making facilities in their own bonds. By standing ready to buy and sell their own bonds, they created a liquid market for them. The costs that they incurred in such market making were perhaps more than made up by the lower interest rates that they paid (in some cases lower than that on sovereign bonds). This example once again highlights the fact that borrowers who face the right incentives do end up creating a liquid bond market.[5]

[5] It would take us too far afield to discuss the historical factors in the apartheid era and thereafter which led to the particular institutional structure of the South African financial sector.

What I am trying to drive at is that if a critical mass of infrastructure developers had access to fundamentally profitable projects, then the lack of a debt market would not prove to be much of an obstacle. Chances are that, armed with strong incentives, they would simply go about creating the required market.

Of course, governments can make a big difference in this process of market development.

• On the negative side, the government can destroy the potential for a debt market by pursuing wrong macroeconomic policies and creating regulatory obstacles. In India, governments have done much to impede the growth of the debt market:

– Some state governments have imposed crippling stamp duties on secondary market transactions in bonds and on securitization transactions.

– Market-distorting instruments of monetary policy have also dampened the development of the bond market. A complete shift to open market operations and to interest rate targeting would be beneficial.

– Even more than the large fiscal deficit, the market-distorting manner in which it is financed is a negative factor for the bond market. Despite major reforms, pre-emption of resources by the government has not been entirely eliminated. This reduces the number and diversity of players in the bond market and decreases the liquidity of the secondary market. Moreover, the continued willingness of the central bank to support the government's borrowing programme through direct subscription in the primary market (development) is highly market distorting. Since corporate bonds are priced off the sovereign yield curve, distortions in the government bond market create difficulties for the corporate bond market as well.

– Some of the tax incentives for small savings have the effect of segmenting the fixed-income market. For example, the post-tax yield on the public provident fund is so high that no other instrument can effectively compete with it. This makes bond markets unattractive to a large segment of retail investors.

• On the positive side, the government can facilitate the process of developing the debt market. It can help create that critical mass of borrowers. Credit enhancement and related techniques have a role to play here. For example, if the state were to offer to subscribe to one bond for every two bonds that are placed with the public, developers would have a huge incentive to raise bonds on a large scale. If the government were to provide a partial guarantee, then the fillip to the market would be even greater. A partial guarantee may mean, for example

- a Brady bond-[6] style guarantee of the principal with or without a rolling interest guarantee
- an interest guarantee covering only the gestation period or
- a guarantee covering only a percentage of the holdings of an investor with or without a monetary cap.

It is possible that these techniques need be used only for a few large, high-profile projects in the initial period. Thereafter, if the debt market gathers steam, subsequent projects may well be able to stand on their own feet without much state support.

It is important from a moral hazard perspective to keep the guarantee limited in scope. If the guarantee covers the bulk of the present value of the debt service obligations, the bond holders have little incentive to monitor the project and to make careful assessment of its creditworthiness. For the capital markets to perform their resource allocation function fairly well, it is necessary that bond holders face sufficient residual risk to take their monitoring role seriously. And as I have earlier emphasized, it is even more important that equity holders bear practically all the demand-side risks, technological risks, and operational risks of the project.

## CONCLUSION

Thus, to conclude, the possibility of private financing of infrastructure in India is fairly bright. The difficulties involved are far from insuperable. There is definitely no need for the state to step in with direct or indirect support on such a scale that the private project effectively becomes a privately managed but publicly funded project. Possible government intervention has in this chapter been narrowed down to some limited forms of subsidy and credit enhancement. It has also been argued here that there is little cause for relaxation of financial sector regulations to deal with the alleged peculiarities of infrastructure.

At a fundamental level, it is here argued, most problems in infrastructure financing arise due to weaknesses in the sectoral regulatory structure. For example, the near bankruptcy of the state electricity boards is the key problem in the power sector. Similarly, inappropriate pricing adversely affects canal irrigation and water and sewerage projects. These problems have to be resolved one way or the other, and mechanisms like escrow accounts can only postpone the day of reckoning. It would be a tragedy if it were to be attempted to deal with these deep-seated regulatory problems by creating harmful distortions in the financial sector.

---

[6] Brady bonds, named after the then US Treasury Secretary, were created in the 1980s as part of the restructuring of Latin American sovereign debt. The principal value of these bonds was backed by zero coupon US Treasury bonds, so that the principal was effectively guaranteed by the US government. In some cases, a part of the interest was also guaranteed by a rolling guarantee.

# 5 | STRUCTURAL ISSUES AND CONSTRAINTS

## 5.1 INTERFACE BETWEEN SECTOR-SPECIFIC REGULATORY BODIES AND COMPETITION AGENCIES: A CASE OF THE INDIAN TELECOM SECTOR

*Rakesh Basant*

Regulation and competition policy can be mutually reinforcing but their instruments are different. In deregulating environments the less the regulatory regimes interfere with the working of the market, the more room there is for competition policy. The mutually reinforcing nature of these two sets of policies requires that there be some coordination between the agencies that implement these policies. Issues relating to such coordination are particularly relevant for India today, as it is setting up sector-specific regulatory bodies, along with the liberalization and privatization of these sectors. The country is also in the process of reviewing its competition policy. This part chapter explores the relationship between competition agencies and telecom authorities in order to highlight the key issues relevant for such linkages in India.

The part chapter is divided into five sections. It begins with a discussion of the linkages between competition and sectoral (telecom) authorities in different countries to highlight the variety across geographic locations. The second section explores very briefly how intellectual property rights (IPRs) may require coordination between competition and the industry regulator in the telecom context. The third section summarizes the key aspects of the amended Telecom Regulatory Authority of India (TRAI) Ordinance (Amended), 2000 to bring out the anomalies in the jurisdictions of the sectoral regulators—the TRAI and the Appellate Dispute Settlement Tribunal—and the competition authority—the Monopoly and Restrictive Trade Practices Commission (MRTPC).

Various issues that need to be considered for the allocation of responsibilities between the competition authority and the industry regulator are discussed in the next section. In the light of the discussion in the first four sections, the concluding section suggests some changes in the institutional design of the linkages between sectoral regulation and implementation of competition policy.

### THE EXPERIENCE OF OTHER COUNTRIES

Given contextual realities, each country would probably have to find its own model of the interface between competition policy and sector-specific regulation. However, for any such framework to emerge, links between competition agencies and sectoral regulatory authorities will have to be developed. The Telecom Treaty as a part of the General Agreement on Trade and Services (GATS) at the World Trade Organization (WTO) has gone a long way in achieving such global framework by incorporating a number of competition principles, including bringing to the fore the issue of leveraging monopoly power in one part of the telecom market in another segment.

In the regulation of utilities, different countries have dealt with competition-related issues in a variety of ways. By and large, anti-competitive conduct has been related to abuse of market power by dominant incumbents. Such abuse of dominance has taken various forms like unfair network access charges and interconnection arrangements, cross-subsidy across services (including equipment sale and service provision), and undue price and other discrimination and preference. Prohibition of such arrangements price control or price caps in certain (especially natural monopoly) segments of the utility, accounting separation, publication of prices, and general rules of competition policy have been utilized to reduce or correct such practices. In this broad context, the relationship between regulatory agencies in different countries is now looked at to identify some critical issues in this area.

### The French Scenario: Clear Separation of Functions[1]

The telecom sector in France has been liberalized and the industry opened to competition. France Telecom, the government operator of the telecom system, has partly been privatized; the government still owns the majority share. A regulatory agency for this sector was created before the privatization exercise began. *The regulatory agency is responsible for identifying firms to issue licences and for determining the interconnection rates. The competition authority monitors the actual conduct of firms.* Given the relationship between interconnection rates and the price of services (which will depend on competition), the authority will have to make sure there is no dumping at the level of services.

While this separation of functions, based on a priori determination of who gets into the field and *ex post* verification of firms' behaviour, appears neat, in practice it is unlikely to be so. For example, some constraints that operators have to face are more stringent when they have a dominant position in another sector from which they have diversified into telecom, or if they have a dominant position in the telecom sector itself.

To implement these conditions, the relevant markets and dominant position need to be defined and it is quite likely that the regulatory agency and competition authority may have different views on this issue. And this possibility exists for all those decisions that are at the intersection of regulation and competition. To avoid some of these problems, the two agencies have to cooperate on these decisions. While the regulatory authority in France has the final word with respect to all a priori decisions, it has to seek the opinion of the competition agency and publish it along with its own opinion. This is useful for the operators because the competition agency can intervene *ex post*, and at that stage the opinion of the competition agency will be considered final. The appeal mechanism is the same for both the regulatory and competition decisions; all decisions can be contested at the Paris Appeal Court in

a chamber specialized in regulation and competition issues. In this manner, the French government has sought to incorporate into the law itself a balanced relationship between the two agencies and a cooperating mechanism.

### The Canadian System: Dominance of the Sectoral Authority[2]

The Canadian Radio, Television and Telecommunications Commission (CRTC) is the overseer of the telecom and broadcasting networks. The commission is reasonably independent, but, according to one view, its role is becoming less crucial. One of the most unfortunate aspects of the CRTC is the non-transparency of its appeal mechanism. Any of the decisions of the CRTC can be appealed against to the Cabinet (not in the courts), but the meetings of the Cabinet are held in camera. This secret appeal process implies that one does not know what the other side has presented.

The interface between the regulation and competition authorities has been ensured through a recent revision of competition law. A provision has been put in whereby the Director of Investigation and Research, who is the head of the competition office, has a statutory right to appear before federal regulatory tribunals and commissions as well as parliamentary committees that are to decide on regulatory and competition-related matters. He is also invited by the provincial regulatory bodies. There have been situations where this right has been exercised. For example, the intervention of the director in the early telecom hearings led to what was called the interconnect decision resulting in the dilution of Bell Canada's monopoly. Besides, the director can also intervene in anti-dumping hearings. The Canadian system, therefore, provides for interface among competition, regulatory, and trade agencies. However, despite these institutional provisions, in practice the CRTC deals on its own with most issues of anti-competitive behaviour in the telecom sector and is fairly independent of other institutions.

### The United Kingdom: Privatization Experience is Redefining Boundaries of Control[3]

The industry regulator, the Office of Telecommunications (OFTEL), is responsible for enforcing the regulatory rules contained in the licences of network operators as well as proposing new licence conditions. The modified licence conditions can come into effect in two ways: either the licensee agrees to a modification or the

---

[1] This subsection is based on Basant and Morris (2000), chapter 9.

[2] This subsection is based on Basant and Morris (2000), chapter 9.

[3] This subsection draws on Barnes (1998) and Nuttal and Vickers (1996).

Monopolies and Mergers Commission (MMC) is called in to arbitrate by the Director General Telecommunications (DGT), OFTEL. The MMC investigates and reports whether the licensee's activity operates, or is likely to operate, against public interest and if so, whether modifications of licence can remedy these adverse effects. In cases where the MMC finds that there are adverse effects, it also specifies modifications that could remedy these effects. The DGT OFTEL, can either follow the suggestions of the MMC or make other licence modifications that he thinks are necessary to prevent the adverse effects. Thus the DGT has some discretion as to how any adverse effects specified by the MMC should be remedied, though he can modify the licence only so as to remedy these. Moreover, while the DGT can make a reference to the MMC for licence modification, the Secretary of State has unlimited power to direct the MMC not to proceed with the reference if it appears necessary in the interest of national security or sensitive relations with foreign governments.

Policy on entry into the industry (that is awarding new licences) is made by the Department of Trade and Industry, although OFTEL has an advisory role here. The licence conditions relate to many aspects of service provision, including the prices the licensee may charge. Several of these conditions relate to competition, for example accounting separation, prohibition of undue discrimination and preference, prohibition of cross-subsidy, access charges and interconnection agreements, and publication of charges.

Given the long experience of privatization and associated regulatory processes, OFTEL has argued that even the provisions mentioned above do not provide it with sufficient control over the transition to competition. It has been suggested that a new licence condition for telecom operators prohibiting behaviour that has the object or the effect of preventing, restricting, or distorting competition in telecommunications needs to be added. Besides, the DGT has also proposed that he should be granted anti-competitive practices (ACP) powers which will enable him to determine anti-competitive conduct of operators, and in such instances, intervene and adjudicate without them being able to appeal to the MMC.[4] In effect, the DGT becomes the market referee whose decision is final and subject only to judicial appeal.

[4] In performing this task, the DGT will take into account the principles and practices of European competition law, statements and reports by the UK competition authorities, and non-binding published guidelines. Third-party rights to take action for damages would exist if a licensee violated an enforcement order following a determination that its conduct was anti-competitive, but no powers to fine would exist.

Overall, the regulatory system in the UK seems to be moving away from a situation where competition conditions were embodied in the licence—and in disputes vis-à-vis these conditions, decisions of the competition authority superseded those of the telecom authority—to a situation where more stringent competition-related licensing conditions are imposed. And the telecom authority is seeking wider jurisdiction over such matters.

### The European Union (EU): The Rules of the Game are Still to Emerge[5]

The national competition laws and the Union competition law coexist. The EU law becomes effective as soon as an anti-trust case acquires transborder elements. The European Commission has twenty commissioners, one of them being responsible for competition matters. However, decisions in this field are taken by the commission as a body and the interaction with other policies is in-built through the existence of other commissioners, who are responsible for other policy matters. Similarly, decisions regarding telecom matters are not to be taken by the Directorate General of Competition (DG-IV) alone but in consultation with commissioners of other services. The European Commission also cooperates very closely with member states on these kinds of issues. Consultation with member states is done within the framework of the advisory committees. When a legislation has to be passed, member states play a key role in that decision.

In recent years of significant trade liberalization within the EU, there have been some cases of joint ventures in the telecom and media industries wherein the companies in question applied to the European Commission for permission to go ahead with these ventures. Permission was finally granted after some negotiations with member states to open up markets in some sectors earlier than foreseen. When the European Commission takes a decision in anti-trust cases, it is subject to the jurisprudence of the two European courts, namely the Court of First Instance, which looks very closely at factual matters, and the European Court of Justice, which answers appeals on legal issues.

### The Extreme Case of New Zealand[6]

New Zealand's approach to the regulation of telecommunications differs from that of most other countries. It has attracted considerable attention in recent years. The most widely known aspect of this approach is the absence of a sectoral authority. Interconnection

[5] This subsection draws on Basant and Morris (2000), chapter 9.

[6] This subsection is based on Klein (1998) and Webb and Taylor (1998).

agreements, access pricing to the telecom network, etc. are supervised by the Commerce Commission, New Zealand's competition policy authority, under its general rules. The New Zealand government expects parties to act in good faith and expedite any court actions. However, as in other countries, there are certain social obligations (for example limits on price increases for residential customers) which find expression through the 'golden share' in the dominant telecom company, Telecom, being retained by the government. Besides, there are information disclosure obligations on the company to reduce information asymmetry and facilitate arbitration of disputes by the Commerce Commission. Finally, the Ministry of Commerce can impose regulatory measures like price controls if it is satisfied that conditions for effective competition do not exist and control is necessary to protect network users or consumers.

In recent years, this 'light-handed regulation' of telecommunications has been criticized. When a new entrant, Clear Communications, negotiated for an interconnection agreement with the incumbent, (New Zealand) Telecom, lack of sector-specific rules and guidelines resulted in high uncertainty about interconnection rules. This led to protracted litigation, with the Commonwealth Privy Council in the UK acting as final arbiter. Consequently, many in New Zealand are now arguing for sector-specific regulatory rules that will clarify things like price-setting principles to reduce uncertainty.

## TELECOM STANDARDS, INTELLECTUAL PROPERTY RIGHTS (IPRs), AND COMPETITION POLICY

Policies on IPRs, standards, and competition interact in a variety of ways. In 1992, the European Commission set out a number of principles to govern the relationship between IPRs and standardization. Although the commission is not directly involved in setting the standards, its views are influential in so far as they affect tender specifications for public procurement. Besides, since the commission is the guardian of European competition policy, its views are of great importance for firms considering the possible effects of a refusal to allow their intellectual property to be incorporated in a standard. The European Telecommunications Standards Institute (ETSI) plays an important role in the standard-setting process in the EU. The two key principles are as follows:

• The standard makers should do everything possible to identify IPRs that could be involved in a proposed standard and consult with the holders of those rights. In general, only if it appears that the relevant rights are available for licensing should they be incorporated into the standard. The IPR owners should also identify any right that might be used in a standard under discussion and indicate if that right can be licensed.

• Intellectual property owners should be treated fairly. They should be given reasonable opportunity to determine whether any of their rights would be required for a proposed standard and to decide whether to agree to that use. If they do agree to licence their rights, there should be a clear mechanism to arrive at fair royalty rates for use by those operating under the standard.

In principle, the intellectual property owner can refuse to licence his right to be used in a standard but in case of such a refusal, the case may be referred to the European Commission's Competition Policy Directorate. Thus a valuable intellectual property that has become a de facto standard due to its commercial success may either be 'compulsorily' licensed or the property owner may face anti-trust action.

## THE TRAI ORDINANCE AND THE DISTRIBUTION OF RESPONSIBILITIES

Given the above background, one can see that the TRAI Ordinance (Amended), 2000 has not explicitly addressed these issues. The role of ensuring competition is being performed by the TRAI, the Telecom Disputes Settlement and Appellate Tribunal (henceforth the Tribunal), as well as the competition authority (MRTPC). The following features of the Ordinance bring out the confusion. For example, the Ordinance provides that the TRAI will make recommendations, either *suo moto* or on request from the licensor, on the following matters:

• Need and timing for introduction of new service provider.

• Terms and conditions of licence to a service provider.

• Revocation of licence for non-compliance with terms and conditions of licence.

• Measures to facilitate competition and promote efficiency in the operation of telecom services so as to facilitate growth in such services.

• Technological improvements in the services provided by the service providers.

• Type of equipment to be used by service providers after inspection of equipment used in the network.

• Measures for the development of telecom technology and any other matter relatable to telecom industry in general.

• Efficient management of available spectrum.

It is obvious that all these activities directly or indirectly impinge on competition. Additional responsibilities of the TRAI suggest that it is also required to implement competition-related conditions. For example, the ordinance provides that the TRAI is also to discharge the following functions:

• Ensure compliance with terms and conditions of licence.

• Notwithstanding anything contained in the terms and conditions of the licence granted before the commencement of the TRAI (Amendment) Ordinance, 2000, fix terms and conditions of interconnectivity between service providers.

• Ensure technical compatibility and effective interconnection between different service providers.

Given the problems of IPRs and standards discussed earlier, these activities also impinge on competition in the telecom market.

Apart from the TRAI, the ordinance creates a separate dispute settlement mechanism for the telecom sector. The Tribunal has been created which will adjudicate any dispute between:

• a licensor and licensee,

• two or more service providers, and

• a service provider and group of consumers.

This is provided that nothing in this clause shall apply in respect of matters relating to:

• monopolistic trade practice, restrictive trade practice, and unfair trade practice, which are subject to the jurisdiction of the MRTPC established under subsection (1) of section 5 of the Monopolies and Restrictive Trade Practices Act, 1969;

• the complaint of an individual consumer maintainable before a Consumer Redressal Forum or a Consumer Disputes Redressal Commission or the National Consumer Redressal Commission established under section 9 of the Consumer Protection Act, 1986; and

• disputes between the telegraph authority and any other person referred to in subsection (I) of section 7B of the Indian Telegraph Act, 1885.

In addition, the Tribunal will hear and dispose of appeals against any direction, decision, or order of the authority (TRAI) under this act.

It is obvious that in the ordinance the roles of TRAI, the Tribunal, and the MRTPC are not clearly defined. Virtually all disputes between licensors and licensees and between service providers will have some competition-related ramifications. Most cases relating to access charges, interconnection arrangements,

simultaneous provision of equipment and services, cross-subsidization of services by the dominant players, etc. impinge on competition in the market. Who will deal with disputes relating to these? For example, if we have a case similar to the one in the UK about number portability, whose jurisdiction will it fall under? Similarly, will assessment of mergers and acquisitions in the telecom sector involve participation of the TRAI or the Tribunal? Such participation may be necessary as many studies have pointed out that while hostile takeover bids can be useful sources of information, consummated mergers, and even conglomerate mergers, are likely to worsen regulatory problems arising from asymmetric information (Nuttall and Vickers 1996).

Given these problems, it is not clear how the Tribunal will deal with various disputes. Prima facie such ill-defined jurisdictions will lead to considerable delays in litigation. Surely their roles can be usefully delineated?

## THE ALLOCATION OF RESPONSIBILITIES: SOME CONSIDERATIONS

In a situation where a monopolistic regulated industry (like utilities) is being privatized and where competitive pressures are being brought to bear, what should be the guiding principles to deal with anti-competitive behaviour? Should problems related to competition be under the jurisdiction of the competition authority or the industry regulator? There are no clear answers to these questions. It is clear, however, that the rules in transition are qualitatively different from those that are adequate to deal with straightforward monopoly problems. They are likely to become less deterministic and more complex (Barnes 1998). Besides, competition related problems are likely to persist in this phase of transition. This will be so because, unless broken up by structural remedies, the privatized utilities (or existing public sector players) will inherit dominant positions in relation to consumers. Such a dominant position will not easily be eroded, as it not only facilitates cross-subsidies but is also sustained by consumer-switching costs. Despite technological change, parts of such regulated industries will remain naturally monopolistic. Moreover, often such naturally monopolistic segments impinge on the competitive environment of related industries which are not naturally monopolistic themselves, but have economies of scope with the former.[7]

Apart from the possibilities of anti-competitive behaviour outlined, the complexity of the interactions between competition and regulation means that the allocation of responsibilities between competition and

[7] See Nuttal and Vickers (1996) for details of these issues.

sectoral regulatory authorities is not without difficulty (Nuttall and Vickers 1996):

• the two are substitutes in so far as sufficient competition might reduce the role of regulation and the associated imperfections;

• they are complements in so far as competition can enhance the effectiveness of regulation, for example by reducing information asymmetries;

• regulation can distort competition due to its effects on the incentives and opportunities of regulated entities.

The received wisdom is that effective sectoral regulation (as against generic competition policy) is needed when rivalry is inadequate within an industry and when general anti-competitive provisions are too weak to safeguard the interests of consumers. As mentioned, the presence of dominant incumbent telecom operators, the multi output nature of these firms, and the existence of large common costs provide opportunities for anti-competitive behaviour. While these conditions exist in the telecom industry and can be used as a justification for the existence of the sectoral regulatory authority, it does not shed any light on the division of responsibilities.

Several characteristics of effective regulation have been identified in the literature. These include independence, accountability, transparency, fairness, simplicity and clarity, speed, and consistency. It has also been argued that the institutional arrangements should have provisions for appeal, penalties, and periodic review. While one can judge an arrangement specifying the links between the competition and industry regulatory authorities on these grounds, in the context of the telecom industry the implications of three features need special attention: (a) technological convergence in telecommunications; (b) trade-off between potential of regulatory capture and sector-specific skills; and (c) regulatory uncertainty.

### Issues Relating to Technological Convergence

Given the natural monopoly characteristics of telecommunications, especially the local loop of networks, ensuring effective competition in this segment has been an important regulatory problem. Since inter-network competition is difficult to obtain, the focus has been on fair access and reasonable interconnection arrangements. The emerging convergence in telecom technology may change this condition. Networks that were highly differentiated in what services they could deliver (for example broadcasting versus voice technology) are now somewhat equivalent in terms of services they can deliver to customers. Different ways of providing the same type of services and the provision of totally new types of services are developing rapidly. These are changing the rules of competition; competition is on the rise not only across networks, with various networks becoming close substitutes, but also in service provision. Broadly, technological changes are leading to growing demand (especially of Internet services) and innovations are significantly modifying the structural features of the telecom industry with emerging convergence across fixed and mobile and across Information Technology (IT) and media sectors.

What implications do these developments have for the relationship between the sector-specific regulatory authority and competition authority? The final impact of the technology convergence is still largely unknown. Meanwhile, these developments cut across the existing regulations and challenge conventional definitions of the telecom industry. In such a scenario, heavy-handed and inconsistent regulation across different delivery mechanisms, arbitrary service classifications, and narrow choices of standards can distort markets. If the regulation is unnecessarily restrictive, it may also result in economic inefficiency with customers failing to get the full benefit of technological convergence.

One can argue that with appropriate provisions, the general competition law can provide the framework within which these new technological developments can be tackled. However, while convergence is bringing different types of networks closer to equivalence, it is not making them the same; at least, not as yet. The particular bottleneck points (for example scarce resources like radio spectrum, incumbency dominance, natural monopoly in some elements in the local loop, or the particular way customers are locked into a specific network by their purchase of equipment) will continue to vary due to economic and technical reasons. Broadly, issues relating to network interconnection will remain very significant in terms of policy due to persistence of (a) fixed costs of a subscriber being connected to a network (both for fixed and mobile networks); and (b) network externalities between subscribers. In other words, anti-competitive behaviour in terms of setting excessive access and interconnection charges will remain a reality and will have to be dealt with.

The ultimate manifestation of convergence will be a single optical fibre cable providing telecom, computing, and media services. The customer premise equipment will sort the incoming signals according to the information carried by them. The convergence of telecommunications, computing and media interests, and the provision of services may lead to future market structures dominated by multimedia conglomerates.[8] Given the technological uncertainty, while one needs to recognize this possibility, there is no need to worry unduly about it and argue for excessive regulation so that such structures do not emerge. As mentioned, such an approach can distort markets and may even retard technological growth. Besides, it is difficult to predict if and when such structures will emerge. In the interim, a more liberal, less regulated policy may be optimal. It has been argued that when technical change is rapid it will be more difficult to circumscribe the domain of natural monopoly and the dynamic benefits of competition are likely to be large.

Competition is often very valuable for the very reason that it is impossible to quantify ex ante that it will be valuable. A review of the deregulation experiments in the United States highlights the role of unexpected new ways of doing business which have followed deregulation and led to welfare gains. [Klein 1998: 70]

Technological convergence brings into sharper focus the issue of jurisdiction of sectoral authorities. In the case of the UK, both the MMC and OFTEL make specific efforts to keep 'competitive markets competitive' (Barnes 1998). The telecom equipment market is fully competitive with a large number of suppliers and no firm has a dominant position. However, British Telecom's (BT's) dominance in network services can result in anti-competitive behaviour in the form of tied or subsidized sales of equipment to its customers. OFTEL sets and maintains rules cutting across boundaries so that the equipment market remains competitive. It is not clear how such anti-competitive conduct cutting across industry boundaries will be dealt with in the Indian context. Firms like BPL which make telephone equipment are already in the telecom services market.

[8] Convergence, if fully realized, can cause a variety of regulatory problems. The primary problem is that the access provider, the organization providing the optical fibre to each and every house and business, becomes a vertically integrated monopoly. Since the difference between long-distance and local disappears, the choice of long-distance operator also vanishes. Since the access-providing fibre is connected to the Internet, the choice of Internet Service Provider (ISP) disappears. Similar to the current option of subscribing to the Internet through cable where it is connected to the ISP continuously, such a situation will exist for video traffic also. This monopoly position is likely to be abused through blocking of sites, channels, and e-commerce sites. Competition is unlikely to be a major regulating device; because of the huge investments involved it is doubtful whether a duopoly can be sustained. The role of regulation becomes more crucial in this environment. Regulation will also be essential due to the huge investments. Cross-subsidization cannot be done away with, in fact the cross-subsidization value may increase in the case of a converged network (Ramadesikan 1999).

It may be useful to incorporate such exigencies in the licensing conditions to prevent anti-competitive behaviour of the kind described here.

Overall, technological convergence brings out two salient issues that are relevant for the allocation of responsibilities. One, industry boundaries are very fluid and it is very difficult to define a 'telecom market'. Two, more and more segments of the 'telecom market' will increasingly become contestable making it difficult to come up with per se prohibitions for any potential anti-competitive practice. The first calls for the extension of boundaries for the 'telecom regulatory authority' and the latter highlights the emerging complexity of competition-related issues in the sector.

## Regulatory Capture and Sector-specific Skills: Is There a Trade-off?

Competition agencies may be less prone to capture as they are more distant from the players in a sector. On the other hand they may lack the detailed technical competence required to deal with some sector-specific issues. For example, it has been suggested that entry restrictions are particularly hard to undo when the boundary of a protected firm coincides with the political jurisdiction that grants the protection. There are obvious benefits from collusion between the political powers and the firm, which would be reduced if the firm operated across jurisdictions and several political entities had to collude to extract monopoly rents. In the same vein a regulatory authority which covers utilities being provided for by a variety of sectors (for example telecom and cable) is less likely to be captured. The key challenge is to strike a balance between these considerations while preserving coherent decision making to reduce uncertainty for investors. An implementation of this general principle may imply empowering the competition authority to deal with fairly generic issues, such as collusion, while asking the regulatory agency to look after more sector-specific issues, such as interconnection rules, pricing, or quality of service. It may also imply that a mechanism to appeal to the competition authority against decisions of the sectoral authority impinging on competition (for example interconnection) is desirable. In many systems, mergers in regulated industries are subject to scrutiny by both industry-specific and economy-wide regulation.

## The Regulatory Uncertainty

The uncertainty embodied in the generic competition law in New Zealand to deal with telecom-related issues has already been mentioned. This created incentives for the dominant incumbent to exploit this uncertainty.

The other key problem relating to the use of competition law to deal with sectoral issues has been delays (and expense) associated with litigation. It has been argued that the New Zealand competition law is incapable of 'effectively handling the complexity of telecommunications access and interconnection disputes and there remains a real prospect of interative disputes about different aspects of the same subject matter and even about the same subject matter'. Consequently, regulatory uncertainty and associated litigation delays and costs may themselves act as a barrier to entry that may be exploited by the dominant incumbent (Webb and Taylor 1998, p. 5).

Whatever framework for sectoral regulation is adopted to tackle anti-competitive behaviour, it should not lead to even more detailed rules. Any regulatory structure, therefore, should not provide a route towards even deeper and more intrusive regulation. The creation of a separate appellate body for telecom and the lack of clarity about disputes that are not related to competition issues makes the structure proposed in the TRAI bill quite cumbersome. This is later discussed in greater detail.

Early and timely action is extremely important in a general sense too; any action necessary to stop anti-competition behaviour must take place fast enough to avoid, if possible, competitors going out of business before any corrective action can be taken. The proposal of OFTEL to add a new licence condition for telecom operators that would prohibit actions that prevent, restrict, or distort competition in telecommunications, with the DGT having powers to determine if the conduct has interesting implications, increases the regulatory discretion of OFTEL. It has several advantages in terms of reducing regulatory uncertainty and delays:

First, it diminishes the incentive for anti-competitive behaviour by reducing delays in stopping behaviour that is found to be anti-competitive. By contrast, general UK competition law has rather weak deterrent effect since, with the exception of radical divestiture remedies, the sanction faced by a firm is just that it will eventually be told to desist from conduct found to be anticompetitive, with no interim measures or third party relief. Second, the proposal is based on the *effect* rather than the form or description of behaviour. No matter how lengthy, a list of proscribed practices is likely to contain gaps, especially in a rapidly evolving industry. Courses of conduct with different descriptions may be close substitutes in terms of their economic effects (and course of conduct that fall under the same description may have very different effects). An effects-based prohibition moreover does away with the need to introduce new licence conditions to fill gaps as they appear, and the associated delays. Third, the new condition would allow a number of detailed monopoly controls, and their attendant costs and inefficiencies, to be removed. [Nuttal and Vickers 1996]

These arguments would suggest inclusion of several effects-based general competition-related conditions in the licence so that the onus of not indulging in anti-competitive conduct is on the licensee. This, along with the inclusion of competition-related issues within the jurisdiction of the sectoral regulator, may reduce uncertainty and delays of litigation. The outcome may be achieved by having more effects-based licensing conditions and a special group within the competition agency (as in the case of the European Competition Commission) to expeditiously deal with telecom-related competition issues.

## MODIFICATIONS IN THE INDIAN INSTITUTIONAL STRUCTURE

Which of these models should India adopt? At one level, the French system seems promising, with the division of roles between the regulation and competition authorities clearly defined. The possible areas of overlap have also been identified. The distinction between authorities dealing with *ex ante* issues (like entry) and *ex post* concerns (behaviour) is sensible. The TRAI ordinance provides such a division of roles between the TRAI and the Tribunal. Unfortunately, the proposed amendment to the TRAI Act does not appreciate the possible conflict of roles between the Tribunal and the competition authority. These conflicts will need to be identified and resolved. Based on the above discussion, the following modifications in the Indian telecom-related institutional structure seem desirable:

• The distinction between disputes relating to anti-competitive behaviour (which are to be dealt with by the MRTPC) and others is very arbitrary. The current structure will add to regulatory uncertainty and will eventually lead to delays with multiple suits filed both with the Tribunal and the MRTPC. Consequently, the advantage of having a sector-specific dispute settlement mechanism to reduce delays will be lost. Therefore, either all disputes should be heard by the MRTPC and the higher courts or the Tribunal should deal with all disputes relating to telecom with a provision of appeal in the Supreme Court.

• If the MRTPC or any other competition authority is to tackle the disputes with the abolition of the Tribunal, a separate cell within the commission to deal with the sector's issues will need to be created to expedite cases and also develop the requisite expertise. The model of the DG-IV of the European Commission is promising in this regard.

• If the sectoral authority is given the powers to deal with competition issues, its coverage needs to be enlarged to encompass all aspects of information, communication, and entertainment services.[9] Such a change will not only take care of some issues relating to technological convergence, it will also mitigate to some extent the problems associated with regulatory capture.

• While inclusion in the licence of clauses prohibiting behaviour that prevents, restricts, or distorts competition in telecommunications is a good idea to reduce regulatory uncertainty, the implementation of competition regulations will have to remain flexible and liberal in order not to distort the market and the dynamics of technological development.

## 5.2 POLITICAL AND BUREAUCRATIC HURDLES IN REFORM AND RESTRUCTURING: THE ELECTRICITY SECTOR

*M. Y. Rao*

It is well known that Orissa took the lead in electricity reforms. The preparations started as early as 1993–4 and by the end of 1994, the broad contours of the reforms had taken shape. The sector was to be unbundled into separate corporate entities for generation, transmission, and distribution. The Orissa Electricity Regulatory Commission (OERC) was to be created as an autonomous body and phased privatization of the corporatized entities was to take place.

Towards the end of 1994 and in early 1995, drafts of the Orissa Electricity Reform Bill[10] were circulated to the various ministries in Delhi and were the subject of heated discussions. Senior officials in the ministry as well as in the Central Electricity Authority (CEA) were not convinced of the need for any reform Act. What is in the reform Act that is not covered by the existing electricity laws? Was not the CEA also autonomous? What is it that the commission can do which the CEA failed to do? What will happen to the supply of electricity to farmers or rural areas? How can we entrust a vital area like electricity to private hands? Would they not simply strip the assets and decamp? After innumerable rounds of discussions, the central government finally cleared the draft with the support of the Union Minister for Power, the Finance Minister, and the Union Finance Secretary.

The scene of the battle then shifted to Bhubaneshwar. The bill was tabled in the legislative assembly and was debated for several days. Legislators agonized over possible loss of control of the House over the privatized successors of the Orissa State Electricity Board (OSEB). Government functionaries were even more exercised about loss of government control over the entities which were, in effect, adjuncts of the government but with

financial latitude not available to government departments. Such parastatals including innumerable state-level public enterprises had been and continue to be convenient arrangements to throw parties or go on foreign jaunts. In Orissa there was the added complication that almost all electrical engineers of the OSEB were technically employees of the state government on deputation. Frequent transfers and postings of the board employees, especially engineers, generated graft and rents. The dual control exercised by the government as the appointing authority, and by the board as the immediate employer, had only exacerbated the confusion. Many exploited this situation for easy postings, postings with scope for rent, etc. The impending loss of control over the electrical engineering cadre and of a cherished fiefdom were perhaps the most important considerations among the decision makers. Even today, several years down the road of reform, these questions still haunt certain sections of the bureaucracy and government. There is much talk about amending the reform act to make the OERC and the privatized companies 'more accountable to the people'.

Orissa, however, was lucky to have the full support of both the two Chief Ministers for the reforms. The bill went through the assembly with only minor hitches. One such hitch was resolved by accepting a wholly unnecessary amendment to the effect that any transfer of assets from the Grid Corporation of Orissa (Gridco) and Orissa Hydro Power Corporation (OHPC) to any other entity could be 'only on lease'. (A subsequent amendment corrected this.) Another hitch related to the service conditions of the members of the OERC. From the very beginning, the OERC was envisaged as a high-powered authority with quasi-judicial powers, which would be able to stand above lobbying and partisan politicians. Indeed, the draft of the bill contained provisions to the effect that the salary and allowances of

[9] Newspaper reports suggest that such an authority is being envisaged.

[10] The Bill marks the first step towards deregulating electricity in India.

members of the OERC and their staff would be 'charged' to the consolidated fund of the state (and not 'voted'); and that the service conditions of members of the OERC could not be varied to their disadvantage during their tenure. When the bill was finally passed, the first provision was re-tained but the second one was 'unaccountably' dropped somewhere between the draft and the printed bill.

Eventually, the rules framed by the state government did include a provision to the effect that the conditions of service of the chairman and members of the OERC could not be varied to their disadvantage during their tenures. But this rule which can be changed by executive fiat does not provide the OERC with the same degree of protection as a provision in the Act itself would have. Reforms in other states, however, learned from this experience. Andhra Pradesh, Rajasthan, and Uttar Pradesh have, for example, included a specific provision protecting the service conditions of regulators in their reform Acts.

Persuading the (Board's) officers' associations to accept reforms turned out to be a tortuous and exhausting affair. To begin with, the associations refused to accept that the Electricity Board was deeply in the red. Part of the reason for this contention lay in the way accounts are maintained by the state electricity boards (SEBs). Under the Electricity Supply Act, 1948, the SEBs are to set their tariffs in such a way that after taking into account government subsidies and meeting all expenses, they should achieve a return of 3 per cent on their fixed assets. This government subsidy, especially in the 1990s, turned out to be only an accounting entry, as the finances of the state governments were also in disarray. But the myth that the Boards were making a nominal profit persisted. More importantly, the cost plus pricing under the Act could technically mean that the possibility of being in the red is ruled out by definition.

Associations were also deeply concerned about the service conditions in the post-reform scenario. The reform Act clearly spelt out that the service conditions of employees in the new set-up would not be inferior to what they had earlier been. This did not satisfy the associations who took the matter to courts, several in fact, from the Bhubaneshwar and Cuttack Benches of the State Administrative Tribunal to the High Court and finally the Supreme Court, where they eventually lost. In the interim period, a 'fitment' exercise gave several hundred officers substantial pay increases by way of compensation for stagnation at various levels.

In sharp contrast to the officers, the non-executive employees belonging to some forty-six unions turned out to be much more amenable. Several rounds of discussions and continuous dialogue with the unions

ensured that the scope for rumours and other mischief was limited. A wage revision agreement signed by the unions with retrospective effect was another important reassuring measure. Unlike the officers, the unions did not tie down Gridco in the courts, and despite several strike threats, Gridco did not lose a single day owing to industrial action during the entire period.

The OERC issued its first tariff order on 12 March 1997, when the assembly happened to be in session (budget session). The tariff order caused a furore in the assembly with several members raising questions of privilege against the commission for what they perceived as the imposition of a tax on electricity without the authority of the House and that too when the House was in session. The Chief Managing Director of Gridco and the Law Secretary to the government were summoned to the Chief Minister's chamber in the assembly for urgent consultations.

It was pointed out that what OERC had done was well within the provisions of the reform Act which had come into force after the same House had passed it. The matter was sorted out after the Chief Minister, the Speaker, and the Leader of the Opposition had a discussion. The Speaker announced on the floor of the House that there was no privilege issue involved. That, however, did not prevent some of the opposition members from walking out of the House.

An important consideration that propelled the state government towards reforms was the cash crunch, with the reforms holding out hope of an end to the need for government support to the power sector. This driving principle had some interesting fallouts. Gridco came into existence on 1 April 1996 when the reform act also came into force. The transmission and distribution assets of the Electricity Board which had a book value of Rs 1201 crore, were taken over by the state government and then upvalued by an additional Rs 1194 crore. The entire assets worth Rs 2395 crore were then vested in Gridco. This upward revaluation was prompted by the need to have a capital base capable of absorbing the loans required for upgrading the system and to have a self-financing ratio of 20 per cent and an adequate debt–equity ratio. However, the upvalued amount of Rs 1194 crore was treated as though it was the government's contribution to Gridco. Against this 'contribution', government dues to the OSEB on account of subsidy and electricity charges, totalling Rs 340 crore, were written off. Gridco was required to issue Rs 400 crore worth of bonds and Rs 253 crore worth of shares to the government.

The state government got out of their obligation to pay Rs 340 crore to the OSEB/Gridco, but the net effect was that Gridco started life with a minus figure of nearly Rs 1000 crore. Even today, Gridco has not recovered from the effects of this upvaluation exercise. However, other states learnt from the Orissa experience and have provided for substantial government subsidy to the reforming entities during the initial transition period of four to five years. For example, Rajasthan, Haryana, and Andhra Pradesh have proposed transitional period support of Rs 4370 crore, Rs 1992 crore, and Rs 12,547 crore, respectively, to their reforming entities.

Senior levels of decision making within the government were never fully reconciled to the autonomy of the OERC, or to the provision of the reform Act stipulating that while the government might issue directions for concessional tariff to specified categories of consumers, it was bound to compensate the distribution companies for the losses they might then have to bear as a result of the government directives. This stipulation is still being viewed as an affront to government sovereignty.

It had been quite usual for the government to agree to many concessions to 'deserving' consumers. At various times, export-oriented units, cooperative textile mills, and ailing public sector units (PSUs) were granted concessions in electricity charges, security deposits, and electricity duty. During one of the board meetings of Gridco in early 1997, the board debated the 'concessions' promised to some industries by the state government and felt that they would need clearance from the OERC so that the cost of the concessions could be claimed from the government as subsidy. A senior bureaucrat on the board exploded at this suggestion but is romoured to currently be an aspirant for chairmanship of the OERC. Whether there has been a change of heart about the Commission is not known.

The Orissa Electricity Reform Act came into force from 1 April 1996 when the transmission- and distribution-related assets, liabilities, and personnel of the OSEB were vested in Gridco. This was done through a transfer scheme framed by the state government under the Reform Act. Under the next phase of Gridco's reform, Gridco's statewide distribution business was reorganized into four zonal entities which were then registered as Gridco's wholly owned subsidiaries. Then came the question of transferring Gridco's distribution-related assets, liabilities, and personnel to these distribution companies.

There were endless discussions in the secretariat about how this was to be accomplished. The oft-repeated questions were: Why not a simple commercial agreement between the companies? Where is the need for a statutory scheme? The realization that the matter was not quite so simple came much later. In addition to assets and liabilities, there were also employees to be transferred which could not have been done with a commercial agreement alone. Workers would require some statutory protection to guarantee them that their service conditions in the new set-up would not be inferior to the old.

There was also a legal hitch. The reform Act continued the stipulation that any transfer from Gridco to any other company could be 'only on lease'. How does one lease out employees? On the other hand, can there be an agreement between the companies which contemplates an arrangement other than a lease of the employees? Would not such an agreement be ab initio null and void? This legal dilemma was finally resolved through an ordinance which did away with the portion of the act stipulating 'only on lease'. The transfer scheme was framed under the amended act in November 1998.

## 5.3 NEED FOR A BOT LAW: GUJARAT INFRASTRUCTURE DEVELOPMENT ACT

*Atanu Chakraborty*

In April 1999 the Governor of Gujarat signed an ordinance to facilitate private sector participation (PSP) in infrastructure in the state. This brought about the first overarching privatization law in the country. Four months later the state assembly unanimously passed a bill entitled Gujarat Infrastructure Development Act, 1999.

The trend towards privatizing infrastructure that was witnessed in Latin America and South East Asia in the 1980s could not be ignored in India after the

balance of payments (BoP) crisis of 1990–1. The impetus for privatization came from the need to bridge the fund gap that the government faced in the provision of infra-structure. In Gujarat alone, the government estimates that fund requirement in eight infrastructure sectors up to the year 2010 will be Rs 117,000 crore, or US $ 29 billion. (Government of Gujarat 1999b). The India Infrastructure Report (1999) estimates a national requirement of about US $ 300 billion. In the earlier stages, achievement of project and delivery efficiency that is possible in a privatized project was a matter of ideological debate. This is a more accepted argument today, though there is still little empirical evidence available.

Private infrastructure projects do not happen automatically. They have to be engendered via a process of equitable risk sharing. Such a mechanism is crucial to PSP.

A frequently asked question was why do we need a BOT law? (The term BOT here is used to represent the entire genre of PSP projects and not in a restrictive sense of build, operate, and transfer.) Would the usual Contract Act, Land Acquisition Act, Arbitration Act, and other sector-specific Acts not be adequate?

Privatizing infrastructure typically involves a large number of players, that is the sponsoring agency, the project developer, the lenders, sometimes even equipment suppliers, the regulator, and consumers of the services, each with its own set of concerns. Even before a contract is entered into, much groundwork needs to be done, right from conceptualizing the project, to preparing feasibility studies, defining the institutional framework, working out the risk allocation, and doing the developer procurement. To lenders and investors, a clear definition of powers and duties of the involved ministries and the public authorities is essential to the success of the project. Experience has shown that uncertainty over which set of officials has the authority to deliver a particular ingredient of the BOT scheme can be a major obstacle (Gulslain 1997). Before the passage of the BOT law, none of the existing laws had clear provisions on the following important aspects:

• appropriate pricing to allow equity investors a competitive rate of return;

• framework for clearly structuring a BOT project, particularly the scope, obligations, and rights of the private developer;

• standardized and streamlined procedures for approval of the project and selection of the developer;

• the norms and kind of support including 'concessions' and subsidies that the government could provide.

• What would be a reasonable security package that was at once acceptable to the lenders?

• Who would be the 'BoT prime mover' within the government to act as the overall coordinator of the privatization programme (Pricewaterhouse Coopers 1999).

Many steps in the privatization of infrastructure are common across the sectors of physical infrastructure. Hence to cover the common dimensions and issues in separate laws for every sector was neither necessary nor desirable. It would only have created confusion. Each sectoral law would not only introduce divergence in the government's approach in different sectors but also sow seeds of confusion in the minds of prospective investors.

A contract can only offer remedies and means for the participating private parties to exercise their rights (Wilde 1997). Thus for example, parties need to be assured against risks emanating from people's protests against environmental risk. The participating sponsoring agencies also need a road map to be able to handle privatization of the infrastructure project. When the size of the project is large, government participation in some manner may be necessary to lower the risk for the developer, especially in the early stages of privatization. A road map showing how to go about a BOT project would be of use to even the public agencies. These issues apart, the impact of a BOT law cannot be understated. To investors the law offers the advantage of explicit political endorsement, which is not negligible given the often politically contentious nature of privatization (Wilde 1997).

The process of the passage of the law through various stages and departments within the department was educational. A priori assumptions pertaining to a particular group/class can be totally misplaced as shall soon be seen. The need for building world-class infrastructure was articulated when Gujarat revised its Industrial Policy in 1995 and set up the Gujarat State Infrastructure Development Board (GIDB). Initiatives were taken to launch port privatization on a large scale as well. Following these initiatives, the need for a clear and transparent framework for privatization was acutely realized.

Senior politicians in the state understood the underlying logic very quickly. This came as a pleasant surprise to those who were engaged in the preparation of the drafts. A BOT scheme tends to be fairly complicated and the dynamics that are covered are not usually easy to understand. Senior politicians even found the right political idiom to sell the idea to their fellow politicians. Most of the senior echelons in the bureaucracy were also receptive to the idea and became active champions for the law.

As a strategy, consensus building was attempted from the start. The executive departments of the government were expected to oppose the proposals, perceiving them as a curtailment of their authority. Therefore the draft of the law was discussed with all executive departments in detail at various round table meetings. Such meetings continued to take place until a few hours before the draft of the bill went to the cabinet for approval! The other potential participants in the BOT scheme, viz. developers, large corporate houses, consultants financiers, and academicians were also involved at various stages.

Significant pockets of resistance emerged from certain middle-level civil servants for a specific instance of the continuing struggle between the GIDB and executive departments of the government, see Box 5.3.1 Surprisingly, their line of argument was that the BOT law would not be flexible! Similarly, strong doubts were expressed about the suitability of bidding as a way to select the vendor. Opponents from the business sector did not like the idea of a priori demarcation of risks. But such resistance soon gave way in the wake of very strong political consensus. The quick passage of the bill in the assembly underscored strong consensus on the liberalization process.

For such a complex process as BOT (in the general sense), the law is rather concise and is a tribute to the rare tribe of legal draftsmen whose understanding of the nuances of each word that goes into the law is considerable.

Some of its salient features are as follows:

• It manifests a clear paradigm shift in the government, as from having been a provider the government becomes an enabler of infrastructure. Section 3 of the law is an unambiguous statement for PSP.

• It allows a wide range of contracts to ensure complete flexibility in structuring the proposals.

• It has both a clearly defined approval process for projects as well as clearly defined contracts. It clearly

---

BOX 5.3.1

**Key Departments Up in Arms Against the GIDB**

After lying low for nearly two years, major project-implementing departments, including roads and buildings, energy, ports, industries, information technology and others, are up in arms against the powerful Gujarat Infrastructure Development Board's (GIDB's) fresh attempts to enhance its role in clearing Rs 117,000 crore worth of infrastructure-related projects planned mainly for the private sector.

Revived in 1998, the GIDB is a top inter-departmental policy body chaired by the Chief Minister. The GIDB executive met the Industries Minister Suresh Mehta, failing to resolve the crucial issue as to whether it should be a facilitator and a guide or also become a regulator for nearly 400 infrastructure projects taken up by the state government for a decade.

The issue at stake was whether the recently passed GIDB rules giving too many powers to the departments be changed. Declaring the discussion on enhancing the GIDB's role as 'inconclusive', Mehta asked heads of all the implementing departments to 'further study' the proposal to allow the infrastructure body to don the role of a regulator too. 'Mehta did not wish to take sides', revealed a senior bureaucrat attending the meeting. 'He was non-committal as the issue was found to be quite complex.'

When it was formed under the first BJP ministry in Gujarat in 1995, all the main departments had declared an open war on the GIDB as they felt their role as project implementors was sought to be curtailed. It remained dormant till 1998 when it was again revived by Chief Minister Keshubhai Patel, in his second tenure, to ensure single-window clearance for all major infrastructure-related projects.

Top policy document, 'Gujarat Infrastructure Agenda Vision-2010', was prepared listing all the 400 projects to be taken up with nearly 75 per cent private participation. The state assembly passed a law, Gujarat Infrastructure Development Act, 1999, to ensure uniformity and transparency in choosing project contractors on a build, operate, and transfer basis after open competitive bids.

With the process of choosing project contractors already on, a tug of war has again broken out between the GIDB and the implementing departments as to who should play the main role.

But the implementing departments were adamant. They said it was not 'worthwhile' for each project to be cleared by the GIDB board even before the prequalification stage. 'Nearly 400 projects have already been worked out by the Vision-2010 document', a bureaucrat said. 'To get each of them cleared by the GIDB board which meets only once in three months, that too when the chief minister has time, would only delay things.'

A bureaucrat gave the example of nine road projects, including Jamnagar–Vadinar worth Rs 400 crore, Bhuj-Nakhatrana worth Rs 150 crore, Bhavnagar–Pipavav worth Rs 400 crore, Magdalla–Palsana worth Rs 250 crore, and Viramgam-Maliya worth Rs 500 crore as having been held up as they would now require GIDB board clearance.

'The situation is not different with several ports, industrial estates, energy and its projects. The wide are a network project, already in the process of being implemented, has been held up as the GIDB board clearance was not obtained at the prequalification stage...', a bureaucrat insisted.

The GIDB, in its defence, cited section five of the Infrastructure Development Act which specifically says that 'the state government, a government agency or a specified government agency' involved in 'financing, construction, maintenance and operation' of a project would need to put forward all the proposals before the GIDB before being taken up. The rules made to implement the Act gave too many powers to departments. These powers should rest with the GIDB.

*Source:* Rajiv Shah, *Times of India*, 27 August 2000 (Ahmedabad).

identifies the agencies and commits to appropriate objective criteria to choose projects.

• It outlines two modes of selection of the developer, one through competitive bidding and the other through a process of direct negotiation that has an inbuilt provision for fairness and transparency. (The negotiated process was to provide the private sector the opportunity to innovate appropriate structures in projects of public interest.)

• It provides for a delicate balance between the nodal agency, that is the GIDB, and executive departments of the government. (The GIDB assumes the role of facilitator while line departments are charged with actual implementation, thus both can use their specific strengths in a clear and non-obtrusive manner.)

• It contains a clause on charging user fees as well

as an introduction of the concept of market-based pricing.

• It contains enabling provisions for lenders to take over projects in cases of default.

• It addresses project maintenance, transfer of technology, and training of the public agency staff.

The law has undergone the test of actual implementation in a couple of projects. The experience gained thereby has been invaluable in drafting the rules for implementing the law. A BOT law is just one of the important pieces in the jigsaw of infrastructure project implementation. Sector-specific legislation that promotes competition and provides for regulation, careful project preparation, and quick decision taking by the government remains central to the theme of private-sector participation in infrastructure.

# 5.4 PROJECT PREPARATION
## THE CINDERELLA OF PRIVATE SECTOR PARTICIPATION (PSP)

*Atanu Chakraborty*

The revival of the private sector in infrastructure projects began in the UK in the early 1980s and soon became a worldwide trend. Deregulation, regulation, independence of the regulator, pricing, rules of access to bring about competition, and the privatization process gathered momentum and came into the limelight.

Much of the discourse was dedicated to regulation, the tussle between regulation and monopolies, and the structure of industry. Tasks like working out the correct scale of projects, or detailed and demanding analysis, did not always get due attention. When the wave of privatization reached third world countries like India, 'regulation' came to be seen almost as a panacea for all problems. No wonder the regulators have been the first to be blighted in the post-privatization phase. In India the so-called 'investment jamborees' compounded the problems. States vied with each other to attract large industrial investments. Large teams organized by state governments either descended on Mumbai, or big shows were held in state capitals to attract 'investment', especially for infrastructure projects. Big melas (fairs) were held, where a couple of sheets of paper masqueraded as a project and memoranda of understanding (MOUs) were signed by the dozen. Obviously, a large number of the projects emanating from these congregations never saw the light of day and spoilt the reputations of state agencies as serious seekers of investment.

The poor rate at which projects are being actively pursued in the course of privatization of infrastructure

is undoubtedly because the agencies do not prepare the projects in a thorough manner. As most of the existing agencies are engineer driven, their concept of project preparation is usually limited to detailed engineering drawings and bills of quantities! To an investor this is unnecessary: he does not expect to be told 'how' to go about the project; that he presumes is his competence. 'What the government wants' is, on the other hand, never clearly stated. Even the more enlightened of the sponsoring agencies still tend to look at the private sector project proponent as a 'works contractor'.

PSP in the infrastructure sector involves a paradigm shift. The sponsoring agency whose job is to provide a particular product/service seeks to make that happen through a private sector agent. Obviously, the sponsoring agency has to know reasonably well what it is that it wants. To illustrate the point, in the case of privatization of a road on build, operate, and transfer (BOT) basis, the material used is of least importance. It is imperative to ensure that the road handles traffic at a certain predefined level of efficiency over the life of the agreement and that safety and environmental conditions are appropriately met. One such agency in privatizing a road over a bridge decided to hand over drawings of the toll plaza instead of specifying the amount of traffic and the maximum permissible waiting time in a specified period. The traffic being heavier than expected, snarls resulted in heavy congestion, leading to increased user side costs for vehicles.

The preparation process in a PSP project involves project definition, analysis and projection of demand determination of willingness of the user to pay the cost at various levels of service, proper sizing, and if need be, phasing. Understanding these dimensions of the project is useful and necessary for the allocation of risks between the private sector proponent and the sponsoring agency, and possibly others. The idea is to ensure that the project is bankable and at the same time no party bears a risk that it should not bear or is not capable of bearing.

The process of doing so involves thinking about the project through its life, and not just at the construction stage, as tends to happen in projects where a works contract is awarded and maintenance is not even considered. The agency is thereby led to critically examine whether the project is truly socially important. The most important change that this brings about in the approach of the sponsoring agency is that it leads the agency to sharply focus on output parameters, which are of utmost importance to the consumer—the *raison d'etre* for the existence of the agency. Delivery of service to the consumer then becomes the core objective. It has been observed that good project preparation drives restructuring in the sector to make it more competitive.

The following are some of the steps in the process of project preparation:

• Outlining the broad contours of the project. This would be largely in terms of the physical dimensions of the project.
• Analysing demand for the service/product that would be provided by the project. This is the trickiest part of the process and one that is often challenged by bidders of the project at a later stage. The level of user fees also sometimes accompanies the analysis of demand.
• Carrying out a brief techno-economic feasibility analysis of the project. This sometimes also involves

'rapid environment impact' analysis, so that at the post-bidding stage of the project, the likely costs to cover environmental damage and displacement are well known.

• Ensuring whether the project is useful to society. This means looking at the economic rate of return (ERR).
• Financially analysing the project, that is ensuring whether the project is bankable.

This process leads to the point where the sponsoring agency takes the primary decision as to whether the project needs to be taken up at location and whether it would be possible to take it up as a PSP project. If this decision is taken, then the risk allocation has to be decided in a manner that ensures financial viability of the project. In fact, government underwriting of part of the risk usually ensures implementation of the project. But such underwriting should be carefully and consciously done.

Carrying out the entire process up front is time consuming and costly. But doing it at a later stage, as has happened in quite a few projects in India, leads to delays which are far more costly both to the project as well as the economy. The project preparation process has to be interactive, iterative, and open so that as far as possible all the stakeholders are involved. This helps to shape a project that is implementable.

Project preparation has to be followed up by quick decision making, otherwise the studies tend to become dated and their relevance becomes questionable.

Project preparation is an activity that needs to be strengthened considerably by the sponsoring government agency. Along with a regulatory regime and sector restructuring, it forms an important aspect of PSP. This is particularly so when market failure in certain infrastructure sectors persists. It is also relevant because the allocation decision is for most governments very difficult to give up. The lead has to be taken by the government agency. Very few governments have understood this need. Fewer still have committed resources to creating such competencies.

## 5.5 HOW MUCH MORE OF THIS INFLICTION? THE CASE OF THE AHMEDABAD–VADODARA EXPRESSWAY[11]

*Amita Gupta and Sebastian Morris*

The quality and especially the carrying capacity of major arterial roads, that is national highways, is of

[11] This is based on Gupta (2000), and draws much on Morris (1990). The authors are grateful to the Shastri Indo-Canadian Institute for financial support for the former and for an updated study of delays and cost overruns in public sector projects.

major concern as these, while constituting merely 3 per cent of total Indian road length, carry almost 40 per cent of total traffic.

State provisioning of roads is a dominant and widespread practice given the major market failures involved in road building and maintenance. Principally the non-excludable character of roads, the long life of the assets created, and the network economies in the use of roads have meant that private appropriability has been a problem. Yet the social return is very high, because without roads a modern economy with an integrated home market is hardly possible. Additionally, in a constrained situation the returns are even greater.

Project implementation by the public sector in India has been a major aspect of state failure. Delays and overruns in public sector investments have resulted in high capital-output ratios economywide, which have reduced the efficacy of investments (Morris 1986).

Government processes for appraisal and approval in India have typically involved multiple agencies and approving authorities, protracted decision making, improper information being available, poor and incomplete appraisal, all of which lead to appraisal and monitoring being more formal and ritualized than functional and critical. Coordination problems between these agencies have been particularly severe. Additionally, inadequate funding, conflicting bureaucratic pursuits, and direct and indirect political influence in not only the choice of projects but also in priority of execution, have been the bases of the massive failure in state provision of infrastructure services in general. Delays and overruns in public sector projects can therefore be understood in terms of the political economy of the public sector itself: the nature of the state and the bureaucracy (Morris 1986).

Delays in project implementation, unlike delays in the approval and appraisal process, result in direct additional costs to the project enterprise, raising its capital–output ratio. This may not only be on account of price escalation but also because expenditures once made have to continue throughout the implementation phase. This would result in 'deadweight loss' in the form of assets locked up for a longer period without potential social contribution during the project phase. The loss is to society as a whole; unlike rents whose first order effect is only a transfer from society or users to the corrupt.

Further, pervasive delays can cause deterioration in the physical state of assets, especially road assets under construction. The cost of bringing them back to a state of repair could be large. Thus earthworks, constructed culverts, cross-drains, etc., when constructed but not used and maintained, would in a year's time definitely lose their value. The deep roots of the present constraints and failures, point to the 'hopelessness' of any piecemeal changes.

The Ahmedabad–Vadodara Expressway, a project of the Ministry of Surface Trnasport (MoST) presents an 'archetypical' case of the delays in public-sector project implementation and the attendant cost overruns. After

more than twelve years since its inception it is, in the year 2000, still only almost 61 per cent complete (as per the Public Works Department [PWD] records), when it was originally expected to be completed in four years, that is in 1991! Since 1996, for almost four years, the project has been deteriorating as the government remains undecided on the mode of its completion. It is worthwhile to note here that, during January 2000, parts of the project road were being used by a municipality's water supply project for dumping soil and also for reinforcing the water pipelines!

In 1986, the contracts for construction were separated into two packages, the bridge package (comprising six contracts) and the road package (comprising seven contracts). The road package was awarded to a joint venture between M/s Continental Construction Limited (CCL) and Belfour Beathy Construction Limited in 1987 which broke up in the year 1989. CCL was rewarded the contract in 1991. Till August 1999, work on the road package was 35 per cent complete (as per PWD estimates). The bridge package was awarded to National Building Construction Company Limited (NBCC) and Uttar Pradesh State Bridges Construction Company Limited (UPSBC). The contract with NBCC was terminated on account of poor progress of work but UPSBC was not reawarded the contract until 1993. Work on the bridge package was 86 per cent complete as of August 1999 (as per PWD records).

The anticipated cost overrun in the project works out to 298.24 per cent and the time overrun to 300 per cent on the basis of the PWD's assessment of completion dates and costs. Such large time and cost overruns necessarily warrant more in-depth analyses. The capital waste[12] in the project, that is the extra 'time X capital', is estimated to be as much as 800 per cent! This means that the resources used in the project could have 'financed' eight more such projects. This is only indicative of the large waste of capital resources that characterizes public-sector project implementation.

Such large delays arose because of problems in land acquisition and utility shifting, a protracted process of reawarding contracts and for obtaining foreign exchange clearances and approvals. Revised cost estimates were being 'approved' only through deferred processes which were not final and hence could and were questioned. The contracts required design approvals and reapprovals of changes and modifications, which again resulted in long delays because of too many sequential stages being involved in the approval process. Besides

[12] For a discussion on the notion of 'capital waste' in a capital-scarce economy, see Morris (1996).

these, the cumbersome procedures involved in the release of funds, which are typical of departmental project implementation were also responsible for delaying the project to the point of unviability.

The concept of rate of return in the Ahmedabad–Vadodara Expressway project had become a ritual 'measure' and had lost its original meaning. The project started with a high economic internal rate of return (IRR) and ended up with a negative one! The IRR in the very first estimate, that is in 1982, before the World Bank (the agency which could have exercised some pressure for task orientation) was 17.39 per cent. For twelve years, starting from 1989, toll on the project highway was to be collected. Working backwards we estimated the likely cost streams. These amounted to Rs 21.57 crore per year for twelve years, with some assumptions. Similarly, benefit streams of the two other estimates at different points of time work out to be Rs 138.4 crore and Rs 118.85 crore per annum over the life of the project respectively. The government overestimated the latter two streams as subsequent data were to show. Claimed economic IRRs were as high as 40.8 per cent, 43.2 per cent, and 30.5 per cent at different points in time and in different reports! In reality the predicted cost streams in 1996, when the BOT proposal was submitted, showed a very different picture. We worked backwards using the actual costs that had been incurred and that had yet to be spent (these include the cost of redoing certain parts of the project road which could not be put to use in the new expressway), and re-estimated the benefit streams work out to be negative. The true IRR was revealed only at the stage when revised estimates for the project were prepared.

A more general perverse process is illustrated by this case. The true costs of the project are usually not revealed at the time of approval. This is done to get the project approved in the first place. This secures the grounds for revision of cost estimates during implementation. Inadequacy in the appraisal shows up only when extra works come up for approval and high quantity variations and price escalations result. Expenditures once made improve the chances of the further estimates being approved. Even after taking into account this 'game playing', the delays and overruns are real enough, and could be more than half the originally estimated costs and time.

According to the government's own norms, the approval of the detailed project report should be completed in six months. For the Ahmedabad–Vadodara Expressway project, the time taken was twenty-five months! The delays in approvals resulted in expiry of the cost estimates, and new estimates were thus required

to be submitted. These in turn resulted in compounding of the delays in project implementation.

The appraisal of public projects is carried out with the help of appraising agencies like the Plan Finance Division of the Ministry of Finance, Project Appraisal Division of Planning Commission, and other 'concerned' departments and ministries, which have to send their comments within a month of receiving the detailed project report. This generally never happens. In the case of this project, it took almost a year for the Planning Commission to sent its queries to the PWD. An interesting clue to the kind of appraisal that actually takes place is revealed by the content of the questions. Of the sixteen queries, half asked for some missing 'vital' information, and another 40 per cent were clarifications on account of ambiguities in the memorandum sent for approval of the cost estimates in 1996.

Appraisal has become a formal process and the content of the project if it is at all contained in the papers is hidden away in the appendices. Improper preparation of agenda papers and too little time being available to high-level government officers making the decision affect the quantity and timelines of appraisal. The time limit of one month is hardly sufficient or meaningful. The actual time taken is much more and that normally lost in formalities and processes is very large. This indicates that the norms and standards that the government has set up for itself are at best procedural rather than functional. In any case, nearly all its norms end up being violated.

Who or what is really responsible for this state of affairs? The project enterprise that is providing incomplete and ambiguous information, the appraising agency/agencies have their own hierarchical and bureaucratically oriented processes, limited technical expertise, or the administrative ministry or department which is responsible for coordination? The system and procedures are such that there is hardly any allocation of responsibility or accountability for delays and slack behaviour, with the result that blame can never be attributed to individuals or small groups, or even to organizations.

The political expedience to fund as many projects as possible tends to increase the number of projects taken up. This results in spreading thin public resources, which in turn results in inadequate funding of any particular project. There was a sanction of Rs 18 crore against the Rs 60 crore originally approved for the financial year 1993-4 for the Ahmedabad–Vadodara Expressway. The ratio between the amount sanctioned and planned expenditure is 3:33, indicating that nearly two more years over and above that planned were at that time required for completing the project at the then rate of funding for the project.

The fact that land was provided piecemeal to the contractor delayed his work and increased his costs. There was a presumption among government officers that work once started would face minimum resistance allowing easy acquisition of the rest of the land. But stay orders from courts and subsequent increments in compensation lead to an increase in the total final cost of the project as well as to delays.

The process of project monitoring in the public sector is again more formal than real and at best helps generate data. The Department of Programme Implementation (DPI) at central government level and the implementation agency (project enterprise)—in this case the PWD—are the important actors. The PWD is answerable to the Ministry of Surface Transport (MoST) while the DPI is an 'independent' body within the Planning Commission which monitors all central public sector projects. The monthly progress reports prepared by the PWD are sent to six different agencies located at different places and the average time taken for one such report to reach the six agencies is about two months, which is too long for any corrective action to be taken. The information provided is ambiguous and is moreover out of date by the time the decision is actually taken.

The DPI's role is purely advisory. Any action, if at all, has to be taken by the Roads Wing at the MoST.

The earnings for the Gujarat PWD were on account of the 9 per cent agency charges for project implementation that it received from the MoST. This fee is not contingent on good performance. Budgetary allocations are not affected even in case of underutilization or underperformance in particular projects. This is because the budgets of the department and the project are not separated, and the project as such is not, or rather cannot be, audited separately. The balance sheet in this case would not reflect the status of the project but that of the department, which typically works on a soft budget, where fund allocation is essentially through grants and not performance based.

The scope for change through internal tensions and measures is weak. Change would be difficult and unlikely as long as rules and procedures are seen as inflexible and punishment for poor performance is non-existent. Corporatization of the involved public entities, performance agreements, management contracts, hardening of budgets, etc. could to an extent help in reforming Indian public enterprise including departments and departmental enterprises. In Maharashtra, for example, a public body called the Maharashtra State Road Development Corporation (MSRDC), which follows commercial principles, has been born out of the trying conditions of rip off prices being quoted by the pioneering private sector. Greater public accountability could quickly come through transparency laws and information access to the public.

# 5.6 LAND ACQUISITION: LAW AND PRACTICE

*Y. M. Shivamurthy and Vinita Sinha*

## INTRODUCTION

The high population density in India means that it is difficult to acquire land without displacing people in large numbers.[13] Even mountainous and semi-arid areas are much more thickly populated than similar areas elsewhere. Most infrastructure projects require large areas of land and/or right of way in or over the land or right to use the land. The provision of infrastructure has in the twentieth century been largely a state obligation, met through budgetary support and utilization. Land for infrastructure and other industrial activities in India has generally been acquired by the 'state' for 'public purposes'. It has been universally accepted that 'eminent

domain' is inherent in sovereignty and does not arise out of the constitution, but independently of it, and may be exercised in respect of all property by the state, for public use. The Constitution of India and the legislative framework governing acquisition of land in India clearly reflect such power of eminent domain in the state. Albeit the state is obliged to follow the principles of natural justice and to pay just compensation to the persons deprived of their land.

The urgency for development of infrastructure for overall economic development of the nation is accompanied by increased resistance and opposition to land acquisition and the resultant involuntary displacement. The struggle by persons whose lands are sought to be acquired (or those who are otherwise likely to be adversely affected by the implementation of the underlying infrastructure project) is sometimes, being espoused or

---

[13] There are few large countries which have comparable population densities: Japan, Korea, and China, excluding its 'desert' areas, come to mind.

otherwise championed by external agencies including the media and the activist groups. There is growing demand for 'sustainable' development. Lack of transparency in declaring the purpose of acquisition, definition of public purpose, identification and enumeration of project-affected persons (PAPs), undue delay in completing the acquisition process, inadequate and/or delayed payment of compensation, lack of rehabilitation and resettlement plans or implementation and, sometimes, serious procedural lapses have been the prime causes of agitation and consequent delay. The non-availability of the required land at an appropriate stage of project implementation is a critical risk to be factored, addressed, and mitigated early on during the process of development of any project, by both the state and project sponsors. It is in this context that an attempt is made herein to take a look at the existing framework for acquisition of land and the paradigm shift that is called for.

## PUBLIC PURPOSE

The principal legislation governing acquisition of land by the state is the Land Acquisition Act, 1894 (hereafter the Act), with the exception of certain special legislations which contain separate provisions for acquisition of land like the National Highways Act, 1956. The power to declare a piece of land as being required for a 'public purpose' reposes with the central government with respect to acquisition for the purposes of the union and with the state government with respect to acquisition for any other purposes. The central government or state government as the case may be is referred to in the Act as the 'appropriate government'). The appropriate government is not ordinarily interfered with by the judiciary in the exercise of such power. The Act provides for acquisition of any land when it appears to the appropriate government that such land is needed or likely to be needed for a public purpose.

Historically, the Act did not define the term 'public purpose', and interpretation has remained contentious. The Supreme Court of India has observed that 'public purpose' has not been defined in a compendious way, for the reason that it is bound to vary with the times and the prevailing conditions, and therefore it would not be a practical proposition even to attempt a comprehensive definition of it. It has, however, consistently interpreted the same as a purpose which is beneficial to the community and in which the general interest of the community, as opposed to the particular interest of individuals, is directly and vitally concerned.[14] This

is not to say that the appropriate government's power to declare a tract of land as being required for a public purpose is unbridled. If such declaration is tantamout to the exercise of legislative power, the same can be successfully challenged. The Supreme Court's response to public concerns not addressed by the Act was exemplified in a matter involving Coal India Limited in which it held that 'no development project, however laudable, can possibly justify impoverishment of large sections of people and their utter destitution'.[15] Consequent to an amendment made by the Land Acquisition (Amendment) Act, 1984 (hereafter the 'Amended Act'), the Act now contains an inclusive definition of the term 'public purpose' whereby certain purposes have been explicitly declared as public purposes. The Act, however, continues to be silent on the criteria for deciding what constitutes public purpose. While it may be true that a precise definition of 'public purpose' will not be able to meet the exigencies of changing situations, the Act must provide certain guidelines and criteria for deciding public purpose that could withstand public scrutiny.

The Supreme Court has held that a change of public purpose after the land has been acquired does not vitiate the acquisition proceedings and that once the original acquisition is valid and title vested in the acquiring authority, how the said authority uses the land is of no concern to the original owner.[16] The Supreme Court has also consistently ruled that land acquired for one public purpose can be used for another public purpose on account of change or surplus thereof and that a particular scheme may serve public purpose at a given point of time but due to change in circumstances it may become essential to modify or substitute it by another scheme.[17]

Thus 'requirement' or a 'likely requirement' for a public purpose is *sine qua non* for acquisition of any land under the provisions of the Act. Such requirement is a sufficient condition to initiate acquisition proceedings. The discretion to decide public purpose has been left entirely with the appropriate government and the judiciary has been reluctant to interfere with the exercise of such discretion except on the limited grounds of malafide. The Act mandates the requirement of a preliminary enquiry to ascertain objections, if any, to the public purpose for which the land is proposed to be acquired and payment of monetary compensation. Except for this limited responsibility, the Act does not

[14] Babu Barkya Thakur's case (1961) 1 SCR 128.

[15] Lalchand Mahto & Ors vs Coal India Limited, Civil Original Jurisdiction, MP No. 196331 of 1982.
[16] Ghulam Mustafa (1976) 1 SCC 800.
[17] Mahadeo Deoman Rai (1990) 3 SCC 579.

enjoin upon the appropriate government any obligation to assess and address the rehabilitation and resettlement and other socio-economic implications.

## ACQUISITION PROCEDURE

The procedure for acquisition envisaged under the Act involves, broadly, a preliminary inquiry by the Collector to ascertain objections, if any, of the interested persons to the proposed acquisition, affording the interested persons an opportunity of being heard, declaration as to public purpose by the appropriate government after considering the report of the Collector, passing of an award by the Collector after determining the true area of the land acquired, and quantification and apportionment of the compensation payable to the interested persons. The Act has conferred a special power on the appropriate government to be exercised in case of urgency, pursuant of which the appropriate government may take possession of the land pending passing of the award but subject to tendering the prescribed compensation. Prior to the enactment of the Amendment Act, there did not exist any time-frame for making declaration by the appropriate government as to public purpose or passing of award by the Collector. Though the Amendment Act provided for a time-frame in these regards, this did not apply to cases of acquisitions under the urgency provisions. Thus ironically, while the time-frame operates for acquisition proceedings in which dispossession has not taken place, it does not apply to cases in which the owner is dispossessed of his land under the urgency provisions. This lacuna in the Amending Act has been highlighted by the Supreme Court which has held that the time-frame prescribed under the Act can have no application to cases of acquisition under the urgency provisions because the land gets vested in the appropriate government and there is no provision in the Act whereby land statutorily vested in the appropriate government can revert to the owner.[18]

The appropriate government is empowered to withdraw from the acquisition proceedings upon payment of compensation for the damage suffered by the owner in consequence of the acquisition proceedings as long as possession has not been taken. The owner's right to damages is restricted only to cases of withdrawal of the acquisition proceedings and does not extend to cases where such proceedings have lapsed due to the Collector's failure to make the award within the prescribed time-frame. This distinction has been upheld by the Supreme Court.[19] Due to this infirmity, the Amendment Act has proved to be futile in benefiting owners whose land is acquired under the urgency provisions.

Besides addressing the issue of delayed acquisition by prescribing a time-frame, the Amendment Act brought about certain other changes in the Act including (a) better means of spreading information about the proposed acquisition; (b) provision for review, revision, and correction of the award before it is made final; (c) payment of 80 per cent of the amount of compensation when possession is taken using the special powers in case of urgency; (d) interest payment at 15 per cent per annum if the deposit of compensation determined by the court is delayed beyond a period of one year from the date of taking possession; and (e) remedy to seek compensation based on determination by the Court even by those who were not party to such determination.

The existing acquisition process however continues to adopt a residual approach to dealing with persons affected by the land acquisition proceedings as it does not involve participation of such persons at the pre-proposal stage. The acquisition process invariably meets with stiff resistance from the affected persons, who see acquisition as not only leading to physical dislocation from their land and loss of income but as also causing social, cultural, and psychological problems in relocation in new and different surroundings.

The process of land acquisition involves, amongst others, hearing of objections and determination of claims of all persons claiming to be interested in the compensation amount. While the legislative intent behind this cannot be faulted, often serious problems arise because of incorrect, incomplete, or inadequate land records that make identification of interested persons difficult, and often protracted, because of rival claims. One of the reasons for the inadequate land records is that land-related transaction costs are onerous. Apart from formal transaction costs, viz. registration fees and stamp duties, there exist informal transaction costs which include the cost of making repeated visits to the tehsildar's and registrar's office, speed money payments, etc. to expedite issuance of relevant documents. Further, the process of effecting mutation in land records often takes decades or longer. This problem gets accentuated with rising activity in land markets and demographic pressure. Though the production of documents of title is obligatory for all such transaction relating to land, these documents are private documents and do not guarantee title. In a large part of India no survey and settlement operations have been undertaken after independence.

---

[18] S. P. Jain (1993) 4 SCC 369, Awadh Bihari Yadav (1995) 6 SCC 31.

[19] Abdul Majeed Sahib (1997) 1 SCC 297.

As a consequence, updating of records has suffered and these records no longer represent the ground realities relating to ownership and possession. A centrally sponsored scheme for computerization of land records has still not been implemented in most states.

## COMPENSATION

The Act envisages relief by payment of monetary compensation, based on the Collector's assessment or as determined by the court upon a reference made to it. While there are certain guidelines for courts to arrive at the compensation payable, the same are absent in case of assessment by the Collector. The guiding factors for courts include a consideration of the market value of the land acquired, damage sustained by reason of taking of any standing crop or trees, damage on account of severance of land from other land of the interested person, damage sustained to other property, movable or immovable, while taking possession, reasonable expenses incidental to change of residence or place of business and damage bonafide resulting from diminution of the profits of the land between the time of publication of declaration and taking of possession. The Act also provides for payment of interest of 12 per cent per annum on market value from the date of preliminary notification to the date of taking possession and payment of 30 per cent of the market value of the land as compensation for the compulsory nature of acquisition.

The compensation determined by the Collector can be objected to by owners on the grounds of measurement of the land, the quantum of compensation, the persons to whom the compensation is payable, or the apportionment of compensation among the persons interested. A reference to the court may be sought for determination of compensation but the Act does not prescribe any time-frame for the Collector to make the reference. This deficiency is significant for it is not unknown that the Collectors take their own time in making the reference prolonging the hardship caused to owners. The Supreme Court has noted that a 'serious view should be taken of the fact that applications for reference are withheld by the Land Acquisition Officers without disposal for time beyond any explanation'.[20] Additionally, Collectors/Land Acquisition Officers do not have the power to condone delay in making the application for reference. Appeals against the Collector's order is not possible. The only remedy left to the owners is to file a writ petition at the concerned High Courts.

The Amending Act that introduced a time-frame for various steps in the acquisition proceedings including a time-frame for the award of compensation, did not provide a time-frame for taking possession of the land or payment of compensation. The issue of delayed compensation was dealt with by the Supreme Court in the case of the Lower Manair Dam Reservoir Project in Andhra Pradesh, wherein the said Court prevented the remand of the matter to District Courts for determination of compensation and observed that with rising inflation, the delayed payment lost all charm and utility and might even get detrimental to the interests of the claimants and that Indian agriculturists wholly depended on land, and if uprooted would find themselves nowhere. In the same matter, the Supreme Court recognized the need for rehabilitation to prevent the impoverishment and starvation of such people.[21]

The compensation awarded by the Collector can be predetermined by him/her on the basis of the award of the court to which a reference is made under the Act (Reference Court). This provision was introduced by the Amendment Act with the objective of removing inequality in the payment of compensation for similar land to different persons and also to provide the remedy of seeking enhancement of compensation to those who had accepted the compensation awarded by the Collector. But this laudable amendment has a restricted scope in as much as the Supreme Court has held that redetermination can be sought only on the basis of the award of the Reference Court and not pursuant to enhancement by the Supreme Court or the High Court.[22]

The Supreme Court, in the early decades, dealt with cases relating to compensation merely to see if the correct method of valuation and suitable multipliers were applied to determine the market value of land. In the last two decades, there has been a change in the response of courts to issues of compensation and the relief given by courts now ensures protection of the rights of the persons affected and aims to include them as beneficiaries of the project. The Supreme Court in the case of acquisition of land for planned urban development by the Meerut Development Authority observed that the wholesome principle contained in the Delhi Development Act, 1957 relating to providing of accommodation on the land developed by the Authority to the original owners should be followed by all Development Authorities throughout the country for acquisition of land in urban areas.[23]

[20] Mangat Ram Tanwar AIR 1991 SC 1080.

[21] (1988) 4 SCC 163.
[22] Bant Ram (1996) 4 SCC 537, Bhagti (1997) 4 SCC 473.
[23] (1986) 4 SCC 251.

This principle was reiterated in the case of acquisition of land for the purpose of setting up New Bombay wherein the Supreme Court went a step further, and directed the authorities to offer alternative sites, as per the scheme framed in 1976, to affected landowners, on the basis of the actual cost of development by charging the cost of acquisition and development and no more, so that the offer of alternative site does not become illusory.[24]

Though the Act continues to mandate the payment of monetary compensation, the Supreme Court has shown a clear shift in looking at compensation as not merely a valuation issue but as a human issue affecting the lives and livelihoods of hundreds of people. In the case of the Pong Dam on river Beas, the Supreme Court expressed its dismay that some of the oustees remained unsettled even twenty-four years after acquisition and observed that oustees who belonged to Himachal Pradesh had been disfavoured in the matter of resettlement. The Court then went on to give detailed directions for awarding the oustees their due in the resettlement package.[25]

## RESETTLEMENT AND REHABILITATION

While the Act continued to remain silent on issues of resettlement and rehabilitation, the courts recognized the issue of displacements caused by development projects. In the matter of resettlement under the dam project over river Karjan in Gujarat, the Supreme Court observed that though it understood the anxiety of the government in acquiring land for building the dam, it could not overlook the human problem arising out of displacement of a large number of tribals and other persons belonging to the weaker section of society. It laid down conditions, in the nature of a *scheme* which permitted dis-possession of land only in the presence of NGOs or the Judicial Magistrate, maintenance of records of the landholders, adequate notice before acquisition, alternative land or employment or payment of minimum wage every fortnight during the period alternative land or employment was not provided, alternative dwelling, etc. It is pertinent to note that the Supreme Court even attempted to monitor the implementation of the scheme by directing the Judicial Magistrate to submit to it a report with regard to the implementation.[26] Recently, the Supreme Court has even touched upon the principle of minimizing displacement in a case relating to acquisition for

construction of a public passage for a religious procession. The Court quashed the acquisition proceedings on the grounds that the route of the procession could easily and conveniently be diverted without disturbing the affected person's shop.[27] This judgement upheld the principle of resorting to displacement only after all other viable means have been considered and rejected. In the case of the Gramin Sewa Sanstha the Supreme Court expressed its inability to understand the reasons for not bringing the Hasdeo Bango Dam Project under the Madhya Pradesh Projects Displaced Persons (Resettlement) Act, 1985 which had been enacted with the objective and purpose of resettlement and rehabilitation of tribals uprooted by the projects undertaken by the state government, and directed the state government to give effect to its policy and to use the guidelines on resettlement and rehabilitation in various reports including the report of the World Bank with regard to the dams being constructed in Gujarat.[28] In another case of acquisition in Mumbai, the Supreme Court upheld the contention that the Government of Maharashtra must implement its policy decision to offer alternative sites to affected landowners.[29]

While judicial activism has played an important role in dealing with the larger issues arising out of land acquisition for public purposes, the absence of any national law or policy on resettlement and rehabilitation of project-displaced persons has led some states like Maharashtra, Madhya Pradesh, Karnataka, Rajasthan, Orissa, and corporations like the National Thermal Power Corporation, Coal India Limited, and Power Grid Corporation of India Limited, to come out with their own Acts/policies on resettlement and rehabilitation. Projects undertaken for development purposes remain meaningless if the local population does not benefit from the development process and continues to get impoverished. It is in this context that a national policy for resettlement and rehabilitation must be formulated with the objective of securing peaceful possession of land with minimum displacement. The policy must introduce a regime of planned rehabilitation and resettlement by enabling the affected communities to assess and react in an informed way to the policy and ensure their full participation in preparing, assessing, implementing, and monitoring the rehabilitation and resettlement schemes. The policy must incorporate the principles of (i) minimizing displacement; (ii) establishment of 'national interest' and 'public purpose'

---

[24] (1993) 3 SCC 634.
[25] (1996) 9 SCC 749.
[26] (1986) Supp SCC 350.

[27] Jnanedays Yogam (1999) 9 SCC 492.
[28] (1986) Supp SCC 578.
[29] (1993) 3 SCC 634.

before formulating the resettlement programme; (iii) expansion of the definition of displaced persons beyond landowners to include those who depend for sustenance on land owned by others or on common property resources; (iv) welfare of displaced persons as a precondition for the project; (v) mandatory rehabilitation leading to better lifestyle after displacement than before it; (vi) advance identification of the persons affected; (vii) replacement value to be the norm for compensation against the present norm of market value; (viii) land for land as preferred compensation for rehabilitation of persons affected and mandatory for tribals; (ix) making acquisition of land cost-effective by minimizing resistance; (x) prevention of misuse of the rehabilitation package; and (xi) implementation and monitoring of the rehabilitation programme.

It is interesting and indeed strange that while we still debate the formulation of a policy for resettlement and rehabilitation, China with a higher population has in place a systematic and democratic resettlement policy. The Chinese policy begins with a preliminary study on resettlement at the pre-feasibility planning stage of the project. At this stage an estimate and description of the scope of the resettlement plan is a necessary component of acquiring state approval to proceed to the feasibility level of the project. At the next, feasibility-level, study, local governments and the affected population are involved in the planning process. The initial survey establishes an administrative framework for planning and administering the resettlement programme and informs the affected persons of the anticipated project. The resettlement programme is then developed as part of the schedule of project construction. Beyond physical relocation, the Chinese policy includes a post-relocation phase of the project and provides for more than the immediate needs of the relocated population within the framework of the resettlement programme. The resettlement policy of China is applied uniformly throughout the country and has now become a benchmark for the rest of the world. (For a rather different and ham-handed approach adopted by the Gujarat government, see Box 5.6.1).

## SUGGESTED AMENDMENTS TO THE LEGISLATIVE FRAMEWORK

The adoption of an appropriate policy for resettlement and rehabilitation should be followed by an equally appropriate change in the legislative framework for acquisition of land and for dealing with issues arising therefrom. In this regard, either a comprehensive amendment to the Act or adoption of an altogether new legislation seems imperative and integral. The changes in legislative framework should include (i) change in the definition of 'persons interested' to include persons who depend for sustenance on the land proposed to be acquired or on common property resources proposed to be utilized for any project; (ii) criteria for deciding 'public purpose'; (iii) resettlement value as the basis for compensation in place of market value; (iv) mandatory resettlement and rehabilitation, the cost of which would be borne by the acquiring body; (v) updation of land records and completion of documentation before initiating acquisition; (vi) proper dissemination of information regarding the acquisition proceedings; (vii) mandatory payment of monetary compensation before taking possession of the land; (viii) guidelines for determination and assessment of compensation; (ix) time-frame for taking possession and making payment of the compensation; (x) provision to check speculative transactions in land after the initial notification for acquisition; (xi) provision to check excessive acquisition of land, and (xii) provisions to address the issues highlighted by the Supreme Court in the catena of judgements discussed earlier.

## CONCLUSION

There is need for a paradigm shift in the policy and legislative framework for acquisition of land. With increasing resistance to compulsory acquisitions and organized movements of people against implementation of projects with vast societal benefits as a whole, any process for acquisition of land has to be democratized and must involve those who are likely to be adversely affected thereby. The objective of the policy for resettlement and rehabilitation should be to minimize displacement and provide relief to not only those who are deprived of land but also to those who are otherwise adversely affected by the project. 'Public interest' should be very clearly defined and in a manner that does not allow governments to cover all uses. Acquisition must be preceded by a complete study of the impact of the project on the persons inhabiting and dependent on the land sought to be acquired, followed by a resettlement programme. The resettlement and rehabilitation of displaced persons should not be seen as a set of palliative measures for welfare and relief but as an integral part of development and implementation of projects. Then those displaced would have the first rights to the benefits from the project. In any case, 'case law' would demand that those affected should not be worse off than they were before. Such a paradigm shift would, while smoothening the process of land acquisition, also facilitate growth of infrastructure development through private sector participation.

BOX 5.6.1

## Land Acquisition Process: The Case of Poshitra Port

*Alice Albin Morris*

The village of Poshitra, with a population of 1500, was little known till eight months ago when the Gujarat Maritime Board (GMB) decided to build a port there. It is located at the tip of Okhamandal taluka in Jamnagar district in the Gulf of Kutchch, near the port of Okha.

Out of the 300 households around 150 own land which they cultivate, largely during the monsoon. Around sixty households cultivate land that, while owned by their ancestors, has not been finally transferred in their name. Therefore there are no records to prove ownership. The livelihood of the remaining households is dependent on the local economy—agriculture labour, livestock, and other services in the village.

Poshitra is one of many ports that the GMB has planned for the state as part of a policy to capture the large hinterland, which includes Rajasthan, Haryana, Uttar Pradesh, and parts of Madhya Pradesh. Poshitra is to be developed into a container and petroleum port. The port will be a joint venture of a consortium of the GMB and four companies: Sea-King Infrastructures, Coatex India Limited, Horizon Battery Technology Limited, and Sumitomo Corporation India Limited. The plan is to turn Poshitra village into the 'Hong Kong of India'. It is reported that a vast network of infrastructure is to be developed, including five star hotels, an airport, schools, roads, a captive power plant, a desalination water plant, gardens, a water park, and water sports facilities. The expected investment in the Poshitra port project alone is Rs 2104 crore in the first phase and Rs 881 crore in the second phase. This project is expected to be completed in three years.

Poshitra village has 11,061 acres of land, of which 6461 acres belong to the government (wasteland, grazing land) and the remaining cultivated by 4600 farmers. The government has helped the GMB acquire 6461 acres of land, which have been handed over to the private consortium. The GMB issued the first acquisition notice to villagers for their farming land in November 1998. The acquisition notice for the land on which the houses are situated has not as yet been issued. The last notification under Section 9 of the Land Acquisition Act was issued on 25 April 2000 in which villagers were asked to put up any objections they have to the acquisition within thirty days.

The villagers have no objection to the setting up of the port at Poshitra but they do object to the process that was followed in the acquisition and the compensation offered to date. They have not been provided with any information on the project, including how it will benefit the local economy. Government officials and businessmen have been visiting Poshitra to measure land, tramping along the coast, and conducting 'impact studies' on the coral and marine life. No study has so far been carried out to examine the possible impact of this project on the local economy.

The government has so far not discussed a compensation package with the community nor have they announced one. The compensation stated in the last notice is Rs 15,000 per acre. The villagers have been told that the project will lead to development of the whole area. However, there is no plan to utilize the local skills and include the local community in the project. The landless and other households that are dependent on the local economy have been totally ignored as far as compensation is concerned.

Following the land proceedings in Poshitra village, in June 2000 the first notice for land acquisition was issued to fifteen more villages adjoining Poshitra. The coastal area around Poshitra (which means 'bad omen' to the local people) has been declared as one of two special economic zones (SEZs) in the country, the other being in Tamil Nadu. The notice states that the land will be acquired by the Gujarat Poshitra Port Infrastructure Limited at a price of Rs 6000 per acre. Even in these villages there is no objection to the plan to develop the SEZ. But they have objected to the amount of compensation and lack of concern on the part of government officials who have not undertaken any discussions with them on the project, the benefits that could possibly accrue, and the provision of an alternative source of livelihood.

The process of land acquisition as per the Act (Sections 4, 6, and 9) is being carried out systematically. However there are some major concerns:

At present the compensation has been arrived at looking at the revenue records for the previous four years. The records indicate an average land value of Rs 5000 per acre. However, discussions with the community and certain institutions revealed that good irrigated land sold for as much as around Rs 30,000–50,000 per acre. Understating the value of land to avoid paying stamp duty is a widely established practice. In these villages too understating has reduced the amount of compensation to the local people.

• When any compensation package is discussed, only those who own land are considered. In most villages about 50 per cent of the households do not own land and, therefore, technically cannot be compensated. However, the takeover of agricultural and common lands affects their livelihood, often to the point of destroying it. In such projects the entire local economy is affected and everyone who is part of this system needs to be compensated. The community sells its land for the project and loses the only earning asset it has. The members of the community are paid a one-time compensation, which can help them survive for a maximum of three years. Only if they are able to find alternative employment would their livelihood be protected.

• There is very little interaction between the community and government officials or representatives of the private sector. Whatever little interaction that takes place is in the form of coaxing or putting pressure on the people to sell their land at the stated price. Such situations create tension and conflict between the parties leading to violence and stalling of projects, the Maroli port project in Umergaon being the most recent example.

- These conflicts can be avoided if the process is made participatory by involving the people. This requires not great investments but a change in attitude, better planning, and efforts to spend more time with the community in sharing the details of the project. All details of the project need to be shared in a simple way so that the community understands the process, which will help them to make an informed choice. There are local institutions willing to help out in this process. This would be required to enable the local people to prepare themselves to take maximum advantage of the opportunities the project could offer. Training the local community in specific skills would also have to be a necessary part of the project.

- There is utter lack of transparency in the project. The Gujarat Industrial Development Board (GIDB) has made plan documents available only to the potential project developers and not the public. These documents are 'confidential'. However, the irony of the situation is that much before (as much as a year and a half) the villagers knew about the project outsiders had the details. These outsiders bought up large chunks of land. Among such buyers were real estate dealers from Jamnagar, politicians, and other speculators. In many villages about 50 per cent of the land has been bought by outsiders. The villagers were happy to sell their lower productivity land, little knowing that in a year's time their land would fetch them more. Only when the notice was issued to Poshitra village did they realize that they had been cheated. The right to information can play a major role here.

- Many general promises have been made to the local community—overall development of the village, employment, better health and education facilities, roads, drinking water, etc. in return for selling their land. As in other cases there is very little chance that these will be fulfilled after the process of acquisition is complete. Though the benefits of development are supposed to percolate down to the local economy, the process of development through land acquisition and displacement of local communities reduces them to mere objects to be shifted to another location where they will be alienated from the development process itself.

Many infrastructure projects end up in dispute/conflict with the local community because the local people, who could have been the stakeholders are not seen as contributors. They have not been provided space to participate in the project and the proposed development process. Today 'public–private' partnerships are public only in the sense of the government and politicians, not the people. There is need to create mechanisms in which local communities can be partners and shareholders in the project. Thus instead of being alienated the community will have a sense of belonging. This will also lead to long-term benefits of the project accruing to the community. The concept of 'development without displacement' can then become more than lip service.

## 5.7 ENVIRONMENT AND SOCIAL RISKS IN INFRASTRUCTURE DEVELOPMENT

*Ajay Narayanan*

Environment-related regulation ought to shield projects and businesses from environmental risk, when the firms in question adhere to all rules and regulations. Nevertheless, in reality even adherence[30] to regulations does not completely shield firms from environmental and social risks in India. I briefly examine the reasons for this state of affairs in this part chapter.

### PUBLIC PRESSURE AND JUDICIAL INTERVENTION

Enhanced public awareness and sensitivity to the environment and social impact of development have led to the increasing role of the public and civil society in opposing development projects. The dams on the Narmada river are a case in point. While there is much rhetoric on the legitimacy and content of these dissensions, clearly the argument is shifting in favour of the critics.

Traditionally, a regulatory clearance for environment was considered as being adequate. However, recent cases have shown that many facilities have been ordered to be closed by courts despite possessing valid environmental permits and clearances[31] (for a shocking case of fraud in environmental clearance of projects, see Box 5.7.1). The mere fact of documentary clearance or a permit will not protect a project from facing public/judicial pressure.

Some reasons why there is increasing interest and involvement of civil society and non-governmental organizations (NGOs) in this process are as follows:

- Post-modernist influences from the West. In the developed countries of the West the value of individual rights and those concerning the environment has increased.

---

[30] Adherence itself has been a problem. Firms may well hold clearance certificates and such formal documents without actually having met the stipulations in the spirit and letter.

[31] Courts are acutely aware that possession of the requisite papers and certificates is no guarantee that laws have not been violated.

---

### BOX 5 7.1
### Hotshot Consultants Copy a Report to Get Project Cleared

Can the environmental impact of two dam projects at different locations and on two different rivers be exactly the same? Can the villages to be submerged, the areas' flora and fauna, even the soil and water analysis data be exactly identical?

Yes, if Ernst & Young, which calls itself 'one of the world's leading professional service organizations' is to be believed.

Although it is only a 20 MW project, experts are calling it a 'serious case of fraud in environmental decision-making in Indian history'. And the green brigade in Karnataka is salivating, for never before has it got such ammunition to campaign against a power project. Especially when the state government gave an 'in-principle clearance' to the project based on this report....

The controversy hinges on an environment impact assessment report prepared by Ernst & Young for its client, the Murdeshwar Power Corporation Ltd., for the Rs 180 crore, 130-mu (million units) Dandeli Mini-Hydel Project (DMH) in Karnataka.

Sixty of the 65 pages of this report have been reproduced ad [sic] verbatim from an impact report of the proposed Tattihalla Augmentation Scheme (TAS), a state government power project. That report was prepared by the Institute for Catchment Studies and Environmental Management (ICSEM), Bangalore.

The only change Ernst & Young have made is to introduce the name DMH wherever the name TAS appear....

Bangalore-based Environment Support Group is now using this 'fraud' in its campaign against the project. The group's Leo Saldanha told the *Indian Express* that the report was 'managed' to get a clearance from the government. And that the project involves the 'submergence of about 87 hectares of moist deciduous and evergreen forests in the Uttara Kannada district in the Western Ghats'.

*Source:* B. S. Nagaraj, *Indian Express*, 27 August 2000 (Ahmedabad).

---

• In the light of the above, the frustration associated with development is growing, given a history of development in India that has generally adversely affected the environment.[32]

• Improved communication and access to information of local communities and the increasing role of NGOs and voluntary organizations who are keen to take up environmental issues. One possible reason for the confrontationist approach is that the people and NGOs

[32] For example, north Chennai and Ennore in Tamil Nadu have been identified by the state as areas for major industrial and infrastructure development. The area already has numerous state-owned power plants and a new satellite port. In a recent public hearing conducted for building a new industrial estate, local communities were clear that they would oppose the project. Their concerns included:

· The poor environmental record of prior development in the area including adverse impact on fishermen's livelihood.
· Poor track record of compensations received for lands acquired.
· Presence of a site of significant ecological importance within 8 km of the development area and the inadequacy of the 'impact' assessment study.

Not only local communities, but also academic institutions, NGOs, and other interested citizens were opposed to the project. A statement from the leader of a local village explained the problem. 'We had accepted the earlier developments in the interest of the state and even sacrificed our land for the same. But we are not willing to do this anymore. We will oppose the project at any cost unless there is a guarantee that our interests will be protected.'

inevitably struggle to obtain information about the impending project.

### INTERNATIONAL PRESSURES

With the opening up of markets and increasing international investment in India, environmental and social considerations are acquiring prominence. Multilateral agencies (MLAs) and donor agencies have long insisted on covenants that ensure compliance with their guidelines that are often quite stringent. Recent experiences of conflict between a large public sector company in India and an MLA tell us that such conditions are becoming even more stringent, and are probably not negotiable.

Multinationals too have insisted upon environmental-liability assessments before investment. These assessments quantify and evaluate the environmental contamination or pollution on account of the planned industrial activity. They also seek to assess environmental compliance. The experience of site assessments in India would indicate that many industrial facilities have caused significant pollution. Poor hazardous and solid waste management practices and improper effluent disposal are widespread. Restorative and remedial measures increase 'land price' significantly over what may have been originally assessed. Past environmental problems today reduce the value of assets for international firms and lending institutions. Privatization of certain public enterprises could be affected by this. This is particularly true of state-level, and infrastructure-related public enterprise.

The Bretton Woods institutions have been much influenced by environmental movements including public protests. The recent disruption of talks at Seattle by NGO groups is a case in point. Environment and social issues, human rights, child labour, social justice, and equity are no longer mere ritual statements in the annual reports of many corporates. The emergence of 'voluntary' environmental reporting standards indicates that environmental concerns and accountability are no longer a matter between the regulator and a company, but one integrally involving the public.

Importantly, the struggle between 'development and environment' in India has generally been a rather inefficient negotiation process. Protests start well after significant investment has been made. Attempts to 'force the construction through at any cost', with a corresponding response to block the project, has become a not uncommon pattern in India. And in the end irrespective of who wins, society as a whole would most certainly have lost.[33] It goes without saying that the environmental issues need to be addressed holistically, at the time projects are conceived.

## REGULATORY FRAMEWORK FOR THE ENVIRONMENT

Environment legislations that are critical in addressing project development risks are as follows:

• The Environment Protection Rules that define emission and discharge standards.

• The Environment Impact Assessment (EIA) notification that requires that every large project's environmental impact be evaluated and mitigated. Such an evaluation and mitigation plan is the basis for the government's clearance for the project.

• The State Air and Water Rules that require projects to obtain permission from State Pollution Control Boards to establish and operate.

There are also a few notifications and legislations that are impractical and are doomed to fail. Prominent among these is the notification that requires that use be made of fly ash, large quantities of which are produced in coal-burning power plants. Use of fly ash in the quantities that typical power plants produce is hardly possible. And the notification therefore would not succeed.

The Land Acquisition Act 1894 (the Act hereafter) and modifications subsequently contain the following pro-visions that make land acquisition contentious, and sometimes unfair to those whose lands are acquired.

• The state has the right to acquire land for any project deemed to be in the 'public interest'. The definition of 'public interest' is unclear and has often been the locus of much controversy.

• There is usually little or no local consultation or participation. Notifications are served more to meet the requirements of the law than to ensure that all concerned have been informed.

• Comments and objections are only permitted with reference to the compensation amount.

• There is also a provision for 'emergency' acquisition of land which does away with the steps wherein public objections could heard. The conditions under which emergency acquisition can be instituted are not well defined, resulting in controversy.

• The Act as such does not provide that compensation necessarily be paid before possession of the land is taken.[34]

• In many cases, after acquiring land, the government is unable to either use it for the original purpose or to do so only partially.[35] Under such circumstances, the

---

[33] Sardar Sarovar has already cost Gujarat state $ 1.5 billion and officials say stoppage of work on the dam is costing the government $ 500,000 a day in interest alone, and delaying power, irrigation, and drinking water projects.

[34] For the Hirakud dam in Orissa, 112,038.59 acres of cultivated land were acquired in the 1950s and today, fifty years later, according to the Orissa government, approximately Rs 6 crore (of the assessed compensation of about Rs 9 crore) has not reached the 3098 affected families.

Land for the BSF training centre near Hazaribagh in Bihar was acquired in the 1960s. Today, thirty years later, only a few land losers have received compensation. There are numerous similar instances where land has been acquired but the land losers have not been compensated. The option available to the land losers in such instances is to approach the courts. Data illustrate that in most cases the courts have enhanced the compensation payable and have directed the government to deposit additional funds as decretal charges on land acquisition. However, these reach only the affluent few because not all the land losers have the resources to approach the courts for redressal.

[35] The propriety of land acquisition has to go beyond the quantum of compensation. Other aspects like the purpose of acquisition, the extent of acquisition, the probable uses of the acquired land are equally questionable. For example, in Orissa 7297 and 12,195.52 acres of tribal land were acquired for two different defence purposes in the 1960s and 1980s, respectively. Today, nearly half of it still lies unused or vacant. This has been a norm rather than an exception, as in the case of industrial estates, where state industrial infrastructural development bodies acquire land, set up an industrial estate, and then search for entrepreneurs interested in using the facilities. More than a third of all industrial estate space has never found use!

land remains with the project or the state, unlike under English law where it reverts to the original owner.

Another weakness in land-acquisition-related legislation in the country is that there is no provision that ensures that the land required for a public purpose is appropriate and not excessive. Different acquisition proposals for similar purposes in different parts of the country have been found to vary to the extent of 1000 per cent. For example, a sugar plant in Andhra Pradesh required 35 acres of land, while another plant in Orissa, of the same production capacity, requested the Orissa government for 350 acres of land. Some tribal districts have protective land alienation laws. It is observed that the overriding character of the Act is exploited to avoid the clauses of the alienation laws. Tribal land is notified to be acquired in such areas either for an undefined or fictitious public purpose. Once land acquisition is over, the ownership of those lands change from 'tribal' to 'government' land. The purpose is then abandoned and the said land transferred to housing cooperatives or other private bodies.

• While there is much case law (that has emerged out of the practice) that seeks to protect the interests of project-affected peoples (PAPs), this has not been incorporated into legislation and the prescribed procedure. Case law can therefore apply only when a matter is referred to court.

• The focus of the Act is on the process of acquisition, not the impact it has on PAPs. As a result the following aspects are largely ignored:

    – loss of livelihood to land owners as well as landless labourers;

    – disarticulation of communities on account of settlements being divided;

    – improper provisions for resettlement where livelihood and access to facilities are not provided in the resettlement sites;

    – loss of common property and resources such as wells, grazing grounds, etc.

The Draft National Policy on Rehabilitation and Resettlement (DNPR&R) that has been under consideration for many years attempts to address most of the above issues but has still not seen the light of day. In the interim there is a Draft 1998 Land Acquisition Bill that is presently under consideration. This Bill largely ignores many of the principles that the DNPR&R had brought out. While the Bill does seek to enhance compensation, it largely follows the framework of the Act and may not be adequate to ensure that project development can take place in a smooth and equitable manner.

## THE WAY FORWARD

Suggestions for improvements in legislation and implementation include:

• Rationalization of legislation and strengthening of implementation and monitoring. Legislation should be viewed in a holistic manner and institutional mechanisms for enforcement should also be defined along with the legislation.

• The penalties for non-compliance, both on industries as well as regulators should be considerably enhanced.

• Financial institutions and insurance companies should own up to being in part accountable for environmental compliance of a project.

• Transparency in all environment-related matters. EIA reports of projects should be easily available for public scrutiny. The public hearing ought to be more transparent, and the provisions of the notification ought to be adhered to in letter and spirit. Penalties for non-compliance by officers of government, may have to be in part personal.

• The Land Acquisition Act could usefully change to ensure that the focus of the law shifts from 'acquisition of land' to 'rehabilitation and resettlement'. From mere compensation for asset loss the law should aim to protect livelihoods. The new framework should take into account the case law that has evolved[36] and provide for a clear and effective process to enable land acquisition for development,[37] while protecting the economic status of PAPs and local communities. Complete transparency and involvement of local communities at an early stage in the project would be necessary.

• Provisions to ensure that land grabbing and speculation are discouraged while genuine landowners are able to realize appropriate values. Protection of not only landowners but also landless labourers and common resource users.

## PAPs AS STAKEHOLDERS IN PROJECT DEVELOPMENT

While it is today fashionable to consider PAPs as stakeholders in projects, in reality they are usually not in a position to negotiate their position. The state, promoters, and lenders are normally the only stakeholders to the development activity, who are able to effectively negotiate their returns commensurate with the risks they accept in the project. The project finance

---

[36] See chapter 5.6 for some interesting rulings by the courts.

[37] For a view that most land acquired for industrial use need not go through the state see chapter 1.

contractual documents essentially serve to allocate risks and returns to these stakeholders. The same is not however true for PAPs, who in a sense bear a stake in the project by involuntarily losing their land to make the project happen. Viewed from this perspective, PAPs are forced to bear a significant risk (of loss of assets and livelihood as well as other environment and social impacts), while not being provided any tangible returns. This is where the potential for project risk arises, often leading to local protests and activism as well as judicial intervention, all of these having direct significant impact on the project.

## 5.8 THE RIGHT TO INFORMATION AS A TOOL OF EMPOWERMENT

*Abha Singhal Joshi*

No society has escaped the evil of corruption in public bodies and government, although the degree varies. In India the common citizen as a consumer of public services is its worst victim. For simple, and the most basic necessities like water, electricity, and sanitation, he has to plead, and bribe, and even then denial is common especially for the poor. Corruption in civic bodies in India is treated with resignation as there is no forum for redressal open to the common man.

Even the media is far more connected with national-level scams and corruption in international deals, and in high places. The issue of routine and mundane corruption which affects the everyday lives of people does not attract media attention. But this corruption threatens the provision of the very basic needs of millions in the country. Take the case of a group of women in a Delhi Basti (resettlement colony) trying to get 6 feet of a water line restored after it was damaged. They visited the Corporation office over twenty times during a period of two years, but were not able to achieve their end. They could not even find out who was responsible and whom they should contact. Similar instances abound whether it is a question of provision of telephones, water, electricity, ration-cards, or access to records of any sort.

It has now been recognized that alternative approaches outside the traditional system of 'checks and balances' are necessary. The 'checks and balances' no longer work. One solution which suggests itself, and which has received quick and almost universal attention as a potent tool for countering corruption, is the simple method of throwing open to public scrutiny, processes within organizations that deal with the provisioning of public goods and services, and governance. The 'right to information' or 'access to information', or 'open government', is the vehicle for such scrutiny.

This right has been viewed primarily in the context of public bodies and in their relationship with the people. However, with the onset of liberalization, access to information of even non-public bodies and organizations like large public corporations becomes necessary. However, since presently the government is the largest provider of public goods and services, it is within government that the change urgently needs to be brought about.

The core of the issue of the right to information is very simple: it presupposes that in a democratic set-up, the government undertakes activities for the benefit of the people. Its actions, therefore, must not only be transparent to the people it works for, but there should also naturally be a high degree of accountability to the people for acts of commission or omission. This in turn presupposes participation of the people in decision-making processes which affect their lives.

The legal and philosophical base of the right to information is in little doubt—no one can deny that these elements are core essentials of a democracy. Moreover, the courts have time and again ruled that government secrecy should be kept to the bare minimum[38] and have pronounced the right to know as inherent in several fundamental rights—whether it concerns print media and broadcasting, civil liberties, or consumer rights.

In spite of court rulings, the need was felt for a legislation which would not only spell out the right to information in concrete terms but would also detail effective methods for implementation. However, the 'Freedom of Information Bill 2000' (hereafter FOI Bill) which was tabled in Parliament in July 2000, has come as a depressing reminder that a law being made without the requisite political will to change the culture of governance will contain in it the seeds of its own failure.

A look at the Bill shows that inspite of its lofty declaration of purpose—'In order to promote openness,

[38] Manubhai D. Shah vs LIC, AIR 1981 GUJ 15, Secretary Ministry of Information and Broadcasting, Govt. of India & Ors. vs Cricket Association of Bengal & Ors., 1995 2 SCC 161, Raj Narain vs State of UP, AIR 1975 SC 865.

transparency and accountability' in administration—it fails to address any of these stated goals. The restricted nature of the proposed law and lack of vision in drafting it are its chief failures.

To begin with, in the introduction of the Bill itself, the assurance to 'provide for freedom to every citizen to secure access to freedom of information' (a curious turn of phrase) is hedged in by the words 'consistent with public interest'. The term 'public interest' itself should be viewed with suspicion, as historically it has been coterminus with 'government's interest', and is used as such to justify appalling misuse of power and expansion or reduction of discretion to suit the ends of those in power. This formulation itself could be used to deny all manner of information. Besides this, all basic elements—that common sense would demand of a freedom of information law—as also the international experience have been ignored. The twin problems of enforcing systemic changes, and of dislodging the culture of secrecy in bureaucracies have completely been bypassed.

The first hurdle is the array of exceptions which are worded widely enough to net out much of the information, which must necessarily be shared with the public for any meaningful assessment of the working of public processes. Sections 8 and 9 of the FOI Bill, operating together, would further lend credence to the always say no approach which has hitherto been adopted by public bodies and governments at all levels. The need was to narrow down broad-based exemptions, making them more specific so that discretion to refuse is limited to the possibility of actual and substantial harm rather than vague conjecture or even a 'likelihood of harm'. For instance, section 8, which allows withholding of information which would prejudicially affect 'security of the state', 'public safety and order', 'the conduct of centre–state relations', could be used to refuse all manner of information to the people. Security of the state has recently been invoked to apply the National Security Act in an innocuous situation where the local populace of the Uttar Pradesh hills was protesting against a publication on AIDS by an NGO! Under the present Bill too, such incidents would receive the stamp of approval quite easily.

The common citizen would also come up against the provisions of section 9 which make it possible to refuse information on the grounds that it is 'to be published at a particular time' or is 'contained in material available to the public'. The difficulties in accessing government documents such as simple notifications and orders, copies of schemes, and even forms for various applications are very real. Gazettes are rarely available or seen. Even if made available, they would cater to only the literate and those who can afford the price of these publications. The section does not take note of the reality of either a poor and illiterate public, or of the breed of middlemen who abound in selling forms and other government documents which are never available at the official outlet. Should not the law make it incumbent upon the public authority itself to make sure that the requisite information is duly published in time in sufficient quantities and made available to the public at a reasonable cost? This would not only ensure the authenticity of the information, but also that all information is available at one source. Had the law really sought to allow the average user access to information, it would have made it mandatory for public bodies to publish certain kinds of educational material, and to have it distributed through channels like post offices and ration shops.

That brings us to the issue of *suo moto* disclosures by government, on which aspect the law is especially weak. Section 4 of the Bill restricts the 'obligation' to give information voluntarily only to some aspects of the structure of departments, details about 'important policies and decisions', and details (as available) of projects and schemes which 'in its opinion' should be known to people. Here again the obligation comes through not as a strong duty which no public authority would be allowed to escape, but as a weak entreaty, wrapped in nebulous terminology of wide discretion.

Taking the recent example of floods in Andhra Pradesh, or the cyclone in Gujarat[39] a couple of years ago, should not the law for ensuring information to people contain a provision, at the least, to give people timely, correct, and sufficient information for safeguarding their lives and property? Moreover, should there not be an attendant duty to give information to people in a manner that it actually reaches them? Such a law, for our country, would build in provisions for mandatory and effective use of communication methodologies, electronic media, and information technology.

Lack of provisions for fixing accountability and imposing penalties for unjustified refusals, delay in giving information, or giving wrong information sound the death knell of an already weak legislation. Moreover, upon refusal, the citizen has the right to 'appeal' only to two governmental authorities. We may describe this more correctly as an 'appeal from Caesar to Caesar'.

[39] The cyclone in Gujarat claimed many lives. A warning about the cyclone was flashed across the screen while the film 'Sholay' was being broadcast on the national channel of Doordarshan—not in Gujarati or Hindi, but in English. The Chief Minister of Andhra Pradesh made a public statement that the Meteorology Department had not given correct and timely information about the amount of rainfall expected when Andhra was under a deluge in August this year.

To add insult to injury, the jurisdiction of the courts has been circumscribed in section 15—an unprecedented step where no alternative judicial forum is provided.

There are further debates on whether the decision-making processes (file notings, opinions, etc.), from local level to cabinet level, should be thrown open or not, but these are at best academic in nature for the moment. One would welcome a provision like the Sunshine Act of the USA, whereby public bodies have to hold open meetings in certain areas of high public interest. Another provision one would like to see, either incorporated into this Act or through a separate legislation, is the protection of whistleblowers—a provision which protects honest and public-spirited employees who disclose facts in their knowledge to protect the public interest.

Freedom of information draft legislations, as are being churned out by state governments, as also the one pending in Parliament, have turned the whole issue around and made the exercise a fruitless one that protects the preserve of government over information, rather than genuinely bringing about the much needed change in the equations between the citizen and the state.

The accounts of local bodies almost all over the world are traditionally open to the ratepayer as an inherent practice in the audit process. It is this 'social audit' or 'public audit', of not only accounts but also of ongoing public works, which gives meaning to the exercise of the right to information. Having accessed the documents and records of a public body as a legal right, a public hearing can be conducted with the local populace as well as government officials and elected representatives. Comparisons can then be made between the expenditure/works shown on paper and the real experience of the people.

This method exposes the misdemeanours and/or misappropriations in a relatively transparent manner. In some rural areas of India, social audit campaigns have been very successful in bringing to light the misappropriation of local funds. But in the absence of a legally recognized formula for conducting such audits and a redressal mechanism following the verdict of these audits, not many public bodies have changed for the better. One solution that appears to suggest itself is to conduct such audits with the 'gram sabhas' in the villages, and with the local electorate in the urban municipal areas, and to ensure the follow-up legal and other actions as decided by an independent judicial body.

# 6 | THE ELECTRICITY SECTOR

## 6.1 MISSING INTERCONNECTIONS IN THE POWER SYSTEMS

*Puneet Chitkara, Rajiv Shekhar, and Prem K. Kalra*

### INTRODUCTION

The electric power system has gone from bad to worse. Power demand outstrips supply by 11.1 per cent during peak periods. Transmission and distribution losses are a mind-boggling 24 per cent of total generation. Tariffs continue to spiral upwards and have risen faster than prices of inputs. Off-peak, the grid frequencies rise to high levels, resulting in large user side costs and sometimes even in inability to use power off peak. The one advantage with few players especially when under state ownership is that merit order is not a worry. Yet the Indian system presents a picture of as bad a deviation from merit order as one can imagine.

Progressive states such as Karnataka and Maharastra face severe power shortages which hamper development. States such as West Bengal have excess capacities which are dumped on the national grid with no arrangements with any other parties for their use.

Successive governments since 1991 have made efforts to streamline and energize the power sector, as manifested by the numerous amendments to the electricity Acts and the Indian Electricity Grid Code (IEGC). For example, generation (in 1991) and more recently transmission and distribution were opened to the private sector to stimulate competition and thereby increase the efficiency and economy of the power sector. But this may in fact have compounded the problem.

Thus independent power producers (IPPs) with full cost recovery at 68.5 per cent but with terms allowing them to operate as base load stations, violate merit order. Similarly, even before the IPP policy, the Bulk Purchase and Sales Agreements (BPSAs) of the National Thermal Power Corporation (NTPC) with the state electricity boards (SEBs) were wrongly crafted. While on the one hand they allowed the NTPC easier norms than may have been correct, the contract creates disincentives that result in the NTPC with usually the lowest unit variable costs being denied the high plant load factors (PLFs) it is capable of achieving. Thus off-peak the BPSAs were such as to result in violation of merit order lowering the PLFs of NTPC stations. Similarly, they allowed the NTPC a return of only 12 per cent on equity when even the average different cost to prime borrowers was higher. In general, the approach has been one of 'correcting' a distortion with another and renewing the same, rather than identifying and removing the source of the distortion. Today many SEBs have 'incentives' for employees that are directly proportional to the PLFs achieved. These result in indiscipline because the SEB units refuse to back down when the loads fall, pushing the grid frequency even to 51 hertz. Nobody cares about the power factor. Such absurdly structured incentives were introduced in the eastern SEBs in response to earlier very poor work practices.

While all these shortcomings and problems with the power sector are widely acknowledged, why have they not been appropriately dealt with? In an attempt to address this question, we briefly examine crucial electricity statutes and current practices in generation and transmission and evaluate their role in affecting the working of the power sector. The efficacy of statutes and current practices in generation and transmission will be examined with respect to the following objectives:

• Promoting efficiency, economy, and competition in bulk electricity supply;

• a tariff structure that (i) is fair to consumers and (ii) facilitates mobilization of adequate resources for the power structure.

Two points need to be made here. First, we envisage competition as a means to attain the twin goals of efficiency and economy, not as an end in itself. Hence the statutes and current practices will be analysed both with respect to their adequacy in providing a competitive market and directly bringing about efficient operations. Secondly, economy and efficiency cannot be viewed in isolation from the tariff structure; in fact, their relationship is circular in a competitive environment.

## BULK TARIFFS

The total installed capacity of utilities stood at 93,245 MW on March 1999. Most of this installed capacity is in the public sector, the states and Centre controlling nearly 57 and 30 per cent respectively of the power-generating capacity. Thermal power, by far, is the predominant source of power in the country. Of the total installed thermal capacity of 23,637 MW in the central sector, the NTPC's share is 75 per cent, amounting to 17,735 MW. The present commissioned capacity of the NTPC is 19,291 MW and its share in total installed capacity of the country was 19.9 per cent on 31 March 2000. More importantly, the NTPC generated as much as 24.9 per cent of total utility power produced in 1999–2000. Recently, the NTPC has taken over Tanda thermal power station (440 MW) from the Uttar Pradesh State Electricity Board (UPSEB). It has also forayed into hydro generation with the laying of the foundation for the 800 MW Kol Dam hydroelectric power project, located in Bilaspur district in Himachal Pradesh. The NTPC plans to augment its capacity through takeovers, joint ventures, greenfield projects, and expansions in the capacity of existing power stations. This indicates the emergence of potential dominance of the market by the NTPC. Consider the following examples:

At the bulk supply level, electricity that is traded is either generated by the NTPC, or is surplus from SEBs. Surplus electricity from SEBs constitutes a very small fraction of the tradable electricity at bulk supply level. Hence, the NTPC wields a great deal of market power at this level.[1]

According to the K. P. Rao Committee (KPRC) report the tariff structure for bulk electricity generation consists of (i) fixed charge and (ii) variable charge. The fixed charge consists of interest payments on debt, return on equity (ROE), depreciation, fixed operations and maintenance (O&M) charges, interest on working capital, and taxes. Fuel costs essentially constitute the variable charge. Calculation of various components of fixed and variable charges is based on certain normative parameters which have to be reevaluated with time. However, these norms were never revised by the Ministry of Power (MoP), except for ROE which was increased from 12 per cent to the current 16 per cent at 68.49 per cent PLF. Furthermore, the KPRC report recommends that power plants be entitled to incentives at the rate of 1 paisa per kWh above the normative PLF of 68.49 per cent. Over the years, the performance of the NTPC has improved considerably. For example, average PLF at NTPC plants is around 80 per cent, a figure comparable with the most efficiently operated plants worldwide, with the Dadri-based plant recording a PLF of over 96 per cent in 1999. Hence if norms related to PLF are not revised, competitive levels of tariffs are not assured to the consumers. The Central Electricity Regulatory Commission (CERC), in its order on Availability Based Tariffs (ABT), to be discussed later, has suggested a target availability (availability is normally greater than the PLF) of 80 per cent for all thermal plants for the recovery of fixed charges. Similarly, norms for other components of the fixed and variable charges may need revision. This is important because the regulator has the mandate to enforce competition in an intrinsically oligopolistic market. Hence tariff design has to simulate the beneficial impacts of competition to extract efficiency improvements for the benefit of consumers. With the incorporation of new technologies and management practices, the cost of operating a power plant, barring vagaries of certain components such as fuel costs, is expected to decrease.[2]

One possible solution to the potential problem of market power of the NTPC could be to let the various NTPC power stations operate as profit centres and compete within each grid. For example, Dadri can compete with Singrauli and Tanda in the northern grid, and Talcher can compete with Farakka in the eastern grid for selling power. Even though most of these stations would primarily be running as base load stations, they could still compete among themselves and with the SEBs, with respect to surplus generation

[1] The NTPC though has not thus far used this monopoly power to its advantage. It has been tied down by adverse BPSAs with SEBs and committed deliveries, at low returns. Yet the NTPC, as also some large IPPs at state/regional level could exercise considerable market power in any future market for wholesale power, unless appropriate restrictions and rules are framed.

[2] IPP contracts are even more adverse from the final consumer's point of view. With returns up to 30 per cent, or full recovery at 16 per cent at 68.4 per cent PLF for base stations huge costs are being borne by consumers. See also case 3, chapter 3.

during off-peak hours.[3] The tariffs can be based on competitive bidding, with a 'price cap' for electricity supply during peak hours. In fact, an order of the CERC, dated 9 March 2000, on a petition filed by the Power Trading Corporation Ltd. (PTC) for the applicability of ABT to the Pipavav mega power project (MPP) signals a shift towards a tariff regime based on competitive bidding. Excerpts from the CERC's order on ABT are reproduced here:

The Commission sees no need to specify target availability as percentage of capacity since it sees no need for PTC to specify the installed capacity of the project. Instead, bidders should make available the required power to meet the demands of the buyers in MW & MWH.

The Commission also sees no need to specify an incentive rate for generation above a target PLF, since the price at which the successful bidder will supply energy beyond the level of off-take assured by the buyer, will be decided through the bidding process itself as has been mentioned by the PTC in the context of the additional cost of fuel supply for energy generation beyond the assured level of off-take.

It is imperative that the Commission's directives be applicable to the NTPC, otherwise India may end up with a heterogeneous system of pricing bulk supply generation with all its attendant disadvantages. It is often argued that the NTPC has long-term contracts with the SEBs and hence needs to be treated separately. However, it needs to be understood that such contracts can be honoured even in a competitive environment. The SEBs can buy NTPC power at market price,[4] determined in the competitive market, and the surplus, if any, can be traded to the deficit customers. This is precisely what the central commission in its order on ABT has envisaged. In fact, this mechanism has the potential to mature into a tight power pool, where individual generators within a state also see an opportunity in the bulk power market and put in extra effort to supply during peak periods to gain a few extra rupees.

## BEING FAIR TO CONSUMERS

A stated policy goal could be 'to bring prices in line with costs to provide consumers with good price signals'. This dictum has two corollaries: (i) buyers should have the opportunity to shop for power on the grid, and (ii) subsidies should be rationalized.

[3] Or even for all power they guarantee if a market is put in place that replaces the BPSA and IPP contracts. See Morris (2000).

[4] The clearing prices in such a market are likely to be much higher than the prices to which the NTPC is tied down under the BPSAs. This is one reason for the reluctance to bring the NTPC onto the market (ed.). See section 6.2.

Suppose a bulk consumer in state A wants to buy electricity from a generating station in state B. This would require that power be wheeled on the network of the distribution companies in states A and B. However, such transactions are restricted under the Electricity Act, 1948 (Amended in 1991), section 15(A), subsection (c), which states that 'the Generating Company shall carry on its activities within such areas as the competent government or governments, may, from time to time specify in this behalf'. Also if there is a transmission distribution licensee serving in either state, then First Schedule, Part (1), section III of the Electricity Act, 1948 becomes operational and forbids such transactions. The legality of the above-mentioned statutes will probably be clarified by the judgement in the Indian Railways versus Uttar Pradesh State Electricity Board (UPSEB) case pending before the Delhi High Court.

The Railways had decided to go ahead with a pilot project for direct purchase of power from the NTPC, following the Delhi High Court's refusal to grant a stay on the project, as desired by the UPSEB. Northern Railway had already spent about Rs 60 crore on the construction of the tower and transmission lines transporting power from the NTPC's Dadri gas power plant. In its order, the Court had, however, said that a final decision on the UPSEB petition was pending, and that the Railways could carry on with the construction activity at their own risk. A UPSEB notice had earlier threatened to demolish the transmission tower and lines on the grounds that such an activity was 'unauthorised and amounted to encroachment on the jurisdiction of the UPSEB' as a licensee. The UPSEB also said that the Railways had no legal authority to construct distribution and service lines on their own. The Railways later obtained a stay on the notice from the High Court.

The Railways maintain that they are legally allowed to 'erect, operate, maintain or repair any electric traction equipment, power supply and distribution installation in connection with the working of the Railways'. Moreover, railway officials point out that direct purchase of power from the NTPC has been approved by the Cabinet. The Power Ministry had allocated 100 MW out of the unallocated central pool of the NTPC's Dadri gas power plant to the Railways.

In its petition, the Railway alleged that though the UPSEB was buying power from the NTPC at the rate of Rs 1.70 per unit, it was selling it to the Railways at Rs 4.15 per unit. This amounted to an annual loss of over Rs 50 crore! The Railways had signed a power purchase agreement with the NTPC in March 1998 at the cost of Rs 2.20 per unit. According to Railway officials, the SEBs do not want a reliable and bulk customer, like the Railways, to bypass them and purchase power directly from the NTPC. The NTPC, on the other hand, finds it more profitable to sell power to the Railways than to the loss-making SEBs at very low prices.

Two important issues emerge from the Railways versus UPSEB case. One, should a consumer be forced to buy power at a higher price when cheaper options are available? Two, the fate of the 'divorced' party, the UPSEB in the above case, needs sympathetic consideration. More specifically, what should be the fate of the UPSEB's 'stranded equipment'? Shouldn't the UPSEB be compensated for the infrastructure it set up to supply electricity to the Railways? If not, in all probability, the O&M costs of the now infructuous infrastructure set up will be passed on to other consumers of the UPSEB.

## Subsidies

Subsidies should be a means to provide power to 'needy' consumers who cannot afford the 'real' price. In reality, subsidies are seldom need based, and are awarded in an ad hoc manner, as a populist election plank. For example, agricultural tariffs (10 horse power (HP), 20 per cent LF [1089 kWh per month]) are lowest in the richer states: free in Punjab and Tamil Nadu and minimal in Gujarat (Re 0.61 per unit), Haryana (Re 0.50 per unit), and Maharashtra (Re 0.38 per unit). Ironically, agricultural tariffs are among the highest in Assam (Re 1.44 per unit), Sikkim (Re 1.72 per unit), and Nagaland (Re 1.50 per unit) where farmers toil under adverse conditions. Agricultural subsidy has always been a sore point since agricultural consumers constitute a third of the total consumers while contributing a miniscule 2.5 per cent towards revenue realization. As a result, other consumers, especially industry, pay very high prices. There is always a danger that in the new, liberalized economy, unseemly high tariffs may unleash a vicious cycle; industries will either migrate to another state or resort to captive power generation, leading to considerable loss of revenue to the SEBs.[5]

Rationalization of tariffs is a must for the health of the SEBs and/or the companies engaged in generation, transmission, and distribution. Recent events in Andhra Pradesh, where the state government reimbursed Andhra Pradesh Transmission Company (APTRANSCO) for subsidizing tariff decided by the APERC were indeed

heartening.[6] In fact, the provision for compensating SEBs for subsidies already exists in the Act of 1948, but has not been implemented by many state governments.

## Resource Mobilization

Giving counterguarantees or opening escrow accounts are not being considered solutions here, given their obvious inadequacy and inefficacy, both conceptual and practically revealed.[7] The incentives for investment should come from the opportunities the market structure provides and the enabling legal environment rather than from economic profits due to regulation or policy.

The Central Electricity Authority (CEA) has formulated a national power policy which specifies optimal location of power plants throughout the country. Unfortunately power plant location has been subject to political considerations even in the era when state coordination was supposedly necessary to choose the lowest cost location. Take the case of the NTPC's Dadri thermal power plant whose location is such that the cost of transporting fuel is 60 per cent of fuel cost.[8] Would it not have been more economical to locate the plant closer to the fuel source, and instead transport energy to the region currently serviced by Dadri? Moreover, how long does the government want to be in the business of planning for the power sector? In a centralized planning model, peak demand forecast and the reliability criterion determine market size and the price of electric energy is considered secondary, whereas in a competitive market prices are set by competition and those prices determine investments in new capacity. Here generation-related reliability criteria are complemented or supplemented by energy prices during generation shortfalls. An enabling legal environment implies the ability to enforce contracts, and should consist of, say, legally enforceable (i) fuel supply and (ii) cash flow agreements.

Three bidders—Siemens-Powergen combine, Vew Energy, and PSEG Global—have pulled out of the race for the 2000 MW Pipavav mega project. It may be recalled that all the thirteen players who had submitted the bids for the first stage had been declared 'qualified' for the second stage in December 1999. According to Indiainfoline industry sources, the three bidders' backing out could be related to lack of policy clarity. The

---

[5] This absurdity is already taking place as industrial tariffs are being pushed through the roof. The obvious need for tariffs to be bounded by the costs of self-generation, at the very least, is sometimes ignored even by regulators, and often by consultants' reports.

[6] The case for direct subsidization on the grounds of moral hazard is very strong. See Morris (2000).

[7] Many IPPs after being so close to financial closure, have given up, or have withdrawn, or have changed hands on this count.

[8] Even if the Railways were to price freight transport correctly it would be a prohibitive 40–5 per cent of the fuel cost.

Power Ministry had earlier announced that land would be procured for mega power projects by the government. It is now understood that the promoters have to procure the land themselves. Land prices at Pipavav have already shot through the roof due to the upcoming power project and speculative purchases. Bidders had not taken such high land prices into reckoning while submitting their bids. There are other ambiguities as well.

The reasons for such ambiguities include *inter alia* the provisions in various electricity statutes. For example, the Electricity Regulations Act, 1998 (chapter III, section 11(d)) mandates the central commission to promote competition, efficiency, and economy in the activities of the electricity industry. But these are subject to the view of the central government (chapter VIII, section 38(1)), which states that 'in the discharge of its functions, the Central Commission shall be guided by such principles in the matters of policy involving public interest as the central government may give to it in writing', and hence could change with a change in governments. Given the politically fluid situation in India, this has worked against the policy goal of mobilization of adequate resources for the power sector. Political and regulatory risks thus continue to remain high.

Many believe that the reforms should start with privatization of generation. Others believe that the government has started at the wrong end by not beginning the reform process with privatization of distribution. This has to be seen as a circular problem. If the government privatizes generation without improving revenue collection, the generators have to take into account highly risky cash inflows, and would typically insist upon escrow/state guarantees. If distribution is privatized it will have to bear significant supply risk because of the current poor state of generators in various states. A possible solution is to let the same entity own generation and distribution. This would require legislation which enables third-party access on a competitive basis, otherwise such a structure could act as an entry barrier for new investments in generation. Moreover, the problem remains whatever be the structure; even state-level regulators cannot change the tariffs charged to various consumer categories without the consent of the state governments. Electricity, being on the concurrent list, all the state governments need to pass a legislation/issue a policy statement enabling the removal of subsidies. But the clause in the existing statute books that the government should make good all the subsidies to the generator's electricity suppliers, should be removed, because no private investor would believe any of the state governments, given their past records. Once this is done, potential investors will have confidence in the future revenue streams and investments could flow in. Then efficient market structure can be thought of in a way that requires minimum regulation and poses minimum anti-competitive problems.

## TRANSMISSION

Transmission is often regarded as a natural monopoly and a case is made for its regulation. One of the criteria in the design of a reform model is the identification of segments where competition can be introduced. In the context of transmission, one needs to identify various services that a transmission company provides. Such an unbundling of transmission services would allow identification of those services where competition can be introduced and pricing of services which need to be regulated. This is widely accepted.[9] The MoP has notified the Power Grid Corporation of India Limited (PGCIL) as the central transmission utility (CTU). The PGCIL operates over 39,000 Ckt km of EHV transmission network across the country and has the distinction of being ranked among the top six transmission utilities in the world. As the CTU it performs the following functions:

(i) provides transmission facilities for interstate transmission of power;
(ii) controls power flow and frequency;
(iii) ensures system reliability and congestion management;
(iv) undertakes energy accounting and billing;
(v) provides reactive power support and voltage control; and
(vi) does investment planning.

We may usefully think of competition as potentially existing at two levels: (1) competition for the market, (2) competition in the market. The Government of India has allowed independent transmission service providers to set up transmission lines for interstate and intra-state transactions, hence India potentially has competition for the market in the provision of transmission services, but once a company has set up transmission facilities, duplication of resources may not be worthwhile, and hence there will not be any competition in the market. However, the CTU has been given extra-ordinary powers by the Electricity Laws (Amendment) Act, 1998 which may act as barriers to private entry. Section 27C (2) of the Electricity Laws (Amendment) Act, 1998 states that 'a transmission license granted under sub-section (1) may authorise the transmission licensee to construct, maintain, and operate any inter-state

[9] See also section 6.2 in this report.

transmission system under the direction, control and supervision of the CTU'. Section 27C (4) further states that the applicant should first obtain the approval of the CTU. *Clearly, the PGCIL simultaneously dons the mantle of both player and controller.* Since the construction of transmission lines has been opened to the private sector, identification of optimal location of transmission lines should also be left to these investors (of course, subject to a transparent system security investigation by the CTU and subject to verification of the same by the CERC. The PGCIL could conceivably prevent the entry of private players in the transmission sector, for example by allotting 'inhospitable', uneconomic regions for setting up and operating transmission infrastructure. Even though the central commission grants a licence for interstate transmission, its decision could still be biased because of information asymmetry between the PGCIL and the CERC.

Section 27(A) of Part IIA of the Electricity Laws (Amendment) Act, 1998 empowers the CTU to exercise supervision and control over the interstate transmission system. The regional load despatch centres (RLDCs), which are mandated to coordinate the integrated operation of the power system in a particular region, are required by the law to be operated by the CTU. The ownership of the RLDCs by the CTU cannot be affected by order of the central commission.[10] Since the cash flows of the PGCIL are linked to the efficient operation of the grid, ownership of RLDCs by the PGCIL may be detrimental to the interests of the other players in the market: In the event of a black/brown out, the responsibility may be shifted to the other players. Practically, it is extremely difficult for the regulator or any third party to analyse the event-related information supplied by the RLDCs. This situation may worsen after the implementation of ABTs. Monopoly problems inherent in the ownership of RLDCs by the PGCIL can be mitigated to a certain extent by developing incentives for performance based on certain transparent parameters. For example, sliding scale incentive schemes could be developed where the target values for costs (of various services, for example reactive power, demand forecasting, rescheduling, and transmission losses) are set in advance. If the PGCIL manages to beat the target by delivering lower costs for each of these services, it keeps a proportion of the difference between the target and actual costs. If the PGCIL does not manage to meet the target, it pays a proportion of the difference between

the target and the actual costs. For the determination of such cost-based benchmarks, the central government could consider creating a separate transmission company in each of the regions and hence introduce 'yardstick competition' between various transmission service providers. A single company, that is the PGCIL, owning and operating the entire country's network may not facilitate such a yardstick mechanism.

The Indian Electricity Grid Code requires the SEBs' distribution companies to install capacitors or provide vott ampere reactive (VAR) support. In the event of a particular state overdrawing reactive power from the grid, it is required to pay charges for reactive power. Ancillary services (which cover reactive power support) can be provided by independent service providers. If the distribution companies pay for reactive power, then it becomes the responsibility of the CTU to arrange for ancillary service providers, and maintain a normal voltage profile throughout the grid.

Demand forecasting is currently being done by the CEA and is a service which is not explicitly priced in the bulk power tariffs. There are three major contentions regarding demand forecasting. (1) This is an extremely useful service for capacity expansion and assumes greater importance in the context of fifteen-minute scheduling (short-term load forecasting) proposed under the ABT system and hence must be explicitly priced. (2) A commercially interested party (in this case the RLDC) should provide all such services. (3) Any errors in forecasting, which may result in the creation of redundant capacity or in transmission congestion due to transmission bottlenecks and hence rescheduling (which generally means switching on costlier generation) must be priced and the cost borne by the agencies involved in demand forecasting. Currently all costs due to switching on costlier generation, in the presence of transmission bottlenecks, are passed on to the consumers. Distributors, generators, and traders are not ideally placed to mitigate this risk, and hence they typically do this job in decentralized and competitive systems.

The Power Trading Company (PTC) has been established with majority equity participation by the PGCIL along with the NTPC, the Power Finance Corporation (PFC), and other financial institutions. The PTC would purchase power from identified private projects and sell it to identified SEBs. A structural arrangement, where a power transmission company has a majority stake in a power trading (which is essentially akin to a generating company), could give it enormous monopoly power. In a competitive market, such a firm could create access problems for an independent generator (that may wish not to trade through the PTC). This

---

[10] The law states that 'until otherwise specified by the Central Government, the Central Transmission Utility shall operate the regional load despatch centres and the State Transmission Utility shall operate the state load despatch centres'.

would then need legislation enabling open access, which is very difficult to monitor. Hence the creation of the PTC, with the existing ownership structure, could pose serious problems for regulation in the future. Moreover, trading is a service where competition is natural and given (there could be many power traders in the electricity market), and this service needs to be opened to competition.[11]

Additional regulatory issues crop up as the PGCIL decides to venture into the telecom sector. To achieve its goal of establishing an integrated national grid, the PGCIL is implementing nationwide a computerized energy management system based on state-of-the-art fibre optic and microwave links which facilitate real time system coordination, data acquisition, monitoring, and control. The PGCIL is also planning to diversify into the telecommunication business by establishing a nationwide backbone network, using its existing infrastructure. The PGCIL already has about 4000 km of optic fibre on the transmission lines connecting various cities, and in the next two years it plans to lay an additional 14,000 km of optic fibre. Some of the links are already ready and others are soon going to be operational. The PGCIL has offered bandwidth capacity on certain routes, utilizing the right of way (RoW) provided by its extra high voltage (EHV) transmission lines which connect the major metropolitan cities/towns, viz. Delhi, Calcutta, Chennai, Bangalore, Hyderabad, Mumbai, and others. The mechanism of allocation of costs (multiple products with independent demands) between power and telecom users would be important. The PGCIL has a monopoly in power transmission (and hence it could increase transmission service charges. Business sense may lead it to charge low prices for bandwidth capacity and hence unfairly compete with other bandwidth providers at the cost of the power system users. The PGCIL further has interests in setting up joint ventures (JVs) with the SEBs to gain connectivity to the smaller cities, towns, and villages in various states. Unless adequately regulated this could lead to it exercising excessively large market power in the telecom business.[12]

---

[11] The logic of a power trading company in the state sector in the current situation of state failure is hardly clear. Earlier the NTPC is known to have strongly resisted this function being thrust on it since it knew that what was truly intended by the government was to buy time from tariff reform and SEB restructuring, with the NTPC's funds and debt capacity. There would be attempts by buyers like the SEBs to not pay the PTC on time, and by IPPs to demand prior payment or security for sales, exposing the net worth of the PTC to erosion.

[12] For a different view see chapter 2 of this report, especially the discussion on Convergence.

## PRICING OF TRANSMISSION SERVICES

Transmission prices should be such as to result in: (1) incentives for new line construction in anticipation of growth in demand and with a view to remove congestion; (2) provide equitable grid access to all its users; and (3) ensure control reliability and adequacy.

### Incentives for Optimal Siting

Chapter 3 of the Indian Electricity Grid Code (IEGC) deals with the planning of interstate transmission. The Electricity (Supply) Act, 1948 orders the CEA to 'develop a sound, adequate and uniform national power policy, formulate short term and perspective plans for power development and coordinate the activities of the planning agencies in relation to the control and utilisation of national power resources'. Given the current interstate transmission pricing policy in India, the entire burden of faulty capacity addition (or 'excess' system redundancies) would fall on the beneficiary states. Logically, a commercially interested party should do the planning so that it may be penalized for faulty planning.[13] Hence it may be difficult for the central commission to ensure 'fair prices' for the consumers of electricity, which it is mandated by the Act to do. Incentives for siting new transmission lines that would allow more competition in electricity generation depend on the revenues recoverable from transmission services. If siting policy is made without considering its effects on pricing, its goals may not be achieved. As opposed to the existing bulk supply transmission pricing policy, if transmission prices were to be based on actual flows (short-run marginal cost-based pricing [SRMC]), it may be argued that SRMC may result in economic losses for the transmission owner. This can, however, be taken care of by two-part pricing of transmission services, which was also envisaged in the Electricity (Supply) Act, 1948. The capacity component could be linked to maximum demand and the variable component could be flow based. Such a pricing mechanism would lead the private transmission owner to optimally locate the transmission lines and ensure their utilization. Chapter 3 of the IEGC recognizes that the interstate transmission system and the associated intra-state transmission systems are complementary and interdependent and the planning of one affects the other's planning and performance. The IEGC further states that the associated intra-state transmission system shall also be discussed and reviewed in respective regional standing committee

---

[13] The probability of faulty capacity addition planning is further increased given the load forecasting techniques used by the CEA (cf: any Electric Power Survey would show this).

meetings on transmission planning before implementation. It is then likely that the final arrangement arrived at in such a meeting may not be in the best interests of all the regional constituents. Revenue-sharing mechanisms need to be designed to ensure materialization of an integrated grid.

*Providing Access Equity Among*
*Various Grid Users*

The functions of the CTU are given under section 27(A) of Part IIA of the Electricity Laws (Amendment) Act, 1998. One of the functions of the CTU is 'to undertake transmission of energy through interstate transmission system'. The PGCIL, at the direction of the Central Commission, prepared the IEGC. Such grid codes have also been prepared at state level by the SEBs/state transmission units (STUs) and approved by the respective state commissions. The Central Commission, in one of its rulings (CERC order on the IEGC) stated:

In para 6.1 on 'Operating Policy', a suggestion was made by GRIDCO to the effect that the operating procedures shall be in conformity with the State Electricity Grid Code as well. This suggestion has not been accepted, as the responsibility of ensuring the required consistency between SEGC and IEGC is with all the respective SEB/STUs. We are in agreement with CTU; for the additional reason that it is impracticable to bring about conformity with differing SEGC. The suggestion of DVC for approval by the constituents of the operating procedures has already been taken care of, since the procedures will be developed in consultation with the constituents.

In addition to reflecting an area of conflict between the Central and state commissions, this also indicates the need for a contract that takes care of the differing economic interests of the regional constituents and the region as a whole. To illustrate the point made, consider section 6.1(c) of the IEGC which states that 'all the regional constituents shall comply with this operating code, for deriving maximum benefits from the integrated operation and for equitable sharing of obligation'. An interstate transaction may maximize benefits of the entire region; it may, however, cause congestion on the lines of the intervening state and lead to higher costs due to rescheduling and redespatch by the state load despatch centre (SLDC) within a particular state (since the IEGC recommends a loose pool). This is a case where a particular transaction is revenue maximizing (or cost minimizing) for the region, but is not economical for the state. This problem needs to be tackled by devising a revenue-sharing mechanism such that the intervening state has no economic incentive to

violate the orders of the RLDCs.[14] This is a classic case where the negative externality problem could be solved through contracts without the need for the intervention of a 'stick' mechanism. Since a state network may be used for interstate transmission, a host state could deliberately raise transmission prices to prevent competition for other generators'/utilities. This could be tackled by formulating a transparent open access policy based on Articles 888 and 889 of the Federal Energy Regulatory Commission (United States).

*Efficient Prices*

Currently transmission charges in India are based on the so-called 'postage stamp' method, that is on average energy drawals from the network rather than on actual transmission resources used in the particular case. Hence these charges do not send the correct signal for optimal use of the scarce resource, that is the transmission network, or even optimal location of generation sources. Also the existing pricing mechanism does not provide any incentive for capacity expansion (at optimal locations, from the point of view of minimizing generation costs and reducing the unmet energy) to the transmission utility. Optimal prices of electricity—as proposed in the literature and as prevalent in some countries, for example US (Pennsylvania, New Jersey, and Maryland (PJM) pool), New Zealand, and Chile—are temporally and spatially distributed. These prices depend on generation and loading conditions of the network, hence they are very volatile. There is an inherent lack of advance price certainty in such a mechanism. Moreover, when power systems are tightly interconnected, such prices have to be calculated many times a day and hence the whole process becomes very cumbersome.

The need is to develop a transmission despatch and pricing model which takes into account the peculiarities of the Indian power system, viz. wide variations in voltage and frequencies in each region, large differences in operating frequencies between regions, generator operation with constrained governor action, and overdrawal by various states. The model may also have to seriously examine the creation of an options contracts market for transmission capacity in India.

An options contracts model would require, in addition to the despatch and pricing model, a short-term load-forecasting model to study the loading conditions on different system buses under various normal and contingency conditions and determine the optimal

[14] In the absence of such contracts, the SEBs/STUs, in their interest, could resort to various means like deliberately declaring a power system component to be faulty, in order to prevent the interstate transaction from taking place.

price (given the objective function) of power flows in various congested segments in the network.

## Engineering Issues

In power systems, the flow of real and reactive power, and control of voltages and frequency are core management tasks. Nationally, we have accepted HVDC (high voltage direct current) transmission as an alternative to HVAC (high voltage alternative current) transmission due to advantages like fast controllability of power and possibility of interconnecting systems operating at disparate frequencies. Furthermore, slow progress has been made to realize advantages of static VAR compensation systems (SVS), and flexible Access Centre (AC) transmission systems (FACTS). We can enhance transmission capacity by installing FACT devices and improve voltage profiles in the distribution system by using modern voltage control devices like SVS. The grid code talks very little of HVDC systems and SVS, and even when it does there is little elaboration. It mainly focuses on AC systems. More elaborate guidelines on reactive power exchange and requirements would help the operation of the system.

It is important for quality of power to have frequency and voltage fluctuations within limits, quick clearance or rectification of faults, minimum level of harmonics in the systems, and least environmental impact of operations. FACTS devices along with other controls make possible fast power reversal. Good power flow control could contribute towards the minimization of power and voltage instabilities. The Indian power system is too far away from such an 'ideal' system which is the norm not just in the advanced capitalist countries but in many developing countries as well. Good control costs money but enhances power quality and loadability of the system, and typically pays for itself.[15]

For good control to operate, the growth in real and reactive power, as also required investments in controls, would need to be estimated for the short, medium, and long terms. Only with reasonably accurate estimates of these can corrective measures be taken. Load management programmes and reactive power compensation mechanisms would not succeed if there were significantly large 'unapproved' loads.

Too little monitoring is done today. Power metres themselves are hardly ever monitored except at key load

despatch centres and switch yards. With present-day technology, it is possible to use networking and Supervisory Control and Data Acquisition (SCADA) to automatically send the readings on hourly basis to the control rooms of substations. Since controls are mostly non-operational, the plants, machinery, and components are pushed beyond their operating ranges. Frequent operation at such levels reduces the life of the plant and equipment. The returns to systems such as SCADA linked to automatic and semi-automatic control mechanism could be very large.[16] There ought to be guidelines which are derived from a suitable national transmission strategy for selecting technologies like HVDC versus HVAC, 400 kV versus 800 kV, SVS versus FACTS, that optimize and make for ease in system interconnectivity.

## ABTs

The proposed ABTs for bulk power users and for that bought by the SEBs, and for generators like the NTPC, consists of three components:

1. A fixed charge component based on capacity allocated to various beneficiary states (of the NTPC's capacity for instance) in a particular region in Rs/MW. The fixed charge is to be recoverable at target-availability level. There is a provision for incentives based on actual generation above a normative level of generation.

2. A variable charge component based on normative fuel costs, in Rs/kWh.

3. A frequency-linked component, which is to be charged based on any player violating the grid discipline resulting in frequency variation. This component is determined based on the costliest generation available, that is diesel generation.

Under an ABT scheme various generators and beneficiary states are required to submit availability and drawal schedules to the RLDCs for every fifteen minutes! These submissions received by the RLDCs may have to be revised until a final schedule of generation/drawal is arrived at. It is claimed that

by bifurcating the method of charging Capacity Charges (fixed) and Energy Charges (variable), the incentive for trading in power is enhanced. The beneficiaries have a claim on the capacity, which they can trade either within or outside the region. By isolating the variable charge, a beneficiary (SEB) can again trade such power depending upon its needs, market

---

[15] In India the poor state of power control arises not only because of inadequate investments, but because of rampant indiscipline and cascading effects pf 'bypassing' cut-off devices. In other words, many safety and control devices are routinely bypassed to allow the system to 'operate' at vastly different grid frequencies and high power factors.

[16] Thus Bombay Suburban Electric Supply Ltd. (BSES), a private company with incentives to minimize its distribution losses and costs and improve the quality of power for its consumers, plans to invest at a furious pace in such systems and also derive the economics of convergence from the joint use of the cables (especially optical fibre) so laid for power data and control and for providing internet and networking services.

demand, and the economics of power in the home state. All this goes to develop the market for power.

Trading of power, however, requires a healthy transmission system. The mandate to plan and construct any interstate transmission line rests with the CEA and PGCIL. Though the opportunities for trading between southern and eastern regions have existed for over ten years now, the 500 MW HVDC link at Gazuwaka came up only as recently as in March 1999. The current transmission-pricing mechanism does not provide any incentive for laying transmission lines. The socio-political constraints on the government do not allow it to let the PGCIL charge an adequate price for transmission services. For example, the PGCIL's investments in the north-eastern region have resulted in huge financial losses to the company.

The problem of low frequency is not only a problem of grid indiscipline by the generators or the SEBs, but also of inadequate transmission and generation capacity. With the linkage of bulk tariff to the frequency, the SEB is left with two options (if it decides not to shed load): (i) to set up its own peak load power station, which may be diesel based; or (ii) to draw excess power from the grid at lower frequency and pay for the same.

If the beneficiary state chooses the second option (which it may do, given the risks and time delays involved in greenfield projects), the grid frequency may still deviate from 50 Hz.

Similarly, a generator may find that backing down the unit is costlier than letting it run under light load conditions. Then the grid frequency may still increase beyond 50 Hz. Consequently, grid disturbances and violent frequency fluctuations may still take place in the system, with resultant inconvenience to all concerned. Grid frequency management is essentially a power systems control problem, which the ABT system proposes to resolve through commercial pricing. Unless the punitive measures are very steep such an approach would not help.

The power of direct controls available with the grid operator is crucial to its operation. During the first week of January 2000 severe deficit conditions were experienced in the northern region. The PGCIL took the following specific measures in order to control the system parameters within the normal range:

1. It brought in additional support from the western region through the PGCIL's back-to-back HVDC link depending on the frequency conditions prevailing in the western region (support up to 350 MW was obtained at 13:30 hrs on 17 January 2000).

2. Further support of around 80 MW from the eastern region on 220 kV Dehri–Sahupuri circuit was mobilized.

3. It ran two units of the Chamera (360 MW) Hydel Station.

4. It persuaded different SEBs to restrict their drawals to within schedules so as to maintain system frequency above 49.0 Hz.

5. It opened (cut off) 220 kV circuits breakers of the states not adhering to their committed schedules even under critically low frequency conditions below 48.5 Hz.

The role of verification and certification of grid indiscipline, which leads to the imposition of unscheduled interchange charge, rests with the RLDC, a unit of the CTU, which itself is a commercially interested party. Though the central commission has noted in the ABT order that 'regarding the claim for payment of UI [unscheduled interchange] charges by transmission utility, specific instances of dereliction on the part of transmission utilities can always be brought up', no rational commercial organization could be expected to adversely affect its own profits by pointing out its own 'dereliction'. Moreover, given that the entire data on systems operation is available only at the RLDC, it may be difficult for anyone outside the RLDC to know the exact nature of the power system failure.

The Central Commission, in the ABT order, notes that

(a) Bottlenecks in evacuation of power due to constraints or limitations etc., in the transmission system in which case RLDC will revise the schedule to be effective from the 4th time block in which the bottleneck occurs, (b) In case of any grid disturbance the schedule of generation and drawals shall be deemed to have been revised for all the time (the) blocks (were) affected by grid disturbance. Certification of grid disturbance and its duration shall be done by RLDC. In this case for the earlier three time blocks also the schedules will be deemed to have been revised to actuals. Bottleneck(s) shall have to be certified by RLDC.

A revision of schedule due to transmission bottlenecks may require cheaper central generation to back down or reduce its loading or the beneficiary states to reduce their generation in the interest of interstate transmission. The question is 'Who shall bear the costs of this rescheduling?' As stated in the grid code, it is the responsibility of the CEA and PGCIL to plan and construct interstate transmission lines. So should these organizations not be charged for poor planning and inadequacy of transmission facilities instead of making the SEBs pay? In addition, in this case because of bottlenecks in the central transmission facilities the schedules will be deemed to have been revised to actuals before the revised schedules are notified. However, if a state is required to change its drawal schedule because of intra-state transmission bottleneck disturbance, the revised schedule shall be effective from the sixth time block. This means that the SEBs will be required to pay UI for the preceding time blocks. This is clearly differential treatment of two players.

ABTs are extremely useful for the current transition phase in electricity generation, where India is trying to move towards a competitive market. The ABT system still requires the regulatory commission to put various generation projects under the microscope for the calculation of various components of the fixed charge. The CERC has noted this in its ABT order. This is, however, necessary under the imperfect competitive conditions in the power markets in India. The NTPC has challenged the ABT order in the Delhi High Court and obtained a stay on its implementation. Currently, NTPC tariffs are being determined in accordance with the recommendations of the KPRC Report. The KPRC recommended that the norms be revised from time to time. Though the CEA had been asking the MoP to change these norms, they were not changed. The recommendations for target availability and other norms had been made by ECC Inc., in collaboration with the Asian Development Bank (ADB) and the World Bank (WB). These were later ratified by the National Task Force and have been discussed for over seven years now.

Table 6 1.1 presents some data to illustrate the performance of NTPC coal-based units.

Competitive Bidding', for both open cycle and combined cycle gas/naptha/liquid fuel based plants, the PLF should be between 85 and 90 per cent. The NTPC claims that it should be provided a level playing field with the private power producers for whom return at 16% ROE is possible at 68.5% PLF. In an evolving system as the knowledge of the regulators about the regulated firms improves, such changes have to be implemented in the interest of efficiency, both from the point of view of consumers and technological progress in the industry. There is enough evidence that the NTPC has achieved and can achieve availability between (85 and 90 per cent) for all its thermal generation (both steam and gas based).

Also, regarding the NTPC's concern on 'Revenue Neutrality', the commission has also observed that this principle has no economic rationale. Besides if this had been allowed no regulator would ever have been able to devise a RPI – X kind of price cap mechanism. The idea is to share the benefits of efficiency improvement with consumers. Certain efficiencies are achieved not due to innovation or technically sound technologies but just through 'learning by doing' and 'scale of operation' (for which consumers pay through fixed charges) which must be identified and passed on to consumers. In fact the idea behind 'X' , in RPI – X, is precisely that. In fact it could mean neutrality in terms of 'return on capital employed' (to be decided

TABLE 6 1.1
Operational Performance of Coal-based NTPC Stations

|  | Unit | 1992–3 | 1993–4 | 1994–5 | 1995–6 | 1996–7 | 1997–8 | 1998–9 | 1999–2000 |
|---|---|---|---|---|---|---|---|---|---|
| Generation | MU | 66,113 | 76,478 | 79,091 | 934,678 | 97,609 | 106,288 | 109,505 | 118,676 |
| PLF | % | 70.00 | 78.07 | 76.57 | 78.80 | 77.00 | 75.20 | 76.60 | 80.39 |
| Availability factor | % | 83.34 | 86.48 | 85.97 | 85.32 | 84.10 | 85.03 | 89.36 | 90.06 |

Even in the case of gas-based units, as noted in the MoP notification dated 30 March 1992 under the section on 'Thermal Power Stations Awarded through

by the commission on the basis of what it perceives to be prevailing in a competitive market) rather than 'revenue neutrality'.[17]

# 6.2 POWER SECTOR REFORMS AND REGULATION: THE ROAD AHEAD[18]

*Sebastian Morris*

## INTRODUCTION

The reform of the electricity sector, especially the decision to unbundle and privatize, has in India been based on the premise that the state (government) does not have adequate financial resources, given its need to control the fiscal deficit. The assumption is that, to bridge the gap between investment requirements

and available public resources, the active and large-scale participation of the private sector is necessary. While this assumption is increasingly being questioned in official circles, the 'reform' thus far, engendered by

---

[17] See chapter 3 in this report for a different interpretation of the NTPC's objections to the CERC's ABT.

[18] Based on Morris (1999), Morris (1996), and Morris (2000).

this perspective, bears all its limitations. I would contend that privatization has its own logic, in terms of overcoming the 'principal-agency' problem, and ushering in incentives for efficiency, especially allocative efficiency. The resources gap argument is not only misleading but is inconsistent, and takes privatization in the wrong direction. This premise is also entirely inadequate as a basis for a privatization programme, since it ignores the underlying reasons for the financial incapacity of the state in general and the electricity sector in particular. It takes as given the current inefficiencies and leakage of resources from the state electricity boards (SEBs), and does not factor in improvements that can contribute a great deal to the investable resources.

Similarly, the hastily crafted independent power project (IPP) programme (especially the so-called fast track projects) has added considerable burden on the SEBs, especially the 'well'-performing SEBs of Maharashtra, Gujarat, and Karnataka. IPP proposals have come down dramatically and many very close to financial closure have been dropped. This has happened because in a situation where *basic* reform was not pursued, private parties had successfully shifted nearly all risks on to the state sector. The contingent liabilities of state governments have as a result swelled. As state governments have woken up to this risk shifting, the basis for IPPs which did not exist stands exposed. While it is privatization of a sort, it can hardly be sustained, and the vast potential benefits of a meaningful possible privatization would go unrealized. These and other problems had been anticipated when the first of the 'reform' initiatives were announced, but the government, especially the Ministry of Power (MoP), had chosen to ignore them. Only belatedly have some of the issues raised been recognized and corrected. Thus the early restriction that limited local financial institutions' (FIs') participation in IPPs to 20 per cent or less of project cost and constrained IPP promoters into tied finance from equipment manufacturers abroad and hence to high cost projects, has given way.

## THE CURRENT PARADIGM

The present paradigm of reform has many other inadequacies. I now very briefly discuss the more significant problems.

### Privatization Not Possible Without Reform

The assumption that large-scale privatization is possible without reform, or delayed reform, of tariffs is questionable. Thus in most private power agreements (PPAs), private generating companies have (expectedly) insisted upon guarantees and counterguarantees, and escrow accounts. The cash flow position of SEBs is, therefore, worsened, since the purchase price per unit of power by SEBs is much higher than the long-run marginal cost of generating the same internally. Profitability too is affected when this purchase price does not leave enough room to recover distribution costs. Equally important, the guarantees only mean that the contingent liability ceiling is either breached or under pressure. The limits of escrowability have already been reached in some SEBs.

### The Economy Cannot Forever be Resource Constrained

'Where are resources for 6000 MW plus capacity addition, equal to approximately Rs 18,000 crore per annum, to come from?' is a question often rhetorically posed with the 'answer' being 'from outside the sector and the country'. This is an obvious fallacy, which even this Infrastructure Report is not free of. If a growing sector cannot generate a sufficient portion of the resources that it invests, then prima facie it is unviable for private capital. And most certainly foreign resources are out because they increase the contingent liability of the state, and would use up the meagre surplus of the SEB sector, driving the SEBs faster to bankruptcy.[19] It has been shown here that at long-run incremental cost pricing and assuming the marginal product of power to be 5, given the power-constrained nature of the economy (as the government claims), the power sector becomes a 'source' of net savings for the economy in less than eight years. This is even less than the period implied by the accelerated depreciation. Vast underutilized capacities in power equipment manufacturing, and in associated works, imply that the social cost of adding capacity through domestic savings and indigenous equipment is far below the private cost.

### IPPs WITH RISK-FREE CONTRACTS ARE NOT THE ANSWER

In privatizing generation alone or first, and in the framework of legally enforceable PPAs, there is no incentive on the part of the generating company to worry about demand. The Pakistan story inspite of being all too familiar, and repeatedly pointed out, has nevertheless been systematically ignored. Competitive bidding for generation projects, while it has the potential to reduce project cost and tariffs, does not correct this problem: overinvestment or incorrect investment can still take place—as when high cost fuels are used for base

---

[19] Thus the Enron Project with watertight contracts continues to be questioned by politicians, the press, regulators, and citizens' groups.

power,[20] or when plants are inappropriately located. The embedding of demand in the risk analysis of private generators has been weak when the state is the intermediary. Considerable demand risk has therefore been shifted on to the state.

Private generators, when operating on return on capital basis (essentially cost plus) have little incentive for making correct choice of technology. If bids are based on lowest total cost of power and not also on the composition between variable and fixed costs, in situations where merit order is not strictly enforced (or when PPAs subvert the same), the socially desired usage of plants across all owners is vitiated. This has several effects. It makes the task of a future regulator very difficult, since he would be burdened with prior socially inoptimal contracts. It would also considerably delay the process of forming a market for wholesale electricity. Equally importantly, the potential for prices to be related to the load on the system (as they must be for a demand side participation in improving system stability and fuller utilization of capital) in the near future would be ruled out, or made difficult. This is because generators being separate from distributors and buyers would not be too concerned about fuller utilization given the two-part tariff.[21]

Policy makers, and especially the bureaucracy, have failed when they have sought and pushed 'options' that at best only shift forward the day of reckoning. In the process, they have not only delayed reform, but have made sustainable reform and basic reform even more problematic. Thus it is quite feasible that private parties with IPPs and PPA contracts in their pockets would be averse to attempts to reform SEBs, that seek to lower the SEBs own marginal cost of generation. They would, for instance, insist on being protected against price cap regulation, or against having to compete.

### Foreign Funding Adds No Value in the Electricity Sector

The earlier insistence that domestic institutional funds should not exceed 20 per cent of project cost, has

deepened the interlocking[22] of markets for foreign capital resources and technology and equipment. Thus most clearly IPPs based on tied finance have ended up choosing high cost equipment. As the policy was amended, more local resources could flow into IPPs. The initial 'fast track' projects with predominantly foreign funding, of which the Dhabol Power Project is a typical case, have imposed as much as a 40 per cent service cost on foreign resources, when the upper bound of cost of foreign resources could have been barely 15 per cent. Indian plant costs are at least 15 per cent less than plants that are tied to foreign credit simply because of lower equipment cost. Using this datum and the typical expected debt and equity returns in the Enron case it is obvious that far too high a foreign exchange cost has been borne in foreign funding and management of IPPs (see Table 6.2.1).

The problem really is that for a country like India, with well-developed capabilities in manufacturing plant and in its operations, an area with not too much technological dynamism, there is little that foreign capital and technology can contribute. The same would apply to a country like China (now), which has the Shanghai Electric Corporation, manufacturing electric plant at a cost 5–20 per cent below that of the Bharat Heavy Electricals Limited. Thus, if foreign capital had to come in, the playing field had to be made partial to the foreign player, and that is precisely what the fast track policy did. Besides the padding of project costs that took place, because the Central Electricity Authority (CEA) was asked to look the other way, the entire mechanism of costing was in error. First high cost fuel-using stations were allowed to operate as base stations. Second, and perhaps more importantly, base load stations were allowed full recovery of cost and earnings at 16 per cent, at 68.5 per cent plant load factor (PLF), when base load stations of many SEBs were already operating at between 70 and 98 per cent PLF. The policy should have allowed recovery of cost and earning at 16 per cent, only at PLFs above the average of *base load* stations of *good* SEBs. Indeed the approach should have been to buy power at a total cost that was least through long-term contracts rather than to worry about PLFs. A utility-buying base power should negotiate for the lowest unit cost of power. It is only when buying

[20] As naptha prices have gone up, certain IPPs that came up with naptha-linked PPAs have stopped working. But the SEBs continue to pay the cost at 16.0 per cent return on equity (ROE) on investments as per the PPAs. The plants could have quickly fitted gas connection kits. But they have no incentive to do so.

[21] The two-part tariff is a good mechanism for a robust, well-diversified utility to contract with a few generators for peaking power (at the margin). It assumes that the utility retains the 'advantage' and sets the terms, and gains from shielding the generator from demand, and variability risks. It cannot have general validity in all situations of bulk power purchase.

[22] Interlocking of markets for credit or funds and equipment is too well known. Earlier, tied 'aid', especially bilateral credit, was important. Today private global institutions like GE Capital have emerged to push GE equipment in global markets particularly in the less developed countries (LDCs). It is inappropriate macro-economic policies that have raised the cost of domestic resources for Indian firms. And the large 'fischer-open' differential between India and international capital markets would mean that neither do they have access to foreign funds.

TABLE 6.2.1

The Internal Rate of Return of the Difference in the Foreign Exchange Flows
Between a Nationalist Alternative and an Enron-like Project

(unless otherwise stated, in Rs cr/MW)

| Item | |
|---|---|
| 1. Average interest on foreign debt on Foreign Project (FP): $i$ | 10.00 % |
| 2. Project cost (FP) : *FPC* | 4.20 |
| 3. Foreign equity (wholly owned foreign project) (Debt:Equity: 2:1) | 1.40 |
| 4. Net project cost of FP »$FPC(1+i/2)/(1+3i/2)$ | 3.83 |
| 5. Plant cost of FP = (4)*0.65 | 2.49 |
| 6. Foreign sourced plant: 0.80*(5) | 1.99 |
| 7. Foreign finance | 3.50 |
| 8. Net foreign finance: (7) – (6) | 1.51 |
| 9. Foreign finance service rate, average on debt and equity | 18.00% |
| 10. Net Indian project cost = 0.85*(4) | 3.26 |
| 11. Indian plant cost: (10)*0.65 | 2.12 |
| 12. Foreign exchange for Indian plant (imported components and cost of technology purchase): (11)*0.20 | 0.42 |
| 13. Interest on above (at an assumed cost of borrowing of 12 per cent during construction) | 0.076 |
| 14. Differential inflow of foreign exchange between the two alternatives (8)+(12)+(13) | 2.01 |
| 15. Equalized annual outflow of foreign exchange on service of debt and equity earnings at an average rate of 18 per cent, being the internal rate of return (IRR) on exchange flows for a foreign financed project, over 30 years | 0.63 |
| 16. Equalized annual outflow of foreign exchange on debt service @ 12 per cent for commercial borowings for financing the foreign exchange component of the Indian project, over 30 years | 0.04 |
| 17. Equity to be retired in the 31st year, for the foreign project | 1.4 |
| 18. *IRR of the differential foreign exchange flows* | *28.31%* |
| IRR of the differential foreign exchange flows at a cost advantage of 20 per cent for the domestic producer, and ceteris paribus | 28.91% |

*Source:* Table 11 of Morris (1996).

peaking power that it should actually buy capacity. It would then have found scope for a mutually agreeable deal only if the IPP could supply it power at a cost lower than what its own marginal or new base load stations are capable of. Any other deal would adversely affect the utility. Introduction of competitive bidding subsequently, and the negotiable 'incentive' above 68.5 per cent PLF, only partly addresses this issue. IPPs who pushed in their contracts before the negotiable incentives, could look forward to 'policy return' between 20 per cent (at the very least) to as high as 28 per cent on equity. If the overdeclaration of capital costs is also to be reckoned with then the combined returns to 'policy and to misdeclaration' could be very high (Mehta 1999).

### Risk Mitigation the Crucial Issue

Risk mitigation (not its shifting), which is the real solution to large-scale privatization, is hardly possible without basic reform of tariffs and collections and appropriate incentives for all involved parties.

In the era of near-exclusive state provision of electricity the risks were high, but the state had a comparative advantage to bear risk.[23] It could also 'bear' the costs arising out of the weaknesses of the administration, protracted approval procedures and modes of tariff whetting, and other dysfunction emanating from political and legal processes. These risks and costs continue without much change. Basic risks emanating from environmental movements, wherein even the Supreme Court's verdict is not final, the softness of the state, and the dysfunctional and contradictory rulings of the environment bureaucracy have considerably increased.

[23] Contracts that shift risks asymmetrically or inappropriately among parastatals or state-owned enterprises (SOEs) still keep the risks internal to the state. Similarly, in the disagreements between government departments and SOEs no litigation is usually involved. As such delays in settlements do not immediately feed back into decision making to enhance the risk perception.

*A Case for Regulation but Not Detailed Regulation*

The central government's initiative to set up a central-level regulator, and urge state governments to set up state-level regulators while undoubtedly a step in the right direction, may unwittingly have introduced considerable 'regulatory risk' instead of resulting in risk mitigation and bringing about transparency. The principal reason is that the regulators have little power. The recommendations of the 'Committee on Distribution Privatization' against price cap regulation are a case in point. Price cap regulation, besides the well-known advantages, has the added merit that its costs are one-time and low, in comparison to cost plus regulation. It brings about significant clarity to potential participants in distribution (and generation), can easily accommodate the long-run 'marginal' cost principle, and shields regulators from undue influence.[24] Besides this, it has sufficient incentives for cost reduction. In a country like India, given its large diversity, there is need is for a 'core price cap formula', with certain parametric values being different for different locations. In the long run, as a national market for wholesale power is possible with (more than) adequate capacity in long-distance transmission, the need for varying regional formulae would no longer be there. This is as it should be, since power is best produced where long-term costs are low (at pit heads, and near the coast, for example), subject to transmission costs. Price cap regulation would leave technology choice to the producer–distributor in the medium term. Given redundant grid capacity in the long run, with competition, technology choice would be internal to the generating companies. Scale, choice of fuel, location, peaking capacity would then be internal decisions, as they should be, driven by cost factors, demand, and willingness to pay.

*Regulation an Economic Rather Than a Legal or Engineering Task*

Unfortunately there are no guidelines for the involvement of experts from various disciplines in regulation.[25] It is not sufficient to involve legal persons and engineers.

Regulation is typically an analytical exercise that demands not only electricity economics, but also the cost of information and policy, transparency, simplicity, the value of time, and most importantly the 'incentive' implications of regulations. In other words, regulators would have to worry about how best they can take the electricity system to the planner's optimality through prices (rather than administrative measures or fiat, though these are not entirely avoidable). If the regulator were to become an authority that examines all aspects in their specific details and has to worry about 'correct' costs and prices of every project, and has to be able to justify its rulings in courts, then the task would be quite beyond the capacity of any reasonable-sized public organization. More importantly the firm and producer side costs that such a regulator would impose would be very large.

*The Particular 'Philosophy' of Regulation Needs Definition*

Thus there is need for a 'strategy of regulation' for the sector as a whole that addresses how transparency can be built into the process, reduces regulatory risk, keeps regulation costs low, and exploits the full potential of competition in generation and improvements that privatization can bring. Otherwise regulation may take us a step backward,[26] even when regulators are honestly attempting to introduce transparency.

*Restructuring of SEBs Would Have to be Derived From the Regulation Strategy*

The restructuring of the SEBs can hardly be addressed without clarity on the role of the regulator and the strategy of regulation. Unfortunately, this has not expressly been realized by the central government. Thus the role of the State Electricity Regulatory Commissions (SERCs) is hardly as yet clear for state governments to go ahead with particular schemes, including privatization for restructuring.

Similarly many regulators have to take suboptimal decisions with regard to tariffs, since there is no overall declared strategy of reform. That has been left to state governments with certain reports, like that of the Committee on Distribution Privatization, providing whatever framework one can infer. Ideally, the Centre should have specified that state governments should restructure towards a market model in generation. (This

---

[24] It is almost certain that in most states the regulator would be captured in due course by a privatized electricity sector, if detailed or cost plus mode were to be the practice. Fertilizer, steel, paper, sugar are all industries that in the control period, and fertilizers even today, generated vast rents out of regulatory prices. In contrast, in states like West Bengal, the political processes could drive the regulator to unviable prices for industry. Buses, trams, and Calcutta Electricity Supply Corporations's (CESC) electricity business are examples.

[25] The 'knee-jerk' reaction of the bureaucracy to translate the need for independence of the regulator to the suitability of retired judges and civil servants, and hardly ever economists, managers, and practitioners is part of the problem.

[26] The US had to go through a major deregulation effort away from return on investment/RONW type of detailed regulation. At one time, more than 50,000 'experts' and their staff were involved in the task of regulation, and regulated industries had effectively captured the regulator, as the fall in retail prices on deregulation, especially in airlines, trucking, and telecom, would indicate.

may happen if the Draft Bill 2000 [NCAER 2000] is accepted.) It should also have provided for total trade in power across the country, with tariffs restricting the role of inter-regional trade for a while whenever stranded assets are large, and complete and unrestricted access to the grid for all generators and consumers above a certain size, if it were truly interested in privatization that enhances efficiency and provides electricity at low cost to the consumer. At the very least it should have cried out against the current captive generation policies of state governments. Additionally, on subsidization it should have ruled out anything but direct subsidization of the agricultural sector. Similarly, it should have taken a clear position with regard to the IPPs and their status in any future competitive model. Only if policy could so have constrained or shaped the direction of reform, could the regulatory and policy risks have been brought down.

### Perverse Incentives for SEB Managers

Low tariffs for agriculture, and more importantly unmetred supply, have resulted in excessive and wasteful consumption and consumption for unauthorized uses, besides creating the basis for moral hazard; The agency (SEB) that sells is the same as the one that reports the identity of the consumer to the principal (the government). Since government lacks the ability to verify the identity of the subsidized consumer, and the amount actually consumed by such consumers, exploiting the agency problem becomes a focus of the agent.

Even incentives that had a functionality earlier have become dysfunctional today. Unfortunately, in the early 1990s and before, when PLFs were low and generation was generally unconstrained by either demand or grid capacity, it made sense to give performance incentives for generation based on achieved PLFs of plant. Some SEBs give the incentives to plants, others to the SEB as a whole. PLFs have gone up generally and today in the eastern region (where capacity had been overestimated[27]), there is a problem of oversupply and high grid frequences, because SEB units refuse to back down, since the incentives tend to be linked to PLFs! So electricity is 'burnt' on the wires and many consumers have to delink to save equipment as frequency goes up beyond 50 hertz. To counter this a frequency-linked availability-based tariff is being proposed, which is an attempt to correct one distortion with another.[28]

### Dysfunctional Tariffs

Tariffs for industry have already reached unsustainable and dysfunctional levels, in most SEBs. Most SEB rates for industry are already higher than the cost of self-generation even at small size (~5 MW). And even within the constraints of the present captive generation policy, it is only the current high interest cost of borrowed funds and generally recessionary conditions that prevent an exodus of bulk consumers from the SEB system. Strangely though, consultants of all hues continue to recommend a linear rise in tariffs even going up to Rs 6 per KwH for industries. The Administrative Staff College of India, Hyderabad for instance recommended a 20 per cent across the board increase which would have taken industrial tariffs to over Rs 5 per KwH in Gujarat! High tariffs affect the competitiveness of Indian industry. In comparison to India's competitors, especially Thailand, South Korea, and China, Indian industry is in a particularly adverse position.

## OVERCOMING THE 'AGENCY PROBLEM'

Restructuring proposals cannot sidestep the agency problem. Any attempt at marketization, privatization, or regulatory reform, and especially restructuring, that does not squarely address the 'agency problem' would not be meaningful. Thus the problem of the SEBs is far more basic than the typical 'inefficiencies of the public sector' noted worldwide. Indian bureaucracies are eminently capable of crafting institutions and rules that in form resemble success stories elsewhere, but in content and behaviour continue to remain dysfunctional.[29]

No piecemeal or stop-gap arrangement that allows the continuation of the agency problem and does not rein in leakages is meaningful. Thus proposals to sell generation assets of SEBs, without a complete reform of distribution are of little use. Similarly, proposals to sell assets, when there is no regulatory or strategic clarity, to state-level public sector undertakings (PSUs) would amount to arm-twisting the few PSUs with the cash reserves to cough up these resources to allow the leakages within the SEB system to continue.[30]

The dead-weight losses that are true social losses, and not just a transfer problem, are very large. They take the form of losses due to unutilized and underutilized

[27] In the past because capacities were estimated assuming the continuation of existing inefficiency and mismanagement. Indeed, the NTPC's capacity expansion in the late 1980s and early 1990s in the east were to cover up for the failure of the Bihar, Orissa, and Bengal SEBs.

[28] See section 6.1.

[29] Thus the oversight of the public sector in India has witnessed all the modalities found successful elsewhere such as the contract form of the French in the MoUs and the holding company form of the Italians in our own holding companies. True success as I have elsewhere observed (Morris 1991) has always eluded us because these modalities or institutions were replicated merely in form, but not in spirit and content.

[30] Apparently such proposals are being 'seriously' considered in Gujarat.

capacity, both within the system (SEB) and outside (other power suppliers and captive generators). Allocative efficiency losses resulting from inappropriate technology choice, violation of merit order, and disincentives that prevent demand from responding appropriately to prices are even more severe, though difficult to estimate.

The independent regulators are already in place and would soon be working. The Gujarat Electricity Board (GEB), Maharashtra State Electricity Board (MSEB), and the inheritor companies of the Haryana State Electricity Board have already asked for average tariff increases that are 20 per cent above current levels. In Maharashtra, the Maharashtra Electricity Regulatory Commission (MERC) has already disallowed the demand for tariff increases, pointing to the need for the Board to plug leakages and minimize the effect of 'sugar-coated' PPAs that have raised costs of purchased power unnecessarily. The Gujarat regulatory authority too is unlikely to grant the heavy tariff increase of 20 per cent asked for since it now has an idea of the vast inefficiencies and leakages. Similarly, the Haryana Electricity Regulatory Commission (HERC) is closely and critically examining the tariff proposals. In Andhra Pradesh, though, the regulatory authority has awarded rather steep increases in tariffs. Thus true reform of the SEB system cannot be further postponed.

### Subsidy Per Se is Not the Problem

The subsidization of agriculture (even after recognizing that a substantial portion of the reported consumption by the agricultural sector is fictitious), is considerable. Central government committees and enquiry reports as well as policy statements have for some time been urging that this subsidization be considerably reduced or even eliminated. Variously it has been stated that tariff should be raised so as to achieve a minimum return of 3 per cent on equity, that agriculture should be charged at 50 paise per unit, Re 1 per unit, etc. Yet no meaningful measures to reduce and contain subsidies have been made. The only meaningful recommendation thus far is that the subsidy cost must be made good by state governments to the SEBs, so that SEBs are able to retain at least accounting independence from state governments. Yet this recommendation in itself if implemented could create a problem of moral hazard. It would result in an incentive for the SEBs to over-report their subsidization costs.[31] This bind of the agricultural sector has coloured the recommendations of the central government on distribution and its privatization. It has

been generally assumed that distribution areas with larger agricultural load would be less amenable to privatization, or that differential costs would have to be recognized. The Report on Distribution Privatization has hardly appreciated the point that differential tariff in principle would be very difficult if not impossible to administer by privatized licensed monopolies without the regulator incurring the impossibly huge costs of producing independently verifiable information on customers' identity. Such measures open the door to faster growth in subsidies, or to a parallel growth of the regulator's back office to ensure the validity of subsidy claims.

### Stepping Stone Solution to Subsidization

It must be recognized, first, that removal or considerable scaling down of agricultural subsidies would be very difficult since electricity-using farmers, comparing themselves with canal water using farmers, would, even now with subsidies prevailing, find themselves relatively discriminated against.[32] Second, there is no way non-agricultural rural use can be separated from agricultural use by the utility; and as non-agricultural use increases, subsidies would in fact become rural rather than agricultural. It is surprising that these simple facts have barely found their way in discussions within the government.

While it is true that 'farmers would chose priced power available regularly rather than free power available just four hours', as many enlightened politicians have stated, it is not widely recognized that farmers would in general disbelieve that the SEBs could in fact deliver quality power. Political entrepreneurship would also be necessary to translate this preference to acceptance. There is a catch-22 situation here, since without tariff and basic reform the system would not be able to add capacity to ensure quality and reliable power. The poor credibility of the state system to do anything about systemized ills is at the root of the problem. And farmers know this. Thus a 'stepping stone' solution of continued but capped subsidization, which provides the opportunity for eliminating leakages and finally makes tariff reform politically acceptable, is necessary.[33]

[31] This is already happening on a large scale in the case of the GEB and there is no doubt at all that in the name of the rural poor and the farmer, vast leakages take place in Andhra Pradesh, Uttar Pradesh, and Madhya Pradesh.

[32] Canal water is provided at low rates that do not even cover the (low) maintenance costs of irrigation systems, leave aside capital or replacement cost. Indeed the rates are far lower than the marginal product of water, and well below private water market rates (Shah 1992; Planning Commission 1992).

[33] Moreover, unlike what all SEBs claim and what the accountants' approach would be, the subsidy is not equal to that revenue that would, when added to current revenues, equal the required return of 3 per cent (or 9 per cent). Even if leakages are accounted for, the problems of differential cost of delivery and time of day the subsidized sector uses power are important. The scattered nature of agricultural or rural demand would mean higher distribution

*Besides Subsidies, Leakages Have Drained the GEB*

Reported agricultural demand for power grew much more rapidly than every other category to become the largest component of demand. In Gujarat it is 40 per cent of total demand. There is obviously misreporting on a large scale going on within the GEB, to the private benefit of GEB engineers and industrial (especially small industry) consumers who are the principal beneficiaries of the misreporting. Real agricultural demand for irrigation is likely to be much less, perhaps not more than half, of what is reported presently. This means that the

need for subsidy is to that extent significantly reduced. Assuming agricultural demand to be 60 per cent of current reported demand, average agricultural realization per unit to be 55 paise, and an assessed Rs 2.75 to be the true standard cost of delivered power today, a subsidy requirement of Rs 1350 crore would be arrived at. This is in fact less than the subsidy actually received by the GEB from the state government! In Table 6.2.2 the upper bound of the leakage from the GEB for the year 1995–6 has been computed. The estimate of course depends upon the two assumptions made: that

TABLE 6.2.2
The Position of the GEB Had Leakages been Plugged 1995–6

| | | |
|---|---|---|
| 1 | Gross generation (m KwH) | 25,979 |
| 2 | Net generation (m KwH) | 20,547 |
| 3 | Purchase gross (m KwH) | 7200 |
| 4 | Purchase net (m KwH) | 7128 |
| 5 | T & D losses (m KwH) | 5549 |
| 6 | Sales (m KwH) | 22,198 |
| | of which domestic | 1927 |
| | commercial | 581 |
| | agricultural | 9383 |
| | industry | 7940 |
| | railway | 345 |
| | outside | 72 |
| | others | 1950 |
| 7 | Tariff average (Rs/KwH) | 1.415 |
| | Domestic (Rs/KwH) | 1.22 |
| | Commercial (Rs/KwH) | 2.91 |
| | Agricultural (Rs/KwH) | 0.27 |
| | Industry (Rs/KwH) | 2.57 |
| | Railway (Rs/KwH) | 2.4 |
| | Outside (Rs/KwH) | 1.65 |
| | Others (Rs/KwH) | 1.79 |
| 8 | Leakage (T&D) assuming half of it can be recovered at industrial tariffs (Rs crs) | 713 |
| 9 | Leakage in misreporting industrial supply as agricultural (Rs cr): assume 40 (20) per cent of agricultural sales | 863 (432) |
| 10 | Total leakages excluding recovery of some auxiliary consumption (8) + (9) | 1576 (1145) |
| 11 | Reported losses of GEB (Rs cr) | 778 |
| 12 | Profits with leakages plugged (Rs cr) (10) – (11) | 798 (367) |
| 13 | Sales revenue (Rs cr) | 3141 |
| 14 | Costs (Rs cr) | 4045 |
| 16 | Reported return (–) on capital (per cent) (without subsidy) | 20.3 |
| 18 | Implied capital (Rs cr) | 3932 |
| 19 | Implied 'return' (+) on capital with leakages plugged (per cent) | 20.3 (9.3) |

cost. On the other hand, since most farmers are pushed to consuming electricity at off-peak hours, the attributable capital charged to farmers is much lower than when a uniform allocation is made. Similarly, how can we trust figures of distribution cost or relative distribution cost as between rural and urban areas (even assuming that SEB data management systems are such as to allow them to undertake this exercise), when rural areas are subject to transformer failure rates of 27 per cent (in Gujarat) when anything above 10 per cent was 'impossible' just a few years ago?

40 per cent of agricultural demand is misreported, and about half of T&D losses are recoverable. These are the estimates obtained from certain knowledgeable sources within the GEB. Others have disputed the figure of 40 per cent and claimed that it is likely to be closer to 25 per cent. It is important to note that at reported agricultural consumption, the average energy drawn per pump set in Gujarat would be between

two and three times higher than in comparable states: Maharastra, Andhra Pradesh, Tamil Nadu, Karnataka, and Madhya Pradesh.

Even ignoring some recovery that is possible from auxiliary consumption, the estimated leakage was double the magnitude of the reported losses in the same year. In that year the GEB reported a loss of 20.3 per cent on capital employed. With the leakage plugged it would have in fact made a profit (including additional duty realization) of 20 per cent on capital employed! With the assumption of 20 per cent (rather than 40 per cent) of agricultural demand being misreported the return would have been as high as 9 per cent.

### Vested Interests the Real Barrier to Reform

Thus the real barrier to reform is not so much, as is usually claimed, the politics of populism as vested interests within SEBs and those outside benefiting from the leakages. The GEB, for example, has estimated the 'effective subsidy to agriculture' to be Rs 2713 crore in 1997-8. In the same year it claimed that 10,089 million KwH of electricity was sold to the agricultural sector. Even assuming for a moment that it is the true figure of actual sales to agriculture, then the subsidy per unit of sales implicit in the GEB's reckoning is Rs 2.689 per KwH, which is untenable. At a more likely 6000 million units of sale to the agricultural sector for irrigation this would be Rs 4.52 per unit! Thus the GEB has been tacking all its inefficiencies and T&D losses, including theft, on to the agricultural sector, treating it as a residual, to claim a whopping Rs 2713 crore from the government. It actually received Rs 1666 crore, the rest being covered by net cross-subsidy from the industrial and domestic sectors.

What we have in effect is the extreme instance of moral hazard in a situation where 'subsidy administration' was not separated from the SEB. This has allowed the SEB to use the excuse of low prices to the agricultural sector to cover up its inefficiencies and more importantly graft.

### Stamps-based Agricultural Subsidy

Agricultural subsidies ought to take the form of an electricity stamps or coupons scheme, which is administered by the Agriculture Department. The scheme would necessitate the use of land records, records related to operational holdings and to the identification of farmers who need subsidy. The government would have to decide to what extent it needs to subsidize rich farmers; the electricity subsidy has thus far been a production subsidy and not poor oriented. Even if it continues to be treated as such, farmers would have to be identified

and matched to their owned and operated agricultural lands, and issued stamps. The annual issuance of stamps through banks can be made a very simple activity through appropriate design to guard against malpractice.

### Should the Stamps be Made Tradable?

As long the subsidy is not poor oriented, tradability would not be desirable. When the subsidy is for farmers, based on their status as poor people, tradability would allow those farmers who want to exchange electricity for food or other consumption items to do so. In effect then it would, as it should, become an income subsidy.

Stamps collected by the distribution companies would entitle them to subsidy revenue from the government. The need for stamps or coupons in the manner described above arises because of the need to target the subsidy better, to cap the same, and to prevent subsidized electricity being used for non-farm activities. Perhaps most importantly, the need for stamps arises because that is one way subsidization can be entirely separated from the business of electricity distribution. Thereby the problem of moral hazard—overreporting of subsidized consumption by the company—is entirely avoided. This would be absolutely necessary for the success and credibility of a privatization programme.[34]

## CREATING THE MARKET

The SEBs could be restructured in several ways. What is feasible and meaningful would of course depend on the regulatory arrangements. Thus a regime of detailed regulation, with the power to licence being in the hands of the regulator, would largely preclude competition in generation, which would otherwise be possible. It would still allow some competition in capacity costs and therefore in capacity addition.

Similarly, recognition of the constraints in transition would mean that proposals would have to consider not only the envisaged end result of reform and restructuring but also lay out a transition path. The reform may be defined as such reorganization and the legal and policy changes which would: (a) solve the agency and moral hazard problem in administration of subsidies; (b) create incentives for cost saving and efficient generation, transmission, and distribution; (c) correct the inversions in the tariff, and lead to a scheme that would allow prices to play their economic role of reflecting costs. The price structure ought also to create incentives for consumers to use electricity optimally. Prices should also signal producers correctly.

---

[34] It is not entirely certain that this problem of moral hazard is not there in the privatized distribution companies of Orissa.

It has already been argued that separation of subsidy administration from the SEBs is necessary. But that alone would not be sufficient to solve the agency problem. In order to neutralize the vested interests, both within and outside the SEBs that have come up around the 'leakages' of revenue, it is necessary that *distribution be privatized*. The culture of tampering with metres, coming to an agreement with the customer, etc. is too well entrenched to be removable by mere administrative, financial, or formal restructuring, such as corporatizing the SEBs or even trifurcating the organizations, while retaining the ownership structure intact.

Quick privatization of distribution, even before regulatory clarity and strategy emerges, is the need of the hour, since with every month the leakages, and continuing inefficiency, accumulate and impose a severe burden on the state budget.[35]

Such quick and revenue-enhancing privatization, that at the same time does not retard the scope of further reform and change, would call for bundling of some generation assets with distribution. This would simultaneously lower the demand risk for generation assets, allowing them to be privatized easily (without creating PPAs, contingent liabilities, etc.) and simultaneously lower the supply risk for distribution entities.

### Some Bundling for Quick Privatization

Thereby, and to the extent that the assets are bundled, their value is not crucially dependent on the ability of the restructuring and regulatory processes to unbundle and put the system back together through elaborate market-creating processes. Thus the '*regulatory* and restructuring risk' can be minimized for partially bundled entities. Resources can then flow from the capital markets if the final tariff awards are consistent with recovery of costs (even if they are in error with regard to recovery of particular costs). Thus the regulatory authority would also have the space to organize and lay out its strategy, including market creation processes in generation, with much caution. It would also be able, in a phased manner, to implement its strategy.

This would allow for quicker privatization of distribution, which is the immediate requirement, because that alone can plug the leakages from the system. Moreover there is a period of learning, when the price cap formulae and the rules are fine tuned and participants learn, and the IT system is set up to allow for quick contracting and settlement and monitoring of power generators and consumers at each of the connection points on the grid. The bundling would allow for a

smoother transition than otherwise. Moreover, the market is familiar with such companies as the Bombay Suburban Electric Supply Limited (BSES), Ahmedabad Electric Company (AEC), Surat Electricity Company (SEC), and Calcutta Electric Supply Corporation (CESC). These companies are licensees under the Electricity Act of 1948, and are subject to annual tariff review by the state governments. Their investment arrangements to expand capacity need not necessarily go through the stand-alone route. They could take advantage of balance sheet financing, for instance, to considerably lower their cost of capital.

### *Public Enterprise would have Problems with Competition*

Let us take the GEB as a case.[36] Currently capacity within the GEB, in the IPPs, in captive generators, and in Gujarat's share from the central electricity companies is together underutilized. There is much scope to shift demand to off-peak hours to raise the systemwide PLF higher and improve power quality. More efficient capacity utilization possibly with workable time of the day tariff (leading to shifting of demand) is not feasible unless distribution and generation company staff have the requisite freedom to offer substantial discounts that depend upon the situation and are essentially unpredictable. Such freedom in government departments and public sector companies given their rule orientation would be difficult, if not impossible. Functional (rather than the usual formal) monitoring of such discounts would be difficult again, unless the entity is privately managed. The scope for shifting to off-peak hours is large in Gujarat given the fact that Gujarat has a large number of power using industries and substantial agricultural demand, which could use off-peak power effectively. Most importantly, bringing back accountability and embedding responsibility in the present SEBs without change in ownership would be very difficult.[37]

### *Transparency of Processes Crucial to Success of Reform*

In moving towards a reformed electricity system wherein privatization of distribution and generation is the crucial aspect, the processes followed to bring about the changes are important. Success would depend upon two critical aspects: It would be necessary to build in complete transparency and information sharing with bidders,

---

[35] At a rough and conservative estimate the leakages per month are in excess of Rs 80 crore per month in the case of the GEB. It is more likely to be at least 50 per cent above that level.

[36] The situation in Maharashtra, Tamil Nadu, and Andhra Pradesh would be quite similar to that in Gujarat. In only a few SEBs is the elastic component of demand small enough to create special problems—Kerala and Delhi and possily the north-eastern states. In, most other states, with some variation, the model that is developed here should readily apply.

[37] Thus even to date GEB management has not been able to install transformer-level metres to bring about some accountability among its commercial staff.

consultants, study groups, concerned departments of governments, power users, captive generators, and citizens in general. Similarly the restructuring process would have to be directed by the appointment of a credible person who not only has the necessary skills, but also independence from the SEB, the government, influential politicians, the bidders, consultants, and advisers. This is vital since incumbent management and staff of the GEB, the government, or influential politicians and bureaucrats cannot be assumed to be uninterested parties.[38]

Equally importantly, complete transparency would result in the best prices from bidders for SEBs' businesses and assets. The true status of most SEBs assets is hardly known[39] and only complete transparency can ensure that bidders do not bring legal claims after takeovers/assets sale. Transparency and the fairness that can come only with independence and expertise would also attract many more bidders other than those who seek to gain out of government failures, or out of their ability to unduly influence the government.[40]

## Transmission the Market Maker

Transmission ought not to be fully privatized. This is to ensure that the option of a complete market solution in generation either through pool prices or contracts is kept open and becomes easier to pursue. It avoids the danger of 'artificial' constraints in transmission segments that give rise to shortages in particular territories, which in turn could result in high realized prices for generators.

Yet since good transmission performance is always in the interest of the consumer the transmission entity could beneficially have substantial participation by consumers, including user industries, while being entirely free of shareholding by generation and distribution interests.[41] Key to enhanced efficiency of the

[38] The Maharashtra State Electricity Board and Tamil Nadu Board Electricity (TNB) have significantly lower leakages and this condition may not be strictly necessary.

[39] Thus in the case of the GEB, auditors had contested or had additional notes to practically every major figure in the annual report, and there were over thirty significant notings (GEB 1997–8).

[40] In the eyes of the people, no government today has the credibility to pose as being corruption free. Thus even if a government is fair, and keeps the disinvestment process free of corruption, nobody would believe it. Certainly not at state level. Competitive politics would ensure that there would be questioning of virtually every decision.

[41] The Draft Bill, 2000 (NCAER 2000) also makes the point about transmission not being interlinked with owners of distribution and generation companies. We would like to go a step further to say that restructuring should actually solicit the participation of industry farmers, and households, in transmission companies.

restructured system is the degree of competition among generators.

## Transmission as a Regulated Monopoly

Transmission is best operated as a regulated monopoly with price cap regulation. A significant but minority shareholding of the government in transmission would be desirable. Transmission business should be confined to system integrity, investments, and operations on behalf of buyers and sellers of power for benefit of consumers. The transmission company should not buy and sell power on its own account, but should facilitate selling and buying of power, in other words be a market maker[42] rather than participant.

## Own Account Trading by Transmission Company Should Be Inadmissible

In principle too if the transmission company (TRANSCO) buys and sells power on its own account, then the generating company is to that extent shielded from demand risk and variability in demand. The TRANSCO then would have to bear these risks, which would be an intrusion into its principle business of transmitting power, which tends to be a natural monopoly.

It is important to realize that large generators would attempt to enhance their returns by creating congestion situations, when connection rights are traded in a market. This has happed in systems where connection rights exclude other competitors. Such artificial congestion could also take place when grid restrictions are significant, even when connection rights are periodically assigned, as would be the case of a regulated transmission monopoly. To avoid or minimize such situations, the ownership structure of the TRANSCO is crucial. Also returns to the TRANSCO in relaxing congestion in the form of line loss charges and connection charges, should be significant. In other words, the TRANSCO should have appropriate incentives to maintain optimal overcapacity.

With less than majority share held by the government, the TRANSCO would not be 'state' in the courts' view and would have the requisite freedom to pay its staff well and in a manner that creates incentives for performance within the organization. Similarly, the

[42] The National Thermal Power Corporation (NTPC), for instance, has resisted enormous government pressure that it become a power trader on behalf of the IPPs, rightly knowing that under the present circumstances, its cash flow would greatly deteriorate with such operations, since the receivables from the SEBs would then mount even faster. The recent decision of the central government to set up a power-trading corporation is inexplicable. The previous section discusses the issue in greater detail.

current constraint of being 'state' in labour management in general would go.

The TRANSCO would have to lay down detailed guidelines and announce connection, congestion, and line loss charges for various types and sizes of loads connected to the transmission network and for use of its facilities, in consultation with the regulator. The assets for sale would have to be valued at replacement cost minus the maintenance costs required to bring them to a state of complete repair. The initial price for services through a price cap, or the return to the transmission company at 16 per cent or more would have to be fixed by the regulator. All distribution-cum-generating companies (DGCs), generating companies (GCs), IPPs or their inheritor companies, and captive producers (CPs) would have equal access to the grid.[43] The TRANSCO would have to, along with the regulator, facilitate and lay down rules for the development of a wholesale market. Surpluses, in the sale of generation and distribution assets of the SEB, and the current capital contributions of the state government if any, could *inter alia* be used to enhance the TRANSCO's network and quality of assets.

## Costs of Immediate and Complete Separation of Distribution and Generation May be too High

To realize the total potential of competition in generation, it would be desirable to separate generation completely from distribution, and ensure that the Herfindahl Index (H-index) of concentration in generation is not too large.[44] Yet the true costs of learning to separate generation entirely from distribution and then put them together through a 'market' would have to be reckoned with. In the initial stages, rather than generation going fully through the market, it may be more appropriate to start only with the market for surpluses and deficits;[45] that is to allow some generation assets to distribution companies.

The possible abuse of vertical integration economies by distribution-cum-generation companies no doubt exists. This can be addressed in part via a price cap

[43] The structure and object of these entities will shortly be defined.

[44] Thus collusive behaviour that raised pool prices in the E&W System by National Power and Power Gen, the two largest players in the UK market in the first few years, when the pool-trading system was introduced, did occur. This had to be corrected by specific regulatory measures including the sale of generation assets to smaller companies and closer oversight of the market by the regulator. There is no merit in having a very large number of small generators. The point is to ensure that the market power of no generator is particularly large.

[45] The Nord Pool of Norway and Sweden is essentially such a market.

on retail electricity prices, ensuring adequate transmission capacity, and in stages by moving towards a retail market for electricity, as I will argue in the following pages.

### Structural Determinants of Competition Potential

The potential for realized competition in generation would depend upon the following: the industrial structure of independent generators, specifically the H-index; the distribution of variable costs, and break-even (cost recovery) outputs of each of the plants. Besides these, the potential for trade, which depends upon the capacity of unattached generators, including exporters, to the system, the deficits and surpluses of utilities with their own generation capacities, and variability in final demanded load and especially its price elasticity, would influence competition in the system. High unanticipated interseasonal and intra-day variability would reduce the potential of market prices to be close to the long-run marginal costs. Another important factor in the potential for competition is the excess capacity in the system; since transmission is in part a substitution for generation, 'excess' transmission capacity and 'excess' generation capacity would tend to keep market prices low. It would most importantly depend upon the ease with which bulk consumers can choose their supplier, including taking up self-generation when they find it most suitable. Variability in market prices would depend upon the variability of demand and the response capacity of the system, especially the extent of hydropower available, the two acting in opposite directions.

### Bulk Consumers Can Provide Significant Competition

I take up the case of the Gujarat electricity system to work out the hypothetical market system. In it the numbers of purchasers and buyers that are obtained, the concentration level, and the overall share of elastic demand are all quite reasonable. Many systems are likely to have values similar to that of Gujarat and as such the proposals are quite general.

Table 6.2.3 reports the average sizes of various classes of consumers, based on officially reported data of the GEB. I have modified the data and reworked the average size of various classes of consumers. Of reported agricultural consumption 40 per cent is assumed to be potentially industrial HT. Similarly, possible savings on account of recognizing that about 12 per cent of T&D losses are really theft and about a fourth of auxiliary consumption could be avoided have also been assumed. This leads to the total supply (or potential supply) to HT to be 14067.6 m KwH rather than the

TABLE 6.2.3
Average Sizes of Various Classes of Consumers of GEB c. 1995–6

| | Type of electricity consumer consumed in m KwH | No. of consumers | Average consumption per year per customer (KwH) | Average implied generation capacity serving each consumer (MW) at 65 per cent PLF |
|---|---|---|---|---|
| *Assuming Correctness of Reported Data* | | | | |
| Domestic | 2176 | 4.951 m | 439.5 | 0.0000769 |
| Commercial | 601 | 0.700 m | 858.6 | 0.0001507 |
| LT (low tension) | 2283 | 0.160 m | 14,268.8 | 0.00251 |
| HT (high tension) | 6325 | 4208 | 1.5031 | 0.26 |
| Railways | 331 | 10 | 33.1 m | 5.82 |
| Agriculture | 10,132 | 0.527 m | 19,225.8 | 0.00337 |
| Public lighting | 94 | 0.017 m | 5433.5 | 0.000955 |
| Public water works and sewerage | 239 | 0.020 m | 11,962 | 0.00211 |
| Licensees | 2675 | 2 | 1337.5 m | 234.92 |
| *Adjusting Reported Data Suitably* | | | | |
| HT | 14,037.6 | 9539 | 1.5031 m | 0.26 |
| Agriculture | 6079.2 | 0.527 m | 11,535.5 | 0.00202 |

*Note:* The adjustments are: About 40 per cent of agricultural demand is assumed to be fictitious and could have been/ is being sold to HT users; half of T&D losses and similarly a fourth of auxiliary consumption could either be saved or could be/is being sold to HT users. This gives the number of HT users to be in excess of 9500. Assuming a log-normal distribution of consumption, with a standard deviation of 2 mu, the number of HT consumers above 1 MW demand would be 476!

reported 6325 m KwH see Table 6.2.4. This means that there are potentially about 9539 HT consumers rather than 4208, with an average capacity requirement of 0.26 MW. Assuming a log-normal distribution of consumption with a standard deviation of twice the mean, it is most likely that there would be 476 or so HT consumers with a capacity requirement of 1 MW or more. Nearly all railway consumers are bulk; as are all public lighting in towns and cities. Only in tiny towns and villages would the load be small. This would give at least 30–50 public consumers whose capacity demand would be in excess of 1 MW. Thus approximately 500 bulk consumers would be able to buy power in the retail market, and their total off-take would likely be at around 1200 MW of capacity. Their presence in the market would constitute a major force to competitive determination of prices. On the supply side, the present captive and co-generators, with a total generation of 4132 m KwH at 40 per cent average PLF today, would be able to raise their PLF[46] to 60 per cent and even more. Assuming a third would wind up operations under a regime of reliable power, they could still contribute up to about 1653 m KwH of net sales. The retiring units

would anyway become bulk consumers, and hence contribute to demand that is price sensitive. The net effect would be to add about 1653 m KwH ~ 270 MW at 70 per cent PLF of capacity implied in the current captive generators' realizable surplus.

Thus we can estimate the amount of power that would be marketed under the proposed scheme of bundling all generation assets within the distribution companies. All 'imported' electricity from the NTPC, Nuclear Power Corporation (NPC), etc. amounts to 10,055 m KwH. Other purchases from captive generators could be ~ 1653 m KwH. Similarly, sales by the GEB to bulk consumers and other utilities would be approximately 8000 m KwH (HT consumers above 0.5 m KwH), and 2675 sales to the Ahmedabad Electricity Company (AEC), Surat Electricity Company (SEC), etc. Thus the traded electricity would be as much as (Purchase + Sales)/(2* throughput); which would be in the range of 35.40 per cent.

*Some Asymmetry in (Zonal) Distribution-cum-generating Companies is Desirable*

Recognizing that the zonal distribution companies could be so structured as to leave all of them with asymmetry between demand, supply, and the planned investments by the IPPs and the NTPC, the trading potential would be in the region of 50 per cent. This

---

[46] Those with marginal cost below market prices would be able to price the power at marginal cost, others would probably have to wind up/retire their operations, since they would find it cheaper to purchase power.

estimate is no doubt crude and could easily be refined with more accurate and reliable information. Thus a market-based reform is consistent and feasible with bundled distribution and generation companies.

In Table 6.2.4 the H-index circa 2002 for all generation and for the traded power that is likely if GEB's

capital assets.[48] The RPI formula could be a weighted average of various prices (fuel, salaries and wages, interest rate, etc.), with the weights being derived from standards and the SEB's present proportions of various costs. R can be based on a desired adjustment period. Thus if the system as a whole can be expected to improve

TABLE 6.2.4
H-index in the Generation Subsector in Gujarat in the Immediate Future, c. 2002

| Producer/supplier | Capacity | Traded capacity | Market share (per cent) | Market share** (per cent) |
|---|---|---|---|---|
| DGC1 | 800 | 0 | 7.7 | 0.0 |
| DGC2 | 800 | 0 | 7.7 | 0.0 |
| DGC3 | 800 | 0 | 7.7 | 0.0 |
| DGC4 | 800 | 0 | 7.7 | 0.0 |
| DGC5 | 800 | 0 | 7.7 | 0.0 |
| Merchant Generating Companies | 800 | 800 | 7.7 | 16.5 |
| Gujarat Industrial Power Corporation | 305 | 305 | 2.9 | 6.3 |
| Nuclear Power Corporation | 125 | 125 | 1.2 | 2.6 |
| NTPC | 1008 | 1008 | 9.6 | 20.7 |
| Indian Oil Corporation | 1000 | 1000 | 9.6 | 20.6 |
| Gujarat Torrent* | 1200 | 1300 | 11.5 | 26.7 |
| AEC (Torrent)* | 900 | | 8.6 | 0.0 |
| Essar Hazira | 515 | 200 | 4.9 | 4.1 |
| Jagadia Chem | 41 | 10 | 0.4 | 0.2 |
| Koraya | 60 | 15 | 0.6 | 0.3 |
| Reliance Jamnagar | 500 | 100 | 4.8 | 2.1 |
| ALL | 10,454 | 4863 | 100.0 | 100.0 |
| H-index | | | 0.1 | 0.2 |
| Share of traded to total capacity | 46.5 | | | |

*AEC and Gujarat Torrent are assumed to be merged, or to coordinate operations.
** For traded power only.

current generation assets are split into six portions, five of which are bundled along with five (zonal) distribution areas to form the DGCs and the sixth sold off as an independent generating company (MGC) is worked out. The H-index for traded power alone is moderate and would permit adequate competition under the right rules.

*Distribution-cum-generation Companies on a Price Cap*
Distribution companies with some generation assets (DGCs) could be subject to a ceiling prices regulation. The maximum price chargeable to any customer would have to be fixed by the regulator in the form of a formula—RPI – X – R. The price at starting year reflects the average present costs of the SEB duly adjusted for avoidable T&D losses,[47] the leakage that can be quickly plugged, and a desirable return of 14 per cent on all

its efficiency at a rate of R per cent per year to reach international standards, say in five years, and if international standards are presently 30 per cent below the SEB's, then R could be as high as 6 per cent for each year. In other words, the regulator expects real prices of electricity to fall with the reform. X may be zero over the period of adjustment and then at a rate that is based on expected improvements in efficiency that follow from technology. Ceterius paribus, in a rapidly growing system, X can be expected to be large as compared to that in advanced countries where expected growth is much lower. Wholesale prices would then continue to be derived from the market, subject to the ceiling on final retail prices.[49]

[47] Thus (SEB's total cost of power generation+purchase)/ (Units sold+A. [T&D loss of units]).

[48] It is desirable to base the return on total capital assets rather than on equity capital. This would allow firms the option of innovatively and efficiently structuring their capital.
[49] In the long run no such ceiling may be necessary as the wires business is completely separated from the sale and purchase of power. But as long as households do have inelastic demand

## Values of 'X'

There has been much discussion on the role of 'X' in price cap regulation.[50] Given that technological change is less unpredictable in power as compared to telecom, which is technology driven, price cap regulation is more suitable in power than in telecom.[51] Some have suggested that a sliding-scale regulation is better, while others have argued that price cap regulation is no different from detailed regulation. The point is to not go back on an 'X' that is agreed upon to be valid for a certain number of years. If 'X' is adjusted *ex-post* after firms make larger than expected profits, then the value of price cap regulation to provide incentives for efficiency and improvements is attenuated. Moreover, with a backward looking 'X', regulatory risk enters into the picture, to raise the a priori expected returns. In the Indian situation, the need of the hour is efficiency, and even if 'X' is in the past known to have been smaller than desirable, there are other ways to overcome the problem than to make 'X' backward looking. Indeed, the regulator would have to announce credibly that 'X' would not be backward looking.

### Investment Tax Credit and 'X'

It would be necessary to allow regulated distribution-cum-generating firms their high profits, provided these are invested in infrastructure, with a sliding scale of investment tax credit linked to an increasing tax scale. Such an arrangement would have the merit of directing investments into infrastructure and especially power distribution itself[52] to relax the present constraints.

---

and would not be able to shift demand over the diurnal cycle, such a cap may be necessary.

[50] We have been told by one of the team members of the Central Electricity Regulatory Commission (CERC) that the CERC rejected the price cap approach to regulation because Professor Littlechild could not give a convincing answer to how he chose 'X'.

[51] In telecom, detailed regulation would be even worse than price cap regulation. Here, beyond a price cap the regulator has to worry about new technology and its diffusion, so that the benefits of technological change (the major source of efficiency gain) lead to expansion of the market, new products, and low prices to the consumer. As such ensuring an industrial structure with low barriers to entry would be of primary importance in telecom. In telecom, it is possible to argue that regulation should be concerned less with tariffs and returns, and more with ensuring that the technological drivers are allowed full play, and that diffusion of cost-reducing technology takes place.

[52] Indeed the investment tax credit could be linked to investments in the rural and sparse component of the distribution system and in investments in equipment like electric metres, that allow time of use (ToU) pricing, etc. if they are envisaged right at the beginning of the reform process.

Moreover, it is not difficult to predict reasonable values for X in the power sector, since much of the power industry in India in the post-reform period would be in a catching up phase vis-à-vis other more efficiently organized countries. As the reform restores managerial incentives for efficiency through both competitive measures and regulation, it would be not too difficult to base X on a comparative study of happenings elsewhere. That would give the regulator enough time to build the necessary skills to arrive at X periodically.

Since retaining generation along with distribution in zonal companies would make such companies marketable, privatization could be very quickly carried out (even with present levels of overmanning). Privatization[53] would be necessary to eliminate theft and restore managerial incentives, which would have to be the immediate concern of any reform.

### Privatization Proceeds Should Go Towards Augmenting Transmission Assets

The considerable proceeds from such privatization (assuming that regulatory clarity has emerged by then), and a price cap regulatory formula that is entirely transparent and valid over the next five to eight years, would release resources for the state government to put into transmission assets. We have discussed earlier why this is important. Analyses of deviation of traded or market prices from generation costs across existing market systems reveal that the 'degree of monopoly' exhibited by generators is a function not only of concentration, but also of grid restrictions, and the proportion of 'near zero variable cost power', typically hydropower, in the system.

Besides price cap regulation for transmission operations in the public sector, transmission companies would have to provide access to all potential users of the transmission: generating companies, distribution companies including those with generators' assets, outside suppliers of power, the NTPC or Central Power Corporations (CPCs) from stations outside the SEB in question, or the adjoining SEBs, and large captive

---

[53] We know that many public sector undertakings (PSUs) in Sweden, Norway, US, Korea, and China, to name first a few countries, and even in India (NTPC for example), especially in utilities, perform very efficiently. It is always true that if the SEBs could be corporatized, and truly distanced from government, and dealt with through an annual contract alone, leaving its managers operational and administrative functions, then they would perform efficiently. But this has remained a futile hope in India, since governments in India would never really 'give' this autonomy. In India today, only disinvestment can restore managerial autonomy and bring about ownership of responsibility in PSUs that have veered far from task orientation.

generators. There is considerable potential of large captive generators to offer competition to utility generators, especially in many SEBs with an industrial base, given fairly large installed capacity in captive generation and lower PLFs presently at such stations,[54] under appropriate regulation.

## MARKET CONDUCT

### Captive Producers (CPs) and Bulk Buyers Crucial for Competition

Very early in the market-forming process, bulk buyers of power should be allowed to purchase their power directly from any supplier generating company, another distribution company not in its area, a party outside the state, a captive generator, or any combination of these, subject only to grid restrictions and system integrity requirements. The market for power would be a market for wholesale power to trade surpluses and deficits of distribution companies[55] with generating assets, with generating companies and among themselves, plus a market for bulk retail power.[56] This would mean that access rules to distribution company assets would have to be defined for bulk users, for whom the distribution company's wires business is separate from power purchase.

Allowing all loads at 1 MW or above and all CPs with installed capacity 1 MW or above, the right of access to the transmission/distribution lines would be the key to bringing about competitive pressure. For such customers/entities, the sale and purchase of power is completely separated from its carriage. For them the transmission/distribution companies, including DGCs operate as common carriers (which are regulated).

The rules for market making would have to be spelt out by the TRANSCO, after system and market simulation studies, which would alert it to possible pitfalls. But in the meantime simple rules that insist upon matched contracts by the TRANSCO, for sale and supply with less than 5 per cent variation, before allowing use of the grid to all participants, would serve the purpose. Deviations could then invite significant and asymmetric penalties. They would of course have to be checked for systemic feasibility, given the grid capacities, through a simple simulation programme.

Hydropower stations should be bundled together and sold as a separate generating company (HYGEN). The advantage in such a company is that it could specialize in offering power that caters to unforeseen demand. During monsoons when the run-off is available, the HYGEN would have an incentive to lower its price considerably. This would make coal-using base stations schedule their annual planned maintenance during this period. The HYGEN would then develop as a specialist peak power player and lead market developments in peaking power.

### Export and Import Tariffs

Gujarat has a long-term comparative disadvantage vis-à-vis states like Andhra Pradesh, Madhya Pradesh, Maharashtra, Bihar, and Orissa in generation of power, since it has few hydro assets and hardly any reserves of coal. Lignite remains problematic, and a gas-based strategy is contingent on low gas prices and quick development of coastal infrastructure. Moreover, imported fuels would introduce significant foreign exchange risk for Gujarat-based generators. Similarly, interior states like Punjab and Haryana would be dependent upon the development of internal transport for fuel movements. They would be particularly vulnerable to local pricing by railways and the pricing strategies of oil/gas pipeline companies, since primary energy would have to travel from the coast or from distant gas/oilfields. Given that transport costs continue to be administered and oil pipelines have been suppressed in the past, the relative advantages of the states, for coal- and gas-using power would have to be discovered as liberalization proceeds.

This means that as the national market develops, or even before, when it becomes possible to transmit power

---

[54] Emanating largely out of the present captive generation policy, which places severe restrictions on captive generators attempting to sell 'surplus' power. It is perhaps in the captive power policies of the SEBs that the true extent of the distortions caused by cascading effect of the inverted tariff are revealed. Already tariffs for industrial power are higher than the cost of self-generation. If the costs of unreliability are also included, most bulk users would have be able to install capacities to operate at even PLFs less than 40 per cent. The current captive policy makes it difficult or impossible to sell surplus power. CPs can sell only to related units, at transmission/distribution costs set by the SEB at absurdly high levels, in the hope that by 'force' they can retain their 'best' customers. Indeed, if the captive policy is completely liberalized, the present inverted tariffs' irrationality would be quickly exposed and correct restructuring to put the electricity system on a rational basis can begin to be seriously considered.

[55] At off-peak periods when wholesale prices are below variable costs of expensive distribution-cum-generating stations, they would enter the market to buy power (cheaply) from the pool suppliers.

[56] It is bulk retail power that has created a market for retail power in the UK, which first attempted markets in retail power. Even there, over 95 per cent of the retail consumers, despite choice, buy power from their own regional distribution companies. It is only the bulk users who can actually take advantage of competitive structures.

in larger amounts across regions,[57] there would be a period when generators in states like Gujarat would face competition from outside the state.[58]

There is, therefore, a need to recognize this competitive pressure from outside the state at the outset of the reform process, and to plan for the same. To cap the risk emanating from this future possibility, the regulator would have to impose a tariff on imports of power from outside the state, with a pre-announced schedule to lower the same and ultimately eliminate it altogether. It would be necessary to 'control' imports through such a price-based mechanism rather than through grid restrictions or quantitative restrictions. Besides the well-known advantages of tariffication, this measure would have the added advantage of signalling the generators on location choice. If, for example, imports grow faster than the Gujarat market for retail sales, then it would be clear that generating companies would have to increasingly locate elsewhere to retain competitive potential or use better technology.[59] It would also give the right signals to the transmission company on investment choice.

### Variations in Value of Distribution Assets and Territory are Not a Major Problem in Privatization

To allow even the wholesale market for deficits and surpluses, and a 'bulk retail' market for captive procedures (as both consumers and sellers), the composition of the distribution-cum-generating companies is important. Distribution being a natural geographical monopoly, it is desirable that the current distribution zones that have evolved naturally should constitute the core of the distribution companies.[60] Differences in

terms of consumer mix, ratio of low voltage lines to high voltage lines, of distribution transformers to substations, should be of secondary importance. This is because if subsidization is taken care of externally and not through the distribution companies, then the issue is only one of small differences. Thus a distribution zone with a larger proportion of rural customers and sparse networks and lower consumption per metre[61] would show higher distribution costs per unit of power distributed or sold. Basic asymmetry in the form of large (bulk) power consumers is eliminated by defining such entities as 'bulk consumers' who are able to take part in the power market, using the distribution company's wires for a fee. Despite this measure, it would no doubt be true that the average distribution cost would vary across zones, so that the offer price for purchase of bulk power by a distribution company with high costs of distribution would be lower, given uniform price caps on all consumers.

If the price cap were such as to allow all distribution companies, including one with (structural) high cost, the desirable returns, then those with lower costs would make high profits. This would be so unless the price elasticity of demand (assuming existence of supply) is such as to lower the final effective price to consumers of the favourably disposed distribution company. This is unlikely in the immediate post-reform period, when overall supply restrictions would operate. The way out would be to bundle the generation plants with the lowest marginal costs to the distribution company with high costs, in general, to bundle generation assets and distribution in such a way as to ensure that total costs of generation do not vary by more than 10 per cent. Variation within this range would not be a problem since the market valuation would most certainly adjust to take care of such asymmetry.[62]

---

[57] As the planned investments by the PGCIL materialize the national grid would take shape.

[58] Thus even today a large pithead-based coal station in Madhya Pradesh/Maharashtra, or even distant Orissa, can deliver base power at less than Rs 2.30 per unit (wholesale), with full recovery of cost.

[59] It is presumed that simultaneously reforms that bring about competition in generation would be pursued in most states, and grid capacities developed to allow long-distance transport of power in large quantities. The constraints imposed by the current grid code are discussed in section 6.1 of this report.

[60] There is a tendency among state bureaucracies to show quick privatization of distribution to attempt to privatize a large urban area with much surrounding industrial demand, 'separating' the same from the rural areas to which the urban area is integrally bound. This arises from the myth of 'non-viability' of zones with much agricultural or non-industrial demand. Thus in Gujarat there are moves to pick the Baroda urban and suburban circles and privatize the same, to 'meet' certain conditions of the Asian Development Bank from which Gujarat expects a bigger loan!

Zones have to be largely derived from the grid and distribution networks, their boundaries being such as to minimize the number of segments that interconnect the zones. Otherwise, assignment of responsibility in situations of failure or load backdown would be a nightmare. The current structure of the zones and distribution networks has evolved in a scientific manner, and it is important that the structure is not disturbed in an unnatural carving out of zones based on the market segments! This would amount to creating a structural distortion in response to a prior tariff and agency distortion.

[61] Official data, though, show very high consumption in agriculture per metre.

[62] The important issue here is to make available reliable and detailed information on the status of networks, distribution loss (technical), and such other information vital to the estimation of costs well before the financial bids take place.

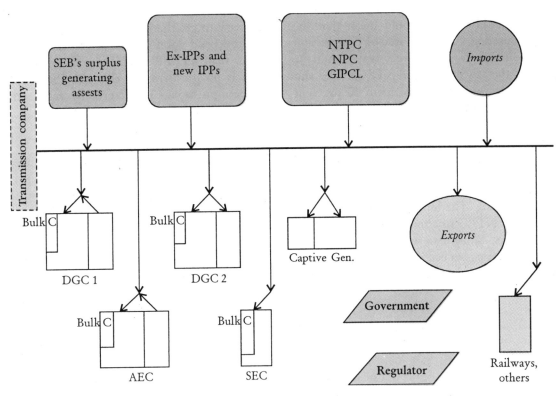

Fig. 6.2.1: The proposed competitive structure of the electric power industry.

### Returns to Scarcity to be Capped Through Demand Backdown Rules

The broader issue really is between generators and distributors, who would be able to mop up the returns to scarcity as they arise. The reform in advanced capitalist countries started from a situation of overall low PLFs (in the range of 35 per cent to 50 per cent), so that generation companies have not been able to mop up the entire value of scarcity. Overriding rules for supply and availability of generators and appropriate rules for market pricing and for demand backdown would be called for. In situations of overall shortage, because some generation assets are bundled with distribution, there is less likelihood of steep market-clearing prices emerging, if the incentive for demand to back down is also sufficiently large.

## PRIOR CONTRACTS

### Retention of Gains of Marketization Within the System Desirable

Typically, SEBs hold contracts with CPCs like the NTPC, National Hydro Power Corporation Limited (NHPC), NPC, Damodar Valley Corporation (DVC), etc. for power purchase. Of these those with the NTPC are most valuable to the SEBs, since the average cost of supply of power of the NTPC under the various Bulk Purchase and Sales Agreements (BPSA) c. 1998 was as

low as 109 paise. Even in the new units like the Simadri Power Project in Andhra Pradesh, where the NTPC has been allowed far better returns that is, 20–2 per cent than the usual 12 per cent, the price of power would be quite reasonable and far lower than that of any IPP.

Presently, the GEB, for example, holds contracts with the NTPC for power supply from the NTPC's coal-based stations at Korba and Vindhyachal, its gas-based stations at Kawas and Jhanor, and with the NPC. The current average cost of power purchase is less than Rs 1.70. Thus the bulk purchase agreement with these central PSUs is an asset of great value to the GEB. The 'market-clearing' prices in the post-reform period, with the arrangements and strategy outlined in this paper, would most certainly be significantly above these prices. Roughly, energy purchases amounted to 49 per cent of generation. Therefore it is vital that the value of these BPSAs with the NTPC and NPC, till they come up for renewal in the cycle after the reform is internalized by the state to a great extent.[63] The NTPC would naturally welcome a change since then it would not have to wait for the expiry of the currently valid BPSAs, if part of the difference between the market prices and NTPC's expected BPSA prices, at current load factors, can in the

---

[63] We know that in England and Wales there were huge benefits of privatization and reform. About a third of these benefits accrued to the Electricitie de France (EdF), which was able to supply to the pool at prices higher than its original contract prices.

future go to the NTPC. This would mean that the NTPC could be used as a major source of competition in the generation sector. The correct way would be to first arrive at the schedule of the NTPC's sales and the prices it realizes over the range from 10 per cent of its current maximum supply to full supply. The schedule would obviously be such as to decline with supply. The NTPC can then be offered a schedule as given in Fig. 6.2.2 for any particular market price. It is important, nevertheless, that the NTPC does not use its significant market power to its advantage by methods such as grid congesting. The long-term solution would be for units of the NTPC to compete with each other and other generators. Along with such stipulations, if the *regions* rather than states can become the market system, the best results can be had as discussed in detail earlier in the chapter.

necessary to get the full benefits of competition. Much would depend upon market prices. If market prices are higher than the IPP's implicit prices at that time then there is no problem but this is highly unlikely since competition would most certainly reduce the average prices of wholesale power.[64]

### The Problem Can be Overcome

The contracts with the IPPs can be approached in several ways. One way would be to threaten to renege on the contracts by pointing out that they were 'unfair'.[65] Then a negotiated deal which allows the IPPs to quench their contracts and be full-fledged market participants (merchant generators) and earn somewhat lower rates of return then their currently projected returns at 20 to 30 per cent equity capital would be possible. This is an option that would necessitate a

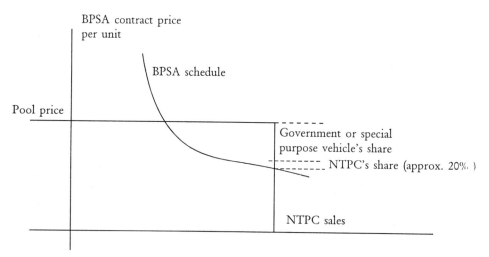

**Fig. 6.2.2:** Extinguishing BPSA contracts of SEBs with the NTPC.

This is one way, and probably the best way, to deal with favourable contracts that the SEBs have with other power producers. The cash flows so generated could be used to enhance transmission infrastructure, finance the on-going expenses of the office of the regulator, carry out a voluntary retirement scheme (VRS), or even extinguish IPP contracts.

### IPP Contracts are a Problem to Competition in Generation

Contracts with IPPs would be a problem to the SEBs attempting reform of generation to make generation competitive. Even in distribution privatization, these 'sweet' contracts would have to be picked up by the inheritor companies, and this they would not do unless appropriate tariff adjustments are made, such as a recovery for 'stranded contracts'. A strategy that addresses this problem and 'extinguishes' IPP contracts would be

political commitment to replace IPPs, and would have, the 'negative' consequences of a state going back on its earlier agreements. On this again many economists have with much logic, argued that the IPP in coming to a deal with the state took a bet that these favourable contracts would continue, and that the regulatory policy regime would continue. The high return then is only a rent to this speculation. Moreover, it has no doubt been proved empirically in similar situations of regulation-created

[64] Only if demand were to grow at rates much higher than those currently envisaged, or those which have obtained in the immediate past, is the contrary situation likely. About a third of all power fed into the GEB system, for example, is purchased from the NTPC at low cost as mentioned earlier. This would keep market prices pretty low, almost certainly lower than IPP's contract prices.

[65] Unlike Maharashtra or Karnataka, Gujarat is not going to be too severely burdened by patently 'unfair' contracts. For many other states this is not an issue.

rents that the market does not, with absolute certainly expect such returns. If events do not turn out as expected, so be it. There is also the issue of whom to compensate if the ownership of these contracts changes, as happens in the case of widely held corporations. Thus it would be wise on the part of a state planning true reform and marketization to begin by insisting upon wide dispersal of at least part of the shareholding. Moreover, this would have the benefit that market price of the stock of IPPs would change to reflect increasing probability of non-realization of rents. Naturally, any attempt to fight back the change that removes rents would be blunted to that extent. On the other hand, if the commitment to a fair market-based reform and restructuring of the electricity sector is strong and credibly pursued, and seen as such, then constituents for change would be strong enough to overcome the difficulties in renegotiating these contracts on the lines outlined here.

A second approach would be to agree to give the IPP a part of the difference in revenues at contract prices and projected market clearing prices (which can be simulated), up front, in capitalized from, negotiating the period thus considered. In exchange the IPP gives up its PPA contract. This arrangement has the merit of ensuring that the capacities of the IPP would result in competition, but has the significant disadvantage that the state, over the life of the PPA as envisaged originally, would pay out to the IPP. In other words, the more the reform succeeds in lowering the generation prices, the greater is the outflow from the state!

## Cajoling IPPs to Trade Political and Regulatory Risks for Market Risk

A third alternative would be as follows: As part of the regulatory strategy the state announces that its policy would be to go in for a competitive market-based solution for generation, and simultaneously imposes upon IPPs the condition that 20 per cent of their stock would have to be traded in the domestic market. The stock price then would reflect the emerging uncertainties with regard to IPPs, and would correctly value the IPP/PPA contracts. The difference between market capitalization of the IPP and the cost of setting up a similar capacity plant as a competitive generator, would be the premium value, if any, of the IPP/PPA contract. The IPP would then be willing to give up its contract and become a player in the market, if a value close to this premium can be transferred to it. This can be done in several ways. One would be to provide this directly from the budget once the bids for privatization and marketization are known. An interesting way would be to offer a bid amount handicap for the SEB

assets-distribution-cum-generation companies and other un-attached generating companies, equal to the premium value. Care would have to be taken to communicate to the market the government's firm intention of going ahead with a market-based competitive solution. In that case, the bid process would have to include the clause that the IPP would be bundled with a distribution company. So a bid from a third party would have to be a joint bid for the IPP (without its contract premium) and the other bids for the two assets separately. Yet this approach would reduce the potential for competition. The best option would be to extinguish one of the contracts in the manner now outlined here. Once again the Gujarat case is used as an example. One way to look at IPP contracts is to recognize that the original policy under which the IPPs came about is the guaranteed 16 per cent return at 68.5 per cent PLF. Returns above these are specific to the project and the government is under no legal requirement to protect the same. These are essentially returns to 'regulatory speculation' and to 'efficiency'. As such only the 16 per cent on equity share capital need be treated as arising out of stranded contracts and provided for. Several options are then available. One would be to buy out the IPP's equity at a value equal to the capitalized value of a stream of returns at 16 per cent for twenty years (the life of the project). Thus for Re 1 of equity, the cost would be Rs 1.21 approximately, at a discount rate of 12 per cent. Since IPP costs per MW are higher than current costs, both because of padding of costs, and fall in turbine and equipment costs since the time the IPPs reached financial closure, the net cost of buying up IPPs and starting on a clean slate is likely to be between 0.8 crore and 1.3 crore per MW. Thus, if competitive pricing of electricity is to be the norm, this loss would have to be covered by the government, unless it wants to renege on IPP contracts. Therefore, a certain provision for 'stranded contracts' would have to be made, but only initially. It would be best to provide for this uniformly across all consumers as a separate charge per KwH of electricity consumed, and the fund so created used to service the financial cost of extinguishing IPP contracts at between 0.8 crore and 1.3 crore per MW, at the very beginning.

Inflow from the BPSA contracts at a rate of approximately Re 1.0 on every unit from BPSA suppliers would accrue to the special purpose vehicle (SPV) set up for privatization. This is the difference between average contract price under various BPSA (Rs 1.38 ~ 1.50) and long-run marginal cost of bulk power at Rs 2.5 per KwH. Thus the actual credit on this account per year for the Gujarat system would be 1293 MW (the GEB's share of CPCs' capacity) * 0.75 (PLF) * (1 – 0.15) (distribution losses) = Rs 849 crore per year. Assuming the BPSAs have an average residual life of five years, this cash flow would have a present value of approximately Rs 3000 crore. This would allow the government (which holds these lucrative contracts) to extinguish up to between 2300 MW and 3800 MW of IPP capacity, if the appropriate SPV for restructuring can be created.

Thus the increase in tariffs that would have to be provided for, for the 'stranded contracts' to be extinguished, may not be particularly large if the value of the BPSAs can be nearly fully internalized.

Alternatively an SPV to recover stranded contracts could be set up, which would buy power from IPPs and CPCs, and market and sell the same to DGCs and bulk buyers. The SPV needs to be constituted so that it has a life of twenty years, is completely transparent, and entirely open to the regulator and the public. It would have the mandate to sell power at the lowest feasible cost to DGCs and others, and shares to the same could be linked to guaranteed access to power in proportion to the shares held by industry and others including the DGCs. This would be only an inferior solution to outright purchase and resale of IPPs, since the SPV would have a life of twenty years, and most importantly would also lock the system firmly to the cost of the inflexibility of fuel choice embedded in PPA contracts. It would also mean major organization effort on the part of the restructuring authority to create the SPV with appropriate incentives structure for its owners and managers to perform their tasks as visualized.

The problem of overcoming the IPP contracts may thus not be as difficult as it appears.[66] A strong and credible commitment to marketization of generation and privatization that is communicated well would be vital to the success of any approach that is finally adopted. Indeed the distinct possibility arises that the IPPs, with a little nudging from the state, may be quite willing to trade political and administration risk for market risk. That the political risks never really disappear in concession-based projects in a competitive democracy like India is obvious. Even as the Enron project after its cancellation and re-examination by the Maharashtra government seemed to be on firm ground, the new government in Maharashtra has announced its decision to re-examine the project (for the second time!), which again introduces fundamental uncertainty into the project. Most companies and promoters would not be able to bear this kind of risk, even if the rewards

were large. It is almost given that, with changes in state governments, IPPs of the previous regime are closely scrutinized. In these circumstances, a credible option to trade such uncertainties with market risk, (which tends to be bounded, at least in the case of electricity) would be welcome.[67] Prior ruling to dilute the shareholding of IPPs in the local market would be very helpful. To sweeten the exchange of political and policy risk for market risk, tax incentives linked to expansion of capacity could also be made available to the IPPs.

## LABOUR AND MODALITIES

The success of the restructuring would crucially depend upon the process adopted and on fixing target dates for significant events in the process much before the process begins.

The first step would be to appoint the disinvestment and restructuring commissioner (RC) with the necessary skills, and the power to operate independently and in the consumers' long-term interest. The next would be to define his terms of appointment, granting him complete insulation from the political process and from day-to-day functioning of government. The government would have to commit to adhere to the overall philosophy of the restructuring and agree to pilot the required bills in the assembly, to amend and repeal such acts as necessary, and bring in fresh legislation. It also has to provide such resources as required for restructuring and for subsidization if it so chooses. The RC would have to have extraordinary powers to supersede the Board of the SEB,[68] and transfer top officials if necessary, so that the process of disinvestment is not hindered by vested interests. His office would need to be provided with funds to cover the cost of studies, preparation of legal documents, negotiations, consultant services, and asset revaluation that may be required.

Demand for power would, in the long term, grow at average rates that can be expected to be no less than 4.5

---

[66] Mr M. Y. Rao, ex-chairman of the Orissa State Electricity Board (OSEB), and the architect of the Orissa Reforms tells me that in the PPAs signed by the OSEB, a clause had been introduced that the contract would not contradict any future rulings by the independent regulator. This may provide a legal loophole to get out of IPP contracts.

[67] Indeed an unwillingness to trade away political risk for market risk by a business should alert us to the propriety of the business. In well-functioning market economies, it is government that should bear the political risk, not business. Business should and would show a tendency (rightly) to reduce the political risk that it bears. The political risk that a company like the Dabhol Power Company Ltd. (DPC) bears is enormous if we admit the possibility that states can rescind on contracts. DPC may itself be well hedged up to a point, given that it would have taken out policies against such risk with the Multilateral Investment Guarantee Agency (MIGA) and other bodies. A high return to political risk is another way of saying that rents are generated in political uncertainty.

[68] This is necessary in the majority of SEBs; but while desirable may not be necessary in the case of Maharashtra and Tamil Nadu, where corruption is not rampant.

per cent, with a GDP growth of 5 per cent, which is the least that one can expect. In all likelihood, with the right macroeconomic policies for growth, the power sector would grow at rates in excess of 6 per cent per annum for many years to come. Current surplus labour can potentially be absorbed within the system in the long run. Yet it would be desirable to quickly shed surplus labour to the extent seen fit by the inheritor companies. This would protect systemic efficiency and remove the distortions (in technology choice, managerial practices, and assessment of costs). Politically though, a median path that allows a liberal VRS for all SEB staff, especially for office and commercial staff and departments where the excess is large, would be appropriate. The government would have to announce upfront that the restructuring would not result in compulsory retrenchment. The actual exercise of implementing the VRS would have to be left to the inheritor companies since they would be best able to assess the potential and value of employees. A fund to cover the VRS of as much as 25 per cent of the current staff would have to be created by the government, and made available to the inheritor companies.

Some crude estimates of the VRS cost could be arrived at for the Gujarat system. The total wage, salary, and terminal benefit costs of 25 per cent of the employees in 1996–7 (the latest year for which the annual report of the GEB was available) was Rs 121 crore or Rs 0.91 lakh per person for approximately 12,130 persons (excess manpower). Assuming a coverage of 50 per cent of current salary for the remaining working life of the employee, and at 50 per cent of the terminal salary for pension, and with a life expectancy of 72 years and retirement age of 58 years, the VRS cost (at 3 per cent real rate of interest) would be Rs 1119 crore, or Rs 8.42 lakh per person. At 70 per cent coverage of salary it would amount to Rs 1567 crore and Rs 11.8 lakh per person. Thus a fund of between Rs 1200 and 1600 crore would be required to operationalize a near complete shedding of excess manpower. A commitment to make available to the inheritor companies up to that amount for the VRS would have to be made by the government. An incentive of about one-tenth the amount should be allowed to the privatized companies that retain manpower in anticipation of future requirements, for a period of five years. A detailed study to assess the actual distribution of excess manpower across various locations and activities would be necessary. The second charge on the privatization proceeds would have to be towards coverage of the VRS, the first being to 'buy' out the stranded contracts.

The actual details of bundling generating assets with distribution zones or territories can be left to the bid process, as long as the overall process and objectives of the reform are clarified early enough and complete transparency is ensured through appropriate processes. Thus the terms covering the appointment of the restructuring commissioner should bind him to transparent processes and to disclosure of information. All relevant information generated by the various consultancy studies and other reports ought to be made public and available to the bidder, and they in turn should be encouraged to make their own investigations and studies, especially with regard to excess manpower, state of assets and equipment, and the extent and nature of demand. There is likely to be much asymmetry in the value of assets and territories to potential bidders depending upon the nature of their complementary assets and skills.

## CONCLUSION

True reform and restructuring of any SEB in India would have to start with putting the consumers' interest foremost. The agency failure in nearly all SEBs, which has resulted in enormous leakage of revenue from the system would have to be addressed first. This would call for privatization of distribution and change in the institutional mechanism for the administration of the subsidy.

Market competition in generation, through the development of a hybrid wholesale and retail (for bulk consumers alone) market is the need of the hour. In this chapter a model for restructuring that would result in market competition in generation has been proposed. It is not a market for all the electricity in the system, but largely a market that would allow distribution-cum-generation companies to purchase power from each other and form pure generators; and would also allow bulk purchasers and captive generators the choice of supply and sale. A market for generation, while allowing distribution companies the comfort of having some distribution assets, would lead to quicker development of the market and facilitate privatization.

The transmission assets of the SEB are best managed by the state with less than 50 per cent shareholding by the state government, all other shares being held by consumer interests including farmers' cooperatives, households and industry associations, and at least 25 per cent of the stock disbursed through the stock market.

The remaining assets of the SEBs are most conveniently split into a few (perhaps zonal) distribution companies, with some generating assets in-house up to about 40–50 per cent of throughput. Surplus-generating assets of the SEBs could be sold as an independent generating company. All hydel capacities need to be bundled and sold as a separate company.

Distribution companies would have to be put on price cap regulation for their distribution business. Without 'light' price cap regulation, marketization would be very difficult. (With detailed regulation, the best that would be possible is to sell the SEBs as near vertically integrated companies. This would introduce considerable regulatory risk over the medium term and a high probability that the integrated companies would capture the regulator. The high regulatory risk in the short term would result in low values being realized for the SEBs' assets. With detailed regulation, it may be better to merely corporatize SEBs and offload some of the stock in the stock market, and attempt a management overhaul. The SEBs or the government on behalf of the SEBs would then have to carry the burden of the PPAs with IPPs that have already been signed.)

Good values would be realized in the privatization of SEBs like those in Gujarat, Maharashtra, Tamil Nadu, and Rajasthan when carried out in the manner described herein. The surplus so generated could be quickly invested in augmenting transmission assets of the transmission company, so that a situation of no congestion, in the normal working of the system, is quickly reached. A key to ensuring that market clearing prices are near long-run marginal costs would lie in having adequate capacity in the transmission system to allow alternative sourcing for each of the segments of load, and in extinguishing IPP contracts, 'forcing' IPPs to operate as competitive generators.

Transparency, especially with respect to information access, including to common citizens, would be important in reducing the hidden risks of change. Once the first stage of the bid process, which checks out the financial and managerial capacities of bidders, is over all shortlisted bidders must be allowed to have complete access to all information with the SEB. Moreover, they ought to be allowed and encouraged to conduct independent studies and investigations with regard to the quality of assets, demand and its growth, consumer mix, and system parameters.

Access to transmission of bulk consumers and of captive generators above a certain size (1 MW for buyers and average sale equivalent to 1 MW for generators, to start with), at standard access charges subject to price cap regulation, would be necessary. This would bring in competition for generation right at the start of the reform process.

Transmission would also have to be operated as a regulated monopoly, desirably on the RPI – X-type formula. Ideally, the transmission charges should be a three-part tariff, each of which is subject to price cap. The three parts would have to be connection charges (which depend on the capacity connected), line-loss or 'distance' charges (based on the current losses in transmission), and congestion charges. The point is that there should be sufficient returns to congestion to allow the transmission company to correctly identify the segments for investments. Yet distortion in the tariff formula that provides an incentive to maximize the returns to congestion should be avoided.

The BPSA contracts with the NTPC or NPC are expected to be beneficial to the system after marketization, since the implied contract prices then are likely to be lower than the market prices that would prevail. In contrast, the IPP contracts are likely to be adverse to the SEBs since the implied PPA prices then would most certainly be higher than the market prices. Both sets of contracts would have to be extinguished in ways that would release the full potential for competition in the system. The BPSAs would pose no basic problem, since doing nothing would mean that the NTPC, given its low costs, would gain from higher market prices. Therefore they could be easily extinguished by sharing part of the price difference (20 per cent) with the NTPC and keeping the rest with the SEBs for subsidies and investment in the transmission company.

The IPP contracts would pose a significant problem which would have to be carefully dealt with. The best strategy would be to nudge them into a willingness to exchange their current high political and regulatory risks for market risk. The presence of both groups in the generation market would be vital to its functioning. And with these players the scope for price formation significantly above costs would be quite small.

The most optimal way to carry out the same would be to communicate effectively and credibly the government's firm determination to move towards a competitive market model in generation of electricity. Simultaneously the government should rule that at least 25 per cent of the shareholding of IPPs be offloaded in the local stock market. Then the market price would reflect the true premium value (if any) of the IPPs' contract with the SEB and the state. As the reform and restructuring takes place in earnest, the willingness of IPPs to trade their political and regulatory risks for market risk would improve. IPPs could also be bought out at an extra cost of between Rs 0.8 and 1.3 crore per MW.

Initially an import tax on electricity from outside the system would have to be imposed even as connectivity with the national grid and the grids of contiguous states is augmented. Yet there must be an upfront announcement of the intention to reduce these tariffs and eliminate them altogether over a specified time period. This would allow some time for adjustment. Such an announcement would ensure that fresh investments and locational and fuel choices are made optimally, since in the long run the comparative advantage of pithead location is likely to be high and generation assets would come up in these locations. Coastal locations too can have advantages and the relative merit of these can only unfold in the future. The commitment that there would be no tariffs, in the long run, would clearly indicate the indifference of the regulator to the location of generation plants, and to the choice of fuel.

Similarly, an export tax would be required in the first few years to have a (second) regulatory handle on market prices. Their removal would have to be based on developments within the state and in neighbouring states. The principle governing the export tax, 'that it would be used to ensure market prices close to long-run marginal costs in a situation of surplus', would have to be announced and widely known.

Possible 'excess' profits accruing to the distribution-cum-generating companies when put on light RPI – X type regulation should be allowed to be appropriated but linked to an investment tax credit on investments in the sector and in other infrastructural areas of priority.

A scheme that subsidizes the farmer through issue of electricity stamps or coupons by the Agriculture/Land Revenue Department, which the farmer uses to pay the distribution-cum-generating companies, is necessary. It would not only allow for capping the subsidies but also overcome the problem of moral hazard in the identification of the consumer. It would also make possible simple price cap regulation for distribution, and for power cost in the early stages before the market for wholesale and retail bulk power has developed. Price differences if any would then be related to cost of supply, time of use, and other aspects such as whether it is interruptible or otherwise. As the reform succeeds and credibility of the system to deliver good quality power is established, the willingness of the farmer to pay would allow a gradual scaling back of subsidies. Stamps would also allow better targeting of the subsidies.

BOX 6.2.1

### California Electricity Markets

ECONIC, N. Y.—*While reporters ogled celebrities at Barbra Streisand's bungalow during the Democratic Convention in Los Angeles, there was a real display of populism 100 miles to the south in San Diego. There politicians have enrolled two million citizens in a scary economic experiment. This year, San Diego became the first city in California to experience the end of state regulation of electricity prices.*

*When California's lawmakers voted to bring the miracle of market competition to electricity, they wrote into the law that homeowners' bills would fall 'by at least 20 per cent'. In fact, bills jumped 124 per cent this August over last. Rather than repudiate this mad market experiment, the federal government and 24 other states, New York included, have rushed to imitate California's lead.*

*Actually, Californians were lucky. Every hour of every day, San Diego Gas and Electric, the local utility, must now buy its electricity at a state auction known as a power pool. On the first hot day this summer, during the noonday heat, the companies that produce the power, newly deregulated, cranked up their bids to $ 9999 per megawatt hour. That's about 5000 per cent more than the once-controlled price of $ 20, but it could have been worse. According to those inside the secretive auction agency, sellers assumed the pool's computers could handle only four-digit bids. In fact, the computers could have accepted bids for seven figures and bankrupted a chunk of the state in a day.*

*One can trace California's electricity market plague largely to a single source, Daniel Fessler. In the early 1990s, Mr Fessler, then president of the state's Public Utilities Commission, developed an infatuation with one of Margaret Thatcher's free-market ventures: the troubled England-Wales Power Pool.*

*How strange. Britons pay about 70 per cent more for electricity than Americans. That's hardly a surprise, as each day around tea time, when England's usage peaks, a small clique of power plant owners take over the electricity auction, bidding up prices by 200 to 2000 per cent.*

*In the United States, utilities vowed they would play no such tricks if California removed the limits on profits that have been at the core of regulation policy for the past 100 years. The promise lasted several months, during which time five giant international electricity sellers—all new to California—imported the techniques they'd learned in Britain: 'stacking,' 'cramming,' 'phantom scheduling' and other maneuvers designed to manipulate the bidding process and in a single month produce profits once permitted for an entire year.*

*....But in San Diego, something extraordinary happened. This month, thousands joined an unprecedented consumers' boycott. The power companies can send out their bloated bills, but the tanned masses won't pay. Refuseniks include the Council of Churches, the school district and—without a hint of shame—Steve Peace, a state senator who sponsored the deregulation law....* [Extracts from Gregory Plaast, 'States Deregulate Energy at Their Peril', *New York Times*, 25 August 2000 (from the web)]

Comments:

Several things have contributed to this mess in San Diego, California. Electricity consumption especially by the rich, is truly price inelastic over a wide range. So a pure price adjustment model can indeed result in vast peak clearing prices. This aspect of supply adjustment needs to be understood when the system is shiftable (industrial demand is low).

The California system while 'single', is actually fragmented because of crucial shortages in grid capacities, a result of earlier return on investment (ROI) regulation which had allowed utilities to set up high cost power locally, since the cost plus regime created disincentives to search for globally optimal solutions. Today the rules are such that the transmission in segments can be congested by suppliers to isolate cities and portions of the system with their large inelastic household demand. And then prices can be made to go through the roof. This had been pointed out by some observers but was apparently ignored by the regulator.

The regulators could have anticipated such a situation by simulation exercises, under the given rules, and realized that, until efficient capacities come up, and transmission links improve, the only solution would be a reasonable peak price (like the stock market breaker) cap at about $ 40–50 per MwH, allowing even diesel-generating sets to operate profitably. This was not done!

The other point is that transmission itself would have to be managed in a non-profit, or regulated profit mode. Alternately, restrictions on ownership of the transmission companies would have enabled other larger segments in the value added chain (generation and distribution) to be commercially directed without the need for regulation. Transmission, even with new-fangled approaches like auction of capacities, remains problematic when marketized. It may be useful to see transmission as in part having a regulatory dimension, like a stock exchange! These niceties have not found much recognition in discussions relating to deregulation.

The industry structure did not get the attention it should have had from the regulator. This is despite the experience of the UK, where the regulator, after the pool scheme came into effect, had to fix Powergen and National Power by asking them to disinvest out of certain assets. (The 'pool' continues to have significantly higher prices than long-run average costs (LRACs.) Large players across all segments continue in the California system. The higher than anticipated growth, especially of California and nearby states, fuelled by the Information Technology revolution and higher overall US growth rates, has created very large demands especially for peaking power.

The more worrisome aspect to the whole marketization of electricity agenda is the practical soundness of the idea that generation can be made competitive in a price auction market. We know that the England & Wales (EW), New Zealand (NZ), and Nord pools have worked with varying deviations of the average clearing prices from the long-run average costs; being always more than the LRAC, but not too far above. The California story calls to question the reasons that many may have assumed to explain success: design, competition among generators and among buyers, and competitive 'structures' to enable the same such as separation of the wires business from trade. Indeed something else, viz. the competition from other sectors, bunker oil, piped gas, and excess capacity in electricity sector may have been more important. While the conditions internal to the sector may have been necessary, are they sufficient?

The clue that competition from other sectors may have been very important is suggested by the developments in California. Summer heat which steps up air-conditioning demand cannot be substituted with direct fuels. But winter demands can be. Among all the large centres of population California, Florida, and Texas would therefore have to be watched carefully in the summer. Indeed, if the competition from other sectors is a necessary part of the success of the marketization model, then on this count the Indian systems are poor candidates for the market model. (This needs recognition.)

Countervailing factors, though, would work in favour of marketization in India. Presently, in India, industrial and agricultural demand shares are very large relative to richer countries. This means that the price-elastic demand component is large, being shiftable on a diurnal cycle, so the market-making processes can build on these specificities. But in the long run if India were as rich as the US, the problems would be more severe since cooling demand would overwhelm all other demands, and seasonally this would also have to be correlated with agricultural demand (diurnal cycle in summer may be less significant.) But in that distant future solar photovoltaic or absorption based air conditioning, using solar heat directly, would have possibly become cost effective. More importantly, much before that day, measurement systems may be able to feed back current clearing prices, and rules could be set up on the home computer to back down systems like air conditioners and water heaters beyond certain prices. The separation of elastic and inelastic components of household demand would then be possible.

Is retail competition worth the effort? Wholesale competition works because a larger part of it is based on price elastic demand, not so much because wholesale markets are easy to craft! But if retail consumers are a large part of the system and do not want interruptible supplies or their price elasticity is very low, then bringing them into the day-to-day market, via 'retail choice', may be counterproductive to the market-making process. After all, inelasticity is a known basis for market failure! Therefore, a separate treatment of power that distinguishes between inelastic and elastic (largely individual and household plus commercial) components may be necessary. While the latter should continue to have some kind of price regulation—the best would be a price cap significantly above the LRAC because the higher the cap, the less probable it is that the ceiling could be hit. Thus in California, and certainly in the cities like San Diego, it should have been no more than 50 per cent above the LRAC. The whole idea that the retail choice is necessary is questionable. Even home based power clearing price indicators and feedback systems to cut off power would not help if power demand is truly price inelastic, as it is in offices and for people who are very rich. Indian systems, with a lot more industrial and agricultural demand and relatively high price elasticities, would actually be more effective for the competition model than the Californian system!

# 7 | INTEGRATED TRANSPORT

## 7.1 THE TRANSPORT SECTOR

*G. Raghuram*

### ESTIMATING DEMAND

The first problem in examining transport infrastructure at the macro level is that there are no reliable estimates of output. Let alone projections, even current estimates of demand for road transport are very weak and are hardly reliable. The problem is quite serious, given that road transport is the primary mode of transportation today.

With the Indian economy expected to grow at around 6 per cent per annum, the transport sector, both passenger and freight, is expected to grow at 7.5 per cent. The income elasticity of demand currently used by the Planning Commission is 1.25. Total freight and passenger traffic was 869 billion tonnes kilometres (btkm) in 1998–9. This has been projected into the future in Table 7.1.1 using the Planning Commission's estimate of elasticity with respect to real gross domestic product (GDP). With the total demand for passenger and freight so arrived at, these are split into rail and road in the ratio of 53:47 for freight and 23.77 for passenger.

Other studies, including one by the Ministry of Surface Transport (MoST), have questioned both the share and absolute figures put out by the Planning Commission, especially for road traffic, claiming that these are underestimates.

The 1991–2 figures so arrived at have been questioned by the World Bank. The World Bank's assessments have been based on demand for expressways (World Bank 1995a). The World Bank also felt that the Planning Commission's figures are underestimates. As per their extrapolation, the rail share in 1998–9 was 33 per cent and 16 per cent, respectively, for freight and passenger. The view of the Indian Railways (IR) is that the rail:road share is closer to 40:60 for freight and 20:80 for passenger today (IR 2000a).

TABLE 7.1.1
Estimates and Projections of Freight and
Passenger Traffic by Rail and Road

*Freight traffic*

| Year | GDP (1980–1 prices) (Rs crs) | Total traffic (btkm) | Rail movement (btkm) | % | Road movement (btkm) | % |
|---|---|---|---|---|---|---|
| 1984–5 | 132,367 | 343 | 182 | 53 | 161 | 47 |
| 1991–2 | 185,503 | 524 | 257 | 49 | 267 | 51 |
| 1998–9 | 281,691 | 869 | 284 | 33 | 585 | 67 |
| *2005–6* | | *1442* | | | | |

*Passenger traffic*

| Year | GDP (1980–1 prices) (Rs crs) | Total traffic (bpkm) | Rail movement (bpkm) | % | Road movement (bpkm) | % |
|---|---|---|---|---|---|---|
| 1984–5 | 132,367 | 966 | 227 | 23 | 739 | 77 |
| 1991–2 | 185,503 | 1477 | 315 | 21 | 1162 | 79 |
| 1998–9 | 281,691 | 2450 | 404 | 16 | 2046 | 84 |
| *2005–6* | | *4065* | | | | |

*Source:* World Bank (1995); IR (1993 and 1999).

This difference in the share of rail in various estimates can partly be attributed to the fact that modes other than rail and road have not yet been formally recognized as being significant! The figures derived by using the multiplier would reflect the total transport demand of all modes, while micro-level studies and the perspectives of IR and MoST are generally limited to rail and road. One way to reconcile this is to estimate the non-rail and non-road modes for freight and passenger. Coastal shipping and pipelines for freight, and airlines for passenger, have gained in significance, especially in the 1990s. The absolute quantities and modal shares for freight and passenger transport for 1998–9 based on my assessments are given in Table 7.1.2.

TABLE 7.1.2
Distribution of Internal Effort for Freight and
Passengers over Various Modes

| | btkm/bpkm | % share |
|---|---|---|
| *Freight* | | |
| Road | 449 | 51.7 |
| Rail | 284 | 32.7 |
| Pipeline (max) | 70 | 8.1 |
| Coastal shipping | 66 | 7.6 |
| Total | 869 | 100.0 |
| *Passenger* | | |
| Road | 2034 | 83.0 |
| Rail | 404 | 16.5 |
| Air | 11 | 0.4 |
| Coastal shipping (max) | 1 | – |
| Total | 2450 | 100.0 |

Air is a maximum of 0.14 btkm.

*Note:* Table 7.1.2 has been derived using documented data for railways and air from CMIE, *Indian Infrastructure*, December 1999. The coastal movement was arrived at from Basic Port Statistics, 1998–9, which give originating tonnes. The lead for coastal freight was assumed as 1600 km (Raghuram 2000a), for coastal passengers towards the islands as 1000 kms, and for the remaining coastal passengers as 100 km. The 100 km is possibly an overestimate, though consequentially insignificant. For pipeline, the capacities and lengths were multiplied and added, with no utilization factor considered. The road figures were estimated to be the balance remaining, based on total transport figures from Table 7.1.1.

For freight transport, total transport effort would be 1442 btkm in 2005–6, given the figure of 869 btkm in 1998–9. For passenger transport, this would imply that the total transport effort would be 4065 billion passenger kilometres (bpkm) in 2005–6, given the figure of 2450 bpkm in 1998–9.

To have more reliable estimates of the output of the transport sector, it would be necessary to make and publish an annual scientific assessment of the road transport tonnes km and passenger km based on reliable sample surveys.

*The 'Golden Quadrilateral' and Spatial Imbalance*
The growth in transport has been, and is expected to be, concentrated on the Mumbai–Delhi–Calcutta–Chennai

'golden quadrilateral', the diagonals of this quadrilateral, a few spurs from the quadrilateral towards certain industrial zones, and the major ports (for both rail and road). This is in keeping with the pattern of industrialization, trade flows, and urbanization. Much industrialization is taking place along the Indian coast, which will always remain an attractive zone for development. Two per cent of road length carries 40 per cent of road traffic in India and one-sixth of the railway network, which forms the golden quadrilateral, carries over two-thirds of all rail traffic. Transport capacity along the key corridors and multimodal handling capacity at the terminals have not kept pace with demand. Traffic congestion, leading to wasteful additional time of travel and environmental pollution, has therefore increased.

The concentration and congestion of traffic also creates the opportunity to relax them. Investments in transport infrastructure can be focused, with high returns, to relaxing the congestion on segments of the quadrilateral. Development of high capacity high speed infrastructure along such corridors, and leveraging alternate corridors for high demand-origin destination links, can then be the investment strategy. This means that no great plans are called for to direct investments to the rail and road networks, at least till such time as congestion is relaxed.

TRANSPORT MYOPIA

Due to insufficient resource allocation and poor management, maintenance of transport infrastructure is poor. This leads to additional wear and tear of transport equipment and further damage to the carriageway. Together they increase pollution unnecessarily and result in avoidable delays in journeys. In addition to the above, due to poor controls or monitoring, safety levels are far below what is desirable.

Fig. 7.1.1 brings out the interlinkages and the feedback effects of this 'transport myopia'.

*Safety*

Safety is adversely affected by the transport myopia. Table 7.1.3 gives a picture of the road deaths in India as compared to developed countries. *India is at least six times worse than the worst of the European countries.*

The true picture of safety on Indian roads may be much worse than what the comparison in Table 7.1.3 would seem to indicate! This is because: (i) many accidents go unreported in India; (ii) nearly 69 per cent of the vehicle population is motorized two wheelers (MTWs), with relatively lower passenger occupancy; and (iii) Indian roads have among the lowest ratio of vehicles to kilometres of roads!

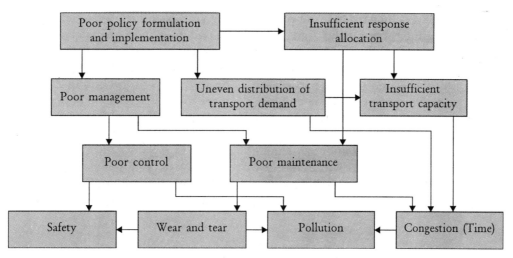

Fig. 7.1.1: Transport myopia.

TABLE 7.1.3
Road Deaths and Vehicles in India and in
Certain Other Countries 1996

| Country | Vehicles/km of road | Road deaths/10,000 vehicles each year |
|---|---|---|
| Britain | 67 | 1.5 |
| Netherlands | 65 | 1.7 |
| Germany | 62 | 2.1 |
| France | 36 | 3.2 |
| Belgium | 32 | 3.2 |
| India | 10 | 20.8 |

*Source*: Bamford (1998); MoST (1998).

The effect of the vehicle profile and increasing indiscipline comes through dramatically if we compare road deaths per bpkm between 1961 and 1996 (Table 7.1.4). The figure for road deaths per 10,000 vehicles was 83.5 in 1961, when the MTW population was 13 per cent, coming down to 20.8 in 1996. This does not mean improved safety on the road. On the contrary, road

TABLE 7.1.4
Road Deaths in India in 1961 and 1996

| | 1961 | 1996 |
|---|---|---|
| Road deaths (no.) | 5547 | 69,800 |
| Vehicles ('0000) | 66.4 | 3355.7 |
| Road deaths/10,000 vehicles | 83.5 | 20.8 |
| Motorized two-wheelers (MTWs) ('0000) | 8.8 | 2311.1 |
| Percentage of MTWs | 13 | 69 |
| Passenger km travelled (bpkm) | 181 | 1368 |
| Road deaths/bpkm | 30.6 | 51.0 |

*Source:* Mohan (2000); Central Institute of Road Transport (2000).
*Note:* The road passenger kilometres have been arrived at using the rail passenger kilometres for 1960–1 and 1995–6, with rail:road modal shares of 30:70 and 20:80 respectively.

deaths per bpkm have increased over the same period from 30.6 to 51.0. Based on a study (Mohan 2000) of eleven locations, amongst the fatalities, over 50 per cent are pedestrians (non-vehicle users) in urban areas, while on the highways 32 per cent are pedestrians, followed by MTW occupants at 24 per cent!

Safety is also a matter of concern for the IR. Compared to the 1960s, IR has improved in safety record. Train accidents per million train km have fallen from 2.7 in 1965–6 to 0.56 in 1998–9 (IR Year Books 1979 and 2000). During the same period, the number of deaths per bpkm fluctuated between 0.0 and 1.2, depending on the number of deaths in a year, which fluctuated between 3 and 406. (It should be noted that the IR only reports the deaths for which it was responsible. There are deaths which occur because of other causes.) Comparing road and rail, it is quite clear that on the parameter of deaths per bpkm, rail is a distinctly safer mode than road.

Air and sea safety are also matters of concern, often critically appraised as 'lesser than desirable' by international bodies such as ICAO and IMO. Apart from deaths in fatal accidents, most accidents result in injuries, damage to vehicles, and loss of cargo. In freight carriage, accidents leading to losses not only happen during transportation, but also during handling and storage necessitated by multimodal movements. The impact of such losses as a proportion of total logistics cost has been estimated for India at 14 per cent (for the year 1987) and is amongst the highest in the world (Raghuram 1992)! (The total logistics cost constitutes 10–12 per cent of GDP). A more recent study by the Ministry of Food and Civil Supplies in 1999 estimated such losses for foodgrains and fruit and vegetables at 10 per cent and 30 per cent of total production, respectively. While 'human failure' is the single largest cause of accidents, the systems and engineering behind the human being are actually responsible in a more meaningful sense.[1]

### Wear and Tear

The wear and tear on vehicles and goods is particularly acute in the road sector. The expert group on commercialization of infrastructure projects estimated the economic losses due to the bad condition of main roads as being of the order of Rs 200 to 300 billion per annum during the late 1990s (Mohan 1996). This is nearly 2 per cent of the GDP! Another way of looking at it is that it is at least about Rs 7000 per road using vehicle per year. Such high wear and tear is also a major cause of pollution and poor safety.

Boxes 7.1.1 and 7.1.2 provides two examples of how poor roads affect vehicle operating costs. One is based on interviews of truckers in Zambia and the other is a more recent statement on Bombay (now Brihanmumbai) Electric Supply and Transport Undertaking (BEST).

### Pollution and Environmental Impact

Pollution is significant on Indian roads, especially in urban areas. Similarly, land acquisition is a problem during, or prior to, construction of transport projects.

---

BOX 7.1.1

#### How Potholes Affect Vehicle Operating Costs

Potholes cause immense damage to vehicles. To better understand the additional costs associated with potholes, the Federation of Zambian Road Hauliers interviewed truckers to compare the running costs of a truck and trailer combination on a road with potholes with those on a road without potholes. The vehicle considered was a lorry and trailer with twenty-two wheels, weighing between 44 and 50 tonnes. The costs estimated are those over and above normal running costs. This excess is equivalent to $ 0.20 per vehicle km.

On a road with bad potholes a driver can either pursue a defensive strategy or ignore the potholes and carry on as usual. If he follows a defensive strategy, he first slows down and changes gears. He then has to negotiate the vehicle through the potholes. This causes extra stress on the tyres, wheel bearings, spring assemblies, spring hangers, chassis, cross members, engine mountings, gear box mountings, brakes, steering assemblies, and shock absorbers. Having negotiated the potholes, he will drive through them at his regular speed, resulting in more damage to the vehicle and tyres and increasing the risk of accidents. The axle pressure on the road now increases by at least three times.

The survey resulted in the following annual expenditures over and above normal running expenditures. It ignores extra fuel consumption, damage to goods, down time of trucks under repair, and accidents caused by potholes and sharp pavement edges.

| Quantity | Item | Unit price | Annual cost |
|---|---|---|---|
| | | ($) | ($) |
| 10 | Extra tyre and tubes | 595 | 5952 |
| 1 | Extra clutch and pressure plate | 1071 | 1071 |
| 4 | Extra wheel bearing | 201 | 803 |
| 1 | Extra set of brake shoes | 1050 | 1050 |
| 1 | Extra set of springs | 1667 | 1667 |
| 4 | Extra spring hangers and bushes | 113 | 452 |
| – | Welding electrodes/oxyacetylene: for body chassis and cross member damage, engine and cabin mountings (repair cost) | 952 | 952 |
| 1 | Extra steering assembly | 1874 | 1874 |
| 4 | Extra shock absorbers | 128 | 510 |
| | Total annual costs attributable to potholes | | 14,331 |

*Sources:* (i) Federation of Zambian Road Hauliers Ltd. (1992).
(ii) Heggie (1995).

---

[1] Poor systems and engineering tax pedestrians and vehicles users alike, increasing the probability of an accident when attention lapses for even a moment. Improper systems, when in place for long, result in a culture of aggressive behaviour. Equally importantly it is systems and engineering that can be improved and leveraged upon.

Road traffic causes air pollution, which is high by international standards, especially in urban areas (Table 7.1.5). The annual premature deaths, due to ambient air pollution levels exceeding the World Health Organization (WHO) standards, are as high as 7491 in Delhi and

BOX 7.1.2

**Deluge, BMC Punch Holes in BEST's Coffers**

They are built for the rough and tumble of Mumbai's asphalted lunar surface. Both the two punishing bouts of rain this year, in quiet collusion with the civic authorities, have left the BEST's lumbering behemoths battered and bruised. Apart from injured chassis, officials emphasize the ground-level is particularly grisly.

Against average 200 punctures per day, sustained by its 3430-strong fleet during the monsoon, the figure has climbed to an alarming 550 since the July 12 deluge. At a cost of Rs 9600 per tyre, officials say the cost of repair and replacement has become prohibitive.

'Potholes have been erupting with unusual enthusiasm this year. May be [sic] it has something to do with the quality of asphalt and tar used by the civic authorities. Besides, the roads near the flyovers under construction are in such bad shape that driving has become hazardous', remarks a senior official of the Brihanmumbai Electric Supply and Transport (BEST) undertaking.

According to V. K. Katdare, deputy chief engineer (traffic), the BEST spends Rs 11.52 crore on the purchase of 12,000 tyres every year. Of these, 8000 are scrapped during the four monsoon months alone. However, this year, the figure is expected to be far higher. Though punctures account for most of the damage, heavy scarring and large tears also necessitate replacement. Outside the monsoon months, the average number of punctures is as small as 50 per day.

According to S. H. Bhatte, chief engineer (traffic), 80 per cent of punctures is caused by cratered roads. The rest is inflicted by sharp objects like nails.

'If the penetration is more than four inches, the tyre is rendered useless.

But if the Island City has turned into a veritable obstacle course in some areas, drivers cringe at the thought of negotiating the distant western suburbs. Identifying four depots as being particularly treacherous, officials say the number of punctures sustained by buses with the Gorai (Borivili-W), Magathane (Borivili-E), Dindoshi (Goregaon) and Mazas (Jogeshwari) depots has trebled, to a staggering 30 per day. The main culprits: the Jogeshwari–Powai Link Road, Sakinaka–Powai Road and roads in Chakala.

In some instances, officials' here say, new tyres sustain punctures after traversing a mere 100 feet!

BEST officials say that they have written to the civic authorities, urging them to improve road conditions but to no avail.

While agreeing that the road conditions generally worsen during the monsoon, A. V. Burute, chief engineer (roads), with the Brihanmumbai Municipal Corporation [BMC] rebuts the allegation that 'most' punctures are due to abysmal road conditions. 'There is no concrete study which shows this. There are many other reasons why tyres are damaged', he says.

Asked to explain why the corporation does not monitor the contractors who undertake the work, he replies: 'When the Civic Roads Department awards a contract, it takes a guarantee of one to five years from the contractor depending on the nature of work. If the road is damaged, the contractor is asked to repair the stretch. A close watch is maintained on arterial and major roads'. He adds: 'Mumbai's traffic is far more than in other cities, making the roads more susceptible to damage'.

'This is worsened by heavy vehicles, especially when traffic congestion makes them brake abruptly and frequently.' He denied, however, that substandard material is used.

*Source:* Kalpana Verma, *Indian Express*, 21 July 2000.

2979 in Ahmedabad. The number of workdays lost per capita annually on account of air pollution is five. MTWs are responsible for 46 per cent of air pollution near the roads.

## Congestion

Average vehicular speeds on Indian roads are amongst the lowest in the world. This is relatively more acute on the highways than in urban areas. A truck in India averages 250 km per day, while in the developed countries the average is closer to 600 kms per day (Mohan 1996).

For the railways, during 1998–9, the average turn-around was 8.2 days, of which only 28 hours was the

TABLE 7.1.5

Premature Deaths Due to Ambient Air Pollution Exceeding WHO Standard c. 1995 in Some Indian Cities

| City | No of deaths per year |
|---|---|
| Delhi | 7941 |
| Calcutta | 5726 |
| Mumbai | 4477 |
| Ahmedabad | 2979 |
| Kanpur | 1894 |
| Varanasi | 1851 |
| Chennai | 863 |
| Bangalore | 254 |

*Source:* World Bank (1995b).

revenue-earning run over an average lead of 669 km (IR 2000a). This reflects congestion and lack of coordination at terminals for multimodal handling. While the maximum speeds for mail/express and freight trains are 100 kmph and 75 kmph respectively, the average speeds achieved are typically 50 kmph and 24 kmph. The average is significantly lower than the maximum, which is indicative of route congestion.

The principal problem with ports is the very large average turnaround time of 5.9 days (MoST Basic Port Statistic 1999). The average comparable turnaround time in ports inter-nationally is only two days. Given the 14,676 port calls during 1998–9 (Indian Ports Association 2000) in major ports in India, at an average ship standing charge of $ 8000 per day, the net cost of the additional 3.9 days spent at ports by ships works out to $ 457.9 million, that is Rs 1623 crore.

*Why is There This 'Transport Myopia'?*

The transport myopia outlined above debilitates the economy. A variety of problems underlie this myopia.

There are problems that arise because of the cadre-based and bureaucratic mindset in the management of organizations which have to create, maintain, or deliver infrastructure. Apart from the deep-rooted hierarchy orientation (which is a complete antithesis to the much required customer orientation), there are additional tensions due to administrative cadres often occupying senior positions in competition with the technical cadres. Examples of such dysfunctional organizations are ports and road transport corporations.

Abdication of authority, or lack of authority at the top, significantly inhibit infrastructure organizations from being responsive to market opportunities, formulating projects appropriately, or managing projects in time and delivering the service effectively. Archetypical of such organizations is the Indian Railways.

Parliamentarians too consider many of the public enterprises providing infrastructure as their fiefdom. For example, the *Times of India* of 8 August 2000 reported that the civil aviation minister was pulled up by the Lok Sabha for the delay of a flight in which the speaker and a few other Members of Parliament from Andhra Pradesh were travelling. The minister assured the Chair that he would take steps to see that no such inconveniences would in future have to be suffered by VIPs (very important persons). This incident brings into focus once again the 'feudal' outlook of governance, which is an anathema to a citizen-oriented infrastructure. It is unfortunate that the plight of 'lesser mortals', the common consumer, did not figure in the discussions. Those affected by VIPs' movements better suffer in silence is the message. The minister himself thought his first responsibility was to serve the VIPs, even to the neglect of the consumer.

*What Next?*

Systems of public management (and governance) in India, though employing some of the best minds and brains in the country, unfortunately do not have the right kind of stakeholding and accountability, nor even the requisite autonomy. There is mismatch between task performance and the criteria for evaluation of managers and officers. There are almost no incentives for performance, or task orientation, or innovations at any level of management. Even the incentives for workers are related merely to hours of work, and never to efficiency or output.

A market-based and customer-oriented approach could change transport infrastructure services and development, removing the 'transport myopia' to result in better service. The crucial challenge then is how to develop structures and systems that would ensure this. The three dimensions of performance are: (1) asset-creation efficiency—nobody wants an expressway that was supposed to have opened in 1988 and is still languishing; (2) asset-management efficiency—an asset, once created, needs to be maintained, but without proper maintenance, roads and most transport infrastructure would deteriorate very rapidly; (3) service delivery effectiveness and efficiency—should an accident on a road hold up traffic for half a day, only because the police is not at the site on time, or the cranes to remove the vehicles are not available?

## SEGMENTING THE MARKET

While it is usual to study the transport sector on the basis of administrative categories, it is more fruitful to look at it from a market segment perspective. One obvious split, which is already recognized, is between freight and passenger. Within each of these divisions, the key geographic segments would be intra-urban, intra-rural and rural to urban, and inter-urban. Urban transportation as well as intra-rural and rural to urban are typically short haul. Inter-urban is typically long haul. Another dimension for segmentation would be the time value of the freight unit or passenger, which could be categorized into low and high. For freight transportation, the segmentation is also influenced by the nature of the user, since freight transportation is part of the supply chain logistics of the user. Fig. 7.1.2 outlines a framework to segment the users as bulk, industrial, and consumer durables and consumer goods manufacturers.[2]

[2] Much of the discussion on the market environment is excerpted from Raghuram (2000c).

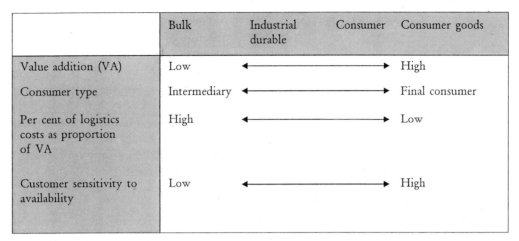

|  | Bulk | Industrial durable | Consumer | Consumer goods |
|---|---|---|---|---|
| Value addition (VA) | Low | ←――――――――――→ | | High |
| Consumer type | Intermediary | ←――――――――――→ | | Final consumer |
| Per cent of logistics costs as proportion of VA | High | ←――――――――――→ | | Low |
| Customer sensitivity to availability | Low | ←――――――――――→ | | High |

**Fig. 7.1.2:** A framework to segment users.

Bulk goods are typically transported in large shipment sizes. Therefore dedicated vehicles, specialized modes of transport, and handling are important. Industrial goods have high value and are often critical. Therefore the need is for speedier transport. Some items require specialized transportation and handling. For consumer durable goods, inventory costs are significant. Appropriate distribution networks that minimize in-transit inventory costs play an important role for such goods. For consumer goods, availability is an important factor. Logistics choices here are governed by better service levels as much as by costs. Appropriate distribution networks and warehouse locations play an important role in both improving service levels and reducing costs, direct and indirect. The users are often willing to pay a premium for superior service.

I consider four key attributes by which these segments can be distinguished. They are value addition (VA), consumer type, percentage of logistics costs as proportion to VA, and customer sensitivity to availability.

The percentage of logistics cost to the total value added signifies the importance of logistics-related activities in the cost of production and sales. It is high for bulk goods manufacturers, while it is low for consumer goods manufacturers. For bulk goods, total logistics cost as a proportion of value addition is about 70 per cent, out of which transportation costs constitute nearly two-third. Such customers are very sensitive to the price of transportation. For consumer goods and durables, total logistics costs as a proportion of value addition do not exceed 10 per cent, out of which transportation costs constitute less than a third. Such customers tend to be sensitive to service. Customer sensitivity to availability would determine the propensity to switching. Such attributes of market segments are most useful and need to be brought into the management of public

transportation systems. Policy making too greatly benefits from the logistics orientation, since that should immediately lead to an integrated perspective with regard to transportation modes and support facilities. And an integrated perspective is the need of the hour.[3]

Thus perishable commodities or hazardous commodities require specialized infrastructure support. Understanding geographic (origin–destination) requirements would enable a focus on appropriate infrastructure investments, especially from the perspective of economies of scale. Segmentation by use would enable an assessment of value addition provided to the customer and the consequent requirements of infrastructural services.

Transportation of hazardous goods assumes great importance for a variety of industries such as petrochemicals, textiles, and dyes and chemicals. Logistics problems arise due to handling requirements and safety aspects. Underregulation, especially with regard to safety and implementation of standard, often leads to accidents with consequential damages and inadequate post-accident measures. On the other hand, overregulation, and adherence merely to the letter of regulations, leads to delays and high costs of transportation.

Similarly segmentation is possible for passenger transportation. The purpose of travel would be a key attribute in the segmentation.

The choice of mode, willingness to pay, and service expectations are governed by the segments. Consequently, transport infrastructure and services need to recognize these parameters while planning service concepts, routing, and scheduling, determining capacity, and in pricing.

[3] De-bottlenecking, reducing consumer side costs, increasing capacity from a multimodal optimality are all constrained today by a lack of the multimodal perspective in transport policy making.

## STRUCTURE OF THE TRANSPORT SECTOR[4]

### Defining Sector Components

While many activities in the transport sector in India are strictly state controlled, there are other significant segments which are almost entirely in the private sector. It would be useful to broadly classify the transport sector into three primary segments, namely infrastructure (hardware), services, and regulation. There are broadly three components of infrastructure with increasing possibility of being attached to the specific services provided: (a) right of way, (b) terminals, and (c) rolling stock and equipment. Services too can be broadly categorized into three types with increasing closeness to the customer: (a) maintenance, (b) operations, and (c) customer services. Both maintenance and operations can be further classified as being for the right of way, or for terminals, or rolling stock. Customer services can be classified into basic and special (value-added) services. Thus, the distinct activities may be seen as under:

INFRASTRUCTURE

1. Ownership and asset creation
   - Right of way
   - Terminals
   - Rolling stock and equipment

SERVICES

1. Maintenance
   - Right of way
   - Terminals
   - Rolling stock and equipment

2. Operations
   - Right of way
   - Terminals
   - Rolling stock and equipment

3. Customer services
   - Basic services
   - Special services

REGULATION

1. Licensing
2. Environmental impact
3. Safety
4. Pricing
5. Service levels

[4] This section is based on Pangotra and Raghuram (1999).

The relative importance of the state and the current structure of provisioning of each of the above activities for all the transport modes are brought in Table 7.1.6. The provider who has primary responsibility and accountability for the infrastructure and services is also identified. Even when activities are contracted (out), the principal continues to bear primary responsibility, though that brings in the principal–agency problem. Hence stakeholding and appropriateness of incentives become important.

### Air

When 'air' is considered as a mode of transport, right of way is not a significant infrastructure. However, the operation associated with it, namely air traffic control, has significant regulatory and safety aspects. The terminals have also never been privatized, though they have been privatized in so far as the terminal buildings or portions thereof are concerned. The rolling stock and equipment, customer services, and other special services (for example reservation) are all privatized.

### Rail

In the case of rail, currently all activities are being handled by one organization, namely Indian Railways. Only recently, certain value-added special services like tourist trains on popular tourist circuits are beginning to be offered through the private sector. The Indian Railways are viewed as providing a robust and bare minimum service, but with poor customer service.

### Road

In the case of road, in contrast to rail, a variety of organizations are involved, with regard to the 'right of way' state governments, the central government (for national highways), and local governments are involved. Apart from these, the Defence Ministry (border roads) and large industries (project roads) too are involved in a minor way. In recent years, some financing for rural roads has come from the Agriculture Ministry. Regarding terminals, for mass passenger transport either State Road Transport Undertakings (SRTUs) or local governments are generally involved. For freight transport, large industries have their own loading and unloading areas while smaller organizations tend to use public roads. Trans-shipment terminals are usually provided by various carriers. A few cities have organized truck terminals under supervision of the local governments. The rolling stock and equipment are manufactured by a few large auto manufacturers, while ownership is diffused across a large number of owners (usually drivers themselves). Many operators often own no more than five trucks.

TABLE 7.1.6
Transport Sector Components and Involvement of the State and Private Sector

| *Physical basis/assets* | Ownership/control | | | |
|---|---|---|---|---|
| | Air | Rail | Road | Water |
| **Right of way** | (State controlled) DGCA, AAI | (State controlled) Indian Railways | (State controlled) NHAI, PWD, urban administrations, local governments, defence | (State controlled) Major ports—Government of India, State Maritime Boards, Port Directorates |
| **Terminals** | (State controlled) AAI, Defence | (State controlled) Indian Railways, large industries for captive sidings | (Open to all) SRTUs, large industries, trucking companies, etc. | (Partly Open) Major Ports—Government of India, State Maritime Boards, Port Directorates, some private and captive ports |
| **Rolling stock and equipment** | (Open to all) IA, AI, other private airlines | (State controlled) Indian Railways | (Open to all) SRTUs, private vehicle owners | (Open to all) SCI, Great Eastern, ESSAR, and others |

| *Maintenance Services* | | | | |
|---|---|---|---|---|
| | Air | Rail | Road | Water |
| **Right of way** | –NA– DGCA, AAI | (State controlled) Indian Railways | (State controlled) NHAI, PWD, urban administrations, | (State controlled) Major ports—Government of India, State Maritime Boards, Port Directorates |
| **Terminals** | (State controlled) AAI | (State controlled) Indian Railways, large industries for captive sidings | (Open to all) SRTUs, large industries, trucking companies, etc. | (State controlled) Major Ports—Government of India, State Maritime Boards, Port Directorates, some private and captive ports |
| **Rolling stock and equipment** | (Open to all) IA, AI, other private airlines | (State controlled) Indian Railways | (Open to all) Innumerable small-scale garages, large organized workshops for SRTUs, few private sector large workshops | (Open to all) Port Dry Docks, HSL, CSL, Chokhani, and others |

| *Operations* | Operations | | | |
|---|---|---|---|---|
| | Air | Rail | Road | Water |
| **Right of way** | (State controlled) DGCA, AAI | (State controlled) Indian Railways | (State controlled) Police Department in case of high traffic density | (State controlled) Major ports—Government of India, State Maritime Boards, Port Directorates, Light House Authority |
| **Terminals** | (State controlled) DGCA, AAI | (State controlled) Indian Railways, large industries for captive sidings | (Open to all) SRTUs, large industries, transport companies, Control and State Warehousing Corporation | (Partly Open) Major Ports—Government of India, State Maritime Boards, Port Directorates, some private and captive ports |
| **Rolling stock and equipment** | (Open to all) IA, AI, other private airlines | (State controlled) Indian Railways | (Open to all) SRTUs, private vehicle owners | (Open to all) SCI, Great Eastern, ESSAR, and others |

(Contd.)

Table 7.1.6 contd.

| Customer Services (associated) | Air | Rail | Road | Water |
|---|---|---|---|---|
| Basic services | (Open to all) IA, AI, private airlines | (State controlled) Indian Railways | (Open to all) SRTUs, private bus operators, TCI, Patel Roadways, forwarding agents, etc. | (Open to all) brokers, chartering agents, forwarding agents |
| Special services | (Open to all) IA, AI, private airlines | (State controlled) Indian Railways | (Open to all) SRTUs, private bus operators, tour operators, TCI, Patel Roadways, forwarding agents, etc. | (Open to all) brokers, chartering agents, forwarding agents |

| Regulation | Controls | | | |
|---|---|---|---|---|
| | Air | Rail | Road | Water |
| Licensing | DGCA | IR | RTO | DG Shipping |
| Environmental controls | DGCA | Department of Environment | RTO | DG Shipping |
| Safety | DGCA | CRS | Traffic Police | DG Shipping |
| Pricing | – | Parliament, Railway Rates Tribunal | – | DG Shipping, TAMP |
| Service levels | DGCA | IR, Railway Claims Tribunal | – | DG Shipping |

*Source:* Excerpted and modified from Pangotra and Raghuram (1999).

In road services, the maintenance of right of way and terminals is vested with the respective governments and organizations providing such infrastructure. The maintenance services for rolling stock and equipment is largely sought from a vast number of small-scale garages dotted over the country by the owners of the rolling stock. Only in the case of mass passenger transport provided by the SRTUs are organized large-scale workshops available. Regarding operations and customer services in mass passenger transport, the SRTUs and private parties provide both. About 20 per cent of vehicle (rolling stock) ownership is under the SRTUs. Special services like school trips and contract services are provided by various organizations who hire buses. In the case of freight transport, operations are largely in the hands of the truck owners, while customer interface and value-added services are provided by trucking companies.

Given this complex web of organizations involved in the road sector, the services are seen to be very competitive, though not always of sufficient quality and reliability. The poor condition of roads has adversely affected the quality and reliability of road services.

## Water

Water transport is another area where a large number of organizations are involved. The right of way (approach channels to port) and terminals (ports) are under the central and state governments. A few private terminals exist for captive use. The rolling stock (ships) ownership is open to private parties. However, nearly 50 per cent of the ship tonnage is owned by one public sector organization, the Shipping Corporation of India. Customer services and special services are significantly privatized. While services are viewed as being competitive, the major bottleneck is in the terminal (port) delays.

## Pipeline

Another mode of transport gaining in significance as a viable alternative to road and railways for liquid bulk is pipeline. This technology is useful for transportation of fluids (crude oil, petroleum products, natural gas, etc.) and other commodities transportable in slurry form (coal, iron ore pellets, etc.). Conceptually, even conveyor belts and aerial ropeways serve the same purpose for transportation of bulk commodities in solid form, though usually for much shorter distances. Currently, all investments in pipelines, belts, and ropeways are for captive use and hence managed by the respective user organizations. However, a 'public' network of pipelines may be useful and even necessary for the oil and gas sector. Two companies, Petronet and Petronet–LNG have been set up with equity participation from the oil and gas companies for this purpose. Questions regarding the actors, the service arrangements, and appropriate regulation of infrastructure investments, maintenance, operations and services still have to be resolved.[5]

## Role of Regulation

It would appear that there is much inefficiency wherever the state has had direct and dominant involvement in transport infrastructure. This is primarily due to lack of accountability in a commercial sense. The state's role is nevertheless essential in regulation and catalysing infrastructure development and services.

The first area for regulation would be licensing, to ensure proper market structuring and competition. Regulating to reduce or mitigate environmental impact is essential in both development and service provisioning. With competition, in many areas for instance pricing of road transport or rail services could be scaled down. But regulations related to ensuring environmental soundness would have to continue.

## Unbundling

Appropriate unbundling would be an important step in attracting private participation in 'smaller' and more manageable businesses. Unbundling would also make transparent the business transactions between those aspects of the market where competition can exist and those where there is a natural monopoly.

In the above framework, the first task of unbundling is to separate the fixed infrastructure (right of way and terminals) from movable infrastructure and services. Further unbundling can be thought of between right of way and terminals, along geographical dimensions, and along well-defined markets with separate characteristics (passenger and freight, urban commuter, long distance and feeder routes, etc.).

While unbundling would increase transaction costs between businesses, they could be offset by the increased value from the focused approach to each business, and from competition. In this context, ensuring market access is very important. A recent counter-example is the Konkan Railway Corporation, structured as a BOT (build, operate, and transfer) project to bridge the

'Konkan Gap' from a place about 120 km south of Mumbai to Mangalore. While the asset creation was successfully carried out due to the autonomy provided by the BOT structure, the operations phase has been far less successful due to market access being less than desirable. Having direct access to the major industrial market of Mumbai would be a key success variable. The project has been flawed from the start since it began from the Railways' idea of bridging the 'Konkan Gap', rather than starting from the needs of the customer.

## Cherry Picking: Cross-subsidies and Subsidy

One of the possible outcomes in seeking private involvement for commercialization of the unbundled businesses is 'cherry picking'. Private interests would naturally be interested in those businesses which are commercially lucrative and less risky. This would leave the not so attractive businesses without any takers. There are two ways of dealing with this. One is to bundle the not so attractive businesses with the attractive ones and view the viable market as cross-subsidizing the unviable ones. This has been attempted in the 'open skies' policy for attracting private airlines. The other is to keep these businesses separate and provide a subsidy to the operator of the commercially unviable business.

The argument for cross-subsidy is not tenable unless a good rationale can be provided for the relationship between markets in terms of network economies and such other considerations. Apart from there being incentive incompatibilities (private airlines are often known to 'drag their feet' in maintaining the committed schedules on the unviable routes), there is also a lack of transparency in the true costs, since there is no longer an incentive to maintain separate accounts. For example, in the IR, it is often stated that freight subsidizes passenger, and the long-distance passenger subsidizes the short-distance and urban commuter. While these facts may be true the degree of cross-subsidization has hardly been estimated. In any case a large part of the costs are allocated costs and much could depend on the basis of allocation. In trains running significantly faster than the average speed of trains there are negative externalities on the other trains which are possibly not being captured. In other words, sensitivity to systemic effects would mean much more careful analysis would have to be carried out. Apart from transparency on cost, the basic issue is that cross-subsidization is highly distortionary in relation to direct subsidization.

The specific unviable business can be offered to that operator who is technically qualified and would manage the service obligations of the business with the least subsidy requirement. This would be a better way of improving service obligations.

---

[5] See section 7.4 in this report for a review of the oil pipeline sector.

*Pricing*

This is an important area, where due to practices of administered and often 'placative' pricing, major distortions have set in. They may have been in existence long enough to have even influenced investment decisions, that is resulted in allocative distortions. The most glaring example is the shift of freight traffic from rail to road due to *inter alia* pricing way above the true economic cost. This has resulted in a significant increase in road traffic along the golden quadrilateral, where large investments are now being channelized.

On the passenger side, there are demand distortions in commuter and short haul traffic, primarily due to concessional season tickets. There are also distortions due to free and subsidized rail travel provided to various segments, including railway employees themselves. With nearly 1.6 million employees, and an average free travel eligible family size of three including the employee, the total number of persons eligible for free travel is 4.8 million. The free travel privileges are available between three and six times a year (depending upon the category of employee). Subsidized travel is also available for a few more occasions. Assuming that three free trips a year are being made, with an average round trip distance of 2000 km, this results in total travel of 29 bpkm. In addition, there were one million pensioners as of 31 March 1998 (Asian Institute of Transport Development 1998) eligible for free travel. Assuming two free trips a year at an average of 1.5 persons per pensioner, with an average round trip of 2000 kms, this works to a further 6 bpkm. Together the 35 bpkms would form nearly 9 per cent of the total IR bpkm! It goes without saying that these distortions in pricing urgently need to be corrected.

With private participation in road development, the following issues need attention: (i) whether and which roads should be tolled, (ii) if to be tolled, what is the appropriate toll and toll-setting mechanism, and (iii) if not to be tolled, what is the appropriate shadow tolling mechanism for providing revenues to private developers. Irrespective of private involvement, many congested road segments, especially in urban areas, could be considered for congestion-based tolling or taxes.

For most other transport infrastructure services where there is reasonable competition (or at least competition can be ensured), pricing could be left to the free market.

*Low Investment Approaches to Improving*
*Infrastructure Quality and Capacity*

Given that congestion and wear and tear are two of the most significant consequences of the current state of 'transport myopia', there is a lot of latent opportunity in activities that would give high returns for low investments in improving quality and capacity of the infrastructure.

For example, simulation runs by the planning group in the Railway Board using the Long Range Decision Support System (LRDSS) software show that a 20 per cent increase in capacity is straightaway possible by improving wagon maintenance (and avoiding breakdowns and accidents). Further increases are possible by improving freight train speeds to reduce the variance in speeds across categories of trains.

The capacity of the IR could substantially increase if the cumulative effect of certain modes of working and certain constraints are removed. The investments required would be very low in comparison to those required to create fresh capacity (see Box 7.1.3).

Bottlenecks on highways and roads reduce considerably the service levels on highways in India, even to the point of reducing the effective capacity of the roads. The potential gains in relaxing these constraints are very large, and the costs very small (see Box 7.1.4).

In the case of road, speed breakers could be located appropriately, not on the higher speed route but on roads joining such routes. Roadside signs have never been given their due role in providing information to road users allowing them to anticipate road conditions. Very often, it is also the case that the 'signage cycle' is incomplete, in that the road user is never informed that the special condition that he was asked to anticipate is over and normalcy has returned.

There is an urgent need to create appropriate incentives that would attract investors and make existing organizations take up these low investment options to relax current constraints. The examples of toll revenue-based maintenance contracts of highway stretches in Madhya Pradesh and Maharashtra are welcome but only small beginnings in this direction.

*Land Acquisition and Management*

Land is an asset valued dearly by everyone in India. This makes land acquisition and land management for transport infrastructure projects a significant issue. It is also clear that land acquisition has to necessarily stay with the government, since it is government alone which has the 'right of eminent domain'.[6] Under this right, the government can take possession of land from private citizens and bodies for infrastructure projects. The only recourse against the government is the court, in which only the compensation amount can be challenged.

---

[6] For a different view see the discussion on land acquisition in chapter 1 of this report (ed.).

Box 7.1.3

**Constraints which Deplete Rail Transport Capacity but which are Removable by Low Investments**

There are significant opportunities to enhance rail transport capacity with soft investments. The best achieved capacity on a double line non-suburban section is 65 trains each way. A spacing of 10 minutes between trains should yield a maximum capacity of 144 trains and an actual of 115 trains at 80 per cent utilization. But the following constraints prevent achievement of this high capacity:

Constraints of flow across stations
- Yard layout, junction arrangements
  - Access to common loops requiring mainline crossover
  - Platforms only on loop lines, especially within smaller stations
- Stop boards in yards
- Diamond crossings on approaches to stations
- Level crossings, especially in station limits
- Provision of washable apron on main lines
- Equipment failures, especially related to signalling

Track-related constraints
- Slow speed of turnouts
- Permanent speed restrictions
- Poor spacing of intermediate block stations
  - Special restrictions at stations due to inappropriate track geometry

Operations-related constraints
- Speed and operating characteristic differential between trains (Rajdhani/Shatabdi, mail/expresses, passengers transport, container trains, freight trains, other operational movements)
- Timetabling with substantial slack
- Frequent crew changes for freight trains
- Attachment/detachment of bankers
- Light running of locos and bankers, sometimes at restricted speed
- Inadequate number of bankers

Rolling stock-related constraints
- Poor braking power
- Inadequate tractive power of engines
- Clamped wagons
- Locos running with deficiencies (like isolated traction motor) affecting speed and acceleration
- Derailments (usually of freight wagons)

*Source:* Based on (i) Raghuram and Rao (1991).
(ii) Thoopal (1998).

Apart from large tracts of land required for ports and airports, the complexity of land acquisition is increased by the need for linear alignments of road and rail routes. There was a time when the government thought that private involvement in transport projects could also result in land acquisition being done by private parties. However, it is now very clear that land acquisition is an activity that will have to remain with the government.

As a result of such acquisition, certain issues arise. The first is the issue of the quantum of land. The Gujarat Industrial Development Board [GIDB] has used a point system for evaluating potential bidders for infrastructure development, in which a bidder with less land

requirement scores higher.) The second is the processes followed by the government in acquiring the land. Lately the large amount of land acquired for Poshitra port in Gujarat has come in for criticism.[7] Similarly, how long can the land be retained if the project is delayed or never takes off. Currently once the land is taken over, it stays with the government. Can extra land (keeping in view a future possible expansion), it be commercially exploited? A Kerala High Court judgement struck down such an ambition of the Kerala PWD, based on litigation by the original landowner. It was ruled that the landowner would have first rights for commercial

[7] See Box 5.6.1 in this report.

BOX 7.1.4

**Low Investment Strategies to De-bottleneck Road Systems**

A section of roadway to which more demand is delivered than can be processed is referred to as a 'bottleneck'. When a narrow road section exists on a roadway, then accumulation of vehicles takes place upstream of this section. Capacity analysis indicates that the best speed and the lowest density is downstream of the bottleneck; the worst speed and the highest density is just upstream of the bottleneck. *Thus an assumption that the section with the poorest speed is actually the bottleneck is wrong and would lead to erroneous identification of the problem, when it is caused by a 'bottleneck'.*

Bottlenecks may occur because of some permanent geometric feature, some construction activity, or as a consequence of some incident. Some bottleneck situations are too trivial to identify. However in many cases, it is necessary to identify both the bottleneck situation and the true demand. A bottleneck situation affects the vehicle-operating cost due to delays and discomforts, and adversely affects safety. Useful descriptive statistics below could be used to estimate the costs imposed by the bottleneck:

- Number of vehicles affected
- Total duration of time
- Maximum number of vehicles queued
- Maximum queue length
- Total vehicle-hours of delay
- Average delay per affected vehicle.

The estimation of the above statistics would be necessary to identify the non-obvious bottlenecks. An understanding of safety implications will also help in benefit–cost analysis of any proposed improvement of the bottleneck.

The following strategies can be adopted to relax the bottlenecks and improve safety:

- realignment of road sections with sharp curves and steep grades, especially where these are below the standard of adjacent road sections
- reducing road roughness
- realignment to improve passing sight distance
- improving intersection geometry
- increasing lane width
- adding auxiliary lanes, especially where traffic demand is higher for a short stretch
- introducing passing lanes at intervals
- providing gentle slopes and removing fixed objects from the sides of the roads
- use of paved shoulders
- installing guard fence to protect hazards
- providing special facilities for runaway trucks on steep downgrades
- improving and controlling roadside development and activity.

*Source:* Marwah (2000).

development, since that was not the purpose for which the land was acquired. The principle behind this ruling has laid to rest all intentions of the IR and road developers. While the principle has its merits, it should not result in a 'dog in the manger' policy resulting in land being idle by which no value is obtained from such land. The IR have used such land temporarily leasing it out for agriculture and horticulture.

There are still opportunities in terms of land management which do not violate the above principle. The land can be used for activities that would directly benefit the infrastructure user (for example petrol pumps, restaurants, garages, and staying places). It is also possible to use the air space above the land for commercial ex-ploitation, since the land is anyway required for the transport activity. Many cities internationally have taken advantage of this possibility. The new suburban stations of Mumbai have been built with multistorey structures to be used as commercial office space. Along the same lines, air space over the existing right of way in all the metropolitan cities would be a valuable opportunity to exploit and make infrastructure development more viable.

*Coordinated Inter-sectoral Development and Centre–State Issues*

Another crucial challenge is to channelize investments to realize multimodal benefits in an environment which has long settled down to a sub-sectoral outlook.

There was an attempt in the mid-1980s to make a unified Ministry of Transport. The experiment failed since in itself it did not lead to any improvement in coordination between the departments. A major opportunity like coastal shipping is underexploited primarily because nobody has taken the onus of coordinated development at ports between various modes. The type of coastal shipping that has taken off is that initiated by large corporates who have invested in the required multimodal logistics of their cargo movement. If an initiative with coordinated development can take place, private investment in various aspects of coastal shipping would naturally flow.[8]

Even if the ministries[9] cannot be integrated, task forces or boards that would look at specific areas of multimodal development would be essential.

In the context of roads and ports, which come under both central and state governments, there have not only been situations of conflict, especially with regard to financing, but also competitive situations to gain control over the activity. An example of the latter is the development of minor and intermediate ports in Gujarat and Orissa. This has no doubt served the purpose of a better industrialization in the states. It could also, however, lead to expensive excess capacity creation.

## Common Carrier versus Captive Infrastructure

If coordinated development does not take place, then more 'captive infrastructure' than required would come about, leading to systematic inefficiencies. This is especially true of ports and pipelines.

While the benefit of captive infrastructure in offering better control and customization for the supply chain cannot be denied (for example the port of Mul-Dwarka for Gujarat Ambuja Cement Limited), the trade-off in terms of better utilization of infrastructure could very well lie in open access and public infrastructure.

In the case of pipelines, two organizations have been set up, namely Petronet and Petronet–LNG, to promote common carrier pipelines for the hydrocarbon sector. Currently, there is debate as to whether the captive pipelines of the petroleum companies should be handed over to Petronet for use in a common carrier mode.[10]

[8] We came across certain urban administrations who would redefine their urban boundaries so that the passenger rail transport system can be kept under their control, and they would not have to involve the IR.

[9] Even if ministries are merged, the older 'departments' once formed have a life of their own and cross-departmental coordination has proved to be very difficult for the Indian bureaucracy.

[10] See section 7.4 in this report.

In the case of project roads developed by specific industrial projects as a primary user, the government has ensured public use by providing land at subsidized rates or even at no cost.

It is thus important that as far as possible, infrastructure development be carried out under the common carrier principle, and preferably with stakeholding by the primary user who would also commercially gain by the public use.

## The Neglect of R&D

One of the important determinants of efficient transport infrastructure is technology, especially that of the 'rolling stock' or vehicle. India suffers from poor technology. The net weight of commodity carried to the weight of the vehicle is among the lowest in the world. The standard truck has a ratio of 1:1 (multi-axle trucks can go up to 3:1 internationally, while in India the best multi-axle trucks have achieved 2.5:1). The best railway wagons in India have a ratio which is slightly higher than 2:1. Ratios greater than 4:1 have been achieved in container flats internationally. As far as ships are concerned, the ratio is typically 1.6:1, both in India and abroad.

The typical bus in India, which does not have to carry more than 4 tonnes, uses the same chassis as a truck, which is designed to carry 10 tonnes. This has been the result of a market oligopoly and a distorted view of economies of scale. Due to these inefficiencies, especially on roads, the nation suffers fuel wastage and road wear and tear. It is important to have a focused effort on appropriate R&D. National-level projects funded by government with contributions from industry to find solutions to such problems, especially those where the social benefits are larger than the private benefits, are required.

## Regulatory Framework

In the context of transport infrastructure, the regulatory framework has been vested in the very same ministry, which also licenses and often is a key player in the activity. To facilitate private infrastructure development, the player must be different from the regulator and the licensor. Even when public enterprise is involved in provisioning, the traditional assumption that the public sector would act in the public interest is not necessarily true, especially when state failure is widespread. This would be relevant in the context of railways, roads, ports, and airports, where the potential for privatization is significant. The licensor has an important role in ensuring proper market structures.

BOX 7.1.5
## Role of Citizens in Monitoring Roads

*Preamble*

Excepting some minor routine maintenance, most road works are contracted out to the private sector with a tendering process.

Quality control cells do exist in many public agencies responsible for roads. Maintenance is an ongoing process and is not given enough attention because it may be politically more exciting to build something new and take credit for it than to fix or maintain an existing system. Lack of proper planning and coordination between the various government agencies and illegal overloading of trucks are two other major constraints that plague road maintenance management in India. All these have contributed to the vicious circle of construction and reconstruction without proper maintenance and management. Other factors are:

• Lack of supervision/poor supervision, ignorance, and unethical work practices.

• The funds allocated for routine and periodic maintenance are not sufficient, in which case it is all the more necessary to be quality conscious.

• Lack of transparency in tendering and contracting process, resulting in collusion and corruption.

• Flaws and loopholes in rules and regulations.

• Absence of records pertaining to construction and maintenance details of each stretch of road.

*Why Citizen Monitoring?*

Safe and motorable roads are important for improvement in the overall *quality of life*. Citizens and taxpayers are the ultimate users and have a right to good quality roads. Rights cannot be divorced from duties. Therefore being vigilant is one of the important duties of citizens. It is in this context that citizen monitoring of the quality of road works, which is a culmination of both rights and duties, attains critical importance. They can most effectively mount pressure for a positive change.

*Scope of the Guide*

In this context, the Public Affairs Centre, an NGO based in Bangalore, brought out a Citizen's Guide for roads and related infrastructure monitoring which has become popular.

The most important objective of the guide is to provide the citizens with some information on road maintenance works and quality checks so as to strengthen citizens' voice. The guide describes some of the standard procedures and specifications as may be provided for in the contractual/tender documents. Only those methods of routine maintenance, resurfacing, and overlaying of road pavements which are most commonly being practised in this region have been covered. The coverage itself is, however, not comprehensive, but critical nevertheless. The specifications stated in the guide are based on those given by the Ministry of Surface Transport (MoST) and relevant specifications and code of practices of IRC. The extent to which they are followed and implemented by State Public Works Departments (PWDs) and local governments like Municipalities and Panchayats is a matter, which merits wide spread public debate. This is precisely what the manual aims to achieve in the longer run. Imagine a situation when citizen groups all over the country become quality conscious and begin to demand accountability of public work expenditure from a technical view point. Surely then, positive changes occur?

Though the guide attempts to simplify the 'technicalities' of road quality monitoring, it does not shy away from the same. Unless citizens educate themselves about some essential technical matters pertaining to public works expenditure, unethical practices will prevail resulting in huge wastage of pubic money and deterioration in the quality of life. If, however, some readers find these details too complex, they could seek assistance from civil engineers or other competent persons residing in their neighbourhood to explain these relevant matters.

*Source:* Public Affairs Centre, Department of Science and Technology (1999) mimeo.

In the case of air and water (primarily shipping), the corresponding ministries regulate almost all aspects through the respective Directorate Generals. In the case of the major ports, a Tariff Authority for Major Ports (TAMP) was set up. However, since ports operate in a competitive environment, a body like TAMP was really not called for. In fact, it serves more as a body for recourse than any strategic directions for pricing.

For railways, there are different bodies that look after various aspects of regulation. An interesting concept in avoiding conflict of interest is the Commissionerate of Railway Safety (CRS), which though manned by railway officers on deputation, does not report to the Ministry of Railways, but to the Ministry of Civil Aviation! Furthermore, for recourse on rates and claims, there are tribunals with judicial powers. On the matter of pricing the Railway Budget, which contains the pricing proposals like taxes, is voted annually in Parliament! This makes tariff setting a political process. Typically fares have risen when a 'stable' government does not have to, over the next several years, face an electorate. They have been held back by governments that face an election. Recently though, the politics of coalition have added additional dimensions to the rate-setting process. More importantly, the required flexibility to price differentially through the seasons, or in such a manner as to optimize the use of resources or recover costs is systematically vitiated. It would make sense to delink this role from Parliament and possibly have a tariff authority, as a stop-gap arrangement, before reform and restructuring can begin in earnest.

Similarly, an appropriate mechanism for determining road tolls and ensuring appropriate service levels would be necessary. For example, when an additional bridge is constructed across a river for four laning and a toll is levied, then on days when one of the bridges is closed for maintenance, the toll ought be rolled back since the appropriate service level is not being provided. Today, there is no recourse to such tolling, except through the courts.

*Other Substantive 'Checks and Balances'*

Transport infrastructure development is too important a business to be left entirely to the commercial parties involved. Being as much if not more a public activity as the activities of large widely held corporations, infrastructure development must create the spaces for bringing in other 'stakeholders' and professionals. This would bring about the required 'checks' and 'balances'.

Good examples are the Infrastructure Leasing and Financial Services Limited (ILFS) engineered Gujarat Toll Roads Limited and a few of the projects promoted by the GIDB, where at important stages experts and steering committees of professionals and other stakeholders have been involved.

Involving citizens' groups in an organized manner is an important mechanism. Box 7.1.5 provides an example of an attempt by the Public Affairs Centre, Bangalore, to involve citizens in monitoring road construction and maintenance.

Intellectuals and academics can similarly contribute. Unfortunately, research and development in managerial, economic, socio-political, and even relevant technological issues related to infrastructure are not adequate. Box 7.1.6 excerpts from the 1983 Plan of Action accepted by the Planning Commission, based on the National Transport Policy Committee Recommendations, wherein transport research and training in ample measure are recommended. Unfortunately, they have not been taken further in a meaningful and purposive manner.

---

BOX 7.1.6

**Transport Research and Training**

| | | |
|---|---|---|
| An interdisciplinary centre should be set up to stimulate research, conduct studies, and impart training in transport planning and management. It should enjoy autonomy on the lines of the Institutes of Management and Institutes of Technology. (Para 8.2.1 and 8.2.2) | Accepted in principle. | To start with a separate wing for transport studies may be set up in an institute like the Staff College at Hyderabad and which could later become an independent institute for transport studies. Planning Commission in consultation with transport sector ministries may take further action. |
| Efforts should be made to encourage research and training at the universities and other specialized institutions. Necessary financial support should be provided. (Para 8.2.3) | Accepted in principle. | Further action may be taken by the Ministry of Education in consultation with the Planning Commission. |
| A wing or a unit should be organized as part of the National Transport Commission to function as a central forum for co-ordinating the research and development efforts undertaken by different institutions for various modes of transport. This wing should be appropriately advised by a group of experts. (Para 8.2.5) | Accepted as modified. The specialized group suggested under recommendation No 6.3-6.4 may co-ordinate this function | Planning Commission may take further action. |

*Source:* Excerpts from Planning Commission (1988).

# 7.2 SECTORAL ISSUES IN TRANSPORTATION

*G. Raghuram*

Herein each of the sectors that constitute transportation is examined in detail.

## AIR

Air transport consists of airports, air services, aircraft manufacture, and air traffic control. Since air traffic control is closer to a public good and regulatory in nature, it has been in government hands in most countries. In the aircraft manufacturing sector, India has developed little or no capabilities, except in certain low end defence aircraft. Airports and air services have much scope for private provisioning.

### Airports

There are over sixty airports, either under the Ministry of Civil Aviation and managed by the Airports Authority of India (AAI), or under the Ministry of Defence. The total traffic handled by them in 1998–9 was 37 million passengers and 0.7 million tonnes of cargo, using 0.42 million aircraft movements (Table 7.2.1). The traffic trends over the past four years have not shown any significant growth. What is worth noting is that the cargo traffic has gone up at a compound annual growth rate (CAGR) of 2.5 per cent and the numbers of international passengers have gone up at a CAGR of 3.9 per cent. Forecasts, however, had been estimating the

growth in domestic passengers at 8.5 per cent and international passengers at 6 per cent annually. At those rates, India is expected to handle 63 million passengers by 2004–5.

In 1998–9, Mumbai and Delhi handled 51.1 per cent of passenger traffic (Table 7.2.2), 63.2 per cent of cargo traffic (Table 7.2.3) and 45.0 per cent of aircraft movements (Table 7.2.4). International cargo constituted 67.8 per cent of the total cargo (in tonnes), of which these two airports handled 70.6 per cent. Chennai, followed by Calcutta and Bangalore, are next in order of importance. This is followed by the airports of Hyderabad, Trivandrum, and Ahmedabad, and Goa and Calicut. These ten airports account for 84.9 per cent of passenger traffic, 95.6 per cent of cargo traffic, and 76.5 per cent of aircraft movements.

The key requirement at airports is enhanced service levels and reduction of congestion. Towards this end the AAI envisages an expenditure of Rs 34.21 billion in the Ninth Plan period (1997–2002). A significant share of this is expected through private sector participation. The government formulated a policy on airport infrastructure development in 1997. This policy allows up to 74 per cent foreign equity through automatic approval, and 100 per cent through special permission. It proposes to set up an independent regulatory board to fix tariffs, allot time slots, and allocate space in airports.

In May 1999, the first private sector airport built by Cochin International Airport Limited at Nedumbassery near Cochin was inaugurated. The total project cost was Rs 2.3 billion, financed through equity of Rs 0.9 billion and term loans of Rs 1.4 billion. The Kerala state government has 26 per cent equity participation. New private sector airports at Bangalore, Hyderabad, and Goa have been sanctioned. Privatizing a variety of services at Mumbai, Delhi, Calcutta, and Chennai airports has also been approved. The need now is to pursue these privatization goals proactively. One of the problems has been lack of consistency in the approach of the government. In the case of the Bangalore airport, the contractual conditions between the interested parties and the government were contentious. The contract documents were sent back and forth among the parties. There was much wasted effort, and finally the private parties withdrew. One of the important conditions stipulated by the parties was the closure of the existing airport, which the government after having raised their hopes finally refused to carry out.

TABLE 7.2.1
Traffic at Airports

| Total traffic | Units | 1995–6 | 1996–7 | 1997–8 | 1998–9 |
|---|---|---|---|---|---|
| *Domestic* | | | | | |
| Passengers | (million) | 25.6 | 24.3 | 23.8 | 24.1 |
| Cargo | ('000 tonne) | 212.6 | 201.0 | 218.5 | 224.5 |
| Aircraft movement | ('000) | 314.7 | 303.3 | 291.4 | 325.1 |
| *International* | | | | | |
| Passengers | (million) | 11.5 | 12.2 | 12.8 | 12.9 |
| Cargo | ('000 tonne) | 436.7 | 479.1 | 487.4 | 474.7 |
| Aircraft movement | ('000) | 92.5 | 92.7 | 95.1 | 99.6 |
| *Total* | | | | | |
| Passengers | (million) | 37.1 | 36.5 | 36.6 | 37.0 |
| Cargo | ('000 tonne) | 649.3 | 680.1 | 705.9 | 699.2 |
| Aircraft movement | ('000) | 407.2 | 396.1 | 386.6 | 424.7 |

*Source:* CMIE (2000) and author's analysis.

TABLE 7.2.2
Passenger Traffic at Airports 1998–9

(numbers in millions)

| Airports | Domestic | % share | International | % share | Total | % share |
|---|---|---|---|---|---|---|
| Mumbai | 6.18 | 25.7 | 4.84 | 37.5 | 11.02 | 29.8 |
| Delhi (IGIA) | 4.09 | 17.0 | 3.79 | 29.4 | 7.88 | 21.3 |
| Chennai | 1.79 | 7.4 | 1.74 | 13.5 | 3.53 | 9.5 |
| Calcutta | 1.91 | 7.9 | 0.61 | 4.7 | 2.52 | 6.8 |
| Bangalore | 1.86 | 7.7 | 0.14 | 1.1 | 2.00 | 5.4 |
| Hyderabad (Begumpet) | 1.17 | 4.9 | 0.18 | 1.4 | 1.35 | 3.7 |
| Trivandrum | 0.31 | 1.3 | 0.83 | 6.4 | 1.14 | 3.1 |
| Ahmedabad | 0.63 | 2.6 | 0.14 | 1.1 | 0.77 | 2.1 |
| Goa (Dabolim) | 0.51 | 2.1 | 0.19 | 1.5 | 0.70 | 1.9 |
| Calicut | 0.22 | 0.9 | 0.28 | 2.2 | 0.50 | 1.4 |
| Others | 5.40 | 22.4 | 0.17 | 1.3 | 5.57 | 15.1 |
| All airports | 24.07 | 100.0 | 12.91 | 100.0 | 36.98 | 100.0 |

*Source:* CMIE (2000) and author's analysis.

TABLE 7.2.3
Cargo Traffic at Airports 1998–9

('000 tonnes)

| Airports | Domestic | % share | International | % share | Total | % share |
|---|---|---|---|---|---|---|
| Mumbai | 58.9 | 26.3 | 184.7 | 38.9 | 243.6 | 34.8 |
| Delhi (IGIA) | 47.9 | 21.3 | 150.6 | 31.7 | 198.5 | 28.4 |
| Chennai | 15.4 | 6.9 | 58.7 | 12.4 | 74.1 | 10.6 |
| Calcutta | 26.6 | 11.9 | 22.5 | 4.7 | 49.1 | 7.0 |
| Bangalore | 21.9 | 9.8 | 22.6 | 4.8 | 44.5 | 6.4 |
| Trivandrum | 5.8 | 2.6 | 24.9 | 5.2 | 30.7 | 4.4 |
| Hyderabad (Begumpet) | 8.6 | 3.8 | 4.6 | 1.0 | 13.2 | 1.9 |
| Ahmedabad | 6.4 | 2.9 | 1.5 | 0.3 | 7.9 | 1.1 |
| Goa (Dabolim) | 2.8 | 1.3 | 0.5 | 0.1 | 3.3 | 0.5 |
| Calicut | 2.1 | 0.9 | 1.0 | 0.2 | 3.1 | 0.4 |
| Others | 28.0 | 12.5 | 3.1 | 0.7 | 31.1 | 4.4 |
| All airports | 224.4 | 100.0 | 474.7 | 100.0 | 699.1 | 100.0 |

*Source:* CMIE (2000) and author's analysis.

TABLE 7.2.4
Airport Movement at Airports 1998–9

('000)

| Airports | Domestic | % share | International | % share | Total | % share |
|---|---|---|---|---|---|---|
| Mumbai | 80.9 | 25.3 | 33.1 | 33.2 | 114.0 | 27.2 |
| Delhi (IGIA) | 44.7 | 14.0 | 30.0 | 30.1 | 74.7 | 17.8 |
| Chennai | 20.7 | 6.5 | 11.2 | 11.2 | 31.8 | 7.6 |
| Bangalore | 25.1 | 7.8 | 2.8 | 2.8 | 27.9 | 6.7 |
| Calcutta | 17.7 | 5.5 | 6.7 | 6.8 | 24.4 | 5.8 |
| Hyderabad (Begumpet) | 12.7 | 4.0 | 2.1 | 2.1 | 14.8 | 3.5 |
| Ahmedabad | 10.0 | 3.1 | 0.9 | 0.9 | 10.9 | 2.6 |
| Trivandrum | 2.6 | 0.8 | 6.4 | 6.5 | 9.1 | 2.2 |
| Goa (Dabolim) | 5.7 | 1.8 | 1.1 | 1.1 | 6.8 | 1.6 |
| Calicut | 3.4 | 1.1 | 3.1 | 3.1 | 6.5 | 1.6 |
| Others | 96.3 | 30.1 | 2.2 | 2.2 | 98.5 | 23.5 |
| All airports | 319.6 | 100.0 | 99.6 | 100.0 | 419.2 | 100.0 |

*Source:* CMIE (2000) and author's analysis.

While considering new airports, location and land acquisition are important issues. Location has to be seen in conjunction with urban growth, access to key urban centres and environmental problems, especially pollution, and ease of land acquisition. While considering access to urban centres, an intermodal perspective is important.

For example, it is possible to think of a new international airport location midway between Ahmedabad and Vadodara, with direct access from the Ahmedabad–Vadodara Expressway, rather than upgrading the two airports independently. Also, scheduled coach services and even rail connections could improve catchment areas for airports, thereby allowing them to take advantage of economies of scale. Most European airports are examples of good design.[11] The existing airports at Mumbai and Delhi are connectable by rail, since suburban rail lines go very close to the airport boundary. At Chennai, the situation is even easier, with the suburban rail having a railway station very close to the terminal. However, the systems do not 'feel' integrated. A dedicated covered walkway over a dividing highway would solve the problem.

Both the proposed Bangalore and second Mumbai airports have faced problems regarding location. Apart from local resistance, there are also concerns that locations are being moved around to permit 'insider trading' in land, in view of the expected high land compensation prices.

*Air Services*

One of the first areas of liberalization in the early 1990s was permitting private participation in domestic scheduled air services. Luckily, the country had not forgotten that air services in the country had emerged with private entrepreneurship, until they were nationalized after Independence to form the Indian Airlines and Air India. Though many airlines entered the fray, only two have survived and one of them (Jet Airways) is now a major competitor to Indian Airlines, scoring better on most dimensions of service. Private scheduled airlines now account for more than 40 per cent of domestic air traffic.

Fares and schedules are deregulated. However, the policy of 'bundling', according to which a proportion of seat kilometres operated in the Category I routes (inter-metro routes, expected to be highly commercially viable) must be offered in Category II and III routes,

which constitute the unviable, and metro to smaller city routes respectively.

The policy allows the required offers of seat kilometres in these categories to be traded among the private firms. However, this approach to bundling is problematic because the airlines have been known to drag their feet in operating the less lucrative and unviable routes and operational monitoring by the regulator is weak. In fact, this categorization of routes should really be an approach to unbundling, wherein airlines willing to provide such services are allowed to bid on a minimum subsidy basis for the unviable routes.

The current policy of private investment in domestic air transport permits 40 per cent foreign equity holdings. However, equity participation by foreign airlines is not permitted! This aspect of the policy is questionable since it would imply incentive incompatibility. Surely foreign airlines' 'know-how' would be an important ingredient in upgrading domestic service levels and efficiency.

International air services are controlled by bilateral agreements between countries. However, the route rights are tradable, as in the recent example of Air India offering its unused rights to Virgin Airways of the UK in the India–UK sector. A recent welcome policy decision is that of privatization of Air India (to the extent of 60 per cent equity), in which foreign airlines are also allowed to participate. One hopes that after the hiccups have been ironed out, the privatization would go through.[12]

Cargo traffic is completely deregulated, both in the domestic and international segments. This has given a boost to especially international cargo traffic during the 1990s. In the domestic segment, courier/third party logistics companies entered the fray, and one (Blue Dart) still operates.

As part of the 'open skies' policy of the early 1990s, non-scheduled air taxi operators were allowed free entry. Today, there are over forty operators providing air taxi services, catering to tourist circuits, executives of industries, etc. A fairly extensive infrastructure of landing facilities across the country (thanks to British development initiatives during the Second World War) has come in handy for such air travel operations.

Safety is a matter of serious concern for air transport in India. Maintenance standards, airport landing and take-off facilities, and disaster management need to improve considerably. The recent examples of the air crashes in India (Patna) and in France (Concord) provided a stark contrast in disaster management abilities.

---

[11] As the urbanization pattern in India is shifting away from the 'extreme metropolitan' to the more normal real size mode, many more mid-sized cities are likely to emerge, creating large potential for such strategies.

[12] Newspaper reports would indicate that there is a 'mafia' operating in Air India. Employees at all levels have hijacked the airlines for their private gain.

The Director General of Civil Aviation (DGCA) needs to get tough in implementing safety standards.

## RAIL

Rail transportation is managed by a single organization, the Indian Railways (IR), a 'departmental enterprise' and possibly the largest business in India. As on 31 March 1999, there were 62,809 route kilometres, 81,511 running track kilometres, and 6896 stations. Its total freight traffic was 442 billion tonnes kilometres (btkm) and passenger traffic 404 billion passenger kilometres (bpkm), of which non-suburban traffic was 321 bpkm. Table 7.2.5 gives the investment input and traffic output indices, normalized at 100 for 1950–1. Wagon capacity, number of passenger coaches, tractive efforts of locos, which are the average input indices, had grown by 124 per cent and 156 per cent respectively over the same

This can also be seen by benchmarking with a similar large system like the Chinese Railways (CR) (Table 7.2.6), which has achieved a significantly higher output with almost the same route kilometres. The Chinese Railways have maintained their focus on freight transportation, though water transportation is the market sharewise leader.

Over the period 1950–1 to 1998–9, the market share of Railways has dropped from 89 per cent to 33 per cent (40 per cent as claimed by IR) in btkm and from 80 per cent to 16 per cent (20 per cent as claimed by IR) in bpkm. In fact, over the past four years, even absolute freight traffic growth has been marginal and in fact has fallen over the past two years![13]

The market profile of freight and passenger traffic with a comparison across a decade is given in Tables 7.2.7 and 7.2.8 respectively. The share of coal has gone up and iron and steel has dropped, whatever the measures used.

TABLE 7.2.5
Indices of Growth of Traffic Output and Inputs (1950–1 = 100)

| Year | Traffic output indices | | Fixed capital input indices | | | | |
|---|---|---|---|---|---|---|---|
| | Freight traffic * | Passenger traffic (non-suburban passenger km) | Route km | Running track km | Tractive efforts of locos | Wagon capacity | Passenger coaches |
| 1950–1 | 100 | 100 | 100 | 100 | 100 | 100 | 100 |
| 1960–1 | 199 | 110 | 105 | 107 | 144 | 152 | 154 |
| 1970–1 | 289 | 159 | 112 | 121 | 178 | 226 | 188 |
| 1980–1 | 359 | 279 | 114 | 128 | 201 | 269 | 210 |
| 1990–1 | 550 | 394 | 116 | 133 | 192 | 278 | 219 |
| 1991–2 | 582 | 419 | 117 | 133 | 194 | 286 | 225 |
| 1992–3 | 585 | 400 | 117 | 134 | 194 | 285 | 231 |
| 1993–4 | 583 | 389 | 117 | 134 | 188 | 273 | 233 |
| 1994–5 | 573 | 419 | 117 | 134 | 196 | 260 | 229 |
| 1995–6 | 620 | 448 | 117 | 136 | 196 | 256 | 225 |
| 1996–7 | 635 | 468 | 117 | 136 | 202 | 257 | 229 |
| 1997–8 | 650 | 502 | 117 | 136 | 215 | 258 | 234 |
| 1998–9 | 644 | 535 | 117 | 137 | 224 | 256 | 241 |

* includes non-revenue freight traffic
*Source:* IR (2000b).

period. The route and running track kilometres went up similarly by 17 and 37 per cent respectively. In the 1970s and early 1980s, the productivity gains were rather modest. Much of the productivity gains have been realized in the late 1980s and 1990s. The output indices have gone up sixfold. The above growth in factor productivity has come about due to improvements in technology, improved operating practices, and upgradation of congested infrastructure. However, scope for further improvements, especially in asset utilization, is very large.

Though not presented here, the reason that the market share of finished goods like iron and steel, cement, and fertilizer has gone down for the IR is primarily that the IR has outpriced itself out of this market. In the passenger business, the most noticeable change is the increase in the share of non-suburban upper class, and

[13] The problem is particularly serious, since India is undoubtedly at that stage of development where the need for connectivity between its growing cities is increasing more rapidly than the gross domestic product.

TABLE 7.2.6
Freight and Passenger Traffic (Chinese Railways) 1997

| | | Railways | | Highways | Waterways | Civil Aviation | Petroleum and gas pipelines | Total |
|---|---|---|---|---|---|---|---|---|
| | National | Local | Total | | | | | |
| Freight traffic (mt) | 1618.8 | 78.5 | 1697.3 | 9765.4 | 1134.1 | 1.3 | 160.0 | 12,758.1 |
| Freight km (btkm) | 1304.6 | 5.1 | 1309.7 | 527.1 | 1923.5 | 2.9 | 57.9 | 3821.1 |
| % of freight to total | 34.1 | 0.1 | 34.3 | 13.8 | 50.3 | 0.1 | 1.5 | 100.0 |
| Passenger traffic (million) | 919.2 | 6.6 | 925.8 | 12,045.8 | 225.7 | 56.3 | – | 13,253.6 |
| Passenger km (bpkm) | 354.4 | 0.5 | 354.8 | 554.1 | 15.6 | 77.4 | – | 1001.9 |
| % of passenger to total | 35.4 | 0.0 | 35.4 | 55.3 | 1.6 | 7.7 | – | 100.0 |

Comparison of Indian and Chinese Railways

| | CR (1997) | IR (1998–9) |
|---|---|---|
| Route km | 57,566 | 62,809 |
| Double track route (per cent) | 33.1 | 24.8 |
| % of Route electrified | 20.9 | 21.9 |
| Tonnes (million) | 1619 | 421 |
| Tonne km (billion) | 1305 | 282 |
| Market share of freight (per cent) | 34.3 | 32.7 |
| Passengers (million) | 919 | 4411 |
| Passenger km (billion) | 354 | 404 |
| Market share of passenger (per cent) | 35.0 | 16.5 |
| Total traffic units (btkm + bpkm) | 1659 | 686 |
| Freight % of traffic units | 78.6 | 41.1 |
| Traffic units per route km (million) | 28.8 | 11.9 |

| | CR (1995) | IR (1994) |
|---|---|---|
| Route km/1000 sq km | 5.7 | 19 |
| Route km/million population | 50 | 69 |
| No. of staff (million) | 3.37 | 1.62 |

*Source:* IR Year Book (2000b); Chinese Railways (1997).

reduction in the share of non-suburban ordinary second class. The increase in upper class has come about both due to better service differentiation and a relatively price inelastic market. The reduction in second class ordinary is partly due to competition from bus, and due to reduction in the quantum of services by the IR.

Table 7.2.9 presents the summary statistics of the IR with respect to engine, wagon, and track utilization. On almost all parameters (except for meter gauge, whose share of traffic has been dropping rapidly to insignificant levels due to large-scale conversion), increase in the asset is viewed in the 1990s. Only diesel engine utilization in km per day has come down to 552 km from a high of 673 km in the early 1990s. This is primarily due to diesel losing its prominence on the mainline routes, which have increasingly been electrified. Yet average speeds have increased, as has average wagon turnaround.

The key problem with the IR is its lack of customer orientation and irrational pricing. Customer expectations and competition have grown, especially as alternatives emerged. IR needs is to realize the full scope of its assets through proper use of systems, technology, and information technology, and 'small' investments in balancing equipments.

The IR itself sees the source of most of its problems in inadequate resources. Typically, generating resources tend to be seen more as budgetary support, and there is some justification for such attitudes, since the government has denied the IR the freedom to set tariffs.

TABLE 7.2.7

Freight Business of Indian Railways: 1998-9 and 1988-9

| Commodity group | Coal | Food-grains | Iron & steel | Iron & other ores | Cement | POL (mineral oils) | Fertilizers (chemicals manures) | Lime-stone & dolomite | Stones (including gypsum) other than marble | Salt | Sugar | Total bulk commo-dities | Other goods | Total |
|---|---|---|---|---|---|---|---|---|---|---|---|---|---|---|
| **1998-9** | | | | | | | | | | | | | | |
| Tonnes originating (million) | 198 | 28 | 13 | 50 | 37 | 33 | 28 | 8 | 6 | 4 | 2 | 406 | 15 | 421 |
| (%) | 46.9 | 6.5 | 3.1 | 11.9 | 8.7 | 7.8 | 6.6 | 2.0 | 1.4 | 0.9 | 0.5 | 96.5 | 3.5 | 100.0 |
| Net tonne km (million) | 121,779 | 32,560 | 12,691 | 18,312 | 20,981 | 20,320 | 22,445 | 5238 | 2481 | 5448 | 3024 | 265,279 | 16,233 | 281,512 |
| (%) | 43.3 | 11.6 | 4.5 | 6.5 | 7.5 | 7.2 | 8.0 | 1.9 | 0.9 | 1.9 | 1.1 | 94.2 | 5.8 | 100.0 |
| Freight earnings (Rs crore) | 9051 | 1314 | 1292 | 1214 | 1599 | 2574 | 911 | 334 | 161 | 152 | 161 | 18763 | 913 | 19676 |
| (%) | 46.0 | 6.7 | 6.6 | 6.2 | 8.1 | 13.1 | 4.6 | 1.7 | 0.8 | 0.8 | 0.8 | 95.4 | 4.6 | 100.0 |
| Average lead (km) | 616.3 | 1181.4 | 968.8 | 364.9 | 570.9 | 615.9 | 808.2 | 617.0 | 409.4 | 1464.5 | 1440.0 | 652.9 | 1111.8 | 668.8 |
| Earnings per tonne km (paise) | 74.3 | 40.3 | 101.8 | 66.3 | 76.2 | 126.7 | 40.6 | 63.7 | 64.8 | 28.0 | 53.2 | 70.7 | 56.2 | 69.9 |
| Earnings per tonne originating (Rs) | 458.0 | 476.6 | 986.4 | 242.0 | 435.2 | 780.3 | 328.0 | 393.2 | 265.1 | 409.8 | 766.7 | 461.8 | 625.2 | 467.4 |
| Market share in originating tonne (%) | 64.3 | 13.5 | | 67.2 | 41.8 | 39.6 | 75.8 | | | | | | | |
| **1988-9** | | | | | | | | | | | | | | |
| Tonnes originating (million) | 128 | 25 | 12 | 36 | 26 | 23 | 16 | 9 | 5 | 3 | 2 | 284 | 19 | 303 |
| (%) | 42.2 | 8.2 | 4.0 | 11.7 | 8.5 | 7.5 | 5.3 | 3.0 | 1.6 | 1.1 | 0.7 | 93.8 | 6.2 | 100.0 |
| Net tonne km (million) | 82,694 | 33,436 | 13,284 | 13,131 | 16,895 | 14,135 | 16,267 | 3908 | 2450 | 5476 | 2417 | 204,093 | 18,281 | 222,374 |
| (%) | 37.2 | 15.0 | 6.0 | 5.9 | 7.6 | 6.4 | 7.3 | 1.8 | 1.1 | 2.5 | 1.1 | 91.8 | 8.2 | 100.0 |
| Freight earnings (Rs crore) | 2267 | 535 | 624 | 311 | 491 | 764 | 380 | 105 | 61 | 84 | 64 | 5686 | 511 | 6197 |
| (%) | 36.6 | 8.6 | 10.1 | 5.0 | 7.9 | 12.3 | 6.1 | 1.7 | 1.0 | 1.4 | 1.0 | 91.8 | 8.2 | 100.0 |
| Average lead (km) | 646.0 | 1343.9 | 1101.5 | 368.8 | 652.1 | 625.4 | 1010.4 | 426.6 | 512.6 | 1674.6 | 1190.6 | 717.7 | 975.5 | 733.6 |
| Earnings per tonne km (paise) | 27.4 | 16.0 | 47.0 | 23.7 | 29.1 | 54.0 | 23.4 | 26.9 | 25.0 | 15.3 | 26.4 | 27.9 | 27.9 | 27.9 |
| Earnings per tonne originating (Rs) | 177.1 | 214.9 | 517.4 | 87.3 | 189.6 | 338.0 | 236.1 | 114.7 | 128.3 | 256.1 | 314.5 | 199.9 | 272.5 | 204.4 |
| Market share in originating tonne (%) | 67.9 | 14.7 | | 66.7 | 56.1 | 49.5 | 80.7 | | | | | | | |

*Source:* IR Year Book (1999).

TABLE 7.2.8
Passenger Business of IR

| Particulars | Suburban | | | Non-suburban | | | | | | Grand |
|---|---|---|---|---|---|---|---|---|---|---|
| | Season tickets | full fares | Total | Upper class | Mail/ express | Sleeper | Second class ordinary | Total of mail/ express/ sleeper and second class | Total non-suburban | total |
| **1998–9** | | | | | | | | | | |
| No. of passenger journeys (million) | 1715.0 | 953.0 | 2668.0 | 30.0 | 336.0 | 125.0 | 1252.0 | 1713.0 | 1743.0 | 4411.0 |
| (%) | 38.9 | 21.6 | 60.5 | 0.7 | 7.6 | 2.8 | 28.4 | 38.8 | 39.5 | 100.0 |
| Passenger km (billion) | 53.2 | 29.5 | 82.8 | 17.2 | 109.6 | 88.0 | 106.2 | 303.8 | 321.0 | 403.8 |
| (%) | 13.2 | 7.3 | 20.5 | 4.3 | 27.1 | 21.8 | 26.3 | 75.2 | 79.5 | 100.0 |
| Passenger earnings (crores) | 444.0 | 556.0 | 1000.0 | 1484.0 | 2362.0 | 2328.0 | 1353.0 | 6043.0 | 7527.0 | 8527.0 |
| (%) | 5.2 | 6.5 | 11.7 | 17.4 | 27.7 | 27.3 | 15.9 | 70.9 | 88.3 | 100.0 |
| Average lead (km) | 31.0 | 31.0 | 31.0 | 573.3 | 326.2 | 704.1 | 84.8 | 177.4 | 184.2 | 91.5 |
| Earnings per passenger km (paise) | 8.4 | 18.8 | 12.1 | 86.3 | 21.6 | 26.5 | 12.7 | 19.9 | 23.4 | 21.1 |
| Earnings per passenger journey (Rs) | 2.6 | 5.8 | 3.7 | 494.7 | 70.3 | 186.2 | 10.8 | 35.3 | 43.2 | 19.3 |
| **1988–9** | | | | | | | | | | |
| No. of passenger journeys (million) | 1414.0 | 591.5 | 2005.5 | 14.0 | 322.0 | | 1158.5 | 1480.5 | 1494.5 | 3500.0 |
| (%) | 40.4 | 16.9 | 57.3 | 0.4 | 9.2 | | 33.1 | 42.3 | 42.7 | 100.0 |
| Passenger km (billion) | 36.6 | 15.3 | 51.9 | 7.9 | 121.6 | | 82.3 | 203.9 | 211.8 | 263.7 |
| (%) | 13.9 | 5.8 | 19.7 | 3.0 | 46.1 | | 31.2 | 77.3 | 80.3 | 100.0 |
| Passenger earnings (crore) | 122.7 | 164.4 | 287.0 | 279.8 | 1330.1 | | 557.1 | 1887.1 | 2167.4 | 2454.3 |
| (%) | 5.0 | 6.7 | 11.7 | 11.40 | 54.2 | | 22.7 | 76.9 | 88.3 | 100.0 |
| Average lead (km) | 25.9 | 25.9 | 25.9 | 564.3 | 377.6 | | 71.0 | 137.7 | 141.7 | 75.3 |
| Earnings per passenger km (paise) | 3.4 | 10.7 | 5.5 | 35.4 | 10.9 | | 6.8 | 9.3 | 10.2 | 9.3 |
| Earnings per passenger journey (Rs) | 0.9 | 2.8 | 1.4 | 199.8 | 41.3 | | 4.8 | 12.7 | 14.5 | 7.0 |

*Souce:* IR Year Book (1999).

*Notes:* The average lead is assumed to be the same in case of season tickets and full fares for suburban, to calculate the passenger kilometers.

The number of journeys for a monthly season ticket is assumed to be 50.

Nevertheless, there is increased potential to restructure the organization to make it more commercial in orientation and responsive to the needs of stakeholders, including customers and capital markets. An expert committee, headed by Dr Rakesh Mohan, is examining restructuring of the IR with the view to increasing its resource-generating potential.

A way to restructure the IR is to separate the facilities infrastructure from the provision of services. Thus infrastructure or facility could be kept under a single entity, while services are restructured to bring in competition and private participation. A regulator is essential to oversee the process and ensure equity of access of the service providers to the infrastructure. The British restructuring has been on these lines. But some arguments against a major break up of the IR are that (i) its integrated nature has strengths of better coordination and lower transaction costs, and (ii) unlike the railway companies of Europe, which were restructured, IR is not a marginal player in the transportation business struggling for survival.

It is possible without the break up of the IR, to

TABLE 7.2.9
Utilization of Assets by Railways

(broad guage)

| Year | Engine utilization (kms per day per engine) | | Gross tonne km per kg of tractive effort | Avg. speed of goods train (kmph) | NTKM per engine hr | NTKM per wagon per day (four wheelers) | Wagon turnaround (days) |
|---|---|---|---|---|---|---|---|
| | Diesel | Electric | | | | | |
| 1950–1 | – | 191 | 1525 | 17.4 | 3283 | 710 | 11.0 |
| 1960–1 | 300 | 156 | 1864 | 16.1 | 4170 | 998 | 11.2 |
| 1970–1 | 347 | 316 | 2147 | 17.9 | 4904 | 908 | 13.3 |
| 1980–1 | 303 | 274 | 2372 | 19.7 | 6295 | 986 | 15.2 |
| 1990–1 | 445 | 398 | 3873 | 22.7 | 10,393 | 1407 | 11.5 |
| 1991–2 | 436 | 395 | 4026 | 22.7 | 10,911 | 1439 | 11.1 |
| 1992–3 | 426 | 412 | 4110 | 22.6 | 10,901 | 1457 | 10.8 |
| 1993–4 | 407 | 423 | 4272 | 22.7 | 10,864 | 1506 | 10.6 |
| 1994–5 | 413 | 423 | 4287 | 23.0 | 10,909 | 1590 | 9.9 |
| 1995–6 | 415 | 422 | 4376 | 23.3 | 11,629 | 1792 | 9.1 |
| 1996–7 | 403 | 401 | 4355 | 23.4 | 11,894 | 1840 | 8.5 |
| 1997–8 | 400 | 422 | 4690 | 23.8 | 12,104 | 1894 | 8.1 |
| 1998–9 | 396 | 444 | 4588 | 23.7 | 12,145 | 1904 | 8.2 |

*Source:* IR (1999).

have joint ventures (JVs) and special purpose vehicles (SPVs) for both infrastructure development and service provisioning. These JVs and SPVs would have to be built on the leverage of the complementary strengths and risk-taking capabilities of the partners.

### Resource Generation

Some potential modes of resource generation for the IR are now outlined.[14]

IMPROVEMENT AND EXPANSION OF SERVICES

The present emphasis on increasing freight rates to generate additional revenues has boomeranged, leading to a decrease of market share even in bulk commodities. To improve traffic revenues, the IR should concentrate on attracting traffic through service quality improvement, and possibly even reduce the freight tariffs. Multimodal transport efforts should also be taken up seriously which could divert freight traffic from road to rail.

Focus on value-added services (both in passenger and freight) at premium prices could also generate additional revenues. Recent studies have shown that increased capacity in upper class passenger services would be viable. Reservation for journeys from stations other than from where booking is being made, reservation-related inquiries, tourist train circuits, etc. are services for which customers would be willing to pay premium

charges. Similarly, in the case of freight, time guarantees both for wagon allotment and transit time, transit and handling insurance, etc. are services for which customers would be willing to pay, especially since there would be savings for them on inventories and avoidance of losses in transit.

The IR can expand its customer base to include advertisers, telecom operators, and real estate developers. For these parties, the IR infrastructure and service operations offer valuable inputs to leverage their own businesses. The potential remains underexploited. The IR needs to put up such projects, and possibly even nurture them.

REDUCING COSTS

The IR has made some efforts to cut down costs. The main element of railway costs, which can be brought down in the future, is manpower costs which now account for over half the total working expenses. Wage rates are low, but the numbers employed are far in excess of the requirement, given current technology. Some of the steps taken to reduce manpower are abolishing of posts on retirement, privatization of maintenance activities, and increasing use of contractors for execution of works. But reduction of manpower has not been seriously pursued. An earlier minister of Railways was committed to creating six additional railway zones to 'develop' backward regions and provide employment! Another minister set the clock back on privatization of maintenance services by going back to increased in-house employment merely to create 'government jobs'.

[14] The remaining part of the discussion on IR is excerpted from Raghuram and Babu (1999).

Similarly, asset utilization has much potential to reduce the overall unit cost of output. This is especially so with regard to rolling stock and track, the principal assets of any railway systems. In 1996–7 a broad gauge wagon moved 158 km in a day. With the average goods train speed being 23 kmph, a wagon was effectively running for seven hours a day. Similarly, broad gauge electric and diesel locomotives moved an average of just over 400 km in a day, giving an average utilization of just about 16 hours in a day. Passenger coaches for broad gauge mail/express services achieved a utilization of over 500 km per day, giving an average of ten hours a day at an average speed of 50 kmph. Even if one accounts, for time spent at yards and terminals, and for maintenance, the scope for improving rolling stock utilization is very high. Track utilization can improve on the golden quadrilateral to great advantage. Even though these are high density tracks that presently carry over 70 trains each way on double track sections, the potential to carry at least 100 trains each way can be immediately exploited through improved signalling and information systems! Since the quadrilateral accounts for over 60 per cent of traffic, and there is no shortage of demand (with the right prices), such improvement in asset utilization could result in an increase of at around 30 per cent in turnover!

## MARKET BORROWINGS

Domestic market borrowings are expensive, with interest rates being over 15 per cent. The average return (revenues less expenses, but before dividend payment) on equity (budgetary support) has been 14.9 per cent and 11.7 per cent during 1995–6 and 1996–7, respectively. The average return on total investment has been 10.4 per cent and 8.1 per cent during these years. A study in 1997 by Mckinsey Consultants on behalf of the Asian Development Bank thought railways in India to be a 'sunrise sector' for investments. However, customer and commercial orientation within the IR and the internal organizational structure would have to undergo dramatic changes for the IR to be able to attract large investments.

## BOT

The only experience to date under a BOT (build, operate, and transfer) scheme in the IR is the Konkan Railway Corporation (KRC). While the Special Purpose Vehicle (SPV) set up for this gained from reduced pro-ject financing and completion risks, it was a victim of perverse contracts that enhanced market risk and denied it market access. With no direct access to major traffic originating/terminating points, the KRC is dependent on neighbouring railway zones for traffic. The existing railway zones would like to hold on to their traffic to post better financial results at a time when overall freight market

growth for rail traffic is uncertain or falling.[15] The KRC would certainly have been better off with direct access into the Mumbai area, as also other areas in the south.

A vanilla BOT model can hardly be applied without substantial modification for a part of a large interconnected network. Specific clauses to share revenues, as in originating and distributing demand and interconnect aspects, have to be part of an enhanced BOT. The BOT concept though would have ready application in value-added services like tourist circuits, catering services, terminal operations, multimodal operations, freight forwarding, and consolidation services. In such areas the market can be directly accessed by the BOT operator. In some of these where the life of the assets is not substantially longer than the term of the debt, the projects need not be BOT. BOO (build, own and operate) would be better.

## BOLT

The BOLT (build, operate, lease, and transfer) scheme has not been successful since projects under it are being treated conventionally in awarding and finalizing contracts. The potential of the scheme is difficult to assess since sufficient experience has not yet been built up.

To make BOLT schemes successful, the IR needs to appreciate the fact that the risks faced by the BOLT operator are quite high and different from small contracts. The BOLT operator should also be capable of absorbing the expected down swing in business. The operator should have a long-term interest in the project. The IR should attempt to build long-term relationships with potential BOLT operators based on mutual interest. Case by case approach is best avoided. To offer economies of scale to the operator, especially for his supply contracts, equipment purchase and deployment, either large projects or bundling of smaller projects may be necessary.

The present procedures for obtaining clearances and clarifications from ministries like finance and environment do not, in all cases, explicitly recognize the BOLT operator as a body different from the IR! Matters that could be taken for granted or even dealt with during the project execution stage between ministries would have to be consciously considered prior to the project award stage. Similarly, hidden costs such as use of rolling stock, transport of material and men, and use of captive communication facilities need to be explicitly considered. These could significantly affect project viability.

## BUDGETARY SUPPORT

While it is clear that budgetary support would decrease, the IR should renegotiate an annual contribution

---

[15] Because of absurdly high prices, over which the Railways as such have little control.

towards social obligations imposed on it by the government. The extent of social service obligation during 1996–7 was assessed at Rs 1826 crores on account of:

(i) transport of essential commodities carried at very low rates;

(ii) concessional passenger fares to season ticket holders and a variety of social welfare constituents, including 'forced' operation of certain unremunerative passenger trains;

(iii) investment in uneconomic railway lines on national considerations and 'forced' operation of uneconomic branch lines.

The first step in this exercise would be to develop a robust valuation model that can use various assumptions of alternative use of the capacity. With regular 'subsidy' contribution coming from the government it would be necessary to calculate the same in a manner that is transparent and convincing.

Further, to make a strong case for such contributions, the present costing system of the IR is inadequate and needs to be redesigned. Regarding item (iii) above, there have been situations in which other ministries like Defence, or state governments, have contributed part of the costs. The government has also declared the Rs 2100 crore Udhampur–Srinagar–Baramula line in Jammu & Kashmir to be a national project and has agreed to fully fund the project.

While renegotiating government support, financial restructuring of the capital at charge (which was nearly Rs 31,000 crore by the end of 1996–7 and is likely to be about Rs 35,000 crore by the end of 1998–9) as equity would have to be considered.[16] This would enable the IR to hold back the obligatory dividend payment, which has been of the order of Rs 1500 crore per annum in recent years.

## ROAD TRANSPORT

### Roads

The total road length in the country is 2.5 million km, which represents about a sevenfold growth over the past fifty years. The net outcome of this has been 'extensive connectivity' across the country. However, the quality of the connectivity in terms of reduction of journey times may not have been much. More importantly in com-parison to other countries in East Asia and elsewhere, this achievement is very much below the average!

Roads are classified as national highways, state highways, other district roads (all three of which are maintained by the Public Works Department [PWD]), panchayat raj roads, urban roads, project roads, and JRY (Jawahar Rozgaar Yojana) roads.

Village connectivity still remains a problem. Only 37.5 per cent of villages with population less than a thousand were connected as of 31 March 1994! Besides the capacity and quality of even many national highway segments is very poor. The same is true of many of the state highways and many of the urban roads.

An important aspect of road development is safety. Unfortunately this is not integral to the design of road and highway systems in India (Dinesh 2000). Table 7.2.10 gives statewise data on various safety parameters, for the year 1994–5. Safety indicators with regard to vehicles, such as accidents per 10,000 vehicles or persons killed per 10,000 vehicles are presented. At an all-India level, while the parameters with respect to vehicles have come down, they have gone up with respect to the road length. This is a reflection of both increased traffic on roads and the vehicle profile having changed. The proportion of motorized two wheelers (MTWs) has gone up substantially (Table 7.2.11). MTWs are accident-prone, especially in conjunction with heavy vehicles. Some inter-state comparisons with respect to vehicles would not be valid, since the base is against number of vehicles registered, while accidents could be on any vehicle passing through the state. For example, a state like Arunachal Pradesh, which has fewer registered vehicles, would reflect poorer performance compared to Delhi, Pondicherry, or Chandigarh on the vehicle-related statistics.

Another significant aspect is developing higher capacity roads on key segments, to take advantage of the fact that less than 2 per cent of the roads carry over 40 per cent of the tonne km traffic. Success of private involvement in long stretch road development has been poor, while de-bottlenecking investments in bypasses, bridges, and over/under passes have been more successful.

The late 1980s saw the initiation of discussions over involvement of private players in toll road development. A case in point is the acquisition of land for the purpose. As the government itself was very vulnerable to local political and other forces, and consequent litigation, it was expected that the private sector could 'manage' its way better towards land acquisition!

Much has changed since then, and the government can acquire land and hand it over to private sector road developers prior to the project. It is only the government which can operate under the principle of 'eminent domain', to attempt land acquisition in the larger interest of society. Over the years, project structuring has increasingly provided for greater incentives. These include roadside concessions (for licensing petrol pumps,

---

[16] The idea of an obligatory dividend payment is an anathema to any business, and especially a cyclical industry like the railway.

TABLE 7.2.10
Road Safety Statistics 1994–5

| State | No. of accidents | No. of persons killed | No. of persons injured | No. of vehicles registered* | Road length (km) | Accidents/ 10,000 vehicles | Accidents/ 10,000 km of road | Persons killed/ 10,000 vehicles | Persons killed/ 10,000 km of road | Vehicle density/ 100 km of length |
|---|---|---|---|---|---|---|---|---|---|---|
| Andhra Pradesh | 17,128 | 5561 | 20,122 | 2,212,363 | 171,785 | 77.4 | 997.1 | 25.1 | 323.7 | 1287.9 |
| Arunachal Pradesh | 176 | 85 | 254 | 14621 | 11,860 | 120.4 | 148.4 | 58.1 | 71.7 | 123.3 |
| Assam | 1862 | 914 | 2657 | 352,874 | 68,090 | 52.8 | 273.5 | 25.9 | 134.2 | 518.2 |
| Bihar | 6892 | 2681 | 5120 | 1,246,132 | 87,854 | 55.3 | 784.5 | 21.5 | 305.2 | 1418.4 |
| Delhi | 10,138 | 2074 | 9805 | 2,432,295 | 24,512 | 41.7 | 4135.9 | 8.5 | 846.1 | 9922.9 |
| Goa | 2903 | 231 | 2243 | 192,684 | 7303 | 150.7 | 3975.1 | 12.0 | 316.3 | 2638.4 |
| Gujarat | 30,111 | 4871 | 29,180 | 3,021,166 | 85,768 | 99.7 | 3510.7 | 16.1 | 567.9 | 3522.5 |
| Haryana | 6610 | 2559 | 6717 | 952,434 | 27,180 | 69.4 | 2431.9 | 26.9 | 941.5 | 3504.2 |
| Himachal Pradesh | 1784 | 609 | 3499 | 104,939 | 29,926 | 170.0 | 596.1 | 58.0 | 203.5 | 350.7 |
| Jammu and Kashmir | 2917 | 434 | 3005 | 177,874 | 12,590 | 164.0 | 2316.9 | 24.4 | 344.7 | 1412.8 |
| Karnataka | 30,186 | 5653 | 43,898 | 2,014,141 | 139,768 | 149.9 | 2159.7 | 28.1 | 404.5 | 1441.1 |
| Kerala | 37,980 | 2708 | 53,400 | 1,005,922 | 139,320 | 377.6 | 2726.1 | 26.9 | 194.4 | 722.0 |
| Madhya Pradesh | 27,449 | 4596 | – | 2,069,646 | 211,025 | 132.6 | 1300.7 | 22.2 | 217.8 | 980.8 |
| Maharashtra | 73,085 | 8552 | 48,776 | 3,621,331 | 224,973 | 201.8 | 3248.6 | 23.6 | 380.1 | 1609.7 |
| Manipur | 352 | 111 | 641 | 58,342 | 10,530 | 60.3 | 334.3 | 19.0 | 105.4 | 554.1 |
| Meghalaya | 365 | 152 | 525 | 41,963 | 7721 | 87.0 | 472.7 | 36.2 | 196.9 | 543.5 |
| Mizoram | 78 | 78 | 208 | 16,340 | 6577 | 47.7 | 118.6 | 47.7 | 118.6 | 248.4 |
| Nagaland | 98 | 55 | 238 | 86,376 | 12,880 | 11.3 | 76.1 | 6.4 | 42.7 | 670.6 |
| Orissa | 6202 | 1661 | 7810 | 594,140 | 209,888 | 104.4 | 295.5 | 28.0 | 79.1 | 283.1 |
| Punjab | 2601 | 1897 | 2385 | 1,769,754 | 57,039 | 14.7 | 456.0 | 10.7 | 332.6 | 3102.7 |
| Rajasthan | 16,613 | 4865 | 20,512 | 1,584,776 | 130,085 | 104.8 | 1277.1 | 30.7 | 374.0 | 1218.3 |
| Sikkim | 164 | 46 | 351 | 6876 | 1824 | 238.5 | 899.1 | 66.9 | 252.2 | 377.0 |
| Tamil Nadu | 41,685 | 8773 | 38,312 | 2,423,448 | 204,475 | 172.0 | 2038.6 | 36.2 | 429.1 | 1185.2 |
| Tripura | 421 | 135 | 795 | 32,103 | 14,706 | 131.1 | 286.3 | 42.1 | 91.8 | 218.3 |
| Uttar Pradesh | 16,644 | 8922 | 14,050 | 2,544,215 | 200,010 | 65.4 | 832.2 | 35.1 | 446.1 | 1272.0 |
| West Bengal | 13,050 | 2615 | 7225 | 1,198,733 | 68,316 | 108.9 | 1910.2 | 21.8 | 382.8 | 1754.7 |
| Andaman & Nicobar | 103 | 22 | 133 | 13,283 | 871 | 77.5 | 1182.5 | 16.6 | 252.6 | 1525.0 |
| Chandigarh | 345 | 119 | 347 | 352,308 | 1632 | 9.8 | 2114.0 | 3.4 | 729.2 | 21,587.5 |
| Dadra & Nagar Haveli | 93 | 21 | 99 | 9161 | 509 | 101.5 | 1827.1 | 22.9 | 412.6 | 1799.8 |
| Daman & Diu | – | – | – | 15,872 | – | – | – | – | – | – |
| Lakshadweep | 3 | – | 6 | 1320 | – | 22.7 | – | – | – | – |
| Pondicherry | 915 | 140 | 849 | 119,290 | 2338 | 76.7 | 3913.6 | 11.7 | 598.8 | 5102.2 |
| All states | 348,953 | 71,140 | 323,162 | 30,286,722 | 2,171,355 | 115.2 | 1607.1 | 23.5 | 327.6 | 1394.8 |

*Source:* CMIE (2000), MoST, Motor Transport Statistics in India, various issues.
* MoST.

garages, eateries, and lodges), part financing as equity, debt with lower interest rates, and even commercial development opportunities to tap into the likely increased property value along the road. Despite the willingness to allow similar provisions, the private sector costs were too high in the case of the Mumbai–Pune Expressway which finally had to be undertaken by a state level corporation. Financial closures have been achieved on very few long segment projects; even in these, the segments are in the 40 to 80 km range (for example Vadodara–Halol, Ahmedabad–Mehsana).

Land is a premium resource in urban areas. In this context, parking fees, both to reduce roadside congestion and to raise revenues, should be considered a priority item by urban administrations. As viable alternatives, multistorey parking facilities can be provided as a

TABLE 7.2.11
Total Registered Motor Vehicles in India (Aggregate and per cent)

('000 nos)

| Year (as on 31 March) | Two wheelers | Car, jeeps, and taxis | Buses | Goods vehicles | Others* | All vehicles |
|---|---|---|---|---|---|---|
| 1951 | 27 | 159 | 34 | 82 | 4 | 306 |
|  | 9 | 52 | 11 | 27 | 1 | 100 |
| 1961 | 88 | 310 | 57 | 168 | 42 | 665 |
|  | 13 | 47 | 9 | 25 | 6 | 100 |
| 1971 | 576 | 682 | 94 | 343 | 170 | 1865 |
|  | 31 | 37 | 5 | 18 | 9 | 100 |
| 1981 | 2618 | 1160 | 162 | 554 | 897 | 5391 |
|  | 49 | 22 | 3 | 10 | 17 | 100 |
| 1991 | 14,200 | 2954 | 331 | 1356 | 2533 | 21,374 |
|  | 66 | 14 | 2 | 6 | 12 | 100 |
| 1992 | 15,661 | 3205 | 358 | 1514 | 2769 | 23,507 |
|  | 67 | 14 | 2 | 6 | 12 | 100 |
| 1993 | 17,183 | 3361 | 364 | 1603 | 2994 | 25,505 |
|  | 67 | 13 | 1 | 6 | 12 | 100 |
| 1994 | 18,899 | 3569 | 392 | 1691 | 3109 | 27,660 |
|  | 68 | 13 | 1 | 6 | 11 | 100 |
| 1995 | 20,831 | 3841 | 423 | 1794 | 3406 | 30,295 |
|  | 69 | 13 | 1 | 6 | 11 | 100 |
| 1996 | 23,111 | 4189 | 449 | 1785 | 4024 | 33,558 |
|  | 69 | 12 | 1 | 5 | 12 | 100 |
| 1997(E) | 25,915 | 4682 | 512 | 2265 | 4207 | 37,581 |
|  | 69 | 12 | 1 | 6 | 11 | 100 |

*Source:* Central Institute of Road Transport (2000).
Figures in the second row of the same year indicate the per cent of all registered motor vehicles.

*Notes:* *Others includes tractors, trailers, three wheelers (passengers and goods vehicles), and other miscellaneous vehicles which are not separately classified.

commercial venture. It should also be made mandatory for all urban commercial development projects to assess their impact on parking (given their customer and employee profile) and provide plans for dealing with the same, before they are permitted to do business.

One important reason for recommending private involvement in road development is the need for sound project management. This is a multi-functional task, requiring a high level of coordination and a proactive approach to anticipating and avoiding delays. A live example of poor project management is that of the Ahmedabad–Vadodara Expressway (Gupta 2000). This was originally slated for completion in 1991, but is still incomplete in 2000. The capital waste factor on this has been assessed at 865 per cent, indicating that the deployed resources would have actually financed nearly nine such projects, if on schedule. A mechanism to ensure maintenance so as to avoid capital degradation during the project phase is essential. (The Sardar Sarovar Project canals would be a case in point.)

It may be worthwhile considering a legislation that would prevent reallocation of funds from committed projects, unless that particular project has been given up.

One of the most significant aspects in the measure of capacity on Indian roads arises out of the mixed traffic conditions. The concept of passenger car equivalent units (PCUs), which is used for capacity assessments and road designs in the advanced West, needs a fresh look in the Indian context.

In India it would be difficult to come up with a single PCU measure for each of the vehicle types, since it will depend upon the particular vehicle mix and road geometries (see Box 7.2.1). This measure should be pegged on to the modal vehicle type (the 10-tonne truck on the highways, the passenger car on the central business district (CBD) roads of the metros of Mumbai, Chennai, and Calcutta, the MTW in all the other metros, the tractor or the animal drawn vehicle (ADV) on rural roads, etc.). Even while planning for better flow of motorized vehicles, the interaction with non-motorized vehicles (NMVs) needs to be recognized and dealt with (Tiwari 2000).

So far as de-bottlenecking and better maintenance of roads are concerned, MOT (maintain, operate, and transfer) contracts with (professionally managed) private parties could yield significant benefits. Madhya Pradesh and Maharashtra have already achieved financial closure on certain important stretches under this model. An important element of the MOT contract should be to provide high service levels for post-accident support and breakdown removal.

## Road Freight Transport

While this industry is completely privatized, it is highly unorganized. There is a major divide between trucking companies and truck owners. Trucking companies deal with the customer, bid for contracts, and help consolidate traffic. The truck owners, many of whom are also drivers, are part of entities that typically own less than five trucks each. The only semblance of 'organization' is a few large trucking companies, that provide 'branded' service.

The consequences and the operational dynamics of this industry, structure along with poor road conditions, are that (i) service levels are very poor, resulting in losses and higher logistics costs, and (ii) cut-throat price competition.

The major issues which need a careful review towards sorting out the problems arising out of the highly fragmented industry structure are:

- The special financing incentives offered to the educated unemployed for buying trucks for commercial use, as long as the number of trucks owned is small may have unnecessarily fragmented the industry;

- The Motor Transport Workers Act, which requires provision of proper rest facilities and time limits for drivers is often violated;

- The need for 'side payments' at various checkposts, which add up to a big 'unaccountable' amount for a large fleet owner, but can be managed by the smaller players.

## Road Passenger Transport

Road passenger transport can be categorized into (i) private; (ii) intermediate; and (iii) public. People aspire to move to private modes. This is clearly visible in the vehicle profile of the country, especially in urban areas. However, improving the provisioning of public transport on urban, intercity, and rural routes has emerged as a major challenge to developers. Private stakeholding and competition seem to be potential means of managing the infrastructure. As of 1996-7, nearly 23 per cent of buses were in the public sector, a significant reduction from the 43 per cent in 1980-1. The public sector state road transport undertakings (SRTUs) have not been well managed. As seen in the time-series data in Table 7.2.12, all the SRTUs together have posted a loss of over Rs 1900 crore in 1998-9, up from a loss of Rs 700 crore four years earlier.

The SRTUs offer significant potential for restructuring through private involvement, route rationalization, vehicle size mix, etc. A case study of attempted restructuring of the Delhi Transport Corporation by route rationalization is given in Marwah *et al.* (2000). While it is not addressed here, route rationalization would become even more significant in the context of the Delhi Mass Rapid Transit (DMRT) project. The success of a highly capital-intensive 'backbone' project like

TABLE 7.2.12
Performance Indicators of All State Road Transport Undertakings

| Year | Fleet strength (thousand) | Fleet utilization (%) | Annual km (crore) | Vehicles km/bus (daily) | Passengers carried/day (crore) | Revenue | Expenditure | Profit (Loss) |
|------|------|------|------|------|------|------|------|------|
| | | | | | | (Rs crore) | | |
| 1990–1 | 104.1 | 85.3 | 881 | 240 | 5.9 | 5052.3 | 5731.7 | −679.3 |
| 1991–2 | 107.1 | 87.0 | 941 | 248 | 6.0 | 6054.3 | 6705.1 | −650.9 |
| 1992–3 | 109.7 | 87.9 | 985 | 257 | 5.9 | 6967.6 | 7626.1 | −658.5 |
| 1993–4 | 111.2 | 88.0 | 1018 | 264 | 5.7 | 7936.6 | 8558.2 | −621.5 |
| 1994–5 | 111.5 | 89.0 | 1047 | 271 | 6.1 | 8773.4 | 9475.8 | −702.4 |
| 1995–6 | 111.1 | 87.7 | 1072 | 271 | 6.4 | 9050.2 | 8679.6 | 370.6 |
| 1996–7 | 113.4 | 88.0 | 1074 | 270 | 6.4 | 9599.1 | 10903.9 | −1304.8 |
| 1997–8 | 115.2 | 90.2 | 1129 | 278 | 6.4 | 11556.1 | 12838.4 | −1282.4 |
| 1998–9 | 116.0 | 89.9 | 1176 | 279 | 6.7 | 12367.0 | 14284.9 | −1917.9 |

*Sources:* Central Institute of Road Transport (1998–9); and CMIE (2000).

the DMRT and the bus transport system would depend on how well they complement each other, smoothly feeding into each other, ever if this implies a change in existing travel patterns.

In the sphere of private entrepreneurship, intermediate transportation (chartered buses, taxis, three-wheelers, etc. for public hire) has grown significantly, both in urban and rural areas, providing a much needed transport service. However, strict regulation, especially for licensing, ensuring professionalism amongst the service providers (possibly through required training), and good vehicle condition to protect the customer and the environment, are.

*Vehicle Manufacture*

This sector is open to private participation, and has matured thus. While production capacity is no longer an issue (due to the dismantling of the licence raj), technology upgradation and pollution management are significant concerns. The R&D effort by the industry is far less than desirable and needs to be incentivized. Emission norms and control measures are below international standards (Pundhir 2000). Implementation of policy is a major issue, especially in ensuring that vehicles are properly maintained. States like Andhra Pradesh, Gujarat, and Maharashtra are making progress in this matter (and in related areas of regulation like licensing of drivers) through e-governance, that is use of information technology.

MARITIME TRANSPORT

Maritime transport consists of ports, overseas shipping, coastal shipping, inland water transport, ship building and ship repair, and light houses and light ships. There is ample scope for private involvement in all aspects of the maritime sector, especially because all segments are contestable.

As of now, inland water transport does not seem to have much potential, unless a massive investment programme in 'training' some of the perennial rivers' segments and coastal waterways is undertaken. A discussion on various aspects of ports, overseas shipping, and coastal shipping areas is presented here.

*Ports*

Table 7.2.13 presents traffic and performance indicators at major ports for 1998-9. The total traffic handled at the major ports during 1998-9 was 252 million tonnes (mt) (237 mt excluding trans-shipment), and at the minor and intermediate ports it was 36 mt. Of this, 72 mt and 11 mt, respectively, were coastal traffic. In minor and intermediate ports, Gujarat is the dominant player, accounting for 26 mt of traffic. Gujarat is expected to show significant increase in traffic due to the Reliance Refinery and the private ports, which have started operations during 1999–2000. Traffic is expected to reach 60 mt by 2000-1 and 100 mt within another couple of years. Maharashtra traffic has been growing rapidly over the past four years and is now over 5 mt.

TABLE 7.2.13
Traffic and Performance Indicators at Major Ports 1998–9

| Port | Total | | | Revenue | Expenditure | Revenue/ tonne | Expenditure/ tonne |
|---|---|---|---|---|---|---|---|
| | Total* | Overseas* | Coastal* | | | | |
| | ('000 tonnes) | | | (Rs crore) | | (Rs) | |
| Calcutta Port trust | 5638 | 3297 | 2341 | 905 | 662 | 350 | 256 |
| Haldia | 20,224 | 13,889 | 6335 | ** | ** | ** | ** |
| Paradip | 13,108 | 5282 | 7826 | 173 | 113 | 132 | 87 |
| Visakhapatnam | 28,928 | 18,840 | 10,088 | 274 | 181 | 95 | 63 |
| Chennai | 33,646 | 16,438 | 17,208 | 314 | 219 | 93 | 65 |
| Tuticorin | 10,150 | 4970 | 5180 | 85 | 45 | 84 | 44 |
| Cochin | 12,665 | 7326 | 5339 | 163 | 129 | 129 | 102 |
| New Mangalore | 14,172 | 11,672 | 2500 | 155 | 83 | 109 | 58 |
| Marmugao | 17,996 | 17,090 | 906 | 121 | 100 | 67 | 56 |
| Mumbai | 30,925 | 22,573 | 8352 | 607 | 434 | 196 | 140 |
| JNPT | 11,650 | 10,762 | 888 | 383 | 187 | 329 | 160 |
| Kandla | 37,907 | 32,919 | 4988 | 232 | 86 | 61 | 23 |
| All ports | 237,009 | 165,058 | 71,951 | 3412 | 2241 | 144 | 95 |

* Excluding trans-shipment of 14.7 mt.
** included in the Calcutta Port Trust.
JNPT: Jawaharlal Nehru Port Trust.
*Sources:* MoST (1999).
Indian Ports Association (2000).

## BOX 7.2.1
### A Relook at Passenger Car Equivalents in the Indian Context
*B. R. Marwah*

The composition of traffic must be taken into account in highway capacity analysis. Passenger car equivalents (PCEs) or passenger car units (PCUs), by which the mixed traffic volumes are expressed as an equivalent number of passenger cars, are instruments used for this. The American Highway Capacity Manual (HCM-1985), defines a passenger-car equivalent as the number of passenger cars a single heavy vehicle of specified type displaces in a given traffic stream. The nature of this 'displacement' or 'equivalence' is, however, not uniformly defined or understood.

The PCE value varies greatly depending upon several factors. Trucks have higher PCE value than buses, which have generally better operating capabilities. PCEs decrease as the percentage of heavy vehicle in the traffic increases. This is because as more heavy vehicles enter the traffic stream, they tend to segregate from passenger cars, by concentrating in certain lanes and forming platoons of heavy vehicles. As heavy vehicles have more uniform operating characteristics when operating in platoons, the impact of each vehicle in such circumstances is less than that of an isolated heavy vehicle operating among passenger cars.

Nevertheless, the cumulative effect of many heavy vehicles in the traffic stream is more severe than that of a few. PCEs increase with the severity of terrain and are largest on long sustained upgrades. PCEs are more severe on two-lane highways, where the passing maneuver is more difficult, than on multi-lane facilities. Finally, PCE values may differ depending upon the exact interpolation of 'equivalence' used in their calibration.

The estimation of passenger car equivalents for different types of vehicles in India is of great importance due to the mixed traffic on Indian roads. Very limited research work has been attempted in this area. The PCEs specified by IRC are adopted in estimating the equivalent passenger car demand on the roads. Estimation of this demand is of relevance in planning for benefit-cost analysis of new highway projects.

The PCE values as recommended by Indian Roads Congress (IRC) for rural and urban roads is tabulated here. However, the guidelines do not elaborate as how these values are computed. The guidelines on capacity of urban roads do acknowledge the fact that PCE value of a vehicle is dependent on traffic composition. Yet, only two levels of compositions trucks (less than or equal to 5 per cent and greater than 10 per cent) are taken into account.

- The value of PCE for a vehicle depends upon various road and traffic characteristics: road geometrics, comprising width, shoulder type and width, horizontal curve, longitudinal grades, road roughness etc.; and taffic characteristics, consisting of volume, composition of different types of vehicle, and directional distribution.

- The relative impacts of a vehicle on speed, capacity, overtaking, platoon formation and other traffic characteristics may lead to quite different estimates of its PCE value.

- PCE for a truck based on overtaking delays may be much higher on long steep gradients.

- PCE values vary with the traffic volume and proportion of slower vehicles in the traffic stream. It is found that the incremental effect of the first ten percent trucks in a traffic stream is greater than that of an additional ten percent

- The magnitude of the directional split also affects the PCE values.

- Impact on delays to the traffic stream by an isolated slow moving vehicle may be much higher than when it is moving in a platoon of slow moving vehicles.

- The passenger car equivalents of a slow or heavy vehicle may be considered to have two components: the extra space taken by the vehicle; and the extra delay caused by slower speed and greater difficulty in overtaking. The space component should represent a lower PCE for capacity conditions on level roads where speeds are uniformly low and overtaking is not possible.

An Indian Traffic Simulation Model for two lane and four lane highways was implemented jointly by IIT Kanpur and CRRI, New Delhi, under the sponsorship of MoST.

*Recommended PCE Factors for Vehicles*

| Vehicle type | % composition of heavy vehicle type in traffic on urban roads | | Rural roads |
|---|---|---|---|
| | < 5% | 10% ≤ | |
| Motor Cycle or Scooter | 0.50 | 0.75 | 0.50 |
| Passenger Car: Pickup Van | 1.00 | 1.00 | 1.00 |
| Agricultural Tractor, LCV | 1.20 | 2.00 | 1.50 |
| Auto Rickshaw | 1.40 | 2.00 | 3.00 |
| Light Commercial Vehicle | 2.20 | 3.70 | 4.50 |
| Truck or Bus | 4.00 | 5.00 | 0.50 |
| Bicycle | 0.40 | 0.50 | 2.00 |
| Cycle Rickshaw | 1.50 | 2.00 | 3.00 |
| Horse Cart | 1.50 | 2.00 | 4.00 |
| Hand Cart | 2.00 | 3.00 | 8.00 |

International agencies like the World Bank, Swedish Road Research Institute and Australian Road Research Board participated for in some of the activities. The model was calibrated over a wide spectrum of road and traffic characteristics.

The simulation results were then used to estimate the level of service (LOS) under different operating conditions. This will help estimate PCEs of vehicles under different road and traffic characteristics. The amount of data needed to fully calibrate a set of passenger-car equivalents for different types of Indian vehicles is very large. Hence, no common concept of equivalence emerged and researchers have not agreed on specific calibration techniques.

It is therefore desirable to develop traffic simulation models for Indian traffic and to conduct experiments on the models to predict the behavior of mixed traffic under different conditions. More than PCEs as such, traffic simulation calibrated for various road and traffic conditions especially those specific to India, would be very useful in project analysis.

Of the 252 mt of traffic handled at the major ports in 1998–9, non-POL (petroleum oil and lubricant) (products and crude), coal, and iron ore accounted for 71 per cent traffic, at 107 mt, 39 mt, and 34 mt respectively (Table 7.2.14). This was followed by container handling at 24 mt, fertilizer (finished) at 4.7 mt, fertilizer (raw material) at 4.3 mt, and foodgrains at 3.5 mt. These seven commodities constituted 86 per cent of total traffic.

Soon even the JNPT could be out of reckoning since 6000 plus TEU vessels are expected to come in.

The primary issue in port development is congestion at ports, resulting in unacceptable average turnaround times of 5.9 days (Table 7.2.19). The net cost of congestion at the major ports in India, benchmarking with an acceptable average of two days at ports internationally, was $ 457.9 million, that is Rs 1623 crores for 1998–9.[17]

TABLE 7.2.14
Commodity-wise Cargo Traffic Handled at Major Ports

('000 tonnes)

| Year | POL (%) | Coal (%) | Iron ore (%) | Container (%) | Fertilizer | | Food-grains (%) | Others (%) | Total | of which | |
| | | | | | finished (%) | raw material (%) | | | | Unloaded | Loaded |
|---|---|---|---|---|---|---|---|---|---|---|---|
| 1991–2 | 44 | 14 | 20 | 5 | 2 | 3 | 1 | 12 | 157,598 | 84,853 | 69,327 |
| 1992–3 | 44 | 14 | 18 | 5 | 2 | 2 | 0 | 13 | 166,611 | 95,810 | 67,380 |
| 1993–4 | 43 | 15 | 19 | 7 | 2 | 2 | 1 | 12 | 179,260 | 100,492 | 78,768 |
| 1994–5 | 42 | 15 | 18 | 8 | 2 | 2 | 0 | 13 | 197,262 | 113,776 | 83,486 |
| 1995–6 | 42 | 15 | 16 | 8 | 3 | 2 | 1 | 13 | 215,338 | 126,629 | 88,709 |
| 1996–7 | 43 | 15 | 15 | 9 | 1 | 2 | 1 | 13 | 227,257 | 139,208 | 88,049 |
| 1997–8 | 41 | 15 | 16 | 9 | 2 | 2 | 1 | 13 | 251,659 | 155,977 | 95,682 |
| 1998–9 | 43 | 16 | 14 | 9 | 2 | 2 | 1 | 14 | 251,720 | 164,601 | 87,119 |

*Source:* Indian Ports Association (2000).

The total tonnage of 24 mt through containers was handled across 1.93 million twenty feet equivalent units (TEUs) (Table 7.2.15). Over the eight years preceding 1998–9, container tonnage grew at 14.5 per cent CAGR, while the TEUs grew at 13.9 per cent CAGR. The major portwise containers handled for 1998–9 are given in Table 7.2.16. While container traffic has been growing in India, the total TEUs handled across all the ports are still less than the tenth port among developing countries. The top two ports in the world classified as being in the developing countries handled over 16 million TEUs, that is over 8 times the total TEUs handled at all Indian ports (Table 7.2.17).

Another issue with respect to containers is that most of the containers from/to Indian ports are serviced by feeder vessels for/after trans-shipment at the ports in Colombo, the Middle East, or Singapore. Table 7.2.18 provides data on this, from which we see that except the Jawaharlal Nehur Port Trust (JNPT), all the other ports handle transhipped containers anywhere from 80 to 100 per cent. One of the reasons for this is our inconsistent cabotage policy. Draft restrictions that prevent mother vessels from being directly received at Indian ports is another. Currently the JNPT is the only port that can receive mother vessels of up to 4000 TEUs.

Good multimodal evacuation infrastructure remains a problem. Three of the oldest ports (Calcutta, Chennai, and Mumbai) are located in the city centre, constraining evacuation to and from the port. Each of these ports now has an 'alternate', namely Haldia, Ennore, and JNPT respectively. (Ennore port, the first corporate port under the central government, is nearing completion and is expected to begin operations during this financial year.) The other major ports have scope

TABLE 7.2.15
Container Traffic Handled at Major Ports

('000s)

| Year | Tonnage total | TEUs total |
|---|---|---|
| 1990–1 | 8042 | 681 |
| 1991–2 | 7627 | 683 |
| 1992–3 | 9009 | 799 |
| 1993–4 | 12,249 | 1052 |
| 1994–5 | 15,358 | 1257 |
| 1995–6 | 17,618 | 1449 |
| 1996–7 | 20,590 | 1698 |
| 1997–8 | 23,299 | 1891 |
| 1998–9 | 23,782 | 1932 |

*Source:* Indian Ports Association (2000).

[17] See section 7.2.

TABLE 7.2.16
Container Traffic 1998–9

('000s)

| Port | Tonnage | | | TEUs (nos) | | |
|---|---|---|---|---|---|---|
| | Unloaded | Loaded | Total | Unloaded | Loaded | Total |
| Calcutta | 1159 | 812 | 1971 | 77 | 55 | 132 |
| Haldia | 51 | 376 | 427 | 4 | 24 | 28 |
| Paradip | – | 1 | 1 | – | – | 0 |
| Visakhapatnam | 88 | 84 | 172 | 7 | 7 | 14 |
| Chennai | 1471 | 1471 | 2942 | 146 | 138 | 284 |
| Tuticorin | 428 | 785 | 1213 | 48 | 52 | 100 |
| Cochin | 357 | 620 | 977 | 63 | 66 | 129 |
| New Mangalore | – | – | 0 | – | – | 0 |
| Mormugao | 18 | 19 | 37 | 2 | 1 | 3 |
| Mumbai | 3938 | 3160 | 7098 | 274 | 235 | 509 |
| JNPT | 3795 | 4234 | 8029 | 316 | 353 | 669 |
| Kandla | 394 | 521 | 915 | 33 | 31 | 64 |
| All Ports | 11,699 | 12,083 | 23,782 | 970 | 962 | 1932 |

*Source:* Indian Ports Association (2000).

TABLE 7.2.17
The World's Top 20 Container Ports

| Rank | | Port | TEUs ('000) | | % change |
|---|---|---|---|---|---|
| 1999 | 1998 | | 1999 | 1998 | |
| 1 | 2 | Hong Kong* | 16,100 | 14,636 | 10.0 |
| 2 | 1 | Singapore | 15,900 | 15,100 | 5.3 |
| 3 | 3 | Kaohsiung | 6985 | 6271 | 11.4 |
| 4 | 4 | Rotterdam | 6400 | 6000 | 6.7 |
| 5 | 5 | Pusan | 6311 | 5753 | 9.7 |
| 6 | 6 | Long Beach | 4408 | 4098 | 7.6 |
| 7 | 10 | Shanghai | 4210 | 3066 | 37.3 |
| 8 | 8 | Los Angeles | 3829 | 3378 | 13.3 |
| 9 | 7 | Hamburg | 3738 | 3547 | 5.3 |
| 10 | 9 | Antwerp | 3614 | 3266 | 10.7 |
| 11 | 14 | New York* | 2863 | 2466 | 16.1 |
| 12 | 11 | Dubai | 2845 | 2804 | 1.4 |
| 13 | 12 | Bangkok | 2808 | 2538 | 10.6 |
| 14 | 15 | Felixstowe | 2610 | 2462 | 6.0 |
| 15 | 13 | Tokyo | 2595 | 2495 | 4.0 |
| 16 | 16 | Gioia Tauro | 2253 | 2126 | 5.9 |
| 17 | 17 | Kobe* | 2200 | 2101 | 4.7 |
| 17 | 18 | Yokohama* | 2200 | 2091 | 5.1 |
| 18 | 22 | Bremerhaven | 2181 | 1812 | 20.3 |
| 19 | 19 | Manila | 2090 | 1851 | 12.9 |
| 20 | – | San Juan | 2085 | 1990 | 4.7 |

*Source:* Mundy (2000).      * Port authorities

TABLE 7.2.18
Distribution of International Container Traffic between Direct and Trans-shipment Traffic, 1998–9

| Port | Direct | | Trans-shipment | | | |
|---|---|---|---|---|---|---|
| | Traffic ('000 TEUs) | % | Colombo % | ME % | Singapore % | Total trans-shipment % |
| JNPT | 669 | 80 | 10 | 5 | 5 | 20 |
| Mumbai | 509 | 20 | 30 | 40 | 10 | 80 |
| Kandla | 80 | 5 | 30 | 60 | 5 | 95 |
| Cochin | 128 | 10 | 75 | 11 | 4 | 90 |
| Tuticorin | 100 | 0 | 100 | 0 | 0 | 100 |
| Chennai | 283 | 16 | 50 | 0 | 34 | 84 |

*Source:* Sarosh (2000).

TABLE 7.2.19
Port Statistics 1998–9

| Port | No. of vessels (numbers) | Total DWT ('000 tonnes) | Cargo traffic ('000 tonnes) | Avg DWT ('000 tonnes) | Turnaround time (days) | Vessel days |
|---|---|---|---|---|---|---|
| Calcutta | 1049 | 15,741 | 9163 | 15.0 | 7.1 | 7468.9 |
| Haldia | 1291 | 42,353 | 20,224 | 32.8 | 4.8 | 6248.4 |
| Paradip | 695 | 21,059 | 13,108 | 30.3 | 4.2 | 2891.2 |
| Visakhapatnam | 1514 | 56,191 | 35,653 | 37.1 | 5.5 | 8342.1 |
| Chennai | 1816 | 52,653 | 35,201 | 29.0 | 7.6 | 13,765.3 |
| Tuticorin | 1073 | 18,527 | 10,150 | 17.3 | 4.9 | 5268.4 |
| Cochin | 1113 | 25,040 | 12,665 | 22.5 | 3.6 | 4017.9 |
| New Mangalore | 738 | 24,861 | 14,206 | 33.7 | 3.8 | 2767.5 |
| Mormugao | 483 | 22,839 | 18,020 | 47.3 | 5.4 | 2627.5 |
| Mumbai | 2222 | 46,476 | 30,970 | 20.9 | 6.8 | 15,198.5 |
| JNPT | 974 | 21,112 | 11,723 | 21.7 | 3.4 | 3292.1 |
| Kandla | 1708 | 60,079 | 40,637 | 35.2 | 8.3 | 14,176.4 |
| Total Ports | 14,676 | 406,931 | 251,720 | 27.7 | 5.9 | 86,064.3 |

*Source:* Indian Ports Association (2000).

*Notes:* For 1998–9: International good average for turnaround time was two days. Hence extra turnaround time in India was 3.9 days. Extra vessel days was 57,236.4. At the average standing charges of $ 8000 per day, the cost of congestion was $ 457.9 million, i.e. Rs 1923 crore.

| *Regulator* | *Landowner* | *Utility* |
|---|---|---|
| • Conserving and pilotage | • Manage port estate | • Cargo handling |
| • Vessel traffic management or surveillance services | • Port policy and development strategies | • Passenger terminals |
| • Laws and regulations | | • Towage |
| • Port police | • Civil engineering works | • Linehandling |
| • Emergency services | • Marketing and promotion | • Waste disposal |
| • Licensing port works | • Maintain channels, etc. | • Security |
| • Ensuring competition | • Maintain wharves | • On-dock warehousing |
| • Customs | • Provide land access | • Equipment maintenance |
| • Port planning and monitoring | | |

Fig. 7.2.1: Roles of ports: Regulator, landowner, and utility.

*Source:* Alfred (2000).

for improving the evacuation infrastructure. All the major ports have broad gauge rail connectivity and are expected to be connected through four lane roads with the golden quadrilateral highway project. The evacuation problem is more acute at the minor and intermediate ports, especially those which have tremendous potential for growth, like those in Gujarat, some of which do not even have rail connections.

Minimum of turnaround time and fast evacuation are all the more important in the context of containers. Countries like Singapore, Hong Kong, and the United Arab Emirates (UAE) have made container handling a source of significant national income through the effective use of information technology in improving

productivity at ports for container handling (Ramani 2000). There is scope for the same at Indian ports.

Ports are basically a viable business (Table 7.2.13 shows that average revenue per tonne across all major ports in 1998–9 was Rs 144, while average expenditure per tonne was Rs 94.5). With government encouragement, ports are an attractive proposition for private participation. It would however be important to separate three roles related to ports, namely that of regulator, landowner, and utility (Fig. 7.2.1). The landowner function could involve private participation for infrastructure development and maintenance. The utility function could involve private participation in port-related operations and services. Private involvement of appropriate combinations of the landowner and utility functions can also be considered. The key issues would be the criteria for selection of private parties and the framework for charges.

Recent successful examples of privatization are the container berth and handling at the JNPT by the P&O Australia-led consortium, called the Nhava Sheva International Container Terminal or NSICT Limited, the Gujarat Pipavav Port Limited (GPPL), Gujarat Adani Port Limited (GAPL), etc. A few other projects have also seen financial closure and are expected to be on stream soon. At Poshitra in Gujarat, the private port developer is also planning a large special economic zone complementing the port.

CRITERIA FOR SELECTION

The criteria for selection[18] have been examined here under two heads, namely infrastructure development and port operations.

Infrastructure Development

For investment in infrastructure, we propose the following set of six criteria for evaluation of parties and their organizations.

(a) *Size of the organization*: It should already be a medium to large sized organization.

(b) *Management quality*: The company should be professionally run with proper systems in place.

(c) *Experience with ports*: The organization should have sufficient experience with ports, either as a user or through being involved in port operations in a significant manner.

(d) *Relevant expertise*: The company should have sufficient technological manpower and demonstrated expertise in port infrastructure requirements.

(e) *Financial viability*: The company should be financially viable with sufficient cash for investment as well as a proper financing plan for its scheme.

(f) *Interest in captive commodity*: The organization should be in a position to provide a significant share of the traffic either through commitments of a sister industrial organization or through organizations with whom it has been dealing quite consistently.

FRAMEWORK FOR CHARGES

The current structure of charges levied by a port varies by different factors, either due to the use of private jetties or private services. The most striking of the charges is the wharfage charge, whose rate varies depending upon the use of private jetties. The lighterage charge also varies quite significantly, depending upon whether the ship has berthed directly or not.

[18] The criteria for selection and framework for charges are excerpted from Raghuram (1999).

Based on a comparison of net container handling charges at various ports in India and the nearby Asian region, it is quite clear that the productivity achieved at foreign ports gives them a strong price advantage over Indian ports, even though it is often claimed that labour is cheaper in India. For example, container handling costs at Singapore could be as low as $ 281 per TEU, while in India, at Mumbai, the costs could run as high as $ 530 per TEU. The total charges applicable in the Gujarat Maritime Board (GMB) ports are a little under $ 140 per TEU. This is quite a competitive price and reflects the price advantage that the GMB and other ports in India can enjoy with better management.

Thus the framework of charges should be such that a port can retain the overall price advantage that it can offer to customers. Under privatization, whatever rents/royalties levied should be constrained by the need to keep the port competitive. Of course, the profitability of a port would also be a consideration.

The framework of charges can be examined under two heads, namely infrastructure development and port operations.

Infrastructure Development

In the case of infrastructure development, the party should be willing to pay a minimum periodic (say annual) rent/royalty for the following rights access to waterfront; equipment installation.

This royalty is payable to the port. Apart from this, a per ton rate is leviable on the traffic handled.

Apart from the criteria listed above for evaluating parties, they should be asked to make bids in which the royalty amounts and the per ton rates should be specified. Everything else being equal, the parties bringing in the highest expected revenue should be considered.

Since infrastructure investments would easily run over Rs 100 crore per party, they must be given rights for long periods to enable long-term planning.

Port Operations

Here two kinds of port operations are considered: those in which the port is directly responsible to the customer, but gets the job done through private parties; and those in which private parties are directly responsible to the customer, but are given rights of port operations by the port.

In the first case, which includes essential activities like dredging (maintenance of right of way), pilotage, and maintenance of port infrastructure charges, levied by the port from port users in one form or the other, should pay for 'private contractors' who could undertake the above mentioned tasks. Such contractors must be selected for the lowest bids made for a given service level, which should be monitored by the port.

Such contracts can be given out on a period basis, say annually, or on a target achievement basis.

In the second case, which includes activities specific to each port user's requirements like loading and unloading operations, storage and warehousing, water provision and chandlering, bunkering, and ship repair and dry docking, different parties can be authorized to perform these tasks for a charge which they can directly levy from port users. However, if the service is to be privatized, more than one service provider must be ensured so that competition can control prices. A fixed royalty and a proportion of the earnings could be made payable to the port. The licence to such parties can be given for a period like one year, renewable if the party is providing the service to the port users' satisfaction.

### Overseas Shipping

Overseas shipping is open to the private sector and foreign participation. Though dominated by the public sector company, the Shipping Corporation of India (SCI), which owns nearly about 50 per cent of the shipping tonnage of the country, Indian shipping is open to the private sector. Indian shipping handled about 31 per cent of India's overseas seaborne trade in 1999 (62 per cent of POL, 14 per cent of dry bulk, and 12 per cent of general and container cargo) (INSA 1999).

There is an element of support for Indian shipping companies through an organization under the MoST, called Transchart, which acts as a broker for public sector cargo and provides first right of refusal to Indian companies. Notwithstanding the recent debate as to whether Transchart be wound up, especially since many of the public sector companies prefer to use their own agents, Transchart is among the largest brokers, with an excellent network. With a better marketing approach, and even without the first right of refusal support, Transchart should be able to provide useful service.

### Coastal Shipping

Coastal shipping is an untapped mode of transportation with vast potential, especially because it is environment friendly and operationally inexpensive. Currently, it has a market share of 8.5 per cent of the total domestic transport movement in btkm. Coastal tonnage during 1998–9 was 87.4 mt. It is expected that at least another 50 mt of general cargo traffic can be attracted to coastal movement over the next five years. At present, coastal movement is majorly used by few large corporates as part of their efficient logistics management. Coastal traffic is significant for some of the major ports like Paradip, Chennai, and Tuticorin.

An analytical perspective with policy recommendations is provided in (Raghuram 2000). For growth of coastal shipping, the multimodal infrastructure facilities and the regulatory issues (customs and cabotage laws) need emphasis.

Greater attention should be given to reduction of turnaround times. Ports with sufficient capacity for coastal traffic should be located at a distance of every 300 km (about twenty locations for the Indian coastline) to reduce land leads. These ports should have geared jetties, warehousing, and access to other modes of transport. It is not necessary that the ports be 'big'. Smaller ports (for 3000 to 5000 tonnes parcel size) of about 4 m draft are sufficient for coastal shipping. This would also keep investments low. Further, with the latest relaxations in the cabotage for chartering foreign flag vessels, the scope of coastal shipping has already increased.

All the additional investment at ports should be private investment by appropriate stakeholders. Coordinated development with other modes, and location policy in terms of manufacturing and redistribution facilities are essential.

### Ship Building and Ship Repair

Ship building was attempted to be developed in the public sector, with the hope that India would be able to build modern ships (reliving its traditional role as a maritime nation). Ship repair has largely been in the private sector, but not catering to modern vessels. The ship building industry did not really take off. This was primarily due to a *pari passu* clause, which required all Indian shipping companies importing modern vessels to place a formula-based equivalent order on public sector companies. This clause effectively killed the industry by offering protection through a captive market. These companies did not invest in R&D, nor did they even work towards matching international standards on order delivery. Distortions against exports confined them to the small home market.

This clause has since been removed and the order book position has gone down. The ship-building companies are trying to reposition themselves as offering ship repair services also. Success is uncertain, even though there is a cost advantage, as there is absence of adequate knowledge about modern vessel technology. Also, the existing private players confined to building small ships and ship repair.

## PIPELINES

In the context of freight movement, pipelines is a growing segment; it is environment friendly, with low operating costs. The primary use of pipelines is for transporting oil (crude and products). Gas is gaining as another major user.

No data are available on the tonne km movement of water through pipelines. However, for oil, one can arrive at such a figure using the data provided by Barua and Madhavan in this report.[19] Assuming that maximum capacity exists throughout the pipeline and capacity utilization is 100 per cent, the total btkm would be 70.2 (51.5 btkm of crude and 18.7 of products). This would amount to about an 8 per cent share of total domestic movement. In terms of share of originating tonnes of product from refineries/imports, pipelines currently account for 20 per cent of the mode primary movement. This is expected to reach 40 per cent in the next couple of years.

The crucial issue in pipeline development is enabling it to become a 'common carrier', as opposed to a captive carrier. This requires appropriate institutional infrastructure and regulation. Petronet and Petronet–LNG are two companies which have been set up as holding SPVs, with equity participation from the oil companies. While each new pipeline being developed has stakeholding by the primary user in its specific SPV, the issue of making it a common carrier is still not resolved. Further, the issue of opening up the existing not-so-insignificant pipeline network from its captive format still remains. Issues related to government policy, regulation, and tariff gain significance in this context. This chapter criticizes the current SPV route for pipeline development and recommends that the oil majors should be allowed to build the infrastructure and a regulator kept in place to ensure common carrier access. The underlying issue is that of incentive compatibility for driving infrastructure development.

## MULTIMODAL TRANSPORT

Unless the movement is by road all the way, almost every commodity and passenger would require to use more than one mode, since at least the 'first' and the 'last' miles would be by road (or on foot). Ensuring smooth inter-modal transfer is essential. Today, multimodal transport gains even more importance with more than one mode constituting significant segments of transportation. Apart from appropriate infrastructure, this requires a 'single window' service interface. For freight movement, containerization as a technology has enabled multimodal freight transport substantially throughout the world. India is catching up, but has a long way to go.

During 1998–9, out of 1.93 million export/import TEUs handled at major ports, 0.58 million (30 per cent) originated at container freight stations (CFSs) other than

port sites. Out of this, 0.33 million (17 per cent) were connected with inland locations by rail through inland container depots (ICDs) (Indian Ports Association 2000). The slow movement towards using networked computer services, especially electronic data interchange (EDI), is also an indication of the growing preference for containerization.

Apart from multimodal transport for the export/import business, the potential for domestic transportation remains far from being fully exploited. Multimodal transport also needs to be a focus area for carrying passengers. It has a significant bearing on development of high speed, high capacity corridors (intercity and intracity), and location of terminals (airports, railway stations, ferry ports, etc.).

Various infrastructural issues[20] were identified in a study by the then Shipping Credit and Investment Corporation of India (SCICI) now a division of the Industrial Credit and Investment Corporation of India [ICICI] in the mid-1990s.

In the first place, the container handling facilities at the ports are not adequate to attract main line container vessels who continue to rely to a large extent on feeder services entailing additional cost. Secondly, the cost of moving a container through an Indian port is comparatively higher than the cost in other South-East Asian ports. Thirdly, both road transport and rail transport have not been adequately developed as yet for the inland movement of containers. The national highways are already overburdened to cope with the increasing volume of container traffic. The position in regard to rail transport is not satisfactory either. The quality of rail service for catering to container traffic needs improvement. More regular scheduled rail services carrying containerized cargo connecting ICDs and gateway ports are necessary. Besides, the progress in the modernization and technological upgradation of Railways in several areas such as electrification, track renewal, conversion of narrow gauges into broad gauges, signaling system computerization, etc. have been slow, obviously due to resources crunch. Apart from these factors, the trade appears to be besieged with a number of problems relating to documentation, handling and more importantly lack of coordination among the agencies involved such as ports, customs, Railways, carriers agents, etc. As a result, most shippers, consignees and shipping lines are still wary of patronizing ICDs to the maximum extent. There are several inter-related and complementary elements—procedures and formalities—at different points in the multimodal transport chain which need to be coordinated preferably under the overall control of a single authority in order to ensure smooth and efficient operations. The need for establishing such a high powered national coordinating body for the purpose has been emphasized at several forums in the recent past.

---

[19] See section 7.4.

[20] The following issues are modified excerpts from Raghuram (1999).

Multimodal transport requires significant investments in the following:

- Ships (container ships, pallet ships, roll-on–roff-off (ro–ro) ships, barge carriers, multipurpose ships, etc.).
- Cargo units (pallets, containers, wheeled units, barges, etc.).
- Port facilities (container berths/multipurpose berths, gantry cranes, mobile cranes, forklift trucks, straddle carriers, etc.).
- Transport vehicles (trucks, trailers, etc.).
- Inland transport facilities (roads, railways, inland waterways, etc.).
- Inland container depots with handling and storage facilities.
- Container freight stations, warehouses, packaging organizations, etc.

All the above would be attractive for private investment and operation. Ensuring of coordinated development would be the only responsibility of the state.

IR has the potential of becoming a major player in the multimodal (export/import and domestic) transport system in India. The following are some of the areas which would need examination:

- Development of non-containerized multimodal transport through appropriate rail–road and rail–water

trans-shipment facilities, under a single transport document. Joint ventures could be a possible organizational form to ensure this.

- Development of containerized multimodal transport by:

  – improving service levels to the Container Corporation of India (CONCOR) through guaranteed departure and transit times and associated incentives and penalties;

  – providing unutilized and strategically located railway land for ICD and CFS use, both for international and domestic trade;

  – manufacturing and maintaining railway wagon flats for carrying containers;

  – offering innovative 'bridge' routes, possibly in collaboration with CONCOR (for example tea exports to the Middle East and Europe from the northeast could be minibridged to Mumbai port rather than being exported through Calcutta which involves feedering via Singapore);

  – nominating certain routes for 'no electrification' so that double stack container trains can be run on high container traffic routes, exploiting cost economies;

  – appropriate pricing strategies, as a function of service levels and value offered to the customers.

## 7.3 PORT AND SHIPMENT MANAGEMENT AT SINGAPORE PORT: THE REVOLUTION IN THE USE OF ELECTRONIC DATA INTERCHANGE

*K. V. Ramani*

Singapore had its humble beginnings as a riverine port on the banks of the Singapore river in 1819. Today Singapore port is the busiest seaport in the world, handling more than 15 million containers per year. In the last few years, international trade handled annually by the Port of Singapore Authority (PSA), valued at US $ 300 billion, has been almost four times the gross domestic product (GDP) of Singapore itself. The PSA, which is a major trans-shipment port, serves as a super logistics hub for the entire Asia–Pacific region.

Dubai is another example of a port that serves an entire region. The Dubai Ports Authority (DPA), which operates the twin terminals of Port Rashid and Jebel Ali, is positioning itself as one of the most prominent players on the economic scene in Dubai and the Middle East. The DPA does more than channel goods to and from the domestic market. It acts as the distribution hub for the whole region which includes the Organization of the Petroleum Exporting Countries (OPEC), Iran,

the Indian subcontinent, and the Commonwealth of Independent States. It is worthwhile to mention here that Jebel Ali Port in Dubai is a man-made port, strategically constructed by the DPA to promote the economic development of the Gulf region.

India has several natural ports but has not been able to attract a significant level of the international cargo traffic. Several other countries such as Sri Lanka, Malaysia, Indonesia, and the Philippines offer much better port facilities. If India is to actively participate in international trade, and get even a share of international shipping proportional to its trade, it has to modernize its seaports and improve working efficiency.

Port planning has undergone several fundamental changes over a period of time; some of these are described here. Traditional ports were designed to serve the local community around the port, while modern ports are designed as trans-shipment ports to serve the needs of a geographically larger dispersed community. Port configurations and operations in the past were influenced by the demand for multipurpose cargo handling. As a result, most traditional ports handled all types of cargo, though not very effectively. Today's trend is to build dedicated ports or at least terminals for handling each type of cargo (such as containers) effectively and efficiently, thereby offering high quality of service.

Developments in ship technology, port technology, and information technology (IT) are providing new insights into port planning and configuration. Container traffic is rapidly gaining popularity on account of security, safety, and cost effectiveness. Bigger and bigger ships, such as Post-Panamax vessels carrying 6000 containers, demand sophisticated port facilities. Even countries like India which have policies and modes of operation that discriminate against containerization and multimodal traffic are forced to containerize due to the pressure of exports and imports. Port operations have perhaps seen the sharpest fall in labour intensity, especially blue collar work. Indeed, the handling technologies and port work flow organization have changed enough to render the older intense labour-using modes absolutely inefficient. The logistics and systemic gains possible with containerization are denied if an efficient factory shopfloor-like organization of ports is not maintained.

Non-POL (petroleum oil and lubricant) bulk includes fertilizers, coal, foodgrains, and other such cargo usually assumed to be not amenable to containerization. POL handling almost from the very beginning, has been through dedicated terminals. POL handling has technological characteristics very different from that of containers. Many bulk items like ores, fertilizers, and foodgrains have characteristics of material handling and may impose negative externalities on other more general cargo and container operations, when carried out close to container berths.

Container traffic has been growing rapidly since its introduction in the US coastal services in 1957–8. The Australian coastal trade was containerized in 1959; the Europe–North America trade in 1966, the Far West–North American trade in 1967, and the Europe–Far East trade in 1971. By the mid-1970s container traffic had become very popular on all the three arterial trade routes of the world, namely the Pacific, Atlantic, and Asia–Pacific routes. Today, more than 90 per cent of international cargo moves through seaports and 80 per cent of seaborne cargo moves in containers through major seaports.

## Management of Container Terminals

The most important tasks in the management of a container terminal consist of berth allocation, yard planning, stowage planning, and logistics planning of container operations.

Information regarding the status of a ship, which indicates whether the ship is a priority ship or not, besides the nature of its cargo, is an important determinant in berth allocation. Berth allocation is extremely important since it has significant influence on the performance of both the ship and the berth. Most international seaports use computer-based expert systems for berth allocation, which assign berths to ships by matching the ship and the port characteristics.

Yard planning thus involves optimal allocation of storage areas for import, export, and trans-shipment containers. Most major international seaports use computer-based expert systems for yard planning. While yard planning assigns storage locations to the containers in the yard, stowage planning assigns storage locations to the containers in the bay of the ship. Stowage planning is also usually done with the help of expert systems which match the ship's bay characteristics with container details and marine considerations. Logistics planning deals with assigning and coordinating the operations of port equipment such as quay cranes, prime movers, and yard cranes in the transportation of containers between the ship's bay and the storage yards. Logistics planning and its execution are the most challenging of all the operations at ports. It is here, through appropriate information and communication technology and a disciplined approach, that ports like Jebel Ali or Singapore have been able to take the lead. The challenge for ports is to reduce the overall average time a ship waits in unloading and loading while restricting the maximum time taken by any ship within the given constraints of availability of cranes, prime movers, storage yards, or spaces within ships. Much administration is possible through operations research (OR) and on-line (on time) data generation and use.

The second level of technological change that has the potential to greatly decrease the role of white collar workers and remove dead-weight losses to the economy is in automation of documentation, which is generated in the interface of the port, the customer, and many other agencies. Indeed, ports and countries in this race would be pushed into the feeder and secondary markets. More importantly, such ports would impose huge relative costs on their international traders.

Numerous government bodies usually regulate international trade through ports. In addition, port customs, immigration, health, shipping, security and other governmental authorities or their agents (such as banks), and operators and their agents all claim a need for detailed and repetitive documentation. Although the basic information regarding shipment of goods is quite simple, each of the parties or agencies to the shipment demands this information in its own preferred or traditional format and at particular times and locations.

The extent of this documentation work far exceeds many real requirements. However, the tremendous importance of streamlining this paperwork can be seen from the following excerpts from a report[21] by the Department of Transportation and the National Committee of International Trade Documentation, USA.

• A total of 46 different types of firms and government agencies are regularly involved in international trade in the United States.
• As many as 28 of these parties may participate in an export shipment.
• A total 125 different types of documents are in regular and special use.
• The 125 types of documents represent more than 1000 separate forms.
• A total of 80 types of documents are in regular use, and the remaining 45 types of documents are in special use.
• Average shipments involve 46 separate documents, with an average of over 360 copies of documents in special use.
• US international trade annually creates an estimated 828 million documents and these generate an estimated 6.5 billion copies.
• Average export and import shipments require 64 man-hours to prepare and process.
• Total US international trade documentation annually consumes more than one billion man-hours, equivalent to more than 144 million days of work and equal to 600,000 work years.
• Average documentation cost per international shipment amounted to US $ 351.04 [in 1982].
• On the basis of current shipping volumes, total documentation costs aggregate to almost US $ 6.5 billion a year and represented 7.5 per cent of the value of total US export and import shipments [in 1982].
• The report recommends the elimination of 85 documents. If achieved, this would eliminate over 400 million separate papers (and almost 4 billion copies per year) with an aggregate saving of an estimated US $ 3 billion per year.

It can be seen from this that the port interface with other departments and agencies is governed by a multitude of processes and procedures and requires a tremendous amount of paperwork involving many government and private agencies. Studies by international trade

[21] 'Paperwork or Profits', 1982.

bodies estimate the cost of documentation at 7–10 per cent of the value of goods transacted. Even a possible saving of 1 per cent in trade documentation costs would lead to a substantial saving for any country involved in international trade. Potentially much of these costs can be saved through computerization, including use of the Internet, and the potential excess white collar manpower is large.

Port operations are very complex, especially the management of container terminals. Container terminals are highly capital intensive. They have to be well managed in order to realize their potential capacity and achieve a reasonable level of efficiency and service performance.

Advancements in IT provide a wide range of options for port management to computerize operations to save on capital invested in ports and also costs for clients.

Some of the IT applications for port management are in the areas of:

• Management Information Systems (MIS) to monitor port performance indicators such as ship turnaround time, port resource utilization, and costs for providing services (Holguin-Veras and Walton 1994).
• Executive Information System for investment decisions and port planning decisions.
• Decision Support System to facilitate the logistics planning of port operations for loading and unloading cargo of various types (Ramani 1996).
• Expert Systems for berth allocation, stowage planning, and yard planning.
• Computer simulations to support port operational planning.

Electronic Data Interchange (EDI), to facilitate the port interface with other departments and agencies involved in trade and commerce (Ramani 1995), is the key to the next revolution in port management.

Trade documentation is a complex and expensive activity. The Trade Development Board (TDB), a statutory board responsible for managing all incoming and outgoing trade activities at the Singapore port, was handling about 10,000 declarations daily in 1986 and the number was rising. Yeo Seng Techm, chief executive officer of the TDB, Singapore, explained the situation his agency faced in 1987:

Our agency was loaded with paperwork in 1987 we were handling about 10,000 declarations each day, and the number was rising. And TDB was only part of the system. The trade process involves agencies such as the port authorities, customs, and so on, each with its own rules. Shipping agents and freight forwarders prepared all the documents and physically carried them to service centres where they would be handled manually by government officials and clerks. Two-day turn-around was common. The cost of these transactions was high for all concerned. Swedish and US studies of the costs of trade documentation in those countries estimated the cost at 4.7 per cent of the values of goods shipped. And such transactions are error prone. A British study estimated that half of all Letter of Credit (LoC) applications were turned down on first application due to errors in completion. This seemed like a lot of work with little payoff. It also provided an opportunity for us. Singapore is a small country. We have no natural resources. Our population has stabilised. We know we cannot compete by just bringing in new labour. If we are to be successful, we must improve our competitiveness in every way and especially in external trade, which is our largest business sector. This means cutting costs. That 4.7 per cent was the best place to start.

EDI offers a convenient and cost-effective alternative for processing and exchanging documents and information electronically. For example, Singapore achieved a saving of more than S $ 2 billion with the help of TRADENET, an EDI application (King and Konsynski 1990).

TRADENET, an electronic network to facilitate international trade, integrates all the processing procedures for import, export, and trans-shipment documents and licences. It uses a single document to satisfy all the trade documentation needs of Singapore. The same document is routed electronically through all the parties associated with trading such as traders, freight forwarders, shipping lines, and the various government and controlling agencies. All these parties[22] are linked to each other electronically under a large IBM mainframe computer system owned and operated by the Singapore Network Services (SNS) Pvt. Ltd.

The host computer at SNS acts as an electronic clearing house for TRADENET. It receives and transmits trading papers and forwards them to the relevant government agencies for processing and approval. For example, a trader can obtain approval from the TDB by filling up a TDB declaration form available on his Personal Computer (PC). The TRADENET software then automatically establishes communications with the TRADENET computer at SNS, transmits his declaration to the TDB and receives the TDB approval in his electronic mailbox. Subsequently, this approval is transmitted to other parties such as customs and shipping lines for further processing. The software also ensures

confidentiality and integrity of all the communication between trading partners and the approving authorities. It permits all payments for government duties and fees for TDB, customs, and other controlling agencies to be made electronically. It also offers an on-line enquiry system, which gives the status of any trade declaration at any point in time, twenty-four hours a day. Under TRADENET, most of the transactions are processed within 15 to 30 minutes.

TRADENET also provides a comprehensive information service. Direct access to critical company and business information such as company and business information and trade opportunities facilitates users in making key decisions quickly so as to gain an edge over their competitors. Traders can gain access to third-party databases owned by PSA, the Civil Aviation Authority of Singapore (CAAS), etc. on shipping schedules, airline schedules, and related information. Its electronic bulletin board has eliminated the need to subscribe to multiple information providers. With information services, TRADENET subscribers are able to enjoy effective business communication and speedy information.

Starting with a pilot group of 50 users in 1989, TRADENET has more than 2000 users today accounting for almost 90 per cent of the traders. Several freight forwarders have reported savings of 25 to 30 per cent in handling trade documentation on account of TRADENET. The total time for documentation processing has been reduced from an average of two days in 1987 to less than half a day in 1991. Governmental agency duties, such as customs and excise, are paid even before the cargo arrives. But the biggest pay-off from TRADENET is perhaps the enormous growth in international trade over the last few years, making the Singapore economy very competitive.

PORTNET, another EDI network of the PSA, provides an on-line computer service to support the daily operations at the port. For example, the shipping lines/agents can input the sailing schedule of their vessel into PORTNET and obtain information on services they need, such as identifying a second carrier for their transshipment cargo. The TRADENET–PORTNET link provides an interface between the maritime and trading communities to electronically exchange real-time operational and trade information.

To better serve the maritime and trading communities, a new system called Maritime Information System (MAINS) is currently under development. MAINS will generate cargo manifests, match them against import/export permits electronically and eliminate some manual procedures, such as storage/despatch of paper manifests to TDB and customs and endorsing

---

[22] These are the Trade Development Authority (TDA), the Port of Singapore (PSA), customs, controlling bodies, the Civil Aviation Authority of Singapore (CAAS), Changi International Air Services (CIAS), for passenger traffic, Singapore Airlines Transport Services (SATS) for cargo, air cargo agents, traders, freight forwarders, shipping agents, among others!

of customs permits by ship masters. It will provide instantaneous confirmation to shippers about their import/export consignments. Shipping lines will receive their bills of lading electronically from their shippers. Above all, MAINS will have an on-line real-time comprehensive database of shipping schedules and cargo consignments to meet almost all the needs of the maritime and trading communities.

Why should a port be concerned with cost and time reduction for shippers and others? Clearly, the port itself would not be able to internalize all or even a great deal of the gains. The gains would be largely external. Yet the port, of all institutions involved in international trade, is crucially placed to bring about this revolutionary change. Are Indian ports ready to begin thinking about this next round of technological change?

# 7.4 AT THE CROSSROADS: PIPELINE INFRASTRUCTURE FOR OIL PRODUCTS

*Samir K. Barua and T. Madhavan*

## INTRODUCTION

There are two types of oil pipelines: crude oil pipelines and product pipelines. While the former carry crude oil to refineries, the latter transport refined products such as gasoline, kerosene, jet fuel, and heating oil from refineries to the market. Offshore (submarine) pipelines are needed for transporting oil from offshore wells to overland pipelines, which further transport the oil to a refinery. They are more expensive and difficult to build than overland pipelines. Several developments in the last fifty years such as the use of 'pigs' to clean the interior of pipelines, the use of 'batching' to transport different petroleum products through the same pipeline, the use of cathodic protection to reduce corrosion of pipelines, and the use computers and communication technologies to monitor and control pipeline operations have seen pipelines emerge as the preferred mode of transport. Pipelines are safer and more convenient and reliable and environment friendly than other modes of transport for bulk liquids. Although most countries have an extensive network of pipelines, its contribution and importance to the economy goes unrecognized by the general public. These are now discussed.

## OPERATION

Modern long distance pipelines operations are largely automated. The various flow parameters are automatically monitored and the requisite feedback sent to operate the valves and pumps attached to pipelines. Manual intervention is essentially needed to direct different batches of liquids to different temporary storage tanks or when the systems must be shut down or restarted.

## ADVANTAGES OF PIPELINE TRANSPORTATION

• Transit losses are also lower in pipeline transportation vis-à-vis other modes.

• Pipeline transportation consumes the least energy; hence it has lower energy intensiveness (see Figs 7.4.1 and 7.4.2).

• Pipelines also offer large-scale economies in transportation.

• It is a reliable mode.

• As the handling of products is minimal, it is a safe mode.

• Environmental impact during construction, operation, and maintenance is negligible and reversible. Thus it is environment friendly (see Box 7.4.1).

• Unlike other modes, in which different containers may be required for different products, pipeline transportation can handle multiple products.

• Pipeline transportation is flexible, as the volume transported can be increased/decreased quickly and at negligible cost.

• Additional energy consumption for transportation of dead-weight of containers is not incurred in pipeline transportation.

## OIL PIPELINES IN INDIA

Despite a well-established industrial base, India's consumption of oil and gas as primary sources of energy (Table 7.4.1) is well below world percentages.

The growth rate in the consumption of oil products in India over the last three decades, however, has been among the highest in the world (Table 7.4.2). The consumption of oil products has grown at the rate of about 5.5–6 per cent per annum over the thirty-year period. In contrast, world consumption of oil grew at the rate of about 1.5 per cent per annum in the 1990s. In India per capita consumption at 93 kg per annum is about one-tenth that of the world, which is 920 kg. A comparison of growth rates of oil consumption and gross domestic product (GDP) shows that the elasticity of oil consumption has declined over the years. It is currently less than 1.

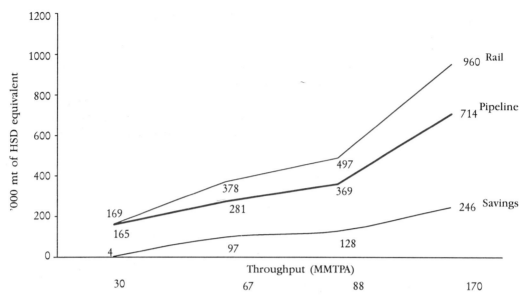

**Fig. 7.4.1:** Energy conservation in pipelines fuel consumption
(pipeline vis-à-vis rail).

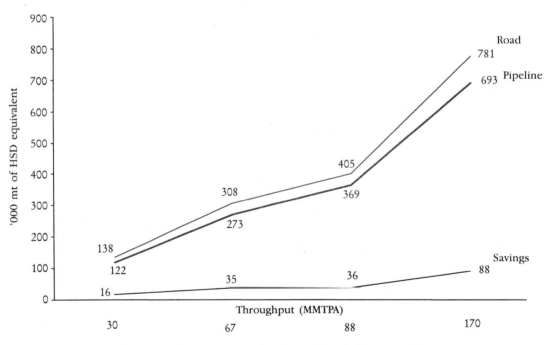

**Fig. 7.4.2:** Energy conservation in pipelines fuel consumption
(pipeline vis-à-vis road short distance).

The Subgroup on Development of Refinery, Marketing and Transportation Infrastructure Requirement (of the main group on Hydrocarbon Vision 2025) assessed the demand for oil products at about 370 million metric tonnes per annum (MMTPA) as against current consumption of 94 MMTPA. This projection is consistent with an annual growth in oil consumption at the rate of 5.5 per cent per annum. Even if there were a shift towards natural gas and coal, the oil consumption would grow very rapidly if the economy grew at rates similar to or better than those for the 1990s. At a pessimistic growth rate of 4 per cent per annum, the projected consumption would rise to about 250 MMTPA in 2025. Given the pressure on road and rail transport, safe transportation of crude and oil products would pose a huge challenge to the country. However, as is clear from the figures in Table 7.4.3· the share of pipelines has remained stagnant. If further additions are not made to pipeline infrastructure in India, the percentage share of pipelines in transportation of oil would go down substantially by 2025. There is therefore an urgent need to plan and implement a network of pipelines for distribution of crude and oil products.

### BOX 7.4.1
### Ambient Air Quality and Noise

| Parameter | Ambient air quality standrads ($\mu g/m^3$) | Performance of pipelines ($\mu g/m^3$) |
|---|---|---|
| $SO_2$ | 80 | 14.3–17.1 |
| $NO_x$ | 80 | 7.4–8.0 |
| Suspended Particulate matter (SPM) | 360 | 156–168 |
| Noise (continuous 8 hours) | 75 db | 69–72 db |

Exhaust emission is localized in pump stations where large diesel/crude oil engines are operated.

### TABLE 7.4.1
### Primary Sources of Energy: India and World
(per cent)

| Source | India | World |
|---|---|---|
| Oil | 32 | 40 |
| Gas | 8 | 23 |
| Others | 60 | 37 |

### TABLE 7.4.2
### Growth Rates in Consumption of Oil
(per cent)

| Period | Compounded annual growth rate in oil consumption | Compounded annual GDP growth rate |
|---|---|---|
| 1971–80 | 5.63 | 3.20 |
| 1981–90 | 6.13 | 5.60 |
| 1991–9 | 5.64 | 5.80 |

The growth rate in demand for pipelines is likely to increase more rapidly than that of oil for several reasons. Given the environment friendly nature of pipeline transportation, 60–70 per cent of transportation of oil products is done through pipelines in most developed countries. A comparison of the shares of various modes between India and the United States (Table 7.4.4) clearly shows that with increasing urbanization and greater concern for environment and safety, the share of pipeline transportation is likely to increase in India. The growth in pipelines stagnated to accommodate the demand from railways to use oil tankers for transportation of oil. With the dismantling of controls in the oil sector, the formal and informal restraints on adding pipelines would cease. There is therefore likely to be an explosive addition to pipeline capacity in the near future.

The major existing crude and oil products pipelines in India are listed in Table 7.4.5. The projected addition to capacity, based on the plans of various companies, is presented in Table 7.4.6.

The 11,500 km of pipelines under consideration or conceptualization would require an investment of over Rs 15,000 crore. These pipelines have been conceived to create a network that could be connected to form a grid. As of now, the density of pipelines in southern India is distinctly low.

### EXISTING POLICY

While energy consumption varies between 50 and 135 British thermal units (BTU) per tonne km for transportation of oil products by pipelines, movement by rail consumes about 320 BTU per tonne km. The railways are facing increasing constraints in movement of oil products due to saturation and mismanagement of track capacity and non-availability of locomotives and tank wagons. The utilization of tank wagons has shown little improvement. Recognizing the importance of creating oil pipeline infrastructure, the government formed a working group of general managers from

### TABLE 7.4.3
### Shares of Alternative Modes for Transportation of Oil in India

| Mode | 1993–4 | | 1994–5 | | 1995–6 | | 1996–7 | |
|---|---|---|---|---|---|---|---|---|
| | MMT | per cent share | MMT | per cent share | MMT | per cent share | MMT | per cent share |
| Road | 15.3 | 25.2 | 17.9 | 27.3 | 22.2 | 30.6 | 23.4 | 30.3 |
| Rail | 26.1 | 42.9 | 28.1 | 42.9 | 29.3 | 40.4 | 29.1 | 37.7 |
| Pipeline | 14.5 | 23.8 | 14.9 | 22.8 | 15.5 | 21.4 | 18.9 | 24.5 |
| Coastal | 4.9 | 8.1 | 4.6 | 7.0 | 5.5 | 7.6 | 5.8 | 7.5 |
| Total | 60.8 | 100.0 | 65.5 | 100.0 | 72.5 | 100.0 | 77.2 | 100.0 |

TABLE 7.4.4
Mode-wise Distribution of Petroleum Products

(per cent)

| Mode | India | USA |
|---|---|---|
| Rail | 37.50 | 3.20 |
| Road | 27.50 | 5.10 |
| Coastal | 7.50 | 33.70 |
| Pipeline | 25.00 | 59.00 |

TABLE 7.4.5
Major Crude and Product Pipelines in India*

| Pipeline | Length (km) | Capacity (MMTPA) | Owner |
|---|---|---|---|
| *Crude oil* | | | |
| 1. Nahorkatiya–Barauni | 1156 | 5.5 | OIL |
| 2. Salaya–Mathura | 1881 | 21 | IOCL |
| 3. Ankleshwar–Koyali | 95 | 2 | ONGC |
| 4. Kalol–Navagam–Koyali | 127 | 2 | ONGC |
| 5. Bombay High–Uran (offshore) | 203 | 15 | ONGC |
| 6. Haldia–Barauni | 506 | 4.2 | IOCL |
| Total (Crude) | 3968 | 49.7 | |
| *Products* | | | |
| 1. Guwahati–Siliguri | 435 | 0.818 | IOCL |
| 2. Koyali–Ahmedabad | 116 | 1.1 | IOCL |
| 3. Barauni–Kanpur | 669 | 1.8 | IOCL |
| 4. Haldia–Barauni | 525 | 1.25 | IOCL |
| 5. Haldia–Mourigram–Rajbandh | 277 | 1.35 | IOCL |
| 6. Mathura–Jalandhar | 526 | 3.7 | IOCL |
| 7. Kandla–Bhatinda | 1443 | 7.5 | IOCL |
| 8. Digboi–Tinsukhia | 75 | 0.73 | IOCL |
| 9. Bombay–Pune | 161 | 3.67 | HPCL |
| 10. Mumbai–Manmad | 252 | 4.33 | BPCL |
| 11. Vizag–Vijayawada | 356 | 4.1 | HPCL |
| Total (products) | 4835 | 30.348 | |
| Grand total | 8803 | 80.048 | |

*Excluding about 2300 km of sub-sea and about 7600 km of on-land oil and gas pipelines of small diameters in the oil fields of ONGC.
*Note:* OIL is Oil India Limited; IOCL is Indian Oil Corporation Limited; ONGC is the Oil and Natural Gas Commission; HPCL is the Hindustan Petroleum Corporation Limited; and BPCL is Bharat Petroleum Corporation Limited.

TABLE 7.4.6
Projected Growth of Pipelines in India C. 2000

| Description | Length | Cumulative length |
|---|---|---|
| Existing pipelines | 8803 | 8803 |
| Pipelines under construction | 3630 | 12,433 |
| Pipelines under consideration | 5000 | 17,433 |
| Pipelines under conceptualization | 6500 | 23,933 |

various oil companies in December 1994 to examine the issue of infrastructure creation for distribution of oil products through pipelines. The report prepared by the group recommended setting up a financial holding company, Petronet India Limited (PIL), to expedite development of pipeline infrastructure. PIL would promote each pipeline as a separate joint venture company (JVC) owned by PIL and a group of oil companies. The actual operation of the pipeline would be one of the public sector oil companies, especially that having the largest stakes in the JVC.

The Government of India approved the establishment of the holding company on 10 April 1996. PIL was duly incorporated on 26 May 1997, with equity contributions of 16 per cent each by the Indian Oil Corporation Limited (IOCL), Bharat Petroleum Corporation Limited (BPCL) and Hindustan Petroleum Corporation Limited (HPCL), 2 per cent by Indo-Burma Petroleum Limited (IBPL), the balance 50 per cent to be warehoused by Infrastructure Leasing and Financial Services Limited (ILFS). In the long run, the oil companies are expected to have a 50 per cent stake in the equity of PIL, while the balance 50 per cent is to be offered to private companies with the proviso that the holding of any individual entity shall not exceed 10 per cent. As stated earlier, PIL is to function as a financial holding company with the mandate to create JVCs for construction, operation, and maintenance of oil products pipelines in the country. PIL would retain adequate equity stake in each JVC to ensure a decisive say in the functioning of the JVCs.

Each JVC would function as an independent business entity with equity ownership distributed among potential users of the pipeline. Each entity would have complete freedom of operation. The rate to be charged would be decided by each JVC based on factors such as structure of the company, expectations of the JVC partners, demand and supply scenario, and the cost of alternate modes of transportation.

The government has already given, in principle, clearance to eleven such pipeline projects. The total outlay at the time of conception of these projects (early 1996) was Rs 3220 crore. The debt to equity mix for funding these projects was assumed at 2:1.

## ON-GOING PROJECTS OF PIL

PIL identified five product pipelines for implementation. The status of these five projects is as follows:

Vadinar–Kandla pipeline: The appraised cost of the project was Rs 410 crore. The pipeline would essentially evacuate products from the Reliance Petroleum Limited (RPL) refinery in Jamnagar and would join the existing

Kandla–Bhatinda pipeline of the Indian Oil Corporation Limited (IOCL). The project, being implemented by the IOCL, has been completed.

Chennai–Trichi–Madurai pipeline: The appraised cost of the project is Rs 539 crore. It is to be completed by July 2001 and the IOCL is the lead company for the project. In view of the proposed refinery at Cuddalore, the viability of the project is being re-examined.

Environmental and right of way (ROW) clearances have been received for the Mangalore–Hasan–Bangalore pipeline (Rs 667 crore) and the Cochin–Coimbatore–Karur pipeline (Rs 535 crore). Engineers (India) Limited (EIL) has also completed the detailed route surveys and the processes and design for these projects. The Bina–Jhansi–Kanpur pipeline is still in the preliminary stages of implementation.

Though, in principle, financial institutions have agreed to fund these projects, they have held up the actual disbursement of funds pending the signing of 'take or pay' contracts. The institutions insist on such contracts to eliminate uncertainty associated with cash inflows. However, given high commercial and operational uncertainties, potential users are unwilling to sign long-term 'take or pay' contracts at rates that would be attractive for the pipeline projects. The government is yet to take a final view on issues connected with tariff. PIL has therefore put these projects on hold, pending resolution of the above issues.

## TARIFF

The tariff regime prevailing under the administered pricing mechanism (APM) for the petroleum sector essentially guarantees a 12 per cent return on net worth. Operating costs are reimbursed under a predetermined formula. The compensation paid by the Oil Co-ordination Committee (OCC) today for investment in pipelines is quite inadequate:

• The return provided is less than 1 per cent based on the replacement cost of the assets; as a result, the margins are inadequate to plan replacement of existing pipelines.

• The norms for cost computations are unrealistic. There is no compensation for escalation in the costs of chemicals and power tariff. The actual working capital required is much higher than the normative working capital used for reimbursement of expenses.

• The compensation is based on quantity delivered and not received; transit losses, if any are borne by the pipeline operators.

• There is no compensation if pipeline usage decreases because of non-availability of products.

It is absolutely imperative to evolve a new sensible tariff structure to ensure that requisite investments are made in the creation of pipeline infrastructure. The tariff structure will have to balance the requirements of different constituencies. Users would prefer a competitive tariff structure that is transparent and devoid of intractable cross-subsidization. They would be reluctant to sign long-term 'take or pay' contracts as that would constrain both their distribution and marketing activities. Lenders would look for stable and guaranteed cash inflows to ensure repayment of debt. They would obviously prefer long-term 'take or pay' contracts with credible parties. Shareholders would look for returns that justify the various risks to which they are exposed. They would obviously prefer pipeline companies to charge rates based on the market capacity to pay. Regulators would be interested in ensuring that monopoly gains do not accrue to the owners of pipelines. They would also like to ensure that equitable rates are charged so that the customers do not suffer.

## PIPELINE PROJECTS REMAIN UNBANKABLE

Like other infrastructure projects, pipeline projects also require large investments and have long gestation periods. The risks associated with these projects arise from time and cost overruns, high uncertainty in demand over the long operating life of the projects, limited possibility of alternative uses of assets created, and uncertainty about the regulatory regime in which the projects would have to operate.

The chief sources for delays in completion of a pipeline project are delays in acquisition of ROW. Despite parliamentary sanctity in the form of the Petroleum and Pipeline Act, 1975, protracted litigations do arise while acquiring land. Heightened concern about the environment, particularly in situations where there could be permanent displacement of a population due to non-reversible changes in land use pattern can also be a major source of delay in completion.

In India, pipelines have operated at 100 per cent capacity since these are captive pipelines of oil companies. However, if pipelines were to be operated under a common carrier principle, they would face uncertainty in utilization arising from demand–supply dynamics. The viability of a pipeline project crucially depends on the demand for the facility in the future. Since these are projects with long lives, high capacity utilization over long periods becomes a prerequisite for financial viability. Demand may many a time be affected by developments outside the control of the pipeline company. A case in point is the poor utilization of the Kandla–Bhatinda pipeline till demand picked up from the Panipat refinery. The setting up of the Panipat Refinery has also had an impact on the utilization of the Mathura–Jalandhar pipeline which serves the Delhi–Ambala consumption zone. The throughput in the Vadinar–Kandla pipeline, specifically set up to evacuate products of RPL, would also be seriously affected if RPL were to resort to exporting products as a result of oversupply in the country. These uncertainties about sustained demand for capacity are a major concern of financiers of pipeline projects.

In the Indian context, financiers also have to contend with regulatory risk. The regulatory regime that would be in force in the post-APM era is still unclear. To attract investments it would be necessary for the government to frame stable and credible guidelines for tariff determination and disclose its regulatory and restructuring intentions.

## TARIFF DETERMINATION IN THE US AND UK

In the United States, no approval is required for construction of pipelines. Pipelines have to be operated under the 'common carrier' principle. Tariff is fixed by the pipeline company every year through negotiations with users. It is subject to a ceiling based on the oil price index. The Federal Energy Regulatory Commission regulates the tariff and practices of oil pipeline companies. In the UK, pipeline companies are assured a fixed return by the government. In France and Spain, pipeline companies require government approval for operation. A two-part tariff structure is followed for compensation of fixed and variable expenses.

## THE ROAD AHEAD

In India the government appears to have gone wrong from the very beginning. The creation of PIL as a financial holding company, and the setting up of a separate JVC for each pipeline, is an incorrect policy choice. The supply–demand scenario is so uncertain that each JVC would face enormous commercial risks. Since financing is being done independently, the stakeholders in each JVC would demand compensation for the risks assumed which would be quite high. Instead, if these pipelines belonged to one or a fewer number of companies, the risks would be considerably reduced due to the portfolio effect. The losses incurred on some pipelines could have been off-set by profits realized on the others. But with each pipeline as a separate company, all projects are ex ante exposed to the demand risk. It would therefore be very difficult to achieve financial closure of these projects. In addition, even if

funds were available, the interest rate demanded would be high to reflect the high risk. As is already evident for the projects conceived by PIL, lenders are justifiably demanding tariff contracts which provide them the required protection. A better policy would be to permit the major refining and marketing companies such as the IOCL, BPCL, and HPCL to expand their existing pipeline infrastructures such that a grid is created for the entire country, and simultaneously to set up a pipeline regulatory authority to ensure equitable operation of the network. These companies have the necessary resources as well as the experience to quickly set up the network.

## REGULATORY FRAMEWORK IS NECESSARY

Since pipelines create natural monopolies, a comprehensive regulatory framework is required. The role of the regulatory authority would include ensuring adherence to stipulated safety and quality norms, ensuring that facilities are not needlessly duplicated, and determining the tariff that is attractive to investors and yet does not exploit consumers. The issue that would require resolution is the demand by financial institutions that the projects should enter into long-term 'take or pay' contracts. Acceding to this demand would largely violate the common carrier principle that attempts to ensure equitable access to all users. If 'take or pay' contracts are to be permitted to a limited extent, then should the tariff be different for those who sign such contracts and those who do not? How should this difference, if any, be determined?

The principles governing the tariff structure should ensure adequate competition among various mode combinations, fair return to investors, that is returns commensurate with the risks assumed, equitable access to all users, and equitable costs to consumers. While it is easy to enunciate the broad principles, implementing them would be an extremely complex task given the peculiarities of the situation. Since the pipelines would essentially be links in a multimodal network of paths for transportation of oil products, a change in the tariff of any one pipeline or segment would change the flow pattern in the entire network with sometimes significant consequences for the other links (pipelines) in the network. For example, reducing the tariff for one pipeline could make several other pipelines financially unviable. The authors have experimented with a comprehensive optimization model for production, import, and distribution of oil products and found that the tariff structure creates significant interdependencies in the financial performance of various pipelines and modes. In addition, as was discussed earlier, setting up of a new refinery (source) also significantly impacts the fortunes of pipeline segments. The regulatory authority would have to be given a say in the establishment of supply points to ensure that pipelines assessed as financially viable do not become unviable due to unexpected change in the source structure.

It is thus clear that if the government is serious about creation of pipeline infrastructure, it must without delay set up a regulatory authority to frame the tariff structure and norms for operation of the pipeline companies. Such a move would remove the regulatory uncertainty and encourage investments in pipelines. Given the complexities involved, the tariff structure would have to be decided based on supply and demand of products for the entire country. Such simultaneous determination of the tariff structure for different pipelines and pipeline segments would require use of a comprehensive mathematical model which would be able to faithfully capture the actual behaviour of users in response to tariff rates fixed.

# 7.5 INTEGRATING COASTAL SHIPPING WITH THE NATIONAL TRANSPORT NETWORK[23]

*G. Raghuram*

## A REVIEW OF TRENDS AND PATTERNS

Coastal shipping constitutes about 30 per cent of the total traffic handled at our ports. Table 7.5.1 gives data for the past years for the major ports, the Gujarat Maritime Board (GMB) ports, and non-GMB minor and intermediate ports. We see that the total coastal traffic for 1998-9 was 87.4 million tonnes (mt). Out of this, 75.8 mt (86.7 per cent) was handled at major ports, 6.4 mt (7.3 per cent) was handled at GMB ports, and the remaining 5.2 mt (5.9 per cent) at non-GMB minor and intermediate ports.

1998-9

| Port | Coastal traffic (mt) | per cent |
|---|---|---|
| Major ports | 75.8 | 86.7 |
| GMB ports | 6.4 | 7.3 |
| Non-GMB minor and intermediate ports | 5.2 | 5.9 |
| Total | 87.4 | 100.0 |

TABLE 7.5.1
Cargo Traffic at Major and Minor Ports and the Share of Coastal Shipping

('000 tonnes)

| Year | Total | | | | per cent of coastal to total | | | |
|---|---|---|---|---|---|---|---|---|
| | Unloaded | Loaded | Trans-shipment | Total | Unloaded | Loaded | Trans-shipment | Total |
| *Major Ports* | | | | | | | | |
| 1997-8* | 142,468 | 94,764 | 14,727 | 251,659 | 24.8 | 35.2 | 27.5 | 28.9 |
| 1998-9* | 150,780 | 86,229 | 14,711 | 251,720 | 26.5 | 37.1 | 26.4 | 30.1 |
| *GMB Ports* | | | | | | | | |
| 1997-8** | 15,409 | 10,215 | 0 | 25,624 | 24.8 | 22.4 | 0.0 | 23.8 |
| 1998-9** | 16,927 | 8082 | 0 | 25,009 | 20.7 | 35.4 | 0.0 | 25.4 |
| *Non-GMB Minor and Intermediate Ports* | | | | | | | | |
| 1997-8*** | 8556 | 4427 | 0 | 12,983 | 16.4 | 43.8 | 0.0 | 25.7 |
| 1998-9*** | 5076 | 5565 | 0 | 10,641 | 53.5 | 44.1 | 0.0 | 48.6 |
| *All India Traffic* | | | | | | | | |
| 1997-8 | 166,133 | 109,406 | 14,727 | 290,266 | 24.4 | 34.3 | 27.5 | 28.3 |
| 1998-9 | 172,783 | 99876 | 14,711 | 287,370 | 26.7 | 37.4 | 26.4 | 30.4 |

*Sources:* * Indian Ports Association (1998-9). ** Gujarat Maritime Board (1997-8 and 1998-9) Administration Report. *** MoST (1998-9) Basic Port Statistics.

[23] Assistance by Deepa Kheskani is acknowledged. This part chapter has benefited by inputs from Partha Mukhopadhyay of the IDFC, based on earlier drafts. Financial assistance was provided by the IDFC through the 3iNetwork.

The time series data for major, minor, and intermediate ports of overseas, coastal, and total cargo, split as unloaded, loaded, and trans-shipment are given decadally from 1960–1 till 1990–1 and annually therefrom till 1998–9 in Tables 7.5.2 and 7.5.3.

Table 7.5.2 shows that for major ports in 1960–1, coastal traffic constituted a similar share (27 per cent) as now, but it fell to about 15 per cent until 1980–1, primarily due to the growth in overseas traffic. In the 1980s, coastal traffic grew rapidly to regain about a 33 per cent share, which has declined marginally during the

1990s. The compounded annual growth rate (CAGR) over 8 years (between 1990–1 and 1998–9) was nearly 5.6 per cent (the growth actually occurred in spurts in 1994–5 and 1997–8). This was less than the growth in total port traffic, which was 6.5 per cent for the same period.

For minor and intermediate ports, coastal traffic constituted over 50 per cent of total traffic in 1960–1. Since 1970–1 it has fallen to around 30 per cent. The variance around the 30 per cent share has been significant, primarily because the total volumes are small. The

TABLE 7.5.2
Cargo Traffic at Major Ports and the Share of Coastal Shipping

('000 tonne)

| Year | Total | | | | per cent of coastal to total | | | |
|---|---|---|---|---|---|---|---|---|
| | Unloaded | Loaded | Trans-shipment | Total | Unloaded | Loaded | Trans-shipment | Total |
| 1960–1* | 22,581 | 10,542 | NA | 33,123 | 21.6 | 39.8 | NA | 27.4 |
| 1970–1* | 25,557 | 30,022 | NA | 55,579 | 15.9 | 11.5 | NA | 13.5 |
| 1980–1* | 46,816 | 33,454 | NA | 80,270 | 16.5 | 14.8 | NA | 15.8 |
| 1990–1** | 85,088 | 66,577 | NA | 151,665 | 30.6 | 34.5 | NA | 32.3 |
| 1991–2** | 84,844 | 69,304 | NA | 154,148 | 31.0 | 36.2 | NA | 33.3 |
| 1992–3** | 95,351 | 67,526 | 3373 | 166,250 | 25.1 | 36.2 | 26.8 | 29.6 |
| 1993–4** | 96,671 | 76,634 | 5925 | 179,230 | 22.4 | 30.6 | 32.7 | 26.2 |
| 1994–5** | 109,717 | 81,419 | 6126 | 197,262 | 26.7 | 36.1 | 32.3 | 30.8 |
| 1995–6** | 120,634 | 85,675 | 9017 | 215,326 | 23.5 | 33.7 | 33.6 | 28.0 |
| 1996–7** | 129,089 | 87,411 | 10,757 | 227,257 | 23.6 | 33.9 | 24.6 | 27.6 |
| 1997–8** | 142,168 | 94,764 | 14,727 | 251,659 | 24.8 | 35.2 | 27.5 | 28.9 |
| 1998–9** | 150,780 | 86,229 | 14,711 | 251,720 | 26.5 | 37.1 | 26.4 | 30.1 |

*Sources:* * MoST Basic Port Statistics of India (1994–5).
**Indian Ports Association Major Ports of India—A profile (1992–3).

TABLE 7.5.3
Cargo Traffic at Minor and Intermediate Ports and Share of Coastal Shipping

('000 tonne)

| Year | Total | | | per cent of coastal to total | | |
|---|---|---|---|---|---|---|
| | Unloaded | Loaded | Total | Unloaded | Loaded | Total |
| 1960–1* | 1332 | 3075 | 4407 | 77.1 | 47.3 | 56.3 |
| 1970–1* | 1740 | 4948 | 6688 | 50.1 | 31.5 | 36.3 |
| 1980–1* | 2498 | 4234 | 6732 | 23.1 | 20.1 | 21.2 |
| 1990–1* | 7677 | 5105 | 12,782 | 25.6 | 24.5 | 25.2 |
| 1991–2* | 7781 | 5477 | 13,258 | 38.8 | 25.1 | 33.1 |
| 1992–3* | 9327 | 6076 | 15,403 | 33.2 | 22.0 | 28.8 |
| 1993–4* | 11,424 | 8046 | 19,470 | 33.6 | 17.7 | 27.0 |
| 1994–5** | 14,973 | 8309 | 23,282 | 42.5 | 22.7 | 35.4 |
| 1995–6** | 15,067 | 10,643 | 25,710 | 34.0 | 23.2 | 29.5 |
| 1996–7** | 16,884 | 10,948 | 27,832 | 36.2 | 29.9 | 33.7 |
| 1997–8** | 23,965 | 14,642 | 38,607 | 2108 | 28.8 | 24.5 |
| 1998–9** | 22,003 | 13,605 | 35,608 | 28.2 | 38.8 | 32.3 |

*Source:* Same as Table 7.5.2.

CAGR over 8 years (between 1990–1 and 1998–9) was nearly 17.3 per cent (the growth occurred in spurts in 1994–5, 1996–7, and 1998–9). To that extent, the share of minor and intermediate ports (including GMB ports) of total coastal traffic has increased from 6.1 to 13.2 per cent.

As seen in Table 7.5.1, for the all-India traffic, the coastal tonnage that was unloaded was greater than what was loaded during both 1997–8 and 1998–9. The difference could arise because of time lag between loading and unloading, and other inaccuracies in the data.

It is interesting to note from Table 7.5.1 that for major ports in 1998–99, the share of coastal cargo for unloading (26 per cent) was less than the share for loading (37 per cent), even though for absolute tonnage it is the reverse. This is simply due to the fact that our total cargo has a significantly greater overseas import

component than export. For non-GMB minor and intermediate ports, the shares cannot be interpreted since the volumes are small.

There was more passenger traffic at minor and intermediate ports than at major ports. It is further evident that most of the passengers were coastal. Passenger traffic is important for short hauls near ports and to and between the offshore islands of the Union Territories of Andaman & Nicobar and Lakshadweep. Tourism-based coastal passenger traffic could have potential. As such, for coastal movement the commercial potential of passenger traffic is not high compared to freight traffic at ports. The discussion here focuses on freight traffic.[24]

In 1998–9 coastal traffic constituted 87.4 mt out of a total port traffic of 288 mt. Out of this, 3.9 mt was trans-shipment cargo (Table 7.5.1) at major ports, primarily Vishakhapatnam (Table 7.5.4). GMB ports and the

TABLE 7.5.4
Portwise Cargo Traffic 1998–9 and the Share of Coastal Shipping

('000 tonne)

| Year | Total | | | | per cent of coastal to total | | | |
|---|---|---|---|---|---|---|---|---|
| | Unloaded | Loaded | Trans-shipment | Total | Unloaded | Loaded | Trans-shipment | Total |
| *Major ports** | | | | | | | | |
| Calcutta | 4497 | 1141 | 3525 | 9163 | 47.1 | 19.4 | 0.5 | 25.7 |
| Haldia | 13,600 | 6624 | 0 | 20,224 | 3.2 | 89.0 | 0.0 | 31.3 |
| Paradip | 4507 | 8601 | 0 | 13,108 | 12.6 | 84.4 | 0.0 | 59.7 |
| Vishakhapatnam | 15,377 | 13,551 | 6725 | 35,653 | 19.1 | 52.7 | 45.4 | 36.9 |
| Chennai | 24,313 | 9333 | 1555 | 35,201 | 67.9 | 7.6 | 50.0 | 51.1 |
| Tuticorin | 8485 | 1665 | 0 | 10,150 | 60.6 | 2.2 | 0.0 | 51.0 |
| Cochin | 10,358 | 2307 | 0 | 12,665 | 36.7 | 66.7 | 0.0 | 42.2 |
| New Mangalore | 6894 | 7278 | 34 | 14,206 | 5.0 | 29.7 | 55.9 | 17.7 |
| Mormugao | 2536 | 15,460 | 24 | 18,020 | 30.8 | 0.8 | 0.0 | 5.0 |
| Mumbai@ | 19,139 | 11786 | 45 | 30,970 | 8.5 | 57.1 | 0.0 | 27.0 |
| JNPT | 7347 | 4303 | 73 | 11,723 | 11.4 | 1.1 | 34.2 | 7.8 |
| Kandla | 33,727 | 4180 | 2730 | 40,637 | 14.3 | 3.8 | 0.0 | 12.3 |
| All Major Ports | 150,780 | 86,229 | 14,711 | 251,720 | 26.5 | 37.1 | 26.4 | 30.1 |
| *GMB*** | | | | | | | | |
| Magdalla | 7596 | 1273 | 0 | 8869 | 40.6 | 55.1 | 0.0 | 42.7 |
| Mul-Dwarka | 414 | 1656 | 0 | 2070 | 0.0 | 73.5 | 0.0 | 58.8 |
| Jafrabad | 524 | 2347 | 0 | 2871 | 0.0 | 25.6 | 0.0 | 20.9 |
| Other Ports of GMB | 8393 | 2806 | 0 | 11,199 | 5.0 | 12.2 | 0.0 | 6.8 |
| All Ports of GMB | 16,927 | 8082 | 0 | 25,009 | 20.7 | 35.4 | 0.0 | 25.4 |
| All Major Ports and GMB Ports | 167,707 | 94,311 | 14,711 | 276,729 | 25.9 | 37.0 | 26.4 | 29.7 |
| Non-GMB Minor and Intermediate Ports*** | 5076 | 5565 | 0 | 10,641 | 53.5 | 44.1 | 0.0 | 8.6 |
| All India Traffic | 172,783 | 99,876 | 14,711 | 287,370 | 26.7 | 37.4 | 26.4 | 30.4 |

@ Break-up of trans-shipment cargo is not available.
*Source:* * Indian Ports Association (1998–9).
** Gujarat Maritime Board (1998–9).
*** MoST, Basic Port Statistics of India (1998–9).
[24] For details, see Table 4 of Raghuram (2000).

non-GMB minor and intermediate ports reported nil trans-shipment, raising doubt as to whether it is a classification category. The total originating traffic during 1998–9 was 37.3 mt, subject to limitations of available data.

The tonne km (tkm) of coastal movement is now estimated. Average traffic moved during the year is taken as 41 mt (average of unloaded and loaded traffic). Over 70 per cent consisted of thermal coal and POL (petroleum oil and lubricant), whose average coastal lead has been estimated as 1600 km (Raghuram and Chaudhary 1994). Assuming a lead of 1600 km for all coastal traffic, total tkm would be 65.6 billion. The corresponding figure for Indian Railways was about 284 btkm (1998–9), which is 40 per cent of railroad share. Total land movement was thus 710 btkm and total domestic movement (including coastal) about 775.6 btkm. Thus coastal movement had a market share of 8.5 per cent of domestic movement. (Pipeline and inland water transport have not been considered here. While inland water transport is insignificant, the pipeline is a growing mode of freight movement.)

Examining portwise data from Table 7.5.4, the share of coastal cargo can be seen as varying across ports and within ports between unloading and loading. For example, in 1998–9, more than 50 per cent of the cargo at Paradip, Chennai, and Tuticorin was coastal, while at Marmugao and Jawaharlal Nehru Port Trust (JNPT) less than 8 per cent was coastal. At Haldia 89 per cent of loaded cargo and only 3.2 per cent of unloaded cargo was coastal. At Chennai 7.6 per cent of loaded cargo and 67.9 per cent of its unloaded cargo was coastal (The loading and unloading shares are expanded upon later in the discussion.) Thus the significance of coastal cargo as a business varies across ports and would be important in determining the interest of a port in servicing coastal traffic (See Table 7.5.5).

The hinterland of the port, the volume of cargo, and multimodal and port infrastructure play significant roles in determining port traffic. These aspects are later elaborated upon.

It is widely felt both by the industry and policy makers that coastal shipping has been underexploited in India, especially since the country has over 6000 km of coastline catering to the direction of significant flows of traffic. Further, coastal shipping is more environment friendly, less expensive, and has the potential of relieving congestion in land transport. (The market share of coastal shipping and inland water transport in the United States is nearly 40 per cent of the tkm freight movement). Historical reasons for not exploiting coastal shipping have been many and varied, including that the Industrial Revolution missed India under the colonial

yoke. Today the reasons are primarily infrastructural and regulatory. It is thus important to examine what can be done to increase coastal shipping by integrating it with the rest of the transportation system.

TABLE 7.5.5
Share of Coastal Cargo at Various Ports 1998–9

| Port | % share of cargo to total cargo of each port | Coastal cargo (mt) |
|---|---|---|
| *Major ports* | | |
| 1  Paradip | 59.7 | 7.8 |
| 2  Chennai | 51.1 | 18.0 |
| 3  Tuticorin | 51.0 | 5.2 |
| 4  Cochin | 42.2 | 5.3 |
| 5  Vishakhapatnam | 36.9 | 13.1 |
| 6  Haldia | 31.3 | 6.3 |
| 7  Mumbai | 27.0 | 8.3 |
| 8  Calcutta | 25.7 | 2.3 |
| 9  New Mangalore | 17.7 | 2.5 |
| 10  Kandla | 12.3 | 5.0 |
| 11  JNPT | 7.8 | 0.9 |
| 12  Marmugao | 5.0 | 0.9 |
| Total major ports | 30.1 | 75.8 |
| *GMB ports* | | |
| 1  Mul-Dwarka | 58.8 | 1.2 |
| 2  Magdalla | 42.7 | 3.8 |
| 3  Jafrabad | 20.9 | 0.6 |
| 4  Other GMB ports | 6.8 | 0.7 |
| Total GMB ports | 25.4 | 6.4 |
| Non-GMB minor and intermediate ports | 48.6 | 5.2 |
| All India traffic | 30.4 | 87.4 |

## COASTAL TRAFFIC PROFILE

Cargowise coastal movement data are available for 1997–8 from *Basic Port Statistics of India, 1998–9*. Out of 37.6 mt of originating coastal traffic during 1997–8, 14.2 mt was accounted for by thermal coal, 8.6 mt by POL crude, 8.4 mt by POL products, 2.9 mt by iron ore and pellets, 0.8 mt by cement, and 0.7 mt by clinker.

1998–9

| | Commodity | Quantity (mt) |
|---|---|---|
| 1 | Thermal coal | 14.2 |
| 2 | POL crude | 8.6 |
| 3 | POL product | 8.4 |
| 4 | Iron ore and pellets | 2.9 |
| 5 | Cement | 0.8 |
| 6 | Clinker | 0.7 |
| 7 | Others | 2.0 |
| | Total | 37.6 |

Tables 7.5.6 and 7.5.7 give the details of various coastal cargoes loaded and unloaded at different ports. The major coastal cargo flows are as follows:

• Thermal coal (from Haldia, Paradip and Vishakhapatnam to Chennai and Tuticorin). This traffic is driven by the Tamil Nadu Electricity Board (TNEB).

• POL products (between major ports, with sources being Mumbai, New Mangalore, Cochin, and Haldia, where the refineries are situated. Jamnagar will become an important port for loading and unloading POL products, from 2000–1, with the Reliance Petroleum plant coming on stream. The key destinations are Calcutta and Marmugao. Chennai and Vishakhapatnam, which also have refineries, seem to be using their capacities for distribution by land); POL crude (from Mumbai (Bombay High) to Chennai and Cochin); Imported crude obviously moves directly to the refinery ports. This traffic is driven by the petroleum companies, that is, the Indian Oil Corporation Limited (IOCL), Bharat Petroleum Corporation Limited (BPCL), Hindustan Petroleum Corporation Limited (HPCL), and Reliance.

• Iron ore and pellets (Vishakhapatnam and New Mangalore to Magdalla). This traffic is driven by Essar.

From the minor and intermediate ports the principal cargoes are:

• Cement (Mul-Dwarka to Magdalla and Maharashtra minor ports)—This traffic is driven by GACL;
• Clinker (Jafrabad to Magdalla and Maharashtra minor ports)—This traffic is driven by Gujarat Narmada Cement Limited (GNCL).

Tables 7.5.8 and 7.5.9 give the profile of ports where coastal movement (loading and unloading) is significant. For major ports and GMB ports, commodity-wise performance indicators including average turnaround time, pre-berthing time, and parcel size.

Much of the traffic is driven by large corporates that view coastal movement as a part of their logistics management. They themselves have invested in the necessary multimodal evacuation infrastructure and in some places even port infrastructure (Gujarat Ambuja Cements Limited [GACL] at Mul-Dwarka and Essar at Magdalla). Reliance has invested in its own port

TABLE 7.5.6
Cargoes Loaded at Major, GMB, and Minor Ports 1997–8

(mt)

| Port | Coal/ coke | POL- product | Iron ore/ pellets | POL- crude | Cement | Clinker | Others | Loaded | Total loaded | per cent of loaded to total loaded |
|---|---|---|---|---|---|---|---|---|---|---|
| *Major ports** | | | | | | | | | | |
| Haldia | 4.1 | 1.9 | – | – | – | – | – | 6.1 | 6.6 | 92.4 |
| Paradip | 6.1 | 6.4 | 4.2 | – | – | – | – | 7.1 | 8.8 | 80.7 |
| Cochin | – | 1.5 | – | – | – | – | – | 1.5 | 2.5 | 60.0 |
| Mumbai | – | 0.9 | – | 6.7 | – | – | – | 7.6 | 12.7 | 59.8 |
| Vishakhapatnam | 4.0 | 0.1 | 1.9 | – | – | – | 1.4 | 7.4 | 14.2 | 52.1 |
| New Mangalore | – | 2.3 | 0.4 | – | – | – | – | 2.7 | 9.2 | 29.3 |
| Calcutta | – | 0.1 | – | – | – | – | 0.1 | 0.2 | 1.6 | 12.5 |
| Chennai | – | 1.0 | – | – | – | – | – | 1.0 | 10.9 | 9.2 |
| Kandla | – | – | – | – | – | – | 0.2 | 0.2 | 3.9 | 5.1 |
| JNPT | – | – | – | – | – | – | 0.1 | 0.1 | 3.4 | 2.9 |
| Tuticorin | – | – | – | – | – | – | .. | .. | 1.6 | .. |
| Marmugao | .. | – | .. | – | – | – | .. | .. | 19.2 | .. |
| *GMB ports*** | | | | | | | | | | |
| Mul-Dwarka | – | – | – | – | 0.8 | – | .. | 0.8 | 1.4 | 57.1 |
| Jafrabad | – | – | – | – | - | 0.7 | – | 0.7 | 1.8 | 38.9 |
| Others | – | – | 0.4 | – | 0.1 | – | 0.3 | 0.8 | 7.1 | 11.3 |
| *Non-GMB minor and* intermediate ports | – | – | 0.2 | – | – | – | 1.7 | 1.9 | 4.3 | 44.2 |
| Total | 14.2 | 14.2 | 7.1 | 6.7 | 0.9 | 0.7 | 3.8 | 38.1 | 109.2 | 34.9 |

.. Negligible.

*Sources: *MoST (1998–9).
**Gujarat Maritime Board Administration Report (1998–9).

TABLE 7.5.7
Cargoes Unloaded at Major, GMB, and Minor Ports 1997–8

(mt)

| Port | Coal/coke | POL-crude | POL-product | Iron ore/pellets | Clinker | Cement | Others | Unloaded | Total un-loaded | per cent of unloaded to total unloaded |
|---|---|---|---|---|---|---|---|---|---|---|
| *Major ports* | | | | | | | | | | |
| Tuticorin | 5.2 | – | 0.4 | – | – | – | .. | 5.6 | 8.4 | 66.7 |
| Calcutta | – | – | 2.0 | – | – | – | 0.2 | 2.2 | 4.2 | 52.4 |
| Chennai | 8.6 | 2.6 | .. | – | – | – | .. | 11.3 | 24.3 | 48.3 |
| Marmugao | .. | – | 0.8 | – | – | – | .. | 0.9 | 2.0 | 45.0 |
| Cochin | – | 4.1 | 0.1 | – | – | – | .. | 4.3 | 9.8 | 43.9 |
| Vishakhapatnam | – | 3.3 | 2.2 | 0.4 | – | – | .. | 5.9 | 14.7 | 40.1 |
| Kandla | – | 3.7 | 1.5 | – | – | – | .. | 5.3 | 31.5 | 16.8 |
| Mumbai | – | – | 1.7 | – | – | – | .. | 1.7 | 19.0 | 8.9 |
| Haldia | – | – | 0.8 | – | – | – | – | 0.8 | 13.4 | 6.0 |
| JNPT | – | – | – | 0.3 | – | – | .. | 0.3 | 5.3 | 5.7 |
| New Mangalore | – | .. | 0.2 | – | – | – | .. | 0.3 | 7.0 | 4.3 |
| Paradip | – | 0.1 | – | – | – | – | – | 0.1 | 4.5 | 2.2 |
| *GMB Ports* | | | | | | | | | | |
| Magdalla | – | – | – | 2.6 | 0.4 | 0.3 | 0.1 | 3.4 | 7.3 | 46.6 |
| Others | 0.2 | – | – | – | – | – | 0.2 | 0.4 | 8.1 | 4.9 |
| *Non-GMB minor and intermediate ports* | – | – | – | 0.1 | – | – | 1.3 | 1.4 | 8.6 | 16.3 |
| Total | 14.0 | 13.8 | 9.7 | 3.4 | 0.4 | 0.3 | 1.8 | 43.9 | 167.2 | 26.3 |

.. Negligible.

*Source:* Same as for Table 7.5.6.

infrastructure at Jamnagar for receiving POL crude and sending POL products. The shipping capacity is provided as a kind of 'alliance' with traffic guarantees. Examples are the Shipping Corporation of India (SCI) and Great Eastern for oil companies' POL and Poompuhar Shipping for TNEB thermal coal.

The future traffic potential of coastal shipping lies in large corporates shipping bulk products and general cargo in containerized form which is almost non-existent today.

For thermal coal, traffic moves from the collieries at Orissa, West Bengal, and Bihar by rail to Haldia, Paradip, and Vishakhapatnam, as specific berths and loading facilities are provided there. At Chennai and Tuticorin, similar unloading facilities are provided. At Chennai, coal moves by rail to two thermal power stations, one located just north of Chennai and the other at Mettur, about 250 km south-west. At Tuticorin, coal is unloaded and moves directly to the thermal power station by conveyor belt.

Currently, a new port called Ennore, just north of Chennai is in the finishing stages of construction, both to serve the thermal power station located nearby. Ennore also removes the pollution in Chennai, due to coal handling that would have otherwise resulted. Ennore port will supply coal to the neighbouring Ennore Thermal Power station by conveyor belt and to Mettur by rail. This project is funded by the Asian Development Bank (ADB) and takes care of necessary integration with rail as well as the conveyor belt system for proper evacuation.

For POL, appropriate investments in railway sidings, tank farms, pump installations, jetties, buoys and pipelines are in place for integration with the land transport infrastructure. In future, due to investments in pipelines there is a possibility that this traffic might decrease, though the main target is road and rail movement. Almost all the pipelines, including those proposed, are hinterland pipelines from the ports, leading away from the sea. The only 'coastal' pipeline is the one from Vishakhapatnam to Vijayawada, whose lead is, however, too small to be an alternative to coastal shipping. If a common carrier pipeline network of reasonable length and density comes into being, then some of the port-based refineries may be in a position to service hinterland areas directly by pipeline, rather than coastal shipping, rail, or road. Such a network is expected to be in place by 2010.[25]

[25] See section 7.3.

TABLE 7.5.8
Some Aspects of Cargo Handling at Major Ports that Have
Significant Coastal Traffic 1997–8

| Port | Cargo | Coastal loaded (million tonnes) | Average turnaround time (days) | Average berthing time days | Average parcel size (tonnes) |
|---|---|---|---|---|---|
| Hadia (L) | Coal/coke | 4.1 | 8.9 | 2.7 | 22,898 |
| (91.4) | POL (product) | 1.9 | 4.2 | 2.6 | 17,531 |
| Paradip (L) | Coal/coke | 6.1 | 4.8 | 0.8 | 27,766 |
| (83.4) | POL (product) | 0.6 | 4.5 | 3.4 | 9935 |
|  | Iron ore (raw/pellets) | 0.4 | 5.3 | 2.3 | 43,214 |
| Cochin (L) | POL (product) | 1.5 | 4.3 | 2.1 | 29,661 |
| (65.2) |  |  |  |  |  |
| Mumbai (L) | POL (crude) | 6.7 | 5.6 | 2.5 | 33,057 |
| (64.3) | POL (product) | 0.9 | 5.6 | 2.5 | 33,057 |
| Vishakhapatnam | Iron ore (raw/pellets) | 1.9 | 7.0 | 2.4 | 68,220 |
| (54.4) | Coal/coke | 4.0 | 11.6 | 5.2 | 33,286 |
|  | POL (product) | 0.1 | 2.3 | 0.6 | 23,320 |
|  | Other cargo | 1.4 | – | – | – |
| New Mangalore (L) | POL (product) | 2.3 | 2.7 | 1.3 | 22,839 |
| (37.7) | Iron ore (pellet) | 0.4 | 3.0 | 1.4 | 45,062 |
| Tuticorin (U) | Coal/coke | 5.2 | 5.1 | 1.1 | 120,000 |
| (66.3) | POL (product) | 0.4 | 3.0 | 1.4 | 45,062 |
| Calcutta (U) | POL (product) | 2.0 | 4.1 | 1.1 | 8837 |
| (47.7) | Other cargo | 0.2 | – | – | – |
| Chennai (U) | Coal/coke | 8.6 | 13.2 | 6.9 | 19,762 |
| (46.5) | POL (crude) | 2.6 | 7.4 | 5.3 | 30,010 |
|  | POL (product) | NA | 7.4 | 5.3 | 30,010 |
| Cochin (U) | POL (crude) | 4.1 | 4.3 | 2.1 | 29,661 |
| (41.8) | POL (product) | 0.1 | 4.3 | 2.1 | 29,661 |
| Vishakhapatnam (U) | POL (crude) | 3.3 | 2.3 | 0.6 | 23,320 |
| (38.6) | POL (product) | 2.2 | 2.3 | 0.6 | 23,320 |
|  | Iron ore (raw/pellet) | 0.4 | 7.0 | 2.4 | 68,220 |
| Marmugao | POL (product) | 0.8 | 2.4 | 0.9 | 7277 |

*Source:* Indian Ports Association (2000).

*Note:* 'U' and 'L' in brackets refer to unloaded and loaded respectively.

Figures in brackets are percentage of coastal loaded or unloaded to total loaded and unloaded respectively.

TABLE 7.5.9
Coastal Traffic in Certain Commodities
at GMB Ports 1997–8

| Port | Commodity | Loaded coastal mMt |
|---|---|---|
| Mul-Dwaraka (L) | Cement | 0.8 |
| (56.9) |  |  |
| Jaffrabad (L) | Clinker | 0.7 |
| (39.4) |  |  |
| Magdalla (L) | Iron ore | 0.4 |
| (37.3) | Other cargo | 0.6 |
| Magdalla (U) | Iron ore | 2.6 |
| (46.5) | Clinker | 0.4 |
|  | Cement | 0.3 |
|  | Other cargo | 0.1 |
| Okha (U) | Furnace oil | 0.2 |
| (25.9) | Coal | 0.1 |

## ECONOMICS OF COASTAL MOVEMENT

Studies of iron ore, sponge iron (Raghuram and Mathew 2000), and cement movement (Banerjee, Raghuram, and Rangaraj 2000) show that, given the infrastructure at ports and mines for material unload-ing, the operating economics are in favour of coastal movement, whose transport cost per tonne km would be Re 0.25 or less (even for vessels of 3000 tonne capacity). Corresponding rail or road costs, depending on distance, would be Re 0.60–Rs 1.20.

As a proportion of total logistics cost (including transportation, related inventory, handling, and related losses), the transportation cost for low value bulk commodities to high value consumer goods ranged from 90 per cent to 40 per cent for road, 85 per cent to 30 per cent for rail, and 80 per cent to 20 per cent for shipping, for a 1000 km lead.

Despite the fact that coastal shipping would in general require additional land leads, cost differentials favour it even for an east–west movement. In such cases, the sea distances would be 2500 to 4000 km and about twice the port to port direct land lead. More interior the origin/destination, the less the advantage of coastal shipping (see Box 7.5.1).

A professionally run company like the GACL prefers coastal movement, wherever possible, over land transportation. It has therefore made investments to integrate coastal movement with the land leads. While data on its costs for coastal movement are not available, its rail and road freight costs (not total logistics cost) from its plant at Kodinar (served by the port of Mul-Dwarka) to Surat are Rs 600 and Rs 558 per tonne, respectively (GACL 1999). The rail cost by the shortest route would

---

BOX 7.5.1

**Advantages of Coastal Shipping[26]**

The total logistics cost advantage for coastal shipping was over Rs 1 crore for the raw material from Daitari, as compared to rail whose total cost was Rs 3.25 crore. Similar advantages would accrue for other raw material sources. This analysis does not take into consideration the investment cost at the plant end for dealing with sea cargo. This was partly due to the fact that some investments in a jetty had already been made for importing plant machinery during the project stage. The additional investments in the jetty were less than the investments required for constructing a railway siding from the nearest rail access point.

Another interesting dimension for this company was the choice of market based on logistical competitive advantage. The finished product (sponge iron) could use the returning empty vessels to the east coast at an additional transportation cost of Rs 140 per tonne (the inbound full cost of transportation including the empty return of the vessel was Rs 260 per tonne), while rail would have costed anywhere between Rs 382 and Rs 544 per tonne. In this instance, for coastal shipping, the costs due to inventory, handling, and losses would be significant since the inherent value of sponge iron was Rs 4000 per tonne (as opposed to Rs 250 per tonne for iron ore). However, the total costs were still in favour of using the coastal route and servicing a market with competitive advantage over other suppliers who were located closer to the eastern markets. The same was true of markets near Mangalore.[27]

Appropriate infrastructure to integrate with the land movement was key both for raw material and finished goods at the ports which were at the non-plant end. These being major ports, such infrastructure was readily available, including appropriate dumping space. Rail/road connectivity was in place. At the plant end, the key infrastructure was floating cranes to augment the unloading/loading rates of the mother vessel at anchorage and barges to shuttle between anchorage and jetty. Handling and conveyor-based evacuation were required between the jetty and the port-based plant.

---

[26] Here the specific case of raw material sourcing for Laxmi Transformers (LT) is taken up. LT is a company making sponge iron at Alibag. It sources iron ore in pellets and lumpy from Daitari. It has a total requirement of 0.6 mt tonnes of pellets and 0.155 of lumpy ores. One tonne of steel by the direct reduction process than LT uses, requires 1.24 mt of pellets and 0.31 mt of lumpy ore. Daitari is in Orissa. If the pellets and ore were to be routed by rail from Daitari up to Penn and then by road from Penn to Alibag the transport cost per tonne would be Rs 524 per mt (consisting of Rs 5175 for the rail segment and Rs 7.5 for the road segment). The total transport cost would be Rs 3.25 crore. For a 35,000 DWT ship picking up the ore at Paradip, brought there by rail, the transport cost would be Rs 1.99 crore.

In summary the total transport costs are as follows:

|  | Rs crore |
|---|---|
| 1. From Daitari to Penn by rail and then by road to Alibag | 3.2 |
| 2. From Daitari to Alibag by road | 5.52 |
| 3. From Daitari to Paradip by rail and then by 35,000 DWT ship to Alibag | 1.99 |
| 4. Same as above but with a 65,000 DWT ship | 1.84 |
| 5. By rail to Penn and then to Alibag | 3.25 |

The total mode cost per tonne for three of the modes above is as follows:

| Mode | Transport cost (Rs crore) | Inventory cost (Rs crore) | Cost/ tonne (Rs/mt) |
|---|---|---|---|
| (3) Rail + 35000 DWT ship | 1.99 | 0.22 | 356 + extra handling + buffer stock cost |
| (4) Rail + 65000 DWT ship | 1.84 | 0/39 | 359 + extra handling + buffer stock cost |
| (5) All the way by rail upto Penn and road to Alibag | 3.25 | Negligible | 5221 + extra handling + buffer stock |

[27] This analysis uses the given rail freight charges as reflecting the true cost of rail. We know that railways overprice freight to cross-subsidize passenger traffic. Unfortunately, there are no accurate estimates of freight costs by rail either. Similarly, coastal shipping is itself subject to large distortions arising out of the sabotage laws of the country. The question as such remains open.

be Rs 545. However, since this route has restrictions due to the Gir sanctuary, the actual cost works out to be Rs 600, whereas the transportation cost from Kodinar to Surat using coastal movement would not exceed Rs 150 per tonne including the land leads. Part of the saving is also due to the shorter coastal lead across the Gulf of Khambat.

## TRAFFIC POTENTIAL

Given such advantages for bulk movement as in the case of GACL and Laxmi Transformers, the scope for increased use of coastal shipping, with appropriate infrastructure to integrate with the rest of the transport network, is quite large.

It would be difficult to quantify the traffic potential for coastal movement, since much of it would depend on the port and multimodal infrastructure and industrial and distribution centre location strategies. Of the domestic originating tonnes, the railways handled about 420 mt in 1998–9. Assuming that traffic using road as the primary movement had similar leads as rail and given that road share in tkm is one and a half times the rail share, the originating traffic for primary road movement would be about 630 mt. ('Primary' is emphasized since almost every unit of traffic starts its journey by road, but then could be serviced by rail or sea, both coastal and overseas, with very short leads. A primary movement would not include such movements.)

Out of the resultant total of over 1 billion tonnes of domestic originating traffic, a 5 per cent share captured by coastal shipping would amount to 50 mt. This would be in addition to the 41 mt of originating coastal traffic for 1998–9. With a five-year horizon it ought to be possible for coastal shipping to capture 50 mt of traffic. In fact, this figure would be less than the annual growth in originating tonnes in India. This would amount to a 14 per cent annual growth rate compared with the figure of 41 mt in 1998–9 to reach about 90 mt in 2004–5. At a macro level, the transport demand effort multiplier for India has been estimated at 1.5, which means the total tkm of traffic would grow at 1.5 times the gross domestic product (GDP) growth rate. Over the next few years, with an estimated 6–7 per cent gross domestic product (GDP) growth rate, transportation demand would grow at 10 per cent per year. The expectation for coastal movement growth is thus higher.

The scope for increasing coastal traffic would be the movement of coal (along the east coast and from east to west, with port-based distribution centres),• iron ore (east to west and along the west coast), fertilizers, and cement (port-based plant to port-based distribution centres), salt (along the west coast and west to east), foodgrains (north to south, partly by land and coast), and plantation produce (south to north, partly by coast and partly by land).

Projection of additional coal movement from Paradip for power plants in Tamil Nadu by 2004–5 is 13 mt, out of which 8 mt would be to the new port at Ennore, 3.5 mt to Cuddalore, and 1.5 mt to Tuticorin. Another forecast for 2006–7 suggests a total that ranges from 16 mt to 30 mt, covering the thermal coal requirements through Chennai and Ennore (Ennore Port 1999). This compares with the current (1998–9) thermal coal unloading of about 10 mt at Chennai.

Much of the increased tonnage on coastal shipping would be driven by corporates and investments depending on the nature of the cargo.

There is also scope of moving higher value manufactured goods in a containerized manner from industrial concentrations to redistribution centres. The Mumbai area is one possible source; industrial zones which could be developed near port locations are others. There is also the possibility of moving tea from Assam to the west coast consumption points of Gujarat and Maharashtra.

The government of Gujarat has done some work on this issue of joint development of industry and ports (for example Dahej) and has come out with a vision document (Gujarat Infrastructure Development Board 1999).

A study (Banerjee, Raghuram, and Rangaraj 2000) was made of the use of the Konkan Railway Corporation (KRC) to assess the traffic potential along the west coast. Thirteen companies were studied and their inputs closely considered. The study did not quantify the likely market realization but concluded that the KRC should focus on marketing service concepts since customers' willingness to shift modes was a function of the desired services being offered. A study by RITES (RITES 1996) provided a list of commodities and the quantity estimates moving to and from Kerala on the western north–south axis. These were taken up for analysis. (Banerjee, Raghuram, and Rangaraj 2000). For the year 2005–6 the south to north and north to south traffic for Kerala was estimated at 67,000 and 131,000 tonnes per day respectively, amounting to about 25 mt (south to north) and 50 mt (north to south) per year. Coastal shipping could compete for such large and significant movements.

## UTILIZATION OF SHIPS

In terms of number of vessels, there has been a gradual increase in the coastal share, while in terms of gross registered tonnage (GRT) the share has remained steady. The average GRT of a coastal vessel is 2500 while that of an overseas vessel is 26,400. Coastal vessels also include non-cargo-carrying vessels like tugs, dredgers, and offshore supply and service vessels. Coastal tonnage is on average older than overseas tonnage (Raghuram 2000). While coastal is reserved for Indian vessels, it should be noted that non-Indian flag vessels leased to Indian operators are also pressed into service for meeting coastal traffic requirements.

## REGULATORY ISSUES

Customs is viewed as a significant bottleneck, leading to extra paperwork, consequential delays, and corruption. The government thus constituted the Working Group on Coastal Shipping (1993) which recommended that coastal traffic should be removed from the purview of strict day-to-day control of the Customs Act.[28] However, as to whether customs should be completely off coastal traffic, some shipowners said that this would not be appropriate and customs must have the right to inspect any vessel/cargo. Regarding customs control, the paradigm needs to change from 'prove that you are not at fault' to 'beware of the consequences of illegal doings'. To ease customs inspections, streamline coastal cargo flow, and reduce the possibilities of illegal doings, it is suggested that: (i) there be specific ports or jetties earmarked for coastal traffic, and (ii) coast guard monitoring be improved. Indonesia is an example of a country with significant coastal shipping where separate ports and jetties are earmarked for coastal movement.

Ports with bureaucratic orientation are also a major bottleneck especially in turnaround times. This is because they are not stakeholders in this process even though they have a business interest in coastal shipping. Given their present structures and relationship with the government, public sector ports continue to be rule bound. Shipowners have also pointed out that definitions of 'overseas' and 'coastal' vary between customs and ports, causing extra documentation and complexity. This needs to be standardized. The right direction for ports would be corporatization and increased autonomy.

Box 7.5.2 shows how GMB ports are moving in the right direction. The lesson from the GMB is that port development could be more effective if it were market driven, if it leveraged initiatives by major users (captive jetties and ports), and if it were carried out with private participation. Even in the GMB context, one does get the feeling that a lot more can be achieved if the role of the GMB became more and more that of a facilitator, rather than executor.

Cabotage is an international issue, supposedly driven by security, protectionist, and 'others are doing

[28] Based on Recommendations of the Working Group on Coastal Shipping, 1993, as in Ministry of Surface Transport (1993).

---

BOX 7.5.2
**A Relative Success Story**

In the recent past, the GMB can be viewed as a success story in facilitating coastal traffic through faster responses to customer requirements and proactive marketing to traffic. For example, between 1990–1 and 1998–9, coastal traffic at the GMB ports grew from 2.3 to 6.4 mt at a CAGR of 13 per cent. During the same period, the major port coastal traffic grew from 49.0 to 75.8 mt at a rate of 5.6 per cent.

While the GMB has 40 registered minor and intermediate ports, the top six ports account for nearly 72 per cent of its traffic. Of these six ports, five are direct berthing. Two do not have rail connection, but are really ports serving cement plants located closely. Among the remaining four having rail connection, Magdalla (the port with the highest traffic) is least dependent on rail, since most of its traffic either terminates or originates at plants near the port. While traffic in and out of Bedi, Okha, and Sikka uses railways, rail access is not right up to the jetty, thereby requiring extra handling by road.

The relative success of the GMB is attributable both to a strategic vision driven by political will and operational autonomy. The GMB has been successful in facilitating captive jetties and ports and more recently joint venture ports (the Gujarat Pipavav Port Limited (GPPL) at Pipavav and the Gujarat Adani Port Limited (GAPL) at Mundra) which are at the 'take-off' stage.

---

it, why not me' concerns. Cabotage rules in India are relatively liberal compared to many other countries like the United States, Japan, and the EC (European Community) countries. All that is required is 75 per cent Indian ownership in a company providing coastal shipping services.

It is important for coastal shipping that the cabotage regulations stay at the current liberal level which will help bring in the most appropriate shipping capacity and commercial management. An important step, however, would be to change the Indian ownership requirement to 74 per cent, which would permit a foreign partner to seek a board position with 26 per cent equity.

A draft Coastal Shipping Act is under consideration, to put coastal shipping outside the purview of the existing Merchant Shipping Act, 1958 (Gill 1990), with a view to providing less stringent mandatory requirements in respect of design, construction, equipment, manning, and liability without, however, compromising on safety (MoST 1999). The expert committee which drafted this felt that the Act would facilitate the development of coastal shipping.

In my view, however, lack of such an Act has not been a deterrent for the development of coastal shipping.

While the proposed Coastal Shipping Act could lend focus to this transport mode, it should in no way bring in greater controls or bureaucracy in decision making.

## INFRASTRUCTURE FOCUS AREAS

### Turnaround Times

One of the key, if not the most important, concerns of coastal movement is turnaround times at ports. Given that coastal movements would by definition be of short duration (in Europe, similar services are called 'short sea shipping'), the port turnaround times should also be small. With a speed of 10 knots per hour (25 km per hour), distances of 1000, 2000, and 3000 km would be completed in 40 (1.66), 80 (2.33), and 120 (5) hours (days) respectively. However, as per Table 7.5.8, the average turnaround times range from 3 to 5 days at most ports and up to 8 days at Chennai and Visakhapatnam for coastal cargo. At Magdalla, due to lighterage operations, the turnaround time for iron ore and pellets could be as high as 15 days. The pre-berthing detentions range from 0.5 to 2 days at most ports and up to 6 days at Chennai. Greater attention is, therefore, called for in reducing the pre-berthing detention and turnaround times. Priority for coastal vessels including dedicated jetties, direct berthing, and better loading, unloading, and evacuation systems would be essential.

### Parcel Sizes

From Table 7.5.8, it can be seen that the average parcel size for thermal coal is about 30,000 tonnes, for POL products between 8000 and 30,000 tonnes, POL crude about 29,000 tonnes, and iron ore and pellets between 47,000 and 67,000 tonnes. All this cargo is handled at the major ports both for loading and unloading, except iron ore and pellets which are unloaded at Magdalla with a floating crane for lighterage. Cement and clinker movement takes place in vessels and barges with parcel sizes between 3000 to 5000 tonnes.

Other commodities which could potentially use coastal shipping would move in parcel sizes at the smaller end of the range, that is 3000 to 5000 tonnes. This would also be applicable for containerized general cargo, to that extent requiring lesser consolidation efforts. Such vessels would typically run with 150 to 250 twenty feet equivalent units (TEUs).

The smaller parcel sizes are in line with the just-in-time concept of supply chain management. Even though the economies of scale for ship movement would not be fully exploited, the cost advantage over land transport is still significant. Another major advantage is that draft requirements (about 4 m) for such vessels would be low, thereby offering flexibility in locating new ports for coastal traffic.

It is important to think 'small' (3000 to 5000 tonnes parcel size), while considering infrastructure for coastal movement, especially in terms of handling equipment, jetties, and shipping capacity. The draft requirement for jetties/ports handling such parcel sizes would be about 4 m. This is especially so the non-captive coastal shipping. Coastal shipping by captive users could think of parcel sizes most economical to their operations (for example TNEB coal, POL oil companies, and ESSAR iron ore).

Evacuation infrastructure at each of the port sites, both road and rail access, needs to be provided. While thinking of rail and coastal shipping integration, the parcel sizes should be multiples of rake sizes. This will enable quick evacuation, without having to consolidate cargo across vessels.

Even though ports with low draft are being proposed here, in view of the small parcel size approach, the ports need to be geared well to permit quick loading and unloading. The emphasis on gearing is all the more critical since (i) ports are usually not well equipped and (ii) the small parcel size low draft vessels would be more economical with no gear. The ports also need to permit round-the-clock and round-the-year operations. Only then would the desired flexibility and service levels be achieved to ensure a growing market for coastal shipping.

Elsewhere the economies of gearing at ports versus that in ships have been examined (Raghuram 2000). This yields that for a given level of non-bulk originating coastal traffic (say 50 mt), 667 ships of 3000 dwt and 140 jetties are needed. For the same loading/unloading effectiveness, a crane on a ship is more expensive not only in terms of investment, but also in terms of operating costs. Moreover, the numbers of shipboard gearing requirement alone would be more than four times those for port gearing. Thus port-based gearing would be more economical than ship-based gearing and also easier to implement since private sector shipowners would want to keep their investments low.

In Europe and the United States, coastal shipping is also integrated well with inland water transportation for through movement and evacuation. Unfortunately, our potential inland waterways have not been properly maintained and thus cannot really be integrated with the coastal system. If at all, the options are the three national waterways, namely Hooghly–Ganga, Brahmaputra, Kerala coastal waterway, and also the Godavari. Currently, it would be difficult to envisage parcel sizes even as small as 300 tonnes moving in a reliable manner!

## Port Locations

To facilitate coastal movement and reduce land leads, ports would need to be spaced all along the coastline, with a gap of no more than say 300 km. This would require about 20 port locations along India's 6400 km coastline, of which 10 could be at or adjacent to the existing major ports. Locations should be easily accessible from sea and have good land evacuation facilities. Some locations may be captive to industries. Others would serve the purpose of decongesting existing major ports, both in terms of berthing capacity and evacuation access. Chennai and Calcutta would need to be bypassed on account of these criteria. Visakhapatnam and Ennore could be allocatives for Chennai and Haldia for Calcutta. Haldia could be an alternate for Calcutta and Ennore for Chennai. Similarly, alternatives to Mumbai need to be considered.

## Port Economics

For an additional 50 mt of originating coastal traffic, we would need 140 jetties spread over 20 locations, that is, 7 jetties per port. The typical cost of a 4 m draft, seven-geared jetty port would be in the range of Rs 50 to 100 crore, depending on the hydrographics (based on interviews with port executives and shipowners). According to sources from the GMB, a berth for up to seven 5000 dwt ships would need to be 350 m long (50 m per ship). With a 30 m backup area, the total berth area would be 10,500 sq. m. The cost per. sq. m for a 4 m draft jetty would be Rs 40,000, thus amounting to a total of Rs 42 crore. Seven cranes with a 60 tonne capacity would be required to ensure unloading/loading within 24 hours at a 100 per cent peak berth occupancy. Each such crane would cost Rs 2 crore. Thus total crane cost would be Rs 14 crore. Warehousing and rail/road access would cost an additional Rs 4 crore. The total cost of the port, excluding any navigation dredging would be Rs 60 crore.

The annual operating and maintenance costs of such a port would be around 30 per cent of investment cost, that is about Rs 20 crore per annum. Since each additional port is expected to handle about 5 mt per annum, even at the low end revenue per tonne of Rs 100, the total revenue would be Rs 50 crore per annum. The surplus would be more than sufficient for financing costs, thus making ports for coastal operations a viable business. A port business is in general a very viable one. This may have much to do with the fact that all our ports are financially healthy.

## Private Investment

All this additional investment should take place with private investment of appropriate stakeholders (high intensity users, shipping companies, and other organizations with significant multimodal/maritime experience). Tying up investments for industry and/or distribution centres near ports, along with easy integration with land transport would be key requirements for success. What is really important is coordinated development.

## Shipping Capacity and Manning

Shipping capacity as such is not a problem, since vessels required for coastal operations can either be manufactured in India or sourced in through a bare boat charter or even, as per latest relaxations, chartering in of a foreign flag vessel.

Further, depending on the economics of the market, Indian owners can easily change the registration of vessels between coastal and overseas.

The manning requirements of coastal vessels are less stringent than overseas vessels, thereby offering scope for economy. Some shipowners state that there is further room to reduce manning requirements. However, the crucial issue in manning is the quality of manpower, since better take home salaries are available in overseas shipping. In the words of one coastal shipowner, coastal vessels are manned by 'grandfathers'. There does not seem to be any solution to this 'problem' other than being able to pay higher salaries, which would only happen with better market conditions and utilization of vessels.

# 8 | THE TELECOM SECTOR

## 8.1 A REVIEW OF THE INDIAN TELECOM SECTOR[1]

*Rekha Jain*

### INTRODUCTION

Technological changes in telecommunications and computers have radically changed the business scenario. In turn, the new demands of business have spurred many telecom-based technological innovations. In order to exploit these innovations for competing in global markets, the business community the world over has been putting pressure on governments to revise the policy, regulation, and structure of the telecom sector. Several countries across the world have responded by restructuring the state-controlled telecom service provider, increasing private participation, and deregulating service provision. The emergent organizations have attempted to be more responsive to the business needs and have evolved mechanisms to remain competitive even under tremendous pressures (Uehara 1990; Glynn 1992; Kim, Kim, and Yoon 1992; Laidlaw 1994).

Over the past several years, developing countries have also recognized the important role a responsive, business-oriented, and technologically advanced telecom sector plays in the growth of the economy. Many developing countries now see the constraints of a state monopoly in telecom as standing in the way of a response to the twin challenges of spurring internal growth and competing in an increasingly global economy (Donaldson 1994; Jussawala 1992; Melody 1986; Jain 1995; Pisciotta 1994; Tyler and Bednarizyk 1993; Scherer 1994; Wellenius 1990; Wellenius 1994). The process of introduction of new organizational forms and structures

[1] Research assistance provided by Ms Trupti Patel is gratefully acknowledged.

and appropriate policy is complex. In a developing country, resource shortages, lack of technology and trained personnel, and political expediency make the task even more difficult.

Past experience of reform across many countries suggests that the fundamental issue that must be addressed in telecom reform is effective separation of the basic functions of policy making, operational management, and regulation (ITU Report 1989). The second level of consideration is access to capital and human resources. The third level of concern is the introduction of competition for efficiency. Competition is perhaps more important than right ownership, if ever there was anything like it, in bringing about efficiency.

The Indian telecom sector was wholly under government ownership until 1984, and was characterized by underinvestment, outdated equipment, and growth well below the potential of the market. In the mid-1980s, telecom was included by the government as a part of the so-called 'Technology Missions'—a set of dedicated, welfare-oriented, and well focused programmes then implemented at national level (Dhir 1992).

This chapter provides an overview of the various organizations in the Indian telecom sector and assesses policy initiatives from the standpoint of separation of roles, competition, growth, and sequencing of reforms. Have the new organizations that have been created, such as the Telecom Regulatory Authority of India (TRAI), been able to respond better? Have the roles and inter-organizational relationships facilitated or hindered policy implementation? How successful have these attempts been?

BOX 8.1.1

### The DoT and the Precursor to Reform

In one of the earliest steps towards reforms and boosting indigenization efforts, the government set up the Centre for Development of Telematics (C-DOT) in 1984 with the objective of initiating and managing research in the switching and transmission segments. Subsequently, the government separated the Department of Post and Telegraph in 1985 by setting up the Department of Post and the Department of Telecommunications.

In 1986 two new public sector corporations—the Mahanagar Telephone Nigam Limited (MTNL) and the Videsh Sanchar Nigam Limited (VSNL)—were set up under the Department of Telecommunications (DoT). The MTNL, which was carved out of the DoT, took over the operation, maintenance, and development of telecom services in Bombay and New Delhi. The VSNL was set up to plan, operate, develop, and accelerate international telecom services in India. The government created the corporate organizations in order to allow decision making autonomy and flexibility and facilitate public borrowings that would not have been possible under a government framework. However, policy formulation, regulation, and several key decision areas remained with the DoT. A new organization, the Telecom Commission, was created in 1989 with a wide range of executive, administrative, and financial powers to formulate and regulate policy and prepare the budget for the DoT. The Telecom Commission had four full-time members managing technology, production, services, and finance and four part-time members representing the Planning Commission, Department of Finance, Department of Industry, and Department of Electronics.

The creation of the MTNL, its subsequent operations, and the relationship of the personnel employed in the MTNL to their counterparts in the DoT raised questions about the organizational structure most suited for this sector. Therefore, in 1991, upon government initiative, the high-powered Athreya Committee submitted a report on the appropriate organizational structures for this sector. The report recommended: (a) placing both policy and regulatory mechanisms under the Telecom Commission; (b) breaking up of the DoT into zonal corporations under the government; (c) setting up of a corporation, initially in the public sector, to handle the long-distance network; (d) allowing value-added services (VASs) to be provided by the private sector; and (e) indicating general liberalization in production of equipment giving autonomy to R&D and training institutions. Subsequently, other studies for reforms had been commissioned, but in the absence of public debate, and employee and union concerns regarding the consequences of implementation, the government did not formally adopted any report. Table 8.1.1 gives an overview of the reform process. Since 1997, there were several statements in the media by key decision makers and the Communications Minister calling for corporatization of the DoT. However, there was very little public information or debate regarding the sequence of decisions leading to corporatization or the form of corporate structure.

Since 1995, there was increasing pressure from international organizations such as the WTO to review the monopoly status of the VSNL and the DoT's monopoly in international long-distance communication respectively. The government had undertaken to review the monopoly status of the VSNL in 2004 and the possibility of opening of long distance in 1999. The VSNL continued to have a monopoly over international telecom and broadcast transmission. It had planned to enter the long-distance market but the DoT hampered its plans.

In 1999, the government created the Department of Telecom Services (DTS), whose Secretary was appointed from the Indian Telecom Services (ITS) cadre, and the DoT from the erstwhile the DoT, whose Secretary was appointed from the Indian Administrative Services (IAS). This was done ostensibly to separate the service provision component (DTS) from that of policy making (DoT). In reality this was to accommodate the conflict caused by the government's decision to appoint a Secretary to the department from the IAS, as DoT employees wanted the Secretary to be from the ITS. When the DTS Secretary retired, the government appointed an IAS officer in his place, which again led to agitation and further bifurcation of the DTS into the Department of Telecom Operations (DTO) and DTS. The DTS was to be headed by an IAS officer responsible for the MTNL, VSNL, Telecommunications Corporation of India Limited (TCIL), Indian Telephone Industries Ltd. (ITI), and Hindustan Teleprinters Limited (HTL) as well as for formulating the strategy for corporatization. The DTO was responsible for managing the telecom network.

The government's view has been that a person from outside the ITS cadre would be better able to oversee the corporatization of the DoT since in the past senior management of the erstwhile DoT, mostly from the ITS, had resisted any kind of change. Although an outsider Secretary was ostensibly to facilitate corporatization, it is not clear how, without the requisite mandate from the employees and especially the senior managers, he/she would be able to lead such a major task. This is not to say that the ITS cadre was better equipped to handle this task. What was missing was an overall strategy and an indication of the direction of change to inform the administrative changes. The government seemed to view corporatization as an administrative decision rather than a process.

The Athreya Committee report as well as subsequent reports on restructuring may be viewed as the initiation of a process of examining organizational options. The reports, however, did not accord due attention to the need for autonomy in financial and operational decision making. Management incentives that would have allowed these organizations to increase profitability and raise capital from markets had been only very sketchily outlined (Jain and Chhokar 1993). Thus access to capital would have been a problem. Besides the limitations, the suggested changes were superficial since most 'restructured' organizations showed too much of a control and rule orientation and continued to work in much the same manner as before.

Inability of top management and political executives to address the need to make the DoT more competitive could be cited as a failure. Given the large base of employees who had been entrenched in a typical bureaucratic mode of functioning, providing customer orientation and a commercial approach were, and continue to be, the most difficult tasks. The DoT had no specific training policy in this regard. Though there were several training centres, these were not equipped to provide management training. The 'restructuring' was far more concerned with 'form' than content. Areas like identifying the mechanisms for acquiring new core capabilities, developing appropriate incentives, and nurturing a climate in which change could take place were lacking. A major task was to manage unions and to retrain the staff to orient the organization towards a more competitive environment. The opening of basic and value-added services without attempting to streamline DoT operations or review its organization and no apparent articulated statement of change would eventually render DoT vulnerable to competition. Many of its capable and skilled staff at all levels have left to join private organizations which value better such human resources.

The establishment of the TRAI in 1997 separated the regulatory function from all others. However, policy making and operations continued to be with the DoT. But the change did not go uncontested. The DoT saw a potential threat to its position and attempted to evade regulations not in its favour. This had been clearly brought out when some private cellular operators approached the TRAI for contesting the DoT's unilateral revision of tariff. The DoT's initial stand was that the TRAI had no jurisdiction over it, although the TRAI act clearly specified otherwise. Unnecessary litigation could have been avoided by appropriate changes in the Indian Telegraph Act and clear statements from the government. Litigations had most certainly delayed developments in the sector. The DoT and the TRAI continued to have turf wars.

The setting up of the TRAI may have been driven by increasing pressures from private operators and was perhaps not part of a well-thought-out strategy of reform. The TRAI was certainly a positive step, but inadequate legislative reform in other areas of the telecom sector had made the TRAI's task harder. Despite concern from the industry and users at the outdated legislation governing the DoT, the government had not responded and there had been no formal review of the various Acts to determine whether they needed to be reviewed or implemented de novo. Meanwhile, several technological changes made it imperative that the government view IT (Information Technology), telecom, and broadcasting legislation in a coherent and convergent manner. This led to the draft of the Information, Communications and Entertainment (ICE) Bill, which is soon to be presented in Parliament.

Experience of other countries has stressed the need to separate policy, regulation, and operations. Separation of policy, regulation, and operations usually requires changes in legislation especially in those countries that start with dominant state-owned enterprise in the market.

Many countries recognized that the changing technologies and business requirements of this sector required rapid responses in terms of enabling legislation and have thus amended their telecom acts in the past five to six years. Examples of countries where such initiatives have been taken are the US, the UK, Germany, and Mexico.

The Indian restructuring initiative could have drawn significantly from the experience of many other countries such as Indonesia, Malaysia, Japan, Pakistan, Philippines, Sri Lanka, Thailand, and Korea, where at least some degree of organizational restructuring has been introduced.[2]

*Source:* Jussawala (1992); Melody (1986); Jain (1995); Pisciotta (1994); Tyler and Bednarizyk (1993); Scherer (1994); Wellenius (1990); Wellenius (1994).

TABLE 8.1.1
Milestones in Telecom Reforms

| 1984 | Manufacturing of subscriber terminal equipment opened to private sector. |
|---|---|
| 1985 | Telecom was constituted into a separate department with a separate board. |
| 1986 | MTNL and VSNL created as corporations. |
| 1988 | Government introduces in-dialling scheme. PABX services only within a building, or in adjoining buildings. |
| 1989 | Telecom Commission formed. |
| 1991 | Telecom equipment manufacturing opened to private sector. Major international players like Alcatel, AT&T, Ericsson, Fujitsu, and Siemens entered equipment manufacturing market. |
| 1992 | VAS sector opened for private competition. |
| 1993 | Private networks allowed in industrial areas. |
| 1994 | Licences for radio paging (27 cities) issued. |
| May 1994 | New Telecom Policy announced. |
| September 1994 | Broad guidelines for private operator entry into basic services announced. |
| November 1994 | Licences for cellular mobiles for four metros issued. |
| December 1994 | Tenders floated for bids in cellular mobile services in 19 circles, excluding the four metros, on a duopoly basis. |
| January 1995 | Tenders floated for second operator in basic services on a circle basis. |
| July 1995 | Cellular tender bid opened. |
| August 1995 | Basic service tender bid opened; the bids caused lot of controversy. A majority of bids were considered low. |
| December 1995 | LOIs issued to some operators for cellular mobile operations in circles. |
| January 1996 | Rebidding takes place for basic services in thirteen circles. Poor response. The Telecom Regulatory Authority of India (TRAI) formed by ordinance. |
| October 1996 | LOIs being issued for basic services. |
| March 1997 | The TRAI Act passed in Parliament. |
| June 1998 | Several VASs available through private operators. The first private basic service becomes operational. |
| March 1999 | Announcement of National Telecom Policy. |
| January 2000 | Amendment to the TRAI Act. |
| August 2000 | Announcement of Domestic Long Distance Competition Policy. |
| October 2000 | Planned Corporatization of DoT. |

*Note:* Letter of intent.

[2] See Box 8.1.2.

Box 8.1.2

**A Brief Review of Restructuring in Some Other Countries**

The Japanese Nippon Telegraph and Telephone Public Corporation and Kokusai Denshin Denwa was preceded by appropriate changes in the legal framework.

As a part of the Malaysian government's action plan of implementing its liberalization policy, legislation was enacted in 1987 to divide the monopoly service provider Jabatan Telekom Malaysia (JTM), into two parts—the regulatory unit called JTM and an operating company called Syarikat Telekom Malaysia (STM), a government-owned company. STM was issued a licence by the Minister of Telecommunications to operate the basic telecom network as a monopoly for a period of twenty years. Suitable amendments were also made to the Employees Provident Fund Act and Pension Act to protect employees' interests and enable them to continue with provident fund facility in the new organizations. Subsequently, STM was privatized by selling 25 per cent of its share to the public and foreign investors, and renamed Telekom Malaysia.

In Korea, the restructuring initiative was defined by the telecom policy: provision of one telephone per family and switching automation (Kim, Kim, and Yoon 1992). As a first step towards this, telecom operations were separated from the Ministry of Communication and several incorporated public common carriers (PCCs) were made responsible for them. In 1982, the PCCs were placed under a Korean Telecommunications Authority, which had financial and operational autonomy. Subsequently the telecom authority offered specialized services such as data communication, port communication, and cellular mobile communication with active private participation. The Ministry of Communication coordinated policy formation, design, and implementation issues. At this stage the various organizations that provided these services were still monopolies and public entities. In the late 1980s PCCs were privatized, telecom services were further deregulated, and competition existed in both basic and value added services. Both domestic and foreign companies could offer data and VAS, while the VAS providers were allowed to offer services across a number of other service categories. International competition was allowed in manufacturing and some services. The government felt that domestic manufacturers could withstand competition from foreign firms whereas it adopted a more cautious approach for the service providers. There was a stagewise well-defined framework for opening up the market: a tariff rate reduction of 7.5 per cent, greater role of foreign firms in public procurement, and simplification of technical standards. To ensure smooth transition, the government introduced these changes gradually.

In Korea the government consciously decided not to raise money for the telecom sector through tax and bonds, as these mechanisms required consent from the Ministry of Finance and the National Assembly. Government bonds would face increasing pressure for high interest rates (Kim, Kim, and Yoon 1992) and consequently, the customer would have to pay higher tariffs. The government then decided to incorporate the telecom entity as a public corporation, in order to allow it to raise capital and provide management incentives to improve the overall functioning of the organization. Profits from telecom service operations could then be invested back into the sector. This strategy removed financial constraints on investments. In Mexico, the shares of the public telecom companies were sold to private bidders not on the basis of offered price alone but also on the technical expertise of the bidders (*The Economist*, 5 October 1991, p. 34). This ensured not only access to capital but also technical and managerial expertise of the successful bidder.

TABLE 8.1.2

Share of Telecom Sector in National Plan Outlays

| Plan | Period | Total outlay (Rs billion) | Telecom outlay value (Rs billion) | Per cent total |
|------|--------|---------------------------|-----------------------------------|----------------|
| First | 1951–6 | 20 | 0.47 | 2.40 |
| Second | 1956–61 | 47 | 0.66 | 1.41 |
| Third | 1961–6 | 86 | 1.64 | 1.91 |
| Annual | 1966–9 | 66 | 1.59 | 2.40 |
| Fourth | 1969–74 | 158 | 4.15 | 2.63 |
| Fifth | 1974–8 | 287 | 7.81 | 2.73 |
| Annual | 1978–80 | 230 | 5.19 | 2.26 |
| Sixth | 1980–5 | 1097 | 27.22 | 2.48 |
| Seventh | 1985–90 | 2250 | 81.47 | 3.65 |
| Annual | 1990–2 | 823 | 61.0 | 7.40 |
| Eighth | 1992–7 | 3420 | 406.0 | 11.90 |
| Ninth | 1997–8 | 918.39 | 124.34 | 13.54 |
| | 1998–9 | 1051.87 | 137.72 | 13.09 |
| | 1999–2000 | 1035.21 | 197.88 | 19.11 |

*Source*: N. Ravi, 'Telecommunications in India—Past, Present and Future', *IEEE Communication Magazine*, March 1992.

* One US dollar was equal to Rs 18 until July 1991 when the rupee was devalued and was Rs 30 until 1992. It was approximately Rs 37 by November 1997 and had reached nearly Rs 42.50 by June 1998.

Box 8.1.3

## The Telecom Network[3] and the DoT

Unlike the meagre investments that were made before 1990, in the last decade of the century, the government substantially increased the outlay for this sector (Table 8.1.2). This led to more than trebling of telephone lines from nearly 5 million in 1990–1 to 17.8 million by 1997–8. The massive investments required to achieve this connectivity (of the order of nearly US $ 1 billion at 1995 prices) inter alia led the government to seek private participation.

More than 80 per cent of the telephones were in urban areas serving nearly 26 per cent of the population. About 30 per cent of these were concentrated in the four metros of Mumbai, Calcutta, Chennai, and New Delhi. The telephone network had been expanding at the rate of 22 per cent direct exchange lines (DELs) added since 1993–4 and accounted for 178 lakh lines at the end of 1997–8, which at the end of 1999 had grown to 213 lakh lines. Table A.8.1.1 gives various indicators related to the telecom sector since 1991–2. The registered waitlist demand was for nearly 27 lakh DELs. The ratio of registered demand to DELs available was on an average 20 per cent since 1993–4. During 1998, this decreased to 15 per cent, showing improvement. However, the registered demand was not a good indicator of potential demand, as when the connection charges were reduced by the MTNL from Rs 3000 to 1500, 2 lakh more subscribers registered for connections.

Despite this impressive growth rate in India, the waiting list for telephones was 2.65 million which is still about 8 per cent of the installed base. Information on circlewise waiting list data is shown in Table A.8.1.2. This being only the registered demand it does not necessarily indicate full potential demand for basic services. There was a large element of latent demand amply reflected in the immediate bouncing back of the waiting list no sooner than it was wiped out, which was despite sustained high growth in network expansion and provision of new connections.

Although the DoT had set a target of at least one phone per village by 1997, as of March 1996, nearly 60 per cent of the villages still remained uncovered. By March 1999, 310,687 villages were covered (a little more than half the total villages). During 1998–9, 42,855 more villages were covered. Although this represents a growth of 16 per cent over the previous year, it was far below the DoT's own target of 83,000 villages. According to newspaper reports (*Financial Express*, 25 August 1999), this target was likely to be delayed as the DoT had not found sufficient interest in vendors for WLL (wireless in local loop) technology, which it had chosen to deploy in the villages. It is possible that since the third generation of cellular mobile technology had started to be deployed in some of the western countries, vendors were not keen to continue with this technology.[4] There was thus far no available blueprint for third generation deployment.

India's satellite programme had been fairly successful with the development and launch of indigenous multi-purpose satellite systems. The satellites were being used by both the Communications Ministry and the Information and Broadcasting Ministry.

The effective trunk calls per DEL were decreasing until 1998. This could be indicative of slowness of investments in trunk lines, but more importantly could arise because market segments now buying telephone connections have a lower propensity to make trunk calls. Given the impending competition in domestic long distance, DoT increased its investments in the segment from 1998 onwards, expanding net switching capacity from 260.50 lakh lines to 326.45 lakh lines and trunk automatic exchange capacity from 14.70 lakh to 19.47 lakh. On the other hand, examination of the international circuits per DEL revealed that the numbers decreased, showing a slow-down in growth vis-à-vis DELs. This also implies that there were lower revenues due to incomplete calls.

The number of phone faults per 100 stations per month did not show significant decline since 1992–3. The average was 17.4 faults per month per 100 telephones. This indicates that despite the introduction of new technologies, the DoT was not able to enhance the performance of the network and make it more reliable.

The expenditure per employee rose from nearly Rs 1.43 lakh in 1993–4 to 2.57 lakh by 1997–8, a rise of nearly 80 per cent. This, at 15.8 per cent per annum, is significantly higher than rise in the consumer price index for non-manual urban workers at about 8.43 per cent. The conclusion therefore is inescapable that there has been little control over wage increase.

Although employees per 1000 DELs had been decreasing and had reached 24 employees per 1000 DEL by 2000, these need to be reduced significantly, since manning in the DoT in relation to the total value of business is known to be about three times that of progressive state-owned telecos in the nearly industrialized countries (NICs). At the average present rate of decrease (for the last five years), it will be another five years until the DoT reaches ten employees per 1000 DELs.

Although in 1992–3 the revenue per DEL per annum increased from Rs 9120 to 10,304 in 1997–8, the rate increased only 13 per cent, while overall inflation during the same period averaged 6–7 per cent. While total revenues had grown at an average of 24 per cent since 1992–3, expenses grew at an average of nearly 22 per cent. Although the DoT generated

---

[3] Data for this Box are largely taken from the Annual Reports of the Department of Telecommunications, Government of India, 1986–95 and the Rakesh Mohan Committe Report, 1997 on India's infrastructure.

[4] The interlocking international finance and technology and equipment markets at a time when the cost of funds is to high for Indian players is a factor. High licence fees and larger than optimal circles for WLL may have been additional factors. See section 8.2 of this report.

a revenue surplus, potentially its surpluses could have been even more. More importantly, the revenue surplus had a component of net foreign inflow on account of imbalances in international traffic and the consequent accounting rate settlements (Rs 3000–4000 crore or about half the revenue surplus). The component related to net foreign inflow was likely to decrease in the future.

A large number of people in urban areas did not opt for long-distance connectivity (or STD facility) due to fears of wrong or unfair billing by the DoT and preferred to use pay phone booths, especially public call offices (PCOs) when the need to make such calls arose. The proliferation of these booths in urban, rural, high-density, and low-density areas alleviated, to some extent, the need for individual phones. The revenues per line could be enhanced by increasing the reliability of phones in general and particularly that of billing.[5] This becomes even more important if we view the call revenue contributions by different subscriber categories. Nearly 5.2 per cent DELs contributed to nearly 55 per cent of the revenue (Table 8.1.3). Nearly 73 per cent of the DELs provided only 18 per cent of the revenue.

TABLE 8.1.3
Direct Exchange Lines (DELs), Waiting List for Telephones (1985–97), and Demand Estimates until 2006

| Year | DEL (thousand) | Telephone waiting list (thousand) |
|------|------|------|
| *Existing lines and waiting list* | | |
| 1985 | 3166 | 956 |
| 1986 | 3486 | 1125 |
| 1987 | 3801 | 1287 |
| 1988 | 4167 | 1420 |
| 1989 | 4560 | 1714 |
| 1990 | 5074 | 1961 |
| 1991 | 5810 | 2287 |
| 1992 | 6797 | 2846 |
| 1993 | 8026 | 2497 |
| 1994 | 9795 | 2159 |
| 1995 | 11,978 | 2277 |
| 1996 | 14,543 | 2894 |
| 1997 | 17,802 | 2706 |

| *Demand estimates* | | |
|------|------|------|
| | DoT estimate of demand | ICICI estimates of demand |
| 1997 | 13,900 | 17,700 |
| 2002 | 24,500 | 36,000 |
| 2006 | 38,600 | 64,300 |

*Source:* Annual Reports, DoT and The India Infrastructure Report: Policy Imperatives for Growth and Welfare, 1996, p. 121.

[5] Other socio-cultural factors though may have been important. Not all households are private spaces in the sense they are in the West. Phones tend to be shared, and therefore the need to control expensive STD calls makes many households not go in for the facility. Modern exchanges with STD bars and code-based access to STD facility do mitigate this risk to a large extent. Yet the very price of STD—a 6-minute STD call costs more than the second class rail fare between the same two cities—may have been an important factor that has restricted STD demand.

## BASIC SERVICES

Conventionally, telecom penetration has been assessed in terms of teledensity or the number of telephones (fixed and mobile) per 100 population. Indian teledensity as of April 2000 was nearly 2.3 and 2.2, c. 1998. For teledensities in other countries c. 1998, see table 8.1.4. Thus teledensities have been growing rapidly. While in China the number of lines grew at 300 per cent, during the period 1997–2000 in Malaysia the number of lines grew at 200 per cent and India at nearly 140 per cent (1994–8). Mobile densities in India are a fraction of what they are in the East Asian NICs (see Table 8.1.5).

TABLE 8.1.4
International Comparison of Telecom Indicators

| Country | Population (million) 1998 | Per capita (US $) 1997 | Telephone (thousand) 1998 | Tele-density 1998 |
|------|------|------|------|------|
| India | 982.22 | 451 | 21,593.7 | 2.2 |
| Indonesia | 206.34 | 1068 | 5571.6 | 2.7 |
| Philippines | 72.94 | 1136 | 2700.0 | 3.7 |
| Brazil | 165.85 | 5029 | 19,986.6 | 12.05 |
| Chile | 14.82 | 5182 | 3046.2 | 20.55 |
| Malaysia | 22.18 | 4517 | 4384.0 | 19.76 |
| Australia | 18.71 | 21,245 | 9580.0 | 51.21 |
| France | 59.68 | 23,618 | 34,000 | 56.97 |
| Spain | 39.37 | 13,510 | 16,288.6 | 41.31 |
| Germany | 82.04 | 25,625 | 46,500 | 56.68 |
| UK | 58.95 | 21,878 | 32,800 | 55.64 |
| USA | 270.37 | 30,173 | 178,800 | 66.13 |

*Source:* VSNL Annual Report.

However, whether teledensity is an appropriate measure of availability of services, especially in developing countries, is itself debatable. Teleaccess, which may be defined in terms of the percentage of population having access to telecom services within pre-specified distances, is sometimes considered a more appropriate indicator.

TABLE 8.1.5
Fixed Line and Cellular Mobile Teledensity in India
December 1997

|  | Fixed | Mobile | Aggregate |
|---|---|---|---|
| China | 6.0 | 1.2 | 7.2 |
| India | 1.7 | 0.05 | 1.75 |
| Indonesia | 2.1 | 0.6 | 2.7 |
| Malaysia | 18.3 | 11.2 | 29.5 |
| Philippines | 2.6 | 1.8 | 4.3 |
| Thailand | 6.9 | 3.5 | 10.4 |

*Source:* Spectrum Management Report.

*Note:* There is some variation in the data presented in Tables 8.1.4 and 8.1.5.

## RURAL TELECOM SERVICES

Despite an increase in the number of villages connected by phone over the years, rural connectivity remains a matter of concern. Even in villages where telephones have been provided, the general experience has been that many do not function. Many were not accessible to the public nor did they have long-distance facility. Rural public call offices (PCOs) were few, although various surveys had indicated that these as businesses could be good sources of income and could provide a reasonable level of service (Jain and Sastry 1997; Report of ICICI Working group on Telecom; The India Infrastructure Report 1996).

Public pay phones and telecom bureaus provided enhanced access (see Table 8.1.6). However, by western standards and even by standards in many newly industrialized countries (NICs) such as Malaysia and Brazil, access was very restricted. During the Eighth Five-Year Plan (1992–7), the government decided that its objective of development would be accessibility rather than provision of individual phones. It was therefore attempted to provide at least one pay phone per 100 households

TABLE 8.1.6
Telecom Services and Population
in Rural and Urban Areas

| Item | Rural | Urban |
|---|---|---|
| Population (per cent) | 74.0 | 26.0 |
| Teledensity (DELs per 100 people) | 0.2 | 3.4 |
| Number of exchanges (per cent) | 84.7 | 15.3 |
| DELs (per cent) | 17.8 | 83.2 |

*Source:* The India Infrastructure Report: Policy Imperatives for Growth and Welfare, 1996, p. 103.

in urban areas and one pay phone per village. As a result a large number of telecom booths sprang up across the country, providing local, long-distance, and international connectivity, and often fax and telex services.

However, for villages, it was decided to provide phones to the village panchayats. Such phone services were not commercially oriented and often several classes of people, such as women and socially backward classes, continued to have little or no access. The government's schemes were seldom based on consumer preferences or assessment of ground realities. A study that assessed the socio-economic benefits of rural telecom services (Jain and Sastry 1997) showed that beyond voice services, as there was significant demand for information services, villagers were quite willing to pay for the same. Voice when bundled with other facilities like fax could become viable in sparse rural areas. The study also questioned the paradigm of rural obligations being loaded only on basic service providers. Moreover, the Department of Telecom (DoT) continues to identify basic services necessarily as fixed services. Cellular operations could also increasingly provide rapid coverage as costs of 'cellular' services fall more rapidly than those of fixed lines. Certain rural areas are more effectively covered by wireless.[6] Rural obligations on the fixed service provider (FSP) then become redundant or reduced if cellular service can cover rural areas.

## INTERNATIONAL TELECOM SERVICES AND THE VSNL

The VSNL, a state-owned enterprise, was until recently the monopoly international service provider. Until 1999, it was also the sole Internet service provider (ISP). However, in November 1998 the government allowed private participation for ISPs and licensing was made almost free. Private operators initially had to use VSNL gateways, but the National Telecom Policy 1999 (NTP 99) removed that constraint. Some of the operators had plans to set up their own gateways (Table 8.1.7). The VSNL had worked out an exclusive arrangement for access to undersea wideband cable capacity with Fibre Optic Link around the Globe (FLAG), an international telecom carrier in which it had invested US $ 37 million. However, the prime minister's office (PMO) intervened to make the VSNL review these exclusive rights as discussed later in the chapter. Ultimately, other private operators were given the right to work with FLAG and other similar carriers to have access to undersea bandwidth. The VSNL's monopoly status was to be reviewed in 2004. Over a period of time the government had been diluting its stake in the VSNL by issuing global

[6] See section 8.2 of this report.

depository receipts (GDRs). But as of March 2000, the government still held nearly 53 per cent of the equity.

TABLE 8.1.7
Planned Gateways of Private Operators

| Company | Gateways planned |
| --- | --- |
| Satyam | 23 gateways to come up |
| Dishnet | 1 gateway, 7 more to follow |
| Caltiger | 40 earth stations to come up |
| Mantra | 1 gateway, 7 more to follow |
| BSES | 1 gateway to come up |
| BPL | 8 gateways to come up |

*Source: Business Today*, 7–21 August 2000, p. 30.

Far more than domestic networks, international telecom has been affected by declining unit costs and new technologies. This is also because this sector has seen faster deregulation. The VSNL's incoming international traffic grew at an average rate of 24 per cent per annum between 1990–1 and 1999–2000, and over the same period incoming calls grew by 12 per cent per annum. Table A.8.1.3 gives further information on the VSNL. The VSNL's revenue could easily compare with the leading telecom companies of smaller countries like Chile, Pakistan, and Malaysia. Thus the VSNL, MTNL, and DoT do have the size to play independent roles, and could potentially offer effective barriers to entry against MNCs if they geared up to improve efficiencies and expand rapidly enough by 2004, when the sector would be opened up (see Table A.8.1.4).

There is growing imbalance between incoming and outgoing calls in the United States.[7] Therefore in August 1997, the US Federal Communications Commission

[7] The majority of international carriers use the accounting rate revenue division procedure promulgated by the International Telecommunications Union (ITU) for revenue sharing for incoming and outgoing international calls. The international accounting rate system thus consists of three components:

(a) The collection rate, which is the rate charged by an operator to its customers. In theory, the collection charge for the same call should be more or less equal in the two correspondent countries.

(b) The accounting rate, which is the rate agreed between the originating country and the destination country.

(c) The settlement rate, which is the proportion of the accounting rate that determines the actual payment between countries. This is invariably half of the accounting rate. In other words, it is assumed that the cost of terminating the call is the same for each partner, even though this is rarely the case.

Although the collection rate was originally meant to reflect the accounting rate—which is the rate most in line with what a call actually costs to complete—over the years and especially over the past two decades, the accounting rate and collection rate have diverged.

(FCC) issued an order establishing benchmarks with which US carriers must comply in establishing accounting rates with non-US carriers. The order categorized various countries with respect to their levels of development to come up with cost-based benchmarks. The order further specified the transition period for reaching those target rates. As a result, the accounting rate of US carriers with the VSNL has come down drastically. In India, international prices did not fall at the same pace. This resulted in increasing imbalance between incoming and outgoing traffic (see Tables 8.1.8 and 8.1.9). leading to increasing disbursements primarily from the United States through international accounting rates systems. Given the size of payments that needed to be made by the United States to India, review of the accounting rate system and its consequent impact on the VSNL's revenue was important. Traffic from the United States in 1997 was 46 per cent of all incoming traffic. In 1995 the United States' incoming traffic had been 34 per cent. The outgoing traffic to the United States over the same period has decreased from 15 to 12 per cent. Tables A.8.1.5 and A.8.1.6 show the top ten net surplus countries as of 1998. These imbalances meant that the VSNL had 64 per cent of its total revenue coming out of settlements in 1997, up from 54 per cent in 1993–4. Net foreign inflows have been increasing at an average rate between 23 and 72 per cent per annum since 1993–4 (see Table A.8.1.3).

TABLE 8.1.8
Distribution of Incoming Telephone Traffic over
Originating Countries

| Country | per cent of total incoming traffic | | | |
| --- | --- | --- | --- | --- |
| | 1994–5 | 1995–6 | 1996–7 | 1997–8 |
| USA | 34 | 39 | 44 | 46 |
| UAE | 15 | 14 | 14 | 14 |
| S. Arabia | 6 | 7 | 7 | 9 |
| UK | 8 | 7 | 7 | 6 |
| Canada | 4 | 4 | 2 | 2 |
| Others | 33 | 29 | 26 | 23 |

*Source: VSNL Annual Reports, various issues.*

US carriers reduced their settlement rates by about 11 per cent after seeking a 25 per cent reduction during 1997–8. That decline was compensated by a revenue increase of 17 per cent in response to rate declines for international calls.

In part, the VSNL has been protected from changes in accounting, settlement, and collection rates by virtue of its interconnection arrangement with the DoT. The arrangement effectively allows the VSNL to retain approximately Rs 10 per minute for both incoming and

TABLE 8.1.9
Distribution of Outgoing Telephone Traffic over
Originating Countries

| Country | per cent of total outcoming traffic | | | |
|---|---|---|---|---|
| | 1994–5 | 1995–6 | 1996–7 | 1997–8 |
| USA | 15 | 15 | 13 | 12 |
| UAE | 10 | 10 | 9 | 8 |
| S. Arabia | 20 | 20 | 20 | 20 |
| UK | 9 | 7 | 9 | 9 |
| Canada | 2 | 3 | 3 | 3 |
| Others | 44 | 45 | 46 | 48 |

*Source:* VSNL Annual Reports, various issues.

outgoing calls. However, this is only a technicality, since the VSNL passes on the balance revenues to the DoT as network charges and a decline in accounting rate revenues would mean lower revenue surpluses for the DoT.

In May 1997, the VSNL became the first public sector undertaking to offload its equity in the international market. The government, however, remained a majority shareholder with a holding of 65 per cent. Against a GDR issue of US $ 448 million, its receipts were US $ 526.5 million. The VSNL had plans to invest these receipts in other areas, such as opening of more international gateways in metropolitan areas to reduce its dependence on the DoT and increase its quality of service. Due to its monopoly position being under threat and pressures on accounting rates, there could be reductions in the market value of its GDRs unless the VSNL is able to grow fast in other areas.

Regulators and agencies outside our boundaries play a key role affecting our regulations—ITU and OECD countries have put pressure on other countries to review the existing accounting rate regime. Of course, an increase in outgoing minutes implies an overall increase in revenues for the VSNL. Another factor that is going to affect the revenues is the emergence of networks operating on Voice over Internet Protocol (VoIP).[8] (see Appendix 8.1.1)

[8] VoIP networks convert the voice or data that is being transmitted into 'packets' by breaking the communication stream into smaller units and embedding these with origin and destination addresses. Packets allow for better utilization of the transmission channel, as these can be multiplexed, unlike a normal voice transmission (circuit switched) in which the entire channel is reserved for the communication. Another advantage is that the VoIP network can be used for transmitting multimedia and data content. In the future the transmission network will be a data network carrying voice, unlike major voice networks today that carry a small percentage of data. Latency in the packet mode may demand some priority for voice packets as some have argued.

The effect of such networks is to reduce the incoming and outgoing traffic over those networks where it is measured for settlement purposes. This traffic could be routed through the ISP's private leased channel, in which case it is not accounted for in settlements between the telecom operators in the two countries. For example, an analysis of the traffic statistics indicated that

outgoing traffic from the United States rose by only 8 per cent during 1998, compared with a historical growth rate of 20 per cent per year since the eighties. Given that the US economy was experiencing an economic boom in 1998, it is hardly likely that outgoing traffic has really slowed down that much. It is more likely that the 'missing' traffic is simply not being measured. [Kelley 2000]

The emergence of private leased circuits is going to further reduce the traffic volumes for the VSNL for settlement purposes.

Even though telephony accounts for the biggest chunk of revenues for the VSNL (94.70 per cent), value added services (VASs) is its fastest growing segment. The leased line revenue share increased from 2.28 to 4.73 per cent over the period from 1995–6 to 1997–8. Its Internet subscribers have been increasing and it had the largest number of subscribers in India at nearly 400,000 as of 1999. The DoT had constrained the VSNL from extending its ISP services to many more towns. The DoT had also not allowed the VSNL national long-distance operations.

In the future the VSNL needs to examine revenue streams outside the commodity business (such as basic services, bandwidth reselling, ISP customers) and provide VASs such as web farming and possibly seek alliances with other international operators. The opening of the long-distance market could certainly be an opportunity for the VSNL to consolidate its international operations.

The VSNL's monopoly which was to be reviewed in 2004 is already over as international data traffic has been opened up for competition. Its monopoly as a carrier of ISD could go much earlier.

## NATIONAL TELECOM POLICY 1994 AND 1999

Telecom service liberalization started in 1984 with the private sector being allowed to manufacture customer premise equipment. In 1992, service provision was opened for the private sector. At that stage, the government also unbundled basic and value-added services. Private operators were allowed to participate in provision of VASs, especially cellular and paging services. The key driver for change in the sector was the National Telecom Policy announced in May 1994 (NTP 94). It boldly specified as its major objectives telephone on demand, achievement of universal service obligation (USO), assurance of world class service to subscribers, universal availability of basic telecom services, so as to cover all 600,000 villages in the country and provide a PCO for every 500 persons in urban areas by the year 1997. This policy also paved the way for private sector participation in telecom services. Telecom services were categorized into domestic basic (which included basic telephony, telex, and fax), domestic VAS which covered all other services such as paging, cellular, and data services, VSAT, and international basic and VAS. New technologies, rapid growth, and worldwide trends ushering in competition, exposed the limitations of NTP 94. In 1999, NTP 99 was announced to replace NTP 94. Since then, opening up national long-distance services (NLDS) has been another landmark policy, which was announced on 14 August 2000 by the Prime Minister.[9]

Since 1994, private participation in basic, cellular, and VASs has been seen as a vehicle for rapid telecom development. The Rakesh Mohan Committee report hoped that the private sector would invest in telecom Rs 425 billion and Rs 581 billion between 1996 and 2001 and between 2002 and 2006, respectively. Private investment so far has been much more modest. Out of the expected licence fee of Rs 27,408 crore for the six circles, in the revenue-sharing scheme, operators have paid nearly Rs 1600 crore as a one-time entry fee. On the other hand, during the same periods, the DoT was expected to invest Rs 315 billion and Rs 581 billion, respectively. Investment estimates up to 2000 indicated that Rs 354 billion had already been spent, so that the DoT has invested more than it was projected to spend!

Drafted by the DoT, NTP 94 ostensibly facilitated private entry, but the poor design of auctions and the licensing conditions resulted in delays. Subsequent litigation further delayed services. Contentious issues regarding interconnections had to be resolved prior to offtake in services. Consequently, until 1997, provision of basic services by the private sector did not fructify. In effect there was little competition, due to the stipulated duopoly in both cellular and basic operations. While cellular services were a private duopoly, for basic services the DoT and an additional operator were licensed.

NTP 99[10] provided guidelines for managing contentious issues such as high licence fee, interconnections, constraints on service provision (provision of PCOs through cellular operations), and opening up of satellite services to foreign companies.

[9] Developments in India promise to be very exciting with the PMO's initiative. Essentially, the approach of the PMO would indicate that it understands that telecom in increasing segments is contestable, and as such the 'licence' mode is inappropriate.

[10] See http://www.trai.gov.in/npt1999.htm.

The key objectives of NTP 99 were as follows:

- Availability of telephone on demand.
- Teledensity of 7 per cent by 2005 and 15 per cent by 2010.
- To provide Internet access to all district headquarters by 2000.
- To provide high speed data and multimedia capability using technologies including ISDN (integrated services digital network) to all towns with a population greater than 2 lakh by the year 2002.
- Provision of world class services at reasonable rates.
- Emergence of India as a major manufacturing/exporting base of equipment.

NTP 99 changed the competitive scenario by liberally reviewing licence conditions. The highlights of NTP 99 are as follows:

- It allowed operators to carry their own intra-circle traffic without seeking an additional licence.
- Operators could interconnect to any other service provider including another cable service provider (CSP), which was not earlier allowed.
- Direct interconnectivity to the VSNL was also possible, after domestic long distance was opened up (target date 1 January 2000).
- Operators were eligible for licences for any number of areas.
- Licence fee was to restructured as a one-time entry fee and recurring revenue share (later fixed at 15 per cent).
- Entry of more operators would be based on the recommendations of TRAI and the situation would be reviewed every two years.
- Licences were to be available for 20 years, and were extendible by 10 years.
- Both voice and data traffic could be carried by the service provider.
- Direct interconnectivity between the licensed service provider and any other type of service provider in their area of operation and sharing of infrastructure with any other type of service provider was possible under NTP 99.
- Interconnectivity between service providers of different service areas was to be reviewed in consultation with the TRAI and the same was to be announced as part of the structure for opening up NLDS.
- Providing services would require a payment of a one-time entry fee (as a percentage of the original licence bid) and licence fee, based on revenue share. The number of

players, their mode of selection, appropriate level of entry fee, and percentage of revenue share were to be recommended by the TRAI.

There was to be free entry in basic services FSP and cellular mobile service provider (CMSP) for each area of operation. FSPs were required to pay an additional one-time fee for using frequencies for the Gas Authority wireless in local loop (WLL) provision. In addition, FSP operators using WLL were required to pay additional licence fee in the form of a revenue share for spectrum utilization. The TRAI would have to suggest the fee.

NTP 99 also envisaged the participation of CSPs in providing last mile linkage and switched services within their areas of operation. It permitted direct inter-connectivity between CSPs (who would be required to acquire an FSP licence) and any other type of service provider including sharing of infrastructure within their areas of operation.

A key fallout of NTP 99 was the development of a migration package according to which all FSPs would pay their licence dues as of 31 July 1999 as a one-time entry fee as well as a stipulated percentage of their revenue as licence fee. Potential licensees were required to bid for the entry fees.

Earlier the TRAI had recommended free competition in national long distance, with open entry. Revenue share at 5 per cent or less of the licensee's revenue and a fee in the form of a bank guarantee were additional features of the TRAI's recommendations. However, the Telecom Commission recommended restricting the total number of players including the DoT to four and increasing the revenue share to 15 per cent. Sub-sequently, the PMO recommended open entry, to which the Telecom Commission responded by placing restrictions on carriage of intra-circle traffic saying that it would hurt the revenues of existing basic service providers. However, there are only three significant basic service providers with very limited operation. Moreover, when the switch to revenue sharing was made, the operators had agreed to open entry.

Licensing criteria for the recently announced National Long Distance Policy are as follows:

• one-time entry fee of Rs 100 crore;

• bank guarantee of Rs 400 crore which will be re-funded in phases on fulfilment of network obligations;

• paid-up capital of Rs 250 crore of the applicant company with a total networth of the promoters at Rs 2500 an Indian registration with a maximum foreign equity of 49 per cent;

• network roll-out obligations covering all the districts in seven years;

• revenue sharing fixed at 15 per cent;

• DTS spared from paying entry fee, but will be sharing revenue.

Two types of competition are envisaged, facilities based and service based. In the first type, infrastructure providers who only provide end to end services for carrying traffic may be licensed.

Cellular traffic and the potential introduction of Internet telephony have been ignored in the TRAI consultation paper as discussed later. Alternative scenarios should have been generated. The TRAI con-sultation paper also did not take into account conver-gence. In the future, networks such as Bharti Telecom or new players like Zee may use the existing cable TV network to provide connectivity. Capacity or network provision by government bodies like the Gas Authority of India Limited (GAIL) and the Railways will lead to increased capacity and therefore a fall in rates. As a result, traffic is expected to increase at the rate of about 20 per cent per annum. Some companies are already planning alternate revenue streams (such as the export of software services) so that cross subsidization of long-distance services is possible in case of a future price war.

The TRAI has not specified a framework for equal access and interconnections. This has implications for the extent to which the DoT can exercise its monopoly power. If intra-circle long-distance traffic had not been opened to the private sector, the DoT would have re-tained a monopoly of over 65–70 per cent of the market. Moreover, since the national long distance operator (NLDO) is required to follow network roll-out condi-tions, such as coverage of all districts within seven years, carrying of intra-circle traffic should be allowed. In theory, NLDOs are allowed to seek interconnections with exist-ing service providers in basic services at circle level on mutually agreeable terms for onward carriage to the private operators' network. However, in reality, private operators' have a minuscule presence. This implies that NLDOs would have to rely on carrying DoT traffic unless they spread their own networks into the circles.

NTP 99 leaves several issues unresolved. Would infrastructure lease be considered a facility? Could one infrastructure player be allowed to sell facilities to more than one player? Could an infrastructure builder sell facilities, and also be a player in the national long distance market?

## PRIVATE PARTICIPATION

### Basic Services

As per NTP 94, basic service provision had been planned as a duopoly between the DoT and a selected service provider. Several service providers, one for each of the twenty 'circles'[11] into which the entire country had been divided would compete with the DoT for basic services. The bidders were evaluated using both financial and technical parameters. Permissible network technologies were specified and basic service providers were required to base their services on fibre optic cable and wireless in the local loop as far as possible. Licences had been granted for an initial period of 15 years and could be extended by another 10 years. Private services operators were allowed to provide intra-circle long distance services that contributed most to revenue.

The government had made it mandatory for all private basic service operators to provide 10 per cent of all new lines in rural areas. A weightage of 15 per cent was given at the time of bid selection for service provision in rural areas. A penalty on a per day basis for each telephone not installed sought to prevent companies from delaying meeting rural targets. At the same time, the government encouraged new emerging technologies including local loop wireless, cellular telephony, and satellite-based communication systems that could help develop rural telecom in a cost-effective manner.

Inter-circle communication remained under the DoT. The VSNL was to maintain an exclusive licence for international services at least until 2004. Other communication services like cellular, paging, e-mail, fax, data transmission over telephone, and leased circuits were increasingly being made available by private operators.

Private sector investments have been far below expectations, but these need to viewed in the light of delays in signing licences and contentious interconnection issues. Only one company, Bharti Telecom, was able to or chose to roll out services fast, and within three years it had a subscriber base equal to 11 per cent of the DoT's (see Table 8.1.10). It had obviously chosen to wire those customers who paid higher bills, as monthly revenue per DEL from Bharti Telecom was Rs 1200 against Rs 800 from DoT. Given the high costs of providing fixed services, changes in the technology, and opening up of the NLDS market, companies such as Bharti Telenet and Tata Teleservices, which were providing basic services, reconsidered their plans for expansion. Bharti Telenet and Tata Teleservices, for example, planned to limit their expansion to a few major cities. Hughes planned to provide broadband network to corporate houses through its fibre optic link in Mumbai.

[11] Circles are administrative boundaries usually co-terminus with a state boundary.

TABLE 8.1.10
List of Basic Service Providers in India and Their
Areas of Operation

| Service area | Name of service provider |
|---|---|
| (a) Operational | |
| All India | DTS |
| Delhi and Mumbai | MTNL |
| Madhya Pradesh | Bharti Telenet Ltd. |
| Maharashtra | Hughes Ispat Ltd. |
| Andhra Pradesh | Tata Teleservices Pvt. Ltd. |
| (b) Licensee yet to be operational | |
| Gujarat | Reliance Telecom Pvt. Ltd. |
| Punjab | Essar Comvision Ltd. |
| Rajasthan | Telelink Network (India) Ltd. (Shyam Telecom) |

## Cellular Services

In May 1991, the government announced its intention of awarding licences to private operators for providing cellular phones in the 4 metro cities: New Delhi, Calcutta, Mumbai, and Chennai, and paging services in 27 cities across India. Cellular services were viewed as a lucrative segment by the industry and there was enthusiastic response to the call for bids. Cellular service was planned as a duopoly between two selected service providers, with the DoT keeping the option of being the third service provider open. For paging services, a maximum of four players in each circle were proposed. For both cellular and paging services, separate licences were issued for the four metropolitan cities: Mumbai, Calcutta, Chennai, and New Delhi.

The bidding guidelines mandated foreign collaboration, and evaluation was based on financial consideration such as net worth of partners, licence fee quoted, and technical aspects such as the subscriber base experience of the foreign collaborator and network roll-out plan. Despite the initial legal hurdles, by 1997 cellular and paging services were established in the metropolitan cities and several other cities in different service areas. The selected bidders, the licence fee, and areas of operation are provided in Table 8.1.11. The growth of subscriber base in cellular connections is provided in Table 8.1.12.

The metro licences that were on fixed fee for the first five years were the first to take off. Although there were several initial problems, similar to those faced by basic service providers, cellular services have shown significant growth. There were 2 million subscribers to cellular services at the end of 1999. Since NTP 99 also allows operators to provide services in other service

Table 8.1.11
Licence Fee Payable under 'Migration Package'

| Circle | Licensee | Total licence fee payable for the year (Rs crore) | Licence fee amount payable up to 31 July 1999 (Rs crore) |
|---|---|---|---|
| Madhya Pradesh | Bharti Telenet Ltd. | 655 | 38.50 |
| Andhra Pradesh | Tata Teleservices Ltd. | 4200 | 241.10 |
| Maharashtra | Hughes Ispat Ltd. | 13,909 | 759.02 |
| Rajasthan | Shyam Telelink Ltd. | 655 | 160.65 |
| Gujarat | Reliance Telecom Ltd. | 3396 | 195.13 |
| Punjab | Essar Commvision Ltd. | 4593 | 265.23 |

TABLE 8.1.12
No. of Cellular Subscribers c. 1999

| | |
|---|---|
| Mumbai | 319,000 |
| Calcutta | 90,000 |
| Chennai | 54,000 |
| Gujarat | 146,000 |
| Karnataka | 127,000 |
| Kerala | 106,000 |
| UP | 113,000 |

*Source:* India Infrastructure Report, June 2000.

TABLE 8.1.13
Subscriber Base of Private Basic Service Operators

| Circle | Operator | Subscriber base (nos) |
|---|---|---|
| Madhya Pradesh | Bharti telenet | 117,000 |
| Maharashtra | Hughes | 28,000 |
| Andhra Pradesh | Tata teleservices | 40,000 |
| Rajasthan | Shyam | 1500 |
| Gujarat | Reliance | Just started |
| Punjab | HFCL | Yet to launch |

*Source:* Various Operators, *Economic Times*, 14 August 2000.

areas, several operators are spreading their networks across more than one state. For example, Bharti is operating in the Andhra Pradesh and Karnataka circles. Birla AT&T have sought a merger with Tata Teleservices, thus consolidating the Maharashtra and Andhra Pradesh regions. There could be several mergers and acquisitions in the future as operators and newer players find synergies with their existing or potential networks. Further, the government recently liberalized norms for telecom companies to acquire stakes of their foreign partners.

## EMERGENT ISSUES

While cellular services' privatization has had some success, basic services' privatization has been an absymal

failure. With just about 200,000 direct exchange lines (DELs) in five years, clearly NTP 94 was not adequate. It remains to be seen whether NTP 99 will be more successful (see Table 8.1.13 for the subscriber base of private FSPs).

Due to the high licence fee, cellular and basic services were slow to take off initially. There were several other problems, mainly relating to interconnections with the DoT and various clearances required. The cellular licences did not specify the interconnection terms, as these were left to operators to work out with the respective circle authorities. But the government and the TRAI need to evolve an interconnection framework that is equitable to both incumbent and private operators. The cost of interconnection needs to be explicitly quantified, and distribution of this cost across the various parties needs to be worked out. Similar issues will arise when private parties begin to participate in NLDS. Another issue closely related to interconnection which also needs to be examined is co-location.

Although in evaluating licences, indigenization plans were given due weightage, the subsequent monitoring of this aspect has been insufficient. This has resulted in the almost total absence of a manufacturing base for key cellular equipment, whether handsets or switching stations. In China, the government has insisted on foreign collaborators setting up manufacturing bases, ensuring for example much lower prices for handsets.

Should the government be specifying technology or mode of coverage of villages, or in meeting USO? As per the TRAI report dated 3 July 2000, FSPs had provided only twelve village phones! But several cellular operators have plans to install cellular phones in the rural areas. For example, Escotel plans to cover nearly 2500 villages in its area of operation. The government envisaged that the FSPs would be the primary agents for network expansion and that the CMSPs would cater to a small population that would use them as VASs. This perspective resulted from projecting its own role into the future without taking technology and market trends into account. Falling costs of cellular service make it worthwhile for CMSPs to expand the network possibly into smaller towns and villages. China's experience of the faster growth of cellular services to reach an installed base comparable to that of fixed lines should perhaps have informed government telecom policy.

Spectrum availability for rapid expansion is another constraint in India. While operators in metros have been given 7 MHz each in the Group Special Mobile (GSM) band, circle operators have been given barely 5 MHz. In most countries, nearly 25 MHz has been provided to operators for roll-out of GSM based networks.

The decision on the implementation of the calling party pays (CPPs) regime was long awaited. A drop in customs duty on handsets from 25 to 5 per cent and the low figures per line for the MTNL's proposed GSM network augur well for the cellular industry.

The auction of 3G licences abroad may reduce the number of players for the remaining vacant circles, as players would want to assess the new technology before service roll-outs in India.

There is a need to bring about coherence and convergence regarding policy making with respect to various services. For example, while NLDOs are required to submit a rather hefty licence fee, ISP licences are virtually free. With VoIP, in the future, licence for the NLDOs could be an anomaly.

Before NTP 94 developments in data communication were rather modest. NTP 94 provided a major impetus for growth in this area (see Appendix 8.1.2.).

NTP 99 provided for more liberal terms to VSAT service providers, for example:

• granting of licences on a non-exclusive basis for an initial period of 20 years extendible by 10 years;

• unrestricted entry based on a one-time entry fee and a revenue share;

• connectivity to other service providers;

• interconnectivity outside the service area to be reviewed upon opening up of long-distance service.

## STRENGTHENING THE TRAI

The TRAI was a regulatory body set up without teeth. It was set up to 'independently' decide upon the mode of interconnection between the cellular networks and the fixed network of the DoT. Its judgements could be challenged in the High Court, even though it was headed by a retired High Court Chief Justice. DoT officials were members of the apex committee and there were inevitable turf wars between the DoT and TRAI. The TRAI had to be headed by an individual with judicial background and was precluded from regulating

broadcast services and had no role in the allocation of the spectrum.

Over a period of time, the TRAI established a participative style of functioning by making the issues under consideration public, seeking comments from a variety of sources, and having open house sessions. It made a review of tariffs with the objective of bringing them closer to costs. However, the implementation of the interconnection regime, in which the calling party would pay for calls between the fixed and mobile services, led to a review of the TRAI's structure.

In January 2000, to strengthen its regulatory powers the government amended the TRAI Act and bifurcated its adjudicating powers to the Telecom Disputes Settlement and Appellate Tribunal to be headed by an individual with a judicial background. The Tribunal was also authorized to adjudicate disputes 'between a licensor and a licensee', unlike the earlier TRAI Act that precluded the TRAI from doing so. Moreover, the decisions of the Tribunal could only be appealed against in the Supreme Court, unlike earlier when appeals against TRAI orders could be made in the High Court.

Under the amendment, the TRAI's composition was streamlined, reducing total membership from seven to five. Moreover, the chairperson no longer had necessarily to have a judicial background. Further, the TRAI also acquired the power to fix interconnection rates between service providers. The central government was given the right to notify other services as telecom services, including broadcasting services. The recommendatory role of the TRAI was expanded to include efficient management of spectrum, timing of local and long-distance service provision, and need and timing and terms and conditions of new licences (to be awarded by the government). (The details of the functions are provided in Appendix 8.1.3.)

With the separation of the regulatory aspects that deal with the spread of the network, increased access, etc. from the adjudicating role of the TRAI, increased powers, and reduction in the steps in appeal against TRAI decisions, regulation has been considerably strengthened. This has been welcomed by the industry, as given the dominant position of the DoT, it feels that fair terms of operation can only be worked out within a well-functioning regulatory framework.

However, the TRAI needs to be able to stand on its own and avoid regulatory capture by the DoT. Its spineless recommendations for opening long-distance competition may be viewed as inability on its part to exploit the flexibility provided to it. The earlier TRAI had recommended open entry, while the Telecom Commission subsequently recommended only four players. The new TRAI reviewed these recommendations and suggested five players. The PMO had to intervene to remove restrictions on the number of players. The PMO's intervention shows that the Ministry of Communications is unable to deal with contentious issues vis-à-vis the department and, further, that the TRAI needs to more aggressively push for consumer interest.

While it appears that the institutional framework is in place, ground realities are somewhat different. All decisions of the TRAI that could have significant bearing on the growth of the sector are examined and reviewed by the Telecom Commission, staffed by people from the DoT. While it is only to be expected that an incumbent would not easily give up its turf, as exemplified in the cases of China Telecom, British Telecom (BT), and several others. It is for the top management of the DoT and the administrative ministry to take the steps to strengthen the DoT, so that when the inevitable competition comes about the organization can respond positively. Another actor that has stepped into the picture is the PMO. Increasingly, the PMO has issued policy directions that are more open than those formulated by the Telecom Commission. The National Long Distance Policy was announced by the PMO rather than the Telecom Commission. The Telecom Commission had to accept the free entry provision announced by PMO but insisted on restricting the market only to inter-circle calls. It is expected that the PMO would see through the holding out operation of the Telecom Commission and insist on removing this and other restrictions now being pushed by the Telecom Commission. The purist would no doubt be concerned about the several points of decision making that have emerged. But the PMO's initiatives are far reaching, and do not attempt to protect either the incumbent or those who had entered in the first flush of reforms. These initiatives are based on the understanding that technology and competition would be important drivers, as contestability improves with the high growth that is possible.

With the introduction of the ICE bill soon, it is hoped that a review of the TRAI's powers within the 'convergent framework' will be provided.

## ISSUES IN LICENSING

Telecom licensing as a mechanism to bridge fiscal deficit was first implemented in the United States. The large amounts of revenues generated there lent a great deal of visibility to this mechanism. However, one must recognize that these licences were for additional services over a large customer base already using basic services of high quality. When governments are driven by the need to manage fiscal deficits, entry fee and licence fee appear suitable instruments. Ultimately, subscribers pay the licence fee as costs in terms of higher prices. In developed markets where different service providers have existing large bases, paying a high licence fee would imply spreading the cost of licence over a large number of customers and the ability of customers to pay may no longer affect subscriber growth. Companies paying licence fees would naturally recover the same from consumers, or through efficiency gains. In any case the price to consumers would be higher than otherwise without license fees but with competition. In India higher prices would retard the growth of the network.

While auctions are viewed as instruments for assigning licences to those who value them most, the first mover advantage in attracting customers and potential revenue from VASs invariably drives up the licence bids.

Another mechanism could be to award the licence to the bidder who would charge customers the lowest rates for a specified basket of services. This would, however, not lead to revenue maximization. In Brazil, bidding for the poorly developed areas was based on willingness to accept the lowest subsidy. The payment of subsidy was contingent upon completing roll-out conditions as specified.

To make the licences attractive, ability to bundle a variety of services such as broadband on the same network is important. However, until NTP 99, licences were exclusively for voice. NTP 99 provides for data services (to be separately licensed over the same networks). In an era of convergence, such inequities should be removed.

## BUNDLING

The TRAI is considering whether to bundle the unattractive category C licences along with other more attractive licences. This would immediately raise the issue of which circles to bundle together. Since basic services per se are not seen as being commercially attractive, this may also lead to private capital shying away from the more attractive circles. If some operators choose category A with C because of geographical contiguity or the ability to exploit the network infrastructure in category C for national long distance, then that circle is not unattractive. For example, Bharti Telenet views operations in Madhya Pradesh (category B) as attractive because Madhya Pradesh borders seven other states and in a competitive long-distance scenario, putting backbone infrastructure in place for basic services would be commercially attractive. Bundling also leads to issues of determining the quantum, revenue potential, and so forth—attributes that are difficult to assess, especially over a twenty-year time horizon.

## UNIT OF BIDDING

It has been argued that the unit of bidding (that is, a circle) is too big to licence to private operators. Comparisons are made with cable operators who have spread rapidly within geographically small areas. Together, their 60 million plus customer base achieved in less than a decade remains unmatched. However, in cable there is no need to interconnect networks nor is there need for billing software. Similarly, quality and price are tradeable to some extent. These characteristics as well as lack of regulation of any kind allowed small operators to enter and run their businesses successfully. The potential for convergence, and ability of cable to carry voice and Internet, has led to cable consolidation among cable operators, especially in the metros and large cities.

A feasible small operator model could consist of players who cover any particular area unconstrained by administrative notions of boundaries, but who would naturally avoid each other's turf, at least to start with. As they jostle each other, and with competitive pressures in and around their boundaries, the need for interconnection would drive them to consolidation. Smaller areas are feasible for certain types of telecom services as was exemplified by the personal communication service (PCS) licence in the United States in which the entire country was divided into 51 major and 493 basic trading areas. In India the unit of licensing has been selected on the basis of administrative simplicity from the DoT's perspective.

## BID DESIGN

Until now the government has chosen the single round, sealed highest bid form. This has been fraught with problems such as too high bids, subsequent winner's curse, and inability to share information regarding other players' estimates. Based on its own experience in the past, the TRAI has now come out with a new mechanism involving multi-stage bidding preceded by a pre-qualification round. All information regarding the bidders, bid prices, etc. is to be made known to other bidders. This design is similar to the US PCS auction that has been adopted by several other countries such as the UK for its 3G licenses. One key learning across all countries has been that such a design works well when there are a large number of bidders and the details for the conduct of the auction are well thought out.

## INTERCONNECTION ISSUES

Interconnection has emerged as the major contentious issue between the DoT/MTNL and Cellular Mobile Service Providers (CMSPs) due to the absence of an interconnection agreement. (Most calls in the early stages of development of cellular services are fixed to mobile or mobile to fixed, with few being mobile to mobile. This is only natural.) In India the receiver pays for cellular calls. While CMSPs were required to pay the DoT for carrying calls on the fixed network, the DoT did not pay any interconnection charges for carriage of fixed to mobile calls to CMSPs.

In the early years of CMSPs, the DoT insisted on providing a single point of interconnection in each service area as this enabled it to charge STD rates for carrying CMSP traffic. From the CMSP's perspective, having multiple points of interconnection would enable it to minimize the traffic carried on the DoT network, leading to lower payments to the DoT. The DoT increased the per minute peak time charge payable by CMSPs for interconnection to an amount that was equivalent to twenty-four local calls! As with a single point of interconnection, a fixed to mobile call often had to travel 100–200 km. The CMSPs went to the High Court, which stayed the DoT order. The court order led to the setting up of the TRAI, which, upon close examination of the issue, mandated multiple points of interconnection.

Subsequently, in 1999 the TRAI came up with revised tariffs for the CMSPs, which decreased the connection charges from Rs 600 to Rs 475 per month as well as the per minute usage charges. It also recommended the implementation of the CPP regime and sharing of revenue between CMSPs, the DoT, and the MTNL. While the CMSPs felt that the CPP would lead to an increase in revenues because of an expansion in subscriber base as well as interconnection revenue share, the DoT and the MTNL felt that they would lose revenue through having to share it, and that it would increase the load of payment on fixed line subscribers to the benefit of cellular subscribers. Several rounds of negotiations took place between the DoT, MTNL, and TRAI. Subsequently, the MTNL and consumer organization, Telecom Watchdog, went to the High Court with the plea that the TRAI did not have the authority to review already existing interconnection agreements, as this would entail change in the existing licence conditions that the TRAI was not empowered to make. Moreover, it was argued that the MTNL would not only lose revenue, it would have to bear the cost of implementing the CPP. Telecom Watchdog pleaded that the CPP would lead to an increase of 100–200 per cent in the fixed line subscriber bill.

The Delhi High Court examined whether the TRAI had the power to issue any regulation that would affect the rights of individuals under contract or would override terms and conditions of government-issued licences. It ruled that the TRAI had no authority to issue the tariff order implementing the CPP, as this would effectively change the licence conditions, thus striking down the Tariff Amendment and the Interconnection Amendment Orders as they related to the CPP regime. However, it suggested that the TRAI should take suitable steps to ensure that the benefits arising out of changes in the licence fee structure are passed on to consumers, even if the CPP regime is not implemented. Cellular operators agreed to implement the reduced tariffs without the CPP features. This judgement also led the government to review the TRAI's mandate. It came up with an amendment to the TRAI Act, 1997 that gave the TRAI the power to fix interconnection charges. The amendment also increased its regulatory scope to recommend steps for efficient management of the spectrum.

## UNIVERSAL SERVICE OBLIGATIONS (USOs)

Since infrastructure generally, and telecom specifically, is regarded as a 'public' service, there are usually obligations imposed on the private (and public) players to 'serve' some of the low paying, or high cost to serve, subscribers. The private players in basic services were expected to provide 10 per cent of their coverage in rural areas. However, with the coverage of a mere 12–15 villages that has so far been achieved a serious effort in this direction can hardly be said to have begun. The DoT's own record in this regard has also been dismal. Its rural coverage as a percentage of total coverage is 1.75. As cited earlier, its plans for rural coverage are likely to be delayed due to changes in the DoT's specifications for rural telecom from WLL to 3G services. Innovative approaches that do not distinguish on the basis of the mode of access are necessary to make a significant dent in rural coverage.[12]

The TRAI has brought out a consultation paper on universal service obligations. In that paper NLDOs are required to contribute 5 per cent of their revenue to the proposed Universal Access Levy Fund. But questions such as who would administer the fund, on what basis would the allocations be made, and how the selected service areas would be chosen remain to be addressed. Would this fund receive 5 per cent of the revenue from the basic and cellular service provider as a part of the 15 per cent revenue sharing that is already in place?

The DoT has always vociferously claimed that the high cost of serving rural areas prevents it from expanding rural coverage. In that context, Ram Vilas Paswan's (the Minister of Telecommunications) allocation of free phones to the nearly 300,000 employees of the DoT who do not have a phone needs to be reviewed. The total cost of such a provision would be more than Rs 600 crore, or 10 per cent of its existing revenue surpluses (as per the DoT's estimate, the cost of providing a DEL is Rs 21,000–25,000).[13] Is this pure political expediency to win a vote bank of close to a million people? Or is it the price that 'has' to be paid to get the employees' agreement to a possible reform of the DoT as an organization? Only time will tell. Similar concerns arise regarding the free telecom services available to ministers and bureaucrats whose telephone bills are astronomical! There was a proposal to give a third free phone line to ministers so that they could access the Internet. If the department seeks subsidies for rural coverage, such hidden subsidies that taxpayers provide to ministers and bureaucrats would need to be explicitly recognized.[14]

## DEMAND ESTIMATES

Demand estimates are critical for market assessment. The TRAI has been carrying out such assessments in its consultation papers. The concern here is with the robustness with which such estimates are generated. While it is true that in new service areas it is difficult to assess demand, there ought to be mechanisms to generate alternate scenarios. For example, in assessing demand for basic services, in its consultation paper 'Issues in Fixed Service Provision', the TRAI considered the issue of latent demand. But latent demand has to be linked to the price at which the services would be available. For example, the demand is very sensitive to the one-time connection fee as has often been shown before.

The TRAI has carried out a demand assessment of DELs based on affordability criteria as well as on the DoT's projections. DoT growth rate projections were available only for the two years up to 2001—16 and 20 per cent respectively. Affordability assessments were made on the basis of NCAER (National Council of Applied Economics Research) data. Given the rentals in

---

[12] In section 8.3 *inter alia* a concrete plan to quickly provide very large coverage of this report both voice and data is presented.

[13] The immediate cost could also be less if indeed much of this demand can be accommodated by exchanges with excess switching capacity and outdoor works that are already in place.

[14] Such largesse from the bureaucracy, that controls public enterprise, to the politician have been used to delay and subvert reform and privatization. Air India is another such example.

rural and urban areas and an International Telecommunications Union (ITU) estimate that in developing countries people spend 5 per cent of their income on telecommunications, the TRAI assessed that income categories of Rs 24,000 and Rs 50,000 per annum and above would be able to afford telephones in rural and urban areas, respectively. From the number of households in these categories in various years, the TRAI has projected the demand for DELs. However, there are various assumptions in this exercise that need to be verified and for which alternate scenarios need to be generated. For example, another study[15] estimated that at the current level of costs, basic fixed line services are affordable to less than 1.6 per cent of households. The current expected revenues (based on expected costs) must be reduced to Rs 150–200 per month so that telecom services are affordable to 60 per cent of the households.[16] The point is that data needs to be viewed from multiple perspectives.

Would spending on telecom materialize into demand for new telephones or would the PCO be used by people to satisfy demand?[17]

The TRAI's effort to estimate demand for various services is a commendable exercise, but the quality of this exercise needs to be improved. For example, in estimating the market for domestic long distance, the TRAI's models did not take into account emerging trends such as VoIP and how this could reduce end user or subscriber demand but could increase demand by ISPs for leasing/buying long-distance infrastructure or for reselling minutes of usage. Moreover, its own estimates for domestic long-distance minutes of traffic in its consultation papers on Tariffs and on Competition in National Long-Distance varied from 8–11 billion minutes in the first, to 26 billion minutes in the latter. The DoT's perspective plan of demand is essentially based on the growth rate of expressed demand in each exchange area; once the exchange is upgraded, more demand is manifested. This would be in terms of enhanced usage or extra lines. These estimates, both of the TRAI and the DoT, need to be vetted.

## SPECTRUM MANAGEMENT

Wireless technologies are growing rapidly and are overtaking fixed line growth the world over. Indian mobile

[15] Jhunjhunwala (1998b).
[16] See section 8.2 of this report.
[17] In the long run personal DELs would rule, as incomes rise sufficiently. But in the next several (say five) years, it would be difficult to predict the direction demand will take. Much would depend upon the supply side strategy. Low cost options could help to suddenly improve teledensities, and the resulting larger market would drive costs down.

service providers operate under severe limitations, as several bands are in use by various government agencies and the defence services. Table 8.1.14 provides the amount of spectrum available to various services in different countries. This availability is one of the important reasons why China is able to add nearly 2 million cellular subscribers per month, with a base of 125 million wireless subscribers. There is a similar situation with respect to spectrum availability in several other Asian countries as is evident from Table 8.1.14. In comparison, total cellular subscribers in India to date are 2 million. The needs of the Chinese defence services for spectrum must surely be as much as those of ours. Should we not then question the efficiency with which defence services have managed the spectrum allotted them? Or is it only a matter of time before more bandwidth is released for commercial use?

TABLE 8.1.14
Spectrum Allocation in Some Asian Countries

| Country | Mobile teledensity | Spectrum allocated (MHz) | |
|---|---|---|---|
| | | Mobile (806–960 MHz) | WLL (1710–2000 MZHs) |
| China | 1.2 | 90 | 160 |
| Thailand | 3.5 | 80 | 176 |
| Philippines | 1.8 | 110 | 210 |
| Malaysia | 11.2 | 104 | 150 |
| Indonesia | 0.6 | 98 | 140 |

*Source:* Report of the Spectrum Management Committee (Prime Minister's Council), set up in December 1998 (http://www.trai.gov.in).

While their licences specify the spectrum bands in which operators would be allowed to operate, the amount of spectrum that would ultimately be available is not specified. There has been no review of the spectrum retrieval plan. Spectrum management continues to be under the DoT. Frequency clearances take inordinately long. Removal of spectrum management from the DoT's purview and its review urgently need to be undertaken. The government set up the Review Committee for Spectrum Management, which suggested a review of the existing process of decision making that involves the Standing Advisory Committee for Frequency Allocation (SACFA) (a large committee consisting of various government user organizations). There is a need to restructure the process of spectrum management and allow for greater role of the private sector. While the committee recognized that 'spectrum management and radio regulation has to be an impartial, non-user, non-service provider type of body without any direct or indirect linkages with any user organization', it ruled out jurisdiction by the TRAI, as the TRAI deals with 'commercial public operators'. It recommended an autonomous status for the WPC (Wireless Planning and Co-ordination wing) under the ministry, but that would not be a sufficient measure, as the DoT is a user organization and would hardly be an impartial actor. The committee did not bring forth actionable policy guidelines for spectrum use and management and the appropriate blueprint for making available the already allocated spectrum to various agencies. While citing the experience of auctions of spectrum in the United States, the committee had based its conclusion on factually incorrect data; not all firms that bid for spectrum went bankrupt. Those that went bankrupt did so on account of poor judgement. A very similar auction design to that used in the United States is being used quite successfully by Australia, New Zealand, and UK. This is not to suggest that bidding for spectrum is the recommended method for spectrum allocation.

While on the one hand spectrum was scarce, on the other, government policies did not encourage efficient use of spectrum. For example, spectrum requests were considered on the basis of number of subscribers, rather than allocating a band and letting an operator come out with spectrum-efficient technologies with the growth in number of subscribers.

It is possible that the government wants to address the issue of spectrum management through the ICE Bill. Spectrum management should be within the regulatory agencies' jurisdiction. The recommendation of this report is that the 'convergent' regulator should be responsible for policy guidelines and management of spectrum. New broadcast, telecom and IT applications would require that there be a single agency handling spectrum management. In several countries, including the United States and the UK, spectrum management has been the domain of regulatory agencies.

## ROLE OF COMPETITION

Initially telecom licences were limited to a duopoly, but even now there are few players. Since the policy requires circle-level licences, it is possible that smaller players would not be willing to come forward. Due to the flux in telecom policies, players have desisted from investing in the sector. This is evident from the delays in service provision of basic and cellular licences. For example, Spice Telecom and Bharti Telenet are consolidating and expanding their services beyond their initial service areas by looking at geographically contiguous areas. A few large players are likely to emerge at the circle or national level while niche players would also emerge as VAS providers, or those who have strong regional presence, or those who can provide a bundle of services. Thus limiting the number of players would deprive the Indian

subscriber of the benefits of competition. It could also result in slower growth, if the few players are successful in reaching their target returns on a small customer base with high margins. In other words, the probability of low volume strategies succeeding is high.

China has been creating competition through state enterprises even though they may continue to be under the control of a ministry.[18] In China, top leadership[19] saw competition to China Telecom as an important component of network expansion. It therefore formed United Telecom (Unicom), a new organization from the Ministry of Railways, Power, and Electronics to start telecom services. Its objective was to obtain 10 per cent of the domestic, long-distance, and international market and 30 per cent of the cellular market. China's focus on wireless as the engine of growth has, *inter alia*, resulted in subscriber numbers growing at a phenomenal rate. Recognizing that Internet access through personal computers (PCs) may be limited for a large part of the Chinese population, it is leveraging access through the 320 million television sets and has worked with Microsoft and local IT firms to develop a system to surf the net in the Chinese language. The Chinese Academy of Sciences, State Administration of Radio and Television, and the Ministry of Railways, Power, and Electronics have begun to develop a high speed Internet backbone to directly compete with China Telecom.

China Telecom (Hong Kong) was set up by the Ministry of Post and Telecommunications under its direct control to explore investment opportunities in Hong Kong for the cellular market on the mainland. The Chinese government separated the regulator and operator by forming companies from existing ministries. The principal instrument of regulation is the Opinion of the Ministry of Post and Telecommunications Markets, 1993. The absence of a legislative framework has led to 'problems' especially with the involvement of foreign parties however, the stupendous pace of growth in Chinese incomes and competition enhancing policy have enabled China to expand very rapidly and allowed the Chinese access to cheaper services.

The Chinese telecom sector has focused on internal competition as a mechanism for meeting the challenges of opening up the sector, especially to foreign investment. The Chinese government has not been very open to foreign capital. It has, for example, excluded it from service provision. Yet it has recognized the need to open telecom services to foreign capital to be able to join the World Trade Organisation (WTO). It therefore broke China Telecom into four companies dealing with fixed

[18] *The Economist*, 22 July 2000, p. 22.
[19] In India the fear of loss of bureaucratic privileges and loss of trust remain principal retardants to reform.

telecommunications, mobile communications, paging, and satellite systems with the idea of creating strong entities before the advent of foreign competition.

The DoT, generally, lagged in its level of technology.[20] India's indigenization programme in the switching segment carried out by C-DOT was successful in the introduction of rural exchanges designed specifically for Indian conditions characterized by dust, heat, and humidity. It was also able to licence this technology to private vendors for incorporating in the DoT network. C-DOT's efforts at developing medium and large sized exchanges had been slow (*Business Today*, January 1992) but it has been quite successful lately. C-DOT, which began with government support for its programme, based on the championing of the idea of technology for the masses had support at the highest political level that allowed its mentor Sam Pitroda to cut across red tape. With Sam Pitroda leaving C-DOT, the momentum could not be sustained. C-DOT's initial success demonstrated the capability of Indians in a highly sophisticated technological field and resulted in the government being able to negotiate far cheaper prices for other imported exchanges. Subsequent developments in technology, deregulation in the sector, and the absence of a visionary at the top left C-DOT without focus.

Lessons from Korea's experience of successfully developing indigenous switching technology are worth noting. The key components of this strategy were the alliance between the telecom authorities, equipment manufacturers, and telecom research institutions. Continued and stable financial support from the government and its role in effectively coordinating the interlinkages between business and research institutes were important

instruments in this programme. Further, the government closely monitored the progress and removed bottlenecks during the development phase.

Some developing countries have been able to successfully coordinate the efforts of internal R&D units with those of foreign collaborators. The Korean government not only negotiated for technology transfer but also for a range of auxiliary services such as financing, training, and channelizing for excess output. Monitoring the absorption of technology was incorporated as a part of the negotiation with the foreign supplier. In addition, the government was successfully able to coordinate the efforts of various ministries and was actively involved in the implementation at various stages.

In contrast, the Indian attempt at indigenization[21] suffered from lack of resources, few if any linkages with business and research institutions, delays in absorption, diffusion, and indigenization (Mani 1992), and support based on a single individual's relationship with politicians (*India Today*, 11 January 1991, pp. 115–19). C-DOT's initial success and its ability to recruit high-quality manpower, indicated the availability of professional and technical expertise in the country. The critical issue was harnessing this expertise within an institutional framework and establishing sustainable and responsive high-tech organizations.

Indigenous development of technology and its subsequent commercialization today are hampered by availability of finances and the virtual abdication of the state in R&D. R&D has been pushed on to the Department of Science and Technology. Sector departments do not see any role for cooperative R&D with state funding, to overcome the market failure that is known to exist in R&D.[22] For example, while foreign equipment vendors are able to provide easy credit terms or deferred payments, Indian service providers such as C-DOT or the firms spawned by the Indian Institute of Technology (IIT), Madras, which have indigenized WLL, are not able to do so. Telecom policy needs to recognize this.

[20] For a review of efforts at the Indian Telephone Industries Ltd. (ITI) and Electronics Corporation of India Ltd. (ECIL) see Mani (1992). The organizational constraints of the public sector were strong enough to thwart not only the development of new products, but also adaptation of new technology until Sam Pitroda's efforts in developing the Rural Automatic Exchange (RAX) technology which was productionized by several public sector undertakings (PSUs) including the Bharat Heavy Electricals Ltd. (BHEL) and the ITI. India was at least one age behind other countries, including less developed countries (LDCs), with regard to its exchanges. The ITI's products suffered severely from poor quality and reliability which may have been one more reason for over-employment in the DoT. The monopoly of the ITI in virtually all equipment segments meant that its organization failure ensured the failure of indigenous technological development. The potential of indigenous technology was very high as was to be proved by subsequent efforts by C-DOT and the private sector. Increasing deregulation had also resulted in the ITI being in dire financial straits. The ITI was too poorly organized, lacked vision, and was unduly influenced by its vendors to be able to respond to the challenges of the 1990s. The signs of its failure were already to be seen in the 1980s. See Nagaraj (1984).

[21] For a long time, until the 1990s, the Department of Electronics suffered from the megalomania of trying to indigenize everything from D-RAM chips to full assemblies. Thus efforts at development of calculators, not to speak of entertainment electronic goods, computers, or peripherals, were rendered impossible because basic components like chips and high performance transistors were not easily imported. Even the C-DOT effort was hampered by the absurdity of such policy. C-DOTs CEO, Sam Pitroda, was charismatic enough to enthuse his 'boys to smuggle in chips' to make the RAX possible! That one failure of the department in the 1980s may have cost the nation the lead in manufacturing in electronic goods.

[22] Semantech and the Advanced Turbine Projects of the United States government are recent examples of state-led cooperative success in R&D.

Close to half the foreign direct investment (FDI) inflow in the country since the opening up to foreign investment has taken place in telecom, especially in cellular services. This was to be expected, given the policy to attract FDI and because the cellular industry was entirely new to the economy. In basic services, on the other hand, the dominant status of the DoT allowed it to rapidly expand reducing the need for FDI. The combination of a technology gap between the Indian parties and foreign players and the differential

cost of funds underlies the large flows of FDI into the telecom sector (see Table 8.1.15).

The mode of disinvestment and corporatization of the DoT, VSNL, and MTNL would be crucial to the development of telecom, and for a positive response to the multinational challenge after 2004. While FDI is desirable, the best in FDI can be brought out when there are strong domestic firms that can offer effective competition. Therefore rapid growth of these 'public sector' companies is important. The need to be

---

Box 8.1.4

### STD Calls are Not a Preserve of the Rich

In the 1980s while much of the rest of the world saw telephone call prices falling, as a result of the introduction of modern technology and increased competition, Indian consumers just about began to sense this trend. Even today the cost of a 10 minute call from say Ahmedabad to Trivandrum is comparable to that of second class rail travel between the two places! This is a reflection both of high administered prices of telephone calls, especially long distance calls, and the very low prices in India, for rail travel.

Until the so called public call office (PCO) revolution was ushered in by Sam Pitroda in the latter half of the 1980s through the installation of an network of franchised PCOs, the reach of telephones in the country, especially in rural and semi- rural areas was very limited. Long wait lists in urban areas confirm that the problem was essentially one of the failure of the state to appreciate the 'network' nature of the product. The user side costs in using telephone booths and post offices were large. Personal telephones too were highly unreliable, and imposed large user side costs.

PCOs made long-distance communication easier, but not cheaper. India's monopoly service provider, the Department of Telecommunications (DoT), continued to keep tariffs high, access charges relatively low, and local call charges, low. The profile of the people using the phones was undergoing much change. But no studies appear to have been conducted by the DoT or any other agency to ascertain the profile of the DoT's PCO users.

Users of PCOs and owners of telephones[23] in Ahmedabad city, Nadiad (a large town in the state); and six villages in Nadiad district were studied.

A substantial number of PCO users were found to belong to the lower income categories. Those with income less than Rs 6500 per month accounted for nearly 65 per cent and those with less than Rs 4500 per month for nearly 48 per cent of PCO users. The percentage of PCO users owning telephones was 60 per cent in Ahmedabad and 32 per cent in Nadiad but only 10 per cent in the rural areas.

The owners of telephones were found to be relatively better off than PCO users, but not much better off. About 41 per cent had monthly incomes of less than Rs 6500 and 24 per cent had incomes less than Rs 4500. The similarity of the profiles of PCO users and those who own phones was remarkable. This may be partly because many phone owners are also users of PCOs and a substantial percentage of owners did not use their own phones for making long distance calls. But one thing is clear: phones are not owned or used by the rich alone.

The average number of STD calls made, whether from PCOs or by owners from their homes, was surprisingly high. It was 17.62 calls per month by owners (considering that nearly a quarter of them had their STDs barred, this means that the rest make around 21 calls per month) and 10.07 calls per month by PCO users. Even more surprisingly, it was rural users who made more calls than urban users: 19.84 calls per month by rural owners as against 16.33 calls by Ahmedabad owners and 18.56 calls per month by Nadiad users. A similar pattern was observed among PCO users also: 12.62 calls per month by rural users, 10.89 by Nadiad users, and 8.96 by Ahmedabad users. The average number of calls made per month by the different socio-economic groups were also not too different. They varied between 13.3 and 18.7 with no discernible relationship with income.

We studied the distribution of the purposes of STD calls by users of PCOs as well as telephone owners, categorizing purpose into four types: personal calls, social calls, business calls, and emergency calls. We found that the better off sections used phones for business purposes to a somewhat greater extent than the relatively lower income sections.

However, telephones in general are becoming a need for the 'less affluent' sections too. Gone are the days when people born in a village tended to stay in the village their whole lives; today family members go out in search of work and they would very much like to keep in touch with their relatives through long distance calls. Small farmers and businessmen like to have up-to-date information on markets and prices. Thus the need for long distance communication has percolated to the lower income levels to a greater extent than is perhaps realized. Many in the well-to-do segments, especially in rural areas, may be using their telephones mainly to receive incoming calls. The policy that justifies higher prices for long distance on the basis of richer people having a higher propensity to use the same is therefore fallacious.

*Source:* S. Manikutty (1997).

---

[23] Many owners of telephones still use PCOs, especially for long distance calls, for various reasons, the most important of which being fear of high bills due to irresponsible usage by family members, and arbitrary billing by DOT.

TABLE 8.1.15
Actual Inflow of FDI in the Telecom Sector from
August 1991 to October 1999 (sector-wise)

| S. no. | Service/item | FDI (Rs million) | Percentage |
|---|---|---|---|
| 1. | Basic telephone service | 2665.9 | 6.32 |
| 2. | Cellular mobile telephone service | 20,823.5 | 49.33 |
| 3. | Radio paging service | 909.9 | 2.16 |
| 4. | E-mail service | 687.5 | 1.63 |
| 5. | VSAT service | 137.7 | 0.33 |
| 6. | Cable TV network | 514.5 | 1.22 |
| 7. | Satellite telephone service | 481.2 | 1.14 |
| 8. | Radio trunking service | 61.6 | 0.15 |
| 9. | Manufacturing | 6688.49 | 15.85 |
| 10. | Holding companies | 9241.2 | 21.89 |
| | Total | 42,211.5 | |

*Source:* India Infrastructure Report, June 2000.

completely free of bureaucratic and ministerial interference that is dysfunctional and parasitic is most urgent. Their managers would need the requisite freedom to bring about major organizational changes, including a fairly large voluntary retirement scheme (VRS). All this would not be possible without quick disinvestment reducing government share to below 50 per cent. The disinvestment/restructuring process could itself throw up incentives for employees to work efficiently and towards the primary task. The freedom to reward and punish differentially is also essential in the three 'public sector' telecom companies in order to achieve efficiency.

With the PMO's initiatives, policy is irreversibly headed towards competition and liberalization. The Indian consumer's fortunes, especially in basic and cellular services, would depend a great deal on how the DoT and MTNL are able to, and allowed to, respond.

There are vast gains to be made by national R&D efforts with fixed schedules on modes similar to that which gave us the RAX and PARAM (the series of parallel super-computers of the Centre for Development of Advanced Computing or the C-DAC). The ITI, DoT, and VSNL, which have failed woefully in the past in their R&D, are unlikely on their own to initiate much R&D. The efforts from China and Korea are especially worth imitating. India's very low coverage of villages and absymal teledensities would continue to remain much as they are if policy cannot imaginatively address R&D, standards, and industry structure and regulation in ways that break the existing constraints. The fact that close to 50 per cent of all exchanges the DoT uses are RAXs should give policy makers the requisite confidence in domestic R&D as being integral to the reform process.

The tendency for regulation and policy to be trapped in the means such as fairness, competition, revenue rebalancing, and neutrality, besides being constrained by the bureaucratic stranglehold and the 'need' to be fair to players of an earlier policy, is strong in India. Can this be overcome? Can policy and regulation serve the consumer interest?

# 8.2 LOOKING BEYOND NTP 99

*Ashok Jhunjhunwala*

## INTRODUCTION

India today has barely 20 million telephone connections and less than half a million Internet connections for a billion people. With less than 2 per cent teledensity, telecom and, Information Technology (IT) cannot play a major role in the nation's development. Recognizing that Internet Access could result in a divide deeper than any existing so far between the haves and have-nots, the government wishes very quickly to reach 100–200 million telephone and Internet connections. It has long been recognized that this would not be possible without participation of the private sector.

Until around the end of the 1970s the sole telecom operator in India, the Department of Telecommunications (DoT), procured all its equipments from central government-controlled companies like the

Indian Telephone Industries Limited (ITI) and Hindustan Teleprinters Limited (HTL) (Vittal 1999). In the early 1980s the liberalization process began, first with the procurement of telecom equipment through state government enterprises. It took another four to five years before the private sector was allowed to manufacture telecom equipment. The late 1980s saw a major initiative when STD public call offices (PCOs) were allowed to be opened. The STD PCOs quickly spread to all parts of the country and today net about 20 per cent of total telecom revenue. The process continued when, in mid-1992, operation of VASs was opened up to allow private participation.

The next major turning point came in 1994. First, cellular licences were issued to the private sector. At the same time, NTP 94 laid the foundation of allowing private sector into the operation of basic services (one operator in addition to the DoT for each circle or state). This policy document attempted to clearly enunciate the goals of the liberalization process. Universal and reliable service was the principal goal to be singlemindedly pursued.

In itself NTP 94 was a momentous step but subsequent developments left much to be desired. The high licence fees bid by operators initially created euphoria but later a great deal of confusion. Long-distance service was not opened up as expected and remained a DoT monopoly. With the interconnection, spectrum utilization, and right-of-way policies lacking clarity all efforts slowed down. Further, the expected corporatization of DoT never took place.

But despite being dogged by these problems the reform process moved ahead and the establishment in 1997 of the Telecom Regulatory Authority of India (TRAI) was a major step forward, though once again there was much subsequent confusion about its role and power. The next major initiative was the 1998 Internet Policy. This freed Internet operation completely, with Internet service providers (ISPs) being allowed to establish their own access networks.

The year 1999 saw a major initiative from the TRAI. For the first time, it talked about the *cost* of establishing a telecom network and corresponding *prices* that provide a minimum return. Over the years there had been drastic reduction in the cost of setting up a long-distance network, but the increase in cost of providing an access network had nullified this reduction. The TRAI suggested significant reduction in long-distance charges and a simultaneous increase in rentals and local call charges to bring prices closer to cost. Unfortunately the step was not popular politically.[24] The second major initiative of the TRAI was to reduce leased circuit charges which enabled significant development in Internet and Intranet services.

But by 1999, the major problem for the reform process was that the basic and cellular licensees were unable to pay their licence fees. There was fear of large-scale collapse. The operators pleaded with the government to do something so that the telecom liberalization process would not be totally derailed. It is in this environment that NTP 99 was born. The key features of NTP 99 are:

• licence fees for basic and cellular operation converted to revenue sharing plus entry fee;

• removal of the restriction earlier imposed on multiple operators in the same circle;

• existing operators allowed to shift to revenue sharing; the payments already made by them to be taken as entry fee;

• national and international long distance operation to be opened up in 2000 and 2003, respectively.

It is unfortunate that NTP 99 was born as a reaction to imminent private telecom sector collapse. But even so it is part of a twenty-year process; a process typically consisting of a step forward, new problems resulting therefrom, and steps for the correction of these problems. The process had and continues to have the aim of providing everyone a telephone and Internet connection. On the whole, the NTP takes us forward. But will NTP 99 take us more rapidly towards the main objective? This chapter analyses the limitations of NTP 99, particularly in the area of basic services operation.

## WHERE DID THE OPERATORS GO WRONG?

The operators, both mobile as well as basic service operators (BSOs), bid very high licence fees—operators for some of the circles bid in excess of Rs 100 billion to be paid for a fifteen-year licence—payable by them in return for duopoly rights.

It is this high licence fee which has rendered private telecom operation unviable within just three to four years. Today's evaluation is that the bid amount was high—by a factor of five! It is important to understand the reasons for such an error. The high bids were based on (a) the assumption that India is a very large market with over 100 million middle-class customers; and (b) the assumption that this large number of potential subscribers has a reasonable ability to pay.

In fact, the first assumption was not too far off the mark. Most cellular licensees received more subscribers in the first two years than they had hoped for. But it is in the estimate of the ability to pay that the error seems to have been made.[25] India is indeed a large potential market, but with *very limited ability to spend*.

The issue today is whether the reform process is now indeed more market savvy, or is going to continue to blunder its way forward?

## SOME IMPLICATIONS OF REVENUE SHARING

The most important aspect of NTP 99 is that the operators have a revenue sharing rather than licence fee

---

[24] The day after the announcement of new rates by TRAI, there was a hue and cry in Parliament, with some of the parties supporting the ruling coalition threatening to walk out. The government withdrew the revised tariff, which was brought back after some revision a few weeks later.

[25] Almost all cellular operators in the country, except those operating in Delhi and Mumbai, have a revenue income from each subscriber far less than was envisaged. There are many people who keep cellular phones, but use them only sparingly. Even the upper middle class find the cellular airtime charges too high.

arrangement. This, of course, solves the immediate problem of operator insolvency. But why revenue sharing instead of simply a lowering of the licence fees? Perhaps it may have been politically suicidal to accept lower licence fees.

The more serious implication, however, is that licence fee bidding, unlike revenue sharing, requires solid understanding of the market. The switch from license fee bidding to revenue sharing is a sort of acknowledgement of the inability to accurately estimate the market and, in fact, points to the major uncertainties therein.

The obvious question now is, what prevents private operators from concentrating on providing service to only a few high-paying subscribers? It makes perfect business sense as less than 20 per cent of subscribers today contribute 80 per cent of revenue. Even if high cost technology and systems are used to provide service to these few subscribers, operators are likely to make a profit. In a fixed licence fee regime, as the subscriber base is expanded, gains (vis-à-vis licence fee payment) are likely even with marginal revenue from new subscribers. This is not the case with revenue sharing. Why bother to provide service to subscribers who are small consumers, at least to begin with? In fact a few of the BSO today refuse to provide service to all but corporate subscribers—a direct consequence of using high-cost imported technology. Is revenue sharing going to encourage this further?

BSOs taking high-paying subscribers away from the DoT could hardly have been the goal of the country's telecom policy and privitization process.[26] The entire privatization process started with a promise of universal service (providing telephone and Internet to all).

In the light of this, the removal of universal service obligation for the BSOs in NTP 99 is likely to be very problematic. A universal service tax (a certain percentage) is to replace this universal service obligation. Does this imply that private companies are to serve the high-paying subscribers, from whom a nominal tax will be collected and used to provide service to the masses?

At best, NTP 99 is not a comprehensive policy towards telecom and IT for all. It has addressed an immediate problem and found the best available means to solve it. One has to go beyond NTP 99 to look at several of these problems afresh.

### What Does It Take to Rapidly Expand the Network?

It is often believed that vital for network expansion are:
- technology and
- finance.

There is a prevailing assumption that both these components are not available in India. The national policy is therefore naturally designed to attract multinational corporations with their technology and finance. This is considered crucial at the current stage of infrastructure development for the country.

However, the above assumption has a basic fallacy. Mine is not an argument against multinationals, but market and affordability in India have unfortunately not been considered basic starting points; and *market and affordability* are key if one wishes to install hundreds of millions of telephone and Internet connections in India.

### Technology

Today it costs about Rs 32,000 to install a telephone line in India (Annual Report, DoT 1996–7; Jhunjhunwala, Ramamurthi, and Gonsalves 1998). For Internet access a telephone is a must. If one takes 15 per cent as the finance cost and 15 per cent as operation, maintenance, and obsolescence cost (the operation and obsolescence cost will in fact be higher), it requires an income of 30 per cent of Rs 32,000 per year from each line for the operator to just break even (this does not include licence fee, interconnectivity charges, or spectrum charges). This amounts to Rs 9600 per year or Rs 800 per month and less than 2 per cent of the population in India can spend this amount. Thus at the current cost, even with cross-subsidy, not more than 3 per cent could afford telephones. This simple computation stares one in the face, but is often ignored.

Will foreign technology help to overcome this problem? The cost of installing a telephone line in the West is US $ 1000. It is unlikely to drop substantially in the coming years. A US $ 1000 investment requires an income of US $ 300 per year taking into account finance, operation, and obsolescence. At US $ 25 per month, it is affordable to about 95 per cent of the people. Therefore there is no incentive to reduce cost. Instead, to stay in the market, telecom companies in the West have to attempt to provide a larger basket of services at the same cost. The emphasis of technology is therefore on providing more services and features, keeping the cost constant. Similarly, the cost of the personal computer (PC) has stayed constant for the last fifteen years in spite of major technological developments.

In India, we require telecom technology that is affordable to the majority. Of course, sharing of lines enhances affordability significantly.[27] But to provide

[26] Unfortunately, however, all private operators are aiming at exactly this, particularly in the first few years of operation. One cannot fault them as it is sound business policy.

[27] An example of such sharing is the STD PCOs, which are available today at in every nook and cranny of at least urban India. Around 15 per cent of population finds this affordable, and

telecom service even to 25 per cent of homes would require technology costing no more than Rs 10,000 per line, for which a revenue of only about Rs 250 per line per month would be needed to break even. With cross-subsidy, the revenue required could go down to Rs 100 per month; and this would be affordable to about 20 per cent of the population.

It is true that such technology is not available today. Would such a drastic reduction (from around Rs 32,000 to Rs 10,000 per line) ever be possible? The answer to such a question is why not? The R&D community in the West have had a totally different focus. But many of their innovations and inventions may be useful to R&D groups with the goal of cost reduction. The goal may be tough and not achievable immediately, but there is no reason to believe that it would be impossible in the long term.

Appendix 8.2.1 briefly describes the efforts in this direction of the Telecommunication and Computer Network (TeNeT) group. This group at IIT, Madras, along with several companies formed by its alumni, has been carrying out R&D to develop telecom and computer networking technologies for developing countries like India. The aim is to significantly reduce cost such that 100 to 200 million telephone and Internet connectivity becomes a reality in India. With about five years (and about 1000 man-years) of effort behind it, the group is currently planning citywide telecom and Internet network for operators, such that cost per line is close to Rs 18,000. It provides simultaneous voice and Internet service for over 50 per cent of the connections. The cost is likely to drop to about Rs 15,000 per line in about a year. Beyond this, new technological developments will be required to further reduce costs. What is important is that costs are not much higher in rural areas. It costs only about Rs 3000–4000 more per line to provide voice plus 35/70 kbps Internet in rural areas. (Jhunjhunwala 1998).

A note of caution is in order. The efforts of the TeNeT group demonstrate that it is possible to significantly reduce cost and create a basis for providing telecom and Internet connectivity to large sections of people. If the dream of 100 to 200 million telephone and Internet connectivity is, however, to materialize, several similar yet innovative efforts would be required.[28] Fortunately,

there are a large number of companies in India that have the technical ability to take up such a task. Most of them today concentrate on providing services to companies in the West and thus work for the Western market. They do not believe that this large Indian market can really be tapped because of the enormous bureaucratic wrangling in the country. The success of TeNeT group in large-scale deployment of its technologies is therefore crucial to confidence building; the process of Indian IT and telecom companies looking inwards and developing products affordable in India (and other developing countries) could then easily take off.

To sum up, availability of affordable telecom and Internet solutions is the basic requirement of universal connectivity in India (and most other developing countries). As such products are not available in the West, the development of these products becomes a key priority.

## WILL THESE TECHNOLOGIES BE ACCEPTABLE TO OPERATORS?

Is availability of these cost-reducing technologies the only bottleneck to fast expansion of the telecom network in the country? Would such technologies be acceptable in the country and can adequate financial resources be generated?

Let us look at the switches developed by C-DOT. This organization designed and developed switches in India in the late 1980s. It faced serious obstacles in its initial years, with the multinational lobby, along with a few officials, running down the product using all kinds of arguments. However, the persistence of those who believed that indigeneous development is the key to affordability paid in the long run. By the end of 2000, 10 million of the total of 20 million installed telephone lines in India will use C-DOT exchanges. C-DOT exchanges are working in rural areas, small towns, and even in large cities. The product has been proven in time to be not only as reliable as any imported exchange but in fact better adapted to the harsh Indian environment. Today, the exchanges have been exhaustively tested for up to 40,000 line capacity. The exchanges have been upgraded with signalling software for SS7, V5.1 and V5.2, ISDN, and even intelligent network (IN) services. The most important thing is that today a C-DOT line costs Rs 2700 as opposed to Rs 4300 for imported exchanges; in fact, if C-DOT exchanges were not available, the cost of an imported exchange would probably have exceeded Rs 6000 per line.[29]

---

even make long-distance calls at late nights. It generates around 20 per cent of total telecom revenue.

[28] For example, bringing Internet connection to home still requires massive investment in a computer, which well over 95 per cent of families in India cannot afford. Low cost Access terminals using TV or an integrated telephone, TV, and Internet Access terminal definitely need to be developed.

[29] For a year or two in the mid-1990s C-DOT exchange manufacturers were in financial trouble as the DoT was not buying CDOT exchanges, the multinationals took advantage of this and significantly increased the per line price of their exchanges.

However, the C-DOT exchange has so far not been used by even one BSO. Why is this so even though any field-level DoT engineer will swear to its reliability and its costs are less than two-thirds those of imported exchanges?

The first reason is that often the foreign partners of the BSOs, would like to sell their own or their partner company's products. They therefore prevail on the BSOs to buy the more expensive product.

The more important reason is finance. Multinational companies offer vendor financing for their products. They are ready to provide even equity financing, if the BSOs are willing to use their products. The finance terms they offer are attractive—LIBOR (London Inter Bank Offer Rate) of around 6 per cent plus 0.5 per cent interest rate and, more importantly, a five-year moratorium on all payments. Most of the BSOs are short of finance, and a five-year moratorium on payment implies that payment starts only after they are likely to break even and are in a position to pay. Thus the more expensive imported products get the go ahead. But where does this leave the goal of universal access? With more expensive inputs BSOs are likely to be further oriented away from market expansion.

*Finance*

WHAT ARE THE FINANCING OPTIONS?

Some of the most innovative initiatives that have been taken in India over the last ten years include the launching of STD PCOs, cable TV operation, and computer training institutes. These have mushroomed all over the country. Cable TV operation is probably the most widespread. Today cable TV reaches some 35 million homes in India, even more remarkable when one remembers that it was non-existent in 1992. The important thing is that this happened without any initiatives from the government or any R&D institute, multinational, large Indian corporate house, or the World Bank or Asian Development Bank. It happened because a couple of youngsters in each locality would put in Rs 300,000–500,000 by borrowing money and even mortaging family jewellery. They provide service in a neighbourhood, going house to house to sell connections and returning to collect the Rs 50–150 monthly fee from each. They live in the neighbourhood and are known people. When something goes wrong, one has only to go down the street corner and complain. Service is provided round the clock and on weekdays and weekends. If the service is not good enough, the subscriber can opt for another operator; one pays at the end of the month at one's doorstep only if one is

satisfied. This is what Mahatma Gandhi referred to as face-to-face society.[30]

Leaving aside the implications this has in terms of service quality, let us examine the financing issue. With about 35 million cable TV connections existing with an average cost of Rs 300 per connection, the total investment in this operation is around Rs 10 billion (1000 crore). Where has this investment come from? Is it not an excellent example of internal resource mobilization?

This is not to argue that telecom in India does not need international finance. In fact, all financial resources need to be tapped and international finance may be key. *But financing must not be allowed to force expensive network choices.* Having viable alternate sources of local finance will ensure that international finance is also deployed cost effectively.

NTP 99: SOME SPECIFIC ISSUES

Having discussed some of the key issues which need to be tackled to enable rapid expansion of the telecom and Internet network in India, let us get back to NTP 99. What needs to be done now in terms of policies? We take up some specific issues.

*NTP Must Focus on Reduction of Network Cost*

It is clear that the national telecom policy must focus on reduction of network cost if universal communication is to be made possible in India in a short time. How is this to be done?

Can incentives be provided to operators for using low-cost indigenous products? And what kinds of incentives and to what extent? The incentives could be in terms of better revenue-sharing terms to operators for using such products. For example, operators using CDOT's exchanges and IIT, Madras (TeNeT) group's access product could be given a more favourable revenue share as compared to those not doing so. Alternatively, incentives can be provided in terms of lower or deferred entry fee or deferred revenue-sharing payments. But can the incentives compensate favourable vendor financing terms available for imported equipment?

One has to look at World Trade Organization (WTO) agreements and other commitments that the country has made while proceeding on these lines. But as the incentives are only to compensate an attractive vendor

[30] This is a running theme in several works of Mahatma Gandhi. He contrasted this face-to-face service with the service provided by a beauracratic faceless body, to which you can only petition for a service. The methods advocated by Gandhiji definitely need a closer look, specifically in view of a situation where service from the organized sector in India is either becoming too expensive or is totally breaking down.

finance package available for imports, it should be possible to find a way.

### Import Bill

If 100 million lines are to be commissioned over the next 8–10 years and even if we assume a modest equipment cost of Rs 15,000 per line, the total cost works out to Rs 1500 billion. What will be the source of all this equipment? Will this go on the import bill? Going by the current volume of manufacturing in India and the trend adopted by the BSOs, it appears that all equipment will be imported. Can India afford this?

If not, what kinds of incentives can be provided for local manufacturing? Can such incentives be built into licence agreements? Once again, it requires detailed study of the WTO regulations to find a way. With such import-based developments of the network 100 million telephones and Internet connections will simply never be a reality.

### Why Only Large Operators?

NTP 99 did attempt to make the operations of CMSPs (cellular mobile service providers) and BSOs viable by converting the committed licence fees to revenue sharing. But the reasons behind it having recommended an entry fee barrier for new operators are not at all clear. Why have such barriers at all? Why not use the same policy as adopted for Internet service? Second, why continue to think in terms of statewide (circle-wide) operators only? Why not in terms of smaller operators?

As discussed earlier, some of the most successful operations in India have been cable TV and STD PCO operations. Why not allow similar operations in telecom? Why not allow small operators (franchise operators) providing 500 to 1000 line connections in a neighbourhood?

Today, the access network costs 65–70 per cent of the total per-line cost of the telecom network. Further, it is the access part of the network that requires maximum care and maintenance. As this kind of service is best provided by a local person in a neighbourhood, it is best to have a franchise operator put up the access network and provide the service. The backbone networks could be provided by a statewide operator (the DoT or a BSO). As such a franchise operator puts up 65–70 per cent of the cost, he/she must get at least 50 per cent of the revenue.

### Incentives for Universal Service

There should be specific incentives to encourage an operator to provide service as widely as possible. Some suggestions are as follows:

• Incentives should given to provide service in small towns and rural areas:

– revenue share accruing to the government for operation in *small towns* should be *zero*;

– revenue share accruing to the government for operation in *rural areas* should be *negative*, implying that the operator can offset part of the revenue share that he/she has to pay to the government for operation in urban areas by providing more telephones in rural areas.

• To discourage an operator from focusing only on high-paying customers in urban areas, the revenue share to be paid should decrease as teledensity provided by the operator in a city increases.

It is important to point out that universal service tax cannot compensate for universal service obligations. Instead incentives to widen customer base would greatly help.

### Incoming and Outgoing Calls

In the international arena, the difference between call-minutes originating from one country to another and call-minutes terminating in the first country from the other are used for settlement. In other words, as many more call-minutes originate from the United States to India as compared to the other way around, the VSNL gets paid for by US operators.

The reasons why more calls originate in one country rather than another vary. Of course the reason is often lower tariffs in one country. The other important reason is that income levels in one country may be higher than in the other. For example, when Indians leave India and settle in the United States, they earn in dollars and therefore much more in absolute terms as compared to their relatives in India. Even if tariff in the two countries were the same (in absolute terms), many more calls are likely to be made from the United States to India than the other way round. However, it requires a telephone in both countries to complete the call. Recognizing this, the international settlement is carried out.

Similar situations exist within India between rural and urban areas. Very often the family breadwinner leaves the village and comes to a town to work. It is he/she who has much more money to make the call to the village.

It is imperative that settlement between the incoming and outgoing call-minutes in rural areas be carried out. Otherwise, the operators who serve rural and backward areas of the country will be at a disadvantage.

### CONCLUSION

Some policy initiatives to strengthen NTP 99 and render its goals more achievable have been highlighted. There are several other specific policy decisions that need to be taken as one moves beyond NTP 99. For example, it is surprising that NTP 99 did not try to resolve the mobile versus fixed wireless service tangle. NTP 99 did what was imperative at the time. The point is to move on. The principal goal of telecom policy needs to be underscored once again—to provide reliable telephone and Internet connectivity to all.

Such a goal is achievable only with clear policy initiatives. A push is required such that Indian companies and institutes take up the task to design and develop such telecom and IT that is affordable to people in India. Initiatives need to be taken to encourage large-scale efficient manufacturing in India. Finally, policy instruments need to be used to provide incentives to expand telecom and Internet operations in small towns and rural areas and to provide service to lower-income groups in urban areas. Only such explicit policies will enable India to expand its network to the required extent.

---

BOX 8.2.1

### Enabling Telecom and Internet Connectivity in Small Towns and Rural India

*Ashok Jhunjhunwala and Bhaskar Ramamurthi*

There are a little over 300 Class I towns (over 100,000 population in the 1991 Census) in India. These are the only towns in which the DoT makes a profit on its services. In other places (Class II, III, IV towns and rural areas), the DoT either barely breaks even or loses money. Private BSOs today are putting up their operations in the largest cities and have very little interest in going beyond. At most, a few may cover some larger Class II cities. The ISPs also largely confine their operations to the larger Class I cities.

The world over, telephone revenue continues to significantly exceed revenue obtained from Internet connections. Telecom revenue has been used to build the Internet. However, in the future the Internet is likely to yield large revenues and also change ways of living and doing business.

The IT taskforce took a very bold step in freeing the setting up of Internet service anywhere in the country virtually licence free. It has led to the emergence of a large number of ISPs all over India. But today, they largely depend on the telecom network to provide access to subscribers. Not only are they denied a part of the resulting telecom revenue, but in fact subscribers have to pay Rs 26 per hour to the DoT (or BSOs) as access charges in addition to paying Internet service charges. Such a low revenue share for an ISP out of the total amount paid by a subscriber for Internet access implies that an ISP can be successful only in larger cities.

Development of telecom and Internet in smaller towns and rural areas requires telecom and Internet revenue to be *combined* to make the operation commercially viable. Further it requires a *local* business focusing on the region to optimize its costs.

The following measures are therefore recommended:

Telecom operations *in all areas of the country other than Class I cities be entirely licence free.* A local service provider (LSP) could set up a telecom network and provide telephones in all such areas (in addition to Internet service which is today virtually licence free) by simply registering itself. The region of operation could be small or large—one town, one district, one block, or even one neighbourhood. The local operator be allowed to connect to the nearest statewide telecom operator (the DoT/BSO) by paying *connectivity charges* as per norms similar to those applicable for BSOs today.

A BSO today pays (a) a revenue share (15 to 20 per cent) to the government for licence in addition to a one-time entry fee for the entire state (circle); (b) for physical connectivity to the nearest DoT (digital E1 connections) exchange; (c) thirty-three per cent of STD charges for all calls routed through the DoT network; (d) fifty per cent of international STD charges for calls routed through the DoT/VSNL network.

To help the telecom and Internet network grow in small towns and rural areas, licence fee and revenue share (as in (a) above) should be zero for fifteen years. The charges as in (b), (c), and (d) for a LSP should be the same as for a BSO, or even less, in order to encourage LSPs. However, for connections in rural areas, the LSP should get the universal service (USO) benefits that the DoT and BSO would.

The interface between exchanges used today in India is digital E1 lines. The signalling used is R2-MF or SS7; R2-MF signalling dominates though it is progressively being changed to SS7. The LSP should be allowed to connect to the DoT/BSO on E1 lines with R2-MF signalling. As and when the DoT/BSO as well as LSP have the capability to upgrade the connection to SS7, the upgrading should be allowed. The LSP should require only this E1 interface approval for connection to the DoT/BSO.

Frequency spectrum is a valuable resource and frequencies must be used and reused efficiently by the country. The frequency charges must be such as to encourage this. However, in small towns and rural areas, where usage is less, charges should be made zero for the first ten years in order to rapidly enhance telecom and Internet services in these areas. The target for such connections in these areas should be at least 30 million in the next five years.

The charges stated in (b), (c), and (d) are reasonable, as the access part of the telecom network is 65 to 70 per cent (the percentages are even higher in rural areas) of the total cost of installing a telephone line. The backbone network is only a small percentage of the total cost. This policy will enable tens of thousands of small local operators to come up, providing telecom and Internet service in small towns and rural areas. The operating costs of these small entrepreneurs would be much less than those of the DoT and BSOs. Further, being local, they would provide better services. India's phenomenal cable TV expansion in small towns and rural areas is an example of the success of this approach. The DoT and BSOs do not lose by this policy, as currently they do not profit financially when they provide connections in small towns and rural areas.

# 8.3 NUMBER PORTABILITY: WHY DO WE NEED IT?[31]

*Dheeraj Sanghi*

Many countries that have opened up their local telephony markets have found that the incumbent local exchange carrier (ILEC) continues to dominate the market long after a competitive local exchange carrier (CLEC) starts providing local service in the same market. This is true even when the CLEC provides better service at similar or lower rates. For a CLEC, the cost of entry is typically very high. Besides the high initial capital costs, marketing costs are also huge. It is typically much costlier to acquire a new customer than to keep an existing one. Inertia of customers preventing a switch to a new carrier may be one reason. But there is another significant reason. Customers will lose their original telephone numbers if they switch to a CLEC. This will cause hardship as they will have to inform all their friends, relatives, businesses, and everyone else who may need to contact them of the change. They will have to discard their business cards and other stationery. Customers will not be willing to switch their telephone service if the cost of the switch in terms of both hardships and actual economic cost is going to be substantial. Hence it is clear that true competition in the local market cannot develop without number portability.

The Telecommunications Act, 1996, in the United States was instrumental in promoting competition in the telecom market. It made it obligatory for all ILECs to open their networks to competitors. It removed legal and regulatory barriers to entry and specifically mentioned number portability as a mechanism to promote competition in the local access market. The Act defined number portability as 'the ability of users of telecommunication services to retain existing telecommunications numbers without impairment of quality, reliability, or convenience when switching from one telecommunications carrier to another'.

[31] This article has references to the Federal Communications Commission (FCC), FCC–95–284, 1995; FCC 96–286, July 1996; FCC–97–074, March 1997; FCC–97–289, August 1997; FCC–98–082, May 1998; The Number Portability Site, www.ported.com; www.fcc.gov; OFTEL, www.oftel.gov.uk; Office of the Telecommunication Authority (OFTA), Honkong, www.ofta.gov.hk; Australian Communications Authority, www.aca.gov.au; Telecommunications Standards Advisory Council of Canada, www.tsacc.ic.gc.ca; America's Networks magazine, www.americasnetwork.com; N. Mulachy and P. Waters (1997); Telephone Number mapping working group of IETF, www.ietf.org/html.charters/enum-charter. html; International Telecommunication Union, www.itu.int.

The first example of number portability was the freephone service in the United States (800-NXX-XXXX numbers, where the party who receives the call pays for it). For a long time, carriers were allocated specific three-digit codes (NXX) and were free to assign the last four digits of the freephone number. So each code meant a block of 10,000 numbers. The three-digit code determined the routing of the freephone call to the appropriate carrier. If a subscriber wanted to change the service provider, then the three-digit code (and hence the freephone number) would also change. Companies invest large sums of money in advertising their freephone numbers. Therefore, they would not opt to change their number and would rather use the same provider.

In May 1993, the United States switched to a system whereby a database was created for all freephone numbers. In this database, each freephone number was associated with the public switched telephone network (PSTN) number, the name of the carrier, and some other details necessary for routing the call. Every time a call was to be made to a freephone number, a query was first sent to this database and based on the information returned the call was handed over to a particular carrier. As a result the numbers became completely portable. Switching a carrier was as simple as changing the database entry without changing the number. This database was managed by an independent party (BellCore at that time) and not by long-distance operators.

This allowed even the smallest of carriers or resellers who did not have presence in all areas to offer this service. This increased competition. And it resulted in drastic improvement in the quality of service at much lower costs. Enhanced services included routing the call based on the time of day and originating number. It was also possible to state in the database that a portion of the traffic could be carried on one carrier and the rest on another. The companies started providing guarantees on uptime and fault tolerance. Meanwhile the cost of the call was decreasing.

There are three aspects of a telecom service, viz. geographical location, service (like ISDN [integrated-switched digital network] versus PSTN), and service provider. There are three types of corresponding portability that affect competition. Service provider portability implies that the customer retains the same number if she switches the service provider but location and the type of service remain the same. Service portability implies that the customer retains the same number if she switches the type of service (for example PSTN to ISDN) at the same location and with the same service provider. Finally, location portability implies that the customer retains the same number if he/she changes his/her location but continues to receive the same type of service from the same service provider. Ideally, one would like to have all three types of portability, that is freedom to change all three and still keep the same number. But in the immediate context of providing a level playing field to the CLECs, service provider portability is the most important. It is also referred to as local number portability (LNP). If wireless service becomes significantly cheaper to the extent that a subscriber may switch from fixed line service to wireless, then service portability will become important to enhance competition. This type of portability is called wireless number portability (WNP). (WNP is quite similar to LNP except that the rate areas of wireless service and fixed line service are different. If one switches from wireless to fixed-line service, the numbers that one could call free of charge earlier may no longer be free to call. Between two fixed-line service providers, this problem rarely arises since the rate areas are usually identical.)

There are four mechanisms to implement LNP. In the simplest case, the donor network (the previous service provider) simply routes the call to the new routing number (all phones/terminal devices have an internal routing number that is used to route the call through the telecom network). The donor network will maintain a mapping between the old telephone number and the new routing number. This is simple and easy to implement, but the resources of the donor network are being used throughout the duration of every call. The donor network will demand substantial compensation for providing this service. The second problem is the delay, particularly if the number is ported more than once.

The second mechanism involves the donor network dropping the call and informing the source network about the new routing number. This requires the donor network to keep the mapping between the telephone number and the new routing number for all times to come. The mechanism will require simple enhancements in the signalling protocol. Overall, this is an improvement over the previous scheme, but the delay in setting up the call could be slightly higher.

Another obvious problem in this scheme is the requirement that the donor network keep the mapping for all times to come. This continued dependence on the donor network even after the customer has switched to a new service provider is not very desirable, except in

the interim period. Also it continues to reinforce the belief that the numbers are owned by service providers. Ideally, an independent authority should deal with numbers (assign numbers, keep the information about portability, etc.).

In the third scheme, called 'query on release', the call connection request goes to the donor network, which only replies that it no longer serves the number. It need not provide (or even have) the current routing information. Now the source network queries the database and finds the latest routing information and then establishes the call. This scheme requires setting up additional database infrastructure and upgrading signalling on all telecom switches to permit querying this database. But setting up such an infrastructure is the next logical step for providing all kinds of portability, or 'one number for life'.' The problem is the delay involved in setting up the call. There is one roundtrip time delay with respect to the donor network, another roundtrip to the database, and a third roundtrip to the new network.

The fourth scheme cuts down on this delay by always sending the request to the database first. This reduces the delay for ported numbers by avoiding the first roundtrip time to the donor network. But it increases the delay for non-ported numbers, which now have an additional query and response time. However, querying for all calls can have additional advantages, such as the ones noted in the case of freephone service. This will be a precursor to the 'one number for life' goal in telecommunications. The additional benefit is that the donor network is not at all involved in the operation.

All four schemes have different costs involved, both in terms of investment in upgrading the network and switches as well as in maintaining and running the system. There is a need to study the advantages and disadvantages of these schemes, conduct a cost–benefit analysis of different schemes and finally decide the model to facilitate cost sharing between different service providers and customers.

The costs of implementing LNP are usually shared between all service providers and customers. Each service provider will upgrade its own network at its cost. The cost of database or shared infrastructure is paid for by the service providers. It can be based on actual usage (number of queries, for example), but it is more likely that the ILEC would need to pay a larger share of the cost. The argument given is that the ILEC has benefited the most from the monopoly situation, and now it should be made to promote a level playing field. Service providers will in turn charge customers some additional money. This additional charge cannot be solely paid for by those who actually port their numbers, since it will be enormous in that case. The charges to a large extent have to be shared by all customers, because everyone benefits from the increased competition made possible by LNP. Thus the benefits of LNP are in its availability, not necessarily in its use by a large number of customers. There are a large number of cost-sharing models in place in different markets and India will have to find its own when it implements LNP.

The cost of implementing LNP (including upgrading all switches and creating a database) is estimated at around US $ 10 per telephone line in urban areas. Considering that the cost of setting up of a new network is around US $ 400 per line, it is very small by comparison. The US Federal Communications Commission (FCC) has allowed initial cost recovery from all existing customers. The per month charges vary from 23 cents in the case of Bell Atlantic customers to 48 cents for Sprint Local customers. These charges are expected to come down further and in any case will disappear when the initial costs are fully recovered. The saving to customers in the medium term, because of efficiency enforced by competition, is expected to be much higher. The estimates of saving on account of not having to print new stationery upon changing the service provider are upwards of US $ 1 billion per year.

There are several countries that are implementing LNP. In fact, almost all countries that are opening up their basic telecom services are making it mandatory for operators to implement LNP. The United States, for example, has already implemented LNP in most of its markets and has also started implementing WNP. In the UK, Australia, and Hong Kong too LNP is being implemented. There are at least thirty other countries, where the regulatory bodies are looking at issues related to LNP and are likely to mandate it soon.

Besides enhancing competition in the local telecom market, number portability has other benefits. It had already been stated that this is the path towards a single lifelong number. It also conserves number space. The FCC has mandated number pooling in all areas where LNP implementation is complete. When LNP is not supported, then each CLEC is allocated a block of numbers in each rate area where it intends to provide service. Each block may be as large as 10,000 numbers, even though the number of actual customers may be very small. This wastes the numbering resource and forces an increase in the size of telephone numbers sooner than would otherwise be necessary. With number pooling, each exchange code is shared between different local exchange carriers (LECs), thereby effectively allocating smaller blocks of addresses to different LECs. Number pooling requires LNP, since routing

information will be retrieved from the number database.

Having said all this, it must be mentioned that number portability is not immediately relevant to the current Indian telecom scenario. The Telecom Regulatory Authority of India (TRAI) is currently planning to completely change the national numbering plan. The nine-digit numbers (including the national destination code and the subscriber number but not counting the initial 'zero' of the STD code) will soon be insufficient in the country. Cellular and paging services have already been allowed 10-digit numbers. Last year the TRAI published a discussion paper on the new numbering plan for the country. It is likely that the new numbering plan will be adopted within about a year. LNP should be taken up only after the new numbering plan has been adopted and implemented.

But implementing number portability is a tricky business. The TRAI needs to discuss different possible schemes to implement LNP. It needs to decide whether WNP should also be adopted. It then needs to give sufficient time to carriers to implement LNP and test their networks. Another important regulatory issue will be the allocation of costs. Who pays for the network upgradation as well as the running cost? Should this be shared by all existing telecom customers, since they will all eventually benefit from the competition even if they do not actually switch their service. Should it be paid largely by those customers who actually switch their service? Should this cost be forced upon the ILEC, since it should be the responsibility of the monopoly carrier to support competition? ILECs have long benefited from monopoly. And is it the time for them to pay back? All three ideas of cost sharing have some merits and perhaps all three will share some parts of the cost. But who should share how much is a difficult question that the TRAI will have to determine.

The experience of other countries shows that it takes at least two years to decide on the regulatory aspects of LNP and two more years to implement and test it. Even if the process can be speeded up by learning from others' experience, it will still take a minimum of three years. India certainly will be ready for LNP in three years. So the discussion on number portability has to start today. Also, it is to be noted in the proposed numbering plan that fixed-line service has been given a different number space from wireless telephony. It is likely that India might consider WNP to be more important. Having two different number spaces for wireless and fixed line phones will be an impediment to WNP. Therefore, portability issues should be carefully discussed before deciding on the numbering plan.

# APPENDICES

## APPENDIX 8.1.1

### NOTE ON IP TELEPHONY AND VOICE OVER INTERNET PROTOCOL (VoIP)

*What is Packet Telephony?*

Packet telephony is a transport service providing voice communication on a packet-based data network. Real time voice communication refers to standard telephone calls where maintaining accurate speech structure is critical. Other types of potential packet communications include fax, voice messaging, e-mail, video, and data. Other terms used to describe packet telephony are: voice over Internet protocol (VoIP), Internet telephony, voice over frame relay, voice over Asynchronous Transfer Mode (ATM).

*How Does Packet Telephony Work?*

The circuit-switched telephone conversation is converted to a format suitable for transmission over a data network. The signal is first encoded, then it is compressed, and finally it is packetized. The final converted signal can be transported over a frame relay, ATM, or Internet protocol (IP) network.

*Why is Packet Telephony Getting So Much Attention in the Industry?*

Packet telephony is less expensive and more efficient than circuit-switched telephony. It takes advantage of several significant trends in technology. The first trend deals with the development of digital signal processor (DSP) products. DSP products perform the signal conversion process and are doubling in processing power every eighteen months (this is referred to as Moore's Law). The second is that since 1997 more data have been transmitted on the 'network' than voice. The third is the ability to use one infrastructure to transport voice, video, and data (convergence).

*How Does Packet Telephony Work With the Circuit Switched Network?*

There are several ways packet telephony can work in conjunction with the public-switched telephone network (PSTN). Our current implementation will provide a gateway device attached to the host digital terminal (HDT). From the HDT, the service provider has the ability to utilize either network. To what degree the PSTN is used depends on where the IP conversion process takes place and to what extent an alternative service provider can carry the packets on a managed backbone. In all instances, a gateway device is required that performs voice conversion.

*Will Current Customer Premise Equipment (CPE) Work with an IP System?*

For the near term, packet telephony will be transparent to the end user. Any subscriber can place packet telephony calls with his/her standard telephone. In this topology, the IP conversion process will take place within the network via gateways. Future products will migrate the conversion functionality towards the subscriber.

*What are the Growth Projections?*

IDC (International Data Corporation—an organization engaged in research in information technology and telecommunication) predicts that by the year 2002, the Internet could carry 11 per cent of the US and international long-distance traffic. Continued growth will be determined by a combination of standards, regulation, and the availability of a managed backbone where delay will not effect voice quality. Market estimates regarding the future share of IP telephony vary considerably. Tarifica's Internet Consultancy Practice estimated that by the year 2003, IP telephony could take as much as 43 per cent share of the total global market. The market is expected to reach US $ 290 million, up from US $ 130 million in 1998. By 2003, IDC believes the total worldwide market will exceed US $ 1.8 billion. As per Yankee Group's estimate (1995), IP minutes of usage would be 9 per cent by 2004 and 15 per cent by 2006.

*What Benefits does Packet Telephony Offer Compared to Circuit Switched?*

The benefits are as follows:

• combines voice, video, and data on one transmission network;

• eliminates wasted bandwidth by not transporting silence (about 60 per cent of normal speech is silence);

• can achieve greater compression (64 kbps to as little as 6 kbps);

• is currently unregulated and offers a viable means of bypassing the existing PSTN at a significant saving.

*Who Will Deliver Services Using Packet Telephony?*

Multiple service operators (MSOs) that want to offer three or more simultaneous services to their subscribers would benefit from packet telephony. The services offered need to be full featured, low cost, and provide custom local area signalling services (CLASS). The MSOs would be able to offer lifeline/primary service at a significant discount and combine voice, video, and data communications on a single point of presence. This offering fits well with the residential customer, whose service demands are currently driven by price and additional features in the future.

*Are There International Applications for Packet Telephony?*

A variety of companies around the world have announced plans for IP deployment:

• SouthNet Telecom & Deutsche Telecom to use Ascend gear for VoIP service

• Telestra uses NetSpeak for VoIP trials

• Telnor signs contract with Ericsson to include Ericsson's Gatekeeper in Telenor's Public H.323 Network

• Bezeq to use VocalTec equipment for phone to phone Internet trial

• Exit2Europe to offer Internet telephony using VocalTec's equipment

• TVS to use Array Telecom's gateways for IP network in Japan

• Digitcom teams with providers to offer IP Telephony in Egypt and Russia

• Swisscom testing Inter-Tel's technology for VoIP service

• ITXC announces global connectivity for IP Telephony calls.

*What Standards are Relevant for Packet Telephony?*

H.323 is one of the primary standards for packet telephony. SGCP is the interface standard for the interaction between a cable client and the circuit switch-network gateway. ADC fully supports both of these standards.

There are additional standards that cover the specific functions of transmission. G.723.1 is one of the International Telecommunications Union (ITU) standards for encoding voice. H.323 Rev 2 for wide area networking recommends G.723.1 for voice/video and G.729 for voice only.

*Which Organizations are Involved with Creating Standards?*

The following is a list of the organizations:

1. European Telecommunications Standards Institute Telephone.

2. Internet Protocol Harmonization Over Networks (TIPHON).

3. International Telecommunications Union (ITU).

4. Internet Engineering Task Force (IETF).

5. Intelligent Network Forum (INF).

6. Forums also exist for voice over frame relay/ATM/IP.

7. Managing Cisco Network Security (MCNS)/Data Over Cable System Interface Specification (DOCSIS).

*Does Packet Telephony Offer Toll Quality?*

Factors affecting packet telephony voice quality include the voice conversion process, the delay associated with getting from point to point, and the variable delay at the far end gateway as it reconstructs the signal (jitter). Digital signal processor (DSP) products embedded in the gateway device have the processing power to handle the voice conversion with toll quality. The principle issue today involves the delay associated with transmission. The more routers or 'hops' that the packet experiences on the network, the more delay.

*What are the differences between Voice over ATM, Frame Relay, and IP?*

ATM is a connection-based protocol similar to circuit-switched service. ATM was designed to support multimedia applications and will see future implementations as a backbone application. Frame relay and IP are connectionless-based protocols. Frame relay has its strength in the corporate environment as it evolved from X.25 technology. IP is geared more to the residential market with its ties to the Internet and its global acceptance. Most gateway manufactures are designing products to support multiple protocols.

*Will Packet Telephony be Regulated?*

It is not really a question of whether packet telephony will be regulated but when, and what form the regulation will take. It is important to note that even if it becomes regulated, there are still significant advantages to combining voice, video, and data on the same transmission platform.

*Will Web Browsers Have an Effect on My IP-Based Phone Calls?*

Using the Internet or an Internet protocol-based network there will have to be some method to prioritize voice packets over others. IPv6 has been developed to address this issue along with Resource Reservation Protocol (RSVP), a protocol that ensures minimal delay for voice packets.

*Source:* http://www.adc.com/Education/HFC/topics/voiceIP/pg3.html#4

## Non-Compressed Voice

In order to compare the cost implications of IP telephony with long-distance communications, we need take into account the generally falling costs of long-distance voice communications, decrease in deficit of access charges which Internet service providers (ISPs) in the United States are exempt from paying to local service providers (but long-distance providers are not), and decreasing costs of billing and administering the traditional voice networks to recognize that the differential is becoming smaller. Various simulation studies for comparison indicate the following:

Total of All Costs
(Cost in cents per minute, average for all long-distance domestic calls)

|  | Circuit switched | Packet switched | Packet/ circuit switch adv. |
|---|---|---|---|
| Access | 5.0 | 5 | |
| Operation | 2.5 | 1.47 | |
| S & GA | 3.5 | 3.5 | |
| Total | 11.0 | 9.97 | 10 per cent |

*Source:* Quoted in Policy Approach to Internet Telephony, G. Ramadesikan, Workshop on 'Telecom Policy Initiatives: The Road Ahead' held at Indian Institute of Management, Ahmedabad, 28–9 August 1999 in Martin B. H. Weiss & Junseok Hwang (1998), Internet Telephony or Circuit Switched Telephony: Which is Cheaper?, presented at Telecom Policy Research Conference Alexandria, Virginia October 1998.

The reduced capital expenditure is attributed to reduction in switching and transmission equipments and the capacity required. In a circuit-switched network, multiple levels of switches (Class 1 to Class 5) are required to complete a call whereas such is not the case in packet switching. Transmission capacity required is lower in the latter because communication channels can be utilized by multiple calls simultaneously.

As competition will increase for basic ISPs, most face declining revenue from their traditional subscribers. After IP infrastructure is in place, ISPs can begin to offer value-added services (VASs), such as voice mail, fax store and forward, and virtual second line.

International carriers such as World Com and China Telecom want to route some of their long distance calls over net-based networks because it is cheaper, and are partnering with telephony carriers such as Internet iBasis and ITXC.

## Appendix 8.1.2

### Data Services Before NTP 99

India's first public data communication network, INDONET, was started in 1985 by CMC Ltd., a public sector computer organization. However, due to poor service quality and lack of revenues for expansion, this effort was not very successful. Though a large number of studies had shown that networks enabled organizations to become more competitive (Parson 1987), Indian organizations had little or no imperative to use networking as they operated with fewer challenges and slower growth than in dynamic countries like the newly industrialized countries. Therefore, there was no pressure to hone up organizational competitiveness.

In 1992, I-NET, the data communication network owned and operated by the Department of Telecommunications (DoT), also became operational. It initially linked up eight metropolitan cities in India through 9.6 kbps and 64 kbps data links. However, there were delays in service provision and often the quality of service was poor, resulting in poor growth of the network. The National Informatics Centre (NIC), a government agency, had set up a nationwide network, NICNET, employing VSATs for the use of various ministries and government agencies. It linked nearly 450 districts of India. The NIC provided system design and implementation support. In most cases, the system was basically used for generating fixed format reports. There was little flexibility in querying or report generation. Since the mid-1990s the NIC had attempted to get into telecom service provision, but its efforts were thwarted by the DoT. An educational network, ERNET, set up by the Department of Electronics with funding support from the United Nations Development Programme (UNDP), linked several universities and research and educational institutes and was successful in providing e-mail, inter-national connectivity, and other network services. However, its services were not generally available to commercial organizations.

Setting up privately owned data communication networks was an expensive exercise for Indian organizations since rental of leased lines was very high and continues to be so. The tariff policy also seemed to discourage networking. For example, if the leased line was connected to more than one terminal, then the tariff was doubled. In addition, the DoT provided very little choice in the transmission media it leased out.

Subsequent to NTP 99, Internet service provision by private players took off. There are reportedly 2 million or more Internet subscribers today. The VSNL, Satyam, and Bharti are some of the large players. The DoT too provides Internet services. With NTP 99 having removed constraints on setting up private international gateways, several private players have plans in this area. This will bring down the cost of international services by breaking the VSNL's monopoly over international gateway services provision.

Although the DoT allowed private VSAT (very small aperature terminal) provision, it regulated the tariffs. Besides the DoT did not allow leased private networks or VSAT-based networks to be connected to the PSTN. There was a 64 kbps data rate limit for private VSAT provision. High cost of imported equipment, due to the high import duties, high licence fee, and non-recognition of VSAT as infrastructure excluded VSAT service providers from tax reliefs available to other infrastructure providers and made it expensive for Indian organizations to use VSATs for data communications.

## APPENDIX 8.1.3

### SCOPE AND FUNCTIONS OF THE TRAI

*Scope of Recommendatory Role of the TRAI*

i. Monitor the need and timing for introduction of new service provider.

ii. Lay down terms and conditions of licence to a service provider.

iii. Lay down the standards of quality of service to be provided by the service providers and ensure the quality of service and conduct the periodical survey of such service provided by the service providers so as to protect the interest of the consumers of telecommunication services.

iv. Lay down and ensure the time period for providing local and long-distance circuits of telecommunication between different service providers.

v. Maintain register of interconnect agreements and of all such other matters as may be provided in the regulations.

vi. Ensure effective compliance of universal service obligations.

vii. Revoke licences for non-compliance with terms and conditions.

viii. Lay down measures to facilitate competition and promote efficiency in the operation of telecommunication services so as to facilitate growth in such services.

ix. Try to ensure technological improvements in the services provided by service providers.

x. Decide on type of equipment to be used by service providers after inspection of equipment used in the network.

xi. Lay down measures for the development of telecommunication technology and any other matter relatable to telecommunication industry in general.

xii. Ensure efficient management of available spectrum.

*Functions of the TRAI*

i. Ensure compliance with terms and conditions of licence.

ii. Notwithstanding anything contained in the terms and conditions of the licence granted before the commencement of the Telecom Regulatory Authority (Amendment) Ordinance, 2000, fix the terms and conditions of interconnectivity between service providers.

iii. Ensure technical compatibility and effective interconnection between different service providers.

iv. Regulate arrangement amongst service providers for sharing their revenue derived from providing telecommunication services. Levy fees and other charges at such rates and in respect of such services as may be determined by regulations.

v. Perform such other functions including such administrative and financial functions as may be entrusted to it by the central government or as may be necessary to carry out the provisions of this Act.

## APPENDIX 8.2.1

### EFFORTS OF THE TELECOMMUNICATION AND COMPUTER NETWORK (TeNeT) GROUP

In recent years, developments in the area of fibre optics and microwave radio technology have reduced the cost of the backbone telecom network to Rs 1000–1500 per line. Similarly with the access network getting separated from the exchange, the cost of the main exchange today is only around Rs 1200 per line. The key contributor to the telecom network cost today is the cost of access network, which is sometimes as high as Rs 22,000 in some urban areas. The cost in rural areas may be much higher.

The TeNeT Group and its associates, which include Midas Communication Technologies, Banyan Networks, Vembu Systems, and Nilgiri Networks, have developed a fibre-access network (optiMA), wireless in local loop system (corDECT WLL), and a direct internet access system (DIAS), which aim to significantly reduce access cost and at the same time enable large-scale usage of Internet. Using these technologies it is possible to set up a total network today at an average cost of Rs 13,500 per line. These systems flexibly enable rapid expansion of the telecom and Internet network both in urban and rural areas.

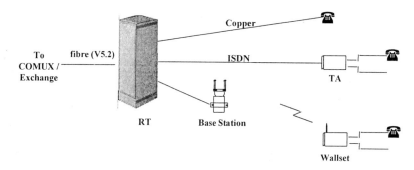

**Fig. A.8.2.1:** Remote terminal at the curb serving subscribers on copper or wireless.

### optiMA Fibre Access Network

This fibre-to-the-curb (or street-corner) system provides one of the most cost-effective means of deploying telephones especially in dense urban areas. The system consists of a remote terminal (RT) deployed at street-corners as shown in Fig. A.8.2.1. The single cabinet with a built-in power plant and battery, serves about 500 subscribers and could be located at a PCO or street-corner kiosk. The subscribers are connected to the RT on copper (either plain old telephone system [POTS] or integrated-switched digital network [ISDN]) or on wireless (the last 500–800 m). The RTs on street corners are connected to a central office mux (COMUX), located at the main exchange premises using a fibre-optic ring as shown in Fig. A.8.2.2. The ring network enables the system to withstand any single failure of fibre link. The COMUX is connected to the main exchange on standard E1 lines using V5.2 protocol and to the radio exchange (DIU) to serve wireless subscribers. As shown in Fig. A.8.2.1, a remote access switch with modems (RASM) connected to the main exchange on E1 would ensure that Internet traffic from different users is statistically multiplexed before entering the backbone telecom network. The

RASM also enables a guaranteed 56 kbps Internet connectivity as the analog portion of the loop is now reduced to 500–800 m. The cost of the POTS-access solution using optiMA is astonishingly low, approximately Rs 7000 per line, including Rs 5000 for copper cost in the last 800 m. The wireless connection would cost around Rs 13,000 and the use of multiline unit providing connections to four subscribers in a building would bring cost down to around Rs 8000 per line.

### corDECT WLL

corDECT WLL, based on the Digital Enhanced Cordless Telecom or DECT standard, has an interesting architecture, especially for its fixed part. The fixed part consists of a DECT Interface Unit (DIU) acting as a 1000-line wireless switching unit providing a V5.2 interface towards the main exchange, and weather-proof Compact Base Stations (CBSs). These are connected to the DIU either on three pairs of copper wire carrying signal as well as power, or fibre/radio using E1 links through a base station distributor (BSD). The subscriber terminal is a wallset (WS), with either a built-in antenna or a rooftop antenna providing a line-of-sight link to a CBS.

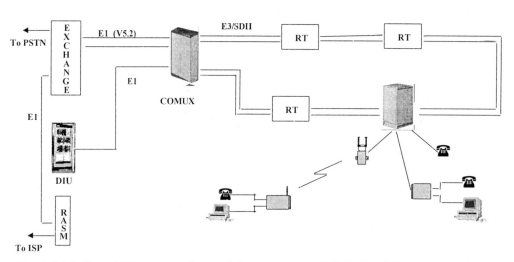

**Fig. A.8.2.2:** Several RTs connected on a ring network to a COMUX and then to an exchange.

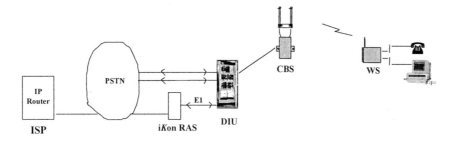

**Fig. A.8.2.3:** corDECT WLL.

The WS has an interface for a standard telephone (or fax machine, modem, or payphone) and an additional RS232 interface for a computer, enabling Internet connection at 35 or 70 Kbps. No modem is required for Internet access, since all links between the WS and DIU are digital, as shown in Fig. A.8.2.3.

Efficient transmission of packet-switched Internet data on a circuit-switched network is achieved by combining a remote access switch (RAS) with the corDECT system. The connection is digital all the way from subscriber to internet service provider (ISP). The Internet call from a WS to a RAS *does not enter the exchange at all*, but terminates in the access network itself. Only the concentrated IP traffic from the RAS to the ISP traverses through the exchange and PSTN (public switched telephone network).

All subsystems are built primarily using digital signal processors (DSPs), with the DIU having nearly 100 DSPs. This soft solution, while cutting down development time and providing design flexibility, also ensures that the cost of the fixed part is no more than 15 per cent of total per-line cost in a fully loaded corDECT system. This allows deployment flexibility for both dense urban and sparse rural areas.

A new operator who wishes to initially deploy lines in a mid-sized town or city in the very first year would use the deployment scenario using a cluster of about 12–15 CBSs (each serving 50–70 subscribers at 0.1 Erlangs each), along with the backhaul microwave equipment, mounted on a 15 m rooftop tower to serve an area of 2–3 km. This deployment uses no cables and can be made operational in two to three months at a total deployed cost of Rs 15,000 per subscriber.

Later, the operator could increase the number of lines by using an optical fibre grid to connect BSDs to the DIUs. A CBS cluster now serves 1000 subscribers within a 700 m to 1 km radius. Here, many subscriber installations may not need line-of-sight links to the CBS. Once again, the total deployed cost of the access solution is under Rs 15,000 per subscriber, including the cost of optical fibre cable and cable laying.

The corDECT system also offers an excellent deployment opportunity for a small town and its surrounding rural areas at a similar cost. The mode of deployment uses DIU at the tower base. To serve about 1000 subscribers, an operator needs a tower (about 35 m high) in the town centre. The microwave link connects the DIU to the nearest trunk exchange. The base stations now serve subscribers within a radius of 10 km using wallsets with rooftop antennas providing line-of-sight links.

Deployment in sparse rural areas is possible using the corDECT relay base station (RBS). A two-hop DECT link is used to provide connection to the subscriber as shown in Fig. A.8.2.4. One link is from the WS to the RBS, which is mounted on a tower typically 25 m in height. The other DECT link is from the RBS to CBS, which is also mounted on a tall tower (say 40 m). Both the RBS and CBS use high-gain directional antennas, making a 25 km link possible. The 5 km maximum link distance due to the guard-time limitation of DECT is overcome by the use of auto ranging and timing adjustment. This technique is used in the RBS to support a 25 km link, and to enhance the CBS range to 10 km. This provides subscriber density as low as 0.5 subscriber/km$^2$ at a total cost of Rs 18,000 per line.

*Direct Internet Access System*

The direct internet access system (DIAS) allows service providers to provide high bandwidth Internet access to residential and corporate subscribers, in addition to voice services, *without any changes to the existing cabling infrastructure*. In contrast to current residential PSTN and ISDN dial-up access, the DIAS provides an *always on Internet access* that is permanently available at the customer's premises. Using Digital Subscriber Looper (DSL) techniques, seamless voice and data connectivity is provided to the customer over the same pair of copper wires.

This system is implemented using the existing cable plant. All that is required is the installation of the IAN (integrated access node) at the exchange and a DSU

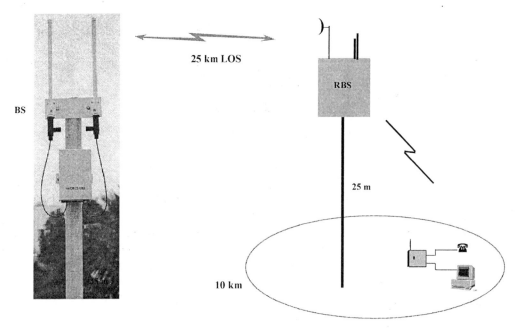

**Fig. A.8.2.4:** Relay base station.

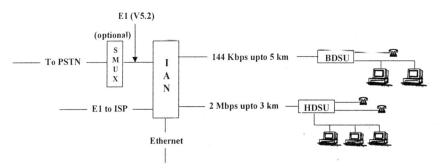

**Fig. A.8.2.5:** Direct internet access system.

(digital subscriber unit) at the customer's premises as shown in Fig. A.8.2.5.

The DIAS has a DSU that combines voice and data packets on a single twisted-pair wire at the subscriber's premises. At the service provider's premises, an IAN separates the voice and data traffic from a number of subscribers and routes it independently to the PSTN and the Internet respectively. The IAN is connected to the PSTN via the E1 V5.2 port, and to the Internet either through two E1 data ports or through the Ethernet port. Alternatively, PSTN connectivity can be achieved through the POTS ports of the exchange with the addition of an optional subscriber multiplexer module, that converts a single E1 line into multiple POTS lines.

The DIAS system provides two types of voice and data services:

• The BDSU (basic digital subscriber unit) is designed for the SOHO (small office home office) and residential Internet user. It provides a permanent Internet connection at a maximum data rate of 144 Kbps, which drops to 80 Kbps when the telephone is in use and transparently goes back to 144 Kbps when the telephone is not in use.

• The HDSU (high bitrate digital subscriber unit), which is designed for corporate subscribers, can provide voice connectivity for up to eight telephones and a permanent data bandwidth of up to 2 Mbps, which drops by 64 Kbps for each telephone call.

*The Internet Tangle and Access Centre*

Before proceeding to describe some of the deployment scenarios using these technologies, let us look at a problem associated with accessing the Internet. The most common way of accessing Internet today from home and office is through the telephone network. One just has to connect a telephone modem and a computer to a telephone line and dial to a modem bank at the ISP as shown in Fig. A.8.2.6. The modem bank connects the user's computer to the ISP router, which is connected to other routers on the Internet. This simple-looking scheme has a few problems.

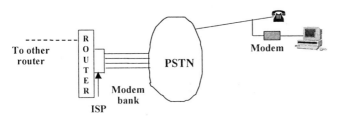

Fig. A.8.2.6: Internet usage today.

Telephone calls are usually for a few minutes each and the average traffic from a telephone is about 0.1 Erlang. The telephone network in most places, but especially in developing countries, is designed to handle just this much traffic. Internet calls, however, are usually of much longer duration, typically lasting 30 to 60 minutes. The traffic that Internet calls inject on the PSTN, especially during busy hours, is much more than 0.1 Erlang per Internet subscriber. Fortunately only a very small fraction of telephone users in developing countries use Internet today. As more and more people get on the Internet, increasing traffic beyond 0.1E/ subscriber, the network would get congested and collapse.

The solution to this Internet tangle lies in recognizing that even though Internet usage is for long hours, the traffic is 'bursty'. With long silence periods between traffic bursts, rarely does average traffic on the Internet exceeds more than 10 to 15 per cent of peak traffic. If one could only statistically multiplex Internet traffic from multiple subscribers, total traffic from the Internet (with peak access rate less than 64 kbps) is unlikely to significantly exceed the voice traffic. The access network framework that therefore emerges is shown in Fig. A.8.2.7.

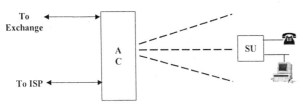

Fig. A.8.2.7: An AC serving subscribers through a SU.

An access centre (AC) placed in an area provides services to the subscribers in the vicinity. The subscribers premises have a subscriber unit (SU) providing a standard telephone interface (RJ-11) and a port (either serial port or Ethernet port) to connect a PC. It is assumed that the access at the subscriber's premises would be a digital access, providing direct digital connectivity to the personal computer (PC) (without an external modem). The interconnection between AC and SU could use any of the multiple mediums—copper, DSL on copper, (Cioffic 1999), digital wireless, fibre (Burpee 1994) coaxial cable, or even power-line (Perkins 1999). The AC could in fact combine the line interfaces for these various mediums. The key task at the AC is to separate the voice from Internet traffic. The voice traffic is to be sent to an exchange usually using one or more standard E1 interfaces with V5.2 signalling. The Internet traffic is statistically multiplexed and transmitted to an ISP on usually one or more E1s.

How large an area and how many subscribers should an AC serve? Ideally the area should be small, as it is the access from AC to SU that may dominate cost. Also, small distances, especially on twisted-pair copper, imply that higher bit-rate DSL can be used and upgradations will be possible in future. However, installation of an AC requires some infrastructure (especially power back-up) and the cost of this infrastructure must be taken into account.

ACs need to be connected to the central-switching centre where the main exchange and routers are located. This interface is best provided by a fibre backhaul. As multiple ACs are to be located in an area, it would be desirable that a fibre loop connect ACs to the central switching centre. However, in order to get quickly started or for interfacing an AC in a rural area, an operator may prefer digital microwave radio. Costs of such Plesiochronous Digital Heirarchy or PDH as well as Synchronous Digital Heirarchy or SDH radios have come down by a factor of about 5 in the last five years due to developments in the area of Microwave Integrated Circuits or MMICs and Digital Signal Processors.

In urban areas, fibre backhaul is the obvious choice. A PDH or SDH fibre-ring network with Drop and Insert as shown in Fig. A.8.2.8 could be used. At each Drop and Insert, multiple E1s are dropped to connect an AC to both the main exchange as well as to the router. The dual ring architecture provides the redundancy and a single point failure does not bring down an AC. The optiMA fibre in the loop system is an ideal choice to provide this connectivity.

*The Last Mile*

As discussed earlier, there are multiple options for the so called last mile—the interconnection between the AC and the subscriber unit. If POTS service is all that is required, and the distance between AC and SU is less than 800 m, the most inexpensive access solution is provided by plain old copper. Wireless access is the

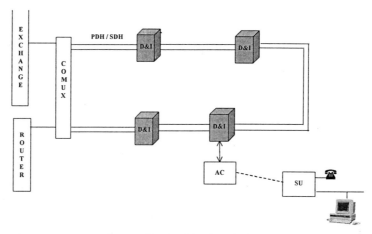

Fig. A.8.2.8: PDH/SDH Fibre backhaul with drop and insert (D&I).

next best solution. The DSL on copper provides high quality service at slightly extra cost. A DSL solution that is becoming popular is the one using basic rate DSL (BDSL) which provides 144/80 Kbps Internet connectivity plus telephone. Of course, High bit rate Digital Subscriber Loop or HDSL and Asynchronous Digital Subscriber Loop or ADSL provides access at much higher bit-rates.

The co-axial feeder could provide excellent access solution with telephone, Internet, as well as video. However, the experiments undertaken in India have not been very encouraging. The problems are the poor quality of cables and connectors used, higher man-made noise in 5 MHz to 45 MHz frequency band, and illegal taps which significantly adds to the noise in the uplink direction. Further experiments are under way. The fibre in the last mile is too expensive currently for most developing countries.

The solution now being widely deployed employs an AC as shown in Fig. A.8.2.9 using access products developed by TeNeT Group. The AC provides POTS, wireless, and DSL services. The wireless subsystem, referred to as corDECT, provides 35 Kbps Internet plus simultaneous voice connectivity on Wallset with Internet Port or WS-IP. A multi-wallset (MWS) provides telephones to four subscribers in a multistorey unit, bringing down the cost significantly. The DSL subsystem, referred to as DIAS, provides 144/80 Kbps Internet connectivity plus voice using BDSU and 2 Mbps Internet connectivity plus 8 telephones using HDSU. In addition, POTS connectivity is provided at low cost.

A complete access network providing 1100 WS-IP subscribers, 400 MWS subscribers, 180 BDSU subscribers, and 480 POTS subscribers at each AC costs around Rs 13,500 per line. The cost includes about 4 km of fibre associated with each AC, SDH COMUX, and Drop and Insert as well as the cost of fibre laying, copper layingm and installation. Further, the cost includes about 25 per cent taxes.

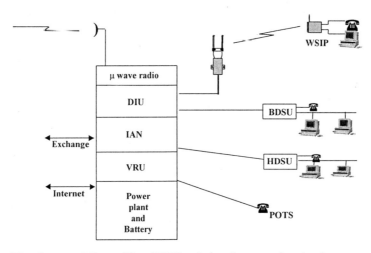

Fig. A.8.2.9: AC providing POTS, wireless internet plus simultaneous Voice connectivity and DSL connections presiding Internet plus voice.

## Deployment Examples

The deployment of Access Centres varies widely depending upon the area that needs to be served. Fig. A.8.2.10 shows a plan to provide sixteen ACs in the city of Chennai in India. Each AC would typically serve an area of 1.6 km by 1.6 km, but wireless connection can be given to a much larger area when required. The SDH fibre connects the ACs to a central switching unit. Each AC will serve about 2000 subscribers. Fig. A.8.2.11 shows deployment in a rural area, the district of Thanjavur, in Tamil Nadu. Here the backhaul links could be either by microwave radio or a fibre. The objective here is to provide at least 35 kbps Internet connectivity in addition to voice in every village. An RBS is used to extend the reach of wireless to 30 km. The cost of serving about 15,000 subscribers spread over the whole district is around Rs 20,000 per line. The network can be set up in about a year.

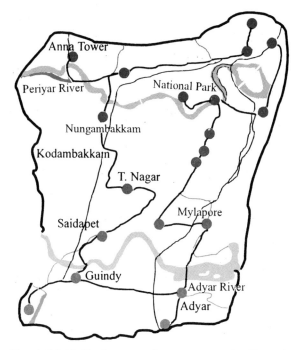

Fig. A.8.2.10: Deployment of access centres in Chennai.

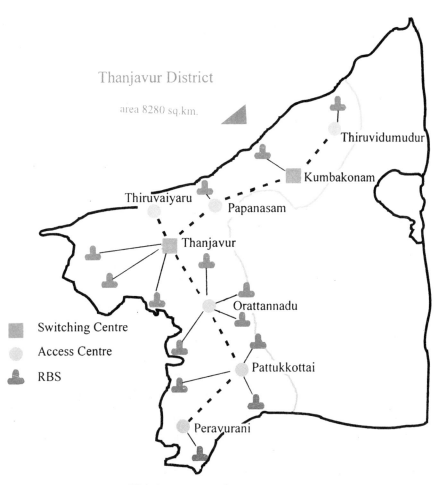

Fig. A.8.2.11: Deployment in a rural area.

TABLE A.8.1.1

Indicators of the Telecom Network in India

| Items | 1986-7* | 1987-8* | 1988-9* | 1989-90* | 1990-1* | 1991-2* | 1992-3* | 1993-4* | 1994-5* | 1995-6* | 1996-7* | 1997-8* |
|---|---|---|---|---|---|---|---|---|---|---|---|---|
| DEL (no. in lakh) | 34.86 | 38.01 (9.02) | 41.67 (9.62) | 45.90 (10.15) | 50.75 (10.57) | 58.10 (14.49) | 67.97 (16.98) | 80.26 (18.08) | 97.95 (22.05) | 119.78 (22.29) | 145.43 (21.41) | 178.02 (22.41) |
| Revenue (Rs lakh)** | 177,039 | 242,407 (36.92) | 340,558 (40.49) | 401,315 (17.84) | 444,743 (10.82) | 496,658 (11.67) | 619,891 (24.81) | 820,518 (32.36) | 1,020,639 (24.39) | 1,251,777 (22.65) | 1,548,003 (23.66) | 1,834,225 (18.49) |
| Revenue per DEL (Rs lakh) | 5078 | 6378 (25.60) | 8174 (28.16) | 8744 (6.98) | 8764 (0.23) | 8548 (-2.46) | 9120 (6.69) | 10,224 (12.10) | 10,420 (1.92) | 10,450 (0.29) | 10,645 (1.86) | 10,304 (-3.20) |
| Expenditure (Rs lakh) | 140,950 | 175,844 (24.76) | 219,048 (24.57) | 253,243 (15.61) | 304,122 (20.09) | 353,558 (16.26) | 415,856 (17.62) | 566,038 (36.11) | 638,249 (20.71) | 658,861 (-3.57) | 906,598 (37.60) | 1,094,791 (20.76) |
| Expenditure per DEL (Rs lakh) | 4043 | 4626 (14.44) | 5257 (13.64) | 5518 (4.96) | 5992 (8.61) | 6085 (1.54) | 6118 (0.54) | 7053 (15.27) | 6975 (-1.10) | 5500 (-21.14) | 6234 (13.34) | 6150 (-1.35) |
| Revenue surplus over expenses (Rs lakh) | 36,089 | 66,563 (84.44) | 121,510 (82.55) | 148,110 (21.89) | 140,621 (-5.06) | 143,100 (1.76) | 204,035 (42.58) | 254,480 (24.72) | 337,390 (32.58) | 592,916 (75.74) | 641,405 (8.18) | 739,434 (15.28) |
| Telephone waiting list (no. in lakh) | 11.25 | 12.87 (14.45) | 14.20 (10.29) | 17.13 (20.70) | 19.61 (14.45) | 22.87 (16.62) | 28.46 (24.44) | 24.97 (-12.27) | 21.53 (-13.77) | 22.77 (5.76) | 28.94 (27.11) | 27.06 (-6.51) |
| Registered demand (no. in lakh) | 46.11 | 50.88 (10.34) | 55.86 (9.79) | 63.03 (12.83) | 70.36 (11.63) | 80.97 (15.08) | 96.43 (19.09) | 105.22 (9.12) | 119.48 (13.55) | 142.56 (19.31) | 174.37 (22.32) | 205.07 (17.61) |
| DELs added annually (no. in lakh) | 3.21 | 3.14 (-1.93) | 3.66 (16.32) | 4.23 (15.67) | 4.85 (14.70) | 7.35 (51.53) | 9.87 (34.22) | 12.29 (24.53) | 17.70 (44.01) | 21.83 (23.35) | 25.64 (17.46) | 32.59 (27.10) |
| Telephone exchange capacity (no. in lakh) | | | | | | 11.86 | 18.27 (54.05) | 22.28 (21.95) | 26.02 (16.79) | 31.15 (19.72) | 35.19 (12.97) |  |
| Telephone exchange capacity per DEL | | | | | | 0.17 | 0.23 (30.46) | 0.23 (-0.08) | 0.22 (-4.50) | 0.21 (-1.39) | 0.20 (-7.21) |  |
| Number of effective trunk calls (no. in lakh) | 2290 | 2090 (-8.73) | 2040 (-2.39) | 2200 (7.84) | 2240 (1.82) | 2060 (-8.04) | 2060 (0.00) | 1620 (-21.36) | 1220 (-24.69) | 764 (-37.38) | 683 (-10.60) | 562 (-17.72) |
| Long-distance circuits ends speech# (equipped capacity) (no. in lakh) | 1.51 | 1.63 (8.22) | 1.80 (10.10) | 1.90 (5.51) | 1.99 (4.69) | 2.09 (5.09) | 2.47 (18.40) | 2.95 (19.18) | 2.97 (0.92) | 3.09 (4.10) | 3.66 (18.13) | 4.17 (14.15) |
| Capital investment during the year | 98,232 | 135,301 (37.74) | 204,747 (51.33) | 259,613 (26.80) | 277,222 (6.78) | 340,026 (22.65) | 460,585 (35.46) | 557,912 (21.13) | 681,386 (22.13) | 821,526 (20.57) | 841,549 (2.44) | 873,357 (3.78) |
| Capital investment per DEL added annually (Rs lakh) | 30,640, | 43,035 (40.45) | 55,988 (30.10) | 61,374 (9.62) | 57,136 (-6.91) | 46,249 (-19.05) | 46,675 (0.92) | 45,399 (-2.73) | 38,501 (-15.20) | 37,631 (-2.26) | 32,819 (-12.79) | 26,797 (18.35) |
| Progressive capital investment (Rs lakh) (at the end of year) | 638,996 | 774,297 (21.17) | 1,002,094 (29.42) | 1,231,275 (22.87) | 1,511,268 (22.74) | 1,851,294 (22.50) | 2,311,879 (24.88) | 2,869,791 (24.13) | 3,551,177 (23.74) | 4,372,603 (23.13) | 521,425 (19.25) | 6,087,609 (16.75) |
| Personnel (at the end of year) (no. in lakh) | 3.49 | 3.50 (0.29) | 3.62 (3.43) | 3.70 (2.21) | 3.75 (1.35) | 3.73 (-0.53) | 3.85 (3.22) | 3.95 (2.60) | 4.19 (6.08) | 4.21 (0.48) | 4.29 (1.90) | 4.25 (-0.93) |
| Expenditure per employee (Rs) | 40,620 | 50,313 (23.86) | 61,530 (22.29) | 69,192 (12.45) | 81,099 (17.21) | 94,788 (16.88) | 108,015 (13.95) | 143,301 (32.67) | 145,622 (1.65) | 163,131 (11.99) | 211,328 (29.54) | 257,598 (21.89) |

(Contd.)

Table A.8.1.2 contd.

| Items | 1986-7* | 1987-8* | 1988-9* | 1989-90* | 1990-1* | 1991-2* | 1992-3* | 1993-4* | 1994-5* | 1995-6* | 1996-7* | 1997-8* |
|---|---|---|---|---|---|---|---|---|---|---|---|---|
| Staff per 1000 DEL (no.) change | 104 | 96 (-7.69) | 87 (-9.38) | 81 (-6.90) | 74 (-8.64) | 64 (-13.51) | 57 (-10.94) | 49 (-14.04) | 43 (-12.24) | 35 (-18.60) | 29 (-17.14) | 24 (-17.24) |
| No. of telephone calls per DEL (no.) | 4956 | 5306 (7.06) | 5090 (-4.07) | 4920 (-3.34) | 4709 (-4.29) | 5267 (11.85) | 5904 (12.09) | 5822 (-1.39) | 5982 (2.75) | 6546 (9.43) | 6415 (-2.00) | 6612 (3.06) |
| No. of faults per month per 100 phones (no.) | 28.50 | 23.40 (-17.89) | 21.20 (-9.40) | 19.30 (-8.96) | 18.50 (-4.15) | 19.00 (2.70) | 18.20 (-4.21) | 18.30 (0.55) | 17.60 (-3.83) | 15.80 (-10.23) | 17.20 (8.86) | 17.40 (1.16) |
| No. of telephones per employee (no.) | 9.60 | 10.40 (8.33) | 11.00 (5.77) | 11.80 (7.27) | 13.50 (914.41) | 15.60 (15.56) | 17.70 (13.46) | 20.30 (14.69) | 23.40 (15.27) | 30.60 (30.77) | 35.90 (17.32) | 43.80 (22.01) |

*Source:* Annual Report 1997–8, Department of Telecommunication, Ministry of Communication, Govt. of India.

* includes MTNL.

** Excluding network charges received from MTNL.

# Includes Analogue and digital long-distance circuits Ends Speech (Equipped Capacity in '000) 188 and 166 respectivly.

Figures in brackets are per cent change over previous year.

TABLE A.8.1.2
Circle-wise Status of DELs and Waiting List 1998–9

| S. no | Name of unit | Equipment capacity | DELs (nos) | Waiting list (nos) | Waiting list as per cent of DELs | Teledensity DELs per 100 persons |
|---|---|---|---|---|---|---|
| 1. | Andaman & Nicobar | 17,440 | 12427 | 410 | 3.3 | 3.12 |
| 2. | Andhra Pradesh | 1,623,695 | 1,412,059 | 150,695 | 10.7 | 1.85 |
| 3. | Assam | 224,289 | 182,790 | 42,271 | 23.1 | 0.69 |
| 4. | Bihar | 555,158 | 449,214 | 81,183 | 18.1 | 0.46 |
| 5. | Gujarat | 1,630,448 | 1,396,625 | 262,939 | 18.8 | 2.91 |
| 6. | Haryana | 572,138 | 472,359 | 120,385 | 25.5 | 2.41 |
| 7. | Himachal Pradesh | 241,606 | 196,663 | 53,610 | 27.3 | 2.03 |
| 8. | Jammu & Kashmir | 127,028 | 101,703 | 37,883 | 37.2 | 1.07 |
| 9. | Karnataka | 1,576,246 | 1,368,436 | 168,631 | 12.3 | 2.65 |
| 10. | Kerala | 1,476,474 | 1,214,891 | 673,711 | 54.2 | 3.82 |
| 11. | Madhya Pradesh | 1,149,310 | 868,057 | 54,338 | 6.3 | 1.12 |
| 12. | Maharashtra | 2,025,156 | 1,697,547 | 260,777 | 15.4 | 2.19 |
| 13. | North East | 174,782 | 132,853 | 17,349 | 13.1 | 1.11 |
| 14. | Orissa | 350,445 | 306,466 | 34,424 | 11.2 | 0.84 |
| 15 | Punjab | 1,143,488 | 981,241 | 217,845 | 22.2 | 4.04 |
| 16 | Rajasthan | 1,022,580 | 841,599 | 147,865 | 17.6 | 1.59 |
| 17 | Tamil Nadu | 1,510,208 | 1,327,670 | 294,490 | 22.2 | 2.33 |
| 18 | UP (East) | 1,029,209 | 786,540 | 31,891 | 4.1 | 2.7 |
| 19 | UP (West) | 903,549 | 740,416 | 90,349 | 12.2 | 1.36 |
| 20 | West Bengal | 428,771 | 363,556 | 121,698 | 33.5 | 0.65 |
| 21 | Calcutta | 924,790 | 825,580 | 6624 | 0.8 | 6.48 |
| 22 | Chennai | 676,735 | 562,635 | 70,279 | 12.5 | 8.95 |
| 23 | MTNL, Delhi | 1,843,346 | 1,578,934 | 0 | 0 | 12.23 |
| 24 | MTNL, Mumbai | 2,199,176 | 1,973,772 | 0 | 0 | 13.56 |
| | Total | 23,426,067 | 19,821,033 | 2,939,647 | | |

*Source:* Annual Report, Department of Telecom Services (1998–9).

Table A.8.1.3
Key Network and Performance Indicators of VSNL

| Description | 1990-1 | 1991-2 | 1992-3 | 1993-4 | 1994-5 | 1995-6 | 1996-7 | 1997-8 | 1998-9 |
|---|---|---|---|---|---|---|---|---|---|
| International telephone circuits (no.) | 2109 | 3331 (57.94) | 4789 (43.77) | 8520 (77.91) | 11,525 (35.27) | 12,873 (11.7) | 14,184 (10.18) | 15,431 (8.79) | 17,922 (16.14) |
| International telecommunications traffic telephone paid minutes (in millions) | 369 | 474 (28.28) | 614 (29.61) | 743 (20.94) | 942 (26.81) | 1148 (21.82) | 1385 (20.68) | 1685 (21.63) | 1935 (14.87) |
| Transit telephone paid minutes (no. in millions) | | | | | 5 | 7 (44.40) | 5 (-21.79) | 8 (51.72) | 9 (13.84) |
| Data transmission (GPSS) minutes (no. in thousands) | 989 | 1977 (99.9) | 3522 (78.15) | 4868 (38.22) | 8673 (78.16) | 7725 (-10.93) | 7982 (3.33) | 8920 (11.75) | 7929 (-11.11) |
| High speed data cicuits (no.) | | 2 | 38 (1800) | 85 (123.68) | 161 (89.41) | 245 (52.17) | 402 (64.08) | 603 (50) | 661 (9.62) |
| Inmarsat traffic telephone (thousand mts) | | | 754 | 1808 (139.77) | 2250 (24.4) | 2597 (15.44) | 3307 (27.33) | 2660 (-19.56) | 1961 (-26.28) |
| Internet access customers (no.) | | | | | | 4151 | 28,042 (575.55) | 90,042 (221.1) | 213,045 (136.61) |
| Leased voice/data circuits (no.) | 78 | 98 (25.64) | 91 (-7.14) | 81 (-10.99) | 72 (-11.11) | 54 (-25.0) | 44 (-18.52) | 35 (-20.45) | 25 (-28.57) |
| Leased 64 Kbps data circuits (no.) | 0 | 2 | 38 | 85 | 161 | 245 | 402 | 603 | 661 |
| Satellite circuits (no.) | 1430 | 2465 (72.38) | 3749 (52.09) | 6937 (85.04) | 7702 (11.03) | 8573 (11.31) | 9220 (7.55) | 9266 (0.50) | 10,609 (14.49) |
| Cable circuits (no.) | 679 | 866 (27.54) | 1040 (20.09) | 1583 (52.21) | 3781 (138.85) | 4300 (13.73) | 4964 (15.44) | 6165 (24.19) | 7313 (18.62) |
| International automatic services ISD telephone service to countries (no. of countries) | 210 | 212 (0.95) | 233 (9.91) | 237 (1.72) | 236 (-0.42) | 236 | 236 | 236 | 236 |
| *Revenue* | | | | | | | | | |
| Total revneue (Rs million) | 9712 | 14,830 (52.7) | 20,270 (36.68) | 29,284 (44.47) | 36,068 (23.17) | 44,731 (24.02) | 52,853 (18.16) | 64,361 (21.77) | 71,756 (11.49) |
| Fixed assets (Rs million) | 2706 | 3658 (35.18) | 6217 (69.96) | 8141 (30.95) | 10,283 (26.31) | 11,887 (15.6) | 15,273 (28.48) | | |
| Forex inflow (FI) (Rs million) | | | | 16,048 | 20,936 (30.46) | 28,563 (36.43) | | | |
| Forex outflow (Rs million) | | | | 11,240 | 11,920 (6.05) | 13,251 (11.17) | | | |
| Net forex earnings (Rs million) | | 1754 | 2819 (60.68) | 4808 (70.56) | 9016 (87.52) | 15,312 (69.83) | 18,939 (23.69) | 23,978 (26.61) | |

Figures in brackets are per cent change over previous year.

TABLE A.8.2.4
Telecom Companies in Top Emerging Market c. 1998

| Company | Market Value (US $ million) | P/E ratio | Sales ($ million) | Profit US ($ million) | Assets US ($ million) | ROE (per cent) |
|---|---|---|---|---|---|---|
| Telebras | 20,740 | 15 | 8635 | 811 | 35753 | 5.1 |
| Telekom Malaysia | 18,209 | 29 | 2102 | 629 | 5897 | 16.4 |
| Telefonos de Mexico | 15,023 | 9 | 5610 | 1249 | 12,523 | 17.3 |
| PT Telekomunikasi Indonesia | 14,205 | 37 | 2189 | 389 | 503 | 12.2 |
| Telecommunicacoes de Sao Paulo (Telesp) | 11,237 | 26 | 2466 | 302 | 11,333 | 5 |
| Hellenic Telecom-Indosat | 7022 | 17 | 1999 | 393 | NA | 18.7 |
| Telefonica de Argentina | 6910 | 16 | 2733 | 458 | 5375 | 12.7 |
| Pakistan Telecom | 5936 | 12 | 950 | 484 | NA | 29.2 |
| Korea Mobile Telecom | 5521 | 24 | 1678 | 230 | 3525 | 25.5 |
| Telecomasia | 4873 | 130 | 189 | 51 | 2221 | 2.7 |
| Compania Peruana de Telefonos | 4627 | 15 | 991 | 292 | 1397 | 23.8 |
| Telecom Argentina Stet-France Telecom | 4589 | 16 | 1933 | 307 | 4651 | 12.5 |
| Portugal Telecom | 4579 | 20 | 2574 | 230 | 5618 | 10.2 |
| Telecommunicaciones de Chile(CTC) | 4502 | 16 | 1033 | 267 | 3646 | 16.2 |
| Advanced Info Service | 3937 | 30 | 393 | 118 | 606 | 40.1 |
| Mahanagar Telephone Nigam | 3730 | 19 | 851 | 165 | NA | 31.9 |
| Indo Sat | 3563 | 18 | 448 | 197 | 698 | 24.6 |
| VSNL | 3369 | 32 | 1016 | 85 | NA | 38.5 |
| United Telecommunication | 3308 | 30 | 541 | 111 | 763 | 15.1 |

*Source:* VSNL, Annual Report, 1999.

TABLE A.8.1.5
Top Ten Net Settlement Countries, as Indicated by Estimated
Net Settlements to Rest of the World 1998

| Country | Outgoing traffic 1998 (million minutes) | Incoming traffic 1998 (million minutes) | Imbalance (outgoing minus incoming) | Imbalance as a per cent of total (incoming and outgoing) | US settlement rate 1998 (US cents per minute) | Estimated net settlement 1998 (US $ in million) |
|---|---|---|---|---|---|---|
| United States | 24,300 | 7146 | 17,154.3 | 54.6 | 26 | −5309.5 |
| Canada | 4286 | 4635 | −349 | −3.9 | 10 | −2333.1 |
| UAE | 874.8 | 280 | 594.8 | 51.5 | 100 | −1211 |
| Saudi Arabia | 932.6 | 445 | 487.6 | 35.4 | 103.5 | −500 |
| United Kingdom | 8225 | 6400 | 1825 | 12.5 | 7 | −235 |
| Switzerland | 1901 | 1779 | 122 | 3.3 | 14 | −190 |
| Qatar | 119.2 | 71.5 | 47.6 | 25.0 | 100 | −115.7 |
| Israel | 661 | 424 | 237 | 21.8 | 29.5 | −70 |
| Singapore | 1235 | 1090 | 145 | 6.2 | 26 | −40 |
| Austria | 1250 | 1011 | 239 | 10.6 | 0 | −30 |

Figures shown in italics are estimated. All figures are as reported by the country concerned.
*Source:* ITU/TeleGeography Inc. 'Direction of Traffic Database'. FCC (Federal Communication Commission) quoted in Kelly T. and Woodall M. 'Telecom traffic Indicators', Telecommunication Policy, vol. 24, Table 1, p. 156.

TABLE A.8.1.6
Top Ten Net Settlement Surplus Countries, as Measured by Estimated
Net Settlements to Rest of the World 1998

| Country | Outgoing traffic 1998 (million minutes) | Incoming traffic 1998 (million minutes) | Imbalance (out going minus incoming) | Imbalance as a per cent of total (incoming and outgoing) | US settlement rate 1998 (US cents per minute) | Estimated net settlement 1998 (US $ million) |
|---|---|---|---|---|---|---|
| India | 436.2 | 1498.8 | −1062.6 | −54.9 | 64 | 680 |
| Mexico | 1307.6 | 3060.5 | −1752.9 | −40.1 | 35 | 620 |
| Philippines | 286.4 | 681.2 | −394.8 | −40.8 | 36.5 | 505 |
| China | 1711.5 | 2400 | −688.5 | −16.7 | 70 | 480 |
| Pakistan | 87.5 | 640 | −552.5 | −75.9 | 60 | 330 |
| Vietnam | 56 | 334 | −278 | −71.3 | 55 | 240 |
| Lebanon | ·70 | 300 | −230 | −62.2 | 85 | 201.3 |
| Egypt | 127.3 | 475.3 | −348 | −57.7 | 57.5 | 150 |
| Poland | 602.4 | 1144.4 | −542 | −31.0 | 65 | 145 |
| Dominican Rep. | 157.5 | 730.5 | −573 | −64.5 | 10.5 | 130 |

See Notes to Appendix Table A.8.1.5.

TABLE A.8.1.7
Call Revenue Contribution by Different
Subscriber Categories

| (A) Number of metred calls made every two months | (B) Proportion of total DELs in the category mentioned in A (%) | Contribution of DELs in B to call revenue (%) |
|---|---|---|
| More than 10,000 | 2.7 | 46.1 |
| 5001–10,000 | 2.5 | 9.8 |
| 2001–5000 | 7.9 | 13.4 |
| 001–2000 | 14.0 | 11.6 |
| 500-1000 | 21.3 | 10.0 |
| 0–500 | 51.0 | 8.1 |

*Source:* DoT, Singh, H. V.,'Trade in Services: Opportunities and Constraints', Table 17, p. 19.

# 9 | THE SPATIAL CONTEXT

## 9.1 FINANCES AND FUNCTIONING OF URBAN LOCAL BODIES: A SITUATION REPORT

*M. P. Mathur*

### INTRODUCTION

The urban population of India has rapidly increased in recent years. In 1961 about 79 million persons lived in urban areas of the country; by 1991, their number had gone up to over 217 million, an increase of over 250 per cent in the last three decades. Almost all population projections indicate that India has entered the twenty-first century with an urban population of about 300 million, which will increase to over 400 million by the year 2011 and 553 million by the year 2021 (see Table 9.1.1).[1]

Studies conducted by the National Institute of Urban Affairs (NIUA) suggest that most urban areas in the country have in recent years witnessed a deterioration in the standard and quality of public life. In 1995, for which countrywide data are available, approximately 15 per cent of India's total urban population had no access to safe drinking water and approximately 50 per cent had no access to basic sanitation (NIUA 2000). The position with respect to the collection and disposal of garbage was worse. The coverage was very low. About 30–40 per cent of garbage was left on the city streets uncollected.

TABLE 9.1.1
Urbanization Trends in India 1951–2021

| Census year | Total population (million) | Urban population (million) | Percentage of urban population to total population | Decadal urban growth rate (per cent) | Annual compound growth rate | |
|---|---|---|---|---|---|---|
| | | | | | Total | Urban |
| 1951 | 361.08 | 62.44 | 17.29 | – | – | – |
| 1961 | 439.23 | 78.93 | 17.97 | 26.41 | 1.98 | 2.37 |
| 1971 | 548.15 | 109.11 | 19.91 | 38.24 | 2.24 | 3.29 |
| 1981 | 683.32 | 159.46 | 23.34 | 46.15 | 2.23 | 3.87 |
| 1991 | 846.30 | 217.61 | 25.71 | 36.47 | 2.16 | 3.16 |
| 2001* | 1048.15 | 296.97 | 28.33 | 36.47 | 2.16 | 3.16 |
| 2011* | 1298.15 | 405.26 | 31.22 | 36.47 | 2.16 | 3.16 |
| 2021* | 1607.77 | 553.04 | 34.40 | 36.47 | 2.16 | 3.16 |

* Projected figures.
*Source:* NIUA (2000).

[1] The projections are based on an assumed total population growth rate of 2.16 per cent and urban population growth of 3.16 per cent. The total population growth rate could decline sharply especially after 2011, if the present trends are any indication (ed.).

Municipal bodies (urban local bodies [ULBs]) which are statutorily responsible for provision and maintenance of basic infrastructure and services in cities and towns are under fiscal stress. To even operate and maintain existing services, let alone augment them, would be difficult. There has been little or no increase in their revenue base; user charges continue to be low or non-existent. Faced with such a situation the ULBs, barring a few exceptions, are becoming increasingly dependent on the higher levels of government for their operation and maintenance requirements. What is worse, many ULBs have accumulated 'large' debts and face serious problems in servicing them.

According to the Planning Commission's estimates, the share of municipal expenditure in total public sector expenditure declined from nearly 8 per cent in 1960–1 to 4.5 per cent in 1977–8 and was estimated to be roughly 3 per cent in 1986–7 and 2 per cent in 1991–2 (Planning Commisson 1983, NIUA 1989, National Institute of Public Finance and Policy 1995). A study conducted by the NIPFP revealed that the finances of municipal bodies are in a mess; a majority of them are not able to raise adequate resources to meet increasing expenditure on services. As indicated in Table 9.1.2, municipal bodies raised approximately only Rs 3900 crore on their own during the year 1991–2, which constituted a mere 4.7 per cent of revenue raised by the central government and 8 per cent raised by state governments. This amount is estimated to be only 0.6 per cent of the country's gross domestic product (GDP). In per capita terms, own sources of funds of municipal bodies works out to be nearly Rs 205 per capita as against Rs 987 per capita for the centre and Rs 574 for the states. Although urban centres contribute nearly 60 per cent of the country's GDP, the structure of taxes is such that municipal bodies have not benefited from the economic activities that take place within their own jurisdictions, and thus remain peripheral to the Indian economy (NIPFP 1995).

TABLE 9.1.2
Revenues of the Centre, States, and Municipalities 1991–2

| Unit | Revenues (Rs crores) | Per capita (Rs) |
|---|---|---|
| Centre | 83,320 | 987 |
| States | 48,660 | 574 |
| Municipalities | 3900 | 205 |

*Source:* Finances of State Governments, RBI Bulletin, February 1994, as quoted in NIPFP (1995).

Besides the restriction to a small resource base, ineffective local governance, inefficient management practices, poor planning process, lack of periodical revision of municipal tax rates/user charges, and poor information system and records management are some of the basic weaknesses in the present municipal administration. Many municipalities in India, particularly those of small- and medium-sized cities are poorly staffed, staff responsibilities are unclear and often fragmented, and their capabilities and motivation to deal with the increasingly complex urban needs are limited.

As per certain conservative estimates, the municipal bodies of India would require an additional investment in basic infrastructure and services of about Rs 74,000 crore if the deficiencies in the existing level of services are to be eliminated and all sections of urban population are to be provided basic access by 2020. In addition, approximately Rs 18,000 crore annually would be needed to operate and maintain these services at the barest minimum levels. At the present rate of municipal taxation, user charges, and efficiency, it is expected that only two-thirds of the total operation and maintenance (O&M) requirements will be generated by the municipalities themselves (Mathur 1999a).

A number of committees and commissions have looked into the finances of municipalities with a view to improve them. The Constitutional (74th) Amendment Act of 1994 (CAA74) is the culmination of a prolonged debate in post-independent India for a democratic system of municipal government in the country. In constitutionally recognizing municipal governments a significant beginning has been made. The Act has introduced some fundamental changes in the system of local governance. It has provided for the regular and fair conduct of elections to municipalities by a statutorily constituted State Election Commission. A framework is provided for the assignment of appropriate civic functions to urban local bodies through the Twelfth Schedule of the Constitution. Besides the traditional core functions, municipalities are now expected to play a crucial role in preparation and implementation of local development plans and social justice programmes. The states are required to constitute finance commissions once every five years, to recommend measures to improve the financial health of municipal bodies. The CAA74 has provided for the constitution of ward committees in municipalities with a population of three lakh or more (with the scope for such committees in smaller cities too), in order to ensure people's participation in civic affairs. The states are also required to constitute metropolitan planning committees (MPCs) and district planning committees (DPCs), for the preparation and consolidation of development plans for their respective territories.

## ULBs

According to Census of India 1991, there are 3255 ULBs in the country,[2] classified into four major categories of municipal corporations, municipalities (municipal council, municipal board, municipal committee), town area committees, and notified area committees (see Table 9.1.3). The municipal corporations and municipalities are fully representative bodies, while the notified area committees and town area committees are either fully or partially nominated bodies. As per CAA74, the latter two categories of towns are to be designated as municipalities or nagar panchayats with elected bodies. Until amendments in state municipal legislations, which were mostly made in 1994, municipal authorities were organized on the basis of the *ultra vires* principle and the state governments were free to extend or control the

TABLE 9.1.3
ULBs in India 1991*

| State/Union Territory | Municipal corporation | Municipal council | Municipal committee/city committee | Municipal board | Municipality | Town committee/township/town area committee | Town/nagar panchayat | Notified area | Total |
|---|---|---|---|---|---|---|---|---|---|
| Andhra Pradesh | 3 | – | – | – | 109 | – | 141 | 2 | 255 |
| Assam | 1 | – | – | 24 | – | 49 | – | – | 74 |
| Bihar | 6 | – | – | – | 70 | – | – | 92 | 168 |
| Goa | – | 13 | – | – | – | – | – | – | 13 |
| Gujarat | 6 | – | – | – | 62 | – | 100 | 10 | 178 |
| Haryana | – | – | 81 | – | – | – | – | – | 81 |
| Himachal Pradesh | 1 | – | 19 | – | – | – | – | 30 | 50 |
| Karnataka | 6 | – | 20 | – | – | 136 | – | 14 | 176 |
| Kerala | 3 | – | – | – | 61 | 2 | – | – | 66 |
| Madhya Pradesh | – | – | 17 | – | 357 | – | – | 7 | 381 |
| Maharashtra | 11 | – | – | – | 227 | – | – | – | 238 |
| Orissa | – | – | – | – | 30 | – | – | 72 | 102 |
| Punjab | 3 | – | 95 | – | – | – | – | 11 | 109 |
| Rajasthan | – | 19 | – | – | 168 | – | – | 5 | 192 |
| Tamil Nadu | 3 | – | – | – | 98 | 8 | 212 | – | 321 |
| Uttar Pradesh | 8 | – | – | 228 | – | 418 | – | 33 | 687 |
| West Bengal | 3 | – | – | – | 95 | – | – | 10 | 108 |
| Delhi | 1 | – | 1 | – | – | – | – | – | 2 |
| Andaman & Nicobar Islands | – | – | – | 1 | – | – | – | – | 1 |
| Chandigarh | – | – | – | – | – | – | – | 1 | 1 |
| Pondicherry | – | – | – | – | 4 | – | – | · | 4 |
| Manipur | – | – | – | – | 7 | – | – | 21 | 28 |
| Meghalaya | – | – | – | – | 1 | – | – | – | 1 |
| Sikkim | – | – | – | · | – | 7 | – | – | 7 |
| Tripura | – | – | – | · | 1 | – | – | 11 | 12 |
| Total | 55 | 32 | 233 | 253 | 1290 | 620 | 453 | 319 | 3255 |

*Source:* NIUA (1998).

* Excluding cantonment boards (57) under the Ministry of Defence, established by a separate Act of Parliament.

[2] According to Eleventh Finance Commission Report (2000), the number of ULBs in India is reported to be 3682. Their number might have increased due to reclassification of ULBs in the Constitution Amendment Act of 1992.

functional sphere through executive decisions without an amendment to the legislative provisions.

Most states have amended their municipal laws in conformity with the CAA74. However, variations are found in the definitions of small and large urban areas, as well as transitional areas.[3]

Among all urban local governments, municipal corporations are the most important as they have greater degree of fiscal autonomy, and most urban functions are their responsibility functions. Their local governments have larger populations, more diversified economic bases, and deal with the state governments directly and from positions of much countervailing power. On the other hand, municipalities have less autonomy, smaller jurisdictions, and have to deal with state governments through the Directorate of Municipalities or the collector of a district. These local bodies are subject to detailed 'supervisory control and guidance' by state governments.

## FUNCTIONAL DOMAIN OF ULBs

Municipal bodies are vested with a long list of functions delegated to them by the state governments under the

[3] States like Tamil Nadu have used the income criterion, others only population, and still others additional criterion such as density and percentage of non-agricultural employment to define and identify urban areas. The amended Municipal Act of Andhra Pradesh provides for all three types of municipal bodies, viz. nagar panchayats, municipalities, and municipal corporations. In addition to the population criterion, the Andhra Act uses density of population, percentage of employment in non-agricultural activities, revenue of local body, and economic importance of a city or town for constituting different types of urban local governments. The Andhra Act has further stated that all the district headquarters should be classified as not lower than first grade municipalities while the nagar panchayats should be treated as equivalent to third grade municipalities irrespective of annual income or such other indicators. It may be mentioned that the earlier classification of municipalities in Andhra was largely based upon the income criterion and is still being continued in the state. The amended State Municipal Law also provides for a township committee for specific industrial areas.

Amended municipal laws of Maharashtra have provided classification of municipalities both on the basis of population as well as percentage of employment in non-agricultural activities. According to the Act, municipal corporations are to be constituted in the larger urban areas, only if they have a population of not less than 3 lakh. In case of municipal councils, a minimum of 25,000 population and 35 per cent employment in non-agricultural activities is necessary. For nagar panchayats, the Maharashtra Act No. XLI of 1994 has provided that no area shall be specified as a 'transitional area' unless it has a population of not less than 10,000 and not more than 25,000, is not more than 25 km away from the territorial limits of any municipal corporation or 'A' class municipal council, and the percentage of employment in non-agricultural activities is not less than 25 per cent. Besides the above types of urban local governments, the Maharashtra Act also contains provisions for empowering the state government to notify an industrial area developed by the Maharashtra Industrial Development Corporation or the area of a cooperative industrial estate as an 'industrial township' (Mathur 1999b).

municipal legislation.[4] These functions broadly relate to public health, welfare, regulatory functions, public safety, public works, and development activities. Public health includes water supply, sewerage and sanitation, eradication of communicable diseases, etc.; welfare includes public facilities such as education and recreation; regulatory functions relate to prescribing and enforcing building bye-laws, encroachments on public land, registration of births and deaths, etc.; public safety includes fire protection, street lighting, etc.; public works includes measures such as construction and maintenance of inner city roads; and development functions related to town planning and development of commercial markets. In addition to the legally assigned functions, the sectoral departments of state governments often assign to municipalities unilaterally, and on agency basis, various functions such as family planning, nutrition, slum improvement, and disease and epidemic control.

The Twelfth Schedule of the Constitution (Article 243 W) provides an illustrative list of eighteen functions that may be entrusted to the municipalities. Besides the traditional core functions of municipalities, it also includes development functions like planning for economic development and social justice, urban poverty alleviation programmes, and promotion of cultural, educational, and aesthetic aspects. However, conformity legislations enacted by state governments indicate wide variations in this regard.[5] There is a lot of difference in the assignment of obligatory and discretionary functions to the municipal bodies among states. Whereas functions like planning for the social and economic development, urban forestry and protection of the environment, and promotion of ecological aspects are obligatory functions for the municipalities of Maharashtra, in Karnataka these are discretionary functions (NIPFP 2000).

However, none of the state governments has paid serious attention to the requisite change in the institutional arrangements for urban infrastructure and the role of municipal governments vis-à-vis those of parastatal agencies. Municipal governments in many states are assisted by parastatal agencies, operating either at state or city level to carry out various functions including water supply and sanitation. Parastatal agencies

[4] See section 9.4 of this report.
[5] Whereas Bihar, Gujarat, Himachal Pradesh, Haryana, Manipur, Punjab, and Rajasthan have included all the functions as enlisted in the Twelfth Schedule in their amended state municipal laws, Andhra Pradesh has not made any changes in the existing list of municipal functions. Karnataka, Kerala, Madhya Pradesh, Maharashtra, Orissa, Tamil Nadu, Uttar Pradesh, and West Bengal have amended their municipal laws to add some of these additional functions.

like the Public Health Engineering Department, Water Supply and Sewerage Boards, City Improvement Trusts, Urban Development Authorities usually undertake land acquisition and development works, and take up remunerative projects such as building market spaces and commercial complexes. Municipal bodies in most cases have been left only with the functions of garbage collection/disposal, street lighting, maintenance of inner city roads, and registration of births and deaths!

In terms of the theory of fiscal federalism, functions whose benefits are largely confined to municipal jurisdictions and which are subject to heterogeneous preferences are suitable for municipalities. These may be termed the 'essentially municipal' functions. Services with large spillover effects, distributional and stabilization attributes, and services providing uniform benefits and not typically spatially localized need to be entrusted to higher levels of government. Similarly, functions that involve substantial economies of scale or are of national interest may not be assigned to small local bodies. For valid reasons, certain functions of higher authorities are appropriate for entrustment to the municipalities—as under principal–agent contracts. These may be called 'agency' functions that need to be financed by inter-governmental revenues. Thus instead of continuing the traditional distinction between obligatory and 'discretionary' functions municipal responsibilities may be grouped into 'essential municipal', 'joint or shared', and 'agency' functions. The assignment of functions to municipal corporations, municipalities, and nagar panchayats that follows from such a

## FISCAL DOMAIN OF ULBS

The fiscal domain of municipal governments in India consists of a large array of tax and non-tax sources of revenue. They also receive funds from state governments in the form of grants-in-aid as also shares in taxes collected by state governments. The various sources of tax, non-tax, and transfer revenues of ULBs are given in Table 9.1.4.

There is little variation among states in the matter of taxation powers granted to ULBs. However, significant variation exists across states in their application. Taxes on the entry of goods (octroi), which are among the most buoyant and elastic of local taxes, are currently levied only in six states, namely Gujarat, Haryana, Maharashtra, Manipur, Orissa, and Punjab. The inclusion or exclusion of this tax has an overwhelming impact on the revenue base of municipalities.[6] Many municipalities in Rajasthan do not levy property taxes. The Punjab government has recently abolished the levy of property taxes on domestic properties. Similarly, there are inter-state differences with respect to taxes on entertainment and taxes on professions, trades, callings, and employment. The differences in tax jurisdiction, the degree of control exercised by state governments in terms of the fixation of tax base, rates, and exemptions have a direct impact on the finances of municipalities.

The revenue income of ULBs is presented in Table 9.1.5. It shows that 'own sources' of municipal income which comprise tax and non-tax revenue form an important part of the total revenue receipts of municipal

Table 9.1.4
Major Sources of Income for Municipal Bodies in India

| Sources | Major Components |
| --- | --- |
| *Internal/own sources* | |
| Tax revenue | Property taxes; tax on vehicles, animals, trade, and callings and professions; theater tax/show tax; tax on advertisements, boats, etc. |
| Non-tax revenue | Rents from municipal assets; income from municipal undertakings; user charges; fee and fines; income from municipal investments; etc. |
| *External sources* | |
| Grants-in-aid | General purpose; specific purpose; grants in lieu of taxes |
| Shared taxes | Entertainment tax; motor vehicle tax; land revenue; stamp duties; profession tax; etc. |

guiding principle would mean that much of the current responsibilities of parastatals should devolve on to municipalities or these bodies should be brought under their control (see Mohanty 1995). The functional domain of municipalities has direct impact on the volume and structure of municipal finance.

[6] Notwithstanding the importance of octroi for municipal finance, a large number of committees and commissions have recommended its abolition, for example, committees set up by the Government of Maharashtra (1987) and Rajasthan (1992). In their opinion, it is an obnoxious, vexatious, and wasteful tax and needs to be replaced with a suitable alternative. In 1993, the All India Motor Transport Congress (AIMTC) went on a

bodies. This is particularly so in the octroi levying states such as Gujarat (87.5 per cent), Haryana (80.5 per cent), Maharashtra (95.4 per cent), Punjab (89 per cent), and Manipur (98.3 per cent).

From the viewpoint of financial autonomy, it is desirable that own sources should be the major source of revenue for the ULBs and dependency on higher levels of governments as low as possible. One danger of liberal provisions of grants-in-aid is that the efforts of municipal bodies to mobilize their own resources get slackened. Many of the state finance commissions (SFCs) have recommended performance-based grants-in-aid system to the ULBs. The Uttar Pradesh State Finance Commission, for instance, has suggested that the ULBs should fulfil the responsibilities cast on them, by improving their own resources. It has recommended that whereas 7 per cent of the net proceeds of state taxes

may be passed on to the ULBs during 1996–7, from 1997–8 onwards, when the devolution amount grows with growth in state revenues, initially only 90 per cent of their share may be passed on to the ULBs, the remaining 10 per cent given to them at year end on the basis of performance indicators.

The Himachal Pradesh State Finance Commission has recommended that in case local governments do not collect the statutory levies, the resource transfers from the state to the local body concerned should not be released. The Punjab State Finance Commission has suggested an incentive grant to municipalities for improving their own resources.

## COMPOSITION OF OWN REVENUES

Own sources consist of tax and non-tax sources. Data presented in Table 9.1.5 indicate that in a majority of

TABLE 9.1.5
Source of Municipal Revenues 1997–8

| States | Total revenue (Rs crore) | Own sources (per cent) | | | Transfers (external sources) (per cent) | | | |
|---|---|---|---|---|---|---|---|---|
| | | Tax | Non-tax | Both | Shared taxes | Grants | Others | All |
| Andhra Pradesh | 13,800.1 | 36.37 | 14.80 | 51.17 | 33.56 | 13.03 | 2.25 | 48.84 |
| Assam | 4721.4 | 23.24 | 35.84 | 59.08 | – | 23.37 | 17.55 | 40.92 |
| Bihar | 10,313.3 | 36.86 | 15.91 | 52.77 | 2.99 | 40.31 | 3.93 | 47.23 |
| Gujarat | 10,921.0 | 79.74 | 7.71 | 87.45 | 0.18 | 11.10 | 1.27 | 12.55 |
| Haryana | 5716.8 | 42.80 | 37.71 | 80.51 | 13.44 | 3.95 | 2.09 | 19.48 |
| Karnataka | 11,417.3 | 18.12 | 25.06 | 43.18 | 5.67 | 43.62 | 7.53 | 56.82 |
| Kerala | 7629.6 | 44.69 | 25.63 | 70.32 | 20.65 | 4.74 | 4.29 | 29.68 |
| Madhya Pradesh | 11,472.8 | 22.61 | 24.73 | 47.34 | 11.88 | 39.90 | 0.88 | 52.66 |
| Maharashtra | 21,721.1 | 65.44 | 29.96 | 95.40 | 0.53 | 3.84 | 0.23 | 4.60 |
| Orissa | 5046.7 | 46.92 | 20.20 | 67.12 | 0.93 | 28.59 | 3.36 | 32.88 |
| Punjab | 7074.2 | 69.60 | 19.42 | 89.02 | 6.14 | 3.81 | 1.03 | 10.98 |
| Rajasthan | 8713.8 | 62.90 | 26.90 | 89.80 | 0.17 | 9.30 | 0.74 | 10.21 |
| Tamil Nadu | 13,418.4 | 21.21 | 23.13 | 44.34 | 21.93 | 29.49 | 4.24 | 55.66 |
| Uttar Pradesh | 17,478.1 | 13.50 | 5.95 | 19.44 | 0.36 | 79.14 | 1.06 | 80.56 |
| West Bengal | 9764.41 | 36.51 | 22.82 | 59.33 | 5.05 | 30.53 | 5.10 | 40.68 |
| Himachal Pradesh | 2117.6 | 15.27 | 10.59 | 25.86 | – | 72.04 | 2.09 | 74.13 |
| Manipur | 906.9 | 90.42 | 7.87 | 98.29 | 0.20 | 0.15 | 1.35 | 1.70 |
| Meghalaya | 947.5 | 37.66 | 8.62 | 46.27 | – | 40.09 | 13.63 | 53.72 |
| Tripura | 1130.3 | 27.31 | 15.61 | 42.92 | – | 33.74 | 23.34 | 57.08 |
| All | 163,413.49 | 56.40 | 26.38 | 82.78 | 4.05 | 11.99 | 1.19 | 17.23 |

*Source:* NIPFP (2000).

countrywide strike against imposition of octroi and submitted a memorandum to the Government of India for its abolition in states where it was levied. As a follow up action, the Government of India constituted a committee of Chief Ministers under the chairmanship of Jyoti Basu, Chief Minister of West Bengal, to examine issues related to octroi. The committee submitted its report in 1994, and suggested various measures to streamline the system of levy, assessment, and collection of octroi. The committee, however, did not favour the abolition of octroi in the states where it was levied (NIUA 1999).

states, the share of tax revenues is higher than that of non-tax revenues. It varies from nearly 99 per cent in Manipur (octroi state) to a little over 39 per cent in Assam (non-octroi state).

Among the various taxes, property tax (PT) is the most common and stable source of income for the majority of municipalities in the country. Table 9.1.6 brings out the tax structure of municipalities in India based on the latest available data and shows that the

TABLE 9.1.6
Composition of Municipal Taxes 1992–3

| States | Tax revenues (Rs crore) | % share to tax revenue | | | | | | | | | |
|---|---|---|---|---|---|---|---|---|---|---|---|
| | | Pro-perty tax | Adver-tisement tax | Tax on vehicles, boats, and animals | Better-ment levies | Pro-fession tax | Trade and callings | Entertain-ment tax | Octroi | Show tax | Others |
| Andhra Pradesh | 81.13 | 88.51 | 1.05 | 0.54 | 6.82 | – | – | – | – | – | 3.08 |
| Assam | 2.67 | 63.54 | 0.23 | 2.14 | 6.00 | 8.21 | 8.18 | 0.04 | – | – | 11.63 |
| Kerala | 42.90 | 53.01 | 0.66 | – | Neg. | 6.47 | 0.30 | 39.12 | – | 0.17 | 0.25 |
| West Bengal | 12.82 | 94.10 | 0.13 | 0.80 | 2.00 | – | – | – | – | – | 2.98 |
| Gujarat | 428.09 | 24.84 | – | 0.32 | – | – | – | 0.10 | 74.05 | – | 0.69 |
| Maharashtra | 982.87 | 21.59 | 0.01 | 0.33 | 0.97 | Neg. | 0.01 | 0.07 | 76.01 | – | 0.30 |
| Punjab | 105.63 | 12.06 | 0.38 | 0.05 | 0.38 | – | 0.02 | 0.29 | 86.06 | – | 0.75 |

*Source:* NIUA (1997a).

annual rateable values increased by merely 2 per cent during the period. As current data on composition of municipal taxes are not available, the most recent data on the subject have been used for analysis purpose.

Though PT is the most important tax source of revenue, particularly for the municipal bodies of non-octroi states, its yield in terms of per capita value is not very significant. This tax is not considered to be a buoyant source of revenue for municipalities. In Kerala state data on property taxes for three years, that is 1991–2 to 1993–4, show that the average per capita receipts on constant prices from PT have declined from Rs 28.33 in 1991–2 to Rs 26.37 in 1993–4 (Mathur 1999b). In the Municipal Corporation of Greater Mumbai despite a phenomenal increase in property prices, income from PT has been virtually stagnant in real terms during the period from 1980–1 to 1990–1. Property prices in Mumbai have increased by more than 20 per cent during the same period. In real terms, over the period 1990–1 to 1997–8, yield from property taxes has shown an increase of nearly 6 per cent annually, which is still lower than the massive increase that has taken place in property values (NIPFP 2000). Studies show that on average, only 30–40 per cent of the potential tax is realized, and taxes on property continue to be plagued by problems of narrow base, persistent undervaluation, high rates, poor collection efficiency, and limits imposed on rents of properties under the rent control acts.

Property tax is levied on the basis of rateable value (RV) of the property. The RV is usually defined as the rental value which the property would fetch. In practice, however, the RV is estimated not through market mechanism but through administrative procedures.

Further, large variations are found in the rates of PT not only across states but within states. It ranges from 15 per cent of annual rateable value (ARV) in Lucknow to as high as 160 per cent of ARV in Greater Mumbai. It is observed that in many instances these rates have deliberately to be kept high to maintain the revenue stream from the tax as the taxable base has not been increasing.[7]

It is significant that the Ministry of Urban Development, Government of India has recently issued guidelines to reform PT. These suggest (i) substitution of the existing ARV system of PT by a mix of capital value (CV) and area detail system of PT by decomposing it into land tax and building tax; and (ii) introduction of the concept of user charges for directly chargeable services such as water supply and relation of cost recovery for other services through a building tax on the basis of area details of buildings. Other suggestions of the guidelines concern the modality for relating building tax to cost of services, determination of tax liability, tax exemptions, PT record management, assessment cycle of PT, system of appeals, etc. Building tax is proposed to be levied by adopting an area-based PT system on the Patna and Andhra Pradesh models. Whereas the Andhra Pradesh model uses the values obtained through sample survey of prevailing market rents for different categories of properties in terms of location, quality of construction, land use, age, and physical area, the Patna model uses values arrived at *suo moto*. The guidelines hence suggest a mix of these two models.

[7] These have resulted in severe distortions, and created strong incentives for misreporting and avoidance (ed.).

The proposed reforms in property tax will not only improve the yield from this important source of revenue for the municipal bodies, but may also reduce taxation disputes due to the simplicity of suggested procedures and method of assessment.

The role of transfers in the finance of municipalities is given in Table 9.1.5. It shows that aggregate transfers constitute about 17 per cent of total municipal revenue receipts. This proportion, however, is very high in the case of Andhra Pradesh (48 per cent), Assam (40 per cent), Bihar (47 per cent), Himachal Pradesh (74 per cent), Meghalaya (54 per cent), Tripura (57 per cent), Madhya Pradesh (52 per cent), Tamil Nadu (56 per cent), and Uttar Pradesh (80 per cent). High shares of transfers are a significant feature particularly of the non-octroi states.

Finance commissions of many states have recommended a new system of vertical tax sharing between the state and local bodies, in which state-level taxes, levies, etc. would be pooled together and a proportion thereof devolved to the local bodies of the state. In this system, ad hocism would be minimized and local bodies would know at the beginning of each fiscal year their share in the net proceeds of state taxes; they can then plan their spending accordingly. This would also enable them to select particular expenditures they would have to meet from their own sources of revenues by using various tools of resource mobilization and generation. In the proposed system, local bodies would also benefit from the buoyancy of state taxes. State taxes grow as per growth in the state economy, and the benefits of economic growth in the state would automatically flow to local bodies.

## MUNICIPAL EXPENDITURE

On the whole, the state of municipal finances in India suggests that the present revenues are insufficient to meet the growing expenditure needs of urban areas. Present levels of municipal expenditure are far below the norms suggested by the Zakaria Committee way back in 1963. According to a NIPFP study (2000), of 249 sample municipalities, only 10 met the expenditure norms suggested by the Zakaria Committee. For municipal governments to reach these recommended expenditure norms, their revenue receipts will have to increase significantly.

Municipal governments are legally required to have a balanced budget. Municipal expenditures are thus conditioned by the level of resources available. In states where municipal receipts are very low, municipal expenditures too are low. The quality and nature of services provided by the municipality are limited by these low levels of expenditures. Often repairs and maintenance of services are poor and expenditure on capital works is postponed.

Municipal expenditure could be categorized into three main components: wages and salaries; operations and maintenance (O&M); and interest payments. Wages and salaries constitute nearly 60 per cent of total municipal expenditure, followed by O&M (20 per cent) and interest on payments (7.17 per cent) (see Table 9.1.7).

TABLE 9.1.7
Composition of Revenue Expenditure 1997–8

| States | % of total revenue expenditure | | | |
|---|---|---|---|---|
| | Wages and salaries | O&M | Interest and debt | Others |
| Andhra Pradesh | 49.21 | 49.60 | 0.24 | 0.95 |
| Assam | 42.43 | 54.14 | 1.90 | 1.53 |
| Bihar | 77.21 | 21.13 | 1.03 | 0.63 |
| Gujarat | 53.20 | 30.02 | 6.30 | 10.48 |
| Haryana | 48.76 | 44.49 | 0.00 | 6.75 |
| Karnataka | 20.93 | 78.11 | 0.48 | 0.48 |
| Kerala | 55.04 | 34.57 | 5.19 | 5.20 |
| Madhya Pradesh | 51.01 | 37.67 | 0.61 | 10.71 |
| Maharashtra | 61.50 | 13.29 | 9.89 | 15.31 |
| Orissa | 38.30 | 21.61 | 0.00 | 40.09 |
| Punjab | 52.46 | 28.68 | 4.27 | 14.59 |
| Rajasthan | – | – | – | – |
| Tamil Nadu | 49.13 | 47.49 | 2.53 | 0.86 |
| Uttar Pradesh | 69.18 | 29.62 | 0.00 | 1.20 |
| West Bengal | 71.09 | 18.52 | 1.01 | 9.38 |
| Himachal Pradesh | 46.98 | 52.32 | 0.00 | 0.71 |
| Manipur | 70.69 | 8.73 | 0.00 | 20.58 |
| Meghalaya | 52.28 | 30.37 | 0.00 | 17.35 |
| Tripura | 56.64 | 1.15 | 2.26 | 39.95 |
| Total | 60.32 | 20.00 | 7.17 | 12.51 |

*Source:* NIPFP (2000).

Expenditure on O&M accounts for only one-fifth of the total expenditure of municipal services. The level of spending on O&M of core services is important for maintaining a minimum standard of services in the urban settlements. Recent data on expenditure on core services, viz. water supply, sewerage and drainage, conservancy and sanitation, municipal roads, and street lighting, are presented in Table 9.1.8.

On average, municipalities spend Rs 747 per capita annually on various municipal activities and functions. The break up of expenditure (c. 1997–8) on different core services and activities is as follows:

TABLE 9.1.8
Per Capita Revenue Expenditure on Core Services 1997–8

(Rs)

| States | Water supply | Sewerage and drainage | Conservancy and sanitation | Municipal road | Street lighting | All functions |
|---|---|---|---|---|---|---|
| Andhra Pradesh | 50.52 | 55.12 | 63.37 | 102.53 | 13.19 | 313.38 |
| Assam | 2.98 | 7.46 | 12.60 | 24.17 | 2.49 | 81.77 |
| Bihar | 4.32 | 40.45 | 39.85 | 2.93 | 1.29 | 104.29 |
| Gujarat | 60.40 | 44.28 | 119.37 | 52.23 | 29.76 | 438.21 |
| Haryana | 191.84 | 89.99 | 108.56 | 57.77 | 30.74 | 598.22 |
| Karnataka | 62.56 | 42.91 | 74.19 | 46.46 | 25.92 | 321.05 |
| Kerala | 2.84 | 8.98 | 66.14 | 46.49 | 8.37 | 228.38 |
| Madhya Pradesh | 79.44 | 31.92 | 37.10 | 27.19 | 13.16 | 322.74 |
| Maharashtra | 230.00 | 155.58 | 195.87 | 117.35 | 43.08 | 1750.50 |
| Orissa | 9.66 | 42.58 | 67.91 | 16.29 | 13.08 | 248.29 |
| Punjab | 95.38 | 109.70 | 118.44 | 48.67 | 23.35 | 542.81 |
| Rajasthan | – | 165.07 | – | 12.28 | 5.40 | 497.24 |
| Tamil Nadu | 45.92 | 13.39 | 111.86 | 56.13 | 23.25 | 331.46 |
| Uttar Pradesh | 16.48 | 5.41 | 112.10 | 34.64 | 9.52 | 223.23 |
| West Bengal | 60.01 | 41.58 | 119.48 | 63.71 | 13.72 | 522.83 |
| Himachal Pradesh | 89.57 | 36.67 | 251.76 | 304.90 | 15.62 | 1112.85 |
| Manipur | 0.03 | – | 27.05 | 16.38 | – | 101.42 |
| Meghalaya | 46.57 | 16.66 | 55.98 | 47.32 | 23.03 | 272.10 |
| Tripura | 0.01 | – | – | 2.13 | 4.99 | 255.90 |
| Total | 125.77 | 93.21 | 123.36 | 70.19 | 23.28 | 747.02 |

*Source:* NIPFP (2000).

| Services | Per capita expenditure (Rs) | % of total |
|---|---|---|
| Water supply | 125.77 | 16.83 |
| Sewerage and drainage | 93.21 | 12.47 |
| Conservancy and sanitation | 123.36 | 16.51 |
| Municipal roads | 70.19 | 9.39 |
| Street lighting | 23.28 | 3.11 |
| Other activities | 311.21 | 41.66 |
| Total | 747.02 | 100.00 |

Of the total expenditure, municipalities spent more than 58 per cent on core municipal services.

## TRENDS IN MUNICIPAL FINANCE

The revenue structure of municipalities presented in Table 9.1.9 shows that the relative share of own sources of revenue to transfers has declined. Although the share of tax income to total income declined substantially between 1974–5 and 1979–80, in the following years it went up from 15.39 per cent in 1979–80 to more than

48 per cent in 1997–8. The share of non-tax revenues, however, has been declining over the years, as it has gone down from nearly 22 per cent in 1979–80 to 17 per cent in 1997–8.

TABLE 9.1.9
Trends in Revenue Structure of Municipalities in India

| States | Total receipts (Rs crore) | % distribution | | |
|---|---|---|---|---|
| | | Tax | Non-tax | Transfers |
| 1974–5 | 311.44 | 63.19 | 15.27 | 8.00 |
| 1979–80 | 835.85 | 15.39 | 21.52 | 22.16 |
| 1990–1 | 3930.75 | 49.21 | 20.55 | 30.40 |
| 1996–7 | 10,325.25 | 49.40 | 16.91 | 33.69 |
| 1997–8 | 12,178.79 | 48.37 | 17.46 | 34.17 |

*Source:* NIUA (1997a) and CFC (2000).

Tax revenues have come up against the limits of high rates, and could be highly distortionary. Non-tax sources like remunerative and commercial projects, besides considerably stepping up user charges, are promising areas for revenue generation. The finance commissions of many states have suggested that municipal authorities utilize their properties for commercial purposes in a big way.

Studies show that cost recovery in some of the basic services like water supply is extremely low. On average, local governments recover only 20–30 per cent of the total expenditure incurred on the O&M of water supply. Therefore, rationalization of user charges for services is expected to mobilize substantial revenues for financing urban infrastructure and services. The finance commissions of many states have recommended effective pricing of municipal services with a view to balancing revenue and expenditure of ULBs. The Punjab Finance Commission has suggested that domain of user charges be extended to water supply sewerage, parking, and solid waste management. Tamil Nadu has suggested that charges for water supply may be increased by more than 200 per cent than the existing rates, with a view of having a full cost recovery. Table 9.1.10 provides a picture of revenue and expenditure of ULBs in selected states.

Significantly, the central budget estimate for the fiscal year 2000–1 recognizes the need for large amount of funds to finance urban infrastructure projects. Clause 15 of Section 10 of the Income Tax Act provides for exemption of interest. In order to enable local governments to have access to funds for financing urban infrastructure projects, the Finance Bill proposes to accord a tax-free status to the interest on bonds issued by them each year. These bonds are proposed to be specified by the central government through notification in the official Gazette (Urban Finance 2000).

## GRANTS TO STATES FOR FINANCING LOCAL BODIES: CFC RECOMMENDATIONS

The Eleventh Central Finance Commission (CFC) has not only considered the recommendations of the

TABLE 9.1.10
Trends in Municipal Finances in Selected States

(Rs)

| States | Per capita revenue from own sources | | | | Per capita total revenue expenditure | | | |
|---|---|---|---|---|---|---|---|---|
| | 1974–5 | 1979–80 | 1992–3 | 1997–8 | 1974–5 | 1979–80 | 1992–3 | 1997–8 |
| Gujarat | 67.70 | 98.00 | 486.25 | 618.66 | 85.90 | 119.40 | 501.56 | 438.21 |
| Maharashtra | 103.40 | 149.00 | 775.80 | 1829.00 | 107.20 | 131.40 | 877.20 | 1750.50 |
| Punjab | 41.90 | 78.00 | 275.66 | 444.23 | 40.50 | 55.20 | 298.20 | 542.81 |
| Andhra Pradesh | 37.30 | 38.00 | 89.55 | 210.03 | 28.30 | 53.90 | 163.26 | 318.38 |
| Assam | 13.70 | 11.00 | 43.75 | 47.13 | 18.50 | 20.00 | 59.57 | 81.77 |
| Kerala | 28.30 | 46.00 | 146.62 | 193.70 | 22.30 | 37.00 | 190.95 | 228.38 |
| West Bengal | 33.40 | 28.00 | 44.74 | 337.23 | 41.00 | 54.60 | 121.88 | 522.83 |

*Source:* NIUA (1989) and NIPFP (2000).

It is of interest that in 1997–8, the municipalities of Gujarat and Maharashtra have not only met their expenditures from their own sources but have also been able to generate some surpluses. In the remaining states, a substantial proportion—above 60 per cent—of revenue expenditure is being financed by municipalities from own sources. This picture is, however, highly misleading. The ULBs, in a majority of cases, have devolved a system for financing their regular activities by diverting employees' provident fund/pension fund and also by withholding payment of contractors, debt servicing, etc. Further, under state municipal Acts, municipalities are barred from preparing and presenting 'deficit budgets'. For example section 286(3) d of the Karnataka Municipalities Act, 1964 states that the municipal council shall 'allow for a balance at the end of the said year of not less than such sums as may be required to meet the establishment charges for a period of three months' (NIUA 1987).

finance commissions of states, but has also looked into the following aspects of the ULBs in order to recommend grants to states for financing local governments.

(a) Existing powers of municipalities to raise financial resources including those by way of raising additional taxes by municipalities; and

(b) The powers, authority, and responsibility to municipalities under Article 243 W of the Constitution read with the Twelfth Schedule.

The CFC has recommended grants amounting to Rs 10,000 crore to local bodies of the country during 2000–5. Of this, Rs 1600 crore are to go to panchayats and Rs 400 crore to municipalities for each of the five years, starting from the financial year 2000–1. In per capita terms, the amount recommended for the panchayati raj institutions (PRIs) is higher than that for the ULBs. This amount will be over and above the normal flow of funds to local bodies from states and the amount that would flow from the implementation of SFC recommendations (CFC 2000).

The grants would be untied except that they should not be used for payment of salaries and wages. In order to improve the financial health of local bodies, the CFC has suggested reforms in local taxes and rates including property tax and user charges. It has also emphasized a need for improvements in budgetary and accounting systems beside capacity building of local governments in various fields of municipal administration and management.

The Commission has recommended a special grant of Rs 200 crore for development of a data base on finances of PRIs and ULBs and Rs 98.61 crore for maintenance of accounts. The Commission has recommended the following criteria for distribution of grants to PRIs and ULBs:

| Indicator | Weightage (%) |
|---|---|
| (a) Population | 40 |
| (b) Index of decentralization | 20 |
| (c) Distance from higher per capita income | 20 |
| (d) Revenue effort | 10 |
| (e) Geographical area | 10 |

The Government of India has accepted the recommendations of the Eleventh CFC subject to certain conditions (CFC 2000).

The Eleventh CFC award of grants for local bodies is ten times more than the Tenth Finance Commission's recommended amount of Rs 1000 crore. However, the amount would still not be adequate. Local resources, especially through rational user charges, are the only solution.

The recommendations of the First State Finance Commissions show wide variation between different states on various issues concerning the devolution of functional and financial powers to ULBs. While some SFCs have made clear recommendations about the devolution, others have been quite vague in this regard. The major shortcomings in the recommendations of SFCs are as follows:

• The term-period of the CFC in most cases did not coincide with the tenure of the First State Finance Commissions. As a consequence, the recommendations of the CFC and the SFCs were not for the similar period, leading to problems in allocation of grants.

• While making recommendations for the devolution of funds from state governments to local bodies, most SFCs did not consider the functional domain of the

ULBs and hence the devolutions may not be related to actual needs.

• The grants, to be provided to ULBs out of state government funds, recommended by the SFCs were determined arbitrarily in most cases.

• The grants recommended were mostly made in absolute terms with respect to certain services and not considered as percentages of any particular revenue source of state governments. As such these amounts may remain fixed over the years.

• The gap between income and expenditure as determined by the SFCs to decide about the devolution of funds did not take into account the overwhelming liabilities of the ULBs.

To sum up, the reports of the First State Finance Commissions are silent on several issues concerning sound financial management of the ULBs. The recommendations made have rarely been justified with a detailed analysis of the situation and the sharing formula has not been worked out in many cases for devolution of funds from states to ULBs. Similarly, in many cases, the measures suggested for improving the financial health of the ULBs have been of a very general nature, like the recommendation that property tax assessment should be simplified or made more transparent and scientific. The main objective of the SFCs should be, therefore, to ensure a predictable, practical, comprehensive, and unambiguous system of devolution of funds from state governments to local bodies. The focus should be on achieving 'self-reliance' at local level by addressing issues concerning sound financial health of the ULBs.

Although CAA74 provides full autonomy to the ULBs, state-level functionaries are hesitant about handing over financial and functional powers to these local governments. The CAA74 is also silent on issues concerning financial devolution to the ULBs in line with functional devolution as provided in the Twelfth Schedule. Had the Act given direct financial powers to municipalities commensurate with functions to be assigned to them, real autonomy at local level would have been provided and civic bodies made more responsible and accountable to citizens' need.

## WATER SUPPLY, SANITATION, AND SOLID WASTE DISPOSAL

Urban India presents a grim picture with regard to availability of basic services (Table 9.1.11). At aggregate level although nearly 84 per cent of urban population is reported to have access to safe drinking water, there are severe deficiencies with regard to the quantity of water available to urban residents. Nearly 50 per cent of urban population is covered by sanitation services, but only 28 per cent of urban households are connected to the public sewerage system. Though nearly 300 urban centres have a sewerage system, only 70 of these have sewage treatment facilities. Only 40–60 per cent of garbage is being collected by municipal authorities in urban areas of India. There are, thus, major deficiencies in the provision of urban infrastructure and services, despite major efforts in the past. The state of key urban services, that is water supply, sanitation, and solid waste disposal, is described in detail in this section.

TABLE 9.1.11
Key Indicators for Selected Urban Services

| Service/Indicator | Year | Level/status |
|---|---|---|
| *Water supply* | | |
| Percentage of population covered under safe drinking water supply* | 1995 | 84 |
| Per capita per day supply (litres)** | 1989 | 142 |
| *Sanitation* | | |
| No. of urban centres having sewerage system** | 1991 | 300 (70 with sewage treatment acilities) |
| Percentage of population covered by sanitation facilities* | 1995 | 50 |
| Percentage of households connected to public sewerage system*** | 1991 | 28 |
| Percentage of garbage collected daily*** | 1991 | 40–60 |
| *Roads* | | |
| Km of urban roads per 100,000 of urban population*** | 1991 | 83 |
| Municipal road density (kms per sq. km municipal area)** | 1989 | 6.11 |
| *Public safety* | | |
| No. of lamp posts (street lights) per km. of municipal road length** | 1989 | 155 |

*Source:*
* NIUA (2000).
** NIUA (1989).
*** NIUA (1997a).

*Water Supply*

As a basic principle, cities of smaller size (as per population) do not need the same level of service that a bigger urban centre will need. For example, major urban centres use more water per head as compared to smaller cities and towns. In a small town, some of the non-essential uses such as washing clothes and

utensils could be satisfied by non-protected sources (wells, ponds, etc.), which in a big city have to be met only by piped water sources. Water supply standards will also vary from one region to another, according to functional, climatic, and other characteristics, including habits of the people.[8]

According to the latest data available, against the average designed capacity of 34.3 million litres per day (mlpd), the actual availability of water for distribution is as low as 83 per cent of this amount. States in which the situation is particularly grave are Gujarat, Manipur, Tamil Nadu, and Uttar Pradesh. Non-availability of standby pump sets and inadequate maintenance of the system are the prime factors for low utilization of raw water sources in most cases (NIUA 1989).

Population coverage under piped water supply is an important indicator of levels of water supply.[9] According to the Census of India, 1991, on average more than 81 per cent of population is being served by safe drinking water supply systems in urban areas of the country. Table 9.1.12 gives the statewise consumption.

According to a study conducted by the NIUA in 1989, on average more than one-fifth of the sample cities' population have no access to a protected water supply system. Further, more than 20 per cent of the responding urban centres have less than 60 per cent of the population served by piped water supply. As against this, more than 45 per cent of urban centres provide municipal water supply to more than 80 per cent of their population. Coverage here refers to the number of people who have access to a pipe (a tap) that officially is connected to the network, and has water. It neither takes into account flow nor quality of access, which can vary greatly. Yet it may serve as an indicator of very basic access to the network.

[8] Minimum standards have been set by the Central Public Health and Environmental Engineering Organisation (CPHEEO), Government of India at 125 to 200 litres per capita per day for cities with a population of 50,000 and above. The Zakaria Committee has, however, suggested that a per capita supply of 157.5 to 270.0 litres per day per head would be an ideal goal for cities with a population of 100,000 and above.
The National Master Plan of India has suggested a water standard of 70 to 250 litres per capita per day (LPCD) with an average supply of 140 LPCD irrespective of population size. The Master Plan has also recommended, coverage on an average, of 90 per cent of urban population under protected water supply (Mathur 1999c).
[9] This is not necessarily true. In a rather unique state (Kerala), where most urban households have their own wells, many have invested in their own private pumps and piped systems based on these wells. To a lesser extent this is also not true of several other cities with poor municipal coverage, but with 'easy' availability of good ground water.

TABLE 9.1.12
Levels of Water Supply and Sanitation in Urban India

| State | Population* served by safe drinking water | Per capita** supply (litres) per capita | % population** coverage by sewerage |
|---|---|---|---|
| Andhra Pradesh | 73.8 | 134 | 11 |
| Assam | 64.1 | 30 | 16 |
| Bihar | 73.4 | 61 | 23 |
| Gujarat | 87.2 | 133 | 38 |
| Goa | 61.7 | NA | 13 |
| Haryana | 93.2 | 123 | 28 |
| Himachal Pradesh | 91.9 | 144 | 14 |
| Jammu & Kashmir | NA | 33 | 8 |
| Karnataka | 81.4 | 108 | 38 |
| Kerala | 38.6 | 106 | 28 |
| Madhya Pradesh | 79.5 | 185 | 8 |
| Maharashtra | 90.5 | 175 | 40 |
| Meghalaya | 75.4 | 57 | NA |
| Nagaland | 45.5 | NA | NA |
| Orissa | 62.8 | 239 | 10 |
| Punjab | 94.2 | 170 | 49 |
| Rajasthan | 86.5 | 108 | 10 |
| Tamil Nadu | 74.2 | 94 | 48 |
| Tripura | 71.1 | 251 | 13 |
| Uttar Pradesh | 85.8 | 192 | 14 |
| West Bengal | 86.2 | 106 | 20 |
| Urban India | 81.4 | 142 | 28 |

NA: Not available.

Source: * Census of India, 1991, Series I, Paper 2 of 1993 (Housing and Amenities).
** NIUA(1989).

The notion that water supply is more adequate in the larger cities is not generally supported by the data. Data given in Table 9.1.13 reveal that average per capita availability of water to the citizens of metro cities is about 214 litres per day. In many of the cities, per capita levels are substantially below the average level. These are Hyderabad, Vishakhapatnam, Ahmedabad, Surat, Bangalore, Nagpur, Ludhiana, Jaipur, Coimbatore, Lucknow, Kanpur, the lowest being in Chennai and Madurai.

This average of 214 litres is most certainly overstated, since 30 per cent or more losses are known to be common to nearly all municipal systems. Moreover, supply between locations is also known to be highly skewed, being very little per head in slums and concentrations of the poor.

One striking fact that is evident from the more recent survey conducted by the NIPFP (2000) is that in a sizeable number of urban centres, the availability of water is even less than 100 litres per capita per day, as only 21.7 per cent of the sample municipalities have

reported supplying over 100 litres of water per capita per day. Approximately 28 per cent of the municipalities provided less than 50 litres per capita per day which is less than half the norms recommended by the Zakaria Committee for towns of less than 20,000 persons (see Table 9.1.14). Even these estimates are overstated on account of inclusion therein of water lost in transmission and distribution.

TABLE 9.1.13
Water Supply in Metro Cities

| Metro cities | Per capita water supply (LPCD) | Percentage of population covered by municipal water supply |
|---|---|---|
| Hyderabad | 127 | 90 |
| Vishakhapatnam | 113 | 100 |
| Patna | 297 | 100 |
| Delhi | 341 | 91 |
| Ahmedabad | 182 | 100 |
| Surat | 178 | 66 |
| Vadodara | 233 | 75 |
| Bangalore | 137 | 90 |
| Kochi | 231 | 70 |
| Bhopal | 234 | 95 |
| Indore | 208 | 80 |
| Bombay | 272 | 92 |
| Nagpur | 158 | 100 |
| Pune | 241 | 100 |
| Ludhiana | 175 | 65 |
| Jaipur | 195 | 95 |
| Coimbatore | 104 | 88 |
| Madras | 81 | 90 |
| Madurai | 74 | 86 |
| Kanpur | 200 | 80 |
| Lucknow | 252 | 98 |
| Varanasi | 215 | 100 |
| Calcutta | 200 | 90 |
| Total | 214 | 90 |

Source: NIUA (1997a).

TABLE 9.1.14
Distribution of Urban Centres by Per Capita
Water Supply Levels 1997–8

| Water levels (LPCD) | No. of urban centres | % of total |
|---|---|---|
| No information | 59 | 23.7 |
| 0–25 | 24 | 9.6 |
| 25–50 | 47 | 18.8 |
| 50–75 | 36 | 14.5 |
| 75–100 | 29 | 11.7 |
| 100 & above | 54 | 21.7 |
| Total | 249 | 100.0 |

Source: NIPFP (2000).

According to a NIUA municipal expenditure survey in 1986-7, water supply ranks third in municipal spending outlays. On per capita spending, more than 70 per cent of sampled municipal bodies spend even less than Rs 20 per capita per annum on O&M of water supply systems (see Table 9.1.15). These levels are much lower than the Zakaria Committee expenditure norms updated at 1986-7 prices (Rs 61.30 per capita per annum).

TABLE 9.1.15
Distribution of Urban Centres by Per Capita
Expenditure Levels

| Per capita (Rs) | No. of urban centres | % of total |
|---|---|---|
| Less than 20 | 99 | 71.73 |
| 20–40 | 28 | 20.98 |
| 40–50 | 3 | 2.17 |
| 50 & above | 8 | 5.79 |
| ALL | 138 | 100.0 |

*Source:* NIUA (1989).

## Sanitation

A cholera–gastroenteritis epidemic in which hundreds of people died in Delhi and other areas of the country a few years ago is one of the most tragic indicators of the unhealthy environmental conditions in our cities and towns. The prevailing conditions are indicative of gross neglect of sanitation services by municipal authorities, not just in the last few years but over the decades.

Unlike water supply, specific standards for sewerage and solid waste disposal have not been 'officially' spelt out. Many cities do not have sewerage systems, and even where they do exist, their capacities are not adequate to cope with requirements. The adequacy of sewerage systems depends on the water consumed for industry, domestic, and other purposes. According to the Zakaria Committee Report (1963), 90 per cent of industrial water consumed and 80 per cent of per capita supply in residential areas has to be reckoned as sewage flow and provided for.

In terms of population coverage, the National Master Plan entitled 'International Drinking Water Supply and Sanitation Decade: 1981-90' has recommended almost 100 per cent population coverage with proper sewerage and sewage treatment facilities in Class I urban centres of the country.

According to the mid-term review of water supply and sanitation decade programme 1981–90, at all-India level, the proportionate share of population served by sanitation services (sewerage/drainage) is about 28 per cent! Besides Punjab and Tamil Nadu, only in the states of Gujarat, Karnataka, Maharashtra, and Sikkim

is sanitation coverage above the all-India average. A large number of states, including some of the developed ones, have only partial urban coverage under sewerage services (Table 9.1.11).

An analysis of household amenities in terms of sanitation facilities has data been done in a NIUA study (1997a). The data are presented in Table 9.1.16.

TABLE 9.1.16
Percentage of Urban Households Classified by
Nature of Sanitation Facility 1988–9

| Nature of sanitation facility | Percentage households (to total) |
|---|---|
| Flush system | 26.95 |
| Septic tank | 25.87 |
| Service latrine | 11.74 |
| Others | 4.21 |
| No toilet facility | 31.06 |

*Source:* NIUA (1997a).

## Solid Waste Disposal

Municipal bodies in India are entrusted under law with the obligatory function of conservancy or public cleaning and scavenging work.

The high organic content in the waste and the tropical climate of the country mean that uncollected and indisposed waste would decompose. This is a serious health hazard.

Compared to other, especially richer, countries, solid waste generation in India's urban areas is not large in quantitative terms. It varies between a low of 294 grams to a high of 484 grams per capita per day, the variation being explained by a variety of factors including the size of cities, their functions, household income, and the level of economic development. In most cases however, waste collection is not complete, and on average roughly 40–60 per cent of total waste generated remains uncollected, which is one of the biggest sources of pollution in human settlements (see Table 9.1.17).

In most cities, solid waste is collected from and around bins of inadequate capacity and transported to dump sites at the periphery of the city. The indiscriminate dumping of waste in the nearest available low-lying area often causes damage to the soil. Very few cities practice scientific methods of sanitary landfill or convert the waste into compost or energy. Almost no cities have arrangements to separate garbage before collection. In larger cities, the land fill sites and bins therefore attract a large number of poor people who scavenge for bits of metal, paper and plastic to feed the recycling trade.

TABLE 9.1.17
Solid Waste Collection and Generation in Selected Metro
Centres of India c. 1998

| Metro cities | Solid water per day (tonnes) | | Collection efficiency (%) |
| --- | --- | --- | --- |
| | Generation | Collection | |
| Delhi | 3880 | 2420 | 62.37 |
| Calcutta | 3500 | 3150 | 90.00 |
| Bombay | 5800 | 5000 | 86.20 |
| Bangalore | 2130 | 1800 | 84.50 |
| Madras | 2675 | 2140 | 80.00 |
| Lucknow | 1500 | 1000 | 66.66 |
| Patna | 1000 | 300 | 30.00 |
| Ahmedabad | 1500 | 1200 | 80.00 |
| Surat | 1250 | 1000 | 80.00 |

*Source:* NIUA (1997a).

An important problem of municipal solid waste relates to the mixing of hospital and toxic industrial waste with other wastes. Although, major hospitals by law are required to incinerate their wastes, they often dispose them in municipal bins. Industries are also required to dispose their toxic wastes through prescribed procedures, but they often do not practise them. These wastes create a serious health hazard in urban areas. However, after the plague outbreak in Surat in 1994, there has been greater concern regarding the status of

Urban local bodies in India are mandated to have a balanced budget. This, one would have thought, should have led them to substantial cost recovery of the major services provided by them.[10] However, in practice, most local bodies fail to recover even the O&M costs. Table 9.1.18 indicates that except for Vishakhapatnam, the other three selected cities, namely Bangalore, Aurangabad, and Mangalore, are unable to recover the O&M costs in water supply and sanitation services.

Thus for commercial provisioning average urban water rates would have to rise sharply. Moreover, since the assets would then have to depreciate over a shorter period than is presently the practice under state ownership, there would have to be an additional factor increasing the rates. But the gap is not too large either. This may be deceptive. The bulk of water suppply costs arise out of capital expenditure.

Water tariffs in most cities are much lower than the cost of providing water. Some institutions such as the Bangalore Water Supply and Sewerage Board (BWSSB) have taken the initiative to revise water rates so as to recover costs on a no loss no profit basis. The BWSSB has increased water rates by 20 per cent almost every year since 1991 to recover the escalating cost of procuring and supplying water. Service agencies which have taken loans from the financial institutions like the Housing and Urban Development

TABLE 9.1.18
Revenue Receipts and Expenditures with regard to Water Supply and Sanitation
in Selected Cities 1993–4

(Rs)

| Service | Bangalore | Vishakhapatnam | Aurangabad | Mangalore |
| --- | --- | --- | --- | --- |
| *Water supply* | | | | |
| RE/1000 litres | 3.84 | 1.05 | 1.32 | 1.24 |
| RR/1000 litres | 3.50 | 2.85 | 0.74 | 0.68 |
| Surplus/deficit | −0.34 | 1.80 | −0.58 | −0.56 |
| *Sewerage* | | | | |
| RE/100 litres | 0.87 | 0.68 | 0.28 | 0.49 |
| RR/100 litres | 0.20 | 1.45 | 0.05 | – |
| Surplus/deficit | −0.67 | 0.77 | −0.23 | −0.49 |
| *Solid waste* | | | | |
| RE/tonne | 0.34 | 0.36 | 0.38 | 0.11 |
| RR/tonne | 0.09 | 0.03 | 0.06 | 0.06 |
| Surplus/deficit | −0.25 | −0.33 | −0.32 | −0.05 |

RR: Revenue receipts    RE: Revenue expenditure
*Source:* NIUA (1997a).

urban solid waste in the country, though how long the enthusiasm will last without basic change that relaxes constraints on municipalities to perform services remains to be seen.

[10] More than the imposition of balanced budgets, rational budgets and budgets that are coherent with responsibilities and powers coherent with both are necessary to create pressure for cost recovery (ed.).

Corporation (HUDCO) have also revised their water rates in order to meet the increasing costs on the service (Mehta 1993). Vishakhapatnam, Chennai, Tirupur, Alandur, and Pune are some of the examples of municipalities which have either revised their water tariffs or are in process of doing so. The national conference on water management, organized by the Confederation of Indian Industry (CII) in 1999 made a call for raising water charges to meet O&M expenditure. All the projects commissioned under the Financing Institution Reform and Expansion or FIRE programme have a clear-cut condition for commercialization of urban infrastructure projects (Urban Finance 1999). However, many of the municipalities have not been able to revise water rates as there was considerable local opposition to the same. Thus instances of rationalization of the water tariffs are few, and the service is still highly subsidized.

## MAJOR DRAWBACKS IN THE EXISTING TARIFF STRUCTURE

• There is only partial recovery of capital costs.
• Tariff determined as per existing practices is largely aimed at recovering historical costs rather meeting long-term incremental costs and increased investment needs of an expanding system.

• Tariff structure is not strictly followed due to political interference.
• Attention is not focused on the affordability and willingness to pay.
• It is not linked to the quality of service.
• Minimum *life line* rates not defined.

To get rid of these drawbacks, certain measures are essential. It is important to delink service charges from property tax. A two-part tariff structure for water—one for access and another for use or consumption is essential. Metering in the water supply system, and a limited cross-subsidy mechanism would need to be instituted. Tariff indexation, keeping in view the rising cost of the service provision, is a way out of frequent political and bureaucratic whetting. Improved efficiency in delivery of service including in billing and collection can considerably lower estimates of required tariffs for full cost recovery. There are also economies of scale in expanding and rationalization of coverage, as also in increased supplies of water.

## PRIVATIZATION IN MUNICIPALITIES

Public–private partnerships (PPPs) have resulted in cost savings for most public agencies that have used

TABLE 9.1.19
Private Sector Participation in Water Supply and Sanitation Projects

| City | Services | Management option | Capital finance arranged by | Time (years) | Project cost (Rs crore) |
|---|---|---|---|---|---|
| Chennai | O&M WS&S (pumping stations & tube wells) | Service contracts | Public agency | 1–5 | NA |
| Ahmedabad | Augmentation of water supply & sewerage | Private project consultant | Public agency | NA | 490 |
| Tiruppur | Bulk WS and new sewerage | Joint sector company/BOT | Joint sector company/BOT | 30 | 900 |
| Pune | Augmentation of WS&S | Construction contract Management contract for O&M of new facilities & part billing & collection | Public agency | 5 for O&M | 715 |
| Bangalore | Bulk WS | BOT | Private agency | 25–30 | 800 |
| Alandur | (a) Sewage collection | (a) Construction contract | (a) Public agency | (a) NA | (a) 40 |
|  | (b) Treatment plant | (b) BOT | (b) Private Agency | (b) 15–20 | (b) 8 |
| For Karnataka towns | WS&S O&M, bill collection and augmentation | Management | Private agency | 5–7 | Not known |

NA: Not available; WS: Water Storage; WS&S: Water Storage and Supply; O&M: Operations and Maintenance
*Source:* Urban Finance (1999: 2).
*Note:* The dates of the contracts for these projects are not known. But they would all have been not older than five years.

such arrangements. The extent of savings achieved varies across cities as it depends upon the ability of the public agency to accurately calculate the cost of provision of any given service as well as its ability to invite a sufficient number of private operators for providing the service.

*Role and Responsibilities of Local Bodies in PPPs*

A series of PPPs in provision of municipal services has emerged in different cities and towns. A few examples are given in the following paragraphs.

RAJKOT

The Rajkot Municipal Corporation (RMC) has contracted out maintenance of street lights, solid waste removal and transportation, cleaning of public toilets, maintenance of gardens, afforestation, etc. The RMC has also undertaken various entertainment projects with the help of private entrepreneurs. By using the services of the private sector, the RMC has been able to save a significant amount of money and has been able to close the gap between demand and supply. Huge investments that are needed for acquiring capital equipment such as tractors and trollies have now been given over to private contractors. However, the RMC has not retrenched any of its staff but has stopped fresh recruitment. The RMC continues to use its present manpower as well as equipment in certain areas of the city. This also serves as contingency in case of service disruption due to problems with the private contractors. For its primary solid waste removal in 1991–2 the RMC spent Rs 16.95 lakh. The private agency to which the work has now been contracted out does the same in Rs 14.36 lakh.

PALI

In Pali (Rajasthan), the municipal body has given the maintenance of street lights to the private sector. In doing so it has been able to maintain street lights at one-fifth the cost it would have incurred had it maintained the service itself!

CIDCO

The City and Industrial Development Corporation (CIDCO), a public sector institution in New Mumbai, has had a very successful experience with privatization efforts. The privatization experience includes maintenance of sewerage pumps and water pumps, meter reading and billing, maintenance of parks and gardens, and collection of CIDCO's service charges. CIDCO has given out the collection of its service charges to the Senior Citizens Club (an association of retired

persons) whom it pays 1 per cent as commission. If CIDCO were to collect the charges on its own it would cost it three times more.

Road sweeping, garbage collection and disposal, maintenance of drains, spraying of insecticides, etc. have been assigned (1992–3) to 15 contractors in all of the 7 townships under CIDCO. The work is allotted to different contractors for a group of sectors on yearly basis. The work done by the contractor is supervised by the sanitary inspectors of CIDCO. This system has been functioning for over eight years and has resulted in well-maintained streets. The total cost of all contracts in seven townships is Rs 42.6 lakh per year. If this work had been done departmentally by CIDCO it would have to have at least 400–500 sweepers and 20 trucks. The all-inclusive maintenance cost would have cost around Rs 100 lakh. (NIUA 1997b).

EXNORA

Exnora is an non-governmental organization (NGO) started by non-resident Indians (NRIs) to improve civic amenities in Chennai. The NGO helps in garbage removal not only in well-off localities but also in slums. The households pay a nominal charge of Rs 10 to Rs 20 per month for the service. In the slums, the households pay less but provide labour instead. Exnora has directly employed rag pickers for garbage removal. It has been successful in its attempt to help keep the city clean and has extended its services to many localities in the city.

SRISHTI

Srishti is a Delhi-based NGO using Residents Associations to implement community-level municipal solid waste disposal. It is working in several Delhi colonies with the involvement of about 900 to 1000 households. Garbage which is handled by them reduces the burden of the Municipal Corporation of Delhi (MCD) on the collection front. Srishti's aim is to assist local residents to interact with the MCD and take on much greater responsibility for their garbage.

ALANDUR

The Alandur Sewerage Project is proposed to be implemented in Alandur (Tamil Nadu), on the basis of a PPP. There will be a construction contract for the sewage collection system, whereas the treatment plants will be on a build, operate, and transfer (BOT) basis. In addition, there will be an O&M contract for the collection system as well as treatment plant. The operator is expected to make capital investment for the treatment plant and to recover the same over a period of 15 to 20 years. The local body will recover the costs through a combination of sewerage tax, sewerage charge, connection charge, general revenues, and state government support. The expected gains from more efficient and cost-effective working are likely to be large.

SURAT

Surat suffered an outbreak of plague in 1994. Following from a change in administrative leadership, the Surat Municipal Corporation introduced several innovative measures for improving urban management through PPPs in delivery of water and sanitation services. The private sector has been involved in solid waste collection and transportation, maintenance of street lighting, construction of roads, tree planting, and operation of water treatment plants. As a result of private collection and transportation of garbage, collection efficiency increased from 30 per cent in 1995 to above 90 per cent. By contracting out street-lights maintenance to a private company, the level of service has greatly improved: over 95 per cent of street lights are now in working condition, whereas previously they had been less than 50 per cent at any time.

Local bodies should primarily concentrate on essential urban services such as water supply, sewerage, drainage, and solid waste disposal. They should not involve themselves in provision of other merit goods such as education, which are not locationally constrained, and where state governments and private parties would have the upper hand. The cost of providing these services is substantial and could be better utilized for development and improvement of core civic services.

*Specific Provisions for Involving the Private Sector*

Most ULBs have not seriously thought of private sector participation in the provision of urban services, as there are no 'enabling' legal provisions that facilitate the use of the non-government sector. While the Municipal Acts do not precisely use the term 'private sector', a serious reading of the legal provisions suggests that the Acts do permit the use of any person for delivering specific services. The Hyderabad Municipal Corporation Act, 1955 (No. 11 of 1956), for example, clearly states that 'the Commissioner when authorized by the Corporation can enter into an arrangement with any person for supply of water' (Section 342).

This could include construction and maintenance of water works, purchasing or taking on lease any water works, and storing and conveyance of water. More or less similar clauses are found in the other Municipal Acts.

With the passing of the CAA74 all states are expected to make amendments to their respective Municipal Acts, incorporating the necessary changes to provide a role for the private sector. This has already been done in a majority of states. Amended municipal legislations in Maharashtra contain a provision to the effect that where any duty has been imposed or any function has been assigned to a municipality by law, the municipality may either discharge such duty or perform through any agency. Thus inserting specific clauses enabling the involvement of the private sector will go a long way in improving the quality of services in the urban areas of the country. The finance commissions of some states—Kerala, Madhya Pradesh, Punjab, and Tamil Nadu—have recommended contracting out of certain municipal services to private agencies. The Tamil Nadu State Finance Commission, for example, has suggested contracting out of garbage, maintenance of commercial assets, etc. to private agencies in order to reduce the financial burden on municipal bodies on the one hand and improve the delivery of services on the other. In Punjab, ULBs have been given full powers to get civic amenities delivered through private agencies. Similarly, the Madhya Pradesh Finance Commission suggested that the collection and disposal of garbage should be given out to private agencies.

## INNOVATIONS IN MUNICIPAL ACCOUNTING SYSTEMS

The existing accounting system in a large number of local bodies is based on simple single cash accounting which does not throw any light on the financial status of municipal bodies. It is neither conducive to credit rating nor accessing the capital market. It does not reveal even the expenditure liabilities postponed due to compelling fiscal reasons which is generally a rampant practice and which camouflages the financial status of municipalities. Suitable changes in the accounting system have been an important issue in municipal financial management for many years. The Chennai Municipal Corporation was the first municipal authority in the country to have switched over to a double entry accounting system under the aegis of a World Bank funding of urban development in the late 1980s.

In Gujarat, many cities are in the process of implementing new accounting systems. The Ahmedabad Municipal Corporation replaced the manual cash-based system with a double entry accrual-based computerized system. The Surat Municipal Corporation has also adopted a computerized double entry accounting system. In other states such as Karnataka and Tamil Nadu, attempts have been made in recent years to introduce a new system of accounting and financial reporting system. However, these innovations are on a limited scale.

Considering the need for such an accounting system for efficient functioning of urban local governments in the country, the Institute of Chartered Accountants of India is developing a technical guide for municipal accounting based on a double entry accrual system. This guide is expected to provide financial reporting formats based on generally accepted accounting principles and instructions for preparation of financial statements.

It is important that for accessing the capital market, municipalities develop their creditworthiness. Devolution of additional taxes, rationalized user charges, and fiscal autonomy to set their own rates are necessary changes. Though there is an increasing trend on the part of municipal bodies to go in for credit rating, this is limited to only a few cities in the more prosperous and progressive parts of the country. Proper standards and transparent accounting systems have to be in place before municipalities can go to the market without government guarantees for funds.

## CONCLUSION

The CAA74 aimed in spirit to empower the ULBs in such a way that they function smoothly, efficiently, and effectively as autonomous, self-sustained city governments. To achieve this, there is need to have uniformity in state legislations with respect to tenure and powers of mayors/chairpersons. They should have powers of administration, supervision, and control over all employees of municipalities.

Functions of ULBs should be clearly specified. All the subjects mentioned in the Twelfth Schedule should be transferred to ULBs along with transfer of funds and functionaries.

Property tax is one of the main sources of income for the municipalities. This should be simplified and rationalized. Exemptions from property tax should be minimized and central government properties should also pay service charges in lieu of property tax.

There is scope for improvement in collection and plugging the leakage. In Hyderabad, for example, PT collection during the last three years has doubled as a result of improvement in the PT administration system.

Taxes which are local in nature such as entertainment tax, motor vehicle tax, and stamp duty should either be transferred to local bodies or a reasonable share be given to local bodies.

ULBs should be given autonomy to fix tax rates and user charges.

The state governments should prepare necessary guidelines and enabling legislation to further privatization by the ULBs.

A major problem among the ULBs, as pointed out by many studies and committees, is the lack of expertise.[11] Thus there is need for capacity building and training of municipal officials, particularly to take up the challenges offered by the new functions assigned to them under the Twelfth Schedule. The District and Metro Planning Committees would need to be constituted as per the provisions of the CAA74. Those committees will have to ensure formulation of realistic and effective urban development planning systems incorporating resource mobilization plans, institutional mechanisms for implementation, etc. for which municipal institutions have no expertise. Therefore, there is need to modify the existing recruitment rules of the ULBs to enable them to function as a vibrant and efficient unit of planning at local level. Technical support groups should also be constituted in every municipality to supervise works at local level.

The Municipal Acts of each state differ widely. Thus there is need to replace the existing state Municipal Acts with a model Municipal Act which should be uniformly applicable to all local bodies of the country.

A National Urban Development Fund could be established to extend loans and financial aid to the ULBs for infrastructure development.[12]

Innovative strategies are thus required to be developed by the ULBs to finance urban infrastructure and services. The existing funds available from plan allocation could be supplemented by accessing the capital market. Already the cities of Ahmedabad and Bangalore have accessed the capital market to mobilize funds for urban infrastructure financing. This in turn will mean improvements in the record management and accounting systems beside good governance and urban management systems.

The CAA74 has already provided for strengthening of urban governance and management. This needs to be made operational by ensuring devolution of functions as per the Twelfth Schedule and devolution of adequate financial resources to keep cities running. Box 9.1.1 provides a picture of local governance in small towns in Gujarat since the CAA74.

[11] ULBs need not have such expertise in-house. It would be better to not to since real expertise has it own logic of scale and organization. The point is the ULB's elected representatives should have the right to contract with private parties, and parties other than those imposed upon them by the state (ed.).
[12] The disbursals from such a fund could be linked to the charges and improvements brought about institutionally and in the finances of the ULBs.

BOX 9.1.1

## Local Governance in Small Towns in Gujarat since the CAA74: First Impressions

*Alice Albin Morris and Vivek Raval*

In order to strengthen local self-governments in rural and urban areas, the Parliament enacted the historic 73rd and 74th Constitutional Amendment Acts (CAAs), focusing on Panchayati Raj institutions and municipalities, respectively. Since then, though much interest has been shown in Panchayati Raj, very little has been done to improve municipal governance. Even among NGOs, with the exception of the Public Affairs Centre (PAC) in Bangalore, Exnora International in Chennai, and Foundation for Public Interest (FPI) in Ahmedabad, little interest has been generated by the CAA. Since 1994, when the follow-up legislation was passed in Gujarat, it met with little enthusiasm amongst grassroots institutions, be they municipalities or citizens' groups.

With a view to developing a plan for a larger comprehensive study, Unnati[13] carried out a pilot study of four nagar panchayats (municipalities) in Gujarat: Dholka, Khedbrahma, Dharampur, and Amreli—essentially small and medium sized towns.

Khedbrahma and Dharampur are category D nagar panchayats (with a population of 15,000–25,000); Dholka is category C (with a population of 25,000–50,000); and Amreli is category B (with a population of 50,000–100,000). Some of the issues that emerged from the study are highlighted here.

### Politics of Superseding Municipalities

The CAA74 sought to provide stability to the political existence of local governing institutions. The new law was to discourage supersession of town municipalities which arises out of narrow political interests. However, it has not yet effectively discouraged such politics.

The superseding of the Dholka municipality is one such example. In the municipal elections of 1995, the Bharatiya Janata Party (BJP) and Nagarik Samiti (i.e. Congress in disguise) won 12 and 14 seats respectively; one seat went to an independent candidate. The Nagarik Samiti, with the support of the independent councillor, obtained control of the administration. The opposition BJP sought supersession of the municipality on charges of mismanagement. After the state government superseded the town's elected body, the ruling party, i.e. Nagarik Samiti, obtained a stay order from the High Court against the supersession till the final hearing of the case. In the meantime, certain councillors changed their political alliances and thus the BJP came to govern the municipality. Even though there is an anti-defection law to discourage such politics in municipal bodies, changing the ruling party was not difficult. ·

Similarly, in Khedbrahma the Congress initially had marginal majority in the nagar panchayat with the support of some independents. But later in 1999, the BJP gained a majority after seven independent councillors switched support to the BJP.

### Municipalities and Other Parastatal Bodies

The municipalities depend on parastatal bodies like the GWSSB and the Gujarat Electricity Board (GEB) for infrastructural development. The terms of reference and format of the relationships between these parastatal bodies and the municipality are usually decided by the state government. No transparency or accountability could be discovered in this relationship, since no municipal functionary had any information; all seemed to think that another department was responsible for crucial municipal services. For example, the sewer lines in Dholka were not yet operational. Although much of the work had been completed by the GWSSB, it had yet to hand the facility over to the municipality. The GEB had also not provided the electricity connection to operate the pumping stations because of the municipality's pending dues.

### Empowerment of Women and Weaker Sections

After the CAA74 there has been a definite and welcome change in the composition of municipalities, though caste and community continue to be the principal bases of coalitions. Women, though formally holding positions, have very little involvement in the governance. Very few women councillors were found to spend time in the municipality offices. In one instance, the woman president spent only three hours at the municipality office, but her husband spent the entire day there doing her work! In Khedbrahma, as an effort towards actualizing local governance by popular participation, women councillors had come together to involve the people (largely women) in cleaning up garbage in the town. However, the then president constantly discouraged them and told them not to interfere in the work. The otherwise articulate women were 'forced' to remain quiet by the chairman who insisted that women should not get involved in such 'problems'.

### Citizens' Participation

The CAA74 sought to encourage participation of citizens in town administration. However, unlike Panchayats where there is a provision for holding Gram Sabhas every year, there is no format for contacting citizens for public meetings.

---

[13] An NGO concerned with development education and people's participation in development in Gujarat and Rajasthan.

In Dharampur, officials talked of citizens' contribution in laying of sewer lines. But on closer examination, the citizens' 'contribution' was, in fact, nothing but payment of the connection fee. The estimate of citizens' contribution was therefore merely a projection of the money the municipality would receive if all citizens paid for their connections. The meaning of citizens' participation is not as yet clear. But since it is deemed important in the current development scenario, the bureaucracy tries to pass off anything as citizens' participation.

In the four municipalities in this study, no planning process had yet been initiated. Municipalities were still very unclear about the role that they were to perform. The follow-up legislation in Gujarat did not further devolve responsibilities, nor did it spell out any expectation from local governments to participate in planning and development. Additionally, in the past there had been no efforts to create capacities within municipalities to do the planning, or even to deal with other competent bodies that can do the job.

### Strengthening Municipal Finances

As of local fiscal autonomy, upon the recommendations of the State Finance Commission, principles were to be enunciated for tax assignments, sharing of taxes, and grants-in-aid. All the towns are fiscally stressed. Tax collections have not improved. The practice of octroi collection is corrupt. The dues to agencies like the Gujarat Electricity Board (GEB) have mounted. The time-frame in which the State Finance Commission is to submit its recommendations is not clear. Further delays by the state government could effectively put off the implementation of the Commission's recommendations.

### Devolution of Powers and Responsibilities to Municipalities

The powers devolved to the municipalities through the CAA74 do not give them the autonomy to appoint even one sweeper! These municipalities were seeking permission from the state government to make such appointments. Further, they were making 'ad hoc' appointments irresponsibly to serve narrow selfish political interests of the elected members. Due to lack of actual devolution of power, the elected representatives considered it to be the responsibility of the state government to pay the salaries of employees!

After the CAA74 the term of chairman of the municipality was reduced to one year. This period is barely sufficient for most individuals to even familiarize themselves with the 'system'. In all the municipalities, the presidents during their tenure, had indulged in nepotism through ad hoc recruitment in the municipalities.

### Transparency and Information Availability to the Citizens

Information sharing regarding the town and its development programmes was almost non-existent. The chaotic state of records remains the most problematic aspect of the present system. They had widely varying formats for accounting incomes and expenditures; the documents were cumbersome and often unclear. The multiplicity of development schemes made it difficult even for municipal employees to identify relevant details. We attempted to find how much money had been spent in Dharampur under various schemes. Though the employees could tell us the total expenditure made on roads, drains, water pipelines, etc. in their aggregate, they could not provide details of schemewise expenditure. On the other hand, in other towns, information on expenditure was available schemewise but no functionaries could provide the expenditure either on specific services or in the aggregate!

### Conclusion

Besides reforms related to regular elections, reservations of women and weaker sections, and reorganization of wards, etc. the effect of the CAA74 in terms of day-to-day functioning and the financial status of municipalities is negligible.

## 9.2 URBAN AND INTER-URBAN ROAD DESIGNS IN INDIA: ISSUES CONCERNING MIXED TRAFFIC

*Geetam Tiwari*

### TRAFFIC PATTERNS AND PLANNING ISSUES IN INDIAN CITIES

A high share of non-motorized vehicles (NMVs) and motorized two-wheelers (MTW) characterizes the transport system of Indian cities. Nearly 45–80 per cent of the registered vehicles are MTWs. Cars account for only 5–20 per cent of the total vehicle fleet. The road network is used by at least seven categories of motorized vehicles (MVs) and NMVs. Public transport is the predominant mode of motorized travel in megacities. Buses carry 20–65 per cent of the total trips excluding walk trips.

Because bicyclists and pedestrians continue to share road space with MVs in the absence of infrastructure specifically designed for NMVs, they are exposed to higher risks of road accidents. Unlike cities in the West, pedestrians, bicyclists, and MTWs constitute 75 per cent of the total fatalities in road traffic crashes. Buses and trucks are involved in more than 60 per cent of the fatal crashes. In addition, many indigenously designed vehicles, such as tempos, three-wheeler scooter taxis, and 'Vikrams'[14] are present on the roads of Indian cities because of the absence of efficient and comfortable public transport services. These vehicles operate as paratransit modes, thus serving a useful role in the context of social sustainability. However, they have unique safety and pollution problems, which the West has never experienced.

Unlike the traffic in high-income countries, in India bicycles and other NMVs are present in significant numbers on the arterial roads and inter-city highways, which are designed for fast moving, uninterrupted flow of MVs. All modes of traffic use one-, two-, and three-lane roads. Traffic laws and road designs do not segregate bicycle traffic and enforcement of speed limits is minimal. MVs and NMVs have different densities at peak traffic hours at different locations of cities. The existing traffic characteristics, modal mix, location details, geometric design, land use characteristics, and other operating characteristics present a unique situation where economic and travel demand compulsions not anticipated generally have overwhelmed official plans.

The integration of MVs and NMVs has occurred 'naturally' on city roads. On two- and three-lane roads, bicycles primarily use the outermost lane on the left, that is the curbside lane, which MVs do not use even when bicycle density is low. Bicyclists use middle lanes only when making a right-hand turn. Even at one-lane sites, bicyclists occupy the left extreme, giving space to the MV traffic.

## THE 'CRITICAL ELEMENT' IN THE CITY TRANSPORT FABRIC: VULNERABLE ROAD USERS

If urban transport infrastructure does not meet the needs of vulnerable road users, then the mobility of other modes is adversely affected. Despite a low level of vehicle ownership, a high share of public transport, and the presence of NMVs, in most Indian cities the

[14] These vehicles have the advantage of flexibility, and are even able to match the prices of public bus transport. When traffic speeds are slow enough, they do not impose negative externalities on faster bus transport, which they otherwise do.

concentrations of various pollutants exceed levels laid down in World Health Organization (WHO) standards for ambient air quality.

It is evident that investments in projects that are directed entirely to benefit only car users have not been able to significantly improve urban speeds. Thereby they may not even have benefited car users as much as was anticipated.

Congestion relief has been short-lived due to the impact of latent travel demand. Construction of capital-intensive systems like (MRTS: Mass Rapid Transport System) metros has also not resulted in a decrease in congestion and air pollution. In fact, some of the intended congestion relief measures (construction of flyovers, expressways) may have contributed to greater NMV and pedestrian fatalities due to increased speeds.

Urban transport systems in Indian cities can become sustainable and provide mobility with minimal adverse effects on the environment only if safe and affordable transport for all sections of population becomes available. Nearly 50 per cent of the people in these cities need to live close to places of employment. For survival, they need access to inexpensive modes of travel to work. If the planned transport system does not provide for their travel need, they are forced to operate under suboptimal conditions. In the process, they continue to utilize space that has not been planned for such use. Consequently, land use and transport plans are violated and all modes of transport operate under suboptimal conditions. The experience of past decades of long-term integrated land use transport plan exercises suggests that the existence of the informal sector and its travel needs must be recognized in order to prepare effective plans. This should encourage mixed land use patterns and transport infrastructure especially designed for bicycles and other NMVs.

## AVOIDED COSTS THROUGH INVESTMENTS IN BICYCLE/NMV FRIENDLY INFRASTRUCTURE

Providing a separate bicycle/NMV track would make more space available for MVs and make bicycling less hazardous. Studies in Delhi carried out for this report show that on urban arterials the curbside lane (3.5 m) is used primarily by bicycle and other NMVs. Because of the presence of bicycles and NMVs in this lane, buses are forced to stop in the middle lane at bus-stops. MVs do not use the curbside lane even when bicycle/NMV densities are low.

A segregated bicycle/NMV lane needs only 2.5 m and since most of the major arterials in Delhi have a service road, as do some other Indian cities where planned development has taken place after the 1960s, the existing road space is wide enough to accommodate such a lane. This would not require additional right of way on existing roads. A detailed study completed in Delhi shows how existing roads can be redesigned within the given right of way to provide for an exclusive lane for NMVs (Tiwari *et al.* 1998).

Since a majority of the bicyclists in Indian cities are daily commuters (captive riders—people who use bicycles despite poor facilities due to lack of options) the proposed network must enable direct and safe bicycle travel within a coherent system. The proposed routes must guarantee a coherent network structure, minimize trip length (directness), and minimize the number of encounters between cyclists and MVs (safety). The success of the bicycle/NMV route design depends upon meeting the requirement of convenience for users of bicycles and NMVs. Otherwise they are forced to share the road space with MVs resulting in suboptimal conditions for all vehicles. If the design of arterial roads includes integrated NMV lanes along with dedicated lanes for buses, pedestrian paths and service roads, it would benefit all road users as discussed in the following sections.

### Increased Capacity

If a separate segregated lane is constructed for bicycles, the curbside lane, which is currently used by bicyclists, becomes available to MVs. This relatively small investment in bicycle lanes can increase the road space for MVs by 50 per cent on three-lane roads. Bicycle lanes also result in better space utilization. For instance, a 3.5 m lane has a carrying capacity of 1800 cars per hour, whereas it can carry 5400 bicycles per hour (Replogle 1991). Average occupancy of a car is 1.15 persons (Indian Roads Congress 1990) and a bicycle carries one person. This implies that in order to move the same number of people in cars, we would need 2.6 times the road area that would be required for bicyclists. Given the fact that there is little space available to expand existing roads, the future mobility needs and projected trips can only be met by increasing the capacity of the existing road network. This can only be achieved by encouraging modes that are more efficient in terms of space utilization—bicycles and buses.

MVs benefit because of improved capacity of the road and improvement in speeds. Capacity estimations of a typical arterial road in Delhi (Tiwari 1999) show improvement in corridor capacity by 19–23 per cent through providing an exclusive bicycle track. If the full capacity of the corridor is utilized, that is provision of a high capacity bus lane in the curbside lane, it can lead to 56–73 per cent improvement in capacity

(increasing the present carrying capacity of 23,000 passengers per hour to 45,000 passengers per hour).

### Improved Speeds

Improvement in speeds of MVs will be experienced until the corridor is full to capacity due to realization of induced demand. Major beneficiaries of speed improvement are buses because the curbside lane becomes available to them without interference from slow vehicles. Estimations of time savings experienced by bus commuters, car occupants, and two-wheeler commuters on a typical arterial corridor in Delhi (Tota 1999) show 48 per cent reduction in time costs due to 50 per cent improvement in the speed of buses (increasing the present average speed of 15 km per hour to 30 km per hour) and 30 per cent improvement in the speed of cars and two-wheelers.

### Reduced Congestion

Congestion has long been recognized as an environmental problem. Other than causing delay, it creates noise and fumes and increases health risks of road users and residents. Delhi and other Indian cities have invested in grade separated junctions and flyovers as one of the major congestion relief measures at an average cost of Rs 100 million to Rs 300 million for each intersection. However, detailed simulations of a major intersection in Delhi show that replanning the junction to include separate NMV lanes and a bus priority lane can effect an 80 per cent improvement in the present level of delays. The cost of this measure is 25 times less than the proposed grade separated junction (Karthik 1998).

### Increased Safety

By creating segregated bicycle lanes and redesigning intersections, conflicts between MVs and bicyclists can be reduced substantially, leading to a sharp decrease in the number of accidents and fatalities for bicyclists and users of MTWs. Safety benefits estimated for a typical arterial road in Delhi show 46 per cent reduction in accident costs. This is because a segregated facility reduces injury accidents by 40 per cent and fatalities by 50 per cent.

### Reduced Pollution and Energy Consumption

MVs are reported to be the single largest source of air pollution (70 per cent of total air pollution in Delhi) (Central Pollution Control Board 1998). This is a serious concern to bicyclists, pedestrians, and motorists as air quality is worse in or near built-up roads. Bicyclists suffer the adverse affects of pollution because of heavier breathing whilst exercising close to the source of exhaust pollution. A dedicated infrastructure can reduce this problem to some extent. While motorized transport is one of the most polluting of all human activities, bicycling is the least polluting mode of all, as it generates no noise pollution or toxic emissions. Therefore there is a need to make cycling more popular. A better bicycle infrastructure can play an important role in increasing the modal share of bicycles and thus reduce air pollution and adverse health effects of pollution.

Energy consumption and pollution also decrease because MVs have smoother driving and improved average speeds. Estimations for Delhi corridor show 28 per cent reduction in fuel consumption and 29 per cent reduction in health externalities related to air pollution (Tota 1999).

### Induced Bicycle Trips

There are approximately 1 million households in the middle to high income category in Delhi. If the average trip rate of these households is two per day, at least 10 per cent of these trips, especially by school-going children and young adults, could become bicycle trips for recreation and school journeys. This group benefits by expanding their opportunity space to participate in different activities. It is difficut to express this benefit in money terms.

### INTER–URBAN TRANSPORT ISSUES

On national and state highways speed variation on different types of highways is primarily because four-lane divided highways also have better quality pavements and, therefore, higher average speeds compared to single-lane and undivided highways.

The presence of small towns and villages along the main highways changes the character of Indian highways. Speed, volume, and density data on sections away from villages and towns measure well enough on the parameter. It is the density of villages and towns along the highway that may be considerably slowing down the journey speeds of long-distance traffic. In other words, when long-distance traffic passes through villages and towns along the highway, the presence of local traffic and 'conflict' between local and long-distance traffic results in lower speeds and low level of service. Therefore, one can expect improvement in the level of service of a given highway by resolving the conflict between local and long-distance traffic sharing the carriageway. This may require a different cross-sectional design of the highway that is conventional.

Generally slow-moving vehicles, for example bicycles, tractors, and animal carts, are not present in large numbers (low flow rates compared to other MVs) on our

inter-city highways. However, because of low speeds, they have much higher shares in densities as compared to volume shares. They consume a large capacity of the road because of low speeds. Their presence on the main carriageway, even if it is in small numbers, results in reduced capacity. In a four-lane highway, the curbside lane is occupied by slow-moving vehicles and only the middle lanes are available for fast MVs.

Single-lane and two-lane highways present fewer overtaking opportunities because of the presence of slow-moving vehicles. On four-lane highways, over-taking opportunities also decrease because of a few slow-moving vehicles. The deterioration in the level of service occurs because of mixing of slow-moving and fast-moving vehicles.

Higher average speeds on four-lane highways are explained by the presence of cars and trucks moving at higher speeds. Lower average speed of MVs on single-lane highways is explained by the presence of tractors and trucks moving at lower speeds. Comparison between two-lane highways without shoulders and those with 1.5 m and 2.5 m shoulders shows that the reduction in the average speed of MVs is higher in the former option compared to the latter. Clearly, the presence of shoulders seems to make a difference in traffic performance. Shoulders provide space for slow-moving vehicles and better overtaking opportunities.

Future highway designs must account for the users of different transport modes having conflicting requirements. They must take into consideration MVs' need for clear roads for uninterrupted traffic flow. At the same time they must address the needs of bicyclists and pedestrians for shady trees, kiosks for drinks and food, bicycle repair shops, etc. at shorter distances. Highway planning standards provide for services needed by MV users. However, there are no standards for providing services needed by NMVs. These services mushroom along urban or inter-city highways to fulfil the demands of road users. However, their existence is viewed as 'illegal encroachment' on the designed road space. Rather than view these as illegal, it is important for town and highway planners to incorporate the existence and functionality of such informal services into their models and designs.

MVs are designed to operate at much higher speeds for better fuel economy and emission levels. Roads are also designed to increase throughput of MVs only. These measures decrease safety of NMV occupants and pedestrians sharing the same road space.

Urban arterials passing through commercially developed areas and highways passing through small towns serve multiple purposes. They carry through traffic.

However, the adjacent land use generates cross traffic and demands multiple space usage, for example space for parking vehicles, hawkers, and informal shopping. The existing design standards do not account for the conflicting demand between local traffic and through traffic, resulting in suboptimal conditions for both kinds.

There is a need to accommodate the conflicting requirements of NMV occupants and pedestrians and motorized traffic on our urban and inter-city highways. This includes redesigning the road cross-section setting more exclusive space for pedestrians and NMVs and giving pedestrians and bicyclists priority over cars at certain places.

# 9.3 VEHICULAR AIR POLLUTION IN INDIA: RECENT CONTROL MEASURES AND RELATED ISSUES

*B. P. Pundir*

For all industrial and economic activities, personal mobility is essential. Flexibility, door-to-door convenience, and often shorter total journey time have resulted the world over in the growth of cars and personalized motor vehicles. Even where public transport is available and subsidized, personal motor car demand has grown substantially. In India, between 1987 and 1997 vehicle population grew threefold from 12.6 to 37.2 million. In the West and Japan, actions to control vehicle-generated air pollution started in the early 1970s and very high success has been achieved. The same, however, cannot be said about the third world countries, in spite of the wealth of information and experience available from the advanced countries.[15]

Delhi is one of most polluted cities in the world.[16] This could be attributed to a large number of old and obsolete technology vehicles, a preponderance of highly polluting vehicles, bad maintenance, congested traffic conditions, fuel adulteration, and weak enforcement of traffic discipline and emission regulations. The city of Delhi has a vehicle mix that is typical of some third world countries and common to much of India. It has a large number of two- and three-wheelers.

Table 9.3.1 shows that the number of two-wheelers in the country as well as in Delhi is very large compared

to passenger cars due to their low initial and running costs as a means of personal transport.[17] Throughout India their numbers have risen by more than 37 per cent over the last several years. Cars too have grown at rates exceeding 30 per cent per cent per annum. The corresponding figures for Delhi are 34.7 per cent for two-wheelers and 19.5 per cent for cars. In comparison, the number of buses increased by only 26.7 per cent. Similar trends are likely in most other large cities in India except Mumbai, where two-wheelers are not generally preferred and the number of cars per person is much smaller than in Delhi. The difference in the composition of vehicles between Delhi and Mumbai is striking. The existence of mass transit systems like suburban railways and other efficient means of public transport is an important reason for the much lower vehicle population in Mumbai.[18]

## VEHICULAR AIR POLLUTION AND EMISSION REGULATIONS

In India, to curb growing vehicular air pollution, vehicle emission regulations were implemented for the first time for vehicles registering in 1991–2. Standards for in-service vehicles were already in place even before 1991 in several cities and states. The road transport departments have been issuing certificates to individual vehicles annually or half-yearly in the form of Pollution Under Control (PUC) stickers. Since then, after much deliberation, several ad hoc and other steps have been taken, especially with regard to Delhi. Some of the major decisions have been as follows:

[15] Tokyo was one of the most polluted cities in the mid-1960s. Since the 1970s pollution levels have come down dramatically, as with the sharp rise in incomes the willingness and ability to pay for pollution control measures have increased. In poor cities with lower overall 'value of life' and *inter alia* limited capacity to correct pollution, they remain high.

[16] Thus World Resources (1998–9) reported Delhi to have 415 $\mu g/m^3$ of total suspended particulate matter and over 24 $\mu g/m^3$ of $SO_2$, and 41 $\mu g/m^3$ of $NO_2$. Other cities of India were not significantly better, and most cities of China were as bad as Delhi. Korea and Taiwan have shown reasonable improvement, and China is likely to follow suit as incomes rise. Mexico has continued to show high urban pollution for well over three decades.

[17] Indeed, the scooter is to India what the car was to the United States in the 1920s.

[18] Another reason could well be the income distribution: the very large number of upper middle and middle classes in Delhi could be a factor.

TABLE 9.3.1
Vehicle Population in India, Delhi and Mumbai

(thousands)

|  | Year | Two-wheelers | Three-wheelers | Cars jeeps | Taxis | Buses | Trucks |
|---|---|---|---|---|---|---|---|
| Delhi | 1997 | 1876 | 80 | 706 | 15 | 30 | 141* |
|  | 2000 | 2527 | 133 | 844 | 19 | 38 | 209* |
| Mumbai | 1997 | 329 | 72 | 280 | 49 | 13 | 19.5 |
| all-India | 1997 | 25,693 | – | 4662** | – | 488 | 2260** |
|  | 2000 | 35,319 | 1755 | 6189 | – | – | 3348*** |

\* Registered trucks, but most trucks would be operating outside
\*\* Includes taxis
\*\*\* Includes buses

| April 1991–2 | First set of emission regulations for new registration vehicles was issued. |
|---|---|
| April 1995 | Use of catalytic converters was made mandatory on gasoline passenger cars for metro cities. |
| April 1996 | Revised emission regulations for new vehicles were issued for the entire country. |
| April 1998 | Emission standards for catalytic converter equipped vehicles for metro cities were announced. |
| April 2000 | Euro I regulations for cars and diesel vehicles and new lower revised standards for two- and three-wheelers were announced. Euro II norms for cars in metro cities, as directed by the Supreme Court, are to be implemented. |
| April 2000 | Commercial vehicles older than eight years are to be taken off the road in Delhi. Major programmes for introduction of Compressed Natural Gas (CNG) vehicles are to be developed. In Delhi all new buses are to be CNG operated. |

While these are well-intentioned steps, they have thus far had very little impact because:

• regular and periodic air quality data that is also reliable is rare;

• the inventory of data on pollutants is incomplete;

• inspection and maintenance procedures for vehicles are inadequate;

• limited technology options exist to control emissions from a large number of in-service vehicles;

• little serious attention is paid to developing alternative means of transport, improving traffic flow, or using alternative fuels or energy vehicles.

An integrated long-term approval for control of vehicular air pollution needs to be formulated. This may include effective monitoring of in-use vehicles, traffic improvement, restrictions on the use of vehicles during certain periods of the day or in busy shopping areas, development of a large mass transit system, continuous monitoring of air quality, and linkages with future strategy. Enforcement actions should be derived from such a plan to minimize unacceptable and sometimes costly, unintended consequences. Although the Central Pollution Control Board (CPCB), Ministry of Service Transport (MoST), Ministry of Environment and Forests (MOEF), Ministry of Petroleum and Natural Gas (MoPNG), and other agencies have done considerable work in formulating emission standards and ensuring wholesale supply of the necessary quality of fuels to meet the requirements of new emission controlled vehicles, enforcement is lacking.

While significant progress has been made in formulation and implementation of emission standards for new vehicles, for in-service vehicles there has been little progress.

## EMISSION CONTROL OF IN-SERVICE VEHICLES

Vehicle emission standards were initially enforced for new production vehicles only in the United States and Europe starting in the early 1970s. However, it was soon realized that significant reductions in vehicular air pollution are possible only when emissions are reduced from the in-service vehicles also. Many times, an 80:20 rule is quoted with regard to the contribution of bad in-service vehicles to total vehicle emissions. In other words, 80 per cent of emissions are contributed by the 20 per cent in-service vehicles that are in bad mechanical condition and powered by old technology engines. For Indian conditions, 20 per cent of bad in-service vehicles have been quoted to contribute as much as 60 per cent to total vehicular emissions. Unless these old or badly tuned vehicles are regularly monitored, repaired, or scrapped, no significant gains towards pollution control are likely to emerge.

Emission regulations for in-service vehicles have been in existence since the early 1980s at least in Mumbai, Delhi, and other large cities. For enforcement of these regulations, a large number of petrol/diesel retail stations and some garages have been authorized to carry out PUC checks biannually or annually for a nominal fee. Despite such checks being in force for more than fifteen years, a large number of heavily smoking diesel buses, trucks, and three-wheelers on the road. Petrol cars are expected to be in an equally high polluting condition, but as the pollutants from petrol cars are invisible these do not attract public criticism. The reasons are not far to seek. The principal reasons that make in-use vehicle inspection more or less fruitless or almost farcical are:

• petrol stations and garages that carry out this activity have no incentive to do such work correctly;

• regular and proper calibration of gas analysers and smokemeters is rarely done;

• inspectors lack training;

• the ritual of inspection, rather than the purpose, has taken precedence. Inspection centres are not equipped to, nor are they required to, adjust or correct polluting vehicles.

## REMEDIAL MEASURES

'Centralised Inspection Centres', under direct supervision of the police or other authority, are known to be effective elsewhere. Also, follow-up of failed vehicles to ensure that these are repaired and resubmitted for inspection is far easier when carried out by a centralized inspection. In addition to emissions, these centres carry out safety-related checks, for example wheel alignment, brake tests, and under-carriage inspection, using automated systems. Such centres, in reducing the time for inspection and measurement, also have synergy with other customer needs.

Each well-equipped centre has four to eight test lanes and thus can inspect 1.5 to 3 lakh vehicles every year. Initial investment, excluding land, could be between Rs 10 and 20 crore for a four-lane inspection centre. Five such centres have recently been established in Bangladesh, two in Dhaka and three in other cities. In Mexico, thirty such centres each with eight test lanes have been established for a total vehicle stock of 2.6 million.

Stringent new vehicle emission standards also require better quality fuels. Requirements include lead-free gasoline, low sulphur gasoline and diesel fuels, and upgradation of other properties, for example low aromatics, high diesel ignition quality, narrow range of fuel density, lower final boiling point, and use of multifunctional additives. Use of oxygenates in petrol can reduce pollution.

## BENZENE

Following trends in the United States and Europe, environmental agencies in India too are pushing for lowering the benzene in petrol to a maximum 1 per cent by volume. But with the high incentive to adulterate petrol with benzene and other solvents[19] remaining, there is little hope of the air quality in cities improving. Two- and three-wheelers that constitute the bulk of vehicles in urban areas are particularly polluting because they use two-stroke engines that exhaust almost 15–25 per cent of the fuel unburned outside the engine.

Most of these in-service vehicles are not equipped with catalytic converters. In view of this, the expected environmental benefits of reducing benzene content in petrol would not be obtained.

## OXYGENATES

Various oxygenated compounds, for example methanol, ethanol, and Methyl tertiary butyle or MTBE, have been mixed in petrol to reduce carbon monoxide and unburned fuel emissions from in-use vehicles. However, there has been rethinking on this issue in the United States and other advanced countries. For example, methanol, being toxic, is no longer permitted for blending by the US Environmental Protection Agency (EPA). MTBE is now thought to be carcinogenic and its use is being restricted in certain US states, for example Colorado. Ethanol blending, although acceptable, is agricultural based and thus is not likely to be cost-effective.[20]

## CNG

The Supreme Court of India has directed in its order dated 12 August 1998 that the Delhi government must submit and follow a time-bound plan to switch its city bus fleet over on to a clean fuel mode in the National Capital Region. The Environmental Pollution (Prevention and Control) Authority for the National Capital Region accordingly set the following targets for various agencies with regard to the use of CNG:

[19] The recent large-scale adulteration of petrol with industrial solvents in Gujarat is a case in point.

[20] This would be especially so in a land-scarce economy like India.

| Action | Target Date |
|---|---|
| Replacement of all pre-1990 auto-rickshaws and taxis with new vehicles using clean fuel | 31.03.2001 |
| Financial incentives for replacement of old auto-rickshaws with post-1990 auto-rickshaws and taxis with new vehicles on clean fuel | 31.03.2000 |
| Ban on plying of buses more than eight years old except those on clean fuel | 1.04.2000 |
| Conversion of the entire city bus fleet, both the Delhi Transport Corporation (DTC) and private buses, to a single fuel, viz. CNG | 31.03.2000 |
| The Gas Authority of India Ltd. (GAIL) was directed to submit a time-bound plan for increasing the number of CNG supply outlets from 9 to 80 | 31.03.2000 |

Clean fuel here effectively means CNG. There is now general acceptance that diesel particulates are highly carcinogenic in nature. Internationally, efforts are being made to reduce these levels drastically in urban areas, by switching over to CNG-fuelled buses. In Delhi, two-stroke engine powered three-wheelers are also to be replaced.

For these, conversion to CNG per se does not solve lubricant-related visible smoke. If any reduction occurs, it is entirely due to a separate lubrication pump that is to be necessarily installed on CNG-operated two-stroke engines. This pump regulates the quantity of lubricant introduced into the engine. The same pump would be equally effective on petrol two-stroke engines. The unburned emissions of natural gas (again 15–25 per cent) are, of course, more benign as methane is not photo-chemically reactive.

Thus there are doubts about whether attempting to reduce pollution by converting auto-rickshaws to CNG operation would be cost effective. Four-stroke engines with catalyst equipped three-wheelers powered by petrol or CNG would have been a more environment-friendly option as well as far more cost-effective in the long run.

The CNG solution the world over has been found to be more cost-effective as well as responsible for giving high environmental benefits for medium- to heavy-duty vehicles. On this front, however, the programme in Delhi has made very little progress. According to the Centre for Science and Environment (CSE), New Delhi (18 July 2000), at present Delhi has 7000 CNG vehicles and 44 CNG filling stations in operation. However, it appears the real issue has been entirely missed. Only forty of these vehicles are buses, which ought to be the major CNG-consuming vehicle. This insignificant number is far below what is required to bring about environmental benefits. Again, it is also widely accepted that the dual fuel (diesel–CNG) mode of operation in buses does not provide the expected benefits of CNG fuel.

There is need for an integrated and analysed approach carefully drawn up for strategies to reduce pollution in cities in India. Would the current initiative of the Supreme Court help? It has certainly helped to bring about the newer class of engines with low emissions and the added bonus of better mileage and power! But in-service vehicles would remain a major problem, because effective measurement, incentives for adherence and deterrents remain perverse or insufficient.

## 9.4 IMPLICATIONS OF THE 74TH AMENDMENT ON THE WATER AND WASTEWATER SECTOR

*Anish Nanavaty*

The concentration of political and fiscal power in the upper echelons of the government has led to a near elimination of autonomy at local level. Local institutions set up before Independence have been marginalized and rendered dependent on state governments. It is interesting that the idea of decentralization has gained currency in the last decade and its rise has coincided with the economic liberalization process.[21]

[21] Indeed the two go together more than is generally realized. 'Growing out of the plan', to an incentive- and market-based allocation of resources would, at local government level, mean

Liberalization and the need for higher growth rates have brought into focus the role of cities as engines of economic growth. On the other hand, the spread of media and communications has fuelled the expectations

initiative and the freedom to take decisions. In China, such decentralization of financial and local governments has led to much competition and 'overinvestment' which is one of the important reasons for high growth (Naughton 1996). At municipal levels, the 1980s and 1990s showed a remarkable upsurge in public investments in local infrastructure.

of the people. It is becoming increasingly evident that urban management and governance need dramatic improvement to ensure the efficiency and sustainability of infrastructure. The 74th Constitutional Amendment Act (CAA74) of 1992 has significant implications for the water and wastewater sector. The CAA74 is here viewed in the light of certain key reforms required for the development of the sector, and the extent to which it would aid the reform process is examined.

## KEY FEATURES

The CAA74 has been flaunted as an initiative to decentralize power and strengthen democracy at local level. The CAA74 accords constitutional status to urban local bodies (ULBs) and prescribes a near uniform local governance structure valid across the country. It provides a framework for electing local-level governments and for their 'effective' functioning to ensure provision of urban services and infrastructure.

It envisages certain fundamental changes in local self-government and is apparently a step towards operationalizing the Directive Principles of State Policy. The CAA74 mandates compulsory reconstitution of municipal bodies within a stipulated time-frame, thus ensuring continuity of local representatives. The Twelfth Schedule of the CAA74 suggests specific functions and responsibilities to local bodies. These are:

- urban planning, including town planning;
- regulation of land use and construction of buildings;
- planning for economic and social development;
- roads and bridges;
- water supply for domestic, industrial, and commercial purposes;
- public health, sanitation, conservancy, and solid waste management;
- fire services;
- urban forestry, protection of the environment, and promotion of ecological aspects;
- safeguarding the interests of weaker sections of society, including the handicapped and mentally retarded;
- slum improvement and upgradation;
- urban poverty alleviation;
- provision of urban amenities and facilities such as parks, gardens, and playgrounds;
- promotion of cultural, educational, and aesthetic aspects;
- burials and burial grounds; cremation grounds and electric crematoria;
- cattle pounds; prevention of cruelty to animals;
- vital statistics, including registration of births and deaths;
- public amenities including street lighting, parking lots, bus-stops, and public conveniences;
- regulation of slaughterhouses and tanneries.

Importantly, the CAA74 expressly recognizes a role for the ULBs within the constitutional framework and provides for devolution of financial powers from the state government for strengthening of municipal finances.

## WATER SECTOR IMPLICATIONS

The Twelfth Schedule includes water supply for domestic, industrial, and commercial purposes and public health, sanitation, conservancy, and solid waste management among the recommended municipal functions. The implications of the CAA74 in the light of the key issues facing the development of urban water and sewerage are now examined.

## EXTENT OF DEVOLUTION

Since water and sewerage services are primarily operated and maintained by the ULBs, the actual delegation of this responsibility may not be a significant issue.

In this regard, it needs to be mentioned that while the CAA74 has explicitly outlined the functions to be devolved, it has not been as explicit in terms of fiscal powers. Fiscal devolution has been referred to the respective state finance commissions. Going by the recommendations of the reports already submitted, wide variation has been reported in the extent of fiscal devolution and furtherance of sectoral reform. The extent of devolution has been left open to interpretation, and it is likely to be exploited by state governments to maintain status quo.

However, state governments, through parastatal agencies such as state water supply and sewerage boards, industrial development corporations, and city level boards, have been involved in planning, design, execution, and commissioning of water supply projects. For example, in Maharashtra, the Maharashtra Jeevan Pradhikaran owns, operates, and maintains 35 urban water supply of which 24 involve retail distribution. The Maharashtra Industrial Development Corporation (MIDC) and the Gujarat Industrial Development

Corporation (GIDC) have been supplying water for industrial purposes within their industrial estates. In certain cities such as Chennai, Hyderabad, Bangalore, and most recently Delhi, water and wastewater services have been delegated to a city-level body which is directly under the control of the respective state government.

There is an argument that parastatals exist because ULBs do not have adequate project implementation capacity. This is precisely the stand that state governments would advance in order to persist with parastatal agencies and delay devolution. Thus, to what extent state governments will take this opportunity to re-evaluate the industry structure and promote genuine decentralization is still an open question, in spite of the CAA74.

While the larger municipal corporations and city-level bodies enjoy reasonable autonomy with respect to planning, design, execution, operation, maintenance, and tariff setting for water and waste-water facilities, other local bodies lack the capacity to plan and implement large infrastructure projects. Hence parastatal agencies arrange financing and under-take planning, design, execution and commissioning of the schemes for municipal councils. The schemes are transferred to local bodies for operation and mainte-nance (O&M).

To the extent that the local ULB is responsible for O&M and presumably has the freedom to take decisions relevant to the task, such an arrangement is justified. But the principal failure of governments with regard to water and wastewater is allocative fail-ure—they have not been able to cover as much of the population as they should have. A state monopoly model has failed in sectors such as power, telecom, insurance, banking, and media and is well on its way to being discarded. However, there is precious little debate and thinking on the need for a similar redefinition in the water sector.

The state water supply and sewerage boards are, in effect, monopolist technical and financial consultancy organizations wholly controlled by the government. In the current dispensation, parastatal agencies are the only agencies that ULBs can approach for assistance in project implementation. Given the subsidiary nature of the ULB, the parastatal (as a state government agency) assumes the more powerful position. Such a monopolistic structure contributes to both erosion of resourcefulness and initiative at ULB level and to lack of innovation and the high cost structure in the sector.

Besides these problems the stifling relationship between smaller ULBs and parastatal bodies results in displacement of responsibility. The problem goes beyond water and sewerage to practically all urban functions where an artificial hiatus exists between capac-ity creation and the maintenance of the service. Such a hiatus creates dysfunctions in the task of providing services in a situation of growing demand. Efficient operations can improve coverage and better design has much effect on costs and the scope for efficient opera-tions. But perhaps the organizational failure that thus divided 'responsibility' creates is more serious. Urban councillors and elected members cannot actually be held responsible even when they want to do the right things, since they have to typically depend upon the parastatals. There is no way the elected representatives can hold the (state-level) offices under their control and demand their accountability. Inevitably, organizational stability is reached when the primary task, that of providing the service, is displaced by processes that are rule oriented, even in the absence of corruption. More typically, the displacement of responsibility and the lack of accountability that the relationships en-gender creates the scope for private gain, which can be exploited by both the bureaucracy and the elected members.

The standard argument for giving parastatals the role they currently enjoy is that most urban bodies, except those of large cities lack the expertise! While this is undoubtedly true, the conclusion that therefore mo-nopolist parastatals must exist, with no freedom of choice for the ULBs, and that funds for water develop-ment should be routed through these organizations is fallacious. After all, the capacity to design and build can always be procured from many sources.

My assertion is that such technical and financial expertise (which could include public enterprise dis-tanced from government) should ideally reside in the private sector and can be separated from the govern-ment. Ideally, the ULB, as the client, should be able to choose between competing agencies on the basis of innovativeness, scope for cost reduction, suitability to local conditions, or any such condition and enter into formal contracts for provision of such services. Simultaneously, agencies possessing technical expertise should also be allowed to bid for and execute projects for other utilities in the country or abroad. The industry structure needs to undergo radical change in order to enable such transfer of expertise. The restructuring of these agencies is crucial to development of the water and wastewater sector. The subject still needs further inquiry.[22] It is only when ULBs have the choice to

[22] More is at stake probably than the lack of a correct understanding of how organizational (and inter-organizational)

go to other organizations, including private consultants and developers and even other states' parastatals, that they can be held accountable by the people.

### Industrial Water Supply

Local bodies should benefit from greater decentralization and sustainable revenue sources. However, a significant revenue source in most municipal corporations has largely been retained by state governments. The state industrial corporations have continued to supply water to industrial estates, even within primary urban areas! As a result, cities with a significant industrial base, such as Aurangabad, Surat, Indore, and Nashik, have been deprived of a buoyant revenue source and a significant cross-subsidization opportunity. On the other hand, utilities such as the Brihanmumbai Municipal Corporation and Hyderabad Metro Water Board have benefited in being able to supply to industrial customers within their limits. (It needs to be mentioned that cross-subsidization is not the solution and there are limits to its use.) But, that apart, the mix of consumers that industrial use brings, and the room it creates for a convergence of pricing through the reform process, is being denied to the ULBs. State industrial development corporations in the states of Maharashtra and Gujarat have been generating surpluses on the water supply account. Local bodies deprived of the most lucrative customer segment continue to face resource constraints that prevent them from becoming independent entities.

It is important that the entire gamut of activities with regard to water and wastewater service provision be entrusted to the ULBs. This could also be the case with regard to other municipal functions such as roads, streets, lighting, education, health care, and housing, although the dysfunctionalities in the current arrangements in these sectors have not yet been looked at. Moreover, the CAA74 expressly includes industrial water supply as a responsibility of the local body. Such a transfer of responsibility should enable ULBs to view and develop water and wastewater management (including industrial effluents) in an integrated manner. They should also be able to view city development in a holistic fashion. This should be seen as a step towards giving city councillors and mayors a role in

attracting investment to the city and, perhaps, a step towards the improvement of urban life.

### Financing

Water sector projects have been principally financed through budgetary allocation and state government guaranteed debt. Parastatal agencies have acted as conduits for multilateral agency funds and capital market access. Given the fiscal situation of most of the state governments and recent Reserve Bank of India (RBI) directives with respect to greater disclosures on contingent liabilities and capital adequacy requirements for investee banks, such a financing strategy has become unsustainable. Indeed the rationale for parastatal agencies continuing as monopolies in the state sector can be questioned given the objective of greater decentraliztion and an understanding of market failure.[23]

A second major issue relates to the need for greater emphasis on cost recovery (of both operating and capital expenditure) in project formulation and in credit allocation. Such a shift will help in evolution of municipal financing institutions such as bond banks and other pooled financing mechanisms. In this regard, the ULBs will require independent and sustainable sources of revenue[24] and powers to contract in innovative ways. This is an area that the CAA74 has left for the state finance commissions to devise. Objective criteria for devolution of state government funds, including incentives for financial prudence, would be of immense help in sectoral reform.

---

[23] Water supply and sewerage do not have appropriability (or excludability) problems even in slums if the appropriate organizational innovations of 'Pani Panchayat' like systems can be created. Moreover, the function of design, consultancy, and construction of water supply projects can be completely unbundled and would be entirely a competitive activity. There is little fundamental difference between building a housing colony, a factory, or a water supply scheme. Market failure is largely limited to the distribution segment of the urban water.

[24] Thus far ULBs have not really been free of state governments to decide upon user charges. Where they have had a modicum of autonomy, user charges have been such as to recover as much as 80 per cent or more of cost as in the case of Chennai Metrowater. The point is, what is not possible or difficult at the level of the entire state, viz. to have rational and sustainable tariffs, may well be possible at a smaller level in a few instances. But once the functionality of rational user charges is proved in a few ULBs, others could change by following them. The many ULBs exploring various options in a period of financial stress and increasing expectations are necessary to break the 'all or none' kind of bind that typically holds back state governments, from rational user charges.

---

structures and processes work. As the process of the 'contraction of the state' from economic activities is on, the bureaucracy has been particularly active at state level to promote 'newer' organizations that have the potential to secure and retain certain financial privileges that government offices do not have, but managers of public enterprise (parastatals) can have.

Local bodies in India have still not been exposed to private sector participation, except by way of awarding construction contracts. Access to alternate sources of funding would entail efficient utilization. While such models have been considered by certain ULBs, all of them have been abandoned. A success story still eludes this sector. The CAA74, while it has transferred responsibilities to ULBs, has not given them powers to enter into contracts with other parties to carry these out. An amendment to that effect would greatly strengthen the ability of ULBs to conceptualize and develop projects involving the private sector.

## Tariffs

Inadequate cost recovery has been a major impediment to the development of the water sector in the country. One of the major causes has been low water tariff levels. A fraction of the O&M expenses are recovered through user charges by local bodies. The average recovery, even in progressive states such as Maharashtra and Gujarat, is 68 per cent and 59 per cent respectively and it is probably worse in other states. The deficits are bridged either through state government grants or through octroi revenues (in the case of municipal corporations in Maharashtra and Gujarat). Such a situation is clearly unsustainable.[25]

The setting and revision of tariffs have been subject to the approval of the standing committee (composed of elected representatives) in the case of municipal corporations, and are dictated by state governments in the case of municipal councils. Elected representatives have avoided regular tariff revisions for populist reasons[26] and the local bodies have neglected the O&M of the water supply networks. None of the cities in India has a twenty-four hour water supply and only 48 per cent of the population have access to drainage facilities. The urban populace, for its part, has been reluctant to pay for want of better service. However, the same consumer is willing to pay premium prices for bottled water!

Clearly, the autonomy enjoyed by elected representatives has been inimical to the sustainability of the sector. Experience in other sectors suggests that the political class has been reluctant to take tough measures, while independent regulators have been able to enforce discipline. To correct the situation, it is essential that such an approach be applied to the water sector as well and the tariff revision process be depoliticized. The powers related to setting and revision of tariffs need to be transferred from the elected body to an independent regulatory authority with judicial powers. This apparent curtailment of powers of the local representatives would need to be reconciled with the decentralization envisaged in the CAA74 through a suitable public consultation mechanism.

## Accounting Standards

While complying with the respective Municipal Acts and prescribed formats in recording accounts, the ULBs have been maintaining accounts on a cash basis as against the generally accepted accrual-based accounting. In order to develop a vibrant municipal debt market, it is essential that accounting standards be uniformly and strictly applied across states. However, the task of making provisions with respect to maintenance of accounts and audit has been vested with state governments! A cause of worry is that given the variance in approaches adopted by the various state finance commissions, it is likely that standards may vary across states, which could delay[27] the development of the municipal bond market. The Act has provisions that require ULBs to maintain accounts in accordance with the standards prescribed, and it is hoped that this opportunity will be used by state governments and the ULBs to make their accounting systems and disclosure standards transparent enough to enable investors to analyse them without imposing too high a cost.

---

[25] Octroi is a highly distortionary tax and there are huge dead-weight losses in octroi collections. Replacement of octroi with 'entry' tax as some governments are planning is no solution either. User charges and collection of local taxes need to improve.

[26] An elected body or a group, given the dysfunctionalities, lacks the credibility to ensure quality supplies through a time bound programme of expansion and improvement of the infrastructure. Hence it cannot go to the public with a programme of increased coverage or better quality linked to tariff increases.

[27] Variation in standards impose large costs on the markets, to develop familiarity with the intricacies of several different systems and approaches to accounting.

BOX 9.4.1

## How Low Usage Charges for Drinking Water Act against the Interests of the Poor

*Sebastian Morris*

Consider drinking water from a typical publicly owned municipality, where the supply is limited at a given point in time. The supply is limited either because of 'state failure', or because the parastatals 'lack resources' for adding to capacity, and private parties are circumscribed by policy or regulation. It could also be the case that the geographical and physical conditions make it very expensive to expand supply beyond current levels.

$PP'$ is the demand schedule of the poor, and $RR'$ that of the rich. Water up to a certain level of usage is a necessity hence there is a near inelastic segment of the schedule. The elastic portion of the schedule arises out of inessential use. Abstracting from the reality of a continuity of households over income levels, $PP'$ is the aggregate of all poor households. The poor would have a large inelastic demand given their larger numbers despite lower per head (inelastic) demand. The rich in the aggregate would have smaller total inelastic demand, despite their larger individual demand, given the smaller numbers. The inelastic demand of the poor takes place at a low price. The rich can afford to pay prices up to $Pr$, the poor up to $Pp$. $Pr >> Pp$. The total demand demand schedule is $TT'$ which is only piece-wise continuous. At a supply $Qs^*$ the correct non-rationed price of water is $P^*$, at which price the poor get $Qp^*$ of water and the rich $Qr^*$. The rich could have some elastic demand being served; 'non-essential' demands being met at $P^*$. Now if the government fixes the prices at a low value $Pl$, (as it has indeed done in most cities in India), then the unrestricted demand is very large at $Qd$. The increase in demand from $Qs^*$ i.e. $(Qd-Qs^*)$ is largely on account of the rich, since their demand becomes elastic first; at a higher price. Thus the rich would now like to consume at $Qrd$ and the poor a little higher at Qpd. But supply is limited. In this competition between the rich and the poor, the poor would loose out, given their limited ability to fight for water. Thus the rich, in successfully stepping up their water consumption, would have pushed the poor's consumption from Qp* to Qps. Indeed what we would actually observe would be Qps with the denial that it entails: Qp*–Qps, which would be a very significant part of the poor's consumption at Qps. Higher prices creates an opportunity for the poor to get more water. At Pl, huge costs are borne by the poor as such. First is the 'denial' of the poor who have the purchasing power but cannot get the water. Next, is the large costs that the poor bear in competing with each other in queues, waiting, or organizing access common taps. The real competition between the rich and the poor therefore would manifest as a competition for the resource among the poor! One has only to call to mind the women who have to carry home heavy pots of water, the fish market like situation near community and slum taps, and the low pressure in taps in slum and chawl houses to appreciate the extent of the denial among the urban poor.

Similar analysis would apply for sewerage services, though here the significant money costs that have to be borne by the user would lead to a situation of much greater denial of the poor. The maintenance and operation requirements of publicly accessible sewerage is high and state failure to control and manage 'Class IV' workers makes most public toilets almost completely useless. Indeed, more often than not they are used for altogether different purposes like small-scale gambing and illegal liquor sales. Urinals have a slightly better record. It is in this context that the 'Sulabh' movement, a remarkable organizational innovation that is at once replicable, becomes the only hope for the public (and not just the poor) for public toilets.

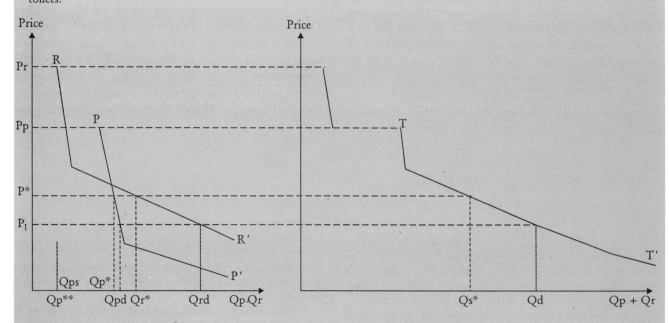

How low prices take water away from the poor.

# 9.5 RURAL DRINKING WATER SUPPLY: ISSUES AND STRATEGIES[28]

*Keshab Das*

## INTRODUCTION

Making available clean and safe drinking water, a basic ingredient for survival and health, has emerged as a major challenge facing development in India, especially in rural regions. The fast rising demand for the resource from the bourgeoning urban dwellers, industrial units, and agriculturalists, mainly large and medium ones, has been exercising tremendous pressure on current availability, not only in the arid and semi-arid regions but also in regions traditionally known to be well endowed with surface and groundwater. With the unmindful exploitation of groundwater, estimated to be providing 80 to 90 per cent of domestic water supply in rural areas, the provisioning of drinking water on a sustainable basis into the future has become an issue of great concern (Bhatia 1992, Nigam *et al.* 1998: 10, and Shah *et al.* 1998: 76–81). (See Box 9.5.1 for means of checking this over exploitation.)

Deterioration of the quality of water bodies, both surface and underground, due to pollution and mismanagement has affected the quality of water available adversely. It may even have affected the quantity in water-scarce regions that have witnessed overexploitation of groundwater. Releasing untreated or ill-treated industrial waste (including harmful chemicals) to rivers or agricultural fields, letting domestic solid and liquid wastes contaminate local sources (including open access sources like stand posts (hand pumps), wells, and streams), and allowing commingling of fertilizer and pesticide particles with field channels are some environmentally most undesirable end serious acts of commission (Murty *et al.* 1999: 1–8). By thus polluting freshwater resources, such practices render potential drinking water supply both unavailable and unsustainable, irrespective of the issue of affordability. Using polluted or unsafe water results in diseases that kill over 1.5 million children (under 5 years of age) every year in rural areas. An annual loss of over 200 million person days of work to the nation (Parikh *et al.* 1999: 2, quoting information from the Ministry of Rural Development) is another result.

As per the prevailing norms (for 'fully covered' or FC habitations) for rural water supply through public safe sources, for 40 litres of drinking water per capita per day (lpcd) are required to be provided, or, in operational terms, a public stand post or hand pump every 250[29] persons. The location of the source of water should not be beyond 1.6 km in the plains and 100 m in hilly areas. Based upon these norms, as on 1 April 1997, whereas as many as 61,724 rural habitations (hamlets) did not have access to any public source of safe water (categorized as 'not covered' or NC habitations), a substantial 3.78 lakh habitations were classified as 'partially covered' (PC). Further, 1.51 lakh habitations suffered from major water quality problems, such as excess fluoride, salinity, iron, and arsenic (Planning Commission 2000:409). At around the same period, it is estimated, a staggering *90 million people in Indian villages* did not have any access to safe drinking water sources!

As detailed in Fig. 9.5.1, there are a number of factors, both endogenous and exogenous, which can and do adversely affect water supply status in rural areas. Given the potential threat of regression of the status of safe water supply, the important issue is whether these set norms of rural water supply are realizable. Also, can an adequate level of provision of the resource be achieved on a sustainable basis?

## STATAL ROLE: CHASING CHANGING TARGETS

In India, although the issue of water supply in rural areas has been assigned importance since the very inception of the five year plans, the actualization of stated goals lacked earnestness. The Rural Water Supply Programme was initiated during the First Five Year Plan and a few years later, in 1954, a programme of water supply and sanitation was taken up in the social welfare sector as part of central health schemes. However, the programme failed to achieve its objectives within the specified time-frame. It was not until 1972–3 that the drinking water issue could be addressed in any comprehensive manner, when the Accelerated Rural Water Supply Programme (ARWSP) was introduced. In 1974–5 with the launching of the Minimum Needs Programme (MNP), which incorporated the rural water supply component,

---

[28] The author is deeply indebted to Sebastian Morris for offering, as always, engagingly critical comments on an earlier draft. Sincere thanks are due to Nikku Bala Raju, Tara Nair, and participants at the Writers' Workshop held at the Indian Institute of Management, Ahmedabad for constructive suggestions and support.

[29] This overestimates the average output of a hand pump set. It means that a hand pump is working eight hours a day at 20 litres per minute, not realizable in any but the most ideal conditions. More typically and especially in regions with groundwater tables hundreds of feet below the surface, a hand pump per 50 or 100 persons may be required.

BOX 9.5.1

## Overexploitation of Groundwater can be Overcome by Correctly Pricing Electricity and Diesel

*Sebastian Morris*

A powerful (political and economic) argument from farmers for continuing with the electricity subsidies emanates from their desire for parity with farmers supplied with irrigation water from surface water schemes—typically dams and barrages. Surface water is supplied at low prices that often cover only a small fraction of the O&M costs. The prices typically are far below the marginal product of water, and certainly below the prices prevailing in nearby water markets. They are also well below the costs of water that can be delivered through efficient construction and management of resources, i.e. the costs for an efficient supplier (without the typical delays and cost overruns of public sector projects, and with efficient operations). The overexploitation of groundwater, resulting out of the government's policy of subsidization of electricity and diesel, has generated much discussion and debate. Dhawan's categorization (Dhawan 1991) of land-scarce and water-scarce systems can be extended to understand the phenomenon of overexploitation appropriately. In Saurashtra, Rajasthan, large parts of the Deccan and Malwa Plateau, and north Gujarat, which are water constrained, it is almost certain that overexploitation has taken place. In other areas like the Gangetic Basin and the East Coast, especially the deltaic areas, and the Punjab, with either much more rainfall or synergistic benefits of large and well-developed surface irrigation schemes, the evidence of overuse is not very strong, despite groundwater tables having receded.

These are areas where relative to easily exploitable water (surface irrigation or groundwater close to the surface) it is land that constrains output; hence additional water exploitation would have lower returns as compared to water exploitation in the water-constrained regions. For land-constrained regions the current constraints to land enhancement and use would have to be overcome before available water is fully utilized. These are principally adverse tenurial relations like sharecropping and interlocking credit and land markets (except in the Punjab), but also such things as drainage, land shaping and bunding, protection from floods, and consolidation of land. Unfortunately their resolution requires state (or collective) action as in bringing about security of tenure or land reforms, or development of drainage and flood control measures. Given state failure and the 'tragedy of the commons' only the slow path of expensive individual and capitalist 'solution' is to be expected. Quite in contrast, the exploitation of groundwater is an individual activity with always lower private than social costs. Therefore, once started it can lead to an accelerated process of exploitation to a point far beyond the social optimal. In other words, relative to the 'water-abundant' regions the marginal product of additional water is much greater. In such areas, therefore, overexploitation results in the 'common resource management problem'. One aspect of this is the suboptimal way the exploitation of the resource takes place. The combined capital assets put into use, and the costs incurred privately in drawing forth a unit quantity of water, are far larger than would need be incurred with cooperation among the exploiters (Shah 1992). The overcapitalization and extra costs that have been imposed thereby still remain to be estimated. In areas like the 'tank' regions of Tamil Nadu and Guntur on the escarpment of the Deccan, the returns to revival of the older tanks and *ayacuts* are large (Shankari, Uma 1991), but the costs are private or state and the benefits public, so in a capitalist world with state failure, unless special organizational (cooperative) initiative is possible, the second best, viz. groundwater irrigation (despite its higher social cost), results. Here the tanks' unintended consequences of synergistic benefits to groundwater helps.

Thus to prevent, reduce, or optimally use groundwater in the water-constrained regions, many measures have been put forward. These range from micro initiatives like encouraging people to form water cooperatives, bringing them together to construct and maintain such things as 'check' dams to improve seepage, regulations by the state as in the current proposals put forward by the Karnataka and Maharashtra governments, removal of subsidies for groundwater exploitation, but more particularly the socially obnoxious Horse Power (HP)-based metering. Other suggestions have been that credit from formal sources such as the National Bank for Rural Development (NABARD) ought to be denied to farmers in areas with overexploitation of groundwater. Still others have argued for complementary subsidies that create incentives for water saving such as for installation of drip systems.

An attack on electricity and diesel subsidies, in a way that limits and redirects the same better, it is here argued, would be a most potent means. The collective initiatives come up against the test of reproducibility, being dependent upon leadership, or the assignment of property rights in new ways. State-based solutions such as regulation would also not work because of the massive state failure at lower executive levels, and possibly very high policing costs with low punitive measures that are there. Neither have credit restrictions worked, since the additional cost of going to private markets including the moneylender is well worth it. A regionally differential subsidization, while seemingly possible, could very well be counter-productive since not all the lands, even in a large area like say North Gujarat, are water constrained. Small islands with good aquifers could actually be 'water rich'.

Electricity and diesel subsidies directly affect in a very large measure the ability of the farmer to lift water. Thus suggestions to replace the electricity and diesel subsidies with an adjustment in the terms of trade through higher purchasing power, while having other problems, would work to attenuate (but possibly not remove) the overexploitation of groundwater in water-constrained systems.

Consider the schedule of private marginal cost $CC'C''P$ as a function of the amount of water drawn to the surface. The private cost beyond a certain point increases more than linearly, since as more water is drawn out one has typically to go deeper. The social cost schedule $CC'C''S$ is at or above $CC'C''P$ since water has a common property aspect. Typically at low levels of extraction, when a farmer's drawal does not reduce the drawal of another farmer, the two are nearly coincident. In water-constrained systems even a drawal at say $Q_n$ would create a significant divergence between the social and private costs. (In systems with abundant water that point of divergence would be at a drawal much higher than at $Q_n$, and may not exist if the marginal product of water declines in water abundant systems. This is not shown in the fig. below). This is because an addition of one tube well to an existing 100 tube wells producing at 100 units of water for a certain cost would now be able to produce say 90 units, and the additional unit would see the effect of his own entry differently, giving him 90 units for his effort. The subsidies particularly the HP-linked small flat charge allow the farmer to increase the production of water at marginal zero energy costs. Since energy has zero price for him, his subsidized marginal cost schedule is much below $CC'C''P$ and may be usefully visualized to go up as $CC'C''U$. With a marginal product of water equal to $M$ and assumed to be constant for simplicity, production takes place at $Q_s$ when there are subsidies, and at $Q_n$ without subsidies. Both involve dead-weight losses to society given by areas DUP and D$D'D''$ respectively. But the latter would be far smaller than the former, since water-constrained regions with overdrawal would be operating in the zone where the private and social costs widely diverge. A removal of all subsidies would take the system from $Q_s$ to $Q_n$. (To take the system to the first best socially optimal $Q_o$, an appropriately structured tax on water extraction would be necessary. This is not discussed here. While this will not guarantee that the system would be below the level of sustainable exploitation, it is likely to be close enough in all except the most water-constrained areas. In some areas like Rajasthan and coastal Gujarat with much lower rainfall or threat of salinity ingress, additional measures (common property management measures or assignable water rights) to take the system to $Q_o$ may be called for. Many scholars have vehemently put forward assignment of water rights as a way out. (Saleth 1994, Moench 1992). Even in such areas where definition and protection of water rights would be necessary, the first measure would have to be to take the system to $Q_n$ from $Q_s$ since otherwise even the specific micro approaches would have to work against adverse individual incentives. If now measures to use the water more efficiently are encouraged via 'proving' subsidies and demonstrations of systems like sprinkler or drip irrigation they could spread very widely, since they would have the effect of raising the marginal product of water. With the distortions created by pumping subsidization in place such measures would hardly be effective.

The measure would most certainly reduce the output of the water in constrained areas, unless $Q_s$ is already at a point where the aquifer is being destroyed, which is rarely the case. (It is not rare though in coastal Saurashtra and Rajasthan [Shah 1992]. But output nationally need not fall at all! The dead-weight losses that are avoided could finance land augmentation in land-constrained areas and water augmentation activities like investments in water conservation, including use of plastic lining, drip and sprinklers systems, wherever appropriate in water-constrained areas. In other words, the marginal returns to both land enhancement and to water extraction would get 'equalized'. If anything, it would be more appropriate for policy to create a bias in favour of land enhancement since the market failures here at the early stage itself prevent their exploitation. (The market failure for groundwater is after a great deal of extraction and is in the nature of overexploitation. The most optimal way to enhance land would be to carry out land reforms which would restore the incentive for the tiller to make long gestation period investments in land shaping, bunding, etc. These in any case would only use largely 'idle' labour.) Indeed, the point is that since there is a national market in agriculture, the adjustments resulting in reallocation of land use from the current distortions would happen. Agriculture output would then rise in the better endowed regions, and the water-scarce regions would shift out of water-intensive crops.

Removing such distortionary subsidies, would have to be accompanied with pricing of surface water to cover costs for distortions between farmers to go. Yet overnight withdrawl of subsidies would not be feasible. What would be most appropiate would be to value the actual subsidy that farmers enjoy and direct it through coupons or stamps. Such stamps should be made tradeable across a variety of input purchases: fertilizer, pesticides, water, electricity, drip systems, and pump sets.

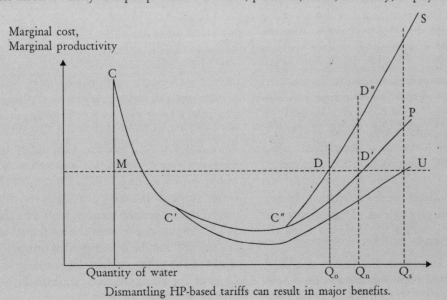

Dismantling HP-based tariffs can result in major benefits.

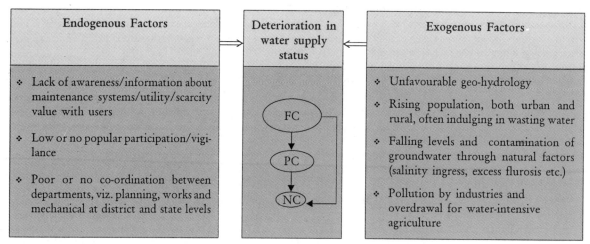

| Endogenous Factors | Deterioration in water supply status | Exogenous Factors |
|---|---|---|
| ❖ Lack of awareness/information about maintenance systems/utility/scarcity value with users<br><br>❖ Low or no popular participation/vigilance<br><br>❖ Poor or no co-ordination between departments, viz. planning, works and mechanical at district and state levels | FC → PC → NC | ❖ Unfavourable geo-hydrology<br><br>❖ Rising population, both urban and rural, often indulging in wasting water<br><br>❖ Falling levels and contamination of groundwater through natural factors (salinity ingress, excess flurosis etc.)<br><br>❖ Pollution by industries and overdrawal for water-intensive agriculture |

Fig. 9.5.1: Factors causing regression of rural water supply status.

the ARWSP was retracted. But in 1977–8, the ARWSP was reintroduced as it was found that 'the progress of supply of safe drinking water to identified problem villages was not up to expectations' (Department of Rural Development 1991: 42).

Solving the drinking water problem, especially in the remote and difficult-terrain rural and tribal regions, continued to be on the agenda of successive governments. In 1980, India became a signatory to the UN (United Nations) Resolution which adopted the International Drinking Water Supply and Sanitation Decade (IDWSSD) programme, and as part of this major initiative, it was decided to cover the entire population by 31 March 1991. Almost midway through the IDWSSD, in 1986, the National Drinking Water Mission (called the Rajiv Gandhi National Drinking Water Mission [RGNDWM] since 1991) was initiated, aiming to provide safe water to problem villages, which were identified as 'no source' villages in a national survey conducted in the previous year. Numerically, it implied covering a total of 161,722 villages by 31 March 1990. Interestingly, another round of survey of 'no source' villages was conducted during 1991–3, which, due to the unsatisfactory estimates that it generated, had to be validated through *one more* round of nationwide census concerning the status of drinking water in rural areas in 1994. The figures, as on 1 April 1994, stood at 140,975 NC habitations/villages (covering a population of 5.3 per cent) and 430,377 PC habitations/villages (covering a population of 45.8 per cent). Sources in an additional 1.51 lakh habitations/villages were reported to be suffering from acute quality problems. These figures, as may be obvious, were substantially different from the target coverage set for 1990.

The statistical maze continues. For instance, according to the Ninth Five Year Plan document as on 1 April 1997 there remained about 0.30 lakh NC, 2.78 lakh PC,

and 1.40 lakh quality problem (QP) habitations/villages to be covered *at the end of the Eighth Plan*. But it also stated that, 'However, *keeping in view the field realities*, Rajiv Gandhi National Drinking Water Mission in consultation with the State Govts, further revised/updated the number of NC and PC villages/habitations and thus the task for the Ninth Plan would be to cover 0.88 lakh NC, 3.91 lakh PC and 1.40 lakh QP villages/habitations' (Planning Commission 2000: 585, emphasis mine).

An important prerequisite to developing any infrastructure, especially in rural areas, is to collect and make available such database and other relevant information which would be both realistic and reliable. The often incongruent statistics on status of sources of water can themselves pose constraints in promoting infrastructure.

It is not clear if the vacillating figures reflect actual progression or regression of status, or problems in survey coverage, or even definitional inadequacies in the field context. Of the three distinct categories describing the status of sources, namely NC, PC, and FC, it may be noted that these refer only to public (belonging to or run by the state) safe water sources and do not indicate anything about the existence of other sources, including private ones, in a given habitation/ village. Hence, as an example, a habitation in Kerala or Assam having several private wells or hand pumps and *no* public source would be recorded as NC, whereas a habitation in the semi-arid Saurashtra or western Orissa region with only one public source (even ad hoc arrangements like supplying water through tankers) providing less than 40 lpcd of water, but no private sources, would be classified PC (or FC, if the source provides above 40 lpcd of water, as per the norms). Similarly, as revealed through the validation study of the status of drinking water in nine districts of Gujarat (including the six Saurashtra districts and Kutch) during May–July of 1994, there were many villages/habitations not covered by any public source, but not included in the original list [of NC habitations of the 1991–3 survey, which were being validated in the 1994 survey] provided by the RGNDWM. Interestingly, from the given RGNDWM list, nothing could be known about the habitations which would have turned NC, from PC or FC status during the 1991–3 survey. Possibly, these unaccounted NC habitations were classified as either PC or FC in the previous survey, when some sources of water still remained active during winter. [Das and Kumar 1995: 4]

It is important to note the period of survey through which the status is assigned. Surveys conducted during non-summer seasons are most likely to come up with gross underestimates of NC habitations, particularly in the large arid and semi-arid regions of India.

Inexactitude in the data on rural drinking water supply status notwithstanding, with the massive backlog in the coverage the Ninth Plan has estimated the required funds for full coverage to be to the tune of Rs 40,000 crore, including the costs of operation and maintenance (O&M) and quality control. On average, as suggested by the RGNDWM, about 6 per cent of the capital investment is required annually for appropriate repairs and maintenance of the systems. It is clear that such resources cannot continue to be provided through the 10 per cent MNP/ARWSP plan funds and limited non-plan resources of the states. Given the economic and financial scenario, it is difficult to visualize public resources of such magnitude coming forth and hence the need for involvement of communities, institutions, and the private sector is urgent.

## THE PROBLEM OF MOBILIZING FINANCE

Irrespective of the fact that water, especially in rural areas, has been viewed and used —largely due to allocative anomalies and also misplaced notions about the copiousness of the resource as often reinforced through political platitudes—as a 'free' good (which the government is obliged to provide), the very phenomenon of emerging scarcity and continuing inefficient use qualifies it as an 'economic' good. However, unlike in urban water supply, where user charges are not uncommon and are acceptable, the concept of charging users for water for domestic use in rural areas has been 'less widely endorsed', as it is held that the large number of people in poverty in Indian villages cannot afford to pay for 'such a thing as water'. But as has been argued perceptively, even the adoption of a 'free' water policy can, in effect, act against the interests of the poorest and vulnerable groups. For this section of the population

such notions as 'free' water bear little relation to their actual situation since they continue to pay a high price for water in

terms of time and energy expended in obtaining sources of drinking water and, in severely affected areas, they buy water from private vendors during water-scarce seasons of the year. [Secretariat for Global Consultation 1990: 42]

It has been observed that in order to improve infrastructure for rural water supply the required capital investment would be very large, also it would involve long periods before pay off. It would hence be difficult to attract private investors to such a sector where returns to investment would not only be uncertain but delayed. 'High-risk, long payback periods and pricing limitations of the Rural Water Supply and Sanitation or RWSS sector as presently structured, serve as serious disincentives to potentially interested parties. Such disincentives discourage even government-sponsored credit facilities' (World Bank 1999: 41). It may not be incorrect to hold that water, at least in rural areas, has the characteristics of both public and open access goods. Whereas its excludability is low because of dual identity, the subtractability is also low, it being a publc good. As has been aptly remarked, 'Private firms do not engage in activities with low excludability because it is difficult to get consumers pay. Where low substitutability exists, market forces will not produce an optimal level of investment' (Easter *et al.* 1998: 581). Towards promoting and sustaining new and existing capital investment, much would, hence, depend upon a demand-driven approach that would reflect the nature and extent of users' willingness to participate in managing the system and, more importantly, to share both capital cost as well as maintenance (World Bank 1999: 45).

So far as plan investment for rural water supply as a proportion of public sector plan is concerned, there has been a gradual, and slow, rise from 0.15 to 2.47 per cent during the eight plans. The persistent low priority (in terms of investment, if not intentions) attached to this sector in successive plans per se makes user financing almost a necessity. The case for recognizing the growing cost and its sharing by the beneficiaries has been getting stronger, especially in concerned global conventions. Demand responsiveness, instead of the conventional supply-driven approach and direct involvement of the local community have been emphasized as the most effective mechanisms to ensure proper management and delivery of water to rural population (Pendley 1997: 10).

Statewise estimates for user charges for water supply in rural India have been calculated by Pushpangadan and Murugan (1997), using Faulhaber's (1975) methodology on cross-subsidization. As may be clear from the estimates, reproduced in Table 9.5.1, in case of the rural poor (defined as those living below the official poverty line) being fully cross-subsidized by the better-off users, the monthly expenditure per family paying user charges

(Rs)

TABLE 9.5.1

Monthly Tariff (Rs per household) to Paying Customers for Cross-subsidizing the Poor 1994-5

| State/union territories | Aggregate sector | | | | Hand pump sector | | Piped sector | | | |
|---|---|---|---|---|---|---|---|---|---|---|
| | Replacement cost | | O&M cost | | Replacement cost | O&M cost | Replacement cost | | O&M cost | |
| | Without subsidy | With subsidy | Without subsidy | With subsidy | | | Without subsidy | With subsidy | Without subsidy | With subsidy |
| Andhra Pradesh | 5.98 | 7.98 | 3.41 | 4.55 | 2.35 | 1.41 | 3.63 | 5.63 | 2.00 | 3.14 |
| Arunachal Pradesh | 49.17 | 83.29 | 29.41 | 49.82 | 2.55 | 1.53 | 46.62 | 80.74 | 27.88 | 48.29 |
| Assam | 15.02 | 32.96 | 8.16 | 17.89 | 2.99 | 1.80 | 12.03 | 29.96 | 6.36 | 16.10 |
| Bihar | 3.94 | 11.30 | 2.11 | 6.04 | 3.06 | 1.84 | 0.88 | 8.24 | 0.27 | 4.20 |
| Goa, Daman & Diu | 22.60 | 38.29 | 13.34 | 22.6 | 2.44 | 1.46 | 20.16 | 35.85 | 11.88 | 21.14 |
| Gujarat | 9.51 | 14.26 | 5.38 | 8.36 | 2.82 | 1.69 | 6.68 | 11.94 | 3.69 | 6.66 |
| Haryana | 51.33 | 62.53 | 26.45 | 32.22 | 3.24 | 1.94 | 48.09 | 59.30 | 24.51 | 30.28 |
| Himachal Pradesh | 42.54 | 55.31 | 22.8 | 29.65 | 2.69 | 1.62 | 39.85 | 52.62 | 21.19 | 28.03 |
| Jammu & Kashmir | 48.66 | 76.07 | 25.68 | 40.16 | 2.77 | 1.66 | 45.88 | 73.30 | 24.02 | 38.49 |
| Karnataka | 9.68 | 15.64 | 5.35 | 8.64 | 2.81 | 1.69 | 6.87 | 12.83 | 3.66 | 6.95 |
| Kerala | 22.53 | 35.00 | 12.14 | 18.85 | 2.66 | 1.59 | 19.87. | 32.34 | 10.54 | 17.26 |
| Madhya Pradesh | 8.20 | 14.87 | 4.29 | 7.77 | 2.81 | 1.69 | 5.39 | 12.06 | 2.60 | 6.08 |
| Maharashtra | 12.32 | 26.46 | 6.44 | 13.83 | 2.69 | 1.61 | 9.63 | 23.77 | 4.82 | 12.21 |
| Manipur | 70.99 | 120.26 | 35.37 | 59.92 | 3.0 | 1.80 | 67.99 | 117.27 | 33.57 | 58.12 |
| Meghalaya | 47.25 | 80.05 | 24.91 | 42.2 | 2.73 | 1.64 | 44.52 | 77.32 | 23.27 | 40.56 |
| Mizoram | 108.35 | 183.55 | 59.59 | 100.96 | 2.97 | 1.78 | 105.38 | 180.58 | 57.81 | 99.17 |
| Nagaland | 84.04 | 142.37 | 38.9 | 65.89 | 2.9 | 1.74 | 81.14 | 139.47 | 37.15 | 64.15 |
| Orissa | 7.81 | 20.43 | 4.25 | 11.13 | 2.65 | 1.59 | 5.15 | 17.78 | 2.66.0 | 9.54 |
| Punjab | 10.64 | 13.00 | 5.83 | 7.13 | 3.03 | 1.82 | 7.61 | 9.97 | 4.01 | 5.31 |
| Rajasthan | 16.47 | 26.11 | 9.14 | 14.50 | 3.0 | 1.80 | 13.47 | 23.12 | 7.34 | 12.70 |
| Sikkim | 110.62 | 187.39 | 59.68 | 101.10 | 2.64 | 1.58 | 107.98 | 184.75 | 58.09 | 99.51 |
| Tamil Nadu | 9.29 | 17.02 | 5.14 | 9.43 | 2.18 | 1.31 | 7.11 | 14.84 | 3.83 | 8.12 |
| Tripura | 25.16 | 42.63 | 13.57 | 22.99 | 2.66 | 1.60 | 22.5 | 39.97 | 11.97 | 21.39 |
| Uttar Pradesh | 7.69 | 14.27 | 4.07 | 7.55 | 3.08 | 1.85 | 4.61 | 11.19 | 2.22 | 5.70 |
| West Bengal | 4.84 | 9.64 | 2.59 | 5.17 | 2.78 | 1.67 | 2.06 | 6.87 | 0.93 | 3.50 |
| UTs* | 86.01 | 145.71 | 25.65 | 43.45 | 2.58 | 1.55 | 83.43 | 143.13 | 24.1 | 41.90 |
| All India | 9.79 | 16.59 | 5.28 | 8.94 | 2.77 | 1.66 | 7.02 | 13.82 | 3.61 | 7.28 |

*Sources:* Pushpangadan and Murugan (1997: 16 and 17, Table 3).

* Includes Andaman & Nicobar Islands, Chardigarh, Dadra and Nagar Haveli, Delhi, Lakshadweep, and Pondicherry.

for piped water supply would be a little over Rs 21 at an all-India level, although these rates could vary as much as between about Rs 9 in Andhra Pradesh or Rs 10 in West Bengal to Rs 280 in Mizoram or Rs 284 in Sikkim. As for water provisioning through hand pumps, the rates are too low to be realistic. The practice of states assigning low priority to O&M of hand pumps, as reflected through allocation of less than required funds for it, can result in 'cost escalation and shortening the life of the system' (Pushpangadan and Murugan 1997: 12).

Despite being a good effort, the rates of user financing and cost recovery suggested by the study, in an operational sense, are incomprehensive and hardly usable. For one thing, as the authors themselves point out, the required data on 'cost of extracting, transporting, storing, treating and distributing water for both joint and separate production' were non-available. For another, the initial capital cost for complete coverage, through hand pumps or metred piped scheme or both, is yet to be properly ascertained. The study, by concentrating on the so-called 'public safe' sources, fails to consider alternative local sources that would substantially influence both the quantum of water use and also the type of system used/required; hence the cost to be borne by users. They also assume the unrealistic norm of 250 people being covered by one hand pump post! Similarly, the cost of adding to the supply could be very different from historical costs, especially since water is a natural resource. In fact, as may be seen from Table 9.5.2, hand pumps and taps in rural areas account for nearly 56 per cent and 21 per cent, respectively, of sources of drinking water; however, there remain a variety of other sources of potable water, not officially classified as 'safe'.

TABLE 9.5.2
Sources of Drinking Water in Inhabited Villages in India

| Sources | Villages (%) |
| --- | --- |
| Well | 69.8 |
| Hand pump | 55.9 |
| Tube well | 21.1 |
| Tap | 18.2 |
| Tank | 14.3 |
| River | 10.0 |
| *Nala* | 3.6 |
| Canal | 3.5 |
| Fountain | 2.6 |
| Spring | 1.7 |
| Lake | 0.1 |
| Others | 4.5 |

*Source: Census of India, 1991: Availability of Infrastructure Facilities in Rural India: An Analysis of Village Directory Data*, New Delhi: Office of the Registrar General, India, 1997. As in Singh (2000: 37, Table 1).

*Note:* Excludes Jammu and Kashmir, where Census was not conducted in 1991.

From a different angle, these user rates (with cross-subsidy) are certain to rise significantly, most probably beyond the stand-alone costs, once the proportion of population below poverty line is restricted and therefore not charged. Such an eventuality is expected as serious reservations have been expressed about the validity of the poverty estimates as brought out by the National Sample Survey Organization. If the criticism, based mainly on the undervaluation of nutritional norms, and recalculated estimates of poverty are any indication, the proportion of rural population below the poverty line would be almost double what the official statistics show (Mehta and Venkatraman 2000; and Suryanarayana, 1990).

So far as the limited piped water system in rural areas is concerned, in the absence of metering, it is difficult to fix user charges. Even the possibility of connecting all or most rural households with piped water system, and, if so, the investment required, are not quite known. The only plausible alternative, without cross-subsidization, could be the provision of hand pumps at household level. But even here, considering only the average cost of a hand pump as between Rs 15,000 and Rs 20,000, the effective demand, as expressed through both willingness and ability to pay, assumes importance.

It needs to be noted that a variety of charging mechanisms and modes of payment have been tried out during the IDWSSD. And the experience has been far from impressive.

Despite the positive role that pricing can play in the mobilization of resources and the delivery of services, the implementation of effective pricing policies has nevertheless proved to be one of the intractable problems facing sector planners during the course of the Decade. Many pricing policies have failed to generate the volume of revenue anticipated or to ensure the long-term sustainability of services. In addition, the poor have in many instances failed to pay for or benefit from expanded services. [Secretariat for the Global Consultation 1990: 42]

Water pricing will undoubtedly become an important policy instrument for mobilizing resources in the future. An implementable and well-thought-out water pricing policy will not only encourage efficient water use in the agricultural, industrial, and domestic sectors but will also provide the much needed and timely revenue to the relevant water authorities (Merrett, 1997; 53–63). Water has been traditionally subsidized to achieve very specific socio-political objectives of food security, provision of clean drinking water, and improvement of income and health of the rural poor. If economic water pricing is to be introduced, other policy instruments have to be developed to achieve the same objectives. The pertinent questions in this context are what criteria should water charges be based on? Should the beneficiaries pay the

O&M costs of the water systems? Or, are they expected to pay total investment costs as well? Should such pricing include external costs like environmental and social damages? If so, how should these costs be calculated?

## MANAGEMENT BY LOCAL COMMUNITY

In order to arrive at pragmatic solutions to these problems of pricing and cost sharing, the most elementary yet vital requirement is that of a comprehensive and dependable database. With the most sophisticated tools of estimating user charges one may arrive at the most ridiculous conclusions if the database used never represented actuality. And even when the realistic costs and prices are known, much remains to be done in terms of maintaining and auditing accounts, timely collection, and also fixing a variable tariff structure locally, if needed. Involvement of local community, preferably through formation of or use of existing habitation/village-level groups, has been found to be the most effective means through which sustainable water supply efforts are possible.

As presented in Fig. 9.5.2, some of the activities that may be taken up by locally active institutions with the help of panchayats, if required, would include mapping of existing and potential sources of water; this would be an important step towards building up a scientific database. Involving these groups in the generation of awareness about the system, both the O&M aspect and also the costs to be incurred for initial capital investment, repairs, and replacement purposes would help create a responsible attitude towards cost sharing, maintaining transparency in accounts and auditing, and, above all, utilizing water judiciously and with concern for all in the habitation/village.

Instances abound wherein local communities have agreed to contribute to the establishment and maintenance costs of regular water supply; such contribution could be in monetary terms and/or in the form of voluntary service, including free labour. A number of successful experiences in rural water supply programmes, documented from many developing countries, including India, attribute their achievement mainly to close participation by local communities in a variety of activities and actual performing of tasks in a group environment (Narayan 1995). In some other instances, the provincial state has come forward to share the financial burden of the initial capital expenditure, and in some, local non-governmental organizations (NGOs) have taken up the responsibility of helping form village groups for managing local water sources and also their expenses. Developing appropriate institutions for successful implementation of user cost recovery and also upkeep of the sources is necessary to promote this significant rural infrastructure (Fig. 9.5.2).

## DESIGN AND TECHNOLOGY

As a design option should one promote the traditional system of water supply or advanced systems like hand pumps/stand posts and piped water supply? Studies have shown that in some places advanced systems have failed and people had to revert to traditional systems and in some others, because of the spread of piped water supply, the traditional systems have become defunct. It is important to determine what combination of these two systems can provide a viable answer in different hydrological conditions. Technology choice(s) will not only affect the costs and organization of O&M but also its sustainability. Eventually, the

| *Management related* | *Technology related* |
|---|---|
| • Encourage awareness about system, utility, and consequences of wasting and polluting | • Mapping of potential alternative sources |
| • Local management of O&M | • Repairing/rejuvenating defunct sources or those fallen into disuse |
| • Financial contribution, if applicable, to be managed locally to ensure transparency in transaction | • Exploring revival of traditional water harvesting systems |
| • Inclusion, by design, of socio-economically deprived and disadvantaged groups | • Introducing new technologies of rainwater harvesting |
| • Prevention of industrial pollution and overdrawal of water for crops through enforcing a system of penalty and punishment, pecuniary or otherwise | • Measures to rejuvenate water bodies through watershed developments etc. |

Fig. 9.5.2: Improving availability and ensuring sustainability: Options.

system(s) that would enhance the availability of water must prevail between competing options. Exploring the economic and managerial potential of traditional water harvesting systems and also encouraging such water harnessing strategies as watershed development are important steps in the context of rural water supply efforts. Fig. 9.5.2 provides a list of technological options to augment water availability and ensure sustainability.

## CONCLUDING OBSERVATIONS

Provision of safe drinking water must ensure both continuous availability and equitable access. An important study by the World Bank (1999) recommends a variety of ways and means through which user cost recovery and private participation are possible, gradually though surely. An important issue, however, remains if the rural poor should also pay for drinking water in order to meet the 'efficiency' criterion, especially in a growth scenario where 'the gains of [even] faster economic growth since 1980–1 have been unequally shared by different sections of the Indian society. [And] Growth has favoured urban India, organised sector, richer states and property owners—against rural India, unorganised sector, poorer states and wage earners' (Nagaraj 2000: 2838).

The major obstacles to achieving equity, efficiency, and sustainability remain quality degradation due to uneconomical exploitation as also overcrowding on the resource. This underscores the need for optimum utilization of water. A comprehensive water policy, to be effective and to have a semblance of concern for equity, must take into account such issues as overdrawal, wastage, and polluting acts by competing sectors and/ or individuals. It is not adequate to merely incorporate the 'polluter pays principle', but to ensure that the priorities are properly defined and strictly enforced. The enormous costs of such unchecked tapping of fresh water bodies and polluting not only amount to shifting the financial burden to the hapless and underprivileged, but also increasing their vulnerability to disease, and even death. Moreover, such irresponsible use of water can actually result in dwindling of the availability of water for the future. Such considerations must precede formulation of any rational pricing structure, especially for the rural poor. The role of community participation cannot be underplayed so far as introduction, and O&M of the appropriate technology are concerned. It may check inappropriate resource discharge and conservation. Further, it may be most useful to consider drinking water as a resource not in isolation but with regard to other basic need resources such as housing, nutrition, and health.

# 9.6 BUS TRANSPORT IN DELHI

*B. R. Marwah, V. K. Sibal, and Sujata Sawant*

## INTRODUCTION

Large cities require large-scale movements of people due to three reasons—increase in total volume because of growth in population, rising per capita trip rate, and increase in travel distance. Additionally, unscientific structures when imposed on cities, under the guise of planning impose unnecessary need for movement.[30] Such large-scale movements, if done by personalized modes of transport create congestion on roads and thus involve high costs, excessive energy consumption, extended journey times, and environmental pollution.[31]

Moreover, most urban residents in Indian cities cannot afford personalized transport. An efficient, reliable, and speedy public transport system constitutes one of the important needs of urban living and acts as a catalyst to the growth of urban economy.

In Indian cities, buses will continue to form the backbone of any public transport system in urban centres in the foreseeable future due to flexible operation and easy accessibility. Even in those cities where high capacity mass rail transit systems (MRTs) are provided,[32] bus transport will still be very important.

---

[30] Delhi would be a prime example, where the inverse density of population and built-up spaces has lengthened travel distances.

[31] This is always true because the private costs of personal transport remain well below its social costs and the two diverge greatly not only because of pollution, but also because of congestion. While in the advanced countries with well-developed public transport, congestion pricing is the only 'solution' to this divergence, in many Indian cities, adequate and correct investments in public transport as also appropriate lane planning, sometimes

---

including separation of slow and 'fast' moving traffic, better signals, and a concerted attempt to identify and relax bottlenecks are necessary, even while congestion pricing ensures that private vehicles are 'priced out' of urban central streets (ed.).

[32] Unless of course such mass transit systems are very large and comprehensive and are designed to take care of a large part of the movement. Today, only the highly congested Mumbai suburban railway system and perhaps the Howrah suburban railway system

## INADEQUACY OF THE BUS TRANSPORT SYSTEM IN DELHI

The National Capital Territory of Delhi covers an area of 1483 sq. km. Delhi is planned on a ring-radial pattern with a hierarchical road network and its total road length is 22,487 km. Ring Road and Outer Ring Road are among the most important arterial roads. Ring Road is connected with most of the important roads and nodal points of the city.

The the population of Delhi has been growing at the rate of about 4 per cent per annum since 1961 and is expected to be 13.2 million in the year 2001.

The total number of vehicles in Delhi is now more than the total number of vehicles in the three other metropolitan cities of Mumbai, Calcutta, and Chennai put together! The number of vehicles in Delhi was about 2.8 million in 1997; about two-third of these are two-wheelers. The sharp increase in the number of vehicles and especially two-wheelers could be attributed to the improved economic status of people and inadequate public transport.[33]

The number of accidents in Delhi has been increasing at an alarming rate with over 11,000 accidents recorded in 1997, 24 per cent of which were fatal! The proportion of fast moving vehicles was 84 per cent in 1994. The average modal composition of traffic on selected arterial roads of Delhi in 1994 shows a 62 per cent share of buses. Average bus speed in Delhi is observed to be only 18 km per hr. The public transport demand in Delhi is expected to increase sharply over the years. In 1997, about 7 million passengers, including passengers using more than one bus per trip, were being carried by stage carriage buses, while 0.7 million passengers were being carried by contract carriage buses, operating as chartered buses. Daily bus passenger demand is estimated to be 11.2 million for the year 2001. The average trip length is over 10 km.

The public transport system of Delhi is primarily road based and the share of rail-based public transport is almost negligible. The bus system in Delhi is a mix of public and 'private'. Public buses are operated by the Delhi Transport Corporation (DTC)[34] whereas private buses are operated mostly by individual agencies based on stage and contract carriage (chartered bus) permits. In 1997–8, the regular (stage carriage) bus system comprised 4000 private buses under the State Transport Authority (STA) and 3870 DTC buses including 1200 private buses under the administrative control of the DTC. About 5000 chartered buses provided point-to-point service during peak hours supplementing the regular bus services. End November 1996, there were over 3900 buses being operated privately, including over 2600 under the infamous Red/Blue Line scheme.

## GROWTH OF THE DTC

In 1985–6, the DTC fleet (including private buses) and manpower grew to 5400 and 41,000, respectively. In 1988, the operation of private buses under the kilometer scheme was discontinued and later, in 1996, the fleet depleted sharply to 2700.

Before 1992, the city bus services in Delhi were mostly state owned. Private sector participation in the stage carriage public transport system was very limited. The revision of the Motor Vehicles Act in 1988 liberalized permit conditions and paved the way for induction of private buses on city routes on a larger scale. In 1992, Delhi became the first city to adopt large-scale privatization of bus services.

The problems of the present bus system from passenger, operator, and management points of view lie especially in the stage carriage system:

- lengthy and zig-zag routes;
- long waiting time;
- unreliable bus service;
- overcrowded buses and uncomfortable journey;
- poor accessibility for newly developed residential/commercial centres;
- unsafe operation;
- absence of published information regarding routes and timings;

---

could quality. All planned MRTs, including Metro rail of Calcutta are not serious contenders because they would only carry a small fraction of total traffic. Bus capacities can be added as the need arises, especially on non-congested roads. This, apart from its flexibility, is an important factor in the growth of bus traffic in cities; and especially so when the organizational and financial capacity to conceive and execute large MRTs is lacking.

[33] While lack of a rail-based public transport system is usually identified as the reason, income distribution, with a larger proportion of middle and upper middle families, is part of the reason. The vast state expenditures and rents which are generated and spent in Delhi are no doubt the underlying reason (ed.).

[34] The nationalized bus services came into existence in Delhi in 1948 with the formation of the Delhi Transport Service (DTS) under the Ministry of Transport, Government of India. In 1950, the Delhi Road Transport Authority was constituted by an Act of Parliament to control the operations of the DTS. In 1958, the Delhi Transport Undertaking (DTU) was established under the control of the Delhi Municipal Corporation. In 1971, the central government took over the DTU and the Delhi Transport Corporation (DTC) was formed. In August 1996, the DTC was transferred to the Government of the National Capital Territory of Delhi (GNCTD)

- unhealthy competition, overspeeding, and non-observance of traffic rules;
- overlapping and meandering routes with long detours, resulting in ineffective control and supervision;
- maldistribution of buses causing unbalanced operation operations, safety, and routes;
- too many operators, resulting in little or no control over operations, safety, and routes;
- inadequate bus supply;
- ad hoc changes in route network as well as frequency of operation;
- inadequate enforcement and regulatory machinery.

The problems that the existing bus system is facing have their origin in large-scale private sector participation brought about in 1992. The very large number of small operators proved to be a regulator's nightmare. Since licences were given on the basis of political connections and graft, little or no regulatory control was exercised and soon enough the operators became an organized vested interest standing in the way of any change for better service.

Ad hoc changes in the routes without going into the principles of route planning resulted in the route network consisting of lengthy and zig-zag routes and wasteful utilization of available resources. The intensity of the problem can be gauged by the example of a route between Deoli village and Nehru Place. The shortest distance between the O–D pair is only 8 km, whereas the route length is 80 km, and traverses through the whole city! The bus completes a single trip in four hours causing tremendous discomfort to the crew and passengers.

Some other problems, which originated from the profiteering behaviour of operators[35] are:

- unauthorized operation on routes;
- non-operation of less profitable routes and trips;
- unscheduled stoppages;
- long waits at the bus stops to get more passengers, imposing large travel times on those already in the bus.

Lack of an institutional set-up for the operation of chartered buses has left their control in a quandary. These buses have contract carriage permits and operate as chartered buses (during peak hours), tourist, and school buses. The nature of operation varies depending upon

[35] There is no logic to the route allocation process. It is largely a function of the pressures the particular route operator is able to bring upon the DTC officials and the rents that change hands. As such violations of the norms of stage operations are more the rule than the exception (ed.).

the purpose of engagement; as a result the STA does not have records related to the number of charter bus routes, origin, destination, paths, or the number of buses operating on these routes and the period of operation. Moreover the present operation of these buses (limited stop special stage carriage) is in contravention to permit conditions.

Private buses on stage carriage follow the same fare structure as that for public buses. Private buses except those under DTC, do not honour the concessional passes issued by the DTC.

## COMPARISON OF OPERATIONAL PERFORMANCE OF DTC AND PRIVATE BUS OPERATION

The operational performance of private buses on all parameters except accidents is much better than that of DTC buses. Table 9.6.1 compares some important aspects of operation by both kinds of buses.

TABLE 9.6.1
Comparable Performance of DTC and Private Buses

| S. no. | Parameter | DTC (1993–4) | Private buses (1997) |
|---|---|---|---|
| 1 | Fleet utilization (%) | 82.6 | 93 |
| 2 | Vehicle utilization (kms/bus/day) | 216 | 246 |
| 3 | Passengers/bus/day | 751 | 1584 |
| 4 | Dead km/day | 107 | 4 |
| 5 | Staff/bus | 9.56 | 4.6 |
| 6 | Fuel efficiency (km/litre) | 3.8 | 3 |
| 7 | Income/bus/day (Rs) | 1321 | 2700 |
| 8 | Income/km (Rs) | 6.12 | 10.97 |
| 9 | Total cost/km (Rs) | 17.15 | 7.73 |
| 10 | Net earning/km (Rs) | –11.03 | 3.24 |

For comparison purposes DTC figures for the year 1993–4 have been taken because after 1993 the DTC fleet started shrinking. Most of the private operators are small fleet owners and bus operation is guided purely by the profit motive. All the performance parameters of private bus operators, as a result, are better than those of the DTC. It can be seen from Table 9.6.1 that fleet utilization of private buses is 10 per cent more than that of DTC buses. The passengers carried per bus per day and consequently income per bus of private buses are almost double those of DTC buses. Labour productivity is also high as staff per bus is almost half that deployed on DTC buses. Dead km per day are low because at night private operators parked their buses on roads near the starting point of their routes. The financial performance of private buses is also far better than that of the DTC. The significant difference in cost per km of the two kinds of operators is mainly because of lower staff cost and less overheads for a private bus operator. Earning per km for private bus operators is almost double that of the DTC. The only operational aspect in which DTC excels over private buses is fuel efficiency. The fuel efficiency of private buses is low mainly because of bad driving habits, overloading, overspeeding, and poor maintenance.

## ACCIDENT SCENARIO

The operation of these individually owned buses encourages competition on the road which has led to a marked increase in the number of accidents. Table 9.6.2 gives the accident scenario in Delhi involving these private buses.

chartered buses is limited to peak hours only. With a view to utilizing the bus to maximum capacity it has been observed that almost all the operators deploy their buses in schools for picking and dropping schoolchildren at non-peak hours. Even then their vehicle utilization is only 120 km, 50 per cent of stage carriage buses (Table 9.6.3).

For the organizer, the average route length is 25 km with a trip time of one hour. On average 40 persons travel on a regular basis as members and 25 travel as casual travellers. These buses operate on flat fare and on average, a regular commuter pays Rs 350 as monthly

TABLE 9.6.2
Details of Accidents by Blue Line/Red Line Buses
(number of accidents)

| Year | Fleet blue/ red line | Accidents by blue line buses | No. of accidents/ bus | Total accidents by private buses | Fatal accidents by blue line | Total fatal accidents by private buses |
|---|---|---|---|---|---|---|
| 1992 | 1100 | 134(16) | .122 | 853 | 89(11) | 842 |
| 1993 | 1800 | 791(50) | .439 | 1580 | 661(46) | 1434 |
| 1994 | 3200 | 983(55) | .307 | 1778 | 910(53) | 1700 |
| 1995 | 3200 | 1072(47) | .439 | 2257 | 964(45) | 2125 |
| 1996 (up to May 96) | 3200 | 290(32) | .091 | 919 | 231(28) | 835 |

*Note:* Figures in brackets are per cent of total accidents.

The awful record of accidents earned a bad name for the Red Line buses. These buses became a terror on Delhi roads and people started calling them 'bloody buses' a parody on their colour. Thus the colour of the buses introduced under the Red Line scheme was changed to blue. Since then, these buses are termed Blue Line buses! But accidents have naturally remained much as they were before.

A study on Blue Line bus drivers revealed that 88 per cent of the bus drivers have got training through informal sources and only 35 per cent of drivers have more than five years of driving experience. Nearly 65 per cent of the drivers are primary or middle level educated and 50 per cent work for 12–16 hours daily making driver's fatigue one of the reasons for high accident rates.

Absence of enforcement of rules and regulations of bus operation as specified by the Motor Vehicles Act and Motor Vehicle Rules by the STA and Traffic Police is the main reason for continuation of dysfunctional and illegal thriving of such practices in private bus operation.

## OPERATIONAL CHARACTERISTICS OF CHARTERED BUSES

About 60 per cent of private operators are small fleet owners, with one or two buses. The operation of

travel charges, and a casual commuter pays Rs 7 per trip. The organizer earns about Rs 19,000 per month, making a profit of approximately Rs 6000.

TABLE 9.6.3
Operational Characteristics of Chartered Buses

| S. no. | Parameter | per cent |
|---|---|---|
| 1 | Fleet utilization | 90 |
| 2 | Vehicle utilization | 120 |
| 3 | Dead kms/day | 17–20 |
| 4 | Daily passengers/bus/day (no.) | 220 |
| 5 | Trips/day (no.) | 4 |
| 6 | Staff/bus (no.) | 2.2 |
| 7 | Fuel efficiency (kms/litre) | 3.3 |
| 8 | Contracting/charges (Rs/month) | 13,000* |

*Income from peak hour trips only.
The owner earns Rs 13,000 per month as contracting charges from the organizer/operator of the peak hour chartered bus trip.

## SUMMARY, CONCLUSIONS, AND RECOMMENDATIONS

The existing bus system suffers from numerous operational problems. The more important of which are:

- lengthy, zig zag, and overlapping destination-oriented routes: route lengths varying from 8 to 80 km;

- long journey hours, including long waiting time at bus stops;

- low frequency of buses on many routes;

- inadequate enforcement and regulatory machinery;

- fierce competition, overspeeding, and non-observance of traffic rules by private operators;

- very high rates of accident by buses, especially private buses, on the streets of Delhi.

Chartered buses are playing an unexpected role in meeting the transport demand and have become an indispensable part of the bus system of Delhi. The ill-planned routes, suiting individual operator's greed rather than consumer needs, have resulted in criss-cross routes. The absences of an institutional set-up to regulate and control their operations have made the management of their operations a difficult task.

Rational route planning and a strong enforcement machinery for ensuring punctual rendering of trips/services would go a long way relaxing some of the harassments that the Delhi user of buses goes through.

# 9.7 DEALING WITH DROUGHT

*Saumyen Guha*

While considering the strategies of drought management, it is necessary to distinguish between different situations of water shortage. Even normally high rainfall areas may occasionally face a failure of rain, consequently upsetting normal human and economic activities. Where such occurrences are not frequent, say less than ten years, part-time relief measures prove to be adequate and separate long-term strategies are called for. But where normal rainfall itself is low, as in the case of the Deccan plateau, the life supporting hydrologic system is always in a delicate balance. Hence more comprehensive and long-term attention is required in such areas for establishing a stronger and more stable economic base. Since Independence the government has invested heavily in water resources development. Its primary concern has been twofold (Agarwal 2000): irrigation development for increasing Green Revolution-style agricultural production; and drinking water supply programmes.

Drinking water supply schemes focused primarily on groundwater exploitation fuelled by the spread of cheap rural electricity and liberal subsidies, with little or no attention to recharge especially in smaller towns and rural areas (Patwardhan 1988; Gadkari 1977; Rakshit 1997). At present, over 90 per cent of rural Indians depend on groundwater for their drinking water supply (Agarwal 2000). Groundwater tables are falling all over the country which poses a serious problem in the years when the rainfall is low. Tube wells and boreholes are constructed primarily by rich farmers and the poor, who depend on dug wells, suffer the most.

The technology of traditional rainwater harvesting has its strengths. The document 'Dying Wisdom', by the Center for Science and Environment (CSE), gives an account of extensive rainwater harvesting cultures that once successfully existed in India (Agarwal and Narain 1997). Even today the technology is relevant for India.

Drinking water requirements of a village can be met with a very small amount of land. The amount of land needed to meet the drinking water needs of an average village will vary from 0.1 ha in Arunachal Pradesh where villages are small (average population 236 people) and rainfall high, to 8.46 ha in Delhi where villages are big (average population 4769 people) and rainfall low (Agarwal 2000). In Rajasthan, the land required will vary from 1.68 to 3.64 ha in different meteorological regions and in Gujarat, it will vary between 1.72 and 3.3 ha (Agarwal 2000). This will leave a lot of land for capturing rainwater for irrigation with a good combination of rainwater harvesting and groundwater recharge. India gets most of its rain during a short period of time. The greatest technological challenge is to store that water. There are basically three options: (a) building large dams and creating large reservoirs with large catchments; (b) creating small ponds with small catchments; and (c) groundwater recharge. Studies conducted by the Central Soil and Water Conservation Research Institute at Agra, Bellary, and Kota, and another study conducted in the high rainfall region of Shillong, have observed that smaller watersheds give higher amounts of water per ha of catchment area. In the light of these findings, it should not be surprising that the large number of medium-size dams that have been constructed in Saurashtra have stored very little water in this drought year and have started going dry by December (Agarwal 2000).

In addition to ponds and tanks, groundwater recharge through percolation tanks, check dams, subsurface dams/barriers, and injection wells will go a long way, especially during drought years, in keeping essential water supply going. This will also help reverse the steady depletion of the water table all over the country. Water management schemes cannot succeed without simultaneous coordinated efforts in land management.

## ISSUES FOR IMPLEMENTATION

Rainwater harvesting may be implemented in any of the two forms : (a) revival of some of the existing structures, (b) building new water harvesting structures. A blanket strategy for reviving old structures may sometimes be counter-productive since in most parts of the country the landscape has been altered significantly due to urban-industrial development. The appropriate technology for rainwater harvesting in different regions has to be developed after considering the local situation. The technological expertise to evolve suitable strategies for various regions exists in the country. However, the economic, social, and managerial factors which are crucial for the successful implementation of rainwater harvesting need to be addressed separately. Some such factors are outlined as follows:

A scheme of individual, community, and state rights over water needs to be defined by planners and legal experts, if community-based rainwater harvesting programmes are to be successful. The government should only function as the facilitator and not the controlling authority. The Pani Panchayat model can serve as the basis. The rights of the landless to water must also be defined.

Unlike large dams, small water harvesting systems are unlikely to have equitable distribution of water. A system has to be evolved by local community participation taking into account the local ecology.

Table 9.7.1
Record of Government Rural Drinking
Water Supply Schemes

| Year of survey | Number of problem villages identified | Number of villages covered till the next survey | Number of not covered the next |
|---|---|---|---|
| 1972 | 150,000 | 94,000 | 56,000 |
| 1980 | 231,000 | 192,000 | 39,000 |
| 1985 | 161,722 | 161,652 | 70 |
| 1994 | 140,000 | 110,371 | 30,604 |
| 1997 | 61,747 | | |

# BIBLIOGRAPHY

Agarwal, A. and Narain, S. (1997). *Dying Wisdom: Rise, Fall and Potential of India's Traditional Water Harvesting Systems*, Centre for Science and Environment, New Delhi.

Akwule, R. U. (1992). 'Telecommunications in Kenya: Development and Policy Issues' in *Telecommunications Policy*, September–October, pp. 603–11.

All India Reporter Private Ltd. (various issues). *All India Reporter*, edited by VR Manohar, Nagpur.

Amann, C. A. (1998). 'The Stretch for Better Passenger Car Fuel Economy: A Critical Look, Part 2', *Automotive Engineering International*, March, pp. 71–6.

*America's Networks* at http://www.americasnetwork.com.

Amreli Nagarpalika (1999). *Citizen's Charter*, Amreli.

———— (various issues). *Income and Expenditure Statement*, 1996–7, 1997–8 and 1998–9, Amreli.

Asian Development Bank and the Ministry of Surface Transport (1993). *Policy Reforms in the Indian Ports and Shipping Sector: Inception Report*, TechEcon, Hong Kong.

Asian Development Bank and Ministry of Surface Transport (1999). *Strategic Development Plan for Ennore Port*, Harris Inc., New Delhi.

Asian Institute of Transport Development (1998). *Greying of IR*, New Delhi.

Asif, Mohammed (1999). 'Land Acquisition Act: Need for an Alternative Paradigm', *Economic and Political Weekly*, vol. 24, no. 25, pp. 1564–6.

Australian Communications Authority, www.aca.gov.au

*Automotive Engineering* (1997). 'Gasoline—Reforming Fuel Cell', February, pp. 151–2.

*Automotive Engineering International* (1998). 'Electric Vehicle Drive Systems', February, pp. 115–17.

———— (1998). 'Electric Vehicle Drive Systems', February, pp. 259–65.

———— (1998). 'NEBUS Fuel-Cell Municipal-Transit Bus', July 1998, pp. 54–5.

Bagchi, Amaresh (1993). 'Financing Urban Local Governments: Issues and Approaches', *Economic and Political Weekly*, vol. 28, no. 37, pp. 1920–3.

———— (1997). 'Reforming the Property Tax Base, Need for a New Direction', *Economic and Political Weekly*, vol. 32, no. 47, pp. 3005–10.

Baird, Alfred (2000). 'Port Privatization: Objectives, Extent, Process, and the UK Experience', *International Journal of Maritime Economics*, vol. 2, no. 3, pp. 177–94.

Bamford C. G. (1998). *Transport Economics*, Heinemann Publishers, Oxford.

Banerjee, Bibek, G. Raghuram and Narayan Rangaraj (2000). 'Konkan Railway Corporation Limited', *Vikalpa*, vol. 25, no. 1, pp. 89–109

Barnes, F. (1998). 'Regulating Telecommunications' in Deiter Helm and Tim Jenkinson (ed.) *Competition in Regulated Industries*, Oxford University Press, UK.

Basant, Rakesh and Morris Sebastian (2000). *Competition Policy in India: Issues for a Globalising Economy*, Report prepared for the Ministry of Industry, Indian Institute of Management, Ahmedabad.

Batra, V. S. and Ajay Mathur (1999). 'Challenges and Promises of Fuel Cell Vehicles' in *Conference on Automobile and Fuel Technologies—Solutions for the Environment*, Tata Energy Research Institute, New Delhi.

Beesley, M. E. and S. C. Littlechild (1989). 'The Regulation of Privatized Monopolies in the United Kingdom', *Rand Journal of Economics*, vol. 20, pp. 454–72.

Benjamin, Solomon and Gururaja Budhya (1999). 'Urban Governance, Civic Society and Local Economic Development: An Agenda Note', mimeo, Bangalore.

Berta, G. L. (1993). 'Engines for Hybrid Vehicles: Requirements and Perspectives', SAE Paper No. 931486, Society of Automotive Engineers, Washington, DC.

Bhatia, Bela (1992). 'Lush Fields and Parched Throats: The Political-Economy of Groundwater in Gujarat', WIDER Working Paper No. 100, United Nations University, Helsinki.

Bhatt, Sanjeev (1990). 'Palace on Wheels', unpublished case, Indian Institute of Management, Ahmedabad.

Bizer, John and Tod Ragsdale (2000). 'The Development of Resettlement Policy in China', http://www.his.com/~mesas/Chinapol

Bond, G. and Carter, L. (1994). 'Financing Private Infrastructure Projects: Emerging Trends from IFC's Experience', International Finance Corporation Discussion Paper 23, World Bank, Washington, DC.

Burpee, D. S. and P. W. Shumate, Jr (1994). 'Emerging Residential Broadband Communications', *IEEE Communication Magazine*, vol. 82, April, pp. 604–14.

*Census of India* (1997). Series I, Paper 2 of 1993 (Housing and Amenities) Census of India—1991, Controller of Publication, New Delhi.

———— (1997). 'Availability of Infrastructural Facilities in Rural India: An Analysis of Village Directory Data', Census of India—1991, Office of the Registrar General, New Delhi.

Central Electricity Authority (various issues), *Electric Power Survey*, 13th, 14th and 15th, CEA, New Delhi.

Central Finance Commission, (2000). *Report of the Eleventh Finance Commission for 2000–5*, Special Supplement No. 3 of 2000, Akalanle Publications, Delhi.

Central Institute of Road Transport (2000). *State Transport Undertakings: Profile and Performance, 1998–9*, CIRT, Pune.

Central Pollution Control Board (1998). *Pollution Statistics in Delhi of 1993*, Ministry of Environment and Forests, New Delhi.

Central Statistical Organisation (various issues). National Accounts Statistics, CSO, New Delhi.

Centre for Monitoring the Indian Economy (2000). *Infrastructure Statistics Report*, CMIE, Mumbai.

Cernea, Michael M. (1999). 'Why Economic Analysis Is Essential to Resettlement?', *Economic and Political Weekly*, vol. 34, no. 31, pp. 2149–58.

Chaloner, W. H. and W. M. Stern (eds) (1969). *Essays in European Economic History, 1789–1914*, Edward Arnold, London.

Chinese Railways (1997). *Annual Statistics*, China Railway Society, Beijing.

Ciofffic, John M. (1999). 'Very High Speed Digital Subscriber Lines', *IEEE Communication Magazine*, vol. 87, pp. 72–9.

Consulting Engineering Services Limited (1987). 'Estimation of Total Road Transport Freight and Passenger Movement in India,' mimeo.

Container Corporation of India Ltd. (various issues). *Annual Report*, 1997–8 and 1998–9, CONCOR, New Delhi.

Crouzet, Francois (1969). In *Essays in European Economic History: 1789–1914*, Edward Arnold, London.

Customs Act, 1962 (2000). 'Provisions Relating to Coastal Goods and Vessels Carrying Coastal Goods', Current Publications, Mumbai, pp 50-1.

Das, K. (1999). 'Underdevelopment by Design? National Planning and Vital Infrastructure in Orissa', Working Paper No. 107, Gujarat Institute of Development Research, Ahmedabad.

———— (1997). 'Politics of Industrial Location: Indian Federalism and Development Decisions', *Economic and Political Weekly*, vol. 32, no. 51, pp. 3268-74.

Das, Keshabananda and B. L. Kumar (1998). 'A Validation Study of Habitations Not Covered Under the Rural Drinking Water Programme in Gujarat', mimeo, Gujarat Institute of Development Research, Ahmedabad.

Datta, Abhijit (1995). 'Municipal Reforms in India: Comparative Models and Processes', *Economic and Political Weekly*, vol. 30, no. 38, pp. 2395–8.

Department of Rural Development (1991). *Annual Report 1990–1*, Ministry of Agriculture, New Delhi.

Department of Telecom Services (various issues). *Annual Report*, DTS, Ministry of Communications, New Delhi.

Department of Telecommunications (various issues). *Annual Report*, DoT, New Delhi.

———— (1991). *Report of the High Level Committee on Reorganisation of Telecom Department*, mimeo, DoT, New Delhi.

Devli, Anil (2000). 'Shipping as Infrastructure: The Coastal Alternative', *Indian Shipping*, vol. 52, no. 3–4, pp. 29–31.

Dharampur Nagarpalika (1999). *Citizen's Charter*, Dharampur.

Dhawan, B. D. (1991). 'Developing Groundwater Resources: Merits and Demerits', *Economic and Political Weekly*, vol. 26, no. 8, pp. 425–9.

Dhir, K. S. (1992). 'The Challenges of Introducing Advanced Telecommunications in India' in Palvia, Palvia and Ziegler (ed.) *The Global Issues of Information Technology Management*, Idea Group Publishing, Harrisburg, PA.

Dholka Nagarpalika (various issues). *Income and Expenditure Statement*, 1993–4, 1994–5, 1995–6, and 1996–7, Dholka.

Dieter, Helm and Tim Jenkinson (ed.) (1998). *Competition in Regulated Industries*, Oxford University Press, UK.

Dobbin, F. (1994). *Forging Industrial Policy: The United States, Britain and France in the Railway Age*, Cambridge University Press, Cambridge.

Donaldson, H. (1994). 'Telecommunication Liberalization and Privatization: The New Zealand Experience' in B. Wellenius and P.A. Stern (ed.), *Implementing Reforms in the Telecom Sector*, World Bank, Washington, DC, pp. 253–60.

Dutta, S. A., and B. Sengupta (1998). 'Air Quality Goals for Delhi: Options to meet Them by Year 2005', paper presented at the Workshop on Integrated Approach to Vehicular Pollution Control in Delhi, New Delhi.

Easter, K. William, Nir Becker and Yacov Tsur (1998). 'Economic Mechanisms for Managing Water Resources: Pricing, Permits, and Markets', in Asit K. Biswas (ed.), *Water Resources: Environmental Planning, Management, and Development*, Tata McGraw Hill Publishing Company, New Delhi.

*Economist* (1991). 'Telecommunications', vol. 3221, no. 7727, p. 34.

———— (2000). 'When India Wires Up', vol. 356, no. 8180, pp. 27–30.

———— (2000). 'Wired China: The Flies Swarm', vol. 356, no. 8180, p. 22.

Eichengreen, B. (1994). 'Financing Infrastructure in Developing Countries: Lessons from the Railway Age', Background Paper for the World Development Report 1994, Policy Research Working Paper 1379, World Bank, Washington, DC.

Electricity (Supply) Act 1948: Act No. 54 of 1948 (1979). As amended up-to-date by Act 23 of 1978, Ram Narain Lal Beni Prasad, Allahabad.

Enos, J. L. and W. H. Park (1988). *The Adoption and Diffusion of Imported Technology: The Case of Korea*, Croom Helm, London.

Evenari, M., L. Shanan, and N. Tadmor (1982). *The Negev: The Challenge Of A Desert*, second edition, Harvard University Press, Cambridge, MA.

Faulhaber, G. R. (1975). 'Cross-Subsidization: Pricing in Public Enterprises', *American Economic Review*, vol. 65, no. 5, pp. 966–77.

Federal Communications Commission (1995). Telephone Number Portability: Notice, FCC–95–284, Washington, DC.

————— (1996). Number Portability: First Report and Order, FCC–96–286, Washington, DC.

————— (1997). Number Portability: Second Report and Order, FCC–97–289, Washington, DC.

————— (1997). Number Portability: First Reconsideration Order, FCC-97-074, Washington, DC.

————— (1998). Number Portability: Third Report and Order, FCC-98-082, Washington, DC.

Federal Communications Commission at www.fcc.gov.

Federation of Zambian Road Hauliers Ltd (1992). *Annual Report,* Road Hauliers Ltd., Harare.

Fernandes, Walter (1998). 'Land Acquisition (Amendment) Bill, 1998', *Economic and Political Weekly*, vol. 33, no. 42–3, pp. 2703–6.

Ferreira, D. and K. Khatami (1996). 'Financing Private Infrastructure in Developing Countries', World Bank Discussion Paper 343, World Bank, Washington, DC.

Foundation for Public Interest (1998). *Performance Rating of Municipal Services in Nagarpalikas: Case Study of Gujarat,* Ahmedabad.

Frankel, Ernst G. (1986). *Port Planning and Development,* John Wiley & Sons, New York.

Gadkari, A. D. (1977). 'Groundwater Potential in Drought Prone Areas of Maharashtra', *Journal of Indian Water Works Association*, vol. 9, no. 4, pp. 323–9.

Garg, Pooja (2000). 'The End of Monopoly', *Business Today*, vol. 9, no. 15, p. 30.

Gill, J. S. (1990). 'Control of Indian Ships And Ships Engaged in Coasting Trade' in *Manual of Merchant Shipping Act, 1958*, Bhandarkar Publications, Bombay.

Glynn, S. (1992). 'Japan's Success in Telecommunication Regulation: A Unique Regulatory Mix', *Telecommunications Policy*, pp. 5–12.

Godbole, Madhav (1999). 'Right to Information: A Long Way to Go', *Lokayan Bulletin*, Special Issue on the Right to Information, vol. 16, no. 3, p. 11–28.

Government of Gujarat (1964). *The Gujarat Municipalities Act, 1963*, Gujarat Act No. 34, Gandhinagar.

————— (1999a). *Gujarat Infrastructure Development Act, 1999*, Gandhinagar.

————— (1999b). *Gujarat Infrastructure Agenda: Vision 2010,* Gujarat Infrastructure Development Board, Gandhinagar.

————— (1999c). *Final Report of Gujarat Infrastructure Development Board (GIDB) on Institutional Strengthening,* mimeo, Gandhinagar.

Government of India (1983). *Recommendations of the National Transport Policy Committee*, Planning Commission, GoI, New Delhi.

————— (2000). *Report of the Group on India Hydrocarbons Vision 2025*, Prime Ministers Office, GoI, New Delhi.

————— (1997). *The India Infrastructure Report*, volumes I, II and III, The Rakesh Mohan Committee, NCAER and GoI, New Delhi.

————— (1995). *Hydrocarbons Perspective 2010,* report of the study group, Ministry of Petroleum and Natural Gas, GoI, New Delhi.

Guislain, Pierre (1997). *The Privatisation Challenge: A Strategic, Legal and Institutional Analysis of International Experience,* World Bank Regional and Sectoral Studies, World Bank, Washington, DC.

Gujarat Electricity Board (1997). *Annual Report*, Gujarat Electricity Board, Gandhinagar.

Gujarat Government Gazette Extraordinary (1993). *The Constitutional (Seventy-Fourth) Amendment Act, 1992*, vol. 34, 17 August.

Gujarat Maritime Board (various issues). *Administration Report,* Gandhinagar.

Gujarat Municipal Finance Board (1999). *A Report on the Services in Municipalities and Need Assessment,* GoI, Gandhinagar.

Gupta, Amita (2000). 'An Investigation into Delays and Overruns in Public Sector Projects: A Case of Ahmedabad–Vadodara Expressway', Masters dissertation, School of Planning, Center for Environmental Science and Technology, Ahmedabad.

Heggie Ian G. (1995). 'Management Financing of Roads: An Agenda for Reform', Working Paper No. 8, Sub-Saharan Africa Transport Policy Program, World Bank, Washington, DC.

Holguin-Veras, Jose and Michael Walton (1994). *An Annotated Bibliography on the Performance Analysis of Port Operations*, Center for Transportation Research, University of Texas, Austin.

HUDCO (1995). *Report of the Sub-group on Commercialization of Urban Infrastructure Projects*, Expert Group constituted by the Government of India, New Delhi.

Hyun, D. and J. A. Lent (1999). 'Korean Telecom Policy in Global Competition: Implications for Developing Countries', *Telecommunications Policy*, vol. 23, no. 5, pp. 389–401.

*Indian Infrastructure* (1999). 'Petroleum Transportation: Creating a Common Grid', vol. 1, no. 6, pp. 26–8.

Indian National Shipowners' Association (various issues). *Annual Review*, Mumbai.

Indian Ports Association (2000). *Major Ports of India: A Profile—1998-99*, New Delhi.

Indian Railways (various issues). *Year Book,* Ministry of Railways, New Delhi.

————— (2000). *Draft Corporate Plan: 2000–2012*, New Delhi.

Indian Road Congress (1990). *Guidelines for Capacity of Urban Roads in Plain Areas*, New Delhi.

Indira Gandhi Institute of Development Research (1999). *Clean Water: Environmental Governance-1*, Mumbai.

International Finance Corporation (1996). *Financing Private Infrastructure: Lessons of Experience*, World Bank, Washington, DC.

International Telecommunication Union, www.itu.int.

———— (1989). 'The Changing Telecommunications Environment: Policy Considerations for Members of the ITU', *ITU Report*, Report of the Advisory Group on Telecommunication Policy, Geneva.

Jain, K. C. (1984). *Land Acquisition Act*, Jain Publishers, New Delhi.

Jain, R. (1995). 'A Review of Regulatory Issues in Developing Countries', paper presented at the conference on *Regulatory Frameworks: The Lessons of Experience for Developing Countries*, Commonwealth Telecom Organisation, Kuala Lampur, Malaysia.

———— (1997). 'Operationalizing a Regulatory Framework in India', *Vikalpa*, vol. 23, no. 3, pp. 29–37.

Jain, R. and J. Chhokar (1993). 'Reorganisation of the Telecom Sector: Past and Future', *Economic Times*, 3 February.

Jain, R. and T. Sastry (1997). 'Rural Telecom Services in India', paper presented at the Telecom Policy Research Workshop, Indian Institute of Management, Ahmedabad.

Jhunjhunwala, Ashok (1998b). 'Can Telecom and Information Technology be for the Disadvantaged?', *Journal of Rural Development*, vol. 17, no. 2, pp. 321–7.

Jhunjhunwala Ashok, Bhaskar Ramamurthi, and Timothy A. Gonsalves (1998). 'The Role of Technology in Telecom Expansion in India', *IEEE Communication Magazine*, November.

———— (1999). 'Indian Telecom and Internet Tangle: What is the way out?' in *Emerging Communication Technologies and Society*, Narosa Publishing House, New Delhi.

Joshi, S. (1990). Keynote address at the Seminar on Traditional Water Harvesting Systems of India, Centre for Science and Environment, New Delhi.

Jussawala, M. (1992). 'Is the Communications Link Still Missing?', *Telecommunications Policy*, vol. 16, no. 6, pp. 485–503.

Kanpur Development Authority (2000). *Swarna Jayanti Vihar Scheme*, mimeo, Satabari.

Kanpur Development Authority (2001). *Financial Report 2000–1: Income and Expenditure*.

Kartik, V. (1998). *Comparison of Alternate Measures at AIIMS Intersection*, B. Tech Thesis, Department of Civil Engineering, Indian Institute of Technology, Delhi.

Kelly T. and Woodall M. (2000). 'Telecom Traffic Indicator', *Telecommunications Policy*, vol. 23, no. 3, pp. 155–9.

Khedbrahma Nagarpalika (various issues). *Income and Expenditure Statement*, 1993–4, 1994–5, and 1997–8, Khedbrahma, Gujarat.

Kim, C., Y. K. Kim, and C. Yoon (1992). 'Korean Telecommunications Development: Achievement and Cautionary Lesson', *World Development*, vol. 26, no. 12, pp. 1829–41.

King, John and Benn Konsynski (1990). 'Singapore Tradenet: A Tale of One City', case material, Harvard Business School, MA.

Klein M. (1998). 'Network Industries' in Dieter Helm, and Jenkinson Tim (ed.) *Competition in Regulated Industries*, Oxford University Press, UK.

Kumar, Neeraja (2000). 'DoT may drop WLL in Fixed Telephony', *Financial Express*, 23 August, p. 1.

Laidlaw, B. (1994). 'Evolution of Telecommunication Policy in the United Kingdom in Implementing Reforms in the Telecom Sector' in B. Wellenius and P. A. Stern (eds), *Implementing Reforms in the Telecom Sector*, World Bank, Washington, DC, pp. 285–92.

Landes, D. (1956). 'The Old Bank and the New: The Financial Revolution of the Nineteenth Century', translated into English by Max A. Lehmann in W. H. Chaloner and W. M. Stern (eds) (1969), *Essays in European Economic History: 1789–1914*, Edward Arnold, London.

Le Blanc, N., R. Larsen, and M. Duoba, (1996). 'The 1995 HEV Challenge :Results and Technology Summary', SAE Paper No. 960741, Washington, DC.

Lewis, C. (1938). *America's State in International Investments*, quoted in B. Eichengreen (1994), 'Financing Infrastructure in Developing Countries: Lessons from the Railway Age', World Bank, Washington, DC.

Leys, Colin (1975). *Underdevelopment in Kenya: The Political Economy of Neo-colonialism*, Heinemann, London.

Mahanagar Telephone Nigam Ltd. (1991). 'MTNL Completes Five Years', mimeo, New Delhi.

Mahapatra, L. K. (1999). *Resettlement, Impoverishment and Reconstruction in India*, Vikas Publications, New Delhi.

'Maharashtra', *Journal of Indian Works Association*, vol. 9, no. 4, pp. 323–9.

Mani, S. (1992). *Foreign Technology in Public Enterprise*, Oxford & IBH, New Delhi.

Manikutty S. (1997). 'Telecom Services in Urban and Corporate Segments: A Consumer Perspective', *Vikalpa*, vol. 22, no. 3, pp. 15–20.

*Manubhai D. Shah Vs. LIC* (1981). All India Reporter, GUJ 15, Secy.

*Maritime Monitor* (2000). 'A Survey on Coastal Shipping in India', April.

*Maritime Monitor* (2000). 'Sabotage Law in India: An International Comparison', April.

Martin, B., H. Weiss, and Junseok Hwang (1998). 'Internet Telephony or Circuit Switched Telephony: Which is Cheaper?', paper presented at Telecom Policy Research Conference, Alexandria, VA.

Marwah, B. R. (2000). 'A Relook at Passenger Car Equivalents in the Indian Context,' mimeo, Indian Institute of Technology, Kanpur.

———— (2000). 'Strategy for Identification and Evaluation of Bottlenecks on Road System', mimeo, Indian Institute of Technology, Kanpur.

Marwah, B. R., V. K. Sibal, and S. Savant (2000). 'Bus Transport in Urban India: A Case Study of Delhi', mimeo, Indian Institute of Technology, Kanpur.

Mathur, H.M. and David Mardsen (1998). *Development Projects and Impoverishment Risks*, Oxford University Press, New Delhi.

Mathur, M.P. (1995). 'Financial Requirements for Municipal Services: Need for Alternative Arrangements', paper presented at the Seminar on Finances of Local Bodies in *Kerala*, State Finance Commission, Trivandrum.

———— (1999a). 'Upgrading Municipal Services: Financial Needs and Strategies for Resource Generation', paper presented at the National Seminar on Resource Mobilisation for Urban Services at Decentralized Level, DTUDP, Centre for Development Studies and UP Academy of Administration, Nainital.

———— (1999b). 'The Constitution (74th) Amendment Act and Urban Local Governments: An Overview', *Urban India*, vol. 19, no. 1.

———— (1999c). 'Norms and Standards of Infrastructure and Services in India: A Review and Methodological Assessment', FIRE (D–II) Working Paper Series, no.1, National Institute of Urban Affairs, New Delhi.

Mathur, O. P., P. Sengupta, and A. Bhaduri (2000). *Option for closing the Revenue Gap of Municipalities*, 2000-1 to 2004-5, National Institute of Public Finance and Policy, New Delhi.

Mehta, Abhay (1991). *Power Play*, Orient Longman, New Delhi.

Mehta, Jaya and Shanta Venkatraman (2000). 'Poverty Statistics: Barmecide's Feast', *Economic and Political Weekly*, vol. 35, no. 27, p. 2377.

Mehta, M. (1993). 'Pricing of Water Supply', *All India Housing Development Association Journal*, February.

Melody, W.H. (1986). 'Efficiency and Social Policy in Telecommunication: Lesson from the US Experience', *Journal of Economic Issues*, September.

———— (1991). 'Telecommunication Reform: Which Sectors to Privatize', paper presented at the ITU Conference, Geneva.

Mendler, Charles (1997). 'Taking a New Look at Hybrid Electric Vehicle Efficiency: A Critical Look', *Automotive Engineering*, February, pp. 67–70.

Merrett, Stephen (1997). *Introduction to the Economics of Water Resources: An International Perspective*, UCL Press Ltd., London.

Miller, N. P. (1994). 'Regulation: Reconciling Policy Objectives in Implementing Reforms in the Telecom Sector' in B. Wellenius and P. A. Stern (eds), *Implementing Reforms in the Telecom Sector*, World Bank, Washington, DC, pp. 485-504.

Ministry of Information and Broadcasting (1995). *Government of India and Ors. vs. Cricket Association of Bengal and Ors*, 2 SCC 161.

Ministry of Surface Transport (various issues). *Motor Transport Statistics of India*, Government of India, New Delhi.

———— (various issues). *Pocket Book on Transport Statistics of India*, 1997 and 1998, Government of India, New Delhi.

———— (1993). *Report of the Working Group on Development of Coastal Shipping*, Government of India, New Delhi.

———— (1997). *Report of the National Shipping Policy Committee*, Government of India, New Delhi.

———— (1999). *Basic Port Statistics of India: 1998-99*, Government of India, New Delhi.

———— (1999). *Report of the Expert Committee on Draft Coastal Shipping Act*, Government of India, New Delhi.

Moench, Marcus (1992). 'Drawing Down the Buffer: Science and Politics of Ground Water Management in India', *Economic and Political Weekly*, Review of Agriculture, 28 March, pp. A7–A14.

Mohan, Dinesh (2000). 'Accidents on Indian Roads', mimeo, Indian Institute of Technology, Delhi.

Mohanty, P. K. (1995). 'Reforming Municipal Finances: Some Suggestions in the Context of India's Decentralization Initiative', *Urban India*, vol. 15, no. 1.

Morris, Alice (2000). 'Land Acquisition Process: The Case of Poshitra Port', mimeo, Unnati, Ahmedabad.

Morris, Sebastian (1990). 'Cost and Time Overruns in Public Sector Projects', *Economic and Political Weekly*, vol. 25, no. 47, pp. 154–68.

———— (1991). 'Holding Companies, Performance Contracts and Task Orientation in Public Sector', *Economic and Political Weekly*, 30 November, pp. M137–44.

———— (1996). 'The Political Economy of Electrical Power in India', Parts I and II, *Economic and Political Weekly*, vol. 31, nos 20 and 21.

———— (1997). 'Why not Push for a 9 per cent Growth Rate?', *Economic and Political Weekly*, 17–24 May, pp. 1153–65.

———— (1999). 'GEB Reforms: A Note on Regulatory Strategy and an Approach to Privatisation', WP No. 99–11–04, Indian Institute of Management, Ahmedabad.

———— (2000). 'Restructuring Gujarat Electricity Board: Outline of a Strategy and Proposal for Action', WP No. 2000–03–12, Indian Institute of Management, Ahmedabad.

———— (2000a). 'Regulatory Strategy and Restructuring: Model for Gujarat Power Sector', *Economic and Political Weekly*, vol. 35, no. 23.

*Motor Vehicle Emission Regulations and Fuel Specifications* (1996). Part 1, Report No 5/97, CONCAWE Publications, Brussels.

Mundy, Mike (2000). 'Containership Markets', *Global Shipping Digest: Industry in Perspective*, Mike Mundy Associates.

Murty, M. N., A. J. James and Smita Misra (1999). *Economics of Water Pollution: The Indian Experience*, Oxford University Press, Delhi.

Nagaraj, B. S. (2000). 'Hotshot Consultants Copy a Report to get Project Cleared', *Indian Express*, 27 August, Ahmedabad edition.

Nagaraj, R. (1984). 'Subcontracting in Indian Industries: Analysis, Evidence and Issues', *Economic and Political Weekly*, vol. 19, nos 31, 32 and 33, pp. 1435–53.

———— (2000). 'Indian Economy since 1980: Virtuous Growth or Polarisation?', *Economic and Political Weekly*, vol. 35, no. 32, pp. 2831–9.

Nalatwadmath, S. K., M. S. Rama Mohan Rao, and M. Padmaiah (1997). 'Joladarasi Model Watershed Development Programme in Bellary District of Karnataka: A Diagnostic Evaluation', *Journal of Rural Development*, vol. 16, no. 2, pp. 313–28.

Nanjundiah, Y. N. and J. M. Barot (1989). 'A New Dimension in Rural Watersupply Programme', *Journal of Indian Water Works Association*, pp. 239–43.

Narayan, Deepa (1995). 'The Contribution of People's Participation: Evidence from 121 Rural Water Supply Projects', Environmentally Sustainable Development Occasional Paper Series No. 1, The World Bank, Washington, DC.

National Council of Applied Economic Research (2000). *The Draft Electricity Bill 2000*, version 5, NCAER, New Delhi.

National Institute of Public Finance and Policy (1995). *Redefining State-Municipal Fiscal Relations: Options and Perspective for the State Finance Commissions*, NIPFP, New Delhi.

National Institute of Urban Affairs (1983). *A study of the Financial Resources of Urban Local Bodies in India and the Level of Services Provided*, NIUA, New Delhi.

———— (1986). *Management of Urban Services*, NIUA, New Delhi.

———— (1987). *The Nature and Dimensions of Urban Fiscal Crisis*, NIUA, New Delhi.

———— (1989). *Upgrading Municipal Services: Norms and Financial Implications*, vols 1 and 2, NIUA, New Delhi.

———— (1995). *Norms and Standards of Expenditure for Municipal Services*, paper prepared for the National Workshop on the Role and Functions of the State Finance Commissions, NIUA, Mussoorie.

———— (1997a). *Financing Urban Infrastructure in India*, NIUA, New Delhi.

———— (1997b). *Scope and Practice of Privatization of Urban Services in India*, NIUA, New Delhi.

———— (1998a). *A Compendium of Municipal Legislations in Conformity with Constitution (74th) Amendment Act, 1992*, NIUA, New Delhi.

———— (1998b). *Project Development Experience in Urban Environmental Infrastructure*, vols I and II, compiled by Gangadhar Jha, NIUA, New Delhi.

———— (1998c). *Strategy for Capacity Building of Urban Government Institution in India*, , NIUA New Delhi.

———— (2000a). 'First State Finance Commissions: Recommendations Regarding Transfers, Sharing and Devolution of Taxes', background paper prepared for the *National Meet on Approach to State–Municipal Fiscal Relations*, NIUA, NIPFP and Indo-US FIRE Project, New Delhi.

———— (2000b). *Urban Statistics: Hand Book 2000*, NIUA, New Delhi.

———— *Synthesis Report of the UBSP Benchmark Survey*, vols I and II, New Delhi.

National Telecom Policy (1999) at http://www.trai.gov.in/ntp1999.htm

Naughton, Barry (1996). *Growing out of the Plan: Chinese Economic Reform, 1978–1993*, Cambridge University Press, UK.

Nigam, Ashok, Biksham Gujja, Jayanta Bandyopadhyay and Rupert Talbot (1998). *Fresh Water for India's Children and Nature: Learning from Local-Level Approaches*, UNICEF and WWF, New Delhi.

Number Portability Site at www.ported.com.

Nuttall R. and Vickers J. (1996). 'Competition Policy for Regulated Utility Industries in Britain', Regulation Initiative Discussion Papers Series No 1, Oxford University, UK.

Oei, D. G. (1997). 'Fuel Cell Engines for Vehicles', *Automotive Engineering*, February, pp. 115–17.

Office for Telecom Authority, Hong Kong, at www.ofta.gov.hk.

Office for Telecommunications at www.oftel.gov.uk.

Operations Research Group (1989). Delivery and Financing of Urban Services, Mumbai.

Pangotra, Prem (1999). 'Resource Mobilization Strategies for Financing of Transport Infrastructure and Services', in G. Raghuran *et al.* (ed.), *Infrastructure Development and Financing*, Macmillan India, New Delhi.

Parikh, Kirit (ed.) (1999). *India Development Report 1999–2000*, Oxford University Press, New Delhi.

Parson, G. L. (1987). 'Strategic Information Technology', in E. K. Somogyi and R. D. Galliers (ed.) *Towards Strategic Information Systems*, Abacus Press, Cambridge.

Patwardhan, S. S. (1988). 'Urban Water Supply during Drought Conditions: Case Study of a Town', *Journal of Indian Water Works Association*, pp. 15–20.

Paul, Samuel (1993). 'Bangalore's Public Services: A Report Card', *Economic and Political Weekly*, vol. 28, no. 52, p. 2901.

Pendley, Charles (1997). 'A Demand-based Approach to Rural Water Supply and Sanitation', in K. Pushapangadan (ed.), *Proceedings of the National Seminar on Rural Water Supply and Sanitation*, Centre for Development Studies, Trivandrum.

Perkins, Stephen, and Alan Gatherer (1999). 'Two-way Broadband CATV-HFC Networks: State-of-the-art and Future Trends', *Computer Networks*, vol. 31, pp. 313–26.

Pisciotta, A.A. (1994). 'Privatization of Telecommunication: The Case of Venezuela in Implementing Reforms in the Telecom Sector' in B.Wellenius and P. A. Stern (eds), *Implementing Reforms in the Telecom Sector*, World Bank, pp. 185–94.

Plaast, Gregory (2000). 'States Deregulate Energy at Their Peril', *New York Times*, 25 August.

Planning Commission (1983). *Task Force on Housing and Urban Development: Financing Urban Development*, Planning Commission, Government of India, New Delhi.

———— (1992). *Report of the Committee on Pricing of*

*Irrigation Water*, Planning Commission, Government of India, New Delhi.

———— (1998). *Perspective Planning for Transport Development: Report of Steering Committee*, New Delhi.

———— (2000). *Compilation of Ninth Five Year Plan: 1997–2000*, Nabhi Publications, New Delhi.

PricewaterHouseCoopers (1999). *Report On Institutional Strengthening of GIDB*, Asian Development Bank Technical Assistance No.2716-IND, mimeo.

Public Affairs Centre, (1999). *Monitoring the Quality of Road Works: A Citizen's Guide*, Department of Science and Technology, Bangalore.

Pundir B. P. (2000). 'Vehicular Air Pollution in India: Recent Control Measures and Related Issues', Indian Institute of Technology, Kanpur.

Purswani, R. (1988). 'Need of Reservoirs to Meet Droughts and Floods', *Journal of Indian Water Works Association*, pp. 11–13.

Pushpangadan, K. and G. Murugan (1997). 'User Financing and Collective Action: Relevance for Sustainable Rural Water Supply in India', Working Paper No. 274, Centre for Development Studies, Trivandrum.

Raghuram G. (1992). 'Logistics Management: An Introductory Note', *Vikalpa*, vol. 17, no. 1.

———— (1996). 'Towards a National Shipping Policy: A Study of the Indian Shipping Industry', PSG Monograph, Indian Institute of Management, Ahmedabad.

———— (2000a). 'Coastal Shipping: Scope of Integrating with the National Transport Network', Working Paper No. 2000-10-04, Indian Institute of Management, Ahmedabad.

———— (2000b). 'Experiences of Various Forms of Commercial Partnerships in Indian Railway', mimeo, Indian Institute of Management, Ahmedabad.

———— (2000c). 'Logistics Infrastructure in India and its Implications for Supply Chain Management' in G. Raghuram and N. Rangaraj (ed.), *Logistics and Supply Chain Management: Cases and Concepts*, Macmillan India Limited, New Delhi.

———— (2000d). 'Regulation and Privatisation: A Comparative Case Study of Gujarat Maritime Board and Jawaharlal Nehru Port Trust', Indian Institute of Management, Ahmedabad.

Raghuram G. and V. V. Rao (1991). 'A Decision Support System for Improving Railway Line Capacity', *Public Enterprise*, vol. 11, no. 1.

Rai, Kuldip and D. K. Bhalla (2000). 'Computerisation of Land Records in India' at http://www.csdms.org/magazine/ April 2000

*Raj Narain vs. State of UP* (1975). All India Reporter SC 865.

Rakshit, R. N. (1977). 'Development of Groundwater Resources for Drinking Water Supply in The Rural Water Areas of Maharashtra State', *Journal of Indian Water Works Association*, vol. 9, no. 4, pp. 315–21.

Ramadesikan, G. R. (1999a). 'Policy Approach to Internet Telephony', paper presented at the Workshop on Telecom Policy Initiatives: The Road Ahead, Indian Institute of Management, Ahmedabad.

———— (1999b). 'Technological Convergence: A Note', mimeo, Indian Institute of Management, Ahmedabad.

Ramani, K. V. (1993). 'IT Applications in Transportation', *CSI Communications*, October.

———— (1995). 'Port Management: Some EDI Applications in Singapore', *CSI Communications*, May, pp. 25–7.

———— (1996). 'An Interactive Simulation Model for the Logistics Planning of Container Operations in Seaports', *Simulation Journal*, vol. 66, no. 5, pp. 291–300.

———— (2000). 'Port Management: India's Preparedness to Face Global Challenges', mimeo, Indian Institute of Management, Ahmedabad.

Replogle, M. (1998). 'Nonmotorised Vehicles in Asia: Issues and Strategies', World Bank, Washington, DC.

*Report of the Spectrum Management Committee* (1998). Prime Minister's Council at http://www.trai.gov.in.

Reserve Bank of India (1994). 'Finances of State Governments', *RBI Bulletin*, February issue, Mumbai.

Roth, Gabriel (1996). *Roads in a Market Economy*, Ashgate Publishing Ltd., London.

Saleth, Maria R. (1994). 'Towards a New Water Institution: Economics, Law and Policy', *Economic and Political Weekly*, Review of Agriculture, 24 Sep, pp. A–147–55.

Sapte, Wilde (1997). *Project Finance: The Guide to Financing BOT Project*, Economy Publication, PLC, UK.

Sarkar, P. K. (1998). *Law of Acquisition of Land in India: Including Requisition and Acquisition of Immovable Property*, Eastern Law House, Calcutta.

Sarosh, Bana (2000). 'Young Port in a Hurry', *Business India*, 7–20 August.

Satyanarayan, G. (1999). *Development, Displacement and Rehabilitation*, Rawat Publications, New Delhi.

Scherer, P. R. (1994). 'Telecommunication Reform in Developing Countries' in B. Wellenius and P. A. Stern (eds) *Implementing Reforms in the Telecom Sector*, World Bank.

Secretariat for Global Consultation (1990). 'Global Consultation on SafeWater and Sanitation for the 1990s', Background Paper, Government of India, New Delhi.

Seshan, T. N. (1990). Speech at the Seminar on Traditional Water Harvesting Systems of India, Centre for Science and Environment, New Delhi.

Shah, Mihir, Debashis Banerji, P. S. Vijayshankar and Pramathesh Ambasta (1998). *India's Drylands: Tribal Societies through Environmental Regeneration*. Oxford University Press, Delhi.

Shah, Rajiv (2000). Times of India, 27 August, Ahmedabad edition.

Shah, Tushaar (1992). 'Sustainable Development of Groundwater Resource: Lessons from Junagadh District', *Economic and Political Weekly*, 7–14 March, pp. 515–20.

Shankari, Uma, (1991). 'Tanks: Major Problems in Minor Irrigation, *Economic and Political Weekly*, vol. 26, no. 39, pp. A115–A125.

Shetty, S. L. (1978). 'Structural Retrogression in the Indian

Economy since the Mid-sixties', *Economic and Political Weekly*, annual number.

Shipping Corporation of India Ltd. (1999). *Annual Report 1997–8*, Mumbai.

Shivji, Issa (1976). 'Class Struggles in Tanzania' Monthly Review Press, New York.

Shu, Jet P. H., Wei-Li Chiang, Bing-Ming Lin, and Ming-Chou Cheng (1997). 'The Development of the Electric Propulsion System for the Zero Emission Scooter in Taiwan', SAE Paper No. 972107, *Society of Automotive Engineers*, Washington, DC.

Singh, J. P. (2000). 'Availability of Potable Water in Rural India', *Kurukshetra*, vol. 48, no. 12.

Singh, P. K., J. Singh, S. C. Mahnot, and S. Modi (1995). 'Watershed Approach in Improving the Socio-economic Status of Tribal Areas: A Case Study', *Journal of Rural Development*, vol. 14, no. 2, pp. 107–16.

Singh, R.P. (1993). 'Dryland Agriculture and Technological Options: Issuesand approaches for Watershed Development', *Journal of Rural Development*, vol. 12, no. 1, pp. 21–3.

Sinha, S. K. (1990). Speech at the Seminar on Traditional Water Harvesting Systems of India, Centre for Science and Environment, New Delhi.

Sreenivas, J. (2000a). 'Forget the Sensex for a Second, Look what Else is Going Down', *Indian Express*, 19 April, New Delhi, p. 1.

————— (2000b). 'Once a Fortnight, They get a Few Drops and That too for Twenty Minutes', *Indian Express*, 19 April, p. 1, New Delhi.

Superstratum (1997). *Proceedings of Euroforum conference on Telecom Regulation*, Frankfurt.

Supreme Court Cases (various issues), SCC, Eastern Book Company, Lucknow.

Supreme Court Reports (various issues), SCR, Government of India, New Delhi.

Teagon, P., C. Ross, N. Whitton, and D. Arthur (1999). 'Impact of New Generation Vehicle Technology on Oil Industry', paper presented at the Third International Petroleum Conference and Exhibition, New Delhi.

Tee, Kam U. (1995). 'Commercialization and Privatization of Water and Sewage Supplies: The Case of Malaysia', UMP-Asia Occasional Paper No. 23, Kuala Lumpur.

Telecom Regulatory Authority of India (1997a). 'Consultation Paper on Tariff', TRAI, New Delhi.

————— (1997b). 'Telecom Regulatory Authority of India Act 1997', no. 24, TRAI, New Delhi.

————— (1999a). 'Consultation Paper on Competition in Domestic Long Distance', TRAI, New Delhi.

————— (1999b). 'Telecom Tariff Order, 1999, Annex A, Explanatory Memorandum', TRAI, New Delhi.

————— (2000). 'Consultation Paper on Licensing Issues Relating to Fixed Service Providers', TRAI, New Delhi.

Telecommunications Standards Advisory Council of Canada at www.tsacc.ic.gc.ca.

*Telematics India* (1991). 'The C-DOT Baby Matures', pp 24–6.

Telephone Number Mapping Working Group of IETF at www.ietf.org/html.charters/enum-charter.html.

Tewari, Vinod K. and M. P. Mathur (1999). 'Octroi Issues and Alternatives', National Institute of Urban Affairs, New Delhi.

Thoopal, R. K. (1998). 'Strategy for Increasing Throughput on High Density Routes', OSD West Central Railway, Jabalpur.

Thukral, Enakshi Ganguly, 'The Displaced and the Dispossessed'.

Times Research Foundation (1998). *Municipalities in India: The Devolution Paradox*, study supported by USAID, TRF, Delhi.

Tiwari, G. (1993). 'Pedestrians and Bicycle Crashes in Delhi', paper presented at theWorld Injury Conference, Atlanta, GA.

————— (1998). 'Bicycle Master Plan for Delhi', Final Report submitted to Transport Department, Delhi Government, TRIPP, Indian Institute of Technology, Delhi.

————— (1999). 'Planning for non-motorized traffic: A prerequisite for sustainable transport system', *IATSS Research*, vol. 23, no. 2, pp. 70–7.

————— (2000). 'Urban and Inter-Urban Designs in India: Issues Concerning Mixed Traffic', TRIPP, Indian Institute of Technology, Delhi.

Tota, Katarzyna (1999). 'The role of non-motorised transport in sustainable urban transport systems: A preliminary analysis of costs and benefits of non-motorized and bus priority measures on Vikas Marg', TERI, Delhi.

Tyler, M. and S. Bednarizyk (1993). 'Regulatory Institutions and Processes in Telecommunications: An International Study of Alternatives', *TelecomPolicy*, December, pp. 650–76.

Uehara, T. (1990). 'Privatization and Reorganisation of Nippon Telegraph and Telephone' in *Restructuring and Managing the Telecommunication Sector*, pp. 67–9.

Ulmer, M. J. (1960). *Capital in Transportation, Communications, and Public Utilities: Its Formation and Financing*, NBER Study, Princeton University Press, NJ.

United Nations Conference on Trade and Development (1985). 'Operations Planning in Ports', monograph no. 4, UNCTAD, New York.

————— (1987). 'Measuring and Evaluating Port Performance and Productivity', monograph no. 6, UNCTAD, New York.

*Urban Finance* (1998). 'Urban Infrastructure Finance: Need for a Change in Strategy', vol. 1, no. 3.

————— (1999). 'Private Sector Participation in Urban Water Supply and Sanitation Sector in India', vol. 2, no. 3.

*Urban Finance* (2000). 'Budgetary Incentives for Urban Infrastructure Financing', vol. 3, no. 1.

Vani, M.S. (1990). 'Role of Panchayat Institutions in Irrigation Management in Tamil Nadu and Karnataka', paper presented at the Seminar on Traditional Water Harvesting Systems of India, Centre for Science and Environment, New Delhi.

Varma, J. R. (1998). 'Asian Crisis and Finance Theory', *Vikalpa*, vol. 23, no. 4, pp. 23–34.

Verma, Kalpana (2000). 'Deluge, BMC Punch Holes in BEST's Coffers', *Indian Express*, 21 July.

Videsh Sanchar Nigam Ltd. (various issues). *Annual Report*, VSNL, New Delhi.

Vittal, N. (1999). 'The Course, Content and Consequence of the Reforms in Indian Telecommunications', *Journal of the CTMS*, vol. 8, no. 6, pp. 13–21.

Webb M. and M. Tayler (1998). 'Light-handed Regulation of Telecommunications in New Zealand: Is Generic Competition Law Sufficient?', paper presented at the International Telecommunications Society Twelfth Biennial Conference, Stockholm.

Wellenius, B. and P. A. Stern (1994). *Implementing Reforms in the Telecom Sector*, World Bank, Washington, DC.

Wellenius, B. (1990). 'Beginning of Sector Reform in the Developing World' in *Restructuring and Managing the Telecommunication Sector*, pp. 89–98.

——— (1994). *World Development Report 1994: Infrastructure for Development*. Oxford University Press, New York.

——— (1995a). *India Port Sector: Strategy Report*, South Asia Regional Office.

——— (1995b). *India Transport Sector: Long Term Issues*, report no. 13192-IN, Infrastructure Operations Division Country Department II, India and South Asia Regional Office, Washington, DC.

——— (1995c). *World Health Organization Report*, Asian Environment Division.

——— (1999). *Rural Water Supply and Sanitation*, South Asia Rural Development Series, Washington, DC.

——— (2000). *World Development Report 1999–2000: Entering the Twentieth Century*. Oxford University Press, New York.

World Resources Institute (1999). *World Resources*, Oxford University Press, New York.

Yankee Group (1995) at http://www.adc.com/Education/HFC/topics/voiceIP/pg.3.html#4

Yoon, C. (1999). 'Liberalisation Policy, Industry Structure and Productivity Changes in Korea's Telecommunications Industry', *Telecommunications Policy*, vol. 23, nos 3–4, pp. 289–306.

Zakaria Committee (1963). *Augmentation of Financial Resources of Urban Local Bodies*, Report of the Committee of Ministers constituted by the Central Council of Local Self-government, Government of India, New Delhi.